THE ECONOMICS OF INDUSTRIAL ORGANIZATION

William G. Shepherd

Professor of Economics
University of Massachusetts

 PRENTICE HALL, *Englewood Cliffs, New Jersey 07632*

Shepherd, William G.
    The economics of industrial organization / William G. Shepherd. —
3rd ed.
        p.   cm.
    Includes bibliographical references.
    ISBN 0-13-223694-X
    1. Industrial organization (Economic theory)   I. Title.
HD2326.S46   1990   89-72160
338.6—dc20

Editorial/production supervision: *Edith Riker/Jeanne Sillay Jacobson*
Interior design: *Jeanne Sillay Jacobson*
Cover design: *Edsal Enterprises*
Manufacturing buyer: *Laura Crossland*

**For Helen, in sociology,
Fred, in political science,
and George, in economics**

Printed in the United States of America

10 9 8 7 6 5 4 3 2

ISBN   0-13-223694-X

Prentice-Hall International (UK) Liimited, *London*
Prentice-Hall of Australia Pty. Limited, *Sydney*
Prentice-Hall Canada Inc., *Toronto*
Prentice-Hall Hispanoamericana, S.A., *Mexico*
Prentice-Hall of India Private Limited, *New Delhi*
Prentice-Hall of Japan, Inc., *Tokyo*
Simon & Schuster Asia Pte. Ltd., *Singapore*
Editora Prentice-Hall do Brasil, Ltda., *Rio de Janeiro*

CONTENTS

PREFACE

Competition and market power have always been among the most important conditions of economic life. Who shall control markets and gain riches? Is the playing field level or slanted? Is there open, effective, creative competition, or instead monopoly, with its controls and exclusions?

These are deeply embedded human conditions, at the heart of economic striving and progress. They were decisive in primitive times, in pharaonic Egypt and classical Greece (note Aristotle's example in Chapter 1), in all intervening cultures, and on down to the modern industrial era.

The subject has great depth and human drama, even though it now arises mainly in impersonal, complex corporate settings. Behind the cool concepts of market shares and profit rates lie hot issues of power and human conflict.

These issues remain so intensely controversial partly because they involve the very largest commercial interests. Students are amazed and delighted with this big-league subject, where a "gigantic" IBM or General Motors becomes just another big company, to be assessed skeptically.

Moreover, the field itself has been undergoing strenuous and dramatic changes. "New" schools, offering ideas and techniques which challenge the mainstream concepts, have been bubbling up in the field especially rapidly since 1970. The debates between the mainstream and the "new" schools have been sharp, and they seem to be widening rather than resolving.

In this textbook I have sought to offer a full range of choice among the topics and a carefully balanced coverage among the viewpoints. I also stress the need for students to think independently in judging complex issues that do not have definitive research answers. Mastering the concepts and techniques is Task 1; applying them skillfully, to form independent judgments, is the mature Task 2.

The book lays out the core topics in their natural order, in a format tested over many years of teaching at the University of Michigan, the University of Massachusetts, Yale University, and Williams College. All subjects in the usual "business and government" course are covered, but the primary focus is on the industrial organization side.

The book's emphasis on independent judgment is one of its distinguishing features. Another is the basic format, which presents the forms of competition and monopoly in Chapters 1–4 and then moves immediately to monopoly's effects on performance in Chapters 5–7. That tight sequence highlights the crucial structure-performance link, while leaving open the central question of which causes which.

This edition restores the higher level of technical detail that characterized the first edition. New are the presentations of compact case studies of actual U.S. industries in Chapters 17 and 18. Chapter 17 discusses four firms that dominate their markets (Eastman Kodak, AT&T, Boeing and IBM) and leading newspapers, while Chapter 18 presents four tight oligopolies (cereals, sports, beer, and airlines). These case studies show students how the concepts explored throughout this text work in actual markets. Chapters 19 and 20 summarize public policy in the areas of antitrust, regulation, deregulation, and privatization.

In a two-term sequence of industrial organization and public policies, this book will nicely fit the first term. For the second term, my *Public Policies Toward Business* (7th edition, 1985) covers policy details in depth. The present volume can be used in many course settings, from basic coverage in sophomore courses up to senior-level and business-school courses. Teachers will find that they have much choice in topic emphasis, order of subjects, and the depth of detail.

For example, Chapters 8 and 10 can be read early in the course, to stress the role of "the enterprise" and its capital markets setting. For a "behavioralist" emphasis, Chapters 11–16 can be covered earlier and in more detail. The two case study chapters (17 and 18) can even be assigned at the beginning of the course to give students a real-world focus from the start.

In revising this textbook, I have made extensive changes. To keep the text as lucid as possible, some technical details have been consigned to footnotes and appendixes. As noted, the sequence spotlights the structure-performance issue, letting the student focus directly on the basic question of causation. That permits addressing debates between the mainstream and the Chicago-UCLA School with a maximum of clarity. The coverage of contrasting schools of thought has been broadened to ensure balance in assessing both the mainstream and the "new" schools.

As for the new chapters of industry case studies (Chapter 17 on dominant firms and Chapter 18 on tight oligopolies), they can be covered in sequence or read in parallel with the earlier chapters. Some teachers may, as I do, ask students to read in the case studies right from the beginning of the course. Alternatively, Chapter 17's dominant firms could be covered simultaneously with Chapters 11 and 12, and Chapter 18's tight oligopolies could be read with Chapter 13 on concepts of oligopoly.

In any event, the format, the ways of posing the mainstream and "new school" issues, and the case-study chapters are distinct among textbooks in this field.

Five appendixes which provide technical material without cluttering the body of the text. An appendix to Chapter 2 covers the design and sources for student research papers. It has been expanded to include a general bibliography of monographs in the field, so that students will have the leading research sources in one place. Appendix 1 at the end of the book gives a deeper historical coverage, to enlarge the historical perspective presented in Chapter 1. Other appendixes deal with the SIC system (Appendix 2), the internal choices about financing, accounting, and discounting by companies (Appendix 3), and the interpretation of statistical analyses (Appendix 4). The review questions at the ends of the chapters have also been improved, and a separate *Teacher's Manual* discusses the range of possible answers to the essay questions. The *Manual* provides a variety of assistance for teachers, in dealing with specific topics.

To students, I always insist that the goal is to learn to think skillfully and maturely, *but also independently,* about the matters within the covers of this book. All of the issues are still open, even the most fundamental questions of causation and the nature of effective competition. The recent discord and debates among competing schools can be seen as healthy ferment, as long as you think for yourself in evaluating them.

I am pleased to acknowledge the help of many people in the evolution of this book. First are the many hundreds of students at the University of Michigan, the University of Massachusetts, Yale University and Williams College. For this edition, Professor Joseph Shaanan of Oklahoma State University, Professor Kambiz Raffiee of the University of Nevada at Reno, and Professor Mark McBride of Miami University provided helpful advice about all aspects of the volume.

Over the years, I have learned much from discussions with such gifted colleagues as James R. Nelson, Shorey Peterson, Henry W. de Jong, Richard E. Caves, Walter Adams, Donald J. Dewey, Leonard W. Weiss, William J. Adams, Alexander Cairncross, Kenneth D. Boyer, Lee E. Preston, Donald F. Turner, William S. Comanor, Oliver E. Williamson, Takao Nakao, Alfred E. Kahn, George J. Stigler, Frederick M. Scherer, John S. Heywood, Alister Sutherland, Eleanor Fox, and many others. I am also indebted to Susan Fischer, Edie Riker, and Jeanne Jacobson for their excellence in editing.

If the book falls short of the attainable despite all this help, the fault is mine. If readers will be kind enough to let me know where changes are most needed, I will endeavor to make the next edition more useful. Your advice has been helpful with earlier editions, and it will continue to be warmly received.

William G. Shepherd

BOOKS WRITTEN BY THE AUTHOR

The Treatment of Market Power
Market Power and Economic Welfare
Public Policies Toward Business
Microeconomics
The Ultimate Deterrent
Economic Performance Under Public Ownership

BOOKS EDITED BY THE AUTHOR

Mainstreams in Industrial Organization (with H. W. de Jong)
Public Policies Toward Business: Readings and Cases
Utility Regulation: New Directions in Theory and Policy
Economic Regulation (with K. D. Boyer)
Regulation and Entry (with M. W. Klass)
Public Enterprise: Economic Analysis of Theory and Practice

1 INTRODUCTION

com·pe·ti·tion: . . . **1:** the act or action of seeking to gain what another is seeking to gain at the same time and usually under or as if under fair or equitable rules and circumstances: a common struggle for the same object especially among individuals of relatively equal standing . . . **4b:** a market condition in which a large number of independent buyers and sellers compete for identical commodities, deal freely with each other, and retain the right of entry and exit from the market. . . .

Merriam-Webster *Dictionary of the English Language*

For over a century, scholars in the field of industrial organization have studied competition and monopoly power in markets. From corporate boardrooms in gleaming New York skyscrapers to gritty factories in Ohio and humble stores along countless Main Streets, the struggle to gain economic power courses daily through thousands of U.S. markets. Companies contend for advantage, seeking profits and control over their markets.

When competition is effective, it drives this activity to be efficient, innovative, and rich in opportunities. Monopoly power usually leans the other way, undermining efficiency, slowing innovation, transferring wealth from ordinary citizens to wealthier ones, and reducing freedom of choice. The issues are ancient and timeless. From the earliest human eras, economic exchanges have been the focus of struggles for control in which the winners capture wealth and power. The process continues, and it continues to fascinate and baffle even the most learned scholars.

Competition and monopoly are not simply opposite extremes, like red and black squares on a checkerboard. Markets contain all degrees and varieties of competition, and the very concepts for assessing whether it is effective are debatable. It is precisely because these conditions shape the highest orders of industrial values and power that they are packed with controversy. This book is your map through the minefield of explosive debates.

Effective competition is the central concept of the field. This book assesses the mainstream methods that scholars have used in defining effective competition, measuring it, and tracing its effects. We also review other schools and views, especially the new theories advanced since 1970. The mainstream is now paralleled by a largely separate field commonly called "new IO" theory," which explores pure cases of duopoly and entry. Chicago-UCLA theorists also hypothesize that monopoly merely represents greater efficiency. The contrasts are stark: mainstream analysis shows that monopoly usually imposes harms, while many "new" theorists welcome monopoly as beneficial! Indeed, some of them say that *monopoly* can really be *competition!*

For more than a century, "industrial organization" has been an evolving set of concepts dealing with fascinating phenomena at the core of modern capitalism.[1] Section IV of this chapter reviews the history of the field, and Appendix 1 at the end of the book gives a larger historical perspective on the issues. Industrial organization is a branch on the main stem of microeconomics: it is the applied economics of supply. In popular terms, IO covers "big business," "corporate power," and "the monopoly problem." Often it is presented as "the case for competition" or "antitrust economics."

Whatever the label, the field of industrial organization, like other scientific fields, exists on two planes. First, the field involves *logic:* concepts and analytical methods that may clarify markets. These tools are relatively few and powerful. Second, the field is about *facts,* the data of those actual markets that teem with the drama and follies of real, struggling firms. The combat has occurred daily in numberless markets, throughout virtually every economy. For example, Aristotle mentions an early example in 347 B.C.[2]

> There was a man of Sicily who, having money deposited with him, bought up all the iron from the iron mines; afterwards, when the merchants from the various markets came to buy, he was the only seller, and without much increasing the price he gained 200 percent.

In modern markets, the patterns are complex and the stakes are often immense. Leading American families, such as the Astors, Vanderbilts, Rockefellers, Mellons, and du Ponts, drew much of their immense fortunes from monopolies.[3] Monopoly

---

[1] The field began in the 1880s, with leading early discussions by Alfred Marshall, Henry Carter Adams, Richard T. Ely, and John Bates Clark. The 1890s trust wave and 1901–1915 antitrust movement generated more intensive debate and research, and by 1933, Knight, J. M. Clark, Chamberlin, and Robinson had advanced the issues far; see Frank H. Knight, *Risk, Uncertainty and Profit* (New York: Harper & Row, 1921); John M. Clark, *Studies in the Economics of Overhead Costs* (New York: Macmillan, 1922); Edward H. Chamberlin, *The Theory of Monopolistic Competition* (Cambridge, Mass.: Harvard University Press, 1933; 8th ed., 1962); and Joan Robinson, *The Economics of Imperfect Competition* (London: Macmillan, 1933).

The 1930s saw an amplification of the debates, techniques, and empirical evidence, and major new gains occurred in the 1950s; see George J. Stigler, *Business Concentration and Price Policy* (Princeton, N.J.: Princeton University Press, 1955); Joe S. Bain, *Barriers to New Competition* (Cambridge, Mass.: Harvard University Press, 1956); Edward S. Mason, *Economic Concentration and the Monopoly Problem* (Cambridge, Mass.: Harvard University Press, 1957); and Carl Kaysen and Donald F. Turner, *Antitrust Policy: An Economic and Legal Analysis* (Cambridge, Mass.: Harvard University Press, 1959). Empirical research was greatly extended in the 1960s, including Edwin Mansfield, *The Economics of Technological Change* (New York: Norton, 1968) and related volumes.

Two helpful recent surveys of the field and its literature are F. M. Scherer, *Industrial Market Structure and Economic Performance,* 2d ed. (Boston: Houghton Mifflin, 1980), and Stephen Martin, *Industrial Organization* (New York: Macmillan, 1988). See also Section IV of this chapter for a more detailed discussion.

[2] Aristotle's *Politics,* Book 1, Chapter 12.

[3] In addition to Vanderbilt University, the Rockefeller Institute, and Carnegie-Mellon University, Duke University and Stanford Universities were also named after monopolists (James B. Duke in cigarettes and Leland Stanford in California railroads).

impacts on efficiency can also be large. For example, General Motors, Ford, and Chrysler dominated the U.S. automobile industry from the 1920s to the 1970s, and they became sluggish and inefficient, turning out inferior cars. Japanese automakers moved in strongly after 1978, taking over 25 percent of the U.S. market. Therefore the earlier market power cost over 100,000 U.S. autoworkers their jobs and U.S. stockholders many billions of dollars in losses. Other cases of market power will be noted in these pages, along with other examples where effective competition has yielded gains.

This chapter presents the basic concepts of the field in Section I. Next Section II summarizes the real markets and trends of competition in the U.S. economy. Section III introduces the concept of "effective competition," and Section IV reviews the history of the field and its new "schools." Section V explains the format of the book.

I.   BASIC CONCEPTS AND TRENDS

The core issues, in concise form, are these:

1.   Firms seek higher market shares in order to gain higher profits.

2.   When these firms' mutual strivings hold each other in check, then effective competition exists. It restrains prices, forces firms to be efficient, and stimulates innovation.

3.   But if one or several firms gain high market shares, they can obtain high profits by setting prices above costs and restricting output. Their monopoly power imposes social costs: a degree of inefficiency, a slowing of innovation, unfair shifts in income and wealth, and less freedom of choice.

4.   These costs of monopoly power may be offset if there are large enough scale economies or superior performance by the dominant firms.

1.   The Degree of Monopoly

The *degree of monopoly* is critical. It is embodied in the demand for the firm's product, as illustrated in Figure 1.1. A highly elastic demand curve means that the firm has little scope for raising its price. Curve 1 in Figure 1.1 illustrates that: with even a small price rise, the firm will sell nothing at all. If demand is highly inelastic, as shown by Curve 3, the firm can raise its price sharply and still sell large amounts. Its profit-maximizing price will be well above the competitive level (Chapter 2 will clarify this). Little wonder that all firms' officials yearn for inelastic demand and go to great effort and expense trying to achieve it.

Demand elasticity can be of any degree between infinite and zero. This is not a binary yes-or-no matter, a checkerboard world of pure monopoly versus pure competition; the degree of monopoly is a matter of shading. Ideally, demand curves would be accurately measured, and the degrees of competition could be recorded simply as elasticities of demand, as easily as reading temperatures with a thermometer. But elasticities are devilishly hard to measure, and in most situations the actual elasticity is simply unknown. Other, indirect evidence is used instead, and often it is not very accurate.

Each market has three main categories of conditions: *structure, behavior,* and

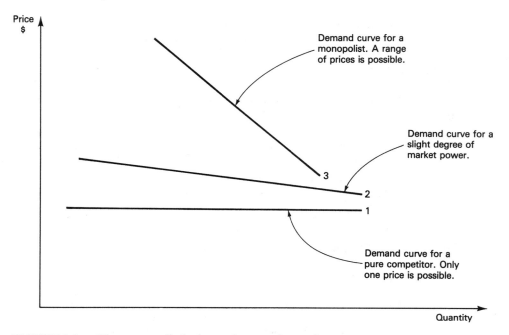

FIGURE 1.1.   The monopolist's demand curve slopes down.

The monopolist can set the price anywhere that it chooses along its demand curve. A pure competitor, by contrast, has no control over price. When the demand curve is horizontal, only one price is possible.

performance. They include most of the concepts and facts of the field, and each of them can vary with the degree of monopoly. Economists have usually focused on market structure as the key indicator of market power, but behavior and performance can also be used to infer it.

2.   The Meaning of Structure

Consider structure first. It is embodied in the size distribution of firms. Imagine that the extent of the market can be exactly defined (a key problem—see Chapter 3), and that each firm's share of the market can be precisely measured. One arrays the firms in order of their market shares, starting with the top firm. Figure 1.2 shows such an array, in this case for a dominant-firm market such as parts of the U.S. computer industry.

The main feature of each firm's market position is its own *market share*. Firm 1 with 50 percent is in a different market situation from firm 4 with 6 percent, and firm 10 with 2 percent, and so on. Though they are in the same market, firm 4 is under more severe competitive stress than is firm 1.

Concentration in the market is usually indicated by the summed shares of the largest four firms, as shown in Figure 1.2. Such a "concentration ratio" helps to describe the degree of horizontal market power held by the leading firms in this market. But the shares within any given four-firm concentration ratio can be roughly equal or sharply unequal (as they are here).

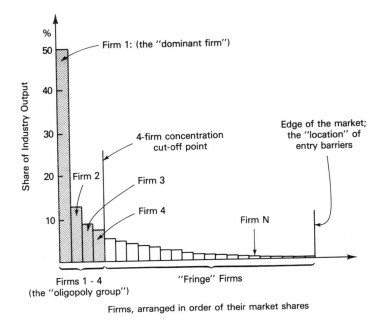

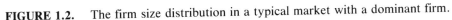

Firms, arranged in order of their market shares

FIGURE 1.2.   The firm size distribution in a typical market with a dominant firm.

At the edge of the market—at the end of the array of firms—there may be *barriers to entry* that keep out whatever potential competitors might be waiting outside the market. The height of the barrier ranges between vanishingly low to high enough to prevent any entry. Height is shown here roughly as the size needed to get permanently established. (See Chapters 4 and 11 for analysis of barrier height.) The group of "most likely potential entrants" may be large and strong or small and weak.

Figure 1.2 shows a market with a dominant firm. All other structures can also be shown by size distributions.

In *effective competition,* no market shares are large enough to permit strong influence, and entry barriers are low. The largest market shares may be 15 or 20 percent, with the rest tapering off from there.

Between effective competition and the dominance shown in Figure 1.2 lie many markets. Assessing them is complex, and the methodology for doing so is debatable. In any event, structure is not a simple, one-dimensional matter. Just counting firms is not enough, because their market shares can vary so sharply.

3. Cause and Effect

In every market, structure is usually related to behavior and performance; where monopoly is found, so is reduced performance. Yet there is much debate about how this *causation* runs. As the field of industrial organization developed and matured in the decades from 1890 to 1970, the mainstream scholars reflected common sense and business experience in assuming that each market's structure tends to influence how firms behave and how well they perform.

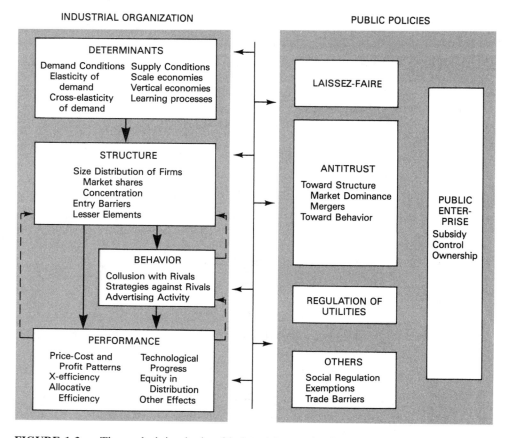

FIGURE 1.3.   The underlying logic of industrial organization and public policy.

The typical industry is on the left-hand side. Causation runs mainly downward, as shown by the thick arrows, from determinants to structure, behavior, and performance. On the right-hand side are the public policies that may be taken toward industries with monopoly power. The arrows in the middle of the figure go in both directions, because policies not only apply to industries but are also affected by them.

This pattern of cause-and-effect is illustrated in panel I of Figure 1.3. (Panel II shows the main U.S. public policies that are used to control market power. They are summarized in Chapters 19 and 20.)

The Mainstream View.   The causation flows mainly downward, as illustrated by the thick arrows in panel I of Figure 1.3. At each point in time, the market's structure usually influences the behavior of the firms as they decide how strongly to compete or collude with each other. For example, higher concentration encourages a greater degree of collusion. The structure and behavior then affect the market's performance, as reflected in the firms' prices, cost-cutting efficiency, rates of innovation, and so forth. Good performance is usually promoted by a competitive structure and behavior.

Reverse causation can occur also or instead, as illustrated in panel I by the thinner dashed arrows pointing back up from performance to structure. For example, a firm that has a run of good luck and high profits will generally increase its market share: its performance will affect the market's structure. Careful mainstream researchers have always recognized that cause and effect are mixed to some degree, but logic and business experience have strongly suggested that the causation usually flows mostly downward, as in Figure 1.3.

This can be expressed in a simple formula, with the causative (independent) variables on the right-hand side. We assume that they influence the performance variables, such as profits, innovation, and the like. For each firm:

$$\text{Performance} = \text{a function of (Structure; Behavior;} \qquad (1.1)$$
$$\text{Internal Organization; and External Conditions)}$$

where *structure* includes the several elements, *behavior* covers a range of firms' actions; *internal organization* includes such things as diversification and owner-managers; and *external conditions* includes changes coming from outside the industry, such as shifts in demand, changes in adjacent markets, and new opportunities for better technology.

A more specific, widely followed line of research has focused on profits as a key performance variable. The following is a common model for testing the effects of structure on firms' profitability:

$$\text{Rate of profit}_i = f \text{ (Market share}_i, \text{ Concentration}_j, \qquad (1.2)$$
$$\text{Entry barriers}_j; \text{ Growth rate}_i)$$

where i is the firm and j is the industry. As in Figure 1.3, the causation here is assumed to run mostly (but not exclusively) from the right-hand variables to the left-hand (dependent) variable. Chapters 3 and 4 will present statistical results from fitting this sort of model to data about a variety of U.S. corporations.

Underlying this triad of conditions (structure, behavior, and performance) are the *determinants* that may shape structure itself. These include economies and diseconomies of scale. At one extreme is "natural competition," where economies of scale are small, so firms can be or must be small. At the other pole is "natural monopoly," with very large economies of scale. If a market's technology gives rise to large economies of scale—as, for instance, in electric power and telephone service at the local level—then there is room for only one firm, which will be a monopoly. But if technology favors small sizes of firms, and there is room for many firms, competition can be intense. Economies of scale can shape structure: the factual question is how closely they *do* shape structure. Chapter 9 will assess that.

The mainstream premise about causation is often called *structuralist* because it accords structure an influential role. But "structuralists" (who include a wide variety of scholars with a range of views) have regarded structure as only an influence, never as an airtight determinant of performance. Firms are human organizations, with much room for variety, historical chance, and contrasting motives.

The basic set of relationships in equation (1.1) is central to the field. Our job is to formulate its details more fully. Is causation strong? Which specific variables have the most influence?

The Chicago-UCLA School.   An opposite, self-consciously "antistructuralist" view came to prominence during the 1970s. Often called the "Chicago School" hypothesis, it is actually a "Chicago-UCLA" view, because UCLA economists have been among its most active proponents.[4]

This hypothesis reverses the direction of causation. Each firm's relative efficiency is said to be the real determinant of its position in the market's structure and behavior. Thus a firm's superior innovations may generate large profits and enable it to take over 40, 60, or 80 percent of a market. Indeed, some Chicago-UCLA analysts attribute *all* structural monopoly to superior performance (or to scale economies), as Chapters 2 and 9 will explore.

This view of causation is illustrated in Panel I of Figure 1.4, which reverses Figure 1.3. For those who visualize it as a formula, equation (1.1) becomes:

$$\text{Structure} = f \text{ (Performance; Behavior; External conditions)} \qquad (1.3)$$

The version relating profits to market structure now reverses equation (1.2) to read:

$$\text{Market share}_{ij} = f \text{ (Rate of profit}_i; \text{Behavior}_j; \text{External conditions}_j) \qquad (1.4)$$

Chapters 4 and 5 consider this version of causation as a model, suitable for fitting to real data.

Note how the Chicago-UCLA premise also reverses the usual belief about the harms caused by monopoly. Instead of exacting economic costs, any existing monopoly is merely an inocuous side effect of the monopoly firm's superior performance. So this view about causation, which is illustrated in panel I of Figure 1.4, has strong normative lessons, indeed. If it is correct about most or all markets, then monopoly is to be embraced and encouraged rather than resisted.

Behaviorists.   Still other variants of causation are possible. Rather than structure, behavior may be the really powerful influence. This possibility is illustrated in panel II of Figure 1.4. For example, two firms may control all of a market, so that structure is extremely tight. But whether or not monopoly results may depend entirely on how the two firms behave toward each other, either fighting or colluding, and the outcome may be impossible to predict. If so, then structure matters little, while the directions of behavior are critical.

---

[4] The history of this school is complex and ironic. Members of the *original* Chicago School in the 1920s and 1930s were deeply opposed to monopoly of every kind, which they saw as widespread, powerful, and very harmful. The leaders were Frank H. Knight, Henry C. Simons, and Jacob Viner. See especially Simons, *Economic Policy for a Free Society* (Chicago: University of Chicago Press, 1948).

Then, in the 1950s, George J. Stigler arrived at the University of Chicago and led a complete reversal: competition was seen as ubiquitous, while monopoly was said to be limited, transient, and weak. In the 1960s and 1970s, his followers, led by Harold Demsetz and J. Fred Weston at UCLA, John McGee at the University of Washington, and Yale Brozen, Richard A. Posner, and Sam Peltzman at Chicago, carried the point further, saying that any monopoly *probably* reflected superior efficiency.

Still other disciples then carried the argument to the extreme, saying that any monopoly *surely* reflects superior efficiency. They include Robert H. Bork, Dominick T. Armentano, and M. Bruce Johnson.

More details about the Chicago-UCLA School are given later in this chapter and throughout the book.

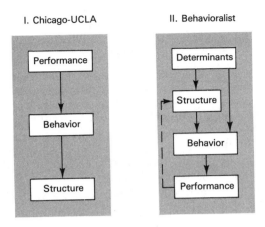

I. Chicago-UCLA

Performance → Behavior → Structure

II. Behavioralist

Determinants → Structure → Behavior → Performance

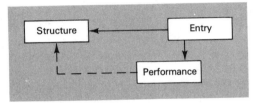

III. Entry ("Contestability")

Structure ← Entry → Performance → Structure

FIGURE 1.4.   Alternative views of causation.

Potential Competition.   In still another variant, entry from outside the market may be decisive, rendering irrelevant the market's internal structure. Scholars who emphasize the importance of entry can be termed the "entry" or "contestability" school (they are discussed in Section IV). This approach stresses that potential entry by newcomers is the main force, which is limited only by entry barriers. If the barriers are low, it does not matter that the existing firms have large market shares or try to behave collusively because actual or threatened entry will force them to perform at optimum, competitive levels. Panel III of Figure 1.4 illustrates this approach.

Each of these views has internal logical consistency, and each may be valid for one market, for many, for most, or even for all markets. The question is one of proportion: what share of actual markets actually fits each of these competing theories? The answers cannot be deduced by pure logic, no matter how brilliant the theorist. Indeed, the theories are a babble of conflicting assertions.

The resolution of this discord turns on real conditions and evidence in real industries. Which way, in fact, does causation mainly run? Which elements are most important in most markets? The field has long grappled with these questions, and views will undoubtedly continue to evolve and shift. Later chapters will summarize the research results that bear on these questions.

Your own judgment will develop as you learn, and you may adopt any position among these alternatives. Your specific views are likely to change and mature as you continue studying. What matters most is the degree of skill with which you think and study. The aim is to grasp the concepts and logic firmly, and then use care in weighing the evidence, so that you can explain your views persuasively. That is what distinguishes professional quality from mere ideology.

4.   The Costs of Monopoly

A second question also requires your careful judgment: What are the net effects of monopoly? The costs naturally occur, as market power reduces efficiency and slows innovation, in some degree. But there may also be benefits. If scale economies are large—in production, innovation, or other activities—then a high market share may yield benefits that offset some or all of monopoly's costs.

This *logic* is clear; the real questions, then, concern *degree:* How strong are the monopoly impacts? How big are the economies of scale, if there are any? Answering these questions requires a careful reading of the evidence, as summarized in Chapters 5, 6 7, and 9.

5.   Alternative Sources of Monopoly

Monopoly and dominance may arise from "good" causes, such as economies of scale and superior performance, but they may also arise from causes that are neutral or anticompetitive. Competitors may simply merge to capture more of the market. Or one of them may take strategic actions that prevent other firms from competing fairly. From 1880 to 1970, the field emphasized these anticompetitive causes. Since 1970 many Chicago-UCLA writers and other "new IO" theorists have denied the imperfections and said that only good causes are at work.

Assessing the possible *non*efficiency sources of monopoly, as reviewed in Chapters 8 and 10–16, will be another main task for you, as it is for all specialists in the field.

II.   REAL-WORLD MARKETS AND TRENDS

Now we turn to real conditions in real markets.

1.   Industries and Sectors

The economy is composed of a vast array of individual markets in a number of major sectors. Their variety is suggested by Figure 1.5 and summarized in Table 1.1.

Farming and natural resource industries feed their products into manufacturing industries. In turn, manufactured products flow to other industries or out through distribution to final consumers. Utilities and construction sectors provide basic services such as electricity, transport, and communications. Labor markets channel workers' skills and effort. Service markets cover a wide range of activities, from serving hamburgers to providing health care or a college education. Over them all lie the financial sectors, which provide funds and exert control.

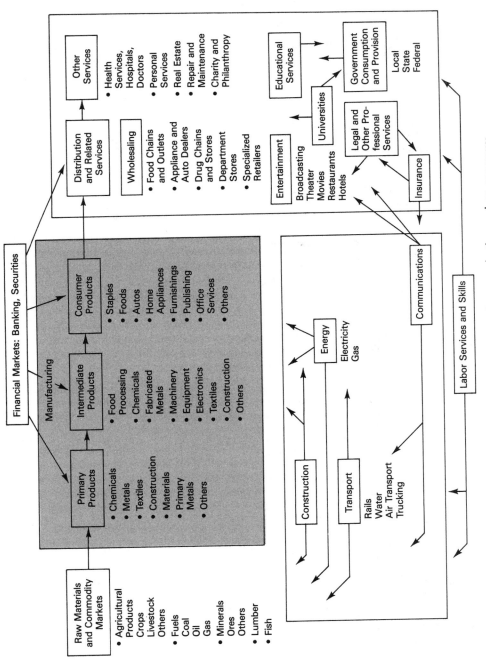

FIGURE 1.5. A schematic outline of sectors in the modern economy.

TABLE 1.1   Gross National Product, by Industry: United States, 1986

Industry	Billion $	Percent	
Gross national product	**4,235.0**	**100.0**	
Domestic industries	**4,201.3**	**99.2**	
Private industries	**3,699.6**	**87.4**	
Agriculture, forestry, fisheries	93.0	2.2	
Farms	76.4		1.8
Mining	95.3	2.3	
Construction	197.9	4.7	
Manufacturing	824.3	19.5	
Durable goods	478.5	11.3	
Lumber and wood products	24.8		0.6
Furniture and fixtures	13.4		0.3
Stone clay and glass products	25.3		0.6
Primary metal industries	34.8		0.8
Fabricated metal products	56.9		1.3
Machinery, except electrical	85.9		2.0
Electric and electronic equipment	88.2		2.1
Motor vehicles and equipment	49.5		1.2
Other transportation equipment	54.3		1.3
Instruments and related products	31.4		0.7
Nondurable goods	345.8	8.2	
Food and kindred products	71.1		1.7
Tobacco manufactures	12.7		0.3
Textile mill products	18.5		0.4
Apparel and other textile products	20.7		0.5
Paper and allied products	35.0		0.8
Printing and publishing	54.4		1.3
Chemicals and allied products	64.4		1.5
Petroleum and coal products	38.9		0.9
Rubber and misc. plastics products	27.1		0.6
Leather and leather products	3.0		0.1
Transportation, public utilities	391.4	9.2	
Transportation	144.1	3.4	
Railroad transportation	21.6		0.5
Trucking and warehousing	60.9		1.4
Air transportation	29.8		0.7
Communications	115.3	2.7	
Telephone and telegraph	102.6		2.4
Radio and TV broadcasting	12.7		0.3
Electric, gas, and sanitary services	132.0	3.1	
Wholesale trade	294.6	7.0	
Retail trade	407.9	9.6	
Finance, insurance, and real estate	695.0	16.4	
Banking	69.0		1.6
Security, commodity, brokers' services	32.9		0.8
Insurance carriers	53.6		1.3
Real estate	483.2		11.4

TABLE 1.1   *(continued)*

INDUSTRY	BILLION $	PERCENT	
Other services	700.2	16.5	
Hotels and other lodging places	31.9		0.8
Personal services	31.1		0.7
Business services	162.8		3.8
Auto repair, services, garages	34.3		0.8
Motion pictures	8.5		0.2
Amusement, recreation services	21.4		0.5
Health services	198.6		4.7
Legal services	52.3		1.2
Educational services	26.7		0.6
Government and government enterprises	506.6	12.0	

SOURCE: *U.S. Statistical Abstract, 1988,* p. 408.

Services now make up about half the economy, as Table 1.1 shows, while manufacturing has dwindled to only about one-fifth of economic activity. Yet most of the data about monopoly problems are for manufacturing industries. The "utility" sectors (including railroads, communications, and electric, gas, and sanitary services) are important and fascinating, but they account for only 6.3 percent of total production. Finance, despite its pivotal role (see Chapter 8), is an even smaller sector, accounting for less than 3 percent of national income.

For further perspective, consider the following major industries: steel, automobiles, all publishing (newspapers, books, and magazines), banking, airlines, all broadcasting, motion pictures, and sports (amusement, recreation services). These are very prominent industries, and they will be discussed frequently throughout this book. But their total contribution to GNP in 1986 was only $227 billion—a mere 5.4 percent.

In short, the economy contains a vast array of ordinary industries that draw little attention because they function reasonably well under competitive processes.

2.   Categories of Markets

Each sector contains many industries, and each industry usually embraces many individual markets, as defined by their *specific products* and *geographical areas* (see Chapter 3 for the methods of defining genuine markets). Each of these thousands of U.S. markets has its own structure, behavior, and performance, ranging from pure competition to pure monopoly, with infinite gradations and variations in between.

The field has defined six main categories of markets to reflect the degrees of competition and monopoly. They are summarized in Table 1.2, with examples of each kind.

Pure monopoly is one extreme; here there is just one firm (electricity, telephones, and postal service, for example) and demand is often highly inelastic. The next category is the "dominant firm," which has a majority of the market and no close

TABLE 1.2   Types of Markets, Shading from Pure Monopoly to Pure Competition

MARKET TYPE	MAIN CONDITION	FAMILIAR INSTANCES
Pure monopoly	One firm has 100 percent of the market.	Electric, telephone, water, bus, and other utilities
Dominant firm	One firm has 50–100 percent of the market and no close rival.	Soup (Campbell), razor blades (Gillette), newspapers (most local markets), film (Eastman Kodak), aircraft (Boeing)
Tight oligopoly	The leading four firms, combined, have 60–100 percent of the market; collusion among them to fix prices is relatively easy.	Copper, aluminum, local banking, lightbulbs, soaps, textbook stores, breakfast cereals
Loose oligopoly	The leading four firms combined, have 40 percent or less of the market; collusion among them to fix prices is virtually impossible.	Lumber, furniture, small machinery, hardware, magazines
Monopolistic competition	There are many effective competitors, none has more than 10 percent of the market.	Most retailing, clothing
Pure competition	There are over 50 competitors, all with negligible market shares.	Wheat, corn, cattle, hogs, poultry

rival (IBM and Kodak are instances). That category shades into "tight oligopoly," in which the leading four firms have a combined market share of over 60 percent. They, too, enjoy some inelasticity of demand, and are often able to cooperate in setting prices.

"Loose oligopoly" has a combined four-firm share below 40 percent and little real chance to hold prices high by means of price-fixing. Each firm's relatively elastic demand tempts it to cut prices, so prices are pressed down close to the level of cost. Moving further down in the degree of monopoly, "monopolistic competition" has many competitors, each with a slight degree of market power. Then comes the extreme case of pure competition with many competitors, none of which has any influence on the market at all.

These last three classes (from loose oligopoly on down) are all *effectively competitive;* their results consistently approach the competitive ideal of efficiency and innovation. The other market types will frequently, or usually, deviate markedly from that ideal. Only if there are large economies of scale in production or innovation will a substantial degree of monopoly be efficient.

3.   The Extent and Trend of Competition

These market categories can be applied to all markets in order to estimate the relative extent of competition and monopoly in the U.S. economy. This pattern is helpful background in approaching the main issues.

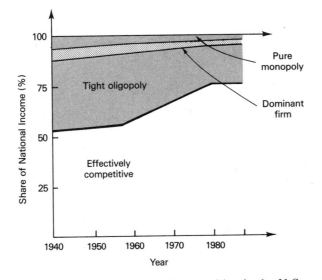

FIGURE 1.6.   The trend of competition in the U.S. economy, 1939 to 1988.

In 1939, just over half of all national income arose in markets that were effectively competitive (they were either loose oligopoly, monopolistic competition, or pure competition). The competitive share rose to 56 percent in 1958, and then to 76 percent in 1980. Much of the rise occurred in the 1970s.

SOURCE: From data in W. G. Shepherd, "Causes of Increased Competition in the U.S. Economy, 1939–1980," *Review of Economics and Statistics*, 64 (November 1982), 613–626. See Table 4.9 below.

The larger picture is shown in Figure 1.6, covering the U.S. economy since 1939.[5] There are three main lessons. First, the economy contains widely varying degrees of monopoly, from the 2 percent of national income in pure monopolies to the roughly 70 percent in effectively competitive markets. Second, the U.S. economy has become predominantly competitive. In the 1980s, only about 25 to 30 percent of total production has been in pure monopolies, dominant firms, and tight oligopolies combined. Third, competition rose sharply during 1960–1980, compared to the glacial pace before 1960.

The rise occurred in scores of markets, including automobiles, steel, cameras, aircraft, banking, telephones, legal services, and even professional sports. During the 1980s, there were a lot of individual shifts, and some industries reverted toward higher market power. But competition rose in others, and on balance the slippage was light.

In a nice coincidence, the field began being influenced more by Chicago-UCLA views in the 1970s, just as competition in many real markets was indeed rising. The 1980s have been an era of aggressive confidence in competition, with claims that monopoly has become rare and weak. This opinion may persist or fade, as scholars continue rethinking and testing the issues, and as the economy continues to evolve.

---

[5] It is from W. G. Shepherd, "Causes of Increased Competition in the US Economy, 1939–1980," *Review of Economics and Statistics,* 64 (November 1982), 613–26. For a contrasting view, stressing that monopoly power continues to be highly important and harmful, see Walter Adams and James W. Brock, *The Bigness Complex* (New York: Pantheon Books, 1988).

III.   EFFECTIVE COMPETITION

1.   The Meaning of "Effective"

Now we turn to focus directly on the meaning of *effective competition*. It involves a striving among comparable rivals, who exert a mutual pressure so strong that all competitors must apply maximum efforts. None of them is able to raise price above costs by very much, or to remove rivals except by superior efficiency.

When competition is *ineffective,* one or several firms dominate the market, and competitors are not evenly matched. Mutual pressure is not strong: dominant firms face only light stress, while their little rivals face extreme pressure and risks. Accordingly, the dominant firms can raise prices and, if they wish, take actions that will remove their smaller rivals from the market.

Effective competition therefore requires two *internal* conditions, that is, conditions inside the market: (1) a reasonable degree of parity among the competitors, and (2) a high enough number of competitors to prevent effective collusion among them to rig the market. Ten comparable competitors will usually give a high probability that competition is strong; five will usually give a lower probability, though in some cases they may compete effectively. But some types of markets may require fifteen or more comparable firms to make competition fully effective.

As for *external* conditions, free entry reinforces effective competition. Even if rivals are few, a strong threat of massive entry from outside may frighten them into behaving competitively. In general, such external entry conditions can substitute for internal competitive conditions to some degree. In other words, low entry barriers can make a monopolist behave more competitively. But is potential entry a strong force or largely a minor one?

These questions of degree will occupy much of the rest of the book. They involve judgment rather than simple formulas. Notice that effective competition does *not* require a very high number of tiny firms in purely competitive markets. The real questions concern the middle range, where markets have two to twenty comparable firms and less-than-free entry.

2.   Unity Among Models of Competition

Whatever the specific conditions may be, the essence of competition is always the same: the mutual exertion of pressure to perform well. Even when models of competition seem to differ sharply, they share this meaning. To see this, let us examine some of the divergent views of competition.

Two centuries ago, Adam Smith noted that competition spurs efficiency by preventing "indolence," and also that competitors are always tempted to collude: "People of the same trade seldom gather together, whether for merriment or diversion, but the conversation ends in a conspiracy against the public or some contrivance to raise prices" (*The Wealth of Nations,* 1776). For a century after Smith, classical economists inveighed against monopoly and state controls.

The Neoclassical Equilibrium Model.   As neoclassical analysis developed after 1870, economists began to carry the concept of competition to an extreme in order to derive precise conclusions about efficiency (see Chapter 2).[6] Perfect competition was eventually defined to require numberless competitors, with their horizontal demand curves. Their choices yielded an equilibrium state of strictly efficient allocation.

A Realistic Process of Rivalry.   This abstract model gave precise results, but many economists and business managers rightly pointed out that it was unnecessarily farfetched. The mainstream concept of competition is quite robust even when there are large departures from perfect conditions. Markets with relatively few rivals are often intensely competitive, in a dynamic process of struggle over time. Schumpeter's process of "creative destruction" was the most colorful of these versions of rivalry, but they all suggested that the pure neoclassical model was misleading.[7] Various schools have suggested a variety of models of competition, which differ in important ways. Which ones are best?

In fact, all versions of competition share a fundamental unity: competition leads toward certain basic kinds of economic results, by a process of mutual pressure. Competition narrows the firm's choice over price by lowering its demand curve, forcing costs down, and inducing innovation. Monopoly and dominance, to the contrary, distort the process.

Competition is, as noted, a robust concept: it applies over a wide range of market conditions. For the market types listed in Table 1.2, competition is usually effective even when concentration rises to substantial levels. Only when conditions approach very high degrees of monopoly does competition lose most of its force and become *ineffective*.

Competition can be a complex phenomenon, taking a variety of forms. It also has an important cultural role. The United States, especially, relies on it as a fair and efficient process. This reliance derives from a number of roots, such as the cultural fluidity caused by large-scale immigration during 1880–1910, the rigors of frontier life, and the Protestant ethic of effort and reward.

Competition is commonly seen as a basic test of the ability of people and firms: if competition is effective, it permits superior talents to prevail and to gain appropriate rewards. Competition does have its dark side, which we will go into in Chapter 2. But competition "on the merits" is a sound general basis for seeking good performance.

3.   The Paradox of Competition

The competitive process can pose a dilemma. Each competitor strives to win, so as to gain higher rewards. But if one of them wins in a big way, then competition is replaced by a substantial degree of monopoly. Even a partial victory giving a market share of 50 percent will usually create a high degree of monopoly power.

---

[6] See George J. Stigler, "Perfect Competition, Historically Contemplated," a chapter in his *The Organization of Industry* (Homewood, Ill.: Irwin, 1968).

[7] See Joseph A. Schumpeter, *Capitalism, Socialism, and Democracy* (New York: Harper, 1942). The process is presented in full in Chapter 3 below. Alfred Marshall, Edward S. Mason, and other mainstream scholars of industrial organization generally adhered to realistic ideas about the degrees of competition. It is only some Chicago-UCLA writers who claim that the mainstream has been preoccupied with the pure, atomistic model. See especially Robert H. Bork, *The Antitrust Paradox* (New York: Basic Books, 1978); Yale Brozen, *Concentration, Mergers and Public Policy* (New York: Macmillan, 1982); and John S. McGee, *Industrial Organization* (Englewood Cliffs, N.J.: Prentice Hall, 1988).

In such cases, competition seems to be self-destructive, because the new dominant firm will prevent future competition from being effective. Effective competition requires parity so that rivals can put strong pressure on one another. Victory by any competitor destroys parity. Yet to restore parity by limiting the new monopolist could be criticized as "penalize superior efficiency." Indeed, officials of monopolistic firms denounce any resistance to their market dominance for threatening the incentive to succeed.

This problem has arisen frequently in real markets. A Standard Oil, IBM, or Eastman Kodak will attain a dominant market position (with a market share of over 50 percent) and then exert control to extract monopoly profits. Critics of their dominance are attacked for allegedly wanting to "punish success" and for being anticompetitive by rejecting the outcome of a competitive struggle.

The paradox is solved in the sports world by dividing competitors into leagues on the basis of age, size, sex, and so on. Thus parity is carefully guaranteed. Moreover, competition *recurs* again and again in a series of episodes, during distinct games, seasons, and yearly championships. No loss is permanent; play begins anew at each tourney or season, with every person or team given a fresh start on an equal footing. Also, players are mortal, and as leading athletes grow older and decline, the way is opened for others. Competition is continually renewed and is usually effective.

In industrial markets, of course, there are no such careful divisions, processes, and balancing factors. Once competition becomes lopsided and ineffective, it can stay that way indefinitely. When dominant firms gain high profits, they can use those extra resources to reinforce their position and suppress effective competition. In fact, once a firm *begins* to attain dominance, it may naturally accumulate greater profits, which then enable it to enlarge its dominance and to retain it.

The paradox of competition is therefore real and often urgent. Genuinely superior competitors need to be given sufficient rewards. But it must be remembered that dominance can be gained through *non*efficient methods. How to distinguish and guard against these cases while renewing the competitive process is a central problem.

Fortunately, competition in most actual markets remains effective and balanced. Still, it can be an unstable and fragile condition, easily lost and hard to regain. Just how fragile or self-renewing competition is will be an underlying topic in the rest of this book.

IV.   THE FIELD EVOLVES

Like every field of study, this one evolves and changes. You are entering it at a time when certain concepts and research results are prominent, but they are subject to change. By considering the history of the economics of industrial organization up to now, you will better understand how to evaluate the field's current content and anticipate future changes. The main lines are given here; Appendix 1 at the end of the book surveys the field's history in greater detail.

1.   Debates That Are Embodied in the Literature

"The field" is created by the thinking and writing of specialists, most of whom are professors at leading universities. What they write becomes "the literature," as you will see in the footnotes of this book and the bibliography in the appendix to Chapter 2. Each article and book is really part of an ongoing debate in which experts try to promote their own research views (and, of course, their own careers!).

The research is published in professional journals and book-length monographs, and these papers and books comprise the core of "the literature of industrial organization." Far from being dry articles and tomes, many of them are weapons hurled against the opposing side in the ongoing intellectual battles of the field. Authors seek to disprove earlier ideas or results and to establish their own points.

The debates in the literature thrash out the conflicting ideas and evidence, so that in the flow of things sound concepts and evidence should prevail. The research and writings are influenced by what is happening in the economy—for example, merger waves or a general trend to higher competition. So reality shapes research and the academic notions of markets. Public policies toward industry also interact with the ongoing research. If, for instance, U.S. officials encourage a merger boom, as they did in the 1980s, that will stimulate research into the effects of mergers (see Chapter 8). And the deregulation of airlines has spawned a wave of new research into that experiment (see Chapter 18).

The process of debate is intensely human, with clashes among "schools," ideologies, and vested interests. With luck, the best ideas endure, and the literature evolves a core of sound concepts and methods for testing them. But remember, these are merely people's ideas, not immutable laws or engraved truths. They often lag many years behind events, and some topics are neglected for decades. Moreover, dubious "new" ideas can crowd out solid older concepts as fads and fashions come and go.

The "best" specialists are few: perhaps 10 or 15 scholars are most influential in each decade, but they are constantly engaged in controversy with one another. All writers, both the leading and the lesser ones, are fallible, often making errors of logic and facts. Indeed, since their writings clash so repeatedly, they obviously must be incorrect much of the time. The urge to make a name for themselves or win debating points can lead scholars to press ideas that are shallow or empty.

The debates sometimes lead the field astray, causing it to retrogress or go on detours, rather than progressing steadily. That has probably happened since 1970, when the "new IO theory" began to crowd out valid, established research knowledge with untested ideas. Still, there is room for widely differing views on nearly every issue, so long as they are plausible.

Consequently, industrial organization is a lively, contentious, and changing discipline that is still being hammered out in a rugged setting of powerful vested interests. Each student must think the issues through independently, developing a keen sense for what is mainly valid, possibly biased, or even merely wrong.

2.   Main Lines and Periods of the Debates

Understanding industrial organization's rich history is crucial to evaluating the merits of current ideas. That history is a long and distinguished one, with important contributions beginning over a century ago.

Origins.   The modern study of competition and monopoly began in the 1880s.[8] Some of its concepts were deeply and firmly set by 1901 through the work of John Bates Clark, Henry Carter Adams, Richard T. Ely, and Charles J. Bullock, among many others. The spectacular wave of dominant-firm-creating mergers during 1897–1901 merely intensified the debates and gave them major industrial applications.

Most of the current ideas at the center of the field—degrees of monopoly, actual and potential competition, the efficiency and other effects of monopoly, economies and diseconomies of scale, oligopoly, price discrimination, first-mover advantages, the importance of innovation, dynamic processes, overhead costs, risk and uncertainty—had been discussed extensively by 1925.[9] Not only Alfred Marshall in England but also J. B. Clark, Ely, Adams, Bullock, Knight, J. M. Clark, and other economists in the United States had advanced the literature far, and the concepts had been applied to a large number of major industries.[10]

The 1930s.[11]   The modern technical field began in the 1930s, with more complex theoretical study of "the oligopoly problem" (e.g., Chamberlin, Robinson), extensive statistical research on concentration, costs, and profits, the Temporary National Economic Committee investigations of 1939–1941, and the formation of the field's basic conceptual design.[12] Structure was seen as influencing behavior and performance, though not rigidly or hermetically. There was much anxiety that corporate power was increasing and causing higher economic instability, as Karl Marx had predicted in *Das Kapital* (see Chapter 7).

The 1940s and 1950s.   Research increased rapidly, generally showing the serious dimensions, anticompetitive sources, and harms of monopoly power.[13]

[8] See John Bates Clark, "The Limits of Competition," *Political Science Quarterly*, 2 (1887), 45–61; Henry C. Adams, "Trusts," in American Economic Association, *Papers and Proceedings,* December 1903, Vol. 5, pp. 91–107; Richard T. Ely, *Monopolies and Trusts,* New York: Macmillan, 1900; and Charles J. Bullock, "Trust Literature: A Survey and Criticism," *Quarterly Journal of Economics,* 15 (February 1901), 167–217;

[9] See Alfred Marshall, *Industry and Trade* (London: Macmillan, 1920); Knight, *Risk, Uncertainty and Profit;* John M. Clark, *Studies in the Economics of Overhead Costs* (New York: Macmillan, 1922).

[10] Major studies and antitrust actions occurred in the first wave of Sherman Act, Section 2, cases against Standard Oil, American Tobacco, U.S. Steel, Du Pont gunpowder, International Harvester, the meatpackers' oligopoly, ALCOA, and even AT&T. See Philip Areeda and Donald F. Turner, *Antitrust Law,* 7 vols. (Boston: Little, Brown, 1978 et seq.); Hans B. Thorelli, *The Federal Antitrust Policy* (Chicago: University of Chicago Press, 1954); and William Letwin, *Law and Economic Policy in America* (New York: Random House, 1965).

[11] Chamberlin, *Theory of Monopolistic Competition;* and Robinson, *Economics of Imperfect Competition.* Another influential book was Adolph A. Berle and Gardiner C. Means, *The Modern Corporation and Private Property* (New York: Macmillan, 1932).

[12] In the 21 TNEC reports and extensive hearings, Congress explored the dimensions of corporate power and its effects. Among much chaff, see the two superb report volumes: Walton Hamilton and Irene Till, *Antitrust in Action,* Vol. 16, and Clair Wilcox, *Competition and Monopoly in the American Economy,* Vol. 21 (Temporary National Economic Committee, Washington, D.C.: U.S. Government Printing Office, 1940).

[13] See William J. Fellner, *Competition Among the Few* (New York: Knopf, 1949), for a major formulation of the oligopoly problem; and George W. Stocking and Myron W. Watkins, *Monopoly and Free Enterprise* (New York: Twentieth Century Fund, 1951). See also Morris A. Adelman, "The Measurement of Industrial Concentration," *Review of Economics and Statistics,* 33 (November 1951), 269–96; and Fritz Machlup, *The Political Economy of Monopoly* (Baltimore: Johns Hopkins Press, 1952), and *The Economics of Sellers' Competition* (Baltimore: Johns Hopkins Press, 1952).

A major summary of the field as it stood is provided by George J. Stigler, ed., *Business Concentration*

Stocking and Watkins assembled detailed assessments of cartels and monopoly conditions, both in foreign and domestic markets. Fritz Machlup published comprehensive, sophisticated assessments of monopoly, strategic actions, and public policies. By 1955, Stigler could assemble a wide range of scholarship on major branches of the field. Joe S. Bain's work on barriers emerged in 1956, Simon Whitney surveyed some 20 industries in 1958, and Kaysen and Turner provided a comprehensive, subtle analysis of the tight-oligopoly problem in 1959. Many case studies of important industries accumulated, both from scholarly treatises and antitrust cases.

The 1960s.   Next came many broad-scale econometric studies of structure and performance, by Weiss, Scherer, Comanor and Wilson, this author, and others. Williamson developed further the study of internal complexities of firm behavior.[14] Leibenstein's X-efficiency concept debuted in 1966.[15] Edwin Mansfield and his associates prepared extensive studies of innovation, and Scherer's work in the mid-1960s was important.[16] Scherer's survey treatise on the entire field appeared in 1970.[17]

Moreover, public-utility economics—with lengthy study of profit and price-cost criteria—had undergone sharp changes in the 1960s, and Alfred E. Kahn's classic volumes on the subject appeared in 1971.[18] Stigler had fostered a series of studies seeking to show that regulation had few good effects, and the Chicago-UCLA challenge to mainstream ideas was developing.[19]

In short, there was a large accumulation of knowledge and technical skills, combining theory, econometrics, cases, and policy issues. There was vigorous debate among many schools and research methodologies, and no orthodoxy prevailed. Meanwhile, antitrust and regulatory policies were quite moderate (for example, the prospect of a Bell System divestiture was scarcely conceivable, and the deregulation of railroads and airlines was only a faint hope).

Since 1970.   After 1970, the mainstream continued to develop, including a

and Price Policy (Princeton, N.J.: Princeton University Press, 1955). Joe S. Bain, *Barriers to New Competition* (Cambridge, Mass.: Harvard University Press, 1956), started the systematic study of entry barriers.

Other influential works in the 1950s include Mason, *Economic Concentration and the Monopoly Problem;* Simon N. Whitney, *Antitrust Policies: American Experience in Twenty Industries,* 2 vols. (New York: Twentieth Century Fund, 1958); Morris A. Adelman, *A & P: A Study in Price-Cost Behavior and Public Policy* (Cambridge, Mass: Harvard University Press, 1959); Kaysen and Turner, *Antitrust Policy: An Economic and Legal Analysis;* Martin Shubik, *Strategy and Market Structure* (New York: Wiley, 1959); and Walter Adams and Horace Gray, *Monopoly in America: The Government as Promoter* (New York: MacMillan, 1955).

[14] See Oliver E. Williamson, *The Economics of Discretionary Behavior* (Chicago: Markham, 1967); and Richard M. Cyert and James G. March, *A Behavioral Theory of the Firm* (Englewood Cliffs, N.J.: Prentice Hall, 1963).

[15] Harvey J. Leibenstein, "Allocative Efficiency vs. 'X-Efficiency,'" *American Economic Review,* 56 (June 1966), 392–415; and *Beyond Economic Man* (Cambridge, Mass.: Harvard University Press, 1976) by the same author.

[16] See Edwin Mansfield, *Industrial Research and Technological Innovation* (New York: Norton, 1968); and Edwin Mansfield and others, *Research and Innovation in the Modern Corporation* (New York: Norton, 1971); and the papers by F. M. Scherer gathered in his *Innovation and Growth* (Cambridge, Mass.: MIT Press, 1986).

[17] F. M. Scherer, *Industrial Market Structure and Economic Performance* (Boston: Houghton, 1970).

[18] Alfred E. Kahn, *The Economics of Regulation,* 2 vols. (New York: Wiley, 1970).

[19] See papers collected by Stigler in his *The Organization of Industry* (Homewood, Ill.: Irwin, 1968).

renewed focus on market share as a main indicator of market power. Other important research directions include Scherer and associates on the economies of scale, Williamson on transactions costs, Leibenstein and others on X-efficiency, Michael Porter on enterprises' competitive strategies, many econometric studies of profitability and structure, Dennis Mueller and Ravenscraft and Scherer on mergers, my assessment of the trend of competition, and scores of case studies.[20]

But three schools of "new IO theory" gained influence: (1) pure theoretical strategic modeling, (2) the full versions of Chicago-UCLA theory about monopoly, and (3) "contestability" theory.

"NEW IO THEORY:" COURNOT-NASH MODELING OF STRATEGIC CHOICES. Rising numbers of theorists began to develop pure theoretical models to try out interesting propositions about duopolies. This "strategic analysis" is usually based on very abstract (short-run, Cournot-Nash) assumptions (see Chapter 13), using only static consumer surplus as the criterion for assessing the benefits of competition.[21] The analysis is usually strictly theoretical, with little effort at empirical testing or fitting to real cases.

Some of this work could clarify real markets, but most of it should be considered a new, separate field, often called "new IO theory." Although these theoretical models are characterized by increasing rigor, they often lack a grounding in real competitive processes. The resulting theories (see Chapter 13 for a summary) have provided many "insights," but they have modest practical uses.

CHICAGO-UCLA ANALYSIS. Meanwhile the Chicago-UCLA movement to minimize the costs of monopoly came to full flower.[22] It urged four main hypotheses:

---

[20] For excellent reviews of "new IO theory," see Jean Tirole, *The Theory of Industrial Organization* (Cambridge, Mass.: MIT Press, 1988): Michael Waterson, *Economic Theory of Industry* (Cambridge: Cambridge University Press, 1984); Lester Telser, *Theories of Competition* (Amsterdam: North-Holland, 1988); Joseph E. Stiglitz and C. Frank Mathewson, eds., *New Developments in the Analysis of Market Structure* (Cambridge, Mass.: MIT Press, 1986); and Alexis Jacquemin, *The New Industrial Organization* (Cambridge, Mass.: MIT Press, 1987).

[21] On economies of scale, see F. M. Scherer et al., *The Economics of Multiplant Operation* (Cambridge, Mass.: Harvard University Press, 1975); and Leonard W. Weiss, "Optimal Plant Size and the Extent of Suboptimal Capacity," in Robert T. Masson and P. David Qualls, eds., *Essays on Industrial Organization in Honor of Joe S. Bain* (Cambridge, Mass.: Ballinger, 1976). On transaction costs, see Oliver E. Williamson, *Markets and Hierarchies* (New York: Free Press, 1975). On X-efficiency, see Harvey J. Leibenstein, *Beyond Economic Man* (Cambridge, Mass.: Harvard University Press, 1976). On competitive strategies, see Michael E. Porter, *Competitive Strategy: Techniques for Analyzing Industries and Competitors* (New York: Free Press, 1980); and Porter, *Competitive Advantage: Creating and Sustaining Superior Performance* (New York: Free Press, 1985). For summaries of profitability and structure studies, see Scherer, *Industrial Market Structure*, chapter 9; and Chapters 3, 4 and 5 below. On mergers, see Dennis C. Mueller, ed., *The Determinants and Effects of Mergers: An International Comparison* (Cambridge, Mass.: Oelgeschlager, Gunn and Hain, 1980); and David J. Ravenscraft and F. M. Scherer, *Mergers, Sell-offs and Economic Efficiency* (Washington, D.C.: Brookings Institution, 1987). On the trend of competition, see my "Causes of Increased Competition in the US Economy, 1939–1980," *Review of Economics and Statistics* 64 (November 1982): 613–26. Examples of case studies are given in the Appendix to Chapter 2 below.

[22] Leading writings include Stigler, *The Organization of Industry;* Brozen, *Concentration, Mergers and Public Policy;* John S. McGee, *In Defense of Industrial Concentration* (Seattle: University of Washington Press, 1971), "Predatory Pricing Revisited," *Journal of Law and Economics* 23 (October 1980), 289–330, and *Industrial Organization;* Harold Demsetz, "Industry Structure, Market Rivalry, and Public Policy," *Journal of Law and Economics,* April 1973, pp. 1–9, and "Two Systems of Belief about Monopoly," a chapter in Harvey J. Goldschmid, H. Michael Mann, and J. Fred Weston, eds., *Industrial Concentration: The New Learning* (Boston: Little, Brown, 1974).

(1) Monopoly reflects superior efficiency. (2) The costs of attaining monopoly commonly use up any possible monopoly profits. (3) Market dominance has only minimal harmful effects. (4) Collusion is the only pure form of market power, and it quickly collapses from cheating by the colluders.

These ideas were asserted largely without evidence, but their optimism was catching. In 1981, the Reagan administration came into office ready to use these doctrines as a rationale for eliminating most antitrust policies and continuing to deregulate many sectors.

"CONTESTABILITY" THEORY.   During 1975–1982, a third school developed, the Baumol-Bailey-Willig "contestability school," which focused on free entry.[23] These theorists argued that internal structure was secondary in importance to possible entry from outside, and therefore that their new theory of entry was more fundamental than the established theory of competition and should displace it. This approach was still being debated as the 1980s ended.

Altogether, the 1970–1985 period brought marked changes in the field, in the economy, and in policies toward market power. As the economy grew more competitive, many economists embraced pure-theory modeling, the Chicago-UCLA view that monopoly was beneficial, and the assumption that entry nullified the dangers of monopoly. The anticompetitive ways to gain monopoly power were denied or neglected, as if the field's core research had suddenly vanished. Indeed, most "new IO theory" writers cite only one another's papers (all written since 1975), ignoring the rich, accumulated research in the mainstream.

Not only has the U.S. economy become a vast practical experiment in enhanced competition. The field has also experimented in the 1980s with extreme doctrines, which simply deny the importance of monopoly power. IO economics is in turbulence, with no clear outcome. For you, as for scholars in the field, these doctrines pose a special need for careful judgment, using logic and weighing facts.

One of the few Chicago-UCLA attempts at empirical verification of the basic position is in Sam Peltzman, "The Gains and Losses from Industrial Concentration," *Journal of Law and Economics,* 20 (October 1977), 229–63. See also Richard A. Posner, *Antitrust Law* (Chicago: University of Chicago Press, 1976), and "The Social Costs of Monopoly and Regulation," *Journal of Political Economy,* August 1976, pp. 807–27.

For more extreme views, see John Carter, "Collusion, Efficiency and Antitrust," *Journal of Law and Economics,* 21 (October 1978), 435–44; Bork, *The Antitrust Paradox;* and Dominick T. Armentano, *Antitrust and Monopoly: Anatomy of a Policy Failure* (New York: Wiley, 1982).

The papers have mostly appeared in one Chicago journal (the *Journal of Law and Economics*), rather than in a variety of leading mainstream journals.

For a parallel view, see Franklin M. Fisher, "On the Misuse of Accounting Rates of Return to Infer Monopoly Profits," *American Economic Review,* 73 (March 1983), 82–92; and Franklin M. Fisher, John J. McGowan, and Joan E. Greenwood, *Folded, Spindled and Mutilated: Economic Analysis and US vs. IBM* (Cambridge, Mass.: MIT Press, 1983).

[23] See especially William J. Baumol, John C. Panzar, and Robert D. Willig, *Contestable Markets and the Theory of Industrial Structure* (San Diego, Cal.: Harcourt Brace Jovanovich, 1982), and Baumol and Willig, "Contestability: Developments Since the Book," *Oxford Economic Papers,* special supplement (November 1986).

For critical reviews, see W. G. Shepherd, " 'Contestability' versus Competition," *American Economic Review,* 74 (September 1984), 572–87; and Marius Schwartz, "The Nature and Scope of Contestability Theory," *Oxford Economic Papers,* special supplement (November 1986).

V.   THE SEQUENCE OF TOPICS

This book is organized to convey the fundamentals and details in a logical sequence that shows how they relate to one another. First come the basic theories of competition and monopoly in Chapter 2. This chapter is followed by an appendix surveying the methods and topics typically involved in writing student research papers; a summary bibliography for the entire field is included. Then come the four major topic areas: Part II, Market Structure; Part III, Performance; Part IV, Determinants of Market Structure; and Part V, Behavior and Related Topics.

After much experimenting, I have found that putting Structure and Performance back to back is extremely valuable for showing their fundamental linkage. It enables readers to see directly the effects of the normative properties of structure. It also permits me to present more fully the issue of causation, so that students can assess mainstream, Chicago-UCLA, and "contestability" evidence more clearly.

Chapter 3 presents the important topic of defining markets, and then surveys the four intermediate categories of competition. Chapter 4 shows how to assess evidence about the actual structure of the U.S. economy. Part III, the Performance chapters, consider the effects of monopoly on prices, profits, and efficiency (Chapter 5), on innovation (Chapter 6), and on fairness and other elements (Chapter 7).

In Part IV on Determinants, Chapter 8 covers all influences on structure *other than* the economies of scale. Chapter 9 then rounds out the coverage by treating the methods and results of research on scale economies and diseconomies.

Part V, Behavior and Related Topics, covers a wide range of subjects. First is the nature of the firm as the building block of the economy in Chapter 10. Monopoly and dominant firms are covered in Chapter 11. The closely related topics of price discrimination and "predatory" (that is, anticompetitive) actions are treated in Chapter 12.

Next, Chapter 13 presents theories of oligopoly, with special attention to barriers to new competition and "contestability." Chapter 14 turns to the main evidence about oligopoly collusion and strife in real markets. Chapter 15 moves to quite different topics: vertical ties between stages of production (e.g., between smelting and fabricating metals), and conglomerate ties that link wholly unrelated types of production (e.g., rubber tires and coffee). Finally, the fascinating topic of advertising is taken up in Chapter 16: Does it generally suppress competition or sharpen it?

Next, in Part VI, Chapter 17 presents five case studies of dominant firms, and Chapter 18 gives four case studies of tight oligopolies. These chapters have two purposes. One is to demonstrate how the elements of the analysis fit together in real cases; the other is to show how a variety of industries, from cereals and aircraft to newspapers, electricity, and sports, can be clarified by the concepts of industrial organization.

Two chapters on U.S. public policies round out the text. Chapter 19 summarizes antitrust policies, while Chapter 20 covers (very briefly) regulation of utilities, deregulation, public enterprise, and privatization.

Several appendixes give further details on topics that may particularly interest some teachers and students. A fuller history of the field is presented in Appendix 1. Appendix 2 discusses the SIC (Standard Industrial Classification) system used by the U.S. Census Bureau. Appendix 3 covers a variety of problems that arise in using data in this field, including structure, profits, costs, and simple accounting issues. Finally, Appendix 4 provides guidance in interpreting statistical evidence.

So: Welcome to the dramatic and intriguing world of industrial organization! It treats fateful matters, as well as many strange and amusing ones. It illuminates modern capitalism, from the arcane realms of high finance and high corporate power to the humble shops along thousands of Main Streets.

QUESTIONS FOR REVIEW

1. Explain how the inelasticity of demand for the firm governs the degree of monopoly, by controlling the range for raising price.
2. "To assess the degree of competition, simply count the number of firms. More firms, more competition." Explain the problem with this.
3. Explain the basic logic of causation in the triad of structure-behavior-performance.
4. Explain how the Chicago-UCLA view reverses the logic of the structure, behavior and performance. Show how it makes monopoly appear to be valuable and desirable.
5. Has competition been rising or falling in the US economy since 1960? By a little or a lot?
6. Which categories of markets have generally ineffective competition? Please give real examples of each kind.
7. What conditions make for effective competition?
8. Explain the "paradox of competition." Does the aim of efficiency conflict with the need to renew competitive parity?

2 THEORIES OF COMPETITION AND MONOPOLY

Recall the three basic points: (1) Competition enhances performance; (2) monopoly power distorts it; but (3) monopoly power may have offsetting benefits, from economies of scale or superior performance. Now we consider the standard theories about these truths, especially using the standard neoclassical analysis.

The chapter is about *logic and concepts*. Later chapters will develop the concepts in more detail and deal with the questions of *facts and degree,* using statistics and cases.

First come the criteria for "good" performance, in Section I. Next, Section II presents competition's role as an "invisible hand" guiding the market system toward efficiency and progress. But this hand does not reach everywhere; Section II also shows its limits. Section III introduces monopoly power and shows its several effects. Finally, Section IV compares monopoly's costs to its possible benefits.

Many readers will find the material familiar from introductory economics or intermediate microeconomic theory. But this chapter contains additional points, which need careful reading. This is, after all, a different field.

I. PERFORMANCE VALUES

Economic performance has many dimensions, but economists commonly focus on three main elements: efficiency, innovation, and fairness in distribution.[1] Chapter 1 noted them briefly, and they are summarized in Table 2.1. Moreover, the competitive process itself has important intrinsic values. In addition, competition can affect other, broader values, including freedom of choice, the avoidance of insecurity, and social diversity.

---

[1] Which values to include, and how to rank them, are old and important issues lying at the heart of economic science. Among important sources are Alfred Marshall, *Principles of Economics,* 8th ed. (London: Macmillan, 1920); and Joe S. Bain, *Industrial Organization,* rev. ed. (New York: Wiley, 1968).

For two sharply contrasting views, see John M. Blair, *Economic Concentration* (New York: Harcourt, Brace, Jovanovich, 1972); and Robert H. Bork, *The Antitrust Paradox: A Policy at War with Itself* (New York: Basic Books, 1978). Blair presents an expansive view that embraces broad values, including the value of competition itself. Bork subscribes to the narrow view, in which only the maximization of consumer surplus, in static terms, is relevant.

TABLE 2.1   Performance Values

1. *Efficiency in Resource Allocation*
   a. *Internal efficiency* (also called "X-efficiency," or "business efficiency"). Firms evoke maximum efforts from their employees and avoid all slack in operations.
   b. *Allocative efficiency.* Resources are allocated among markets and firms in patterns that maximize the value of total output. No revision of production could raise the total value. In all firms, prices are set equal to long-run marginal cost and minimum average cost.
   c. *Avoiding resource waste.* Simple wastes of resources are avoided, including persuasive advertising, which only alters consumer preference.
2. *Technological Progress*
   There is speed in the invention and innovation of new products and of new production methods.
3. *Equity in Distribution*
   There is a fair distribution (in line with the society's standards of fairness) of wealth, income, and opportunity.
4. *The Competitive Process*
   Competition itself provides social values.
5. *Other Dimensions*
   Such values as individual freedom of choice, security from extreme risk, and cultural diversity are provided.

1.   Efficiency

Efficiency's basic meaning is simple: a maximum total value of outputs from any given set of inputs. Any simple waste of inputs is to be avoided, of course, so that there is no idleness or functionless use of resources. Beyond that, efficiency is traditionally divided into two main categories: internal efficiency and allocative efficiency.

Internal Efficiency.   Good management minimizes the firm's costs for attaining each level of output. This condition of X-efficiency, as it is often called, is reached when (1) the use of inputs is kept to a minimum and (2) all employees put forth maximum effort.[2]

Though this goal is obvious, managements often slip from it, as the detailed discussion in Chapter 5 will show. Like all human beings, managers tend to perform better when they are under some pressure and to relax when pressures are reduced. In very large companies, which have large profit flows, it is often easy for internal efficiency to slacken.

X-inefficiency occurs in two main forms: (1) in buying more inputs than are necessary, and (2) in low effort levels by employees. It is the excess of actual costs over minimum possible costs. As shown in Figure 2.1 by points *A* and *B* for output

---

[2] The phrase was coined by Harvey J. Leibenstein in his "Allocative Efficiency and 'X-Efficiency,'" *American Economic Review*, 56 (June 1966), 392–415. The full theory is in his *Beyond Economic Man* (Cambridge: Harvard University Press, 1976).

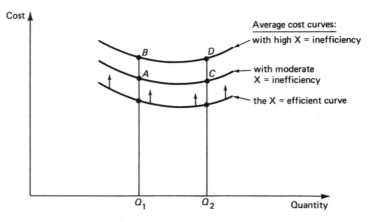

FIGURE 2.1.   Illustrations of X-efficient and X-inefficient cost curves.

Q_1, and C and D for output Q_2, it means being above the lowest possible average cost curve. Its amount is:

$$\text{Degree of X-inefficiency} = \frac{\text{Excess cost}}{\text{Actual cost}}$$

X-inefficiency is a routine occurrence, and many actual cases of X-inefficient firms are freely discussed in the business press. The amounts of excess costs are hard to measure, so each case is debatable. Most cases probably fall in the range of 1 to 10 percent of costs, as Chapter 5 will discuss.

Allocative Efficiency.   This is a set of general equilibrium conditions, in which the net value of production cannot be increased by changing the allocation. Each output is at the level where marginal cost equals price for each product of each firm, throughout the economy. Price will also equal the minimum level of long-run average cost. These and other Pareto conditions apply throughout the economy. Even if they are reached only approximately, the result can be close to maximum efficiency.

As a result, consumer surplus is maximized. Consumer surplus is the excess of value that consumers receive over what they must pay for a good. It is shown by the area under the demand curve but *above* the price paid for the good, as illustrated in Figure 2.2. It occurs whenever a consumer buys more than one unit of a good.

The size of the consumer surplus depends on the elasticity of demand. Low elasticity means that consumer surplus is large (panel I of Figure 2.2); it occurs for goods that are "urgently wanted," like life-giving drugs and other "necessities" such as water, food, and housing. With high elasticity (when there are close substitutes), consumer surplus is small (panel II of Figure 2.2).

An efficient outcome will maximize consumer surplus by forcing prices down to costs. The total of all shaded areas under all demand curves in the economy is then as large as possible. Even if the result is reached only approximately, it is a powerful one.

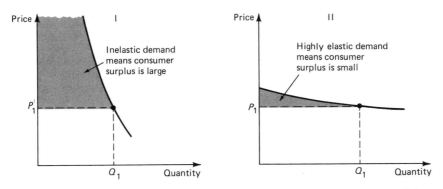

FIGURE 2.2. The amount of consumer surplus depends on elasticity of demand.

Avoidance of Waste.   One added element of allocative efficiency is the avoidence of certain functionless activities. Economists usually point to advertising as partly functionless. When it *provides information,* advertising promotes efficiency. But when it merely attempts to *persuade,* altering consumer preferences rather than adding to consumer information, advertising is a cost that does not improve efficiency. Actually, much advertising may have no effect, so both the preference-changing and ineffective parts of it are possible inefficiencies.

2. Technological Progress[3]

Efficiency occurs within a given state of the art. Innovation raises the state of the art, so that more output can be gotten from the same inputs. That is clearly desirable.

Innovation is also glamorous because it brings new products and processes. Further, its yields can be high. The rate of innovation tends to grow geometrically, like compound interest, so that a sustained high rate of innovation can cumulate to extremely high payoffs over a series of years.

But innovation is seldom free; usually it requires resources to accomplish, often called *R&D* (for research and development). Therefore the correct goal is a rapid rate of innovation, but with only the amount of R&D spending that is efficient for each period.

Innovation also involves uncertainty, for it explores the unknown and untried. For example, the prospects for nuclear fusion power and bioengineering are uncertain. Moreover, even defining and measuring innovation are difficult, as Chapter 6 will show.

Yet the basic criterion is clear, and it is similar to that for allocative efficiency. The current R&D resources devoted to innovation are to be used in each industry and firm just up to the margin at which their expected benefits (discounted for un-

---

[3] For discussions of the basic concepts, see Jacob Schmookler, *Invention and Economic Growth* (Cambridge, Mass.: Harvard University Press, 1967); and Edwin Mansfield, *The Economics of Technological Change* (New York: Norton, 1968). See also John Jewkes, David Sawers, and Richard Stillerman, *The Sources of Invention,* 2nd ed. (New York: Norton, 1969); and Morton I. Kamien and Nancy L. Schwartz, *Market Structure and Innovation* (Cambridge: Cambridge University Press, 1982).

certainty about the outcomes) equals their cost. Moreover, the R&D activities are to be done with complete *internal* efficiency.

3. Equity

Equity means fairness in distribution in three dimensions: wealth, income, and opportunity. Fairness can be separate from efficiency and innovation: an efficient and innovative economy is often relatively fair, but it may be unfair to a small or large degree. Because competition and monopoly can deeply affect distribution, fairness is an appropriate goal to consider.[4]

Fairness is an important value, but unfortunately it cannot be defined simply. It involves ethics, and there are numerous contrasting ethical criteria of fairness. One is *equality,* which is rooted in Western values of sharing and social justice. Another is *effort.* A third is *contribution* (or productivity): this criterion often relates to effort, but it also derives from talent and training. *Need* is still another criterion. There are others, too, but these four are enough to indicate the diversity among possible criteria of fairness.

The criteria may coincide or diverge, from case to case. A provisional summary of traditional standards in the United States might be: a broad preference for equality, modified for clear differences in effort and contribution, with an avoidance of great extremes of wealth and poverty. Opportunity is especially to be made equal.

4. Competition as a Value

The competitive process itself provides value, as part of an open society that is responsive to change. When competition is fair, it provides an array of opportunities, freedom of choice, an outlet for talent, and incentives for superior performance. Sports clearly illustrate how competition energizes and widens the scope of people's abilities. In virtually all categories of human endeavor, at all kinds of work, in the arts, in inventing, and in setting personal ambitions, competition is a powerful stimulus toward excellence and diversity.

Therefore the presence of an effective competitive process is an important element of good performance. Competition on a *personal* level can impose certain costs, especially when competition among people in the workplace is severe. This sort of competition can be divisive and result in stress.

But again, these costs arise mainly in *personal* competition. In the *industrial* arena, there is no reason to seek less than maximal competition—what Chicago-UCLA economists call "hard competition"—so as to generate the highest levels of corporate performance. Effective competition matters in its own right, as well as for the good performance it induces.

---

[4] Some economists take the narrow view that distribution is strictly an ethical matter, outside the competence of economists to analyze. In this view, all distributions are ethically neutral; none (even if one person owns everything) can be said to be better or worse than any other, except by mere personal opinion. There are complex elements to this debate, but in any case, the field has not adopted this position.

5. Other Values

Other values include *freedom of choice*. It cannot be absolute, because in all societies one person's liberties often conflict with those of others. Yet some economies and societies do provide their members with much wider freedoms than others. Competition enhances such freedoms by giving wide access to markets, both for producers and for consumers.

Security from extreme risk is another value. Risks include personal injury, loss of job, and financial ruin from sickness and other random events. Good *content of jobs* is another goal. Jobs define much of our personal identity, and they occupy most of our waking hours. An otherwise optimal economy can impose unpleasant or degrading jobs on many people.

Cultural richness is also a value. People have diverse interests, and good performance includes a variety of goods and services, in the arts as well as in industry. Each society's cultural preferences will differ from those of other societies. Yet the negative extreme is clear—a wasteland in which Gradgrinds and Babbitts rule, perhaps destroying natural and cultural values.

II. COMPETITION AND PERFORMANCE

Under certain conditions, competition will achieve these goals of efficiency, progress, fairness, and other values. Competition's role in reaching efficiency will be shown first, with the metaphor of the "invisible hand."

1. An Invisible Hand?

Perfect Competition.   *Perfect* competition is *pure* competition, plus certain strict assumptions:

1. Perfect knowledge by all participants of all relevant present and future conditions in the market.
2. Perfect mobility of resources and participants.
3. Rational behavior by all participants (consumers maximize utility, producers maximize profits).
4. Stability of the underlying preferences, technology, and surroundings, so that an equilibrium can be reached.
5. No nonmarket interdependencies among consumers or producers.
6. Pure competition on both sides of every market. Each firm's average costs turn up at a very small level, relative to the entire market, so that all firms have small market shares.

Assumptions 1 and 2 are extreme and unattainable, so most neoclassical analysis ignores perfect competition and relies instead on pure competition. It, too, is strict, but its assumptions may be reasonably approximated in many markets: large numbers of sellers and buyers in each market, each operating independently and with little market influence. The resulting process adjusts toward efficient allocation.

Each firm's choices are simple and familiar, as is shown in panel I of Figure

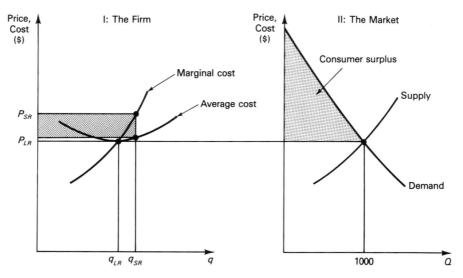

FIGURE 2.3.   Conditions reached under competition.

2.3. Technology is embodied in the production function, which determines the average and marginal cost curves in panel I. Average cost declines at low output levels; there is a point or range of optimal scale where average cost is lowest, and then diseconomies of scale set in. In Figure 2.3, by assumption, the curve has a definite U shape, so that the firm must remain small in its market.

The firm maximizes its profits (a purely commercial, private goal that is much narrower than the many social goals reviewed earlier). The firm has to set output at the level where

$$\text{Price} = \text{Marginal cost} = \text{Minimum average cost}$$

in order to survive in the long run, when price is forced down to P_{LR} in panel I. If price should briefly rise, say to P_{SR}, excess profits will be briefly available, as shown by the shaded rectangle.

The firm's demand curve is a horizontal line at the going market price because this pure competitor has no discretion over price. It is a "price taker," not a "price maker." Its flat demand curve has infinitely high elasticity. To maximize profits, the firm (like all firms) sets output where marginal revenue equals marginal cost. The flat demand curve ensures that *marginal revenue equals average revenue* (which is price itself, by definition), so *price equals marginal cost*. In the long run, the choice lies at the low point of the average cost curve, where *price equals long-run marginal cost and the minimum level of average cost.*

Managers of firms do not make these choices explicitly, using these diagrams, but that does not matter. Rational action, plus the need to survive, drives them to behave usually as if they did make these choices. The end results, in inputs, outputs, and marginal conditions, are the same.

There is no X-inefficiency because inefficient firms cannot survive. Also, the firms use inputs up to the point where each input's marginal contribution to the value of production just equals its price. All elements of the producer's choices are efficient. Consumer choices are also efficient. Each good is consumed to the point where its marginal utility is in line with its price. Under competition in every market, the system is efficient throughout, since no marginal shift could improve allocation: any gain from increasing output of one kind would be less than the sum of losses caused by reductions in other outputs.

This price–marginal cost result has a surprisingly deep meaning. *Price* is the degree of value or esteem for the good that people feel, as shown by what they are willing to pay for it out of their own pockets, in free choices between this and other goods. From Adam Smith, David Ricardo, John Stuart Mill, and Alfred Marshall on, price in free markets has held center stage as the basic measure of true economic value.

Marginal cost is an equally profound index of the true sacrifice made to produce the efficient level of the good. Work is onerous. Tangible resources are scarce, as their prices show. Marginal cost precisely reflects the summed sacrifice made by everybody who participates in producing the good.

Logic and good sense require that value and sacrifice be in line with each other at the margin: price = marginal cost does just that. All resources are used efficiently throughout the economy, without any central direction or plan.

The "invisible hand" of the competitive market system guides allocation in numberless firms and markets. The selfish actors striving to maximize their own good are unconcerned with any social goals. Yet their actions bring about efficiency throughout the economy.

Moreover, the efficient competitive result is robust. Even if there are small or moderate departures from the pure conditions, the main properties of efficiency are retained. Price is still brought quickly toward marginal cost, so that any deviation between the two is small. Consumer surplus is still virtually maximized, consistent with covering the costs of production. Any excess profits are small.

2. Limits

But there are limits to the reach of the "invisible hand." The process may create a universal optimum or, instead, only a small domain of efficiency within a wider realm of nonoptimal conditions. The actual outcome depends on five conditions.

External Effects.   There may be external costs or benefits. Private prices and costs will then diverge from their true social levels. For example, air pollution is a negative effect of production (chimneys emitting smoke, creating acid rain that attacks distant forests) and of consumption (automobiles emitting fumes and particulates). Extreme degrees of externalities may create so-called public goods, such as national defense and primary schooling. The exact, factual scope of real externalities is another topic. Here, note only that in the presence of any externality, competition generates an allocation that is socially inefficient. The invisible hand can create external harms.

Inequity.   Efficient allocation does not ensure fairness. Open competition does usually spread opportunities and wealth widely. But the efficient conditions can coexist with inequity in the distributions of wealth, income, and opportunity, as judged by ethical criteria.

For example, an oppressive, unjust feudal society that develops into a competitive, free market industrial economy may retain all its old structure of wealth and privilege, with factory hands being exploited as ruthlessly by wealthy owners as the peasants were. Or it may shift to a new structure that is even more unjust, or instead it may develop a much fairer set of distributions.

Technological Progress.   Technical change may be outside the pure competitive process. True, small firms may be innovative and flexible under market pressures. But they may be too small to carry out some large innovations. And a "free rider" problem may exist: other firms may be able to copy an innovation so quickly that the potential innovator would be unable to obtain a sufficient reward to make doing the innovation worthwhile.

These problems decrease as conditions move moderately away from pure competition. Therefore effective (but not pure) competition may generate substantial innovation while also providing efficiency.

Producers' Influence.   Producers may influence consumer preferences by advertising and other selling efforts. If producers bend consumers' preferences rather than conform to them, conclusions about efficient allocation "in line with consumer preferences" become circular and meaningless.

Other Criteria.   Competition does tend to maximize freedom, but security, job satisfaction, and culture are outside the competitive system and may be violated. There is a large literature on the desolation that relentless competitive market processes might cause, or have caused, in actual societies, such as Britain during the nineteenth century.

These limits are all matters of degree. There could be a little of each defect around the edges of a largely efficient economy, or the defects could be so large as to dwarf the gains from efficient allocation. The invisible hand remains powerful, as far as it reaches. But it has limits.

III.   EFFECTS OF MONOPOLY POWER

We return to the complete efficient outcome. Set aside the limits; assume competition is causing efficiency throughout. Now consider the effects of converting one market from competition to monopoly. As simple theory and personal experience attest, the main effects in that market are to cut output, raise price, and create excess profits. Yet the act and its effects are complex, and some of the effects are not obvious. We evaluate them step by step.

1.   The Monopolist's Choices

Pure monopoly exists when one seller controls all sales in the market. The *market* demand curve is then *its* demand curve, with whatever inelasticity exists for that product. The inelasticity gives the seller scope to choose the level of price as well as output.

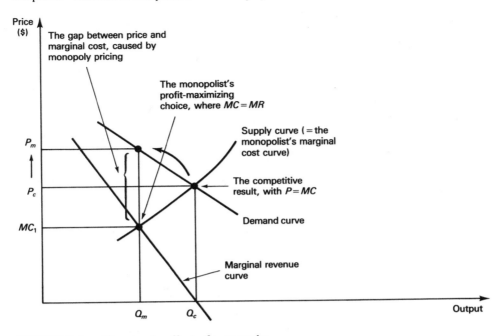

FIGURE 2.4.   The simple effect of monopoly.

Marginal Revenue.   As shown in Figure 2.4, there now materializes a marginal revenue curve, which lies below the demand curve. Marginal revenue is now less than price, because the firm must cut its price in order to sell a higher quantity. It therefore loses revenue that it would have drawn from the infra-marginal units. So its net receipt from an added unit (that is, ιne marginal revenue) is that unit's price *minus* the revenue lost by cutting price on all the previous units. Therefore the marginal revenue curve always lies below a down-sloping demand curve.

The marginal revenue curve is easy to locate: it lies halfway between the demand curve and the vertical axis.

Marginal Cost.   The monopolist's marginal cost schedule is the former competitive market's supply curve. This supply curve was the sum of all the competitive firms' marginal cost curves. Since the single monopolist now includes all those firms, its marginal cost curve is the summation of all the original firms' marginal cost curves.

The monopolist's two crucial curves—marginal revenue and marginal cost—cross at point *A* in Figure 2.4. That is thus the monopolist's profit-maximizing output. As always, the firm produces only up to the level at which the extra unit is just "worth it"; that is, it adds as much to revenue as it adds to costs.

Effects on Price and Output.   The monopolist violates the efficient price-equals-marginal-cost outcome by cutting output and pushing price above marginal cost. There is economic harm in that disparity. In Figure 2.4, people are willing to pay more than twice as much as the marginal cost of the good. The value they place on the good is twice as high as the cost of the resources used to produce the last unit. This is a clear signal that more of the good should be produced. If the marginal car costs $6,000 and is worth $10,000, then $4,000 of net value is lost by not producing it.

The monopolist prevents that good result by prohibiting sales between Q_m and Q_c. Price exceeding marginal cost is therefore a sign of distortion away from the efficient competitive level. The severity of this distortion depends on the elasticity of demand and the slope of the monopolist's marginal cost curve. Compared to elastic demand, inelastic demand gives smaller cuts in output but sharper rises in price. As for cost, the steeper the marginal cost curve, the smaller will be the cutback in output.

Decades ago, this effect was labeled the "Lerner Index of Monopoly."[5] It is a ratio:

$$\text{Lerner Index} = \frac{\text{Price} - \text{Marginal cost}}{\text{Price}} \qquad (2.1)$$

This ratio can be restated using the elasticity of demand:[6]

$$\text{Lerner Index} = \frac{P - MC}{P} = \frac{1}{\text{Elasticity of demand}} \qquad (2.2)$$

As elasticity rises toward infinity, the right-hand ratio approaches zero, indicating a zero level of monopoly power under pure competition. If demand elasticity for the firm is as low as, say, 1.2, then the ratio is 1/1.2, which equals 0.83. The index's minimum value is 0.0 for pure competition. Its maximum value is 1.0, where elasticity is 1.0 and marginal cost is zero. Then $P - MC$ is $P - 0.0$, so the ratio $P - MC$ over P equals simply P/P, which is 1.0.

All this recalls Chapter 1's initial presentation of monopoly power as residing in the inelasticity of the firm's demand curve. Now we have seen more formally how inelastic demand involves monopoly power, as a matter of precise degree. Unfortunately, elasticity is usually virtually impossible to measure, so the Lerner Index is more a conceptual device than a practical indicator.

In Case I in Figure 2.5, demand is inelastic and marginal cost is relatively flat. Because of these two conditions, monopoly drastically changes both output and price. The price is four times the original price and five times marginal cost. The Lerner Index is 0.8. Output is only about half of the competitive level. When people urgently need an item (a life-saving drug, for example), a monopolist can severely exploit them. In contrast, Case II shows only a mild effect: demand is more elastic, and the marginal cost curve is steeply sloped. In this case, price is only nudged up— and output down—by a little. The Lerner Index is about 0.1.

---

[5] After Abba P. Lerner's early discussion of it in "The Concept of Monopoly and the Measurement of Monopoly Power," *Review of Economic Studies,* June 1934, pp. 157–75.

[6] Because marginal revenue equals marginal cost at the profit-maximizing price, *MR* can be substituted for *MC* in equation (2.1). After rearranging terms and changing the value of elasticity to positive, the result is as shown in equation (2.2), incorporating the elasticity of demand.

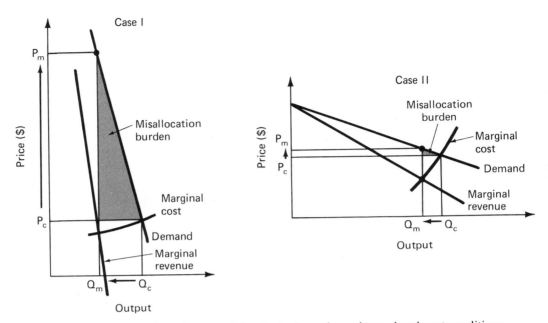

FIGURE 2.5.   The severity of monopoly's effects depends on demand and cost conditions.

2. Monopoly's Effects on Economic Performance

From these effects on price and output flow other effects.

Misallocation.   Because it reduces output, monopoly distorts the allocation of resources. The cutback in output forces some of the inputs into other markets, where their economic value is less. These distortions ripple through adjacent markets into the whole economy. Monopoly in one part of the economy disturbs allocation in the whole system. The larger the monopolized industry and the more severe the direct effects are, the greater is the economic harm.

The *misallocation* is defined as a reduction in consumers' surplus. Recall that pure competition maximizes that surplus (consistent with covering costs). Monopoly's effect stands in contrast. By raising the price, as in Figure 2.6, the monopolist eliminates some of this consumer surplus, which shrinks from *ABC* to *ADE*.

Now suppose for simplicity that average costs are constant (and therefore equal to marginal cost). Then the loss of consumer surplus has two components. (1) The rectangle *EDFC* in Figure 2.6 is the increased payments by consumers because price has been raised. These are taken by the firm as monopoly profits, transferred from the pockets of customers. (2) The triangle *DBF* represents the welfare loss to society resulting from the resource misallocation caused by the monopoly power. This surplus value simply disappears.

The loss is called *the welfare triangle,* and it may range from small to large. Again, slopes of the demand and cost curves are crucial. In Case I in Figure 2.5, the burden is large: about 40 percent of the monopolist's total sales revenue. In Case II in the same figure, the burden is a mere sliver: perhaps 1 percent of sales revenue.

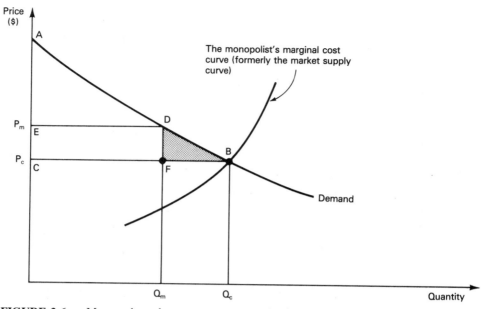

FIGURE 2.6.   Monopoly reduces consumer surplus.

Redistribution.   The monopoly profits shift income and wealth from consumers to the monopoly's owners. The amounts are illustrated in Figure 2.7, where total monopoly profits are calculated by multiplying profit per unit times the number of units sold: $(P_m - AC) \times Q_m$. The magnitude of the excess profits depends on the positions and shapes of the demand and cost curves. In Case I in Figure 2.7, because the steep demand curve is well above average cost, the excess profits are large. But in Case II, where demand is more elastic and is close to average cost, excess profit is small.

The excess profits usually represent a degree of unfairness. They redistribute income and wealth. Many consumers lose income, while the few owners of the monopoly gain sharply. This exacerbates inequality because the consumers usually have lower incomes than the monopoly's owners to begin with. As the monopoly's stock price rises to reflect the flow of monopoly profits, the owners can sell out and put their wealth into other investments. Thus monopoly creates family fortunes for a few at the expense of the many.

Yet Chicago-UCLA economists do not regard this result as a negative, saying only the shift of income and wealth is an ethical matter that cannot be said *a priori* to be bad or good. Most mainstream specialists regard the shift as a social burden, at least in part, but the issue is not closed.

X-Inefficiency.   Freed from competitive pressures, the monopoly firm's management may slacken. Cost controls may loosen and effort may decline, because everyone working for the firm knows that there is a cushion of excess profits. The slack may absorb some or all of the monopoly profit. In fact, the disappearance of

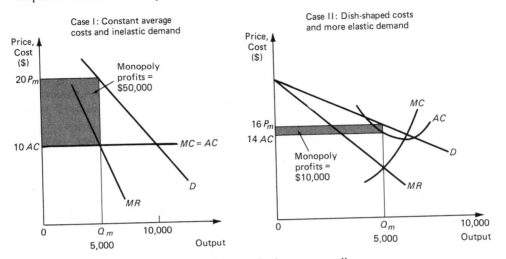

FIGURE 2.7.   The monopoly's profits may be large or small.

Excess profit is the gap between the demand curve (which is the average revenue schedule) and the average cost curve (that is, excess profit per unit) times *the number of units sold. In Case I, excess profit is $20 minus $10 = $10 per unit, times 5,000 units = $50,000. In Case II, excess profit is $16 minus $14 = $2 per unit, times 5,000 = $10,000. The shaded areas show the excess profits. These profit volumes are the areas of the rectangles.*

some profits into X-inefficiency is one reason why profits themselves often understate the degree of monopoly power.

Invention and Innovation.   A monopoly is under no external pressure to invent new products or methods, so the generation of new ideas is entirely voluntary. Neither does the monopoly have strong incentives to translate new ideas into practical innovations. Quite the opposite: the pace of innovation will be retarded because innovations destroy the value of existing products and processes. Thus the incentive structure discourages monopolists from innovating as rapidly as competitive firms do. These incentives are analyzed in Chapter 6.

Other Effects of Monopoly.   The competitive process itself is eliminated under monopoly, and that is a substantial loss of social value.

Monopoly restricts freedom of choice for everyone except the monopolist. Buyers cannot switch to other suppliers, for there are none. Only those goods the monopolist offers are available, and they carry higher prices than they would if there were competitors.

Suppliers also have less choice. Their sales are restricted to what the monopolist will buy, and they have less opportunity to develop new products than they would if there were a variety of firms to sell to. Workers also have fewer choices because the monopolist is now the only employer in the industry.

Democracy may also be adversely affected by monopoly. When there are fewer firms, with less diversity of interests, the monopolist becomes a formidable player with excess profits and market power to protect. It is in a position to use the political process to preserve and enlarge its economic advantage. Culture and society can

40   *Part I   Basic Concepts*

also be affected, for when many markets are monopolized, the economic and social orders become relatively tight and closed, and society is more stratified and rigid.

3.   An Example: Local Student Housing

Imagine that a college town has 10,000 private apartments for students. Competition drives the rent down to the actual level of average cost—namely, $225 per month per person (which includes the cost of the invested capital). At an investment value of $10,000 for each student living unit, this stock of housing is worth $100 million.

Now a group of ten clever economics students pools $10,000 in cash, forms a company (The Student Benevolent Housing Society), and issues one share to each member of the group at a value of $1,000 per share. They get a bank loan of $100 million, enough to purchase all the student housing stock. The interest cost of the loan equals the cost of the capital in the housing stock. Using those funds, the group quietly buys up all 10,000 apartments currently used by students. Then, by certain improper methods, the company persuades the city council to declare all other buildings unsafe and illegal for use as student housing. That political step blocks any entry of new housing capacity, thereby protecting the new monopoly from competition.

This new student housing monopoly has the curves shown in Figure 2.8. The flat marginal cost curve (which is identical to the average cost curve) reflects the constant cost conditions of each housing unit having the same cost of supply at $225 per month.

Benevolent Housing now closes 5,000 of the apartments and raises the rent of the remaining 5,000 to $250 per month. Half the people who maintain, serve, and rebuild apartments—janitors, painters, plumbers, managers—lose their jobs and have to seek work in other industries. The use of paint, furniture, lumber, and other apartment supplies is also cut in half, so that resources in those supplying industries

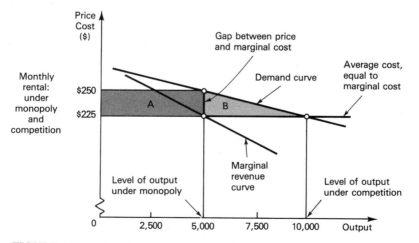

FIGURE 2.8.   The simple monopoly effect.

become partly unemployed. The closed apartment buildings are sold for other uses, such as offices or warehouses. Up to half of the $100 million loan is paid off immediately, and the rest continues, routinely covered as part of normal costs.

The new monopoly will make $25 per month (which is $300 per twelve-month year) in excess profit on each of the 5,000 housing units that remain open. The total excess profits are therefore $300/year × 5,000 = $1.5 million per year. Those profits occur even though rents were raised by only 11 percent, from $225 to $250.

The future flow of $1.5 million yearly in excess profits may well have a capitalized present value in the range of $15 million.[7] (The profits are about equivalent to the interest at a 10 percent rate on $15 million in bonds.) That amount of new wealth divides into $1.5 million for each of the original ten owners, who can now sell out immediately and make a tidy fortune. If they invest their money in 7 percent tax-exempt municipal bonds, they will collect about $100,000 per year in income. They can then live on $50,000 a year, invest the other $50,000, and watch their fortunes grow, without ever having to work again. They, and probably their children, are now in the leisure class.

All this from just one tiny local market in one town! Comparable family fortunes have been created thousands of times in the United States, in local and regional markets. It is evident why the struggle to monopolize continues—the rewards are large, immediate, and lasting. Only effective competition stands between the populace and new monopoly-created drones.

4. Economies and Diseconomies of Scale

In any market there may be economies of scale that justify a degree of monopoly. Their basic nature is summarized here; Chapter 9 defines and estimates economies of scale in detail.

Economies may arise in any of the firm's activities, such as production, marketing, or innovation. They cause the firm's average cost to decline as its size increases. As illustrated by the four alternative cost curves in Figure 2.9, economies of scale prevail where the average cost curve slopes down. Minimum efficient scale (*MES*) occurs where the downslope ends. Diseconomies of scale may then tip the curve up at levels above *MES;* or there may be "constant costs," with the flat range illustrated by curve *A*.

The *cost gradient* is the slope of the curve. It shows how strong the economies are to the left of *MES*. The gradient can be steep or slight. The gradient of *diseconomies* (at outputs above *MES*) can also vary, with important consequences.

Economies may be small (as in curves *A* and *B*) or large (curves *C* and *D*).

---

[7] Any income flow will be capitalized into an asset value, depending on the expected size and duration of the flow and the rate of time discount. If the flow is expected to be constant and long-lasting (over twenty years, say), then the asset value is approximated by the equation

$$\text{Capitalized value} = \frac{(\text{Yearly \$income})}{\text{Interest rate}}$$

where the "interest rate" is the time discount rate applied by investors. In asset markets, the valuation is commonly about ten times the income flow, though it often varies between five and fifteen or even further.

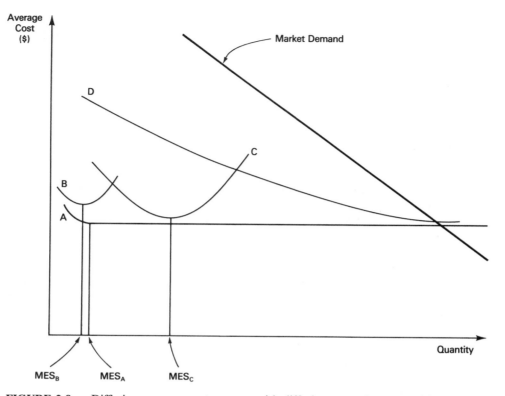

FIGURE 2.9.   Differing average cost curves, with differing room for competition.

Extreme scale economies (curve *D*) cause "natural monopoly"; here there is room for only one efficient firm. Curves *A* and *B* are "natural competition," while curve *C* may be a "natural oligopoly," with room for two or three firms.

Economies of scale can make a degree of monopoly unavoidable. Effective competition is unlikely in cases C and D. Even in case A, firms may capture market share much larger than *MES* and then exert a degree of monopoly power.

Scale economies may also exist in innovation activities, such as R&D, if big laboratories or large-scale projects are needed to create new products. That will add to the downward interval of the long-run average cost curve, but the same concepts of *MES* and the cost gradient will apply.

If the firm holds a market share greater than *MES*, that extra amount is *excess market share*. It exceeds the level needed to obtain minimum costs, and is likely to add to the firm's market power.

Economies of scale may "justify" some portion of monopoly positions by making costs lower. The degree of justification will depend on both *MES* and the cost gradient. Chapter 9 will present evidence about these magnitudes when we test how much the actual level of concentration in U.S. industries is justified by the economies of scale.

Two Basic Cost Curves.   In any event, two kinds of cost diagrams should be kept in mind. One reflects the *industry's* underlying long-run cost conditions (Figure

Average Cost, Marginal Cost $

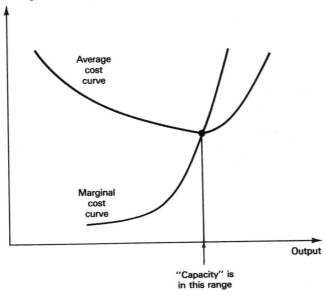

FIGURE 2.10.   Present cost curves of an ongoing firm.

2.9), while the other shows the current cost curves of an *ongoing firm* (Figure 2.10). In those curves, there is a definite capacity where average costs are lowest and equal to marginal cost. Below that capacity, marginal costs are well below average costs; above that level of capacity, marginal costs rise sharply. These two sets of curves will recur frequently throughout this book.

5. Combining the Effects of Monopoly

Figure 2.11 combines the main effects of monopoly, on allocation, X-efficiency, and possible economies of scale. Average cost is initially at AC_1, under competition. Then monopoly achieves some scale economies, as shown by a slight reduction in the level of cost. But X-inefficiency is large, raising costs to AC_2. Given that level of (constant) average and marginal costs, the firm sets the monopoly price, causing the shaded triangle of misallocation loss (labeled B). The shift of income is shown by the rectangle A.

The specifics will differ in other cases. Scale economies may exceed X-inefficiency, or not. Costs may be constant, or not. But the same logic and categories will apply.

6. Gradations of Market Power

Between pure monopoly and pure competition lie many gradations and varieties of markets. The literature has settled on six main categories of markets, as was shown in Table 1.2.

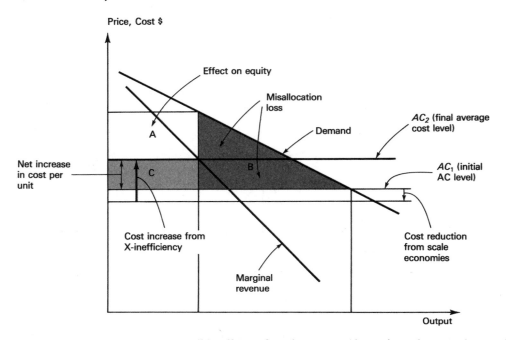

FIGURE 2.11.   The various possible effects of market power (drawn in perhaps exaggerated scale for visual clarity).

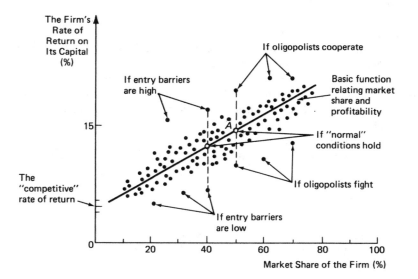

FIGURE 2.12.   The basic relationship between market share and profit rate.

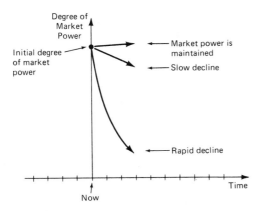

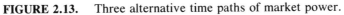

FIGURE 2.13.   Three alternative time paths of market power.

    Combining Market Share and Other Elements.   The fundamental pattern is that a firm's market power varies mainly with its market share. Intermediate market shares cause gradients of intermediate monopoly effects. Figure 2.12 illustrates the basic function relating market share and profitability. Of course, variations around this central tendency may occur. (1) Interactions among oligopolists may push the outcome up or down. For example, a 50 percent market share may yield a profit rate of 15 percent *on average* (at point *A*). But the profit rate may reach 20 percent if the firm is part of a collusive oligopoly; or it may drop to only 10 percent if the oligopolists fight one another. (2) Entry barriers may also make the outcome deviate (this is illustrated in Figure 2.12 for a firm with a 40 percent market share).

    Generally, a firm with a low market share (below 10 percent) has no market power, regardless of the structure of the whole market. That kind of share corresponds to (nearly) flat demand curves. Higher market shares usually give more steeply sloped demand curves, with greater degrees of control over price and quantity.

    The Rate of Decline of Market Share.   The last basic issue we will discuss is the rate at which monopoly power tends to be eroded over time. It may decline swiftly or slowly, or it may persist or even increase, as Figure 2.13 illustrates. Monopoly power that declines rapidly is much less serious than monopoly power that endures a long time.

    This simple matter, easily illustrated by a diagram, holds important lessons, but there is much dispute about exactly what they are. Chicago-UCLA analysts assert that *usually* the rate of decline is rapid; monopoly is not only rare, weak, and justified by efficiency, but also transient (unless it continues to give superior efficiency). More pessimistic and skeptical observers believe that market dominance tends to be lasting, even when the monopoly is not more efficient.

QUESTIONS FOR REVIEW[8]

1. "To measure the whole effect of monopoly on efficiency, just measure the size of the welfare triangle (i.e., the lost consumer surplus)." True?
2. "An efficient outcome may still be unfair." True?

[8] Answers to the true-false review questions are provided at the back of the book.

3. "It takes a large increase in price to yield high monopoly profits." True?

4. "Equality of income guarantees equity." True?

5. If costs are constant, a monopolist will, in theory, reduce output below the competitive level by (1) 10 percent, (2) 20 percent, (3) 50 percent, (4) 75 percent. Which?

6. "High market shares can reflect economies of scale." True?

7. For practice, work through the local housing example of monopolization with different assumptions about prices, costs, and bank loans.

8. How much economies of scale are needed to offset the social cost of a 20 percent rise in price as a result of market power?

9. Can a monopoly have real power and effects even if it has no entry barrier to protect it?

10. Show in diagrams that the less elastic demand is, the sharper the monopoly effect will be.

11. Show in diagrams the net effect of monopoly on price when X-inefficiency is (1) 10 percent and (2) 25 percent; and economies of scale cut costs by (3) 5 percent, (4) 15 percent, and (5) 30 percent.

12. Explain the difference between X-efficiency and allocative efficiency.

13. "By allocating resources so that price equals marginal cost for every firm and every good, the Invisible Hand achieves a deeply meaningful result." Explain why that equality is so meaningful.

14. What main limits are there on the Invisible Hand?

15. The monopolist uses its marginal revenue curve in reaching the monopoly result. Where was that marginal revenue curve before? Why wasn't it used?

16. Does the case of monopoly in student housing apply to your college area? How can you tell?

17. Explain how "minimum efficient scale" can determine the structure of the market, making it naturally competitive or a natural monopoly.

18. Show how a low cost gradient can minimize the importance of a given MES value.

19. If the monopoly output is 100 units, Marginal Cost is zero at that output level, Demand is unit elastic at $100, and monopoly causes X-inefficiency of 5 percent, can you estimate the amounts of allocative inefficiency and X-efficiency?

20. If Chicago-UCLA economists are correct about the rate of decline, is it wise to take policy actions to reduce monopoly?

RESEARCH PAPER
TOPICS AND SOURCES

The purpose of doing a paper is to practice the same steps that professionals do in their research: frame an issue, try to "solve" it with new hypotheses or evidence, and then write up the results. If the student does a first draft about two-thirds through the course, the teacher can then give suggestions for revision or new work. This sequence of drafting, comments, and revision is exactly what expert articles and books (including this text) go through. The paper lets you take a position on an issue and restate it your way. That, too, is what research papers and monographs do. In your paper, the specific conclusions you reach are secondary. What matters is that you treat the issues carefully, with a professional degree of skill.

In research and writing projects, the most direct approach is to take a point from one of the chapters and reexamine it. You can treat a specific issue, do an industry study (on a small scale), or try to use data to test a hypothesis. Suggestions for these three approaches are given below in three groupings. For some topics, I give you specific references as a starting point. Read them, and use their footnotes to trace other references. For other topics, I refer you to the passages in this book where sources are given in footnotes. Usually your teacher can also suggest references or entirely new and timely topics to work on.

1. Issues

You can try (1) restating the issue and taking a position, (2) reviewing the history and current direction of the debate, (3) adding new analysis, or (4) testing the point with data (see below). Nearly all the issues in this book are eligible for critical treatment. A selection of good topics might begin with the following:

1. How large is the burden of misallocation caused by market power? Start with Harberger and other references in Chapter 5.
2. Are price-fixing agreements unstable? What conditions influence the degree of stability? Start with Hay and Kelley (Chapter 14).
3. Estimate the height of entry barriers into three different industries. Start with Bain, Mann, and others in Chapters 4 and 11.

4. Can vertical integration increase market power? Start with Spengler, Bork, and Scherer (Chapter 15), and perhaps analyze a specific vertical merger.

5. What is the true scope of "natural monopoly" in electricity, telephone service, or postal service? Start with references in Chapters 4 and 11.

6. Trace the economic effects of a specific antitrust action, such as *Standard Oil* (1911), *American Tobacco* (1911), *Alcoa* (1945), or the electrical equipment price-fixing cases (1960). Start with Chapter 19 sources.

7. Is Schumpeterian competition relevant to specific parts, or all, of the economy? Which parts?

8. Do dominant firms decline? Trace three dominant firms from 1950 to the present. Analyze the factors that influence the rate of decline.

2. Topics in Theory

Many theoretical topics are excellent term paper subjects. You may try new variations on oligopoly models, or analyze some aspect of strategic pricing. The theory of "contestability" is an interesting area to explore.

Theoretical papers can be much shorter and more concise than those on empirical topics because you do not need to assemble extensive evidence. Among the best books on recent "new IO theory" are:

WILLIAM J. BAUMOL, JOHN C. PANZAR, AND ROBERT D. WILLIG, *Contestable Markets and the Theory of Industry Structure* (San Diego, Cal.: Harcourt Brace Jovanovich, 1982).

TIMOTHY F. BRESNAHAN AND RICHARD SCHMALENSEE, EDS., *The Empirical Renaissance in Industrial Economics* (Oxford: Basil Blackwell, 1987).

ALEXIS JACQUEMIN, *The New Industrial Organization* (Cambridge, Mass.: MIT Press, 1987).

JOSEPH E. STIGLITZ AND C. FRANK MATHEWSON, *New Developments in the Analysis of Market Structure* (Cambridge, Mass.: MIT Press, 1986).

LESTER TELSER, *Theories of Competition* (Amsterdam: North Holland, 1988).

JEAN TIROLE, *The Theory of Industrial Organization* (Cambridge, Mass.: MIT Press, 1988).

MICHAEL WATERSON, *Economic Theory of Industry* (Cambridge: Cambridge University Press, 1984).

3. Industry Studies

Choose an interesting industry. Study its structure and/or behavior and/or performance; emphasize one part or cover all three. Then:

1. Judge how competitive it is. (You may wish to draw contrasting estimates of high and low market power in the industry); or

2. Bring an earlier industry study up-to-date, trying to explain recent changes; or

3. Compare a leading firm and a lesser firm in the industry, showing which one is more profitable, efficient, innovative, etc. Try to explain the difference.

Each industry is usually beset by one or two major questions, which your paper can focus on. For example, in the automobile industry, it might be the quotas on Japanese car exports to the United States. In beer, it might be the real cause of rising concentration in the industry and the effects of exclusive territories for distributors. In health care, it might be the impact of health maintenance organizations: Do they provide for effective competition, and are they "efficient"?

An excellent set of brief industry studies can be found in Walter Adams, ed., *The Structure of American Industry*, 8th ed. (New York: Macmillan, 1990). Following are a number of industry studies and provocative books on other topics in the field. For leading articles, see the footnotes in the pages of this book.

ZOLTAN ACS, *The Changing Structure of the U.S. Economy: Lessons from the Steel Industry* (New York: Praeger, 1984).

WALTER ADAMS AND JAMES W. BROCK, *The Bigness Complex* (New York: Pantheon Books, 1986).

DOMINICK T. ARMENTANO, *Antitrust and Monopoly: Anatomy of a Policy Failure* (New York: Wiley, 1982).

ELIZABETH E. BAILEY, DAVID R. GRAHAM, AND DANIEL P. KAPLAN, *Deregulating the Airlines* (Cambridge, Mass.: MIT Press, 1985).

JOE S. BAIN, *Barriers to New Competition* (Cambridge, Mass.: Harvard University Press, 1956).

ROBERT H. BORK, *The Antitrust Paradox: A Policy at War with Itself* (New York: Basic Books, 1978).

GERALD W. BROCK, *The U.S. Computer Industry* (Cambridge, Mass.: Ballinger, 1975).

KERRY COOPER AND DONALD FRASER, *Banking Deregulation and the New Competition in Financial Services* (Cambridge, Mass.: Ballinger, 1984).

ROBERT CRANDALL, *The U.S. Steel Industry in Recurrent Crisis* (Washington, D.C.: Brookings Institution, 1982).

ANDREW F. DAUGHETY, ED., *Analytical Studies in Transport Economics* (Cambridge: Cambridge University Press, 1985).

RICHARD THOMAS DeLAMARTER, *Big Blue: IBM's Use and Abuse of Power* (New York: Dodd, Mead, 1986).

KENNETH G. ELZINGA AND ROBERT A. ROGOWSKY, ED., *Relevant Markets in Antitrust,* special issue of *The Journal of Reprints for Antitrust Law and Economics* (New York: Federal Legal Publications, 1984).

EDWARD J. EPSTEIN, *The Rise and Fall of Diamonds* (New York: Simon & Schuster, 1982).

DAVID S. EVANS, ED., *Breaking Up Bell* (Amsterdam: North Holland, 1983).

PAUL J. FELDSTEIN, *Health Care Economics*, 2d ed. (New York: Wiley, 1983).

FRANKLIN M. FISHER ET AL., *Folded, Spindled, and Mutilated: Economic Analysis and U.S. v. IBM* (Cambridge, Mass.: MIT Press, 1983).

JAMES FREY AND ARTHUR JOHNSON, *Government and Sport* (New York: Rowman and Allanheld, 1985).

JOHN KENNETH GALBRAITH, *The New Industrial State* (Boston: Houghton Mifflin, 1967).

TIMOTHY GREEN, *The World of Diamonds* (New York: William Morrow, 1981).

JAMES M. GRIFFIN AND DAVID J. TEECE, *OPEC Behavior and World Oil Prices* (London: Allen & Unwin, 1982).

WALTON HAMILTON AND IRENE TILL, *Antitrust in Action,* Monograph No. 16, Temporary National Economic Committee, Investigation of Economic Power (Washington, D.C.: U.S. Government Printing Office, 1940).

J. A. HUNKER, *Structural Change in the U.S. Automobile Industry* (Lexington, Mass.: D. C. Heath, 1983).

JOHN JEWKES ET AL., *The Sources of Invention*, 2d ed. (New York: Norton, 1969).

PAUL M. JOSKOW AND RICHARD SCHMALENSEE, *Markets for Power* (Cambridge, Mass.: MIT Press, 1986).

GORHAM KINDEM, *The American Movie Industry* (Carbondale, Ill.: Sourthern Illinois University Press, 1982).

PAUL W. MacAVOY, *Crude Oil Prices* (Cambridge, Mass.: Ballinger, 1982).

JOHN R. MEYER AND CLINTON V. OSTER, *Deregulation and the New Airline Entrepreneurs* (Cambridge, Mass.: MIT Press, 1984).

JOHN MOODY, *The Truth About the Trusts* (Chicago: Moody Publishing, 1904).

DENNIS C. MUELLER, ED., *The Determinants of Mergers* (Boston: Oelgeschlager, Gunn & Hain, 1980).

WILLARD F. MUELLER, *The Celler-Kefauver Act: The First 27 Years,* prepared for the House Subcommittee on Monopolies and Commercial Law, 96th Congress, 1st Session, 1980.

ROGER G. NOLL, ED., *Government and the Sports Business,* rev. ed. (Washington, D.C.: Brookings Institution, 1985).

MICHAEL E. PORTER, *Competitive Advantage: Creating and Sustaining Superior Performance* (New York: Free Press, 1985).

DAVID J. RAVENSCRAFT AND F. M. SCHERER, *Mergers, Sell-offs and Economic Efficiency* (Washington, D.C.: Brookings Institution, 1987).

STEPHEN A. RHOADES, *Power, Empire Building, and Mergers* (Lexington, Mass.: D. C. Heath Lexington Books, 1983).

EMMANUEL N. ROUSSAKIS, *Commercial Banking in an Era of Deregulation* (New York: Praeger, 1984).

ANTHONY SAUNDERS AND LAWRENCE J. WHITE, *Technology and the Regulation of Financial Markets* (Lexington, Mass.: Lexington Books, 1986).

F. M. SCHERER ET AL., *The Economics of Multiplant Operation* (Cambridge, Mass.: Harvard University Press, 1975).

STEVEN A. SCHNEIDER, *The Oil Price Revolution* (Baltimore, Md.: Johns Hopkins Press, 1983).

WILLIAM G. SHEPHERD, *The Treatment of Market Power* (New York: Columbia University Press, 1975).

HARRY M. SHOOSHAN, ED., *Disconnecting Bell: The Impact of AT&T Divestiture* (New York: Pergamon Press, 1984).

J. TUNSTALL, *Disconnecting Parties* (New York: McGraw-Hill, 1985).

M. A. UTTON, *Profits and Stability of Monopoly* (Cambridge: Cambridge University Press, 1986).

LEONARD W. WEISS AND MICHAEL W. KLASS, EDS., *Regulatory Reform: What Really Happened* (Boston: Little, Brown, 1986).

OLIVER E. WILLIAMSON, *Antitrust Economics* (Oxford: Basil Blackwell, 1987).

4. Empirical Studies

Students often prefer to explore basic sources of empirical evidence, using them to practice doing quantitative research. This gives students a better feel for the meaning of empirical research "results." Here I list several sources and suggest simple questions to try to answer.

Concentration ratios

The basic source is in the U.S. *Census of Manufactures* for 1947, 1954, 1958, 1963, 1968, 1972, 1977, and 1982. The 1982 report is Bureau of the Census, *Concentration Ratios in Manufacturing 1982,* MC82-S-7 (Washington, D.C.: U.S. Government Printing Office, 1985). Topics are in Chapters 3 and 4; see also Appendix 2.

1.   Adjust ratios to reflect true concentration in properly defined markets (examples: drugs, milk, bricks, newspapers, automobiles, computers, sports equipment).
2.   Compute the average degree of concentration.
3.   List the 20 most concentrated and 20 least concentrated industries. What factors explain their differences?
4.   Which industries have changed concentration most sharply over time? Analyze the causes.

Profits

Use the *Fortune Directory of the 500 Largest U.S. Industrial Corporations* (issued yearly in April) and the directories for other groups (banks, utilities, foreign firms) that are published yearly in the summer months. See *Moody's Industrial Manual* (yearly) for more detailed data, and use references in Chapter 5.

1.   Evaluate the most profitable companies. Do they hold market power? Are there economies of scale?
2.   What is the "normal" or "competitive" rate of return?

Company divisions

On the so-called Form 10-K used to report to the Securities and Exchange Commission, firms disaggregate their total sales figures. Use these forms to judge market structure and company positions in more detail.

Mergers

Until 1981, the FTC published yearly a complete listing of mergers involving over $10 million in assets since 1948 (FTC Bureau of Economics, *Statistical Report on Mergers and Acquisitions*). See also *Mergers & Acquisitions* magazine.

1.   Evaluate the trends and volume of mergers.
2.   Check the classification of horizontal, vertical, and conglomerate types, using five selected mergers.
3.   Trace mergers in one industry, appraising their impact on structure.

Advertising

Use *Advertising Age* magazine's summary (yearly in August) of the 100 firms that spend the most on advertising. See other sources in Chapter 16.

1.   Calculate advertising intensity for firms in three industries.

2. Analyze why the firms differ in advertising intensity.
3. Is advertising intensity related to the firms' profitability?

X-Efficiency

The Wall Street Journal and *Business Week* frequently discuss the efficiency of firms. Moody's *Handbook of Common Stocks* (quarterly) gives brief descriptions and performance data for nearly 1,000 firms.

1. Find 10 "efficient" firms and 10 "inefficient" firms.
2. Compare these firms' profit rates and stock price movements.
3. Is market power present?
4. Try to trace whether management undergoes changes in the "inefficient" firms.

3 DEFINING MARKETS; CATEGORIES OF COMPETITION

Now we turn to the middle ranges of competition, where market structure can help in assessing the degree of monopoly. This chapter presents the main concepts of intermediate competition. Chapter 4 will apply them to the data of actual markets, and of course the ideas will recur throughout the rest of the book.

First, Section I presents the methods for defining the extent of the market. Next, Section II considers the three main elements of market structure: market share, concentration, and barriers against entry. Then Section III reviews concepts of three major categories of intermediate competition: dominant firms, tight oligopoly, and loose oligopoly, including monopolistic competition.

I. DEFINING THE MARKET

Defining the market is critical.[1] In order to assess the internal structure of any market, one must first determine its boundaries. "Defining the market" means drawing those edges as accurately as possible, including all products that belong *in* the market and excluding all others that are *outside* it.

The exercise can be controversial because the size of the market affects the apparent degree of monopoly that exists within it. Firms accused of having monopoly power (such as IBM or Eastman Kodak) usually assert that the market is very large in order to make their own share of it seem small. The other side (such as a little

---

[1] Among the large literature on the topic, many leading papers are collected in Kenneth G. Elzinga and Robert A. Rogowsky, eds., "Relevant Markets in Antitrust," *Journal of Reprints for Antitrust Law and Economics,* 14 (1984).

A classic source is the early paper by Robert L. Bishop, "Elasticities, Cross-Elasticities, and Market Relationships," *American Economic Review,* 42 (December 1952), 779–803; see also Philip Areeda and Donald F. Turner, *Antitrust Law* (Boston: Little, Brown, 1978), pp. 346–88; and Kenneth G. Elzinga and Thomas F. Hogarty, "The Problem of Geographic Market Delineation in Antimerger Suits," *Antitrust Bulletin,* 18 (1983), 45–81.

For further variety in viewpoints, see Terry Calvani and John J. Siegfried, eds., *Economic Analysis and Antitrust Law* (Boston: Little, Brown, 1979), Kenneth D. Boyer, "Is There a Principle for Defining Industries?" *Southern Ecoonmic Journal,* 50 (January 1984), 761–70; William M. Landes and Richard A. Posner, "Market Power in Antitrust Cases," *Harvard Law Review,* 94 (March 1981), 937–96; and George J. Stigler and Robert A. Sherwin, "The Extent of the Market," *Journal of Law and Economics,* 28 (October 1985), 555–85.

firm suing a dominant firm) makes the opposite claim, that the market is small and the defendant has a high share of it.

In research, too, the debate can be sharp and bias is always a possibility because researchers often have general beliefs about the extent of monopoly power that shape their views of individual markets. For example, a Chicago-UCLA analyst might write or testify in an antitrust case that a market is big and monopoly power in it is small, while a critic of market power might say that the market is small and the monopoly power in it is high.

A *market* is a group of buyers and sellers exchanging goods that are highly substitutable for one another. Markets are defined by demand conditions; they embody *the zone of consumer choice* for the good.

Markets exist in two main dimensions: (1) *product type* and (2) *geographic area.* In the pure case, there is one distinct product that is sold in a distinct geographic area, such as fresh whole milk in an isolated town. That market's extent is determined by the true zone of consumer choice for that good, as illustrated in Figure 3.1A. In this illustration, the market boundaries are sharply defined, both by product types and by geographic area.

Figure 3.1A also shows adjacent markets for soft drinks, fruit juices, beer, wine, and liquor. If buyers never choose among those drinks, then each market is sharply distinct, as the illustration indicates. But if the drinks are regarded by many or most buyers as close substitutes for one another, then there may be one larger market embracing all drinks.

Now consider Figure 3.1B, a market that contains *submarkets*. The larger market is the U.S. market for new automobiles, and within it are submarkets for low-, medium-, and high-priced automobiles. The larger market is meaningful in assessing broad patterns of choice, since all car buyers make purchases and there is some substantial substitution among these groups as well as within them. But the submarkets are also relevant in defining the main range of choices made by many consumers, who focus on one of the groups of cars.

Substitutability, then, is the key condition for defining markets. Close substitutes

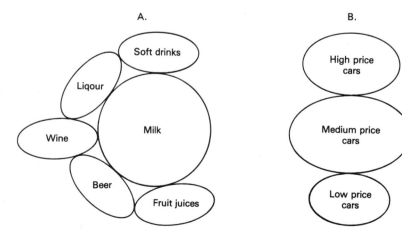

FIGURE 3.1.   Examples of markets.

are in the market together; other goods are outside it. The entire economy can be seen as a honeycomb of these individual markets.

1. Cross-Elasticity of Demand

The correct technical definition of substitutability begins with *cross-elasticity of demand,* which shows how sharply a price change for one product will cause the quantity sold of another product to change. The formula is:

$$\text{Cross-elasticity of demand between goods 1 and 2} = \frac{\%\ \text{Change in quantity of good 2}}{\%\ \text{Change in price of good 1}}$$

For example, let good 1 be red apples and good 2 be green apples. A 20 percent rise in the price of red apples could cause a 40 percent rise in the quantity of green apples sold, as buyers switch. The two goods are therefore close substitutes with a *high positive cross-elasticity of demand,* and so they are in the same market. Comparable pairs would be Coke and Pepsi, Fords and Chevrolets, and different brands of gasoline. By contrast, shoes and ice cream are clearly in different markets; so are houses, pencils, tractors, and popcorn. Their sales quantities do not respond to one another's prices.

Cross-elasticities of demand are also valid for defining geographic market areas. In this case, goods 1 and 2 are the same physical good, but sold in different locations. If beer prices in Illinois closely affect beer sales in Wisconsin, then the two states are in the same geographic market. Otherwise, they are separate markets. On this basis, stock markets and gold markets are international because buyers can easily shift purchases from one area of the globe to another, whereas the markets for bricks, bread, and ready-mix concrete are local because shipping costs are high relative to the value of the products.

Though clear and logical in concept, cross-elasticities have not been of much practical use in defining markets because they are virtually impossible to measure accurately: markets are not laboratories in which neat price-quantity experiments can be performed. Moreover, the critical variables exist along continuums, not in categorical boxes:

> 1. *Time periods.* Responsiveness exists in a time dimension; the length of the period for response between goods is infinitely variable. The shorter the period chosen, the less the responsiveness will be. The choice of time period to examine is arbitrary to some degree: Should it be the short run, the long run, or a period in between? Moreover, the practical length of "short run" and "long run" differs from industry to industry.
>
> 2. *Gradations of product characteristics.* Goods usually have a range of attributes that vary by degrees. This means there are gradations of cross-elasticities rather than a distinct break between close mutual substitutes and all other goods.

So even if cross-elasticity values could be estimated, they would reflect at least two continuums—time and product features—and therefore would vary continuously. There are seldom jumps or gaps in cross-elasticities to show clearly where the market's edges are.

Even when gaps do occur, there are no fundamental criteria for deciding which level of cross-elasticity (.4?, .63? .77?) is the "correct" threshold level for setting the market edges. The choice of threshold is not entirely arbitrary, but neither does it rest on a clear conceptual benchmark.

Finally, cross-elasticities of demand contain two logical problems that make it necessary to use them cautiously. First, they are not helpful in testing two goods that each have small market shares in a highly competitive market. Because so many other goods are also highly substitutable, a price rise in good 1 will not cause a significant rise in the quantity sold of good 2.[2] This problem is not fatal, because it arises only where goods are obviously highly substitutable according to other evidence. But it warns us against the blind use of cross-elasticities alone to determine market boundaries.

Second, the evaluation of substitutability needs to be made at *competitive* prices, whereas the actual prices may be far apart.[3] A leading example of this is the Cellophane case.[4] Cellophane is a transparent film used to wrap cigarette packages and other products. To defend itself in an antitrust suit alleging that it had monopoly power on account of its dominant share of sales of cellophane, Du Pont asserted that the market really included all flexible wrapping materials.

What matters here is that cellophane's price was far above the prices of wax paper and the other materials Du Pont cited as substitutes, and that the Supreme Court evaluated the monopoly charge on that basis. But, in fact, that price differential was a valid indicator that Du Pont *did* hold monopoly power. If the materials had truly been substitutable, the prices would all have been in line. And at equal prices, cellophane would have had far higher sales levels.

Hence the lesson: Substitutability must be judged at competitive (which usually means equal) prices. Price differences may actually reflect the monopoly power that is in question.

(One other possible error is to consider *supply substitutability* in defining market boundaries. That problem will be discussed shortly.)

---

[2] For example, suppose that firm A and firm B each sell 2 percent of the eggs sold in a region, and that all eggs (including theirs) are close substitutes. If A raises its price by 10 percent and consequently loses all its sales, those sales will shift to all other sellers. But since they are only 2 percent of the total, B will gain only a very small addition (namely, 2 percent) of sales. Thus:

$$\text{Cross-elasticity} = \frac{\% \ Q \text{ rise for } B}{\% \ P \text{ rise for } A} = \frac{2\%}{10\%}$$

$$= 0.2$$

This is a low cross-elasticity, which clashes with the fact that everybody's eggs are, in fact, extremely close substitutes.

[3] See Richard A. Posner, *Antitrust Law: An Economic Perspective* (Chicago: University of Chicago Press, 1976), pp. 127–28; and Areeda and Turner, *Antitrust Law*, pp. 346–88.

[4] In a major antitrust case in the 1950s, the Du Pont Company's market position in selling cellophane was alleged to be a monopoly of its market and therefore in violation of the Sherman Act, Section 2. (The case is *U.S. v. E. I. du Pont de Nemours & Co. [Cellophane]*, 351 U.S. 377 [1956].) Du Pont urged instead that the relevant market was much wider, including all "flexible wrapping materials"—wax paper, tin foil, and so on. Estimates of cross-elasticities of demand between cellophane and the others were not calculated, but other kinds of evidence about relative prices and price movements, and about the technical substitutability of the wrapping materials, were extensively discussed. The Supreme Court decided (probably mistakenly) by four to three that such conditions showed all "flexible wrapping materials" to be the relevant market. Other antitrust cases rely on such practical evidence.

TABLE 3.1   Specific Conditions Defining ''the'' Market

Product:
Cross-elasticity of demand among products
Informed judgments by participants
Distinct sellers and buyers
Price gaps between products, and independence of price moves
Geographic Area (local, regional, national, international):
The area within which buyers choose
   Actual buying patterns
The area within which sellers ship
   Actual shipping costs relative to production costs
   Actual distances that products are normally shipped
   Ratios of goods-shipped-into and out of actual areas

---

2.   Other Evidence About Market Edges

Economists usually resort to a variety of other evidence in defining markets. The main types are summarized in Table 3.1.

First is *the general character of the goods,* as tested against experience. Can they be interchanged easily by most buyers? Caviar and hamburgers can conceivably be used in place of each other occasionally, but not by most users under normal conditions. The same is true for bicycles and running shoes. In contrast, many brands of small cars are close substitutes.

Second is an assessment of whether *the goods' prices* are close together and move in parallel or independently. Equal prices often indicate close substitutability, for the competition among the goods naturally forces their prices into line. Sharply divergent prices suggest that the goods are sold to different buyers, for different purposes. A $19.95 motel room on the edge of New York City, for example, and a $220 room at the Waldorf-Astoria in midtown Manhattan may both be the same size. But the price gap indicates that they are in different true markets.

If the two goods' prices move independently, that indicates that they are not closely substitutable. The converse is not necessarily true, however. Prices may move in parallel if one good is an important input to the other—for example, copper ore and copper—but *not* substitutable for it.

Third is *the judgment of participants* in the market, especially the sellers. They know on the basis of daily experience exactly which firms and goods compete in the market. They study the matter continuously because their success depends precisely on knowing the interactions among the firms and goods. Their view will often be a solid consensus, especially when, as in antitrust cases, they testify under oath.

Caution: Learn to handle ''uniform'' products cautiously. Usually they are less uniform than they seem. (An example is electricity. Though kilowatt hours are technically uniform, their cost and demand conditions differ sharply by time of day, time of week, and time of year as well as by the type of user—residence, factory, etc.) Be careful to identify groups within the market who can be charged different prices;

they may form a distinct market of their own. Also define any clear cost differences among groups; these two can create distinct markets and different prices.

Geographic Extent.   The geographic extent of markets can be indicated by other kinds of evidence. One is *the size of transport costs* compared to the value of the good. For example, bricks are a high-weight item, with high shipping costs compared to their value. That alone suggests that market size is limited. Another kind of evidence is *the actual miles shipped.* Cement in bags, for example, is rarely shipped over 150 miles, so that is a good indicator of the maximum radius of most cement markets. A third kind of evidence is *the amount shipped into and out of a given region.* Ten percent is a common rule of thumb. For example, in testing if Missouri is a geographic beer market, one asks if more than 10 percent of its local production is shipped out of the state and more than 10 percent of its consumption is shipped in. If both figures were 50 or 70 percent, then Missouri would be merely part of a multiple-state regional beer market.

The criteria in Table 3.1 are the most commonly used ones, but others have been employed from time to time. All require care and judgment, and none gives simple, definitive answers. Market definition is complex because most markets are complex.

The reason most markets have shaded edges is that the close substitutes are surrounded by a range of partial substitutes. In extreme cases, the shaded edge is very wide, but most markets can be defined at least well enough to permit some judgment about the degree of competition.

Levels of Markets.   Within many industries there are a number of true markets. The drug industry sells at least eight distinct types of drugs, and each type contains specialized subtypes. The chemicals industry includes hundreds of distinct product markets, from sulfuric acid to plastics. Moreover, an industry may have several tiers of product and geographic markets (from local to international), with the same firms operating at *all* levels. For example, banks in large cities usually compete for business clients in local, regional, and national markets. They also compete in local "retail banking" for small depositers. Such banks are operating in several levels of markets at the same time.

3.   An Alternative Method for Estimating Markets

In 1982, Reagan Administration officials at the Antitrust Division of the Justice Department announced a new technique for defining markets in antitrust cases.[5] Although it was offered as more scientific than previously used methods, it is actually based on speculation and arbitrary criteria. It is interesting enough to deserve space

---

[5] The most recent version is U.S. Department of Justice, "Merger Guidelines Issued by Justice Department, June 14, 1984, and Accompanying Policy Statement," No. 1169, *Antitrust and Trade Regulation Report* (BNA), June 14, 1984, S-1 to S-16. For one appraisal of the approach, see Eleanor M. Fox, "The New Merger Guidelines—A Blueprint for Microeconomic Analysis," *Antitrust Bulletin,* 27 (Fall 1982), 519–91.

For a defense of the method by staff members who helped develop it, see David T. Scheffman and Pablo T. Spiller, "Geographic Market Definition Under the U.S. Department of Justice Merger Guidelines," *Journal of Law and Economics,* 29 (April 1987), 123–48; and Gregory J. Werden, "Market Definition and the Justice Department's Merger Guidelines," *Duke Law Journal,* October 1983, pp. 524–79.

here, even though it is probably less practical and less reliable than the conventional approach.

To use it, one begins by selecting the narrowest plausible version of the market in question. (An example might be wool skirts.) Then one hypothesizes a "significant" price rise (usually assumed to be 10 percent) for this good and asks whether within a "reasonable" time period (usually taken to be one year) there occurs a "significant" shift of buyers (usually taken to be 5 percent) to specific substitute goods. If so, then the market is redefined to include these substitutes. (Thus, if buyers shifted to polyester and cotton skirts, these goods would be included in "the" market.) The speculation is continued, product by product (perhaps to dresses and slacks), until there is no further "significant" substitution, as defined. The market is then defined.

If the data were accurate and complete, this method might rival or surpass the conventional methods. But the new technique has several defects. The estimates are speculative, not genuinely scientific. Meaningful tests, using objective data, can rarely be done.[6] All three of the new method's benchmarks (for price changes, time periods, and quantity shifts) are arbitrary and debatable; they have no special justification either in theory or in practice. And adjusting them to plausible other values can make the "defined" markets much larger or smaller.

In any event, the assumed benchmark values would need to be different for each different industry case (e.g., fresh lettuce versus oil-refining equipment), but there is no scientific basis for guiding the selection of "correct" benchmark values. Moreover, the responses may show no sharp break or gap among the products in question that could be used for drawing the market boundary.

As has frequently been the case with the new industrial organization ideas since 1970, this new "scientific" technique is far less valuable than its authors have claimed. It is largely a formalistic restatement of concepts that have long been applied, with more practical value, in other ways. Where really reliable estimates of responses can be made by using the Department of Justice approach, they can, of course, be helpful. But that will be infrequent. In the meantime, markets must continue to be defined somehow, and the standard criteria, used with cautious judgment, are still the most effective way.

4. Supply Conditions

While markets are defined by the zone of choice that *consumers* have, certain conditions of *supply* can also be relevant. Some analysts suggest relying heavily on the cross-elasticity of supply. That reflects the ability of producers now outside the market for good 1 to switch their productive capacity from other goods to good 1. If they are hovering at the edges of the market, then their quick entry when prices

---

[6] In one case involving banks in adjacent small towns in northwest Michigan, customers were asked if they would shift deposits under certain assumed differences in interest rates, etc. Their answers were usually vague and showed no clear pattern. Being hypothetical, they revealed very little about actual depositor choices.

See also Richard J. Wertheimer, "DOJ Tries Out Its 5-percent Geographic Market Test," *Legal Times*, August 30, 1982, reprinted in Elzinga and Rogowsky, eds., "Relevant Markets in Antitrust," 1984, 1079–86, for an example involving Virginia banking.

rise can affect the degree of monopoly. Obviously, the quicker and bigger the entry, the less will be the market power in this market.

The cross-elasticity of supply relates goods *adjacent to* the market for good 1 to the prices of goods *in* this market:

$$\text{Cross-elasticity of supply between good 1 inside the market and adjacent goods} = \frac{\text{\% Change in quantity of adjacent goods}}{\text{\% Change in price of good 1}}$$

Some analysts have gone so far as to give these supply conditions the major role, but that is an error.

Supply conditions deal with entry *into the market*. It is nonsense to mix the definition of the market with the *possible* entry of firms into the market. Instead, it is logical to define the market first, on the basis of demand conditions of consumer choice. After that is done, then any relevant entry conditions can be clarified.

Of course, factories and equipment can often be shifted quickly and costlessly from one product to another, such as from quilts to sleeping bags. Firms not currently making the product may be poised to shift into the market in response even to small price changes. But these are *potential* entrants, and it is erroneous to treat them as if they are in the market already. They are not.

The "supply side" method is frequently used by antitrust defendants trying to draw wide market boundaries, but it poses practical problems as well as logical error. The degree of transferability of capacity is often hard to assess objectively. Transferability of capacity is frequently slower and more costly than is claimed. If capacity is fully engaged in more profitable other uses, as it often is, no transfer into this product will actually occur, even for sizable price shifts.

It is correct and prudent to ignore such potential entrants when defining the market. Once the market is defined, these outside firms can be considered in judging the importance of potential entry, in light of all possible barriers. Potential entry may indeed neutralize market power, in minor or major degrees. But that can only be assessed after markets have been correctly defined.

Taken altogether, the problems of defining markets can be difficult, but the task is basic and unavoidable. It shapes one's view of the degree and trend of competition in the economy. A selection of market definitions drawn from leading antitrust cases is given in Table 3.2. You can test them, and those given in the industry studies in Chapters 17 and 18, against your own judgment.

II.   THE ELEMENTS OF MARKET STRUCTURE

With the market defined, one can assess its internal structure. The structure is embodied mainly in the *size distribution* of the competing firms, as we saw at the outset of Chapter 1 in Figure 1.2. Three of the main types of markets listed in Table 1.1 are illustrated here in Figure 3.2: dominance, tight oligopoly, and loose oligopoly. Firms are arrayed in decreasing order of their *market shares*. The largest firm's market share may be dominant, medium, or small, as shown in the figure. The

TABLE 3.2 A Selection of Markets Definitions from Antitrust Cases

| ANTITRUST CASE (YEAR DECIDED) | ALTERNATIVE DEFINITIONS OF THE RELEVANT MARKET AND THE RESULTING DOMINANT-FIRM SHARES | |
	BROADLY DEFINED MARKET	NARROWLY DEFINED MARKET
1. Aluminum Company of America (Alcoa) (1945)	All ingot and scrap (33%)	New ingot sold (90%)
2. Du Pont "Cellophane" (1956)	Flexible wrapping materials (16%–20%)	Cellophane (75%–100%)
3. Philadelphia National Bank (1963)	National banking (below 4%)	Philadelphia banking (36%)
4. Xerox (1975)	All copying equipment (65%)	Plain-paper copiers (90%+)
5. IBM (withdrawn 1982)	All office equipment (38%)	Mainframe computers sold to private buyers (70%)

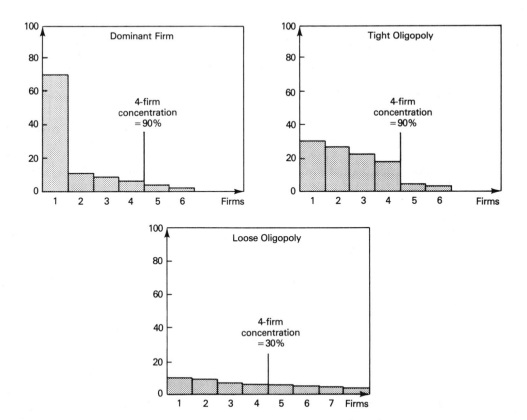

FIGURE 3.2. Market share patterns in three main types of market structure.

market's degree of *concentration* refers to the combined share of the few largest firms (in published census concentration ratios, usually the top four firms). This is the conventional index of the degree of oligopoly.

The *number* of firms in the market might seem important, but it usually tells us little about structure, because market shares can vary so sharply. (Thus four-firm concentration is identical at 90 percent for the dominant-firm and tight-oligopoly cases in Figure 3.2.) If one firm or several firms dominate the market, it may not matter whether there is also one other tiny firm, or fifty of them or five hundred. Of course, whether there is just one firm or two or three in the market may make a difference, but even then, there might be one virtual monopolist with 99 percent, for whom the one or two tiny "competitors" are inconsequential.

These size distributions embody the *internal structure* of *actual competition*. *External* conditions may also matter, as they determine the ability of *potential competitors* outside the market to enter it and become actual competitors. We consider first the main internal elements of structure: market shares and oligopoly concentration. Then we turn to entry barriers and potential competition.

1. Market Share

The firm's own market share is a simple concept. It is the share of the industry's total sales revenue, and it can range from virtually zero up to 100 percent.[7]

Market share is the most important single indicator of the firm's degree of monopoly power in an ordinal sense (compared to higher or lower shares in the same market). Higher market shares almost always provide higher monopoly power, while low shares involve little or none.[8] Within a given market, monopoly power will vary in line with the market shares, rather than be some industry-wide constant that is shared uniformly by all firms. Thus Procter & Gamble, with about 50 percent of the detergent market, has much more market power than Lever Brothers does, with its 10 percent.

A degree of market power usually appears when market share rises from negligible to around 15 percent. At higher shares, such as 25–30 percent, the degree of monopoly may become quite significant, and market shares over 40–50 percent usually give strong market power. The *absolute* degree of market power depends on the firm's demand elasticity, and that is shaped by the market's general conditions, as well as by the firm's own market share. In one market, a 50 percent market share may give higher monopoly power than the same share in another market. But within each market, the degree of monopoly power usually varies ordinally with market share.

The importance of market share has been recognized in the classical and neoclassical literatures, and market share is widely established in business practice as a focus for company motives and strategies. Successes are commonly reported in terms of market shares as well as in profits and stock prices.

Like any element, market share is important mainly as a source of profits to the

---

[7] In odd cases, the share might better be based on other measures, such as assets, value added, or inventories of rental equipment. But sales revenue is the near-universal index.

[8] The exception occurs when entry from outside is so free and powerful that all monopoly power inside the market is prevented. Such free entry is considered in the next section.

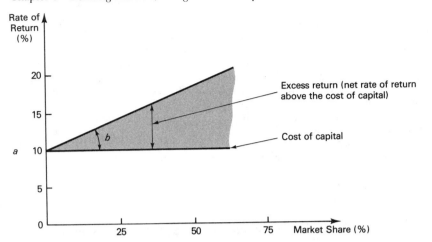

FIGURE 3.3.   The basic relationship between market share and profitability.

firm. There is a general relationship between each firm's market share and its degree of profitability. This relationship is illustrated in Figure 3.3 for any typical market. That line represents a simple formula:

$$\text{Rate of return} = \pi = a + bM$$

where π is the firm's rate of return on its invested capital, a is the competitive rate of return, b is the slope of the line, and M is market share.

The a value is actually the cost of capital to the firm. It must earn the rate a (say, 10 percent on investment) just to pay its investors their opportunity cost: the return they would have gotten on their best alternative investment. Profit rates above a represent excess returns. The shaded area in Figure 3.3 shows what excess profits are available to firms in this market, at varying market shares. If the b slope is high, then market share is particularly rewarding and will be sought more fiercely. This curve is, of course, just an illustration. Actual results would vary from market to market, as Figure 2.12 illustrated.

The actual slope and shape of the curve in real cases will reflect two main conditions.

1. *The firm's demand conditions.* Monopoly power and control over price vary with demand *in*elasticity. Two effects on price are actually possible: the *simple raising of the single price* and *price discrimination*. Firms divide their customers into groups of varying demand conditions, and then charge the inelastic groups higher prices than the others. An array of price-cost ratios is created, aligned with demand elasticities (see Chapter 12 for analysis). This permits higher profits than if only one uniform price were set.

2. *Economies of scale and superior performance.* These are alternative possible causes of excess profits. If economies are large, they alone may cause a steep rise in profit rates as market shares rise. Or if a firm simply is superior in costs or products, its profits and market share may both be large. Indeed, Chicago-UCLA economists credit virtually all high profits to these benign causes. Yet that is a matter requiring evidence (to be reviewed

in Chapter 9.) Also, diseconomies of scale may occur, causing the profit rate line in Figure 3.3 to flatten or even bend down.

In short, the profit yields of market share may be steep or slight, and they may reflect mainly market power (as the firm exploits demand) or greater efficiency (from economies of scale or superior performance). These two sources are independent; there could be high market power yields and large economies. Or diseconomies might be large, but offset by monopoly yields.

In any event, market share is the element most closely related to these possibilities. It is the traditional and logical center of attention in assessing the market power held by any firm. A high market share usually provides high market power; a low market share usually defines the firm as under strong competitive pressure.

2. Concentration

Concentration is the combined market share of the leading firms, which cannot be fewer than two or much more than eight.

Concentration is the degree of oligopoly. Oligopolists may coordinate as tightly as if they were a genuine monopoly; they may compete fiercely; or they may fluctuate in the middle range. *Their combined market power is simply a dilution of the simple effect that a single firm with the same market share would have.* For example, Alcoa (with 90 percent of the aluminum market) was replaced after 1950 by a three-firm oligopoly with a 90 percent combined share. But the three have never exerted as much market control as Alcoa did. Oligopolists have mixed motives, as Chapter 13 explores, while a monopoly exerts unified control.

The degree of this dilution depends on many things, because oligopoly is complex. The complexity has three main causes. First, there are infinite gradients in the degree of oligopoly. It is customary to distinguish between tight and loose oligopoly, but some actual markets lie between those boxes. Often, too, "the oligopoly group" is not distinct from the rest of the market because the firms' market shares shade down by small percentages, as in panel II of Figure 3.2.

Second, the degree and effect of the interdependence need not be strong. Oligopolists may fight, or coordinate, or simply ignore one another and pursue independent policies. If the interdependence has no definite effects, it has no role in market structure.

Third, the group's internal structure may influence the outcome. A symmetrical group (all members equal) may behave differently from an asymmetrical group (dominated by one firm). There are infinite varieties of such internal structures, both in theory and in actual markets.

Accordingly, *the relationship of concentration to profitability is likely to be loose or nonexistent.* Any given concentration ratio may represent a variety of internal structures and degrees of interdependence.[9] The expected relationship is illustrated in Figure 3.4. It may be a continuous line, with a smoothly rising effect as concentration increases. Or there may be a definite stair-step as concentration rises from loose oligopoly to the closer coordination of tight oligopoly (see Subsection III.2). Factual research has not settled this question (see Chapter 5).

Alternatively, oligopoly may simply widen the variation of outcomes between

---

[9] That is why Chapters 13 and 14 treat the matter in such detail.

Rate of Return (%)

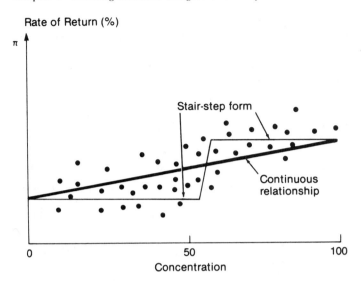

FIGURE 3.4.   The basic relationship between concentration and profitability (illustrated as continuous or stair-step in form).

high profits for a cohesive group and low profits for a contentious group of oligopolists. This would appear as a widened dispersion in the middle and upper ranges of both Figure 3.3 and Figure 3.4.

Even if concentration is too "loose" causally to be a precise, important element of market structure, it remains useful as a descriptive statistic, for it conveys the main shape of an industry reasonably well in one ratio.

Other indexes of concentration have been developed in attempts to portray the entire size distribution of firms in one indicator. Since 1980, the Hirschman-Herfindahl Index (often called the HHI) has gained some popularity and use.[10] Like other "comprehensive" indexes, it incorporates the market shares of all firms. Therefore it requires more detailed information than the standard concentration ratio, which is based on just four firms.

The HHI is quite simple: the sum of the squared market shares of all firms in the market:

$$\text{HHI} = (\text{Market share}_1)^2 + (\text{Market share}_2)^2 + (\text{Market share}_3)^2 + \cdots + (\text{Market share}_n)^2$$

For a pure monopoly, with just one firm holding 100 percent of the market:

$$\text{HHI} = (100 \text{ percent})^2 = 100 \times 100 = 10{,}000$$

In pure competition, with each market share at or below 1 percent, the HHI would be at or below 100.

---

[10] In the Antitrust Division of the Justice Department (one of the two U.S. antitrust agencies). It is embodied in merger guidelines issued by the Division in 1982 and revised in 1984, which are applied in judging whether proposed mergers would reduce competition significantly.

TABLE 3.3   Sample HHI Calculations

The HHI is the sum of the squared market shares. For example, the HHI for four 25 percent oligopolists is 625 + 625 + 625 + 625 = 2,500; for ten 10 percent firms, 100 times 10 = 1,000. Rough equivalents with four-firm concentration ratios are:

Firms' Market Shares	*Four-Firm Concentration*	*HHI*
Ten 10 percent firms	40	1,000
Six 16 percent firms	64	1,660
Five 20 percent firms	80	2,000
Four 25 percent firms	100	2,500
Three 33 percent firms	100	3,300

Roughly, an HHI below 1,000 is loose oligopoly, while an HHI above 1,800 is tight oligopoly.

To measure the rise in the HHI when two firms merge, multiply the two market shares together and then double that number. Examples:

Firm A	*Firm B*	*Multiplied*	*Rise in HHI*
5 percent	5 percent	25 × 2	= 50
7 percent	7 percent	49 × 2	= 98
10 percent	10 percent	100 × 2	= 200
8 percent	4 percent	32 × 2	= 64
15 percent	4 percent	60 × 2	= 120

For a tight oligopoly with market shares of 30, 25, 20, 15, and 10, the HHI would be:

$$\text{HHI} = 30^2 + 25^2 + 20^2 + 15^2 + 10^2$$
$$= 900 + 625 + 400 + 225 + 100$$
$$= 2,250$$

Sample HHI values for middle ranges of concentration are given in Table 3.3. Interpreting the index is difficult because the values are pure numbers, with no direct real equivalent. They correspond roughly to standard concentration ratios, as Table 3.3 shows, but only loosely.

Users have had to rely on the standard ratios to give intuitive meaning to the HHI. Thus HHI values below 1,000 are said to involve no significant monopoly power, while those over 1,800 clearly do. But that judgment has no intrinsic content; it simply refers to loose oligopoly (concentration below 40 percent, and HHIs roughly below 1,000) and tight oligopoly (concentration above 60 percent, and HHIs roughly above 1,800).

Some insight is offered by the "numbers equivalent," which is defined thus:

$$\text{Numbers equivalent} = \frac{10,000}{\text{HHI}}$$

It reflects the fact that if there are N equal-sized firms, then the HHI takes the value of 10,000/N.

For example, for an HHI of 2,000:

$$\text{Numbers equivalent} = \frac{10,000}{2,000} = 5$$

The 2,000 value indeed represents five firms, each with market shares of 20 percent. *If* firms are of identical size, the numbers equivalent is a way of giving more concrete meaning to the HHI. But this is still much like converting the HHI back into market shares and concentration ratios in order to endow it with some concrete meaning.

The HHI, therefore, is one of several "new" tools that remove real content from the monopoly problem.[11] Intrinsically an empty index, it does have the virtue of reflecting all market shares rather than just the top four. It also has interesting properties. It nicely reflects the fact that concentration is a diluted form of dominance. Thus a dominant-firm share of 50 percent has the same HHI for itself—(50) × (50) = 2,500—as four oligopolists each with 25 percent—4 × (25) × (25) = 4 × 625 = 2,500. Intuition suggests that those two situations—50 percent dominance and four-firm concentration of 100 percent—do display about the same degree of monopoly.

Another interesting HHI property is that dominance has very high values. Thus a share of 60 percent has an HHI of 3,600, which is much higher than the tight-oligopoly threshold value of 1,800. This suggests, correctly on the whole, that dominance is a much more serious problem than even tight oligopoly.

At any rate, users of HHIs will continue to have to interpret them in terms of standard market shares and concentration ratios. In practice, the HHI's values are loosely correlated with concentration ratios. Altogether, the HHI is an interesting, but hardly a clearly superior, index.

3. Barriers to Entry

Now we turn to external conditions. At the edge of the market there may be barriers to entry, which impede potential competitors from entering the market to become actual competitors. Anything that decreases the likelihood, scope, or speed of their entry is a barrier to entry.

The ideas are intuitively simple and have been common since John Bates Clark proposed them in the 1890s, followed by Schumpeter's competitive process based on entry in the 1940s and Joe S. Bain's work on barriers in the 1950s (recall Chapter 1 and see Appendix 1). Barriers include all manner of legal devices (e.g., patents, mineral rights, franchises) as well as more general economic impediments.

Bain stressed that barriers rest on fundamental features of the market, especially large size, large economies of scale, and heavy advertising, all of which make it expensive to establish a viable new company. These can be called *exogenous* conditions of entry; they are outside the control of the incumbent firms. At least eight

---

[11] Also, the choice of squaring the market share, with an exponent of 2, rather than applying some other exponent, such as 1.5 or some other value, is arbitrary.

categories of such exogenous barrier conditions have been discussed in the literature, as listed in Table 11.1 of Chapter 11, where there is a detailed analysis.

There are also *endogenous* conditions—under the control of the incumbent firms—which can deter entry. Table 11.1 lists six categories of endogenous conditions, including a variety of strategic actions and retaliations. They are discretionary, chosen freely by the incumbent firms to suit their interests, so they are evanescent rather than fixed and fundamental.

Given so many sources of barriers, it is quite difficult to estimate the "height" of actual barriers, as we will see in Chapter 11. But rough-and-ready estimates made for some industries show a range from no barrier at all (free entry) to very high barriers excluding all entry.[12] The custom has been to classify barriers by three categories of height (low, medium, and high), but the actual variation is continuous.

In short, what seems at first a simple idea actually involves complex, often obscure conditions. Even so, some economists regard barriers as highly important, perhaps more important than internal structure. The Chicago-UCLA School takes the opposite view: barriers are vague and meaningless. A prudent view is that barriers and potential entry are usually secondary to internal conditions, and potential competition rarely disturbs actual competition or monopoly. External conditions are usually (and literally) peripheral.

Incumbent firms are generally more concerned about their existing rivals than about some new firm that might enter the market sometime, with unknown size and impacts. Perhaps some small-town local monopolists, such as a hotel or a lumberyard, may be frightened that a national chain will someday set up a new branch in town. But it is the important national markets, such as automobiles, computers, and aircraft, that pose the central problems of the field.

III. DEGREES AND CONCEPTS OF PARTIAL COMPETITION

All the elements of market structure are combined in judging the degree of competition in a market. No simple formula can be used; one must rely on judgment. First one considers the market share of the leading firm. If it is very high (above 40 percent) and there is no close rival, the market power held by that firm is probably also high. Free entry may nullify the leading firm's market power if potential entrants are powerful and poised to enter. A full appraisal of the market will also consider the behavior of the dominant firm toward the others, and its degree of profitability.

If the largest market share is in the 25–50 percent range, then tight oligopoly probably exists because four-firm concentration is probably above 60 percent. One would also consider pricing behavior and profit rates in assessing the degree of competition.

Finally, if the largest market share is below 20 percent and the combined four-firm concentration is below 40 percent, then some form of effective competition probably exists. Even if entry barriers are high, collusion will probably be futile.

Economists divide the degrees of competition into three main categories: dom-

---

[12] The extreme case of free entry, called "ultra-free entry" or "contestability," may also exist (recall Chapter 1). It, too, is covered in Chapter 11.

inant firm, tight oligopoly, and loose oligopoly (including monopolistic competition). They were presented in Table 1.2. Although the categories shade into one another, each has its distinctive concepts.

1. The Dominant Firm

A firm is dominant when it has over 40 percent of the sales in the market and has no close rival. The higher the dominant firm's market share, the closer it comes to being a pure monopoly. To that extent, the firm's demand curve is likely to be about as inelastic as the total market demand curve. At high market shares, the dominant firm's demand curve tends to coincide with the entire market demand curve.

The dominant firm acts like a pure monopoly, even though its power over the market is less than complete. There is some competition from small competitors, but it is usually not effective. Mainly, the dominant firm just sets its profit-maximizing decisions unilaterally, given the degree of monopoly its demand curve provides.

Persistent Dominance.   Dominant firms are unusual because a high market share is hard to capture and maintain. Yet the firms that do attain market dominance often become household names. Notice the familiar company names in Table 3.4. Many local markets also contain dominant firms. Your local newspaper is probably one, and so perhaps is the biggest local bank, lumberyard, and hospital.[13]

Dominant firms usually impose the two standard monopoly effects on prices: (1) they raise the *level* of prices, and (2) they create a *discriminatory structure* of prices. From both of these effects excess profits usually arise, approximately as illustrated in Figure 2.12. The market share–profit rate relationship is a relatively close one, rising toward monopoly levels as market shares rise toward 100 percent.

Price discrimination is common because dominant firms can usually segment the market and set varying price-cost ratios for customer groups, in line with their inelasticity of demand. For example, IBM has set higher price-cost ratios on the computers that face the weakest competition. Airlines fit their fare discounts thoroughly to differences in demand, especially between business travelers and others (see the analysis of the airline industry in Chapter 18). Chapter 12 explores price discrimination in some detail.

In short, dominant firms are near-monopolies, to be analyzed using the basic concepts of monopoly.

Schumpeter's Competitive Process: Transient Dominance.   But there is an alternative view about dominant firms, often called the Schumpeterian process. Joseph A. Schumpeter (rhymes with "zoom-greater") was a deeply conservative theorist who argued that big businesses, even ones that hold market dominance, could give results even better than the neoclassical competitive outcome. His concept of "creative destruction" (published in 1942) is a dramatic dissent from the prevailing neoclassical view.[14]

---

[13] Cities with leading-newspaper shares over 80 percent include Des Moines, New Orleans, Miami, Milwaukee, Kansas Cit, Atlanta, St. Louis, Phoenix, Los Angeles, and hundreds of smaller cities. See Chapter 17.

[14] See his *Capitalism, Socialism and Democracy* (New York: Harper & Row, 1942), pp. 85–106.

TABLE 3.4   A Selection of Leading Instances of Dominant Firms, Oligopolies, and Monopolistic Competition

1. DOMINANT FIRMS	MARKETS	THE FIRM'S AVERAGE MARKET SHARE (%)	ENTRY BARRIERS
IBM	Mainframe computers	60	High
AT&T	Long-distance telephone service	70	Moderate
Eastman Kodak	Photographic film	80	Medium
Procter & Gamble	Detergents, toiletries	50	Medium
Boeing	Aircraft	55	High
General Electric	Aircraft engines	50	Medium
Campbell Soup	Canned soups	75	Medium
Gillette	Razors, toiletries	55	Medium
Wall Street Journal	Business newspapers	65	High
Washington Post	Washington, D.C., area newspapers	84	High
Many newspapers	Most cities	50–99	High
Federal Express	Overnight mail delivery	60	High

2. TIGHT OLIGOPOLIES	FOUR-FIRM CONCENTRATION RATIO IN RELEVANT MARKETS (%)*	3. LOOSE OLIGOPOLIES AND MONOPOLISTIC COMPETITION	FOUR-FIRM CONCENTRATION RATIO IN RELEVANT MARKETS (%)
Artificial fibers	96	Movie theaters	30
Automobiles	84	Poultry	16
Flat glass	85	Yarns	19
Batteries	89	Commercial printing	18
Glass bottles	54	Knit fabrics	20
Cereal breakfast foods	86	Sheet metalwork	10
Soft drinks	85	Costume jewelry	23
Chewing gum	93	Retail shops	6
Cigarettes	95	Restaurants	24
Beer	77	Wood millwork	14
		Dresses	8

* The four-firm concentration ratio is the share of the market's sales made by the largest four firms in the industry.

It posits competition as a *disequilibrium process*, rather than a set of equilibrium conditions. Competition and progress occur together, he said, but in a series of temporary monopolies. The Schumpeterian process is the exact reverse, point by point, of the neoclassical analysis.

In each time period, each market may be dominated by one firm, which raises prices and earns monopoly profits. But these profits attract other firms, one of which soon innovates a superior product and displaces the first dominant firm. The new dominant firm then has its chance to set monopoly prices, causing the usual distortions and monopoly burdens. But soon it, too, is pushed aside by the next new-comer.

This cycle of "creative destruction" continues: innovation creates dominance, which gains monopoly profits, which stimulate new innovation, new dominance, and on and on. As time passes, the average degree of monopoly profits may be high. Indeed, the profits, disequilibrium, distortions, and market dominance may all be large at each point of time. Yet the process of innovation is rapid, and it might soon generate benefits of technical progress far exceeding any costs of misallocation caused as market power is created and destroyed.

The Schumpeterian process is exciting, and some specialists regard themselves as Schumpeterians because they favor rugged, progressive processes, even if they involve some monopoly power. Moreover, the concept is a refreshing contrast to austere neoclassical theory.

Yet it requires certain doubtful assumptions. Dominant firms must be vulnerable enough to be easily toppled. Entry barriers must be low or weak enough to permit rapid entry on a scale large enough to displace the dominant firm at a stroke. Few entrenched dominant firms will let that happen. The newcomers must attack by launching innovation rather than through other, less glamorous tactics.

Moreover, the contrast with neoclassical analysis is not really so stark. Effective competition also envisions a process of adjustment. It, too, can involve some significant market shares, rather than just swarms of atomistic firms. And monopolies can set prices high enough to attract new competition. Therefore there is a good deal of common ground between the Schumpeterian and neoclassical concepts of competition and monopoly.

Yet they do stress different features: the neoclassical analysis, an efficient equilibrium among many firms; the Schumpeterian analysis, a rugged, creative process involving a sequence of monopolies. As a matter of internal logic, they are equally valid.

Passive Dominant Firms.   Still another view has been taken by several theorists, who since the 1950s have suggested that dominant firms adopt a passive role and let small rivals take away their dominance rather rapidly (see Chapter 11). Passivity in dominant forms is conceivable, as a way of maximizing current profits, even if it lets small rivals move in. But, in fact, many dominant firms are aggressive in using all possible tactics to suppress their rivals. So although the passive-dominance approach may be internally logical—if the assumption of passivity is valid—in practice, it may apply to only a few important dominant firms.

The question about dominance is ultimately a factual one: Which markets actually fit these three alternative concepts? Is most of the economy Schumpeterian, perhaps including computers and other electronics, chemicals, and automobiles, while only a few corners of it (agriculture, possibly parts of retailing) fit the neoclassical version of competition? Or are the proportions reversed, with only a small set of Schumpeterian industries, compared to a wide range of more static competitive and monopolized industries? Are many dominant firms passive, or only some or perhaps none?

Evidence on these questions is given in Chapters 4, 5, 6, 11, and 17. It will emerge that many dominant firms are able to retain their positions for long periods, yielding them up only slowly, if at all. The Schumpeterian and passive-dominance models have only limited scope. But there are exceptions.

2.   Tight Oligopoly

The critical distinction is between *tight* oligopoly, where collusion is likely, and *loose* oligopoly, where it is not.

In all the theorizing about oligopoly since the 1930s, no single solution or model has prevailed. The phenomenon continues to be a riddle, with variations that baffle economists. Only a few of the possible infinite variations have been modeled, as Chapter 13 will show. But the main lines of the topic can be drawn, as follows.

Oligopoly is about *fewness* and *interdependence*. It ranges from pure duopoly, with just two firms, down to loose oligopolies with eight to ten substantial firms. Firms in an oligopolistic market are few enough so that each must consider the others' probable responses to its own actions. Competition is therefore dynamic: a sequence of moves and countermoves.

There is *indeterminacy*. Actions cannot be simple unilateral steps, as they are in pure competition, pure monopoly, and dominance. In those cases, each firm's demand is determinate and known. In contrast, under oligopoly, each firm's demand depends on its rivals' reactions to its actions.

Therefore *strategy* is required. Like chess players, each firm must think ahead strategically over a wide range of actions and possible reactions. What it assumes about its rivals' reactions becomes crucial to its predictions of the outcomes. Those assumptions are developed and used in detail in Chapter 13, where oligopoly models are presented.

Oligopoly also means *a wide range of outcomes,* varying from pure cooperation all the way over to pure conflict. At one extreme, a set of oligopolists may cooperate so fully that they attain the pure monopoly result, with a "joint maximizing" of their shared profits. At the other extreme, they may act strictly independently and hostilely, forcing each other into the purely competitive result. More commonly, they settle somewhere in the middle range; or they may veer between extremes and middle outcomes, as their behavior shifts.

This variety means that there is no single economic model for oligopoly. There are infinitely many possible varieties of oligopoly structures: in degrees of concentration, in asymmetry or equality among the oligopolists, in differing cost and demand conditions for each firm, in long-run and short-run motivations, and so on. Economists have yearned and struggled to develop "the" oligopoly theory, and they have come up with several interesting methods for framing oligopoly choices, which Chapter 13 will explore. But the results are modest: only a number of rather brittle models, based on odd assumptions, and some general "insights" and lessons. Oligopoly is still largely an uncharted jungle.

The fundamental condition is that *the oligopolists always have conflicting incentives to compete and to collude.* And each oligopolist has mixed incentives toward its rivals.

Compete: Each firm could compete intensely, seeking every way to maximize its own profits. Its aggressive actions will stimulate sharp reactions, which cumulate in a process of effective competition.

Collude: Collusion is also attractive. Each oligopolist knows that if they all cooperate, then they can attain higher joint profits, just as a monopoly brings higher profits than a competitive setting.

Mixed incentives: Yet all firms also know that cheating may occur, which will destroy the collusion. Each firm can gain by cutting its price, while all the others cooperate to keep the collusive price up. It is best to be in a market that is rigged collusively, but to be *outside* the price-fixing ring. All firms share the temptation to cheat, so collusion is always prey to cheating and collapse. Yet all oligopolists also know that if only they can make the collusion stick, joint rewards will be high.

Actual markets reflect the intricate mingling and conflicts among these incentives. One oligopoly may settle into snug cooperation, behaving like a total monopoly, while another may be the scene of endless warfare, with low prices and frantic innovation. Chicago-UCLA analysts say that collusion tends to collapse quickly, from its inner conflicts. Others are less optimistic, noting that many cartels have lasted for decades. The actual outcome depends on the specific conditions of each case, a matter of facts rather than mere logic.

Yet there are some general patterns:

1. *The higher the concentration, the greater the likelihood that collusion will be successful.*[15] There are two reasons why concentration promotes collusion. First, high concentration means that there are fewer firms to organize, understand, and enforce mutual agreements. The few leaders, having most of the market, face little pressure from small fringe firms outside the price ring.

Second, price-cutting by any renegade is easier to discover and penalize. If there are only three firms, the other two will quickly know if the first firm cheats. But if ten or fifteen firms are involved, then any one of them will be more strongly tempted to chisel, since it can expect to succeed for a longer time before being discovered.

Accordingly, *collusion is likely to crystallize and persist in tight oligopoly, whereas it is likely to fail in loose oligopoly.* Tight oligopoly tends to become a "shared monopoly," as joint maximizing prevails over independent action. Loose oligopoly tends, instead, toward effective competition, with uncontrollable price-cutting.

2. *Similarity of the firms' conditions.* Tight-oligopoly cooperation is strengthened if the firms have similar demand and/or cost conditions. Because their interests coincide, they can be more confident that cooperation will last.

3. *Familiarity over time.* As time passes, the firm's managers get to know one another and therefore find it easier to predict one another's behavior more accurately. Misunderstandings become less likely, and mutual trust grows. That is why oligopolies in older industries tend to have tighter cooperation. New managers may bring unsettling new attitudes, but again, the differences may fade with time.

The contrast between tight and loose oligopoly is not stark, as Section II noted. Tight oligopolies often undergo bouts of severe competition, while loose oligopolies sometimes manage to collude for a while. Thus there may be no clear break, or stair-

---

[15] A leading discussion, giving rather sensible reasons for the obvious fact that concentration promotes collusion, is by George J. Stigler, "A Theory of Oligopoly," *Journal of Political Economy,* 72 (February 1964), 44–61. But more sophisticated and comprehensive earlier classic discussions are by Edward H. Chamberlin, *The Theory of Monopolistic Competition* (Cambridge, Mass.: Harvard University Press, 1933; 6th ed., 1962); and William J. Fellner, *Competition Among the Few* (New York: Knopf, 1949).

step, in the relationship between concentration and prices. As Figure 3.4 illustrated, there may be a significant rise in prices as concentration shifts from about 40 percent to about 60 percent, reflecting the crystallization of price-fixing in tight oligopoly. Or, instead, the rise may be gradual, because concentration does not hermetically control oligopoly behavior. Chapter 13 will explore the alternatives further.

Types of collusion

The kinds of collusion that may occur in oligopolies range from tight, explicit collusion to informal, loose arrangements.

Direct Collusion.   If price-fixing is legal, then the price-fixing in tight oligopolies can be so complete that it approaches the level a pure monopoly would achieve. A *cartel* (an organization created by companies to manage their cooperation) may be formed to fix prices and enforce penalties against members who violate the agreement. Cartel managers may also set output quotas, control investments, and pool profits. Most cartels have existed in Western European countries and in certain international markets, such as OPEC in the world oil market.

Price-fixing has been against the law since about 1899 in most U.S. industries, under Section 1 of the Sherman Act and various state antitrust laws (see Chapter 19 for details about antitrust). The U.S. antitrust laws therefore shift the margin of choice away from collusion and toward competition in most U.S. oligopolies. Nonetheless, there is some hidden price-fixing, done through secret meetings, phone calls, and other covert ways, as Chapter 14 will survey.

Tacit Collusion.   Price-fixing can also occur in a milder form called *tacit collusion,* or parallel pricing, or price signaling. The oligopolistic firms do not conspire directly or sign binding agreements, for fear of being caught. But a firm can give indirect hints and signals of its preferred price levels. Then all the other firms simply go along with the same price changes. Frequently a fully cooperative price, just as high as if formal collusion had occurred, is reached in this way. Under tight oligopoly, tacit collusion is often nearly as complete as with a full-blown cartel (or even with pure monopoly). Loose oligopoly, in contrast, rarely achieves indirect collusion.

3.   Loose Oligopoly, Including Monopolistic Competition

The realm of loose oligopoly is wide, ranging from moderate concentration to nearly pure competition. There is little formal theory for this category because it simply involves effective competition, with prices forced down near cost, costs forced down toward their minimum levels, rapid innovation, and so on.

But the theory of monopolistic competition, developed in the 1930s, offers some insights into the results that occur when structure is not quite strictly competitive.

Monopolistic competition

As Chamberlin developed the idea, monopolistic competition has low levels of concentration, but each firm has a slight degree of monopoly. Therefore economists treat this market structure as a highly diluted form of monopoly, in which firms'

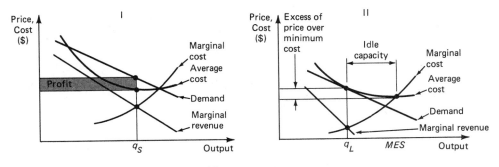

FIGURE 3.5   Monopolistic competition.
Demand is highly elastic. Profits may occur (panel I). But soon demand is forced down until the average cost curve just touches the demand curve (panel II). There is no extra profit, but price is above minimum average cost, and there is idle capacity.

demand curves have only a slight downward slope. No firm's market share is more than 10 percent.

The distinctive features of monopolistic competition are:

1.   There is some product differentiation, which means that consumers can develop preferences among sellers. This slight degree of market power gives the firm's demand curve a slight downward slope, as illustrated in Figure 3.5. The product differentiation can occur either because the products themselves differ physically or in brand images (like various brands of bread, jewelry, or shirts); or because of the sellers' locations (as when a local grocery store, hotel, or restaurant is convenient to a neighborhood).

2.   There is free entry into the market. New firms enter whenever any excess profit (above the normal competitive rate) is being made in the industry.

3.   There is no interdependence among individual firms. No firms have large enough market shares to influence the rest of the market. Each firm merely feels the competitive pressure from all the many other firms in the market.

These conditions are common among retail outlets and in other markets, as shown in the third group of markets in Table 3.4. A typical case of monopolistic competition is a grocery or clothing store, with some clientele centered in its neighborhood but steady competition from many other stores farther away. The firm's demand is highly, but not infinitely, elastic. Because the demand curve is nearly flat, the firm has only a little room for choice in pricing.

In the short run, the situation in panel I of Figure 3.5 may hold. The demand curve may lie above the average cost curve, permitting the firm to earn short-run excess profits, as shown by the shaded box when it chooses the output q_s. But then new firms enter the market, forcing down this firm's demand curve until it is just tangent to the average cost curve. That eliminates the excess profits.

In panel II, none of the long-run demand curve is above the cost curve, so no excess profits are possible. The firm can just survive at output q_L (where marginal revenue equals marginal cost), barely earning the competitive rate of profit. Monopolistic competition eliminates long-run excess profits, even when demand is not perfectly elastic.

Yet monopolistic competition does cause two deviations from the efficient results of pure competition. First, cost and price will both be slightly higher than under perfect competition (which settles at *MES* in panel II of Figure 3.5). This difference is shown by the higher price and by q_L being less than *MES*. This added cost is not just a dead loss, for consumers benefit from the extra price they pay. For example, the local grocery store may charge higher prices, but its neighborhood customers find that the extra convenience can be worth the extra cost of shopping there. Or perhaps brand preferences are at work. For example, suppose a restaurant is regarded as offering more stylish dishes than the other restaurants in town. Some customers will be willing to pay more for these dishes, along the demand curve shown in Figure 3.5, because they get meals they like better than those served in the other restaurants.

The second deviation is a degree of idle capacity. Because output q_L is less than *MES,* some of the firm's capacity (the amount of *MES* $- q_L$) stands idle. In practical terms, most retail shops have near-empty aisles for most or all of every day; most restaurants would like more customers than they have.

You may see significant amounts of these two distinctive features, idle capacity and extra pricing "for convenience," in many stores you deal with. Monopolistic competition is an analytical case that is also a familiar phenomenon in many day-to-day businesses. But monopolistic competition usually comes close to the competitive result.

IV. SUMMARY

Markets can contain infinite gradations and varieties of competition and monopoly. To assess them, one starts by defining the market as the zone of consumer choice among closely substitutable goods. Cross-elasticity of demand is commonly said to define substitutability, but practical judgments must rest on other evidence. General features of the product, price similarity and interactions, and participants' judgments are often crucial. Geographic markets can be defined by transport costs, distances shipped, and shipments among areas.

The two main internal elements of market structures are market shares and concentration. Potential entry is an external element, limited by entry barriers. Though usually secondary to actual competition, potential competition can modify the market outcome to some degree.

Three main intermediate categories of markets are commonly recognized:

1. *The dominant firm* is a diluted version of pure monopoly, fitting the same concepts of pricing, profits, and innovation.
2. *Tight oligopoly* is diluted dominance, with a few firms that are closely interdependent. Although there are mixed incentives, the tendency toward collusion is usually strong and effective, because price-cutting can be readily discovered and punished. Collusion may be direct or tacit.
3. *Loose oligopoly* is a broad category ranging from moderate concentration to nearly pure competition. Because it is unable to make collusion stick, loose oligopoly's outcomes approximate effective competition. The case of monopolistic competition may involve some degree of price-raising and idle capacity, while providing for convenience and brand preferences.

These categories will be analyzed more fully later in the text: dominant firms in Chapters 11, 12, and 17; tight oligopoly in Chapters 13, 14, and 18; and loose oligopoly in commentary in various places throughout the text.

But first we review the broad patterns of actual markets: Chapter 4 analyzes market structures, Part III (Chapters 5, 6, and 7) considers performance, and Part IV (Chapters 8 and 9) examines the determinants of market structure.

QUESTIONS FOR REVIEW

1. "Concentration is the only important element of market structure." True?

2. "The structuralist view is that market structure completely determines market performance." True?

3. "A duopoly is as likely to reach a competitive outcome as a monopoly outcome." Is this a "behavioralist" or a "structuralist" view?

4. "Market definition is simply a matter of calculating cross-elasticities of demand." True?

5. "The relationship between market share and rate of profit may reflect (a) scale economies, (b) concentration ratios, (c) the ability to raise price, (d) diversification, and (e) market power." Which?

6. "Entry is only one of the events that may threaten a firm's market share. Others are small-firm rises and moves by its oligopoly rivals." True?

7. List and analyze five markets with relatively clear edges.

8. What conditions of markets make for relatively sharp market edges that can be clearly defined?

9. List three industries with high entry barriers and explain the evidence that shows barrier height.

10. Explain why substitutability should be assessed at prices that are equal, rather than far apart.

11. Is the Antitrust Division method for defining markets more *realistic* than the traditional one?

12. Markets are defined by considering the range of buyer's substitutability. Why not also include suppliers' substitutability, which shows potential entry?

13. Explain the relative merits of 4-firm concentration ratios and Hirschman-Herfindahl indexes (HHI). Which one requires more complete information?

14. Compute the HHI values for a firm with 70 percent of its market and for a tight oligopoly of four 25-percent firms. Are the relative HHI values a good indicator of market power?

15. Show how the Schumpeterian competitive process is the exact opposite, point-by-point, of the neoclassical perfectly-competitive situation. Can they both be valid?

16. Explain how higher concentration tends to encourage collusion in tight oligopoly.

17. "Monopolistic competition tends toward moderately higher prices and some idle capacity." Please explain, using a diagram.

4 MARKET STRUCTURES IN THE U.S. ECONOMY

With the concepts of structure in mind, we now turn to the structure of real markets in the United States. The appraisal in this chapter will serve as the basis for Chapters 5, 6, and 7, where we assess performance as it may relate to structure.

U.S. markets cover the entire range from pure monopoly (in local electricity supply) to atomistic competition (among many thousands of wheat farmers in the Grain Belt). In this Chapter, we review all sizes and sectors of markets, showing how the degrees of competition and monopoly are appraised.

First, Section I surveys the main types of industries, as determined by their technology, age, and geographic scope. Then Section II notes how the elements of structure fit together. Next, Section III reviews how the economy-wide extent and trend of competition have shifted in recent decades. Section IV rounds out the chapter by reviewing dominant firms and their rate of decay, utility sectors, and foreign comparisons. For further explanation of the industry classifications used by the U.S. Census Bureau, you can consult Appendix 2 at the end of the book.

I. VARIETIES OF INDUSTRIES

Before addressing market structure itself, we need to review several more basic conditions of industries. There are three main features, which are illustrated in Table 4.1.

Technology and Capital Intensity: "Heavy" Industry and Others. Technology varies widely, from capital-intensive industries like oil refining and steel to retailing and personal services.[1] High capital intensity usually imposes a greater degree of risk, for large volumes of assets are frozen in long-lived forms that cannot easily be sold off. Often, too, such heavy industries face extra instability because demand for their producer-goods outputs is derived and therefore subject to the accelerator effect

---

[1] There are several ways to measure capital intensity. One is the capital-sales ratio. Another is the capital-labor ratio. A third is the ratio between capital and value added by the firm. Capital can be measured variously by net total assets, net fixed assets, and so on. Since all the ratios show similar patterns when applied, the definitions are not critical for many purposes.

TABLE 4.1 Three Attributes of Markets, with Selected Examples

	THE TECHNOLOGY OF THE INDUSTRY: HEAVY OR LIGHT (ASSETS PER WORKER, 1986)	THE AGE OF THE INDUSTRY (PERIOD OF ORIGIN)	THE SCOPE OF THE MARKET, FROM LOCAL TO NATIONAL
Upper Levels	Oil $348,000	Textiles 1800–1840	Electronics Aircraft
	Tobacco $136,000	Steel 1860–1880	Cigarettes
	Automobiles $97,000	Electrical equipment 1880–1900	Steel
Medium Range	Chemicals $84,000	Automobiles 1900–1915	Dry cement
	Primary metals $78,000	Chemicals 1910–1925	Bakery goods
	Electrical machinery $62,000	Drugs 1940s	Bricks
Lower Levels	Printing $40,000	Electronics 1950s	Newspapers
	Clothing $21,000	Bioengineering 1970s	Milk

during the business cycle. Innovation is generally limited by the inertia of high capital intensity. Firms have large volumes of capital embodying past and present technology. Therefore the levels of productivity in heavy industries usually cannot respond rapidly to new opportunities.

There is some correlation between "heaviness" of industry and large firm size, but there are many exceptions. Thus, among the largest twenty-five U.S. firms (as ranked by sales), only the oil companies are much above the average capital intensity for all industry. Manufacturing industry as a whole is, of course, much more capital-intensive than other sectors except "utilities."

Age and Growth Phase. Quite a few industries are old, with origins antedating the nineteenth century and some working factories established before 1900. Others are new, with a history of months rather than years. The "normal" life cycle involves slow early growth, explosive expansion as the product spreads toward saturating the market, and then normal growth, possibly followed by displacement and decline.[2] "Mature" industries therefore usually grow at or below the population growth rate. If they are also capital-intensive (as many are, such as steel), then the room for technical change is doubly limited. Structure also tends to be rigid in such cases. By contrast, new industries tend to be formative, flexible, and technically changing.

The economy is an evolving set of such varied industries, with the new often displacing the old. Firms in older industries frequently try to diversify into the new ones. The "normal" life cycle is occasionally broken, as new conditions rejuvenate

---

[2] This is similar to the "product cycle," a basic concept in the analysis of business operations and strategy.

a mature industry. Still, age often explains much of an industry's structure, behavior, and degree of flexibility.

Geographic Scope, from Local to International.   A large share of services and trade is local, and so are many industrial markets (for bread, milk, bricks, ready-mixed cement, etc.). Transportation costs and distinctive local demand are the two reasons for such localism. Transport costs are as high as 20 percent of total costs for some products and, services. This limits the extent of the market, in ways that have been intensively analyzed in theories of location. In some cases, raw materials are focused in small areas, and the transport cost of raw materials is high relative to costs of shipping the final products. Such industries are therefore tied to the area of their resource base. Other industries cluster in areas with low labor costs. Still others are limited to shorelines or rivers, for cooling and disposing of wastes. Technology can change the patterns, but there is some clustering of industries at each point of time.

Thus the textile industry was concentrated in New England, the steel industry in Pennsylvania, meat packing in Chicago, and automobile making in Michigan. All of these industries have recently become more evenly spread. Regional concentration now includes oil in Texas and California, steel in the Chicago-Pennsylvania area, furniture in the Southeast, and food processing in the Midwest. The more advanced technology industries—with smaller ratios of unit transport cost to production costs—have spread more evenly among regions. This gives them variety in economic choices and more independence in political matters.

Apart from this moderate regional clustering, the composition of markets is broadly similar among areas. All areas require certain services (electricity, transport, retailing, repair, construction, etc.), and a range of similar small-scale industry is found in almost every locale.

II. PATTERNS OF STRUCTURE

The several elements of market structure were noted in Chapter 3; we now need to consider how they fit together. Equation (1.2) in Chapter 1 suggested the basic form of possible causation, but did not show the relative importance of the structural elements. Market share seems likely to be the main element, but concentration might also be important, reflecting oligopoly collusion. And in some situations, entry barriers may be the most important element.

1. Estimating the Elements

No clear answer is possible from logic alone, and any of the elements may be the most important for a specific industry. Real patterns can be traced only from concrete evidence, and statistics have supplied that evidence. Equation (1.2) has been fitted to data and tested in a variety of ways, covering a range of actual large corporations. This lets the elements sort themselves out statistically, giving direct evidence about their separate and collective importance.[3]

---

[3] The issues and econometric results that are introduced in this section are covered in much greater detail in Chapter 5, with complete citations to the literature.

The fundamental premise is that a firm's degree of profitability is the basic test of its good performance. That is widely agreed upon as a sound hypothesis.[4] Profitability is, after all, the firm's primary motivation. Each element's importance, then, can be estimated by the amount it adds to the "typical" firm's profitability.

The first studies, in the 1950s, tried to relate *industry-wide* price-cost patterns solely to *industry-wide concentration* or to the *four-firm concentration ratio* because those were the only data available. It was a crude basis for testing, however, since it ignored the specific conditions of individual firms and omitted other elements of structure. Testing done since 1970 has focused with surgical precision on the firm's individual *market shares* and other specific features; those results do clarify the individual elements and their collective role.

One series of inclusive studies has tested these elements on data from the 1960–1975 and 1980–1983 periods, covering various panels of 95 to 245 large U.S. manufacturing corporations. The series has been retested frequently by a variety of researchers, with consistent results. Chapter 5 will go more deeply into the interpretation of the patterns, with references to detailed studies.

For now, the patterns from this research give a reasonably clear picture of how the structural elements fit together. They also give the reader good practice in interpreting what a set of econometric results "really means," for use in later chapters. Appendix 4 provides more detail on econometric methods.

2. The Model

The model "explains" each firm's average profit rate on investors' equity by several variables representing the firm's market position: its market share, concentration in the market, and entry barriers. Thus profit rate is the dependent variable to be explained, and is on the left side of the equation:

$$\text{Profit rate}_{ij} = a + b \text{ Market share}_i + c \text{ Concentration }_j$$

$$+ d \text{ Entry barriers}_j + e \text{ Growth rate}_j$$

The independent variables that may explain profitability are on the right side of the equation. Barriers can be represented by a number of different variables, such as absolute size (S), advertising intensity (A: the firm's payments for advertising as a percent of its total sales revenue), or dummy variables representing estimates of the "height" of entry barriers (HB for high barriers, MB for moderately high barriers, and LB for low barriers). The growth rate is included to filter out external changes that may affect profit rates.

Profits as a percent of investors' equity is the most general measure of the return on the owners' investment in the firm.[5] Each variable suffers from some measure-

---

[4] See F. M. Scherer, *Industrial Market Structure and Economic Performance*, 2d ed. (Boston: Houghton Mifflin, 1980); Joe S. Bain, *Industrial Organization*, rev. ed. (New York: Wiley, 1968); and William G. Shepherd, *The Treatment of Market Power* (New York: Columbia University Press, 1975). To the extent that some reverse causation may be present (recall Chapter 1), this test is diluted.

[5] An alternative measure is profits (plus interest payments) as a rate of return on total assets. But this is not as precise an index of the return to the owners of the firm (the holders of equity capital). Since both measures give similar results, it is sufficient here to report the returns on equity capital.

ment problems (discussed in Appendix 4), so the results should be assessed cautiously. Yet they are consistent and have become fixtures in the literature.

The main results for the several elements are summarized in Table 4.2 and Figure 4.1. A more detailed picture, including several time periods and different variables, will be found in Chapter 5.

The constant term *a* represents the minimum competitive profit rate that a firm with no market power might attain: its market share, concentration, and barriers are all close to zero. This profit rate was in the range 5 to 10 percent in the 1960s, when interest rates were relatively low. The estimated *a* value is therefore about where it is expected to be.

The *b* coefficient (for market share) is $+0.25$, which means that on average there is a 2.5 percent higher rate of return on equity for each added 10 points of market share.[6] A 50 percent market share would usually yield about a 17.5 percent rate of return; that includes about 5 percent from the competitive profit rate, plus an added 12.5 points (50 times $0.25 = 12.5$) from the 50 percent market share. A 25 percent market share would indicate a rate of return of about 11.25 (5 points plus 6.25 points [25 times $0.25] = 11.25$), while a 70 percent market share would tend to give about a 20 percent profit rate.

Not only do high market shares seem to provide very high profit rates, but the *t*-ratio on the coefficient is also high, indicating a tight fit (any ratio over 3.5 indicates strong statistical significance). Market shares, evidently, are closely related to profitability.

Now consider line 2 of Table 4.2, where market share has been replaced by the four-firm concentration ratio. Four-firm concentration is indeed related to company profit rates, but the coefficient and the *t*-ratio are both lower, suggesting a weaker effect. The *c* coefficient is about $+0.10$, which means that the highest possible concentration (100 percent) raises the profit rate only by 10 points. Moreover, the lower *t*-ratio indicates a weaker fit to the data. That is precisely what we would expect, because any given concentration level may involve a wide range of differing structures and outcomes (as Chapters 2 and 3 noted).

The concentration ratio includes the firm's own market share, so the seeming concentration effect may actually reflect mainly the role of market share. Indeed, when market share is subtracted from concentration to give the "rest of the oligopoly group" (variable *G*, which is included in line 1), that variable has alomost no statistical role at all.

In short, concentration appears to be a much weaker element of structure than market share. The correct interpretation appears to be: A dominant firm harvests extra profits by exploiting the advantages provided by its own market share, not because it and several other oligopolists are able to exert a large combined share. The apparent "effect" of concentration by itself (in line 1) may be merely the summed effects of the individual firms' own market shares.

If large firm size results in higher entry barriers, then asset size should show a positive sign in this sort of analysis. Instead, its coefficient is weakly negative in Table 4.2, and in a number of other econometric studies it is also near zero. This suggests that size does not add strongly to barriers; or, possibly, that there is X-

---

[6] In other fittings of the model, the *b* value generally is near 0.25. One would say prudently that it is probably in the range of 0.20 and 0.30.

TABLE 4.2 A Structural Analysis of Profitability of Large U.S. Industrial Firms, 1960–1969

Dependent Variables	Constant Term	Market Share (M)	Concentration (C)	Group (G)	Size (log of assets) (S)	Advertising Intensity (A)	Growth (E)	R^2
				INDEPENDENT VARIABLES				
Profit rate, 1960–1969	5.13 (5.92)*	.250 (12.19)		.028 (1.60)	−.182 (1.34)	.021 (4.39)	.792 (3.93)	.554
Profit rate, 1960–1969	4.38 (4.22)		.105 (5.57)		−.175 (1.06)	.024 (4.04)	1.28 (5.31)	.344

* t-ratios are in parentheses.

SOURCE: W. G. Shepherd, *The Treatment of Market Power* (New York: Columbia University Press, 1975).

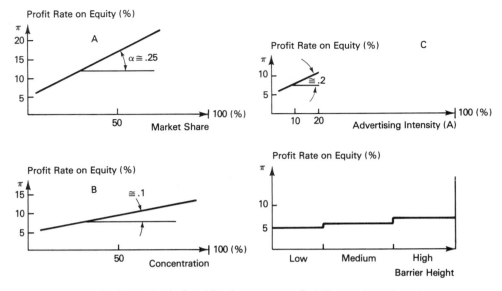

FIGURE 4.1.   Estimated relationships between profitability and market share, concentration, and advertising intensity.

SOURCE: Shepherd, *Treatment of Market Power.*

inefficiency in large firms that subtracts profits, so that the barrier's effect toward higher profits is offset.

Advertising, by contrast, is strongly related to profit rates, as Table 4.2 shows. Only a relatively few consumer-goods industries have intensive advertising: cereals, soaps, toiletries, beer, and jewelry, for instance (see Chapter 16). In these industries, advertising intensity may be a strong element of structure, or also a matter of behavior, since advertising is an activity chosen voluntarily by firms.

Yet advertising's power is limited, as you can see from Figure 4.1. Even the most advertising-intensive industries (where advertising may be as much as 20 percent of sales revenue) show only a 4-point rise in profit rate. This is less than a fourth of the 17.5 percentage points that a 70 percent market share adds to the profit rate.

So far we can say that entry barriers appear to have a significant but secondary effect on profitability, size adds no net effect to profitability, and advertising has only a moderate effect. Another way to test the role of barriers is to use more general estimates of barrier "height" in place of size and advertising intensity. That is done in Table 4.3, where dummy variables are used for low, medium, and high barriers.

The results confirm that the effect of barriers is limited. In line 1 of Table 4.3, high barriers add about 3 points to the profit rate, while medium barriers add about 2 points. Meanwhile, the market share coefficient in Table 4.3 is relatively constant regardless of entry conditions. It is moderately lower in line 3 than in line 2, suggesting that low barriers do reduce market share's effect, but only by a little, compared to higher barriers.

To sum up: Market share emerges as the central element of structure, just as

TABLE 4.3   The Role of Entry Barriers as an Element of Structure

		INDEPENDENT VARIABLES					
DEPENDENT VARIABLES	CONSTANT TERM	MARKET SHARE	GROUP	HIGH BARRIER	MEDIUM BARRIER	GROWTH	R^2
All 245 Large Firms Profit Rate, 1960–1969	4.58 (4.60)*	.251 (11.81)	.001 (0.05)	2.45 (2.84)	1.55 (2.64)	.925 (4.36)	.528
202 Firms with Medium or Low Barriers Profit rate, 1960–1969	4.49 (5.16)	.239 (10.65)	−.001 (0.03)		1.69 (3.03)	.881 (4.29)	.518
71 Firms with Low Barriers Profit rate, 1960–1969	5.39 (4.20)	.175 (5.14)	.019 (0.68)			.807 (3.80)	.461

* *t*-ratios are in parentheses.
SOURCE: Shepherd, *Treatment of Market Power*.

the theory of the profit-maximizing firm suggests. Advertising intensity may also be important in some consumer-goods industries, but the range of its effect is limited. Oligopoly concentration is relatively unimportant, once market share is taken into account, and a "critical" value of concentration does not emerge. Entry barriers can be significant, but are not generally of great importance.

This accords with widespread business experience. Management seeks to increase market share rather than to build up concentration, and managers discuss entry barriers relatively infrequently.

Of course, the reversed Chicago-UCLA causation—from performance to structure—might instead be present. High profit rates might reflect a firm's higher efficiency or innovativeness, or merely random variations, along with (or instead of) market power. The next chapter will address this issue in detail. But whether monopoly power or superior efficiency is the cause, market share is still the main profit-enhancing element of structure.

3.   The Patterns of Structure

Now we turn to the actual patterns of structure in real markets, showing both the average conditions and the range of variation.

Market shares

Market shares span the entire range, from 100 percent to trivial. Unfortunately, no comprehensive set of market shares is published, by any official or private source, mainly because firms go to great lengths to keep such sensitive information secret. Instead, leading-firm shares must be sifted out and estimated from a variety of sources, and in many cases, the estimates are debatable.[7] Every dominant firm insists that its own market be drawn broadly so that its market share will appear to be small. The reverse error is also possible: defining the market so tightly that market shares are overstated.

Reasonably reliable estimates are possible, however. Tables 4.4 and 4.5 list some of the leading dominant firms during the 1910–1973 period, including famous corporate names from different periods in twentieth-century U.S. corporate history. Note how some of these firms persisted for decades, while others receded or abruptly disappeared. We explore the complex causes of that persistence versus decline in Chapters 8 and 9.

By 1980–1985, most of these older dominant firms had yielded to the corrosive forces of competition or to direct antitrust attacks. That is clear from comparing Table 4.5 here with the current dominant firms listed in Table 3.4. Yet many dominant positions remain hidden within conglomerates, which do not report detailed conditions of their individual divisions or products. And new dominant positions are regularly emerging in new markets.

Although the total importance of dominant firms had declined by the 1980s, there

---

[7] Sources include the business press, especially the second section of the *Wall Street Journal*, which frequently reports measures from private market research and other sources. Antitrust cases are often rich sources of data. And there are extensive private sets of market share measures, but they are not published or generally available, except at high fees.

TABLE 4.4   Instances of "Dominant" Firms in Major U.S. Industrial Markets, 1910–1935

	ESTIMATES FOR 1910			ESTIMATES FOR 1935	
COMPANY	MARKET SHARE (%)	ENTRY BARRIERS	ASSETS ($ MILLION)	MARKET SHARE (%)	ENTRY BARRIERS
U.S. Steel	60%	Medium	$1804	40%	Medium
Standard Oil	80	Medium	800	35	Medium
American Tobacco	80	Medium	286	25	Medium
International Harvester	70	High	166	33	Medium
Central Leather	60	Low	138	—	—
Pullman	85	High	131	80	Medium
American Sugar Refining	60	Low	124	35	Low
Singer Manufacturing	75	Medium	113	55	Low
General Electric	60	High	102	55	High
Corn Products	60	Low	97	45	Low
American Can	60	Medium	90	51	Medium
Westinghouse Electric	50	High	84	45	High
E. I. du Pont de Nemours	90	Medium	75	30	Low
International Paper	50	Low	71	20	Low
National Biscuit	50	Low	65	20	Low
Western Electric	100	High	43	100	High
United Fruit	80	Medium	41	80	Medium
United Shoe Machinery	95	High	40	90	High
Eastman Kodak	90	Medium	35	90	Medium
Aluminum Company of America	99	High	35	90	Medium

are still substantial cases. Moreover, some of these, such as newspapers that dominate their local markets (see Chapter 17 for details), are in sectors whose social impact is particularly strong.

These markets contain much of the large-scale "monopoly problem" that remains in the U.S. economy. A skeptic might say that only the top few cases represent a high degree of market power; some Chicago-UCLA economists would say that none of them represents any market power at all! Others would say that all of these cases plus many lesser ones might represent high market power.

Beyond these industrial firms, many "utility" firms and quite a few other non-manufacturing firms hold market shares above 50 percent in large markets. Even so, the entire group of dominant firms probably accounts for less than 3 percent of GNP in the United States. The problem is sharp but limited.

Concentration

Concentration data are more abundant, but they immediately raise special problems of *market definition*. There is no official comprehensive source for correctly defined markets, but the U.S. Census Bureau prepares concentration ratios for manufacturing industries and product groups every four years or so when there is a Census of Manufactures.

TABLE 4.5   Instances of "Dominant" Firms in Major U.S. Industrial Markets, 1948–1973

| | ESTIMATES FOR 1948 | | | ESTIMATES FOR 1973 | |
COMPANY	MARKET SHARE (%)	ENTRY BARRIERS	ASSETS ($ MILLION)	MARKET SHARE (%)	ENTRY BARRIERS
General Motors	60%	Medium	$2958	55%	High
General Electric	50	High	1177	50	High
Western Electric	100	High	650	98	High
Alcoa	80	High	504	40	Medium
Eastman Kodak	80	Medium	412	70	Medium
Procter & Gamble	50	Medium	356	50	Medium
United Fruit	80	Medium	320	60	Medium
American Can	52	Medium	276	35	Low
IBM	90	Medium	242	70	High
Coca-Cola	60	Medium	222	50	Medium
Campbell Soup	85	Medium	149	85	Medium
Caterpillar Tractor	50	Medium	147	50	Medium
United Shoe Machinery	85	High	104	50	Low
Kellogg	50	Medium	41	45	Medium
Gillette	70	Medium	78	60	Medium
Babcock & Wilcox	60	Medium	79	40	Medium
Du Pont (cellophane)	90	High	65	50	Medium
Hershey	75	Medium	62	70	Low

The census *industry* categories are based mainly on the selling companies' conditions: the technology, the groups of firms selling similar products, and the common production features of products. These conditions can deviate substantially from the true basis of *markets,* which is the zone of *consumer* choice among substitutable products. Because the census staff members ignore much of the consumer-choice side, their "industry" and "product-group" categories often stray far from true market edges.

About half of the 450 census industries are seriously wrong, as Appendix 2 explains. Table 4.6 presents examples of the most serious errors. The main sources of error are in the critical elements used for defining markets:

1. *Including Noncompeting Product Types.* In most instances where the census ratios are in error, the census industry category is too broad, including a variety of products that do not substitute for one another. Such *industries* embrace many distinct *markets.* For example (see Table 4.6), SIC code 2834, "Pharmaceutical preparations," probably includes at least ten distinct markets for different drug types, each for strictly different diseases (ulcers, heart disease, kidney problems, blood pressure, AIDS, etc.). Industry 2844—"Toilet preparations"—includes at least five main product categories, from deodorants and hair-care products to mouthwashes.

2. *Geographic Market Divisions.* By geographic areas, too, many census industries are too large. Newspapers are a striking example: the national industry includes hundreds of distinct city-area markets such as Chicago, New York, Los Angeles, and Atlanta, most of which have only one or two newspapers. The national

TABLE 4.6   Comparing Raw and Adjusted Concentration in U.S. Markets, 1982

SIC Number	Name of Industry	Value of Shipments ($ billion)	Census Data CR₄	Census Data HHI	Adjustment Factors	Adjusted Values CR₄	Adjusted Values HHI
Noncompeting Products							
2834	Pharmaceutical prepara-tions	20,314	23	203	P	80	2,800
2844	Toilet preparations	10,437	30	360	P	80	2,500
3444	Sheet metal work	6,573	6	24	P, G	40	900
3662	Radio and TV commu-nications equipment	32,217	21	217	P, I	60	2,000
3573	Electronic computing equipment	34,751	42	754	P, I	85	2,700
Geographic Market Divisions							
2711	Newspapers	20,314	23	203	G	98	6,000
32730	Ready-mixed concrete	7,545	5	16	G	70	2,200
20511	Bread—white, wheat, and rye	4,698	37	478	G	75	2,600
Imports							
3636	Sewing machines	231	66	1703	I	40	1,000
36511	Radios	783	77	(D)	I	35	700

(D) means that census disclosure rules prevented publication of the ratio.
P: Product definitions were adjusted.
G: Geographic market divisions were adjusted.
I: Imports were a factor.
SOURCE: U.S. Bureau of the Census, *Concentration Ratios in Manufacturing, 1982*, MC82-S-7, (Washington, D.C.: U.S. Government Printing Office, 1986), Table 6.

four-firm concentration ratio for all newspapers was recently given by the Census Bureau as 23 percent (see Table 4.6), whereas the true average for most true local markets is close to 100 percent.

These defects make the raw census ratios and HHI values too low. Most researchers regard the 700 *five-digit* product groups (within the 450 four-digit industries) as being much closer to true market boundaries. The five-digit product ratios average about 15 points higher than the four-digit industry ratios—and many of the five-digit product lines are still too broad, such as concrete, bread, and radios in Table 4.6.

Still another fault tilts the ratios the other way, toward being too low:

3. *Imports.* Imports are omitted from the census data. In scores of industries, such as televisions, cameras, and automobiles, foreign imports are important, causing true concentration of all *sales in the United States* (which is the correct basis) to be lower than the concentration of *U.S. production.* As imports have risen (from about 7 percent of U.S. GNP in the 1960s to over 18 percent in the 1980s), this problem has become more severe. Table 4.6 suggests the effects from adjusting the ratios for sewing machines and radios.

Some economists take this point to the extreme, arguing that the recent higher foreign trade activity means that "all markets are worldwide now," so U.S. markets are no longer the correct basis at all for judging concentration in any industry. That is an overreaction. A few U.S. markets have indeed been swept by imports: television sets, radios, and cameras, for example. But in other industries, imports are restrained by strong international quota programs controlling the flow of products into the United States: important examples are steel and automobiles. In nearly all markets, the correct method of adjustment is to merely add imports to the U.S. figures to arrive at an adjusted U.S. concentration ratio.

Adjusting the census ratios to reflect true markets requires care and judgment. There is no simple, mechanical method. Notice, too, that any econometric research that simply uses unadjusted concentration ratios is almost certain to contain gross errors and to give meaningless "results." Moreover, the census concentration data cover only the manufacturing sector, which accounts for just about one-quarter of total U.S. economic activity.

Alternative Indexes of Concentration, Particularly the HHI.   The Hirschman-Herfindahl Index (HHI) has emerged as the favorite alternative to the standard four-firm ratio, as Chapter 3 noted. It is simply the sum of the squared market shares. Data on the HHI are included in Tables 4.6 and 4.7, to illustrate dominance, tight oligopoly, and other situations. Comparing them with the four-firm concentration ratios, you can gain a sense of the equivalent degrees of concentration. The HHI is of little value in the lower ranges of concentration, but it has an uncanny ability to reflect the high market power at market shares over 50 percent.

The HHI ratios are distorted by wrong market definitions just as much as are the four-firm concentration ratios. And although they are provided by the census for most industries, they are withheld for many important dominant-firm industries, such as radios in Table 4.6. Therefore the HHI is often a defective ratio that diverts attention from better indicators of concentration.

For all their limitations, concentration-ratio data are a useful start for establishing the real degree of concentration in an industry, and they have been by far the most thoroughly published data. The careful researcher always adjusts them to allow for their inaccuracies.

The Range of Concentration.   Actual concentration ratios in U.S. industries range from 100 percent down to a mere few percent, as illustrated in Table 4.7. A 100 percent ratio usually does not mean maximum market power: it might indicate four 25 percent market-share firms rather than one 100 percent firm. Maximum concentration, therefore, may mask widely differing degrees of monopoly.[8] The same is true of lesser ratios: a 60 percent ratio may include four 15 percent firms, or one 57 percent, dominant firm.[9]

At the bottom end of the concentration scale there is little such ambiguity. A four-firm ratio below 30 percent rarely indicates significant market power. In fact, loose oligipoly—defined as a ratio below 40 percent—is commonly regarded as effective competition, because market power is usually low both for the leading firm and for the several largest firms together. Effective collusion is also difficult.

Table 4.7 gives the adjustment factors, as does Table 4.6.

---

[8] This is the one area where the HHI can give evidence that is clearer than the four-firm ratios. Four 25 percent firms give an HHI of 2,500 (each market share squared is 625; together they equal 2,500). If there is a 97 percent firm and three 1 percent firms, their combined HHI is 9,412 (that is, 97 squared is 9,409, plus 3 ones). The same 100 concentration ratio indeed masks sharply differing monopoly power.

[9] Here the two HHI values would be 900 and 3,252. Again, the contrast is sharp, and the HHI is useful.

TABLE 4.7 Concentration in Selected U.S. Industries and Products, 1972–1982

SIC NUMBER	NAME OF INDUSTRY	VALUE OF SHIPMENTS 1982 ($ MILLION)	FOUR-FIRM CONCENTRATION RATIOS:				
			BUREAU OF CENSUS		ADJUSTED 1982 (%)	ADJUSTMENT FACTORS	CENSUS HHI
			1972 (%)	1982 (%)			
38615	Photographic film	4,155	(D)	(D)	100		(D)
28412	Household detergents	4,399	84	79	90	P	2735
3795	Tanks and tank components	2,351	99	85	99	P	2515
2823	Cellulosic man-made fibers	1,240	96	(D)			2970
3332	Primary lead	95	93	100			(D)
3211	Flat glass	1,665	92	85			2032
3692	Primary batteries, dry and wet	1,102	92	89			(D)
3996	Hard-surface floor coverings	604	91	99			(D)
2043	Cereal breakfast foods	4,132	90	86			(D)
3511	Turbines and generator sets	2,730	90	86			(D)
3641	Electric lamps	2,072	90	91			(D)
3711	Motor vehicles and car bodies	70,740	93	92	85	P, I	(D)
3632	Household refrigerators and freezers	2,471	85	94			2745
2111	Cigarettes	12,127	84	(D)			2623
3573	Electronic computing equipment	36,767	51	43	75	P, I	793
3251	Brick and structural clay tile	657	17	24	90	P, R	263
2241	Narrow fabric mills	852	20	20		P	209
20262	Fluid milk	9115	19	18	85		179
2341	Women's and children's underwear	2,602	15	22			203
2752	Commercial printing, lithographic	19,442	4	6	25	R	20

(D) means that census disclosure rules prevented pulbication of the ratio.
Adjustment factors were as follows:
P: Product definitions were adjusted.
R: Regional and local markets must be accounted for, within the national "market."
I: Imports were a factor.
SOURCE: Calculated from data in U.S. Bureau of the Census, *Concentration Ratios in Manufacturing, 1982*, MC82-S-7 (Washington, D.C.: Government Printing Office, 1986).

Gradations of Market Shares.   The typical market structure includes a gradation among market shares. Usually there is not a distinct "oligopoly group," as in panel I of Figure 4.2, but rather, the size distribution tapers down from the largest firms to a fringe of small ones (panel II of Figure 4.2). The degree of asymmetry in the oligopoly group varies, but in the average case each firm has about twice the share of the next.

This has suggested to some researchers that a "law" of lognormal distribution and growth governs the formation of industry structure. If the growth of individual firms were randomly distributed by a lognormal distribution, then market shares would fit closely to a rule of two: that is, each firm would be twice the size of the next largest one. For example, General Motors at about 40 percent has twice the

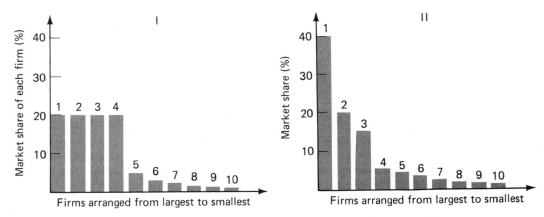

FIGURE 4.2   Oligopolists may be of similar sizes, but they usually vary in size.

Panel I shows a tight oligopoly with four equal-sized firms. In panel II, by contrast, the oligopolists have sharply varying sizes, even though their total concentration, 80 percent, is just the same as in panel I. The tapered pattern in panel II is far more common in actual oligopolies than is the equal-size group in panel I.

share of Ford at about 20 percent, which has almost twice Chrysler's market share, and so on.

This "law" applies loosely: only a few markets have equal-sized oligopolists, with a break between them and the fringe firms. There are many exceptions. Some dominant firms are four or five times larger than their nearest rival (examples are IBM, Eastman Kodak, Campbell Soup, and Clorox).

The Extent of Concentration in U.S. Industry.   To show the general extent of concentration, it is most meaningful to use the standard four-firm ratios. One groups industrial activity as in Figure 4.3, which shows data for a recent year. Value added is used as the measure of economic activity, for weighting the industries. Note that the average of the official four-digit industry ratios strongly understates the true degree of concentration. The weighted-average degree of true concentration was probably about 60 percent, rather than the 40 percent indicated by the raw census ratios.

These patterns of structure are stable. The shape of the distribution has not changed much since the first figures were collected in 1935. There has been some movement by sectors, and some sectors are almost entirely competitive in structure. Others have much higher concentration.

Trends of Concentration.[10]   Lacking data on HHI levels before 1982, researchers used four-firm ratios to suggest the trend of concentration. Since those ratios are defective, only rough estimates are possible. During 1947–1967, there was a significant rise in average (unadjusted) concentration, from 34 to 40 percent. Much of this was in consumer-goods markets, where television advertising is likely to have had an increasing effect favoring the larger firms.

---

[10] Note that *concentration* trends in manufacutring industry may be quite different from the trend of *competition* in the whole economy. Concentration is just one element of structure, while competition is assessed using structure and other conditions, as is explained in the next section.

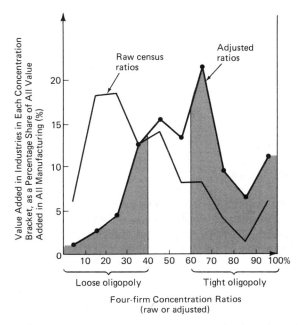

FIGURE 4.3   Concentration patterns in American manufacturing industries in 1972.

Since 1967, the official ratios have shown little change, but note that these ratios do not include imports. Since imports have risen significantly in scores of industries (from autos and cameras to motorcycles and copiers), the true degree of concentration has decreased. The average share of imports has risen from about 4 to 12 percent of manufacturing industry sales since 1967, so the corresponding fall in concentration may be in the range of 5 to 8 points.[11] That would reverse much of the earlier rise in concentration during 1947–1967. The 1950s and 1960s were indeed the high periods of tight oligopoly in the U.S. economy.

Optimal and natural structure

Now we turn to the fundamental comparison between optimal and natural structure. *Optimal structure* gives the best combined performance (efficiency, innovation, and the rest), while *natural structure* is simply the structure that evolves in actual markets. If natural structure tends *not* to evolve toward optimal structure, then society may face difficult choices. Optimal structure is a case-by-case matter, depending on scale economies, technological opportunity, and other specific conditions. Yet, generally, loose oligopoly is the best all-around structure. It provides firms with significant degrees of market presence, continuity, and stability. In most cases (see Chapter 9), it permits the realization of scale economies in production, innovation, and other activities. Because concentration is low, the likelihood of collusion is also low.

---

[11] But when the foreign sellers are among the four largest sellers in the United States, there may be no fall in concentration.

Natural structure may, in contrast, tend toward tight oligopoly. As market shares rise, large pecuniary gains may be achieved in buying inputs at lower prices, even though technical economies of scale are absent. Monopoly pricing will emerge, and collusion will become more effective. Private incentives will draw firms beyond the levels at which technical economies may justify market power.

Unusually clear examples of gaps between optimal and natural structure occurred in the great merger wave of 1897–1901, when scores of dominant firms were created by merger. Most of these new firms had large degrees of excess market share, and many of them quickly shrank.[12] What occurred there in extreme form has continued to occur quietly in many industries. The question is: Is the gap between optimal and actual concentration generally large or small in the common run of markets?

By 1970, there appeared to be a substantial gap between optimal concentration (loose oligopoly) and the average of actual concentration (about 60 percent). This gap probably involved substantial excess market share and lessened pressures for innovation. The resulting diminished performance—particularly in a series of major industries—may have induced the onrush of imports in the 1970s, which supplied the harsh correction of intense competitive pressure.

Thus the gap between optimal and actual structure was reduced in many markets open to strong import competition. Other industries may have escaped import pressures because of high transport costs and other barriers. Moreover, the fall in the dollar's value after 1984 alleviated the stress of import competition. Still, the larger process can be seen as an effective (if delayed) response to the gap between optimal and actual degrees of concentration.

Entry barriers

Because barriers may arise from more than a dozen sources (recall Chapter 3), estimating their height is extremely difficult. One must evaluate each of the sources for each industry, judging how much it adds to the barrier. Then one must combine them, using some sort of weighting. Bain and Mann attempted to do this for about forty industries in the 1950s.[13]

Many industries have changed since then, but one can revise and extend Bain and Mann's coverage, using a variety of sources and exercising rough judgments. The estimates are given in Table 4.8. As Bain has stressed, one must carefully avoid letting the amount of actual entry color one's appraisal of the height of the barriers— the two concepts are distinct, even though they may be related in practice.

Among actual markets, certain utilities have high barriers stemming from both technology and publicly granted franchises. Most retail and other services have low barriers because small size is the rule and little capital is needed to get started. Some minerals are tightly controlled, and some are not. Many professional services have

---

[12] See Ralph L. Nelson, *Merger Movements in American Industry, 1895–1956* (Princeton, N.J.: Princeton University Press, 1959); and Naomi Lamoreaux, *The Great Merger Movement in American Business, 1895–1904* (New York: Cambridge University Press, 1985).

[13] Joe S. Bain, *Barriers to New Competition* (Cambridge, Mass.: Harvard University Press, 1956); and H. Michael Mann, "Seller Concentration, Barriers to Entry, and Rates of Return in Thirty Industries, 1950–1980," *Review of Economics and Statistics,* 48 (August 1966), 296–307.

TABLE 4.8   Estimated Barriers to Entry for Selected Industries

High Barriers to Entry	Moderately High Barriers to Entry	Low Barriers to Entry
Electric service	Bread	Meat packing
Local telephone service	Soft drinks	Flour
Newspapers	Cigarettes	Canned fruits and
Certain drug markets	Periodicals	vegetables
Soaps	Gypsum products	Woolen and cotton textiles
Aircraft and parts	Organic chemicals	Clothing
Mainframe computers	Toilet preparations	Small metal products
Heavy electrical equipment	Petroleum refining	Wooden furniture
Locomotives	Aluminum	Corrugated containers
Beer	Heavy industrial machinery	Printing
Cereals	Large household appliances	Footwear

sizable barriers. Tariffs and import quotas form a special type of barrier, which excludes foreign but not domestic entry. The exact height of such barriers is not known, partly owing to their conceptual complexity, and no survey of them can be presented here.

III. THE EXTENT AND TREND OF COMPETITION

We have considered the elements of market structure, gaining a sense of their relative importance. We have also noted the difficulties in estimating them. Now we broaden the focus to assess the degree of *competition* (not just concentration) in the U.S. economy and its changes over time. Figure 1.6 summarized the trend very concisely. Here we explore it in detail.[14]

No simple method of estimating competition will do, for two reasons. First, adequate data are not available, as we have noted. Second, the degree of competitiveness is in more than one structural dimension, as we have seen in great detail. Moreover, structure itself does not fully determine competitiveness. A range of behavior is possible, and there can be variations in performance (e.g., profits, which also hint at the degree of competitiveness).

The best approach is to use a variety of evidence to assign markets to the main categories of competitiveness. Then one can measure the shares of the economy in each type of market: pure monopoly, dominant firm, tight oligopoly, and "all others." The last group can be considered effectively competitive.

1. Method

The method first uses market share, concentration, and barrier information to fit each industry to a presumptive category. This presumption can then be modified by strong contrary evidence about behavior.

---

[14] This section draws on W. G. Shepherd, "Causes of Increased Competition in the U.S. Economy, 1939–1980," *Review of Economics and Statistics*, 64 (November 1982), 613–26.

The standards used for the four categories are as follows:

1. *Pure monopoly.* Market share at or near 100 percent. Very high entry barriers. Evidence of effective monopoly control over the level and structure of prices. In practice, this category includes mainly certain utilities and patented goods.
2. *Dominant firms.* A market share of 40 to over 90 percent, with no close rival. High entry barriers. An ability to control pricing, to set systematic discriminatory prices, to influence innovation, and (usually) to earn rates of return well above the competitive rate of return.
3. *Tight oligopoly.* Four-firm concentration above 60 percent, with stable market shares. Medium or high entry barriers. A tendency toward cooperation, shown especially by rigid prices. Excess profits are neither necessary nor sufficient to establish the existence of tight oligopoly.
4. *Effective competition.* Four-firm concentration below 40 percent, with unstable market shares and flexible pricing. Low entry barriers, little collusion, and low profit rates.

Many utilities appear to be only moderately restrained by regulation, whereas the effects of government actions in certain other markets (such as milk) have been to intensify price collusion. Such cases are assessed individually, and where appropriate, they are included as tight oligopolies.

2. Patterns and Trends

The patterns in Table 4.9 are broadly consistent with earlier findings about variations among sectors. From 1939 to 1980, effective competition was predominant in agriculture, mining, wholesale and retail trade, and financial markets. About half of the 1939 activity in the manufacturing and services sectors was in markets that were effectively competitive, but that share had risen by 1980. The construction sector began with a low competitive share in 1939, but that share had risen to 80 percent in 1980. Only in the transportation and utility sector did most activity remain in categories 1–3 throughout.

The main trends are immediately apparent. Following a slow rise in competition from 1939 to 1958, there was a sharp rise from 1958 to 1980.

Between 1939 and 1958, the slow rise in competition was focused in the manufacturing, construction, and transportation sectors. Taking all sectors together, in 1958 the markets with pure monopolies and dominant firms accounted for 8 percent of the economy, and the three categories with substantial market power for 44 percent. Tight oligopoly (category 3) was present in over one-third of the entire economy, and a substantial share of the entire economy had either a high degree of market power and/or the presence of ineffective government supervision. Chicago-UCLA economists at the time declared that the economy was virtually all competitive, but the reality did not support that view.

From 1958 to 1980, the degree of competition rose in every major sector, as Table 4.9 shows. In 1980, about 76 percent of national income was produced under effective competition, compared with 56 percent in 1958. Pure monopolies in 1980 accounted for only about 2.5 percent and dominant firms for just 2.8 percent: together, their share shrank from 11 to 5 percent. The share of tight oligopoly dropped by about half, from about 36 to 18 percent.

TABLE 4.9   Trends of Competition in the U.S. Economy, 1939–1980

SECTORS OF THE ECONOMY	NATIONAL INCOME IN EACH SECTOR, 1978 ($ BILLION)	THE SHARE OF EACH SECTOR THAT WAS EFFECTIVELY COMPETITIVE		
		1939 (%)	1958 (%)	1980 (%)
Agriculture, forestry, and fisheries	54.7	91.6	85.0	86.4
Mining	26.5	87.1	92.2	95.8
Construction	87.6	27.9	55.9	80.2
Manufacturing	459.5	51.5	55.9	69.0
Transportation and public utilities	164.3	8.7	26.1	39.1
Wholesale and retail trade	261.8	57.8	60.5	93.4
Finance, insurance, and real estate	210.7	61.5	63.8	94.1
Services	245.3	53.9	54.3	77.9
Total	1,510.4	52.4	56.4	76.7

THE SHARE OF EACH CATEGORY IN TOTAL NATIONAL INCOME		PERCENTAGE SHARES		
		1939	1958	1980
1. Pure monopoly	38.2	6.2	3.1	2.5
2. Dominant firm	42.2	5.0	5.0	2.8
3. Tight oligopoly	272.1	36.4	35.6	18.0
4. Others: Effectively competitive	1,157.9	52.4	56.3	76.7
Total	1,510.4	100.0	100.0	100.0

SOURCE: William G. Shepherd, "Causes of Increased Competition in the U.S. Economy, 1939–1980," *Review of Economics and Statistics,* 64 (November 1982), 613–26, Table 2. Reprinted with permission.

Since 1980, there have been important additional cases of rising competition. These include railroads, buses, and trucking, all of which were freed from regulatory restrictions against entry. Imports have continued to rise in some industries, adding to competitive pressures.

But competition has receded in other sectors, partly because of the lax antitrust policies of the 1980s that permitted major horizontal mergers. Two notable cases of declining competition are automobiles and airlines. Airlines became highly competitive immediately after deregulation in 1978, but by 1986–1988, they had reverted to tight oligopoly conditions with a series of mergers and tightening bottlenecks at major airports (see Chapter 18 for a fuller analysis).

On balance, competition remained roughly stable during 1980–1988, or possibly declined by a few points. But as always, the average masks important shifts in specific cases.

Market power remains high in many markets, such as computers, photographic film, newspapers, soups, and various utilities and city services. Nevertheless, the rise in competition since 1958 is striking. Indeed, the U.S. economy is now a large test case for the functioning of competition in a large-scale industrial economy.

The several forces that have caused much of the trend are antitrust actions, imports, deregulation, and shrinking scale economies. They are discussed in Chapter 8.

IV.   OTHER MAIN CONDITIONS

1.   Rates of Decline of Market Share

Recall that the rate of decline of individual dominance is a critical condition. As is often true, there is little reliable evidence for the most critical points. We first consider oligopoly, and then dominant-firm shares.

Oligopoly.   We can, of course, measure how fast concentration ratios shift as years go by. The simplest method is to make a distribution of the shifts between the two years in question. A more advanced technique is to do a correlation analysis between the ratios for the two years. Both analyses have been done for various year pairs; results show that concentration is highly stable. In any group of industries, only a few ratios change more than 10 points during a ten-year period. Among industries with high concentration, the declines are relatively few and slow. Tight oligopoly, once formed, tends to persist. Only imports seem to make significant inroads in certain trade-vulnerable industries.

Dominant-Firm Market Shares.   Do high market shares usually decline rapidly, or do they persist? The answer is crucial. If they decline quickly, then monopoly power is likely to be transient and slight. If they persist, then monopoly power is more important and may last a long time once it is formed.

The evidence is limited but clear: the natural rate of erosion has been slow. The rate of erosion of dominant-firm market shares in U.S. industries during 1910–1935 was about 1 percentage point per year,[15] and some of it reflected antitrust cases that directly reduced market shares more rapidly than natural forces alone would have.

Pascoe and Weiss observed only a 7-point average decline during 1950–1975 (only 0.3 point per year) in a panel of 23 large U.S. firms with initial market shares above 40 percent. During 1960–1969, another panel of large U.S. firms displayed a higher rate of decline—just over 1 point per year. During the 1970s, the rate of decline may have risen, but it has probably fallen in the 1980s. A panel of 47 U.K. firms studied by Shaw and Simpson showed declines averaging 0.3 to 0.8 point per year.

In Japanese dominant-firm industries during 1952–1966, the leading firms' shares declined by an average of 1 to 1.5 points per year.[16] Conditions in these postwar Japanese industries were probably more turbulent than in either U.S. or U.K. in-

---

[15] Until 1985, the main source of measures of the rate of erosion was my *The Treatment of Market Power* (New York: Columbia University Press, 1975), Chapter 4. Paul Geroski's chapter on "Do Dominant Firms Decline?" in Donald Hay and John Vickers, eds., *The Economics of Market Dominance* (Oxford: Basil Blackwell, 1987), presents and summarizes recent and older research. See also G. Pascoe and Leonard W. Weiss, "The Extent and Permanence of Market Dominance," Federal Trade Commission, Washington, D.C., unpublished paper, 1983; and R. Shaw and P. Simpson, "The Monopolies Commission and the Persistence of Monopoly," *Journal of Industrial Economics*, 34 (1985), 355–72.

[16] See Shepherd, *The Treatment of Market Power*, Chapter 4.

dustries (although the new import competition of the 1970s sharply increased the turbulence of U.S. and U.K. industries). Market shares in the range of 30–50 percent declined more slowly, at about 0.7 point per year. The function is apparently asymptotic, as Geroski (1987) suggests, tending to level off at market shares in the 10–20 percent range.

Geroski concludes that shares do decline, "but only at a glacial pace," possibly 0.3 point per year. My own estimate is closer to 1 point per year. A consensus estimate for general purposes might be 0.5 point per year, subject to wide variations in individual cases. So the retention of dominance for a decade or more is to be expected, and further rises in market share often occur (e.g., in 32 of the 108 firms surveyed by Geroski). On average, a 70 percent market share would take 20 years to decline to 60 percent, and a 60 percent share is still dominant.

Moreover, Geroski concludes that declines occur primarily from "sleepiness" in dominant firms, not because they are overwhelmed by market forces. Dominance can usually be sustained by firms that do not succumb to X-inefficiency and a retardation of innovation.

Thus the evidence for both oligopolies and dominant firms confirms that competitive processes tend to erode high market shares. But the erosion often occurs slowly. And many dominant market shares manage to avoid declining, some (such as General Motors, Eastman Kodak, Gillette, IBM, and Campbell Soup) for decades.

2.   Utilities as "Natural Monopolies"

"Utilities" are at the top end of the market share scale. Certain basic industries have been designated as "public utilities" and are under some form of public regulation. This usually is believed to reflect their "natural monopoly" status, owing to large economies of scale.

Yet many utilities do not fit this simple category. Many evolve through a life cycle comprising four stages: (1) beginning, (2) rapid growth, (3) maturity, and (4) reversion to conditions favoring competition. The large economies of scale last only during stages 1 and 2; during stage 3, they fade. Table 4.10 estimates these stages for many such industries. Actual policies often obstruct natural evolution through these phases. During stage 4, especially, regulation (often under the effective control of the "regulated" firm itself) frequently maintains monopoly well after competition could be viable.

Even during stages 2 and 3, the "utility" often has a "natural monopoly" in only part of its operations, especially local services such as electricity and telephones. Defining this area is usually a difficult task, especially because the utility firm will wish to extend its franchised control to all of the market. Many U.S. railroads (especially those east of the Mississippi River) had passed into stage 4 by 1960, as trucking and airlines spread. Telephones, gas, and electricity may now be viably competitive, in small or large shares of their industries.

Telephones present an especially interesting set of conditions. The local service part in each city has always been a natural monopoly, because having two or more sets of wires along the streets and two or more central exchange offices would be more costly than having just one. Long distance seemed to be a natural monopoly for a long time, but since 1960, the possibilities for competition there have increased.

TABLE 4.10   Stages of Utility Life Cycle: Approximate Intervals

	STAGE 1	STAGE 2	STAGE 3	STAGE 4
Manufactured gas	1800–1820	1820–1880	1880–1920	1920–1950
Natural gas	1900–1910	1910–1950	1950–	
Telegraph	1840–1850	1850–1916	1916–1930	1930–
Railways: All	1820–1835	1835–1910		
Passenger			1910–1935	1935–
Freight			1910–1960	1960–
Electricity	1870–1885	1885–1960	1960–	
Street railways	1870–1885	1885–1912	1912–1922	1922–
Telephone:				
Local	1875–1880	1880–1947	1947–	
Long distance	1880–1890	1890–1960	1960–1983	1984–
Airlines	1920–1925	1925–1960	1965–1975	1975–
Television	1935–1947	1947–1965	1965–1975	1975–
Cable television	1950–1955	1955–1975	1975–	

SOURCE: Adapted from Shepherd, *Treatment of Market Power*, Chapter 4.

The Bell System fiercely resisted such changes, but new regulatory and antitrust policies after 1974 forced it to accept new competitors. Though competition is not fully effective (AT&T still had over 70 percent of the market as of 1988), it may become so in the 1990s. Chapter 17 provides more details.

3.   Highly Competitive Industries

The industries with few or none of the structural elements of market power deserve a separate evaluation, to see what common characteristics they may have and whether they represent a stable condition. Figure 4.3 showed that low concentration is an unusual phenomenon in the manufacturing sector. It is confined mainly to the clothing and wood products industries, most agricultural products, and certain services and trades. The other structural elements fit this basic pattern. Consider the 130 manufacturing industries with 1947 concentration ratios of 25 percent or less. Many of these had rapid shifts in the market shares of the firms, as market forces buffeted them. The same can be said of the mass of small-scale local service trades. Though serious imperfections in information are common in these trades (e.g., the repair services), many of them have low concentration, high turnover, easy entry, and few vertical or conglomerate ties. They are turbulent arenas of competition.

Many of these markets involve rather simple, standardized uniform products or services that are undergoing relatively little innovation. Commonly, as in printing and forging, the size of plants can be small, while improved transportation has widened the intercity competition among local suppliers. This has lessened the potential rewards to large corporations and discouraged their entry into these industries, even as sidelines.

Some of these industries may be evolving toward increased structural monopoly and some degree of oligopoly may emerge even in sectors where it has tended to be uncommon in the past. The net trend of market structure depends on whether such an upward shift occurs, in comparison with the rate of erosion of high market shares.

4.   International Comparisons

Until the 1970s, the degree of monopoly was probably slightly higher in U.S. markets than in their foreign counterparts. The two main reasons for that are instructive, and they help to clarify the more recent trends toward equal degrees of competition in U.S. and foreign markets.[17]

First, most countries are much smaller than the United States; they are roughly comparable to one of our four major regions (Northeast, South, Midwest, and West). Second, foreign competition has long been crucial in most countries, where imports are a larger share of GNP. Imports have strongly affected many markets, ranging from cameras and automobiles to steel and electric generators. In contrast, U.S. markets were mostly insulated from foreign competition until the 1970s.

The two causes combined have given U.S. markets a higher average degree of monopoly than those of most foreign countries. Especially after the European Common Market was formed in 1957 and Japanese exports became important in the 1960s, competition has been more effective abroad. This was true even though concentration ratios in U.S. national industries seemed to be lower on average by 5 to 10 points (before imports were allowed for).

But then, during the 1970s and 1980s, competition increased in U.S. markets, partly because of rising imports. Recently, as many U.S. markets have moved toward merging into international markets, the degree of competition has become more uniform among countries.

Redefining Markets

Including imports in U.S. markets' sales usually has the effect of reducing U.S. concentration, as was noted earlier (unless an importer is among the four largest sellers). But as imports take a ever-larger share of a U.S. market, there comes a point when it is appropriate to redefine the market on a regional or world basis.

The foundation of market definition is still the range of choice of most consumers. This may be limited by product type and costs of transport. A few markets are genuinely global—diamonds, for example, which are universal in type and easily shipped at tiny cost relative to their value. The hard choices are in the middle range. For example, as imports approach 25 percent of new car sales in the United States, are we really looking at a worldwide market, or at least one that includes all Japanese producers? The answer is seldom obvious; there is no simple threshold value for switching from "U.S.-markets-with-imports" to regional or global markets.

The key question is whether *all* production of firms selling any significant share of cars in the United States should be included. For example, Toyota may sell 800,000

---

[17] Among basic studies are Joe S. Bain, *International Differences in Industrial Structure* (New Haven, Conn.: Yale University Press, 1966); Gideon Rosenbluth, *Concentration in Canadian Manufacturing Industries* (Princeton, N.J.: Princeton University Press, 1957); and Frederic L. Pryor, "An International Comparison of Concentration Ratios," *Review of Economics and Statistics*, 54 (May 1972), 130–140.

cars in the United States and 1 million elsewhere. Those concerned with supply substitutability would suggest including all 1.8 million cars in "the" U.S. market, because they could easily be shifted to sales here. The 1.8 million would go in the bottom half of the U.S. concentration ratio, while the 800,000 would go in the top half, because Toyota is the fourth-largest seller of automobiles in the United States. Indeed, all Japanese (and even all European and Korean) car production might be included, on the possibility that all of it is available (in some sense) for sale in the United States.

Against this are two points. First, all foreign production could not conceivably be shifted to the United States under any realistic conditions. Even if volumes of production increased, about the same volumes would be bid away for other countries. Therefore all the "extra" production is not really available. Second, many industries have trade barriers that keep imports out. Automobiles in particular were under informal self-controls by the Japanese during 1980–1988 to limit U.S. sales to about 2 million cars per year. Steel and other industries have comparable cartel restrictions. In these cases, no additional supply should be considered as in "the" market.

Imports may have impacts that go beyond their bare market shares, however. Foreign sellers commonly have different attitudes and objectives from domestic ones. Outsiders do not usually cooperate as readily as home firms do; indeed, they are often notorious for breaking local price-fixing rings. Neither can they be as easily punished or disciplined to force compliance with collusion.

Therefore foreign sellers often enforce competition more strongly than their mere market shares would indicate. Many a U.S. tight oligopoly or dominant firm has felt sharp new pressure from even a modest incursion by new imports. Part of this impact has come from the lower costs that foreign producers have enjoyed. But another part has come from foreigners' willingness to cut prices rather than cooperate in price fixing.

Whether and how to incorporate foreign-trade elements in analyses of competition in U.S. industries is still a formative topic in the field. It is likely to grow in importance and refinements.

QUESTIONS FOR REVIEW

1. "Older industries are likely to be less rigid than new ones." True?

2. "Concentration is not the main element of market structure, but it is useful for describing industrial patterns." True?

3. Many raw census ratios need to be adjusted for true (a) product markets, (b) geographic markets, and (c) imports. Which?

4. "The height of entry barriers is reported by the census every four years." True?

5. Firm A has a market share of 50 percent, while Firm B is in a market with a 4-firm concentration ratio of 60 percent. Assume all other conditions the same. Which firm is likely to have the higher profit rate (using the information in Table 2)? Please explain.

6. "IBM's profit rate reflects both its market share and the barriers against new entry." Is this true? Explain how you might judge which factor is more important.

7. Explain why the 4-firm concentration ratio of 23 percent for "Newspapers" in Table 6

seriously understates true market concentration. How about "Sheet metal work" (6 percent) and "Radios" (77 percent)?

8. "The HHI is empty and obscure, giving little clear basis for assessing the degree of actual market power."

   "The HHI is more broadly based and accurate than simple 4-firm ratios."

   Are they both true? Is one ratio generally better? Explain, please.

9. What are the general conditions of "optimal" and "natural" structure? Do they tend to diverge?

10. Choose three industries and try to estimate the height of their entry barriers. What types of data would you try to use?

11. Japanese and other foreign cars now hold an important share of sales in the U.S. Should we (1) merely include them in calculating US market shares in "the US automobile market," or (2) re-define the market as one world-wide market, including all cars made in the world? What threshhold conditions (import shares, transport costs, similarities of products, etc.) justify switching to the larger market, in this and other cases?

12. Trying appraising these industries as dominant-firm, tight-oligopoly or loose-oligopoly: beer, baseball, automobiles, fast-food restaurants, banking in your town, television broadcasting, newspapers, movie theaters in your area, and long-distance telephone service.

13. Do high market shares usually decline rapidly or slowly? What conditions may speed that decline?

14. Discuss two "natural monopolies," explaining what main conditions give them declining costs within the scope of their markets.

5

MARKET POWER'S EFFECTS ON PRICES, PROFITS, AND EFFICIENCY

We move in this chapter to a direct consideration of how market structure may shape performance in actual markets. Market power is certainly a complex and intriguing subject, but does it really matter to the economy?

If it has only weak effects, market power might be considered a cardboard dragon of little more than academic interest. But instead, monopoly may sharply affect prices and profits, undermining efficiency, innovation, fairness, and other values, and weighing down the economy.

Monopoly's most direct effects would be on financial conditions: prices and profits. They occupy Section I of this chapter. Section II considers several kinds of efficiency: X-efficiency, allocative efficiency, advertising, and the conservation of natural resources. The effects on technological progress, fairness, and other values are held over to the next two chapters.

Causation is the great underlying question, as Chapter 1 noted. Does market power cause the classic monopoly harms, or is it instead mainly a side effect of a prior cause (good performance)? This chapter addresses some aspects of causation, leaving others for later chapters.

Many of the lessons here are based on cross-section studies of statistical data. Appendix 4 at the end of the book presents some basic concepts of research to help readers judge the meaning of statistical results.

I. FINANCIAL EFFECTS

1. Cases of Effects on Price

A monopoly's classic effect is to raise price above cost, as the Lerner Index reflects. That is the practical means to the real end: obtaining a maximum of excess profits, which will translate into capital gains.

These two effects—on price-cost ratios and on profit rates—are both parts of the same basic effect. They have drawn extensive research. The results are consistent with the hypothesis that monopoly's effects are strong, although they do not prove those effects definitively.

Before we review those studies, we will pause to consider a number of specific cases that show dramatically that monopolies can have sharp effects.

No knowledgeable student doubts that some monopolies have raised prices to double, triple, or even much higher multiples of cost. The all-time leading example is the OPEC oil cartel, which sets oil-production quotas for its members, who include many of the world's oil-exporting countries. In 1973–1974, OPEC raised the price of oil from about $3 per barrel to about $14, and then in 1979, it pushed the price up further, to over $30 per barrel.[1] This tenfold rise in seven years brought OPEC members over $100 billion annually in extra profits, and caused severe damage to national production and international economic stability.

In 1985, amid great drama and turbulence, the price was cut to the $13–$18 range, reflecting a mix of Saudi Arabian strategic pricing and a decline in OPEC's control. Whether OPEC can raise prices above $20 again is a matter of endless jockeying among the members. OPEC's colossal impact and gains are all the more striking because the "organization" is a heterogeneous and often divided cartel, as Chapter 14 will explore. Even the chronic "glut" in oil since 1981 has not driven prices down toward truly competitive levels.

Small-scale examples are also instructive. In the 1960s, Miles Laboratories set the price for a medical kit at forty-three times cost. The kits, for prediagnosing mental retardation in infants, were produced under an exclusive licence for about $6 and priced at $262 each.

Soft contact lenses are a similar case, which will be personally familiar to many readers of this book.[2] From 1971 to 1975, Bausch & Lomb was virtually the only seller. The cost was under $5 per pair of lenses, while the price was set at over $60. New competition later drove down Bausch & Lomb's market share and its price for lenses, but then Bausch & Lomb staged a comeback, regained its dominance, and raised the price once again.

The DeBeers diamond monopoly has controlled world diamond prices for over five decades.[3] Its Central Selling Organization can alter the price of diamonds across a wide range.

The leading airlines hold dominance in various "hub" cities; for example, Northwest controls over 80 percent of flights into and out of in Minneapolis, and USAir has a near-monopoly in Pittsburgh (see Chapter 18 for details). The fares on these dominated routes are often roughly double the fares on comparable routes where there is competition.

---

[1] Among the outpouring of writings about OPEC, see James M. Griffin and David J. Teece, *OPEC Behavior and World Oil Prices* (London: Allen & Unwin, 1982); John M. Blair, *The Price of Oil* (New York: Pantheon Books, 1976); Albert L. Danielson, *The Evolution of Oil* (New York: Harcourt Brace Jovanovich, 1982); Steven A. Schneider, *The Oil Price Revolution* (Baltimore: Johns Hopkins Press, 1983); and Paul W. MacAvoy, *Crude Oil Prices* (Cambridge, Mass.: Ballinger Press, 1982).

[2] See "Bausch and Lomb: Hardball Pricing Helps It Regain Its Grip in Contact Lenses," *Business Week,* July 16, 1984; and Roberta Reynes, "New Contact Lens Competition Focuses on Bausch and Lomb," *Barron's,* August 1, 1983.

[3] See David Koskoff, *The Diamond World* (New York: Harper & Row, 1981); Godehard Lenzen, *The History of Diamond Production and the Diamond Trade* (London: Barrie and Jenkins, 1981); and Steve Lohr, "Why a Diamond Cartel Is Forever," *The New York Times,* September 7, 1986, p. B4.

TABLE 5.1   Price Discrimination as a Source of Monopoly Profit

COMPANY-WIDE RATES OF RETURN ON EQUITY (ABOVE THE COST OF EQUITY) (PERCENT)	PERCENTAGE OF COMPANY SALES FROM WHICH MONOPOLY PROFIT IS EXTRACTED:		
	100%	50%	20%
	REQUIRED DEMAND ELASTICITY ON THAT PORTION OF SALES		
(1)	(2)	(3)	(4)
5 percent	40.0	19.6	7.8
10 percent	19.6	9.8	3.9
15 percent	13.3	6.7	2.7

Eastman Kodak, with over 80 percent of film sales in the United States, has been able to price "largely without regard to cost" (in one of its own officials' words) for over 80 years (see Chapter 17).

The drug industry offers many instances in which patented drugs, protected against effective competition, are produced at costs of 10 cents or less per pill but are priced near $1 per pill. In another example, an international cartel was formed in the market for quinine in the 1960s: it more than tripled the price.[4] In Britain, Kodak, Ltd., has held over 75 percent of the market for color film for several decades: it has maintained prices at 35 to 55 percent above competitive levels.[5]

The price of cellophane was raised substantially by duPont during the many years it held a virtual monopoly of this product in the United States.[6] Collusion in a series of tight oligopolies in American electrical equipment markets probably maintained prices about 15 to 20 percent above their long-run competitive levels during the 1950s. In one tiny example among hundreds, a price ring in rock salt for clearing Chicago roads raised the price of rock salt from $8 per ton to about $16 per ton in 1964.[7] When fixed brokerage fees were made competitive on the New York Stock Exchange in May 1975, prices dropped by 43 to 64 percent. Such examples can be multiplied many times over, in many countries, sectors, and specific settings.

Price Discrimination.   Monopoly power also enlarges price discrimination, which sets a structure of differing price-cost ratios depending on differing demand elasticities (recall Chapter 2). Such demand-based pricing can generate surprisingly large volumes of profits. Table 5.1 indicates how much discrimination is required to raise total rates of return to high levels. The third line shows that if a mere 20 percent of a firm's demand has an elasticity as low as 2.7, the firm can have a company-wide profit rate that is 15 points above the cost of capital. The other 80 percent of sales can be at zero excess profit.

Evidently, price discrimination can pack a stiff punch; a little of it can generate

[4] *The New York Times*, March 24, 1967, p. 16.
[5] U.K. Monopolies Commission, *Color Film*, House of Commons, No. 1 (London: Her Majesty's Stationery Office, April 21, 1966).
[6] See George W. Stocking and Willard F. Mueller, "The Cellophane Case and the New Competition," *American Economic Review*, 45 (March 1955), 29–63.
[7] *Chicago Sun-Times*, August 24, 1966.

high profit rates. In many markets, there is quite a lot of it. Chapter 12 considers several detailed cases, but drugs and airlines can be mentioned here.

Drugs are sold to groups with sharply differing elasticities, especially individual patients (who merely buy what the doctor's prescription says) and large hospitals (which shop around and often extract rock-bottom prices). The price-cost ratios to these groups usually differ sharply.

Airline fare-cost ratios also vary steeply among customer groups and city routes, reflecting demand elasticities, as Chapters 12 and 18 will discuss. The same plane may contain customers getting equal service (including scheduling convenience) but paying prices varying by multiples of three or four.

The lesson at this point is that price-*structure* effects are often as sharp as price-*level* effects. They are large when conditions are favorable: inelastic demand, high market shares, entry barriers, few potential entrants, and so on. Then prices can be raised to high multiples of costs.

But these cases might merely be freaks. What is the mainstream experience? Are effects widespread, sharp, and lasting? Evidence is needed across all markets, and that is where past research has focused.

2.   Cross-Section Studies

The task is simple, in logic: to test whether monopoly structure is correlated— as a cause—with either prices or profits. As was defined in equation (1.2) and estimated in Section II of Chapter 4, prices or profits are the *dependent* variable (the effect), while structural conditions are the *independent* variables (the possible causes).

One asssembles data on a cross-section of markets or firms, on all conditions that might strongly affect the prices or profits. Then one runs the statistical regressions, to estimate the coefficients between structure and prices or profits. Chapter 4 used some such regressions to clarify structure. Now we consider more of them in trying to appraise the effects of market power on prices and profits.

Scores of such cross-section studies have been published during the last five decades. They have divided into two main approaches: (1) *industry-based* studies of price-cost margins, and (2) *company-based* studies of rates of profit on investment. The most prominent among some fifty leading studies are summarized in Table 5.2.

Serious research began with Joe S. Bain's 1951 paper. Previously, there had been only a scattering of evidence from specific industries; though strongly suggestive, it was not systematic.

From 1951 until 1968, research focused on *industry-wide* analysis of *price-cost margins,* as explained by *concentration ratios.* That was where the data were. Since then, the research has shifted more to *individual-company* data, in an effort to explain *profit rates* with *market shares* as well as the other structural elements. That reflects the emergence of market share data for companies.

The two main sorts of regression models are shown in Table 5.3, along with some of the most familiar variants. Structure is represented by several variables that reflect the main elements. If complete and perfect data were available, the models would be larger and more complex, possibly including simultaneous equations. But since the data are incomplete and imperfect, the models include only what can be

TABLE 5.2 Some Leading Studies of Market Structure's Relationship to Profitability and Price-Cost Margins

Author and Year of Publication	Profit Measure and Coverage	Variables Representing Structure	Coverage	Period	Main Findings
Joe S. Bain (1951)	Average after-tax return on equity of "leading" firms	8-firm concentration ratio	42 U.S. manufacturing industries; 4-digit	1936–1940	A positive association between concentration and rates of return.
Joe S. Bain (1956)	Average after-tax return on equity	8-firm concentration ratio Estimated barriers to entry	20 U.S. manufacturing industries	1936–1940, 1947–1951	Concentrated industries showed higher returns when entry barriers were medium or high.
David Schwartzman (1959)	Average price-cost margin in the industry	4-firm concentration ratio	61 U.S. and Canadian manufacturing industries; 4-digit	1954	A faint positive association between concentration and price-cost margins.
George J. Stigler (1963)	Average rate of return on total assets, industry-wide	4-firm concentration ratio	All U.S. manufacturing industries; about 80 3-digit industries	1947, 1954	Positive associations in some years, but no associations in others.
H. Michael Mann (1986)	Average after-tax return on equity, "leading" firms	Grouping of "concentrated" and "unconcentrated" industries (by 8-firm ratio; 70% threshold) Estimated barriers to entry	30 U.S. manufacturing industries	1950–1960	Rates of return were higher in concentrated industries when entry barriers were medium or high.
M. Hall and L. W. Weiss (1967)	After-tax return on equity, individual firms	Average 4-firm concentration ratio Asset size	341 large U.S. industrial corporations	1956–1962	Size was more closely associated with rate of return than concentration was.

TABLE 5.2 *(continued)*

AUTHOR AND YEAR OF PUBLICATION	PROFIT MEASURE AND COVERAGE	VARIABLES REPRESENTING STRUCTURE	COVERAGE	PERIOD	MAIN FINDINGS
W. S. Comanor and T. Wilson (1967)	After-tax return on equity, average for the industry	Average 4- and 8-firm concentration ratios Advertising-sales ratio Proxy for "optimal" plant size	35 U.S. consumer-goods industries; about 4-digit level	1954–1957	Advertising intensity was associated with rates of return
N. Collins and L. E. Preston (1968, 1969)	Price-cost margins for the industry	4-firm concentration ratios Asset size Capital-output ratio	All U.S. 4-digit industries	1958, 1958–1960, 1963	Margins were consistently, but not strongly, associated with concentration.
W. G. Shepherd (1972)	After-tax return on equity, individual firms	Market shares 4-firm concentration ratios Asset size Advertising-sales ratio Estimates of entry barriers	231 large U.S. corporations	1960–1969	Rates of return were closely associated with market share, but less closely with concentration and entry barriers.
W. G. Shepherd (1972)	Price-cost margins, industry-wide average	4-firm concentration ratios (raw and adjusted) Size (shipments) Advertising intensity	All U.S. 4-digit manufacturing industries	1963–1967	Margins were consistently associated with concentration and advertising intensity
Almarin Phillips (1972)	Price-cost margins, industry-wide average	3-firm concentration ratios Advertising intensity Price-fixing activity	All U.K. manufacturing industries; approximately 4-digit degree of detail	1948, 1951, 1954	Margins were positively associated with concentration. Collusion variables seemed to play no roles.
H. Demsetz	Rate of return on total assets	4-firm concentration ratio	95 U.S. 3-digit industries	1963	Size and concentration raise profits.
A. Strickland and L. Weiss	Price-cost margin	4-firm concentration ratio	All U.S. 4-digit industries	1963	Size and concentration raise profits.

SOURCE: This table is extracted and adapted from Leonard W. Weiss's excellent survey chapter in H. J. Goldschmid, H. M. Mann, and J. F. Weston, *Industrial Concentration: The New Learning* (Boston: Little, Brown, 1975).

Specific citations for the various studies are as follows:

J. S. Bain, "Relation of Profit Rate to Industry Concentration, American Manufacturing, 1936–1940," *Quarterly Journal of Economics*, 65 (August 1951), 293–94.

J. S. Bain, *Barriers to New Competition* (Cambridge, Mass.: Harvard University Press, 1956).

D. Schwartzman, "Effect of Monopoly on Price," *Journal of Political Economy*, 67 (August 1959), 352–62.

G. J. Stigler, *Capital and Rates of Return in Manufacturing Industries* (Princeton, N.J.: Princeton University Press, 1963).

H. M. Mann, "Seller Concentration, Barriers to Entry, and Rates of Return in 30 Industries, 1950–1960," *Review of Economics and Statistics*, 48 (August 1966), 296–307.

M. Hall and L. W. Weiss, "Firm Size and Profitability," *Review of Economics and Statistics*, 49 (August 1967), 319–31.

W. S. Comanor and T. Wilson, "Advertising, Market Structure, and Performance," *Review of Economics and Statistics*, 49 (November 1967), 423–40.

N. Collins and L. E. Preston, *Concentration and Price-Cost Margins in Manufacturing Industries* (Berkeley: Berkeley University of California Press, 1968); and N. Collins and L. E. Preston, "Price Cost Margins and Industry Structure," *Review of Economics and Statistics*, 51 (August 1969), 271–86.

W. G. Shepherd, "The Elements of Market Structure," *Review of Economics and Statistics*, 54 (February 1972), 25–38.

W. G. Shepherd, "Elements of Market Structure: An Inter-industry Analysis," *Southern Economic Journal*, 38 (April 1972), 531–37.

A. Phillips, "An Economic Study of Price-Fixing, Market Structure, and Performance in British Industry in the Early 1950s," in K. Cowling, *Market Structure and Corporate Behavior* (London: Gray Mills, 1972).

A. D. Strickland and L. W. Weiss, "Advertising, Concentration and Price-Cost Margins," *Journal of Political Economy*, 84 (October 1976), 1109–21.

H. Demsetz, "Industry Structure, Market Rivalry, and Public Policy," *Journal of Law and Economics*, 16 (April 1973), 1–9.

TABLE 5.3 Basic Models for Testing Market Structure's Effects on Profits and Prices

Equation No.	Dependent Variables	Independent Variables*					
		Structural Variables*				Other Variables	
		Constant Term (represents a competitive profit rate or price-cost margin)	Market Share (if available)	Concentration†	Barrier Conditions or Estimates‡	Growth (a background variable)	Capital Intensity (a background variable)
	Industry-Based Analysis						
1	Price-cost margin	Constant		Concentration	Size; advertising intensity	Growth	Capital intensity
2	Price-cost margin	Constant		Concentration	Barrier "height" (high, medium, low)	Growth	Capital intensity
	Firm-Based Analysis						
3	Rate of return on investment	Constant	Market share		Size; advertising intensity	Growth	
4	Rate of return on investment	Constant		Concentration	Size; advertising intensity	Growth	
5	Rate of return on investment	Constant	Market share		Barrier "height" (high, medium, low)	Growth	
6	Rate of return on investment	Constant		Concentration	Barrier "height" (high, medium, low)	Growth	

* Several other structural variables are occasionally added in. These include vertical structure, diversification, leverage, producer–consumer goods differences, foreign control. Various adjustments for regional and product submarkets and for foreign trade can be included. Some studies use HHI or other summary indexes.

† Raw or adjusted ratios.

‡ Proxy variables for economies of scale are sometimes also included, although their role is debatable.

tested reasonably reliably. As always in this field, one has to make trade-offs between the *importance* of the element and the *quality* of the data about it.

The relationships can be assumed to be of a straight-line sort ("linear"), with simple coefficients. Or curved relationships can be tried—for example, by converting some or all variables to logarithms. There may be interaction effects among the independent variables, requiring special techniques. So far, however, most testing has used simple linear models because most of the data are not good enough to justify more complex models. When curves and interactions have been tested, the results of the analysis have not been any better than those obtained from the simpler models.

The "competitive rate of profit" is an important concept. This is the minimum rate of return to capital that will permit a competitive firm to survive. It cannot be less than the true cost of capital to the firm. The "competitive" rate of return ranges between 7 and 11 percent in most markets most of the time. It would be shown by the constant term in items 3–6 of Table 5.3. That is the profit rate earned when all the structural variables reflecting market power are held at zero. "Excess" profit is then the profit that exceeds this benchmark level. Thus a 25 percent rate of return would normally include about 15 points of "excess" rate of return.

3.   Problems of Measuring

Good information is scarce. Each type of data—for profits, price-cost margins, assets, equity, and, of course, the structural data—has its own gaps and idiosyncrasies. We consider them briefly in turn.

Profit Rates.   Profits are usually shown by net income after tax. The degree of profits is then the rate of return, shown by:

$$\text{Rate of return} = \pi = \frac{\text{Net income}}{\text{Equity}}$$

We will use π as the symbol for return on equity in the rest of the book. Equity is stockholders' equity.[8] It is the sum of two items: the money received by the firm for shares of stock when they are issued, and the money retained (or reinvested) by the firm out of its earnings. Equity capital represents the voting control of the *owners*. The return to their interest in the firm is probably the best single basis for judging the degree of profitability: the financial success of the firm.

Yet the return on total assets can also be a valid measure. For this, the profits must also include interest payments, which the accountants treat as a cost. So:

$$\text{Return on assets} = \frac{\text{Net income} + \text{Interest payments}}{\text{Total assets}}$$

This rate of return will usually be lower than the return on equity. If the firm has no debt—that is, a capital structure with leverage of zero—these two measures of

---

[8] *Equity* is virtually identical to "net worth." There are some finer points about measuring it, but the basic concept is relatively direct and consistent.

profitability are identical (because interest payments disappear and assets then equal equity).

Accounting Problems.   In either case, the numbers are often slippery. Accounting is full of controversy and choice rather than simple, uniform bookkeeping rules (See Appendix 3 at the end of the book.) Serious students of industrial organization should examine the main issues in accounting theory and practice with special care.

These complex issues leave much latitude in rendering accounts, and therefore the profit figures reported for identical conditions can vary. Depreciation is particularly tricky. Different methods of setting depreciation can sharply raise or lower the recorded profit levels. (This, too, is shown in Appendix 3.)

Inventories can also be valued several different ways, and again, the methods used can influence the recorded profit levels. Both problems are aggravated if there are strong price trends for inputs and/or outputs. Then firms are likely to resort to special adjustments in order to "normalize" the accounts and reflect the changed values. But there will be several ways to adjust, each giving different results.

Tax treatments can also matter. Tax rules have enabled many firms to pay little or no tax on net income. Other rules permit large profits to be reported as small ones. Whatever the wisdom of these rules, they do affect the comparisons of "true" profitability.

These and other problems should make one cautious when measuring and comparing profitability among firms. Yet the situation is not hopeless. If one covers a number of years and understands the underlying trends in the firm—and any special tax conditions—then the firm's average profitability can be estimated reasonably well. When two firms' rates of return differ steadily by 5 points or more (e.g., between 12 and 17 percent), there is usually a real difference in profitability.[9]

The q Ratio.   Recently, an alternative measure of company success has been proposed to take the place of the faulty rate of profit. It is "Tobin's *q* ratio": *the firm's market value divided by its assets,* valued either at book or replacement value.[10] The *q* ratio can avoid some of the accounting complexities that afflict profit rates.

It also has a somewhat different meaning. The firm's market value is established by its current stock price, set in the stock markets as investors buy and sell. Thus a firm's stock might have a current market price of $100 per share. If there are a million shares outstanding, the firm's market value at this moment is $100 million. If the firm has invested $50 million in its assets (equipment, buildings, inventories, etc.), then its *q* ratio would be $100 million divided by $50 million, or exactly 2.0.

That high ratio shows success: the firm has deployed its $50 million investment to build up a company that is now worth twice as much in the marketplace. The

---

[9] This is the general view, though there are dissenters. Among the most aggressive is Franklin M Fisher, who developed his arguments while helping IBM defend itself against charges of monopoly behavior (and profits) in the computer industry. See Fisher et al., *Folded, Spindled and Mutilated* (Cambridge, Mass: MIT Press, 1983).

[10] See Michael Smirlock, Thomas Gilligan, and William Marshall, "Tobin's *q* and the Structure-Performance Relationship," *American Economic Review,* 74 (December 1984), 1051–60, and the sources cited there.

potential capital gain ($50 million) is no less than 100 percent. A high q therefore shows the same kind of extra profitability that a high profit rate shows. But it is forward-looking, based on investors' evaluations of the likely *future* profitability of the firm (Chapter 10 will explain more about investors' motives and effects).

This forward-looking feature is valuable because it incorporates the firm's current value, as based on the latest collective evaluations by investors of its prospects. But there is a cost to using this method.[11] Inserting the stock market evaluation introduces all the strange things (herd movements, mistakes, manipulations, etc.) that happen on Wall Street. Indeed, when stock prices fluctuate sharply from week to week, it is not clear that they reliably indicate anything.

So although the q ratio is an interesting alternative to the profit rate, it may add large elements of error. Also, it is complicated to measure in practice. Studies using it have had to adopt intricate methods, with arbitrary and debatable steps. The *numerator* usually involves preferred stock and debt, which aren't so easily valued. Actual estimates usually are partly based on book values. The *denominator* is even more troublesome. "Replacement costs" for assets may be tried, but they are nearly impossible to appraise. Book values generally have serious problems of their own, caused by inflation and arbitrary depreciation choices.

Considering that it combines two imperfect parts, the estimated q ratio may be inferior to the profit rate rather than superior. But actual q ratios turn out to give highly similar results to profit rates, so the choice between the two may not be crucial after all. See Table 5.6 later in this section for the results of some tests using q ratios.

Price-Cost Margins.   An "ideal" index of monopoly is the Lerner Index, the relative gap between price and marginal cost.

Yet it is not easy to measure. One usually has to rely on average revenues and costs for whole industries. Such industries often contain many prices, for a variety of specific products. But instead of, say, fifteen specific price-cost measures—for individual products and firms—one has to work with just one price-cost measure for the whole industry.

The cost data blur the picture even more. As a "proxy" for marginal cost, one must use average variable costs. Most researchers now approximate these by the following census categories:

$$\text{Price-cost margin} = \frac{\text{Value added} - \text{Payroll}}{\text{Value of shipments}} = \frac{\text{Price} - \text{Cost}}{\text{Price}}$$

Value added is the value of shipments minus materials, supplies and containers, fuel, purchased electrical energy, and contract work. The *costs* therefore include, roughly, those items bought from outside (including labor) that are "variable." Actually, some of these items are far less variable than others. In fact, some may be less variable than even some of the "capital" items left in. (Example: key specialized employees virtually indispensable to the firm who cannot be freely dropped and rehired.)

---

[11] For a critique of q ratios and their use, see W. G. Shepherd, "Tobin's q and the Structure-Performance Relationship: Comment," *American Economic Review*, 76 (December 1986), 1205–10.

Price-cost margins therefore are oblique and crude. By covering several or all firms in an industry, they average together some highly differing conditions. On the whole, price-cost margins for industries can be expected to understate—perhaps sharply—whatever price effects actually occur in real markets.

X-Inefficiency.   An affluent firm with market power may let some of its profits be absorbed into costs. The monopoly effect on prices would still occur, but the recorded profits and price-cost margins would understate the effect. The tests that follow may therefore understate the role of market power in raising attainable profits.

4. Price Levels and Margins

Price-cost research focuses on concentration and industry-wide average price-cost margins. Because concentration is a crude statistic, the underlying patterns are necessarily loose.

In fact, the price-cost margin approach is quite inferior to studying profits because it is so much cruder. The industry-wide basis masks individual-firm variations; concentration data are faulty; and the data on price-cost margins are quite rough. All findings will contain high degrees of measurment error, and they will omit the crucial role of individual market shares. Still, they are worth reviewing, if only to draw cautionary lessons.

Table 5.4 is typical of many research findings that have fitted these patterns.[12] Concentration is consistently related to margins, but not closely so. The coefficient of about 0.07 to 0.10 suggests that each added 10 percent concentration adds nearly 1 percent to price levels.

Barriers also appear to play a moderate role. Advertising, as a separate factor, seems to have a stronger role, but its range is still narrow, since advertising intensity rarely goes above 10 percent of sales, while concentration ranges up toward 100 percent. Size appears to have a modest association with higher margins. Yet that may instead reflect the role of capital intensity, which the crude capital-output variable has not fully filtered out.

These patterns are broadly similar to those reported by Collins and Preston, Strickland and Weiss, and many others. The dependent variable is the price-cost margin in each case, and the analysis usually covers some hundreds of U.S. manufacturing industries. The information is often for just one year, such as 1963 or 1967. The data contain many errors, and they also mask the variations among individual firms.

Even so, concentration is consistently related to price-cost margins, particularly in consumer-goods industries. A concentration ratio of 100 percent usually implies a price-cost margin that is roughly 10 to 20 percent higher than it is when concentration is minimal. The effect is weaker in producer-goods markets, where advertising and brand loyalty are less intense. Most analyses do not test for a possible stair-step in the relationship at some "critical" level of concentration.

---

[12] The capital-intensity variable is included in order to try to filter out the effect of greater capital intensity on the profit margins. The margins include depreciation as well as profits. Therefore high capital intensity (e.g., in such heavy industries as chemicals and metals) makes the margins higher, apart from any true monopoly effect. Though the variable used here is imperfect, it is the best there is. It may filter out most of this extraneous effect. Bear in mind that the concentration data are also highly imperfect.

TABLE 5.4 Analysis of Market Structure and Price-Cost Margins, U.S. 4-Digit Industries

			INDEPENDENT VARIABLES				
DEPENDENT VARIABLE	CONSTANT TERM	CAPITAL INTENSITY	CONCEN- TRATION	SIZE	ADVERTISING INTENSITY	REVENUE GROWTH	R^2
A. *General Panel of 336 Industries*							
Price-cost margin	9.045 (4.20)	$.011K$ (7.36)	$.089C_r$ (5.24)	$1.051S_r$ (3.03)	$.017A$ (9.20)	$2.723E$ (2.16)	.403
B. *114 Consumer-Goods Industries*							
Price-cost margin	1.936 (.51)	$.009K$ (1.97)	$.012C_a$ (3.91)	$2.262S_a$ (3.17)	$.014A$ (5.48)	$3.272E$ (1.16)	.539
C. *222 Producer-Goods Industries*							
Price-cost margin	16.313 (7.25)	$.011K$ (6.50)	$.007C_a$ (2.78)	$.008S_a$ (.02)	—	$2.809E$ (1.87)	.255
D. *32 Mature, Homogeneous- Goods Industries*							
Price-cost margin	11.408 (2.38)	$.018K$ (6.07)	$.001C_a$ (.02)	$.018S_a$ (.19)	—	$3.443E$ (.97)	.658

T-ratios are shown beneath coefficients.
r—raw census data on concentration and size.
a—adjusted census data on concentration and size.
SOURCE: Adapted from W. G. Shepherd, "Elements of Market Structure: An Inter-industry Analysis," *Southern Economic Journal*, 38 (April 1972), 531–37.

Also, the analysis does not distinguish between leading and lesser firms: they are all lumped together in one average. But that distinction may be important. Each firm's degree of monopoly is directly related to its market share, so the top group of firms would have higher price-raising effects—and higher profit rates—than the rest. The possibility calls for tests that split out the leading and lesser firms for separate study. Generally, that has not been accurately done in this line of broad cross-section research.

Two other lines of price-cost research deserve special note. First, the banking industry has been a fruitful target of study because it is a series of geographical markets, all dealing with a uniform product. It is also regulated, so there are abundant data about market shares and interest rates set by banks in specific locales. Repeated studies have shown that interest rates set by banks are strongly related to the degree of concentration in local banking markets. Stephen Rhoades and others conclude that this reflects the exercise of market power.[13]

Second, airlines have been closely studied, especially since deregulation during 1978–1981. They, too, present large numbers of local and regional markets, offering a generally uniform product (passenger air transportation). Recent studies have shown that market concentration is significantly related to price-cost patterns.[14] The finding is a firm rejection of the idea that these airline markets are perfectly "contestable," as discussed in Chapter 3 (see also Chapters 11 and 18).

The sensible interpretation of all this research is consistent with the variety of case study evidence, which was sampled in Section I.2. Degrees of monopoly power are likely to cause degrees of excess profits in a wide range of markets. This causation may be diluted by some instances of reverse causation, with superior performance or scale economies having some effect.

5. Research on Profitability

In 1951, Bain claimed that the leading firms typically have higher profitability than lesser firms. In 1956, he modified this claim: only where entry barriers were high would concentration affect profits. This line of research was extended by Mann in 1966, and by Comanor and Wilson in 1967. In 1968, Hall and Weiss seemed to find that the "capital requirements" barrier was the only real factor; concentration scarcely mattered at all in their data. The present author introduced market share into the analysis in 1972, comparing the roles of the various elements.

Meanwhile, Stigler in 1963, using three-digit industry data, found no relationship between concentration and the industry-wide average return on assets. Such simple regressions were soon superseded by more complete tests employing more precise data. Using price-cost margins, Collins and Preston in 1968 confirmed the positive association between concentration and price-cost patterns.

[13] Stephen A. Rhoades, "Market Share as a Source of Market Power: Implications and Some Evidence," *Journal of Economics and Business,* 37 (1985), 343–63; Rhoades and Jim Burke, "Economic and Political Foundations of Section 7 Enforcement in the 1980s," *Columbia Law Review,* 1989 (in process); and Allen N. Berger and Timothy H. Hannan, "The Price-Concentration Relationship in Banking," Working Paper 88-18, Federal Reserve Board, Washington, D.C., July 1988.

[14] David R. Graham, Daniel P. Kaplan, and David S. Sibley, "Efficiency and Competition in the Airline Industry," *Bell Journal of Economics,* 14 (Spring 1983), 118–38.

By the 1970s, research had advanced to include (1) most of the likely variables; and (2) large sets of relatively reliable data, for various periods and several countries. Such research has repeatedly reaffirmed the structure-profitability association, with increasing precision. This has clarified several specific issues: (1) The relative importance of the various elements of structure—market share, oligopoly concentration, barriers, and others—can be assessed, as we saw in Chapter 4. (2) The strength of the structure-profits association can be estimated. (3) The role (if any) of differential efficiency can be compared.

The basic model of profitability is shown in Table 5.5, with data that most closely fit the research findings. (Recall that Figure 4.1 showed the results in diagrams.) These results can clarify reality; they also give you a chance to practice interpreting what such figures may really mean.

Market share is strongly associated with profit rates. As a rule of thumb, each 10 percent of added market share adds about 2.5 percent to the profit rate.[15] The variables representing the oligopoly group (either C or G in Table 5.5) are quite a bit weaker. Market share therefore seems to be the main source of high profitability. That makes good sense, and it fits well with the broad range of evidence and experience.

Entry barriers appear to be a lesser general source of profitability. Size has no strong positive relation to profit rates; more likely it is *negative*. Advertising has a definite association in some groups of firms, but its role covers only a small range. The general "height" of entry barriers also shows no strong effect on profit rates. Even when barriers are low, market share is still closely related to profit rates.

These patterns have also appeared in regressions that use Tobin's q ratio in place of the profit rate.[16] Recall that q is the firm's market value divided by its asset, or replacement, value. If stock market activity reflects rational, accurate evaluations, then q will be superior to mere backward-looking profit rates. But the q ratios are not easy to derive from company data. Also, their construction inevitably incorporates some of the same errors that infect accounting profit rates.[17]

Smirlock and colleagues have attempted to use the market structure model to explain q ratios, and indeed the two approaches give strongly similar results. Table 5.6 presents comparative results, with the profit rate and q ratio regressions in successive lines. The coefficients are almost identically significant throughout. Apparently, q largely duplicates the results that profit rates give.

McFarland has argued that q is superior in practice, rather than just in theory.[18] He offers tests that suggest q may be slightly more sensitive than profit rates.

But q ratios are not free; they require complex, painstaking, and often dubious methods of estimation. Any gain in sensitivity will probably be slight compared to

---

[15] This is based on the rate of return on equity. Virtually identical patterns hold when one analyzes the rate of return on assets. Other studies confirm the validity of the analysis and the role of market power in raising profitability.

[16] See Michael Smirlock, Thomas Gilligan, and William Marshall, "Tobin's q and the Structure-Performance Relationship," pp. 1051–60, and sources cited there. James Tobin had used the ratio of market-to-book value for macroeconomic analysis, and his name has stuck with the ratio in this use.

[17] See Shepherd, "Tobin's q and the Structure-Performance Relationship," pp. 1205–10.

[18] See Henry McFarland, "Evaluating Q as an Alternative to the Rate of Return in Measuring Profitability," *Review of Economics and Statistics*, 70 (November 1988), pp. 614–22.

TABLE 5.5 Analysis of Structure and Profitability in Large U.S. Firms, 1960–1969

Dependent Variables	Constant Term	Market Share M	Concentration C	Group G	Size (Log of Assets) S	Advertising Intensity A	Growth E	R^2
Subgroups of Firms								
125 Producer-Goods Firms								
Profit rate, 1960–1969	6.41 (6.01)*	.155 (6.00)		−.010 (0.50)	.141 (0.97)	.146 (1.61)	.705 (3.73)	.459
Profit rate, 1960–1969	6.33 (5.11)		.038 (1.82)		.147 (0.87)	.077 (2.36)	1.03 (4.91)	.276
120 Consumer-Goods Firms								
Profit rate, 1960–1969	3.20 (2.53)	.323 (10.74)		.069 (2.61)	−.592 (2.40)	.010 (1.58)	1.99 (4.34)	.649
Profit rate, 1960–1969	2.03 (1.28)		.171 (5.83)		−.548 (1.77)	.005 (0.65)	2.75 (4.89)	.448
50 Firms in "Old Industries"†								
Profit rate, 1960–69	3.70 (0.87)	.524M (2.09)	−.010M^2 (1.36)		−.285S (0.97)		.152E (2.88)	.420

Independent Variables

* t-ratios are in parentheses.
† The industries are steel, meat packing, glass, rubber, oil, and copper.
SOURCE: W. G. Shepherd, *The Treatment of Market Power* (New York: Columbia University Press, 1975), Chapter 5.

TABLE 5.6   Structural Regressions, 95 Large US Industrial Corporations, 1980–1984.*

Constant Term	Market Share	4-Firm Concentration	Log of Assets	Ad/Sales Ratio	Barriers High	Medium	Growth	R^2
1980–1984								
11.6	.303	− .011	− .479	.300			.962	.53
(3.66)†	(6.98)	(− .33)	(− 2.06)	(3.62)			(3.10)	
1980–1984								
8.0	.300	− .066			3.88	2.91	1.19	.49
(3.60)	(6.54)	(− 1.66)			(2.67)	(2.57)	(3.57)	
1982–1984								
12.7	.334	− 027	− 1.66	.333			.535	.48
(3.53)	(6.78)	(− .71)	(− 2.03)	(3.55)			(1.52)	

* Independent variable: the average rate of return on equity for the designated period.
† t-ratios are in parentheses. Ratios of 2.4 are significant at the 1 percent level.
SOURCE: William G. Shepherd, "The Nature of Monopoly," a chapter in Samuel Bowles, Richard C. Edwards, and William G. Shepherd, eds., *Unconventional Wisdom: Essays on Economics in Honor of John Kenneth Galbraith* (Boston: Houghton Mifflin, 1990).

the added costs. In that light, it is often more sensible to use profit rates (cautiously, of course) than to go to great lengths to use q ratios.

Smirlock and colleagues also attempted to use q-based results to claim that market share's role "proves" that the Chicago-UCLA hypothesis of reversed performance-to-structure causation is correct. But that is not permissible. A q ratio can be high because of monopoly power, random chance, or some other reason, as well as because of greater efficiency.

More recent data have also been analyzed; the results are shown in Table 5.7.[19] They use the same methods and models, and the results confirm the earlier patterns. Concentration's coefficient has ceased to be significant in the presence of the market share variable. Market share really does appear to play the main role in company motivation and results.

Other studies have suggested that leverage (in the firm's capital structure) does not play a strong separate role in influencing profitability. Vertical structure and diversification have had only preliminary tests so far; they predictably show little or no relation to profits. Better tests, however, might show real influences. Producer- and consumer-goods conditions do seem to vary, as Table 5.4 indicates. Growth does have a strong role. But, of course, growth is only a background factor, not an element of structure.

Dennis Mueller has recently presented more complex research on models involving market shares, but the models and details are too complicated to present here.[20] The general importance of market share is affirmed, and Mueller finds the standard structure-to-profits direction of causation to be largely confirmed.

[19] They are in William G. Shepherd, "The Nature of Monopoly," a chapter in Samuel Bowles, Richard C. Edwards, and William G. Shepherd, eds., *Unconventional Wisdom: Essays on Economics in Honor of John Kenneth Galbraith* (Boston: Houghton Mifflin, 1990).
[20] See Dennis C. Mueller, *Profits in the Long Run* (Cambridge: Cambridge University Press, 1986). Unfortunately, he always combines market share with other interaction terms, so that the independent role of market share is diffused rather than shown clearly.

TABLE 5.7 Regression Analysis of Profitability and q for 117 Large U.S. Industrial Corporations, 1960–1969*

INDEPENDENT VARIABLES

REGRESSION NUMBER	DEPENDENT VARIABLE	CONSTANT TERM	MARKET SHARE M	CONCENTRATION C	GROUP ($C-M$)	LOG OF ASSET SIZE	ADVERTISING-SALES RATIO	MEDIUM BARRIERS	HIGH BARRIERS	GROWTH	CORRECTED R^2 (F VALUE)
1	Profit rate (π)	+7.69 (3.21)	+0.24 (8.42)		+0.04 (1.55)	-0.56 (1.79)	+0.26 (3.98)			+0.51 (2.09)	0.573 (32.18)
1q	q ratio	+1.09 (1.42)	+0.06 (7.05)		+0.01 (0.79)	-0.19 (1.94)	+0.09 (4.09)			+0.27 (3.48)	0.558 (30.28)
2	π	+7.69 (3.21)	+0.20 (6.27)	+0.04 (1.55)		-0.56 (1.79)	+0.26 (3.98)			+0.51 (2.09)	0.573 (32.18)
2q	q	+1.09 (1.42)	+0.06 (5.64)	+0.01 (0.79)		-0.19 (1.94)	+0.09 (4.09)			+0.27 (3.48)	0.558 (30.28)
3	π	+3.77 (2.38)	+0.23 (6.71)	+0.02 (0.74)				+1.76 (1.88)	+2.99 (2.32)	+0.51 (1.95)	0.516 (25.70)
3q	q	-0.21 (0.41)	+0.07 (5.96)	+0.004 (0.41)				+0.26 (0.86)	+0.59 (1.40)	+0.27 (3.21)	0.475 (21.96)

* t-ratios are shown in parentheses. Profitability is the rate of return on book equity.

SOURCE: William G. Shepherd, "The Nature of Monopoly," a chapter in Samuel Bowles, Richard C. Edwards, and William G. Shepherd, eds., *Unconventional Wisdom: Papers on Economics in Honor of John Kenneth Galbraith* (Boston: Houghton Mifflin, 1990), Table 1. Adapted from William G. Shepherd, "Tobin's q and the Structure Performance Relationship: Comment," *American Economic Review*, 76 (December 1986), pp. 1205–10.

TABLE 5.8   Concentration and Profit Rates, 1963

Number of Industries	Four-firm Concentration Ratio (%)	Rate of Return on Assets (firms with assets over $50 million) (%)
3	60+	21.6
11	50–60	12.2
21	40–50	9.4
24	30–40	11.7
22	20–30	10.6
18	10–20	8.0

SOURCE: Evidence in Harold Demsetz, "Industry Structure, Market Rivalry, and Public Policy," *Journal of Law and Economics,* 16 (1973).

A simpler test was offered by Harold Demsetz in 1973, with results summarized in Table 5.8. The 95 industries are grouped by their degree of concentration, from lowest to highest. But these are *three-digit* industry groups, which are far broader than true markets. Therefore they have only a tenuous connection with genuine competitive patterns.

The small firms (the R_1 column in the table) are separated from the larger ones (the R_4 column). This is a crude basis for separation; it would be better to use *relative size,* to show the largest four, the next four, and the rest. Some small industries have no big firms, while some big industries have no small firms.[21] In any event, the use of raw concentration ratios injects a lot of error, as Chapter 4 pointed out.[22] For all these reasons, no precise results are to be expected.

Yet the patterns do show through: the larger firms, on the whole, do make higher rates of return. That could precisely reflect the greater market power held by firms with higher market shares. Therefore the results tend to confirm the mainstream findings that structural monopoly affects prices significantly.

Demsetz himself offered the opposite conclusion: that the higher large-firm profits reflect economies of scale or superior performance by those firms. The matter is important because Demsetz's study has been cited frequently as the pivotal proof for the Chicago-UCLA School claim that dominance reflects only superior efficiency.

In fact, the higher profitability of leading firms is consistent also with simple monopoly profits, as caused by market power. Only if all imperfections were absent, in every market, would the Demsetz interpretation be permissible. There is no persuasive evidence in the field supporting that strong hypothesis, nor do the figures in Demsetz's study show any such thing. The problem is discussed in Section II of this chapter.

---

[21] Or the small firms are in different submarkets from the big ones, especially if census "industries" are inaccurate or too broad.

[22] Any research that finds only three industries with concentration over 60 percent cannot be very reliable or inclusive.

6.   Return and Risk

There remains the possible role of risk. If investors are generally risk-averse, then the equilibrium rate of return for "risky" firms and industries could be higher than for less risky cases. The existing differences in rates of return might just be "risk premiums." This issue could be important, for risks may differ sharply from industry to industry.

Does this theoretical possibility hold in actual industries? Can one estimate "comparable earnings" among different industries? Research on the issue began in the late 1960s, and so far it has not confirmed risk as a strong element in profitability.

The concept of risk has usually been tied to the variability of earnings. The hazard arises from the chance that a series of low returns could cause bankruptcy and destroy the value of the firm. Yearly profit variance has become a standard index of such risk, especially for empirical tests. Yet the real risk may stem instead from longer-term hazards, such as Schumpeterian inroads by new competitors and changing technology. Quick fluctuations may fail to reflect the true risks. Worse, actual variance may tell little about the risks that were *expected*—and which therefore influenced choices. Finally, variance is half upward as well as downward. Yet it is only the downward fluctuations that are dangerous to the firm. The upward variation means *high* profits and *lower* risk!

Finally, there may be no risk premium at all if risk lovers just balance out risk averters among investors in the capital markets. The intensity of such preferences in the various groups of investors may vary, further complicating the issue.

So the issue is open; risk premiums could be large, zero, or even negative. The framework is general equilibrium analysis, in which all firms are part of the whole pool for investors' choices. Differences among "industry risks" are merely the sum of the differences among the individual firms.

Risk's role may relate to market structure, so one tests for it by adding risk to the broader structural analysis. One uses data for individual companies. There are two basic equations:

$$\text{Rate of return} = f \text{ (Risk, Market structure, Growth, . . .)}$$

$$\text{Risk} = f \text{ (Market structure)}$$

The independent variables may be mutually related ("collinear"), and thus their cause and effect may be impossible to unravel even with perfect data. The available data are not perfect. They are based on the yearly profit variation, and so they may miss true risk.

A recent fitting of these equations suggests that market structure is important in whatever risk-return relation may exist.[23] Many models and groups of firms were tested, using data from 245 large U.S. firms. Yet profit rates and variation were not related in any of them. The structural elements, instead, continue to "explain" profit rates the same way, whether "risk" is included in the analysis or left out. "Risk"

---

[23] It is reported in W. G. Shepherd, *The Treatment of Market Power* (New York: Columbia University Press, 1975), pp. 109–13.

TABLE 5.9   Market Structure and Profit Variation in Large U.S. Industrial Firms, 1960–69

DEPENDENT VARIABLES	INDEPENDENT VARIABLES					
	CONCENTRATION C	MARKET SHARE M	GROUP G	SIZE S	ADVERTISING INTENSITY A	R^2
Profit variation	.242 (5.74)*			.184 (.41)	−.050 (3.05)	.134
Profit variation		.186 (3.02)	.275 (5.49)	.158 (.35)	−.050 (3.01)	.127

* t-ratios are in parentheses.
SOURCE: W. G. Shepherd, *The Treatment of Market Power* (New York: Columbia University Press, 1975).

does not supplant structure as a factor. The "risk premiums" estimated in some earlier studies have probably instead reflected market power.[24]

This is affirmed further in Table 5.9, which is typical of recent findings. The primary relation with "risk" seems to be the degree of oligopoly interdependence (represented by C). A high degree of oligopoly concentration seems to breed ups and downs as price wars alternate with stable shared-monopoly periods.[25] The G coefficient fits this view, too; it reflects the instability of firms that face a relatively large and powerful group of other leading firms.

In short, recent research suggests that (1) true risk has not been measured by the yearly variation in profit rates, and/or (2) risk does not in fact command a large premium.[26] Some calculations of "risk-adjusted rates of return" have been made for twenty or so industries. One needs to treat them cautiously, since the risk premiums they apply may not exist. "Comparable earnings" have not yet been scientifically measured.

Yet these "risk-adjusted" returns can be compared with market structure. From the raw profit rate one can subtract a risk discount equal to the variance in the yearly profit rates that would reflect the lower true value of riskier profit rates. If one does this as a rough approximation, the resulting patterns in Table 5.10 show an especially close relation between structure and profitability. The risk adjustment *sharpens* the measured effect of monopoly on profits; it does not weaken it.

These findings are entirely logical. Dominant firms generally have less risk than their small, more vulnerable rivals. If long-term risk should ever be reliably mea-

[24] See I. N. Fisher and G. R. Hall, "Risk and Corporate Rates of Return," *Quarterly Journal of Economics*, 83 (February 1969), 79–92, and sources cited there; P. Cootner and D. Holland, "Rate of Return and Business Risk," *Bell Journal of Economics*, I (Fall 1970), 211–26; and G. R. Conrad and I. H. Plotkin, "Risk/Return: U.S. Industry Patterns," *Harvard Business Review*, 46 (March–April 1968), 90–99.
[25] This was suggested in Richard E. Caves and Basil S. Yamey, "Risk and Corporate Rates of Return: Comment," *Quarterly Journal of Economics*, 85 (August 1971), 513–17.
[26] A more positive view, based on banking profit rates, is given in Franklin R. Edwards and Arnold A. Heggestad, "Uncertainty, Market Structure, and Performance in Banking," *Quarterly Journal of Economics*, 87 (August 1973), 455–75. Yet their findings are not robust.

TABLE 5.10   A Comparison of "Risk-Adjusted" Rates of Return

Industry	Market Share of the Leading Firm* (%)	Risk-Discounted Rate of Return, 1960–1969 (π minus average yearly shift) (%)
Toiletries	45	25.0
Photographic	75	16.5
Drugs	(50)	17.1
Soft drinks	45	15.2
Office machinery	65	15.2
Automobiles	55	11.3
Tobacco	28	12.6
Electrical machinery	45	11.9
Soaps and detergents	45	12.1
Rubber	25	10.5
Grain milling	28	10.0
Petroleum	(25)	9.9
Containers	23	8.2
Glass	25	8.3
Steel	23	5.9
Meat packing	18	4.2

* Market shares are estimated. Parentheses indicate an approximate average value.
SOURCE: Adapted from W. G. Shepherd, *The Treatment of Market Power* (New York: Columbia University Press, 1975), p. 112.

sured, that, too, would be expected to follow the same basic patterns as short-term variations.

II.   EFFICIENCY

Because monopoly power appears to affect prices and profits, it may also shape real conditions.

We turn first to efficiency. The subject divides in two main parts: X-efficiency and allocative efficiency. We will consider each of them in some detail, in Subsections II.1 and II.2. Then, in Subsection II.3 we will review some evidence for the Chicago-UCLA hypothesis that structure reflects superior efficiency.

In addition, market power may affect efficiency by its role in advertising, as noted in Subsection II.4. Finally, the conservation of certain "open-access" natural resources is also influenced by the degree of competition, as described in Subsection II.5.

1.   X-Efficiency

Criteria.   Internal efficiency—X-efficiency—means keeping costs down to the "minimum" possible level.[27] In a diagram of average and marginal costs, X-efficiency is reached by being *on* the average cost curve. Even a small rise above

---

[27] The leading discussions are by Harvey Leibenstein, "Allocative Efficiency vs. 'X-Efficiency,' " *American Economic Review,* 56 (June 1966), 392–415, and *Beyond Economic Man* (Cambridge, Mass.: Harvard University Press, 1976). See also Richard M. Cyert and James G. March, *A Behavioral Theory of the Firm* (Englewood Cliffs, N.J.: Prentice Hall, 1963).

the curve can increase costs by 5 or 10 percent. Very large rises are not plausible, for the stock market "treadmill" and other pressures usually will not let them last (see Chapter 10). Also, profit is a relatively small margin, often only a 10 or 15 percent sliver above cost; squeezing down a 10 percent margin of X-inefficiency can often double the profit margin. Therefore the incentives against X-inefficiency are very strong.

Against all these pressures is human nature. Managers often have personal objectives that diverge from maximum company profit (see Chapter 10). Excess profits enable these other objectives—including growth, grandeur, an easier life, avoidance of risk—to come into play. Down the line, ordinary employees of a secure firm know that their company's business is lucrative and that there is a cushion. Keeping costs strictly at the minimum becomes difficult. The quality and degree of the work effort itself tend to slip. Leibenstein's broad concept of X-inefficiency embraces this complex process, by which costs rise above necessary levels.

The topic can be quite complicated when analyzed closely, but the simple lesson at this level is clear: X-inefficiency can grow large under "favorable" conditions and persist, even for fairly long periods. Still, the meaning of *efficient* is not simple. One definition is "average" possible costs under normal conditions of human effort. Another is strict minimum costs under the severest levels of effort. Still another is the level of cost under "superior" management and effort. The three criteria can give differing cost levels. None of the three, however, can be defined precisely.

By the strictest criterion, nearly all firms have appreciable X-inefficiency. One's appraisal therefore rests partly on the standard of excellence.

Measurements.   Measuring X-inefficiency is still a primitive art. There is much commentary in the business press about the performance of companies. More directly, studies of performance are frequently done by professional business consulting firms and these "management audits" are occasionally published. Their value lies in their directness and "professional" quality. Yet they are fallible, and often they have been commissioned for purposes other than a broad-scale appraisal. So one considers their lessons cautiously.

There is no other general, practical method for testing X-efficiency in manufacturing industries.[28] Since X-inefficiency can be a large social burden, the lack of a sound technique for measuring it is a serious gap. Pending new research, one can only apply a reasonable judgment to the broad flow of commentary in the business press.[29] Though not "scientific," the published opinions do provide a fairly reliable guide to the general scope of X-inefficiency.

Two lessons emerge. First, X-inefficiency is a common problem, which often

---

[28] A special method has been tried on the 200 or so private electric utility firms. Regression analysis is used to "explain" their average costs, by including size, density, input prices, and other factors. The remaining "unexplained" cost differences are attributed to X-inefficiency. The method works only for this industry, with its special conditions (uniform output, a series of protected monopolies, etc.). Also, it only shows "relative" efficiency, that is, the standing of each firm compared with the whole group. See William Iulo, *Electric Utilities—Costs and Performance* (Pullman: Washington State University Press, 1961). Several more recent applications of Iulo's method have also been made.

[29] Good sources include the *Wall Street Journal* and general-purpose business magazines that report on company affairs and current opinions, including *Business Week, Forbes, Barron's* and *Fortune.* Investment analysts' opinions are circulated in brokerage house newsletters and the financial press. Each major industry has its trade journal, though these journals often reflect the companies' interests instead of taking a critical view.

raises costs by more than 10 percent above their efficient levels.[30] Second, X-inefficiency is closely related to market power. Monopolies, dominant firms, and tight oligopolists are likely to develop marked X-inefficiency. Some avoid it, but many do not.

The following sample of appraisals is meant only to illustrate these patterns and familiarize you with the kind of opinions that appear. The sample is small. Since conditions often change, there is no intention to single out specific firms here for criticism. In fact, X-inefficiency is usually publicized only after the firm has "turned the corner" under new managers.

Recent instances include International Harvester, in the decades before 1970: "We were large, lethargic, lacking in new ideas, and in-bred."[31] Hershey Foods was said in 1975 to have a "structural disease" of complacency.[32] Du Pont "became stuck in an old mold, with too much reliance on historical ways" in the years before 1973.[33] Kennecott Copper was for many years a secure "sleeping giant content to liquidate itself through generous contributions to its shareholders as long as its mines held out."[34] International Paper (the largest U.S. paper firm) and Weyerhaeuser (the largest lumber producer) both became sluggish in the 1960s.[35]

By the 1980s, IBM had become "a giant, calcified institution" with "bad habits and inefficient processes that had taken root over seven decades." "[T]he colossus has one of the world's most luxuriantly thick bureaucracies" with "layer upon layer upon layer."[36] In 1988–1989, IBM was planning to cut its staffing by up to 10 percent, while 20 percent of its factories were to be mothballed.

General Motors, Ford, and Chrysler came under severe new competitive pressure from Japanese imports during 1979–1981. Spurred by that threat, they managed to reduce their costs by 20 to 30 percent, suggesting that their X-inefficiency was that high.

When AT&T consented to be divided in 1984, it kept the manufacturing operations, thinking that they offered high growth and profits. Its old Western Electric equipment company was combined into an "Information Systems" subsidiary. But soon up to half of the former Western Electric capacity and employment were closed down, under the pressure of direct competition in the marketplace, after a century of sheltered monopoly.[37]

---

[30] Leibenstein points out that many instances of X-inefficiency go well above 10 percent; see his "Allocative Efficiency vs. 'X-efficiency'." See also Oliver E. Williamson, "Managerial Discretion and Business Behavior," *American Economic Review,* 53 (December 1963), 1032–57; and F. M. Scherer, *Industrial Market Structure and Economic Performance* (Skokie, Ill.: Rand McNally, 1970), pp. 404–7. Scherer sums up a review of evidence: "My own belief is that padding as high as 10 percent of costs is not at all uncommon."

[31] The quotation is by the executive vice president of the company. See "New Spur for a Sluggish Giant," *Business Week,* March 17, 1975, pp. 50–54.

[32] "Melting Profits," *Forbes,* November 1, 1975, p. 40.

[33] According to its chairman, Irving S. Shapiro, quoted in "Pattern Breaker," *Forbes,* July 1, 1975, pp. 24–25.

[34] *Business Week,* December 7, 1968, pp. 104–8.

[35] "International Paper Sees the Forest Through the Trees," *Fortune,* March 1969, p. 105; and "Weyerhaeuser Fells a Wooden Past," *Business Week,* June 7, 1969, pp. 76–80.

[36] IBM's own chairman, John Akers, was among the company's most caustic critics, and his reorganization program aimed to cut costs by up to 10 percent. See "Akers' Drive to Mend IBM Is Shaking Up Its Vaunted Traditions," *Wall Street Journal,* November 11, 1988, pp. 1, A9.

[37] "AT&T Chairman Sees More Cost Trims but No Further Job Cuts or Restructuring," *Wall Street Journal,* November 1985, p. 4; and "Why AT&T Isn't Clicking," *Business Week,* May 19, 1986, pp. 88–95.

In 1987, Boeing (the dominant aircraft maker: Chapter 17 covers it in some detail) embarked on an arduous reorganization after recognizing that its costs were unnecessarily high. It aimed to cut its employee costs by 25 percent.[38] Caterpillar Tractor Company, long the dominant producer of construction equipment, was hit by new Japanese competition after 1980. It cut costs by over 20 percent, by closing six factories and laying off 19 percent of its workers.[39]

On a much smaller scale, the Harley-Davidson motorcycle company held an overwhelming dominance of the large-motorcycle market in the US until the 1960s. Then it lost that supremacy to new Japanese imports because its costs were high and it had failed to innovate. In the 1980s, it improved its efficiency while under the protection of a tariff that began in 1981 at 45 percent and diminished to zero in 1988. By 1988, the company had cut its inventory by two-thirds, improved productivity by about 50 percent, and reduced the rate of defects by 70 percent. For such large gains to happen, the degree of X-inefficiency in 1981 must have been very large indeed, at least 30 percent.[40]

For companies of this sort, some of the cutbacks were part of shrinkage programs, but most of them simply sought to reduce average costs. Their experience suggests that X-inefficiency can exceed 10 percent of costs for extended periods, even in highly reputed companies.

The list can easily be lengthened by searching further in the *Wall Street Journal* and *Forbes, Fortune,* and *Business Week* magazines. The opinions are often debatable, but they usually express what is widely known in the trade. The firms will, of course, deny the appraisal at the time. Yet they often candidly acknowledge the situation later, after their management has changed.

X-inefficiency also arises outside conventional manufacturing industries. Stockbrokers were less efficient under the fee-setting cartel before 1975. Rate-cutting by the Russian fleet during 1974–1976 exposed excess costs in many private ocean shippers. Regulated utilities have long been recognized as tending toward X-inefficiency. Weapons production in the United States has often been X-inefficient because of the peculiarities of Defense Department purchasing. No market is exempt from the effects of security on efficiency.

Large improvements become possible when a shift to competition and better management occurs. Then the "sleeping giants" wake up and cut costs sharply, and their stock values rise dramatically. In retrospect, X-inefficiency is commonly seen to have been substantial.

No accurate, comprehensive measures of X-inefficiency have as yet been drawn up. Nor has its relationship to market power been precisely tested. A consensus view of "average" X-inefficiency would be roughly in the range of at least 5 percent of costs for monopolists. The extra margin of costs scales down as the firm's market share decreases. This tendency would suggest about 3 percent of extra costs for an "average" oligopoly with concentration of 60 percent. The "true" total amount for the whole economy might range between 2 and 4 percent of net national product. This is a small sliver compared to total costs and to the security that is present in

---

[38] *Wall Street Journal,* September 7, 1987, p. 1.

[39] "A Shaken Caterpillar Retools to Take On a More Competitive World," *Business Week,* November 5, 1984, pp. 91–94.

[40] Drawn from Charles E. Mueller, "'Transformed' Monopoly," *Antitrust Law & Economics Review,* 1988, p. 48.

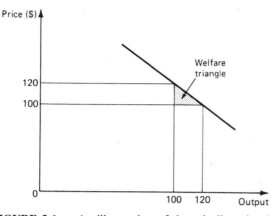

FIGURE 5.1.   An illustration of the misallocation loss from market power.

many national and local markets. Yet it would equal about $50 billion to $100 billion annually. Further research is not likely to change this rough estimate by very much.

2. Allocative Efficiency

The loss of allocative efficiency caused by market power is the "welfare triangle," discussed in Chapter 2. Some economists regard it as *the* traditional "burden of monopoly." To measure it, one needs to know the elasticity of demand, the increase in price caused by market power, and the slope of the average cost curve for each firm exerting market power in each market. The loss, by simple geometry, is:

$$\text{Loss} = \tfrac{1}{2} \, \Delta P \cdot \Delta Q$$

If the demand elasticity were unitary, prices were raised by 20 percent, and average costs were constant, the triangle would be about 2 percent of total revenue. That is:

$$\text{Loss} = \tfrac{1}{2}(.20)(.20)$$
$$= \tfrac{1}{2}(.04) = 2\%$$

(This is illustrated in Figure 5.1, with the initial price at $100 and output at 120 units.)

In actual markets with substantial market power, the average increase in price is often in the range of 10 percent. Scale economies are probably not a strong factor in most markets, as will be noted in Chapter 9. Elasticities of demand will differ sharply across industries, of course. The convention has been to assume that, *on average,* demand is approximately unit elastic.[41]

On this basis, the misallocation effect is slightly under 1 percent of GNP. This is a lower bound on the true value. Some market power is not known, and the data

---

[41] Actually, elasticity would have to be greater than one, for marginal revenue must be positive and equal to marginal cost. The unit elastic assumption is only a rough approximation.

tend to underestimate its effects. The price effect of market power has been conservatively estimated.

Some earlier studies reached varying estimates of the misallocation.[42] Harberger in 1954 used averages of profits from 1920 to 1929 in eighty industry groups. The misallocation burden came out at about 0.2 percent of GNP. His large industry groups masked the range of profits among the true markets. Also, he ignored X-inefficiency. Furthermore, he dealt only with deviations from the average profit rate, assuming that low and high rates would be moved toward the average. The correct method is to assume that all profits are moved down toward the minimum competitive level. As Figure 5.2 shows, Harberger's method in effect split the triangle into two little triangles (*A* and *B*), and this sharply reduced the estimated area (which should also include areas *C* and *D*) below the true area.

Cowling and Mueller have given a contrasting estimate, based on a different approach. They treat monopoly profit itself as a social cost, and they focus on the before-tax levels of profit. To it they add advertising, on the suggestion (by Harberger and others) that advertising is a social cost. The initial level of monopoly profit is therefore:

Monopoly profit = Recorded profit (above the cost of capital) + Advertising − Taxes

The costs spent by the firm in monopolizing activities may absorb some of the monopoly profit, and in that sense, the estimate of actual social loss may be biased.

Cowling and Mueller offer a variety of estimates of the loss, based on varying assumptions, and they use much more complete, refined data than Harberger employed.[43] Their estimates range roughly from 4 to 13 percent of corporate output—an upper-bound set of estimates. The true value probably lies between their estimates and Harberger's, probably between 1 and 2 percent of national income.

[42] See Arnold Harberger, "Monopoly and Resource Allocation," *American Economic Review*, 44 (May 1954), 77–87; and David Schwartzman, "The Burden of Monopoly," *Journal of Political Economy*, 68 (December 1960), 627–30. The downward bias is considered in Ruth P. Mack, "Discussion," *American Economic Review*, 44 (May 1954), 88–92; and George J. Stigler, "The Statistics of Monopoly and Merger," *Journal of Political Economy*, 64 (1956), 33–40. Other estimates since then include David R. Kamerschen, "An Estimation of the 'Welfare Losses' from Monopoly in the American Economy," *Western Economic Journal*, 4 (Summer 1966), 221–36; Frederick W. Bell, "The Effects of Monopoly Profits and Wages on Prices and Consumers' Surplus in U.S. Manufacturing," *Western Economic Journal*, 6 (June 1969), 233–41; William G. Shepherd, *Market Power and Economic Welfare* (New York: Random House, 1970); Scherer, *Industrial Market Structure and Economic Performance;* Paul D. Scanlon, "FTC and Phase II: The McGovern Papers," *Antitrust Law and Economics Review*, 5 (Spring 1972), 19–36; Dean A. Worcester, "New Estimates of the Welfare Loss to Monopoly, United States: 1956–1969," *Southern Economic Journal*, 40 (October 1973), 234–45; John J. Siegfried and Thomas Tiemann, "The Welfare Cost of Monopoly: An Inter-Industry Analysis," *Economic Inquiry*, 12 (June 1974), 190–202; Donald L. Bumpass, "Welfare Loss Due to Monopoly," *Journal of Economics*, 11 (1976), 90–93; Keith Cowling and Dennis C. Mueller, "The Social Costs of Monopoly Power," *Economic Journal*, 88 (August 1978), 727–48; Donald L. Bumpass, "Welfare Loss Due to Monopoly Power: U.S. Manufacturing, 1972," *Industrial Organization Review*, 7 (1979); Malcolm C. Sawyer, "Monopoly Welfare Loss in the United Kingdom," *The Manchester School* (1980), 331–54; and Dennis O. Olson and Donald L. Bumpass, "An Intertemporal Analysis of the Welfare Cost of Monopoly Power," Working Paper, Texas Tech University, 1983. For a critical view, see Stephen C. Littlechild, "Misleading Calculations of the Social Costs of Monopoly Power," *Economic Journal*, 91 (June 1981), 348–63.

[43] Cowling and Mueller, "The Social Costs of Monopoly Power"; see also their "The Social Costs of Monopoly Revisited," *Economic Journal*, 76 (September 1981), 721–25.

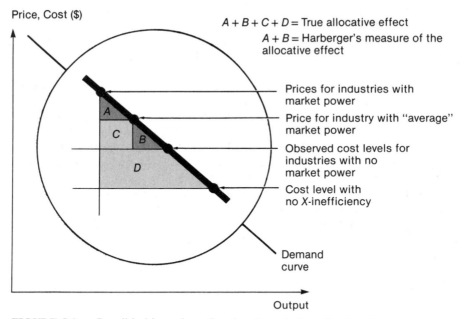

Price, Cost ($)

$A + B + C + D =$ True allocative effect

$A + B =$ Harberger's measure of the allocative effect

Prices for industries with market power

Price for industry with "average" market power

Observed cost levels for industries with no market power

Cost level with no X-inefficiency

Demand curve

Output

FIGURE 5.2.   Possible biases in estimating the misallocation burden.

Note that all estimates are for the existing economy, in which market power has been constrained, to some degree, by antitrust policies. The unconstrained losses, if there were no antitrust restraints, would undoubtedly be much larger.

No definitive study has yet been done. A series of estimates in actual studies done since 1954 is summarized in Table 5.11. The estimated losses range from 0.07 percent of national income up to 13.1 percent, depending on the assumptions and data. Even if the higher estimates are overstated by double, the burden of misallocation has been significant.

Like X-inefficiency, the misallocation burden may have decreased in recent decades as competition has risen. The consensus is that it probably was about 1 to 2 percent of GNP, but that it may be closer to 1 percent now. Of course it is much larger in markets where monopoly power is high. It is almost certainly smaller than the X-inefficiency caused by market power. The misallocation burden is not a large percentage, even if it represents $30 billion per year. It is only one effect of market power, and probably not the largest.

3.   The Chicago-UCLA Efficient-Structure Hypothesis

So the evidence strongly supports the theory and the common observation that market power affects X-efficiency and allocative efficiency. What evidence is there the other way, that differential efficiency shapes structure?

On the whole, very little. Demsetz's 1973 paper interprets profit rate differences as reflecting efficiency differences (as we saw in Section I), but that evidence is fully

TABLE 5.11   A Summary of Estimates of Welfare Loss from Misallocation Caused by Market Power

Estimate by	Time Period	Welfare Loss as a Percentage of National Income
Harberger (1954)	1924–1928	0.08
Schwartzman (1960)	1954	0.13
Kamerschen (1966)	1956–1961	1.87–6.11
Bell (1969)	1954	0.02–0.04
Shepherd (1970)	1960–1969	2.0–3.0
Scherer (1971)	—	1.09
Scanlon (1972)	1967	1.05
Worcester (1973)	1956–1969	0.20–0.73
Siegfried–Tiemann (1974)	1963	0.07
Bumpass (1976)	1967	2.06 (pretax); 0.63 (after tax)
Cowling–Mueller (1978)	1963–1966	0.85–2.81, or 3.96–13.1% of U.S. gross corporate product
Bumpass (1979)	1972	0.30–0.57
Sawyer (1980)	1963 (data for Great Britain)	0.18–4.00
Olson–Bumpass (1983)	1967–1981	1.53–7.53 (pretax); 0.51–4.36 (after tax)

SOURCE: Adapted from Dennis O. Olson and Donald L. Bumpass, "An Intertemporal Analysis of the Welfare Cost of Monopoly Power," *Review of Industrial Organization*, (Winter 1984), 308–23, Table 1.

consistent instead with market power at work. Demsetz's paper offers no method for showing that efficiency is the main influence.

In 1977, Sam Peltzman attempted a statistical test relating growth to cost differences. He tried to correlate changes in concentration with differences in price-cost patterns, as an indirect indicator of efficiency. But the data and coefficients were extremely weak (he used uncorrected census ratios, for example), and a critique by Scherer in 1980 showed that the results indicate little about efficiency.[44]

Econometric Indications.   The other line of Chicago-UCLA research has been simply to reinterpret the econometric research that has shown a close partial correlation between market shares and profit rates.[45] Chicago-UCLA economists merely say that this strong association shows the superior-performance hypothesis at work. The partial correlation of *concentration* with profitability is said to embody the only "real" monopoly power, which is said to arise only from collusion. That correlation is generally weaker than the market share–profit rate correlation. Hence

[44] See Sam Peltzman, "The Gains and Losses from Industrial Concentration," *Journal of Law and Economics*, 20 (October 1977), 229–63; and F. M. Scherer, *Industrial Market Structure and Economic Performance*, 2d ed. (Boston: Houghton Mifflin, 1980), pp. 288–92. See also John S. Heywood, "Market Share and Efficiency: A Reprise," *Economics Letters*, 24 (1987), pages 171–75, for further confirmation that the market share-profit rate relationship reflects market power.

[45] Perhaps the most ambitious empirical claims in this direction have been by Michael Smirlock et al., "Tobin's *q* and the Structure-Performance Relationship," pp. 1051–60.

we get the Chicago-UCLA claim that "the evidence shows" that superior performance is the causative strong factor, while market power has little scope.

That evidence was given in Section I of this chapter. The recent paper by Smirlock, Gilligan, and Marshall claimed that its similar q-ratio results "prove" the Chicago-UCLA hypothesis. But the test does not discriminate among market power, efficiency, and all other possible causes. Even if the close market share–profit rate correlation were entirely caused by superiority, it would take enormous, sustained superiority by *all* firms with high market shares to fit the Chicago-UCLA hypothesis. And that kind of universal sustained superiority does not remotely accord with reality.

The panel of firms used for these analyses includes scores of well-known U.S. firms, few of which have been continually accorded high ratings for management quality and progressiveness. Most have had the usual variations in success that mark all human organizations, and as the previous section noted, some have performed poorly in X-efficiency. Yet an "efficient-structure" appraisal requires that all of them have great superiority at all times.

Cases.   An obvious and prudent approach is to draw on the wide range of past research on market imperfections and on the quality of dominant-firm management. Management slippage is particularly likely as market shares rise and the resulting excess profits encourage the development of X-inefficiency. Recent cases in point are IBM, Eastman Kodak, Campbell Soup, Procter & Gamble, and Kellogg, to name just a few. A brief summary of their performance suggests the obvious: Economies of scale are not crucial: in all five cases, minimum efficient scale appears to be well below the dominant firm's market share. Accordingly, the firms have held substantial amounts of excess market share. Therefore the issue turns on "superior performance."

IBM has dominated the mainframe computer market for some thirty-five years. It gained dominance partly because of nonefficiency advantages, from its 90 percent share of the tabulating machine market.[46] It fell behind its rivals in the early 1960s in rate and quality of innovation, and it retained its dominance only by a series of actions widely regarded as being anticompetitive.[47] At least some of its dominance can therefore be attributed to conditions other than "superior performance."[48]

---

[46] See Shepherd, *Market Power and Economic Welfare;* Gerald W. Brock, *The U.S. Computer Industry,* (Cambridge, Mass.: Ballinger, 1975); and Richard Thomas DeLamarter, *Big Blue* (New York: Dodd, Mead, 1986).

[47] These include anticompetitive price discrimination, the use of money-losing "fighting ships" to drive out specific competitors, and unduly early announcements of new models in order to deter sales of superior computers by Control Data Corporation; see Brock, *The U.S. Computer Industry,* and DeLaMamarter, *Big Blue,* among others. That the U.S. antitrust case based on these actions was eventually withdrawn (in 1982) does not indicate that IBM's actions had no anticompetitive effects. The withdrawal was based on legal considerations and the fact that the case had been going on for so many years. According to knowledgeable observers, IBM's actions were probably anticompetitive.

[48] Indeed, as we saw earlier in the text, IBM's management and structure were noticeably inefficient during the 1970s and 1980s. Since 1987, IBM has been going through major changes. See "Aker's Drive to Mend IBM is Shaking Up Its Vaunted Traditions," *Wall Street Journal,* November 11, 1988, pp. 1 and A9. Five of nineteen plants are being mothballed, 50,000 "indirect" jobs (planners, secretaries, etc.) are being eliminated, and "an entire layer of management, some 9,000 people," is being removed.

Even allowing for possible journalistic overstatement, these changes reflect a firm that has been well below "superior performance."

Eastman Kodak has held over 80 percent of the U.S. amateur film market for about 90 years.[49] It has retained that share partly through its position in the related markets for cameras and film processing. The company's innovativeness has been regarded at times, especially in the 1970s, as mixed, even mediocre (see also Chapter 17, below).

Campbell Soup's share of the canned soup market has been over 75 percent for at least six decades. Its management is frequently characterized as cautious, unimaginative, and unexceptional. Innovations have not been rapid, and there is little evidence that its relative efficiency is unusually high. In earning only about a 14 percent rate of return on equity, Campbell may be adopting an entry-limiting strategy. Or it may simply be inefficient to a significant degree.

Procter & Gamble has held about half of the detergent market for at least 40 years. Even though its record as an innovator has been marked by extreme caution, it has created its share of unsuccessful products. Its strength appears to be in heavy advertising of brand-name products rather than in extreme cost efficiency or rapid innovation.

Finally, *Kellogg* extended its monopoly on corn flakes into other breakfast cereals, holding at least an approximate 45 percent market share for over five decades.[50] Despite a proliferation of brands and cereal variations, Kellogg is not known as a highly innovative or cost-minimizing firm (see also Chapter 18, below).

In all five of these cases, marketing factors—particularly advertising—have been a powerful element in the firms' dominance. Brand loyalties have had important effects in limiting new competition and permitting supra-normal pricing.[51] If the "efficient-structure" hypothesis merely says that advertising to exploit customer loyalty imperfections can support market dominance, then it may be relevant to markets such as these. But that is short of the generality claimed by the hypothesis's authors.

Mainstream research has suggested that a substantial part of the market share coefficient reflects market power. Not only have econometric results been entirely consistent with that view, but leading case studies support it as well.

Variance Analysis.   A newer research tack uses variance analysis to estimate the relative importance of industry, focus, and market share effects on profitability.[52]

[49] William L. Baldwin, "The Feedback Effect of Conduct on Industry Structure," *Journal of Law and Economics,* 12 (April 1969), 123–53; Don E. Waldman, *Antitrust Action and Market Structure* (Lexington, Mass.: Lexington Books, 1978), Chapter 7; James W. Brock, "Structural Monopoly, Technological Performance, and Predatory Innovation: Relevant Standards under Section 2 of the Sherman Act," *American Business Law Journal,* 21 (1983), 291–306, and "Persistent Monopoly and the Charade of Antitrust: The Durability of Kodak's Market Power," *University of Toledo Law Review,* 14 (Spring 1983), 653–83.

[50] See F. M. Scherer, "The Breakfast Cereal Industry," a chapter in Walter Adams, ed., *The Structure of American Industry,* 6th ed. (New York: Macmillan, 1982), pp. 191–217; and Richard Schmalensee, "Entry Deterrence in the Ready-to-Eat Cereal Industry," *Bell Journal of Economics,* 9 (Autumn 1978), 305–27.

[51] See William S. Comanor and Thomas A. Wilson, *Advertising and Market Power* (Cambridge, Mass.: Harvard University Press, 1975), and their "The Effect of Advertising on Competition: A Survey," *Journal of Economic Literature,* 17 (June 1979), 453–76; and Scherer, *Industrial Market Structure and Economic Performance,* Chapter 14.

[52] Richard Schmalensee, "Do Markets Differ Much?" *American Economic Review,* 75 (June 1985), 341–51; and Birger Wernerfelt and Cynthia A. Montgomery, "Tobin's q and the Importance of Focus in Firm Performance," *American Economic Review,* 78 (March 1988), 246–50. For a devastating critique of the Schmalensee paper, see Ioannis N. Kessides, "Do Firms Differ Much? Some Additional Evidence," *American Economic Reveiw,* 1990 (in process).

But its findings are of doubtful relevance to the present issue. In the first place, they show that market share effects are significant, and that conflicts with the categorical "efficient-structure" hypothesis, which rules out any such effects.

More seriously, the method is indirect, applying a rather crude model to estimate conditions that vary within industries in complex ways. The results are doubtful: that industry-specific conditions explain most of the variation among firms' profits. Instead, profitability is known to vary directly with market shares in a wide range of typical industries. These strong *intraindustry* patterns coexist with some *interindustry* variations in profits, reflecting differing industry characteristics.

Indeed, past research and common observation suggest that the intraindustry variation is at least as strong as the interindustry differences. Schmalensee's and Wernerfelt–Montgomery's results are therefore highly suspect, and it is likely that their method is too crude to fit the complexity of the patterns.

Ioannis Kessides found three sources of error, in rechecking Schmalensee's data and calculations. First, a very few observations (55 of the total 1775) had extreme values, strongly affecting the computed patterns. If they are deleted, the expected firm-based effects do become quite strong after all. Second, Schmalensee's results were distorted by heteroscedasticity (differences in the degree of variation, across the size ranges of firms and industries). When that is corrected, the firm-based effects again are strong.

Third, Schmalensee's model constrained the market share effect to be identical among industries, whereas in fact it undoubtedly varies in some degree. Kessides concludes that the model is "misspecified." When that misspecification of the model is corrected, market-share effects emerge from the data.

In the upshot, Kessides finds ". . . that market share is both statistically significant and quantitatively important." This is consistent with the earlier research; market power and/or superior performance is indeed apparently at work, in some degree.

Altogether, there is little systematic evidence for the differential hypothesis, while the indications of market power's effects are widespread and strong. The two are probably mixed in many practical cases, and the proportions are debatable. But a predominance of differential efficiency has little empirical support and is extremely implausible.

4. Advertising

Chapter 16 will show in some detail how advertising usually reduces the degree of competition, although not always. Here we are concerned with another question: How much of advertising is simply wasteful, a subtraction from the resources available for the production of goods?[53]

Advertising comes in two main types: informative and persuasive. *Informative advertising* improves buyers' knowledge so that they can apply their preferences

---

[53] See William S. Comanor and Thomas A. Wilson, "Advertising and Competition: A Survey," *Journal of Economic Literature,* 17 (June 1979), 453–76; Julian L. Simon, *Issues in the Economics of Advertising* (Urbana: University of Illinois Press, 1970); and Richard Schmalensee, *The Economics of Advertising* (Amsterdam: North-Holland, 1972).

more effectively in making choices that will maximize their welfare. By improving choices, informative advertising adds to welfare.

Persuasive advertising instead attempts to change consumers' preferences. Because it interferes with the exercise of innate preferences, it alters choices away from the efficient lines that true "consumer sovereignty" would yield. Thus persuasive, image-instilling advertising is largely a form of economic waste. That applies to both the bulk of television advertising and much magazine advertising, and to some persuasive selling efforts by sales staffs as well.

A subcategory of advertising is "stand-off" advertising among oligopolists. It occurs when each firm would be willing to forgo the expenditure but all are afraid to stop for fear of losing ground to the others. Once one firm has initiated stand-off advertising, the others cannot afford to abstain. Yet the whole process may absorb resources without appreciably increasing sales. Much oligopoly advertising may be of this sort, with no net gain. Indeed, advertisers often say that there is little evidence that *any* kind of advertising strongly affects consumer spending.

No precise measures of the functionless types of advertising have been made, but there is an approximate consensus that perhaps half of all advertising is an economic waste. If that is true, then possibly $50 billion annually represents economic loss.

5. Conservation of Natural Resources

This section departs from the conventional format of industrial organization. Market power does not have a simple relation to conservation. Yet it can influence the use of natural resources in several ways, so some analysis is in order. First we consider the special character of natural resources. Next the role of competition is defined. Then several qualifications are added.

Natural resources

Production and welfare depend on natural resources as well as on other factors of production. Natural resources range across two basic spectrums. One is the degree to which they can be *renewed*. Fish, forests, water, and other resources will renew themselves if not cropped too heavily. Ores, oil, and coal are gone forever once they are taken out. Many resources are intermediate on this spectrum. Topsoil and wilderness, for example, are often renewable, but only at great cost.

The other spectrum is *mobility*. Some resources are fixed and thus are easily allocated among owners. Others, such as fish, can move, so they are open for capture.

For all depletable resources, the social aim is to use them at the rate that maximizes the total value of their use over the whole span of time.[54] Each resource is a stock, which can be used now or held for future use. Decisions about resources rest on speculations about their future values. Thus petroleum can be used at present prices or held in the ground for use at future prices. The choice often is to convert

---

[54] See S. V. Ciriacy-Wantrup, *Resource Conservation: Economics and Policies,* 3rd ed. (Berkeley: University of California Press, 1968); and other sources cited there.

the resource into some other form (such as turning iron ore into steel and thence into a machine) that will give further value in production.

The "optimum" rate of use for each resource depends on (1) the costs of using it, (2) current prices compared with predicted prices, (3) interest rates, and (4) ethical weights used in comparing our use with our posterity's use (Are our needs now more important than those of our great-great-grandchildren in the year 2080?). The predictions will also cover future technology, for new methods can make a resource more valuable or, conversely, obsolete. The whole choice is complex and difficult, for it rests on many factors, some of which are obscure. Yet decisions are often important, for they will shape our own welfare and that of our descendants.

Private choices

Private-market choices, however, may reach the optimum with no special guidance. Owners of resources wish to maximize their assets' value. If markets are perfect, then private choices will bring resource use into line with social criteria. The key variables—interest rates, predictions, relative prices—will emerge in markets and guide decisions by the resources' owners and users. Owners will vigorously seek the best information and then act on it. Present and expected future scarcities will be reflected and balanced in the market result.

Competitive processes may yield conservation, if markets are perfect. If instead the owners are monopolists, they will restrict present usage somewhat by setting prices at higher, monopoly levels. Yet the owners do wish to maximize the long-run value of their resources, and thus their restrictive effect may distort their choices only slightly. At any rate, the resource remains available in larger amounts for future use.

Limits

This powerful hypothesis is valid only if market conditions are perfect. Two important biases may instead be injected.

Future Preferences and Scarcities.   The process can only guess at future conditions. Future preferences are given little or no weight; only present preferences operate directly. Yet future preferences should, in principle, be part of the determination of the long-run optimum path of use.

Open Access.   Mobile resources and certain others will not be optimized by competition. Each firm will have an interest in maximizing its own take. The whole outcome can be to deplete the resource entirely, at far over the optimal rate.

There are many instances. Early oil drilling in the United States gave many owners joint access to unusually large pools. Each owner then tried to take oil as fast as possible. Certain international fishing resources have been cut to one-tenth and less of their sustainable levels by competitive overfishing.[55] There must be a worldwide, unified control of harvesting methods to prevent the elimination of many

---

[55] J. A. Gulland, ed., *The Fish Resources of the Ocean* (Rome: U.N. Food and Agriculture Organization, 1971).

fish populations. Such efforts may ultimately be important for adequate world food supplies. The optimal rates of harvest—for whales, anchovies, tuna, various white fish, and many other major fish categories—are already well known. But shared access distorts the incentives.

Scenic and wilderness areas also involve the shared-access problem. Here the resource is fixed rather than mobile. But if it is open to more than one user, its use will reduce its "natural" character and value. Conversion to a single-owner "park" status (usually under public ownership) has been the usual answer.

The correct general solution is to unitize or monopolize ownership of the resource. Then the optimum rate of use can be applied, using the minimum amount of inputs to harvest the resource at the best rate. Such true "natural monopolies" are rare (as we saw in Chapter 4). The reasons for the condition here differ from the traditional "utility" case.

In short, market structure often affects the use of natural resources. Imperfections can cause competition to depart from optimal patterns, and some of the corrections may seem to require a degree of monopoly. Yet any such monopoly usually needs to be combined with other devices and incentives. And often monopoly is not relevant to the solution. This short section has only hinted at the many complex issues involved in any discussion of natural resources. Still, it shows that market structure is an important part of the subject.

QUESTIONS FOR REVIEW

1. "Pure monopolies can be easily recognized by the high rates of profit they always earn." True?

2. "Because of X-inefficiency, the actual profits may fail to show the full monopoly effect on profits." True?

3. "The mainstream research studies suggest that structure is related to profitability." True?

4. "Though X-inefficiency does not usually reach high levels (such as 30 percent of costs), it does relate fairly closely to market power." True?

5. To estimate the allocative effect of market power, you need to know (a) demand elasticity, (b) the market shares of potential entrants, (c) scale economies, (d) how sharply price is raised by market power, or (e) cross-elasticities of supply. Which?

6. Draw a demand and cost curve diagram to illustrate a firm raising its price 20 percent above the competitive level. Then draw curves to illustrate OPEC's raising of oil prices from $3 to $30 per barrel. Explain the inelasticity of short-run demand that underlay the OPEC case.

7. Explain why *industry-based* studies of concentration and price-cost margins tend to yield much lower correlations than do *firm-based* studies of market shares and profit rates.

8. Try to measure both q and the rate of return for several companies. Then assess the following quotes:
   "The q ratio is theoretically superior to the rate of return in assessing monopoly effects."
   "Perhaps, but in practice its own problems prevent it from improving on profit rates."

9. A close correlation of market shares with profit rates (or q ratios) may reflect market power, or efficiencies, or some of both. Use examples to illustrate the range of these factors.

10. Discuss the forms of short-term risk (fluctuations) and long-term risk (e.g., of technological change) that may afflict firms. Explain how a risk premium may become an element of profit rates.

11. Discuss two instances where X-inefficiency has arisen in firms with market power. What scientific method can be used to assess such cases?

12. How much allocative inefficiency *is* there in the US economy, in your judgment in light of the alternative methods?

13. Explain the difference between informative and persuasive advertising. Locate examples of each and discuss them.

14. Explain how competitive choices will optimize the conservation of natural resources (even "irreplaceable" ones), except when there is open access or some bias in assessing future preferences.

6 TECHNOLOGICAL PROGRESS

Innovation is glamorous, because it can generate large cumulative gains in productivity.[1] A few years' higher rates of innovation can quickly outstrip the best possible results from fine-tuning static efficiency.

Innovation stands outside the neoclassical static-efficiency analysis, in which unrestricted competition is expected to maximize consumer surplus. Innovation is often seen as a cornucopia pouring out creative brilliance and entrepreneurial genius to promote progress and wider consumer choice. And, of course, it is dynamic rather than static.

So innovation may be a major effect—perhaps *the* major effect—of structure. The basic issue is whether competition or monopoly is more favorable to technological progress.[2] The established hypothesis is that competition is the best source of it. But there are reservations and an opposing Chicago-UCLA view. Schumpeter and others have urged instead that monopoly does it best, as Chapter 2 noted.

This chapter reviews the concepts and research that have clarified these possibilities, but the literature is so large that we can only touch on the main points. Many students will wish to read further in other sources.

First, we set the stage in Section I by defining eight main features of innovation.

[1] Robert Solow's seminal article indicated that technological progress was responsible for about 90 percent of economic growth during 1870–1950; see his "Technical Change and the Aggregate Production Function," *Review of Economics and Statistics,* 39 (1957), pp. 312–20.

[2] There are several important books, plus many articles, in the literature. J. A. Schumpeter presents his thesis about entrepreneurs and monopolies as the vehicles of progress in *Capitalism, Socialism and Democracy* (New York: Harper, 1942). J. K. Galbraith's version of progressive oligopolists is in his *American Capitalism: The Theory of Countervailing Power,* rev. ed. (Boston: Houghton Mifflin, 1956). Jacob Schmookler, in *Invention and Economic Growth* (Cambridge, Mass.: Harvard University Press, 1967), explored the processes and sharpened the concepts. Among the best empirical research is Edwin Mansfield, *Industrial Research and Technological Innovation* (New York: Norton, 1968); Mansfield and others, *Research and Innovation in the Modern Corporation* (New York: Norton, 1971); John Jewkes, R. Sawers, and R. Stillerman, *The Sources of Invention,* rev. ed (New York: St. Martin's Press, 1968); National Bureau of Economic Research, *The Rate and Direction of Inventive Activity: Economic and Social Factors* (Princeton, N.J.: Princeton University Press, 1962); John W. Kendrick, ed., *Input, Output and Productivity Change* (Princeton, N.J.: Princeton University Press, 1961); and John W. Kendrick, *Productivity Trends in the United States* (Princeton, N.J.: Princeton University Press, 1961). See also Morton I. Kamien and Nancy L. Schwartz, "Market Structure and Innovation: A Survey," *Journal of Economic Literature,* 13 (March 1975), 1–38; and Albert N. Link. *Research and Development Activity in U.S. Manufacturing* (New York: Praeger, 1981).

Next, in Section II, we review several leading theories about the competitive impacts that may affect innovation. Then we summarize the empirical research and draw the main lessons in Section III. Finally, in Section IV, we examine the effects of the patent system on the rate of invention and innovation.

I. CONCEPTS AND RELATIONSHIPS

Technological progress is divided into eight basic sets of concepts. They need to be grasped at the outset.

1. Invention, Innovation, and Imitation

The procedure of bringing out new processes and products can be divided into three phases. *Invention* is the creation of the new idea. The act is intellectual: perception of a new image, of a new connection between old conditions, or of a new area for action. It can range from basic scientific concepts to strictly practical ideas (such as a new notch in a gear). All inventions, big or little, involve new ideas that are refined for practical use.

Innovation converts the idea to practical use. The innovator establishes production facilities and brings the new product or process to the market.[3] This often (not always) requires displacing previous products or processes.

Imitation then follows as the innovation is copied by others. Diffusion of the innovation across the market may be rapid or slow. It is usually an easier and safer action than innovating. Yet imitation generally gives smaller rewards than innovation, and often the followers act out of necessity, in order to survive.

This triple-I sequence is easy to remember. The three phases require different skills and resources, and the incentives are distinct for each. Invention is usually a lonely activity requiring intensive mental exploration. Eccentrics often do it best, though large-scale "team research" is needed for some inventions.

Innovation, by contrast, is a business act. Financing, arranging of complex engineering details, and risk taking must often be dealt with under difficult conditions. Such "entrepreneurship" goes beyond the "management" of old processes. Though many innovations are small and safe, some are spectacular and require extraordinary innovative skills. By contrast, the imitator copies, often only after the innovation has become safe and routine. The skills and effects are very different.

2. Process and Product Innovations

Changes divide into two categories. Process innovations simply alter the way given products are made. (Examples: a new way to use a drill press, or to lay out the factory floor, or to smelt a metal.) Product innovations create a new good for sale, without any change in process. (Examples: a digital watch, a new kind of

---

[3] Innovation also occurs in nonmarket settings: new public services are prepared and provided, or new charitable activities are developed. Though this text is mainly about commercial improvements, the process is broader than that. The same basic conditions hold for noncommercial applications.

toothpaste, a new body style for an automobile, or a larger model in a line of electric motors.)

The two kinds of changes are distinct in concept, though they often mix in actual cases. They call on different resources, and their incentives and effects often differ sharply. Each kind of change can come in varying degrees, ranging from trivial variations to whole new approaches.

3. Autonomous and Induced Changes

Autonomous changes arise naturally from the onflow of knowledge and technology. Discoveries in areas 1 and 2 often make inevitable an advance in areas 3 and 4, which in turn causes progress in areas 5 and 6. (The automobile, for example, became possible as oil was discovered, motors became small and precise, and rubber for tires was developed. The electric light bulb and telephones were "in the air" in the 1870s and were certain to be developed soon. Hand calculators and digital watches were a natural outcome in the 1970s of new semiconductor technology.) Autonomous inventions also come from the sheer curiosity of creative geniuses.

By contrast, induced inventions occur from the hope of making money. Without that stimulus, they would happen later or not at all. Much commercial R&D activity fits this type. Teams of scientists in company laboratories, working under carefully budgeted plans, are usually seeking inventions that will pay. No payoff, no inventive effort.

Many inventions mingle both features. The advance of knowledge makes them inevitable, but money makes them happen a little sooner. Very broadly, process inventions tend to be autonomous, while product inventions are more likely to be induced. Yet this difference is not clear-cut.

Blurred or not, the distinction helps one appraise social policies toward technical change. A patent system, for example, has no social value if inventions are autonomous.[4] Even if some inventions are induced, one needs to ask (1) what share these are of all inventions, (2) whether they are important or trivial inventions, and (3) how much they are accelerated by money rewards.

4. Several Inputs

Technical progress is the rise in the ratio of total outputs compared with total inputs. Figures based on one input alone are treacherous. (For example, productivity per worker has risen by over 10 percent yearly in electricity supply. Yet this rapid rise mainly reflects a high rate of investment in larger-scale plants. The capital-labor ratio has risen sharply. The total productivity ratio has only been rising at about 3 percent yearly, which is near the average for all industries.) Labor productivity

---

[4] The patent grants a monopoly for some period (seventeen years in the United States) and a free hand in exploiting the invention. The resulting rewards are often high; the dominance of the Bell System, Xerox Corporation, Aluminum Company of America, and many drug firms (among other prominent examples) was built upon key patents. See F. M. Scherer, *Industrial Market Structure and Economic Performance* (Skokie, Ill.: Rand McNally, 1970), Chapter 16; and Alfred E. Kahn, "The Economics of Patent Policy," in John P. Miller, ed., *Competition, Cartels and Their Regulation* (Amsterdam: North-Holland, 1962).

trends are frequently used as rough indexes of technical progress, but you should treat them with great caution.

Some indexes of "total productivity" have been prepared.[5] They usually include figures for labor, capital, and land inputs. However, they are generally incomplete and embody certain biases. There are as yet no perfect measures of technical change.

5. Normative Issues

The distinction between positive and normative knowledge is particularly important in evaluating technical change. The *positive* issues are complicated enough in defining and measuring the various parts of the process—as the points already made in this section show. The *normative* part is even more difficult. Yet the normative lessons are the ultimate purpose of the subject: to judge how "good" the changes have been, compared with what might reasonably have been expected.

One compares the *net gain* in total productivity with its cost. Innovation often destroys the old while adding the new. One might also subtract the autonomous element—the part that would happen in any event—in judging the net gain from innovation in an industry.

The cost is the "R&D" effort—in money, talent, and tangible resources. It often involves a degree of uncertainty, of gambling that a project will "pay off." Also, the efforts cannot neatly be assigned to one innovation or another. Instead, the process often involves a meandering of thought and experiment, from which a variety of possibilities arise.

At any rate, the aim is to compare net gains with costs. Only then can one say whether innovation has been close to "optimal" lines. There may be too little innovation, or too much, in any given industry.

6. "Technological Opportunity."

Industries differ in their potential for raising productivity and designing new products. Some bristle with chances for progress; in others, the state of the art is pretty much fixed. In computers and related electronics, for example, there has been great technological opportunity since 1960. By contrast, brickmaking, papermaking, and ball-point pens have had little chance for progress. Once one compares actual trends with opportunity, the faster changes usually seem normal. Without such a comparison, one simply cannot make intelligent normative appraisals.

Estimating opportunity, however, is a sophisticated task, with an inherent degree of uncertainty and guesswork. Large-seeming opportunities often turn out to be barren (for example, once-glowing prospects of a large net gain from nuclear power have shrunk to virtually zero "opportunity" for progress). Firms in an industry will commonly rate opportunity lower—and claim credit for higher net gains—than outside observers. Opportunity must be included in the evaluation, but one learns to treat it carefully.

In short, normative issues must be kept distinct from positive ones. The net gain must be carefully defined. And it should be compared with technological opportunity.

---

[5] See Kendrick, *Productivity Trends in the United States,* for one important set of measures.

Only then can one judge how well a firm, an industry, or an economy has done in using resources for innovating.

7.   Economies and Diseconomies of Scale

Technical progress may be closely involved with economies (and diseconomies) of scale. There may be a distinct "optimal scale" for the inventing or innovating unit. That scale may be large compared with the market, or it may be small.

Consider inventing first. It is a process of discovery, of forming new images and designs. Much of it is lonely thinking by eccentrics in small laboratories, but some inventions require teams of researchers and large-scale resources. Conditions will differ from industry to industry. Still, the resources are needed only for experimenting and for verifying new ideas. Also, inventions can arise outside an industry and then be sold to the firms that will do the producing. Such economies of scale are not tightly binding upon industry structure.

Innovating uses different skills and resources. It often requires new investment and large engineering changes. The incentives involve (1) net gains from displacing one method or product by another, and (2) chances for sharply increasing the firm's market share, as well as (3) the internal economies involved in the process of change itself. One looks inside the firm to see if its size makes it suited to handle innovations well, *and* one looks at the incentives impinging on the firm from outside (conditions 1 and 2).

These conditions will vary from case to case—and even among differing innovations within a given industry. For example, small firms may be adequate for handling minor innovations, but other innovations may be so large that only a large firm can mass the needed funds, equipment, talent, and sustained effort. Also, the risk may be so high that only secure dominant firms can take the chance. Major new aircraft types are one possible instance where managers feel they have to "bet the company" on a new model; others include large computers, automobiles, and complex communications equipment. These conditions are stressed by Chicago-UCLA writers as reasons for dominant firms.

Yet caution is appropriate here. Among the examples just given, the best large computers are designed and built by a small firm, Cray Research. Small automobile firms (the early Honda, Chrysler) have been at least as creative as General Motors. Large innovations can often be divided into parts that small firms can do, either in parallel or in sequence. Competitive capital markets generate funds for all productive innovations, regardless of size.[6]

Moreover, innovation is often speeded when several firms race to invent or innovate first. The resulting gain in competitive speed may offset any economies of scale in innovation that might exist.

8.   Appropriability and "Free Riders"

The awkward term *appropriability* refers to the ability of the firm to capture enough gains from its new ideas and products to make them worthwhile. New inventions and innovations may be copied so quickly that the inventor or innovator

---

[6] In that sense, the Chicago-UCLA argument implicitly concedes that capital markets are imperfect.

cannot get enough rewards to justify the cost of creating them. Incentives to invent or innovate may then be too low, and progress may dry up.

The gains may instead be reaped by "free riders," who steal the benefits of the original creations.[7] The "free-rider problem" has therefore been posed as a threat to innovation, and the blame is often laid squarely on competition. Innovators need a period of monopoly, it is claimed, so they can reap enough gains to justify their costs before the free riders—who contributed nothing to the original innovation—capture the rest.

This free-rider problem could, in theory, retard or block innovation, as Chicago-UCLA writers have urged. But its net effect is a matter of degree. It does nothing to slow autonomous innovations. The degree of any disincentive depends on the setting; the innovator may reap a significant gain even if free riding is extensive. Indeed, monopoly rewards for innovating may be quite unnecessary, or even too large: *competitive rates of return* may be the efficient rate of reward.[8]

II.   OPTIMAL TECHNOLOGICAL CHANGE

1.   Optimum Choices, at the Margin

Technological progress occurs when the resources for invention and innovation are applied to generating new ideas and products. These resources should be used up to the levels at which their benefits just equal their costs. Each profit-maximizing firm presumably approximates this result in managing its R&D and innovation activities. In fact, most firms do indeed decide continually how much to spend on alternative projects, in light of their likely costs and payoffs.

The cost-benefit setting, and the efficient choice, are illustrated in Figure 6.1 for both invention and innovation. The typical firm has an array of possible projects, which it arranges starting with the best ones. The predicted return on the first project—figured as a rate of return on the R&D expenditures for it—is 25 percent, while that for the next one is 22 percent, and so on, as shown.

This array of decreasing payoffs is in fact the marginal returns curve for R&D expenditure, and it slopes down to reflect the decreasing payoffs as the firm moves down the scale from its best to its worst projects. The returns are only predictions, of course, but they are the best gauge the firm has in trying to make profit-maximizing choices. Many firms actually make such projections, while other rational firms behave *as if* they did.

The payoffs are expressed in rates of return. The cost of the resources is the cost of the funds required to buy the R&D resources. That cost-of-capital value is shown uniformly in Figure 6.1 as 10 percent (in more complex models, the cost of funds might rise at higher levels of spending).

---

[7] The problem has long been recognized, although Kenneth J. Arrow's discussion, "Economic Welfare and the Allocation of Resources for Invention," a chapter in *The Rate and Direction of Inventive Activity,* is usually cited. For a recent discussion, see A. Michael Spence, "Cost Reduction, Competition, and Industry Performance," *Econometrica,* 52 (January 1984), 101–22. See also Jean Tirole, *The Theory of Industrial Organization* (Cambridge, Mass.: MIT Press, 1988), Chapter 10.

[8] See William G. Shepherd, "Efficient Profits vs. Unlimited Capture, as a Reward for Superior Performance: Analysis and Cases," *Antitrust Bulletin,* 34 (Spring 1989).

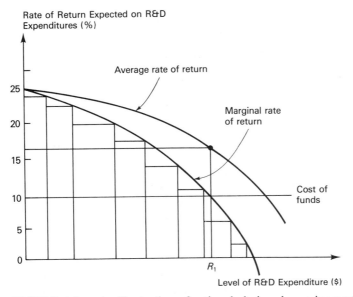

FIGURE 6.1.   An illustration of rational choices by an innovating firm.

The optimal level of R&D activity is at point R_1, where the marginal cost and return on R&D spending are just equal. All projects up to level R_1 should be done; none of those to the right of R_1 should be undertaken because their cost is greater than their predicted returns.

Note that the return on the *marginal* project is just 10 percent, but the *average* yield on all projects at that point is much higher. That is because the average includes all of the superior projects, whose returns are predicted to be above 10 percent. Therefore the firm can make supra-normal *average* returns as part of its efficient choice at the margin.

It is assumed that the R&D resources are being employed with utmost X-efficiency: no bureaucracy, waste, or loss of effectiveness occurs. That is a strict assumption, often violated in practice. Such a violation would appear in Figure 6.1 as a point that is inside and below the marginal returns curve. Only if firms are entirely efficient in managing their R&D will the result be on the marginal returns curve.

R&D is the scarce, costly input to the process of improving technology. *It is not, of course, to be maximized.* Instead, its level is to be optimized in this direction, by this firm, in order to yield the efficient amount of progress. In fact, R&D is to be *minimized* for any given level of yield. It is a common error to suppose that R&D is intrinsically a good thing that ought to be maximized. On the contrary, it is easy to do excessive amounts of R&D in one direction, while holding other directions of R&D below efficient levels.

2. Monopoly's Effects

The fundamental question is: Does competition or monopoly generate more progress for given R&D resources? The basic answer has been that competition generally performs better, because (1) it gives higher rewards (the carrot) and (2) it forces firms to innovate (the stick) even when market power would tilt them toward delay. There are two possible exceptions. Monopoly may deliver superior progress if (1) there are large economies of scale in R&D, or (2) the "free rider" problem discourages innovation by any one firm because it knows other firms will copy it quickly.

Before we analyze these points, note that competition may be superior either in the neoclassical version of effective competition or in the Schumpeterian competitive process of a succession of dominant firms (recall Chapter 2). Both involve fundamentally the same process: the creation of an idea in hopes of gain; then the innovation of that idea into practice; and finally, market gains of some scope.

Competition versus monopoly: Comparing net profits

Competition tends to give a maximum rate of progress for each situation by offering higher rewards to invention and innovation. The basic fact is that *a monopolist directly harms its own asset base by innovating:* the innovation will destroy some or all of the value of its existing technology. This has come to be called the "replacement effect," because the firm's new technology displaces the old.[9]

For example, optical fiber has helped to make copper telephone wires worthless, or at least worth *less,* and new computer models destroy the value of the stock of old models. Knowing that this kind of harm will reduce the firm's gains from innovating, the monopolist will usually bring in new processes and products at below the socially optimal rate.

For the competitive firm, in contrast, the possible gains are unambiguous and possibly very large. It will tend to do the innovation at maximum speed, without restriction, because it wants to capture as much profit from the innovation as it can before its competitors move in. The monopolist, in contrast, is assured of capturing all the value of an invention in its industry. But because it is the monopolist, it has no room to add market share. And from the profit added by innovation will be subtracted the profit that it had earlier obtained from its existing technology. The resulting net gain will be smaller than the competitive firm's gain.

The monopoly will therefore apply the same restrictive policy to inventions as it does to output, using them less fully than they would be used under competition. Competitors cannot apply such controls; therefore they will undertake innovative activity up to the socially optimal level.

The standard analysis of this effect uses a simple demand-and-cost diagram, as in Figure 6.2. Consider first a monopoly that produces the good at a cost of $Cost_1$. For simplicity, $Cost_1$ is assumed to be a constant marginal cost, which (being constant) equals average cost. This monopolist sets output at Q_1, where marginal revenue equals marginal cost, and the resulting monopoly price is P_1.

Now the monopolist considers doing a cost-reducing innovation, which cuts cost to the level $Cost_2$. If it does the innovation, then the new profit-maximizing output is at Q_2, and the price is reduced from P_1 to P_2. Note that the price is only cut half as much as cost, by the geometry of the situation. But consumers do get some benefit, while the monopolist makes the profit shown by the shaded rectangle.

---

[9] See Tirole, *The Theory of Industrial Organization,* Chapter 10.

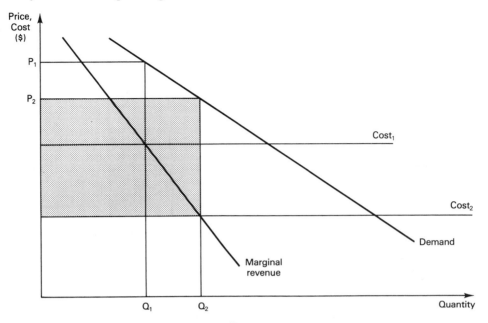

FIGURE 6.2.   Innovation by a monopolist.

Compare this with a competitive situation. Suppose that cost is Cost$_1$ and the total market demand is the same at the outset as the monopolist's demand, as shown in Figure 6.3. But there is no monopolist, only a lot of firms under effective competition. Each one will consider the possible innovation in comparison with its competitive situation, though the first one to innovate will "win" and become a monopolist. Therefore the competitive price, Price$_C$, at the outset is equal to the marginal cost level of Cost$_1$, as shown in Figure 6.3.

Suppose that the competitive firm makes the innovation, reducing cost to Cost$_2$. As a new monopolist, it now would be able to raise the price, but it is limited by the fact that other firms can still use the old technology to produce and sell at a price of Price$_C$. So the innovator raises the price of the innovation to that level, and it reaps the extra profits shown by the shaded rectangle in Figure 6.3.

We can now compare the net profits gained by the two innovators. The competitor in Figure 6.3 gains all of the cost improvement as new net profit. But the monopolist in Figure 6.2 was already making a large extra profit before the innovation. In order to show *the net gains from the innovation,* part of that profit must be subtracted from the (shaded rectangle of) postinnovation profit. That subtraction reflects the *replacement effect:* the degree to which the new innovation destroys the value of the old technology.

The subtraction is done in Figure 6.4. The monopolist's net gain is the odd-shaped area comprising $M_1 + M_2 + M_3$. This will always be smaller than the competitive firm's net gains, which comprise $C_1 + C_2 + C_3$. If the size of prospective profits is a stimulus to innovation, then the competitive firm has a stronger stimulus. *Q.E.D.*

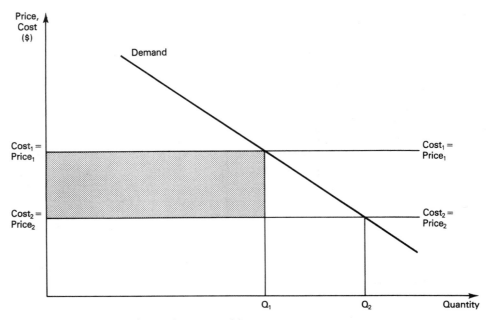

FIGURE 6.3.   Innovation under competition.

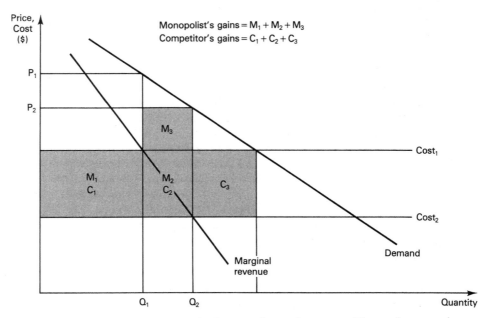

FIGURE 6.4.   Comparing innovation's net gains under competition and monopoly.

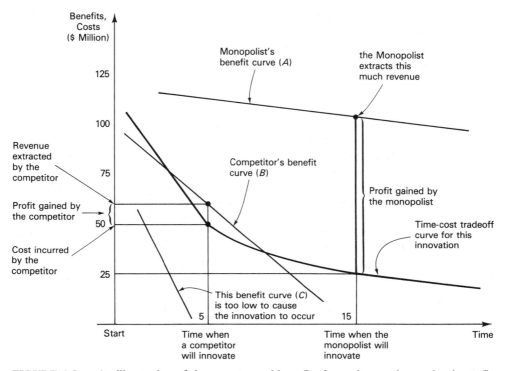

FIGURE 6.5.   An illustration of time, costs, and benefits for an innovation: a dominant firm compared with a competitor.

Note also that the competitive situation provides consumers with the good at lower prices, both before and after the innovation occurs. Consumers receive all possible benefits in both situations.

This conclusion holds generally for a range of more realistic cases, where cost functions are conventionally curved rather than constant. The logic of self-harm by the monopolist is powerful, and it is well recognized in business experience. It is not confined to the extreme cases of pure monopoly and competition. It also affects choices by dominant firms and small rivals. There the contrast is not so stark, but the tendencies are the same: the monopolist gains less from innovation, so it tends to hold back.

Dominant and lesser rivals: The time-cost trade-off

Since innovations involve both time and cost, a time-cost analysis can compare the choices of dominant firms and their lesser rivals. Figure 6.5 presents the essence of the comparison, distilled from a complex discussion by F. M. Scherer.[10]

There is assumed to be a basic time-cost trade-off curve for a given innovation

---

[10] The analysis is adapted from F. M. Scherer, "Research and Development Resource Allocation Under Rivalry," *Quarterly Journal of Economics*, 81 (August 1967), 359–94; see also Scherer, *Industrial Market Structure*, Chapter 15.

in a given industry. Suppose, for example, the innovation is a radically new type of television. It can be done quickly, but only by an enormously expensive crash program of R&D, using hundreds of specialists in a huge effort comparable to the U.S. race to reach the moon in the 1960s. Or it can be done slowly, letting the technology ripen gradually, and only spending modest amounts of R&D resources.

Or it can be done at any speed in between, along a smooth curve such as the trade-off curve in Figure 6.5. Note that the slower, cheaper pace is cheaper partly because it permits *autonomous* innovations to occur in related fields, so that this one becomes easier as time passes. The time-cost trade-off curve will vary for each specific innovation, but its general shape is likely to be as shown in Figure 6.5.

Now consider two alternative innovators, a dominant firm and a competitor with a small share. The dominant firm can expect to gain most of the benefits of the innovation, over a long future period. This is shown by a total revenue curve labeled *A*, indicating the revenues that this firm can obtain from this innovation. The curve is set high, to reflect the large size of revenues. Also, its slope is slight, because the dominant firm has little fear that large rivals will pursue the innovation and capture its future revenues. The dominant firm can do the innovation slowly and still reap most of the revenues.

Not so the small competitor. It can expect to get smaller benefits simply because it starts out as a much smaller firm. And it also must fear that other small firms will innovate first or imitate quickly to capture revenues. Therefore this small firm's revenue curve (labeled *B*) is lower and much more steeply sloped. It is barely above the time-cost trade-off curve for a short interval, as shown in Figure 6.5. An even smaller firm might have curve *C*, which is entirely below the time-cost curve. That firm cannot profitably make this innovation. Only if it can imitate at a much lower level of cost might it eventually adopt the innovation.

Each firm will maximize its profits where the marginal cost and revenue values are equal. That occurs where the slopes of the time-cost and revenue curves are equal. At those points the vertical distance between the curves—the net profits— are maximized. For the dominant firm, this is time T_M, which is shown as 15 years. For the small firm, the time is much shorter, at 6 years. The cost is also greater, $50 million, which is double the $25 million spent by the dominant firm.

Yet the dominant firm is able to reap a larger revenue, $100 million, because it has a high degree of market control. The small firm charges its customers $60 million, making only a $10 million profit. The dominant firm's net profit is much larger, at $75 million.

By the narrow criterion of the amount of resources used to accomplish the innovation, monopoly is less costly. But the innovation occurs much more slowly, and consumers are made to pay much more in order to obtain it ($100 million rather than $60 million). By a consumer-surplus criterion, the small, quick innovator is definitely superior. If this is a radically better product, the extra delay of nine years, plus the consumer payment of $40 million, is a decidedly inferior result.

The revenue curves have been drawn to illustrate the most likely general conditions. They may differ in location, slope, and shape from case to case. Yet the dominant firm would usually have a higher, flatter curve than any small rivals. A variation: the competitive firm might have a lower time-cost curve because it is more efficient at R&D. (Small firms generally have less bureaucracy and stronger incentives to minimize their R&D costs.) If that is true, it would enhance the superiority of the competitive situation compared to dominance.

Dominant Firms and the "Fast Second" Strategy.   The concepts illustrated in Figure 6.5 suggest a general lesson, which is borne out repeatedly in actual markets. Innovations tend to be led by the smaller firms in a market. The dominant firm commonly *invents* actively, discovering the ideas that may eventually prove useful. But it usually chooses to delay the *innovation* phase, letting smaller firms take the risk of trying out the new ideas. When one seems successful, the dominant firm will then move quickly to imitate, trying to catch up and supplant the small innovator. This is sometimes called the "fast second" strategy.

Examples of it abound. Digital watches and personal computers were rejected by the dominant firms when first developed. Small or new firms innovated them instead. Eastman Kodak neglected or opposed many of the major innovations in its markets, including the 35mm camera, compact cameras, cartridge-loading films, and amateur flash devices.[11] IBM rejected plain-paper copying technology in 1946, and it started out slowly in computers during 1945–1953. Gillette hung back from offering a stainless steel razor blade until a small outsider firm, Wilkinson Sword, came out with one. Then Gillette rushed out its own blade.

This pattern is not universal; there are a number of exceptional cases. Also, unusually large innovations might require large firms with large market shares to provide large-scale financing.[12]

But generally, effective competition optimizes innovation. It also passes on the benefits of innovation to consumers, via lower prices set at the levels of costs. Monopolists tend instead to hold back on innovations and to require consumers to pay prices that include a monopoly element.

The same lesson applies to new entry.[13] In duopoly theory, the entrant assumes the same role as an existing rival in applying pressure for innovation. In long-run analyses, the same effect emerges; the fear of an innovating entrant stimulates monopolists to innovate more rapidly.

Indeed, monopolists may often have strong incentives to innovate for strategic purposes; to eliminate a rival or block new entry.[14]

[11] See the scathing evaluation in James W. Brock, "Structural Monopoly, Technological Performance, and Predatory Innovation: Relevant Standards Under Section 2 of the Sherman Act," *American Business Law Journal*, 21, (1983), 291–306.

[12] Though that presumes that capital markets are imperfect.

[13] See Tirole, *The Theory of Industrial Organization*, Chapter 10; and Kamien and Schwartz, "Market Structure and Innovation."

[14] Janusz Ordover and Robert D. Willig, "An Economic Definition of Predation: Pricing and Product Innovation," *Yale Law Journal*, 91 (1981), 8–53, argue that innovations are not predatory if they are profitable when rivals are not eliminated from the market. This argument would justify a number of IBM's product redesigns in the 1970s, which excluded rivals by making equipment incompatible with competitors' products.

Joseph G. Sidak, "Debunking Predatory Innovation," *Columbia Law Review*, 83 (June 1983), 1121–49, rejects this narrow test. He notes that the changes can have the same effect as tie-ins between products (see Chapter 12). They also chill innovation by other firms. The net social effects of such innovations tend to reduce social welfare.

The matter involves complex judgments (see also Janusz Ordover, Alan O. Sykes, and Robert D. Willig, "Predatory Systems Rivalry: A Reply," *Columbia Law Review*, 83 [June 1983], 1150–66), but a reasonable test would probably find that important innovations by IBM and Eastman Kodak (see Chapter 17) had anticompetitive effects.

Monopoly might promote innovation

On the other side of the debate, two main conditions may make monopoly a superior setting for innovation. One is scale economies in R&D. The other is a Schumpeterian process (recall Chapter 2).

Economies of Scale.   As for economies of scale, they may exist in a monopoly, and many dominant firms do support large R&D establishments. For example, AT&T's Bell Laboratories and Du Pont's research facilities have been much praised for their scope and accomplishments. Yet the same doubts apply here as to the economies of scale in production and all other activities (see Chapter 9).

The question is whether large-scale R&D uses proportionally less resources than smaller units. Size may involve diseconomies of scale in R&D because layers of bureaucracy slow down creative actions and promote confusion. Indeed, the 1980s have brought a strong revival of confidence in the small-scale inventors and innovators, as Chapter 9 will note in detail.

Monopoly and Innovative Processes.   The Schumpeterian process is attractive, and it fits some actual cases. But the logic of its superiority is debatable. It does avoid the "free rider" problem, since the entrant-innovator captures large monopoly profits. In contrast, neoclassical competition may lack incentives to innovate. In pure competition, imitation of an invention occurs instantly, because information is fully disseminated. In the pure case, that reduces to zero any monopoly rewards to the original inventor.

If the invention is not autonomous but has to be induced, and *if* the competitive rate of return is not sufficient to induce the invention, then it may be delayed or not done at all. That possibility justifies creating official monopolies over inventions by means of patents (the U.S. patent system, for example, grants inventors a seventeen-year monopoly).

But this only applies in the extreme pure case, which excludes all extra rewards. A realistic degree of competition will permit some excess returns: although limited, they may be sufficient to induce the invention. The same argument applies at the innovation stage. Some degree of competition—possibly quite high—may be superior to monopoly, depending on the balance of conditions in each situation.

Note also that the *entrant* does the innovating in the Schumpeterian process. The incumbent monopolist is assumed to adopt the classic behavior of inefficiency and retarded innovation. In theory, the incumbent may innovate rapidly to escape displacement—but only if entry is a powerful threat. For that to hold, entry must occur frequently.

In short, the Schumpeterian process gives only a slight, hypothetical rationale for monopoly as a source of innovation. The matter is eminently one for empirical evidence.

III.   EMPIRICAL ANALYSIS OF R&D AND INNOVATION

First, some facts will set the issues in perspective. Technical progress has been generating about a 2 percent yearly rise in total output compared with total inputs during the last century. This is not a high rate, even though it does cumulate over many decades into a substantial gain. Certain surface indicators—such as advertising claims or the changing contents of mail-order catalogs between 1920 and 1970—may suggest that change is rapid, even drastic. Yet many of these product changes are matters of style rather than content.

Change varies sharply among industries. Some are virtually static, while others change processes or products rapidly. This primarily reflects differences in "technological opportunity." Often change comes in pulses lasting a few years or a decade or two as an industry develops its basic opportunities. Examples of such waves of innovation are steel in 1860–1880, electricity in 1880–1910, pharmaceuticals in 1940–1960, and electronics since 1960. The pulse often coincides with the early growth stage of the industry, when the new opportunities are large and untapped.

1. Patterns of R&D

Total U.S. spending on R&D has grown rapidly in the 1980s, to a total of $124 billion in 1987. About half of it is market-driven, in private industry, funded by private sources, and devoted to civilian uses. The U.S. government has provided a large share of the total: though the federal government share dropped from 56 percent in 1964 to 30 percent in 1979, it rose to 39 percent in 1987. No less than 40 percent of all R&D is for military and space-related activities.

In short, some one-half of R&D is largely outside the market process. The other half is subject to the competitive-monopoly influences that occupy this chapter.

Tables 6.1, 6.2, and 6.3 show other attributes of R&D in the United States, Japan, and certain Western European countries. The United States has recently lagged behind Japan in R&D growth rates (see Table 6.1, lines 1 and 2), but in 1983, its R&D was about the same percent of gross domestic product as in comparable countries (line 3). R&D workers are a larger share of all workers in the United States than in other countries (line 4). But business-financed R&D—the standard source of commercial progress—is much lower in the United States than in both Japan and West Germany (line 5). A good deal of that difference is attributable to much higher U.S. military R&D (line 6), a category in which Japan spends virtually nothing. Unless the military R&D has astonishingly high civilian payoffs, the United States is simply losing one-fourth of the R&D that could go to industrial progress, and which Japan does apply to its industrial progress.

Table 6.2 shows that basic research is only 13 percent of all U.S. R&D, while applied R&D for development is about two-thirds of the total. Table 6.3 shows the differences among industries in R&D intensity, including both government and privately funded R&D spending. Apart from aerospace, where Uncle Sam provides vast funds, the leaders are electronics and related industries, drugs, automobiles, and chemicals. Most industries actually spend less than 3 percent of revenues on R&D.

Note carefully the problems posed by R&D. First, it is an *input* for innovation, *not* the *output*. High R&D spending may reflect inefficiency or waste in innovation—using "too much" costly R&D resources—rather than high innovativeness. Second, R&D is a slippery category. Some firms put only strictly scientific expenses in it; others include many maintenance and repair costs as well.[15]

---

[15] One old aphorism about R&D concerns efforts to fix a machine. "If the machine works, put the cost in Maintenance. If it doesn't work, classify the cost as Research and Development."

TABLE 6.1   Patterns of R&D

Country	United States	Japan	West Germany	United Kingdom	France	Italy
R&D Expenditure by Country and by Source of Finance, R&D Real Growth and R&D Employment						
Yearly Percentage Growth of Total National (R&D) Expenditures (at constant prices)						
1969–1975	−0.6	8.3	6.2	1.3	2.3	4.9
1975–1983	4.1	8.0	4.3	2.6	4.3	4.7
Total R&D as Percentage of GDP:						
1983	2.7	2.8	2.8	2.8	2.5	1.6
Total R&D Employment per Thousand of Total Labor Force:						
1983	6.6	5.8	4.7	3.6	3.9	2.3
Business-financed R&D as a Percentage of Total R&D: 1983	49.0	65.3	58.1	42.1	42.0	45.5
Military R&D as Percentage of Total R&D: 1983	27.8	0.6	13.5			

SOURCE: Adapted from Giovanni Dosi, "Sources, Procedures and Microeconomic Effects of Innovation," *Journal of Economic Literature*, 26 (September 1988), 1122.

The key question for our purposes is: Does monopoly improve the amounts and yield of innovative activity, or does it restrict and distort it, as theory generally suggests? There are several main ways to analyze evidence on the question: case studies, small samples, large-scale cross-section analyses of data. One can study R&D patterns (the input), or patents (an inventive "output"), or major innovations (another "output"). These and other methods have been tried since the 1950s, and the literature now offers fairly consistent findings. We consider them here for two purposes. One is to give you an understanding of the main patterns. The other is to show that some methods are erroneous, while the best approaches are still not definitive. There is room here to cover only the more prominent studies.

2.   Sources of Invention

Do inventions come mainly from small operators or from large-scale industrial laboratories? Jewkes, Sawers, and Stillerman evaluated the sources of some seventy major inventions from the 1880–1965 period.[16] They were carefully chosen to include the most important ones (some were actually clusters of related inventions). Each invention was researched thoroughly to discern whether its source was an individual, a small firm, or a large company.

The authors concluded that thirty-three of the seventy came from individuals,

[16] Jewkes, Sawers, and Stillerman, *Sources of Invention*.

TABLE 6.2   U.S. R&D: Types and Sources, 1960 and 1983

	1960	1983
Total R&D	100	100
Basic research financed by	8.9	12.6
Federal government	5.3	8.4
Industry	2.5	2.3
University and colleges	0.5	1.3
Other nonprofit institutions	0.5	0.7
Applied research financed by	22.3	23.4
Federal government	12.5	10.6
Industry	9.1	11.6
University and colleges	0.5	0.7
Other nonprofit institutions	0.3	0.5
Development financed by:	68.9	64.0
Federal government	46.8	27.6
Industry	21.8	36.0
University and colleges	0.01	0.02
Other nonprofit institutions	0.01	0.02

SOURCE: Adapted from Giovanni Dosi, "Sources, Procedures and Microeconomic Effects of Innovation," *Journal of Economic Literature,* 26 (September 1988), 1123.

while only twenty-four came from industrial research laboratories, either large or small. Table 6.4 includes a selection of the two groups. Among those accomplished by individuals are air conditioning, catalytic cracking of petroleum, the electron microscope, the jet engine, radio, and xerography—all substantial inventions.

When the authors assessed whether the proportions have changed in recent decades, they found they had not. In short, Jewkes and colleagues discovered no general basis for believing that important inventions come mainly from large-scale laboratories.

Mueller studied the twenty-five main innovations done by the Du Pont Company in the United States between 1920 and 1950. Only eleven of them were initially discovered by Du Pont itself. The rest came from outside inventors.

These and other studies converge on a common pattern, which is suggested by theory. Inventions are predominantly still accomplished by individuals, usually working *outside* of large corporate research establishments in their own facilities or at academic or nonprofit units. Innovations require larger resources, but even so, most are well within the capabilities of small- or medium-size firms. Only an occasional very large innovation seems to require a large-scale corporate setting. And for many of those, the firms are either already receiving U.S. government R&D funding or are actively seeking it as a protection against risk.

Statistical analysis of R&D and patents

R&D intensity may be positively related to concentration. If this hypothesis is true, it could suggest that concentration fosters innovative effort, or that innovative effort causes concentration. Or it might be that oligopoly firms in concentrated in-

TABLE 6.3   Variations in R&D as a Percent of Sales, by Industries, 1983

Sector	United States	Japan	West Germany	France	United Kingdom	Italy
Electric and electronics industries	12.7	8.5	8.8	13.7	16.2	5.7
Chemicals	6.5	7.7	5.8	7.0	6.8	5.5
Organic and inorganic chemicals	4.3	8.0 ⎫	8.4 ⎫	7.6	5.3 ⎫	6.0
Drugs	12.1	10.0 ⎭	⎭		17.8 ⎭	
Petroleum refineries	6.4	3.0	0.6	3.4	2.0	4.6
Instruments	20.5	(8.6)*	8.3	(5.4)*	8.5	(1.2)*
Office machinery and computers	21.7	7.5 ⎫	4.2 ⎫	2.4	19.8 ⎫	2.7
Industrial nonelectrical machinery	2.5	2.9 ⎭	⎭		2.5 ⎭	
Aerospace	32.6 ⎫	7.2	30.8 ⎫	10.0	30.9 ⎫	6.6
Transport equipment	10.0 ⎭		5.5 ⎭		3.1 ⎭	
Motor vehicles	12.6	6.5	5.9	N.A.	4.2	N.A.
Ships	N.A.	7.8	1.2	N.A.	0.8	N.A.
Other transport equipment	N.A.	N.A.	1.6	N.A.	0.0	N.A.
Food, drink, and tobacco	0.7	1.3	0.5	0.3	0.8	2.4
Textile and clothing	2.7	1.3	0.5	0.5	0.3	0.3
Rubber and plastic products	2.5	2.8	1.9	4.4	1.1	1.8
Ferrous metals	1.6	2.9	1.6	1.1	1.1	0.5
Nonferrous metals	2.4	4.3	1.8	2.4	2.1	3.2
Fabricated metal products	1.1	1.2	1.4	1.0	0.8	0.0
Total manufacturing	8.1	4.9	5.4	4.6	6.6	2.9

* Comparable data not available.
SOURCE: Adapted from Giovanni Dosi, "Sources, Procedures and Microeconomic Innovation," *Journal of Economic Literature,* 26 (September 1988), 1124.

TABLE 6.4   Selected Major Inventions, 1880–1965, by Source

By Individuals	By Industrial Firms
Air conditioning	Acrylic fibers
Automatic transmissions	Cellophane tape
Catalytic cracking of petroleum	Continuous hot-strip rolling
Cyclotron	Fluorescent lighting
Electron microscope	Neoprene
Helicopter	Polyethylene
Jet engine	Silicones
Kodachrome	Synthetic detergents
Penicillin	Television
Instant photography	Transistor
Power steering	
Radio	
Synthetic light polarizer	
Xerography	

SOURCE: Drawn from John Jewkes, R. Sawers, and R. Stillerman, *The Sources of Invention,* rev. ed. (New York: St. Martin's Press, 1968), pp. 71–90.

dustries tend to use too much R&D resources through inefficiency or duplication of effort.

When R&D data became available in the 1960s, several tests of the hypothesis that R&D is positively related to concentration were done.[17] Yet all had a basic flaw. R&D is an input. High levels of it can indicate (1) excess amounts of R&D, or (2) sheer waste of R&D resources. So even a tight correlation between R&D and concentration would give no normative lesson. Nor would it distinguish cause from effect.

In fact, the tests mainly suggest a slight negative correlation: R&D intensity declines as concentration increases above about 60 percent. But the concentration data are faulty, and the correlations are faint. One can infer that (1) concentration discourages innovative effort; and/or (2) innovation achieves economies of scale in high-concentration industries; and/or (3) there is no real correlation at all, and no cause or effect.

Patents might serve as a rough measure of "inventive output." One could test whether they are related to company size or concentration. This might suggest which settings foster the most inventive activity.

Unfortunately, patents are a notoriously weak measure. Most of the 70,000 patents issued each year are worthless and are never used. Many others are of moderate value. Only a few are bonanzas. Quite a few have negative social value: they are used as "blocking" patents to stop innovation, or they are developed simply to keep competition out. Various weighting schemes for patents have been discussed, but none works very well. The research has simply counted all patents, assigning them equal value. Most recently a weighting scheme has been developed, which weights each patent by the frequency of its being cited in subsequent patent descriptions. This does give more importance to patents which are related to later inventions. "Key" and important inventions may accurately be indicated by this method. But it is sensitive to the time elapsed, so that it works best for older patents which have existed for many years, rather than for new patents.

Note, too, that patents are only one way to protect new ideas. The other is secrecy. Many—perhaps most—ideas are used secretly rather than revealed in a patent. Patent data miss this process entirely.

There have been some studies comparing company size and patents, along with other factors. Scherer has suggested that, among large firms, patenting activity increases up to moderately large size, and then tails off among the very largest firms.[18] Other researchers have suggested the same for concentration—patenting activity increases as concentration rises toward 40 percent, and then tapers off at higher concentration.

The studies are persuasive, on the whole, yet there could be bias. The larger firms and high-concentration industries (oil, automobiles, computers) might not have

---

[17] They include Edwin Mansfield, "Industrial Research and Development Expenditures," *Journal of Political Economy,* 72 (August 1964), 319–40; Daniel Hamberg, "Size of Firm, Oligopoly and Research: The Evidence," *Canadian Journal of Economics and Political Science,* 29 (February 1964), 62–75; and William S. Comanor, "Market Structure, Product Differentiation, and Industrial Research," *Quarterly Journal of Economics,* 81 (November 1967), 639–57.

[18] F. M. Scherer, "Firm Size, Market Structure, Opportunity and the Output of Patented Inventions," *American Economic Review,* 55 (December 1965), 1104–17.

much technological opportunity. Or inventions might be used secretly rather than patented. Since patent data are so weak, the patterns discovered might be spurious.

3.   Sources of Innovations

One can evaluate the main innovations in a series of major industries and then judge which firms did them. This corresponds to the research on the sources of invention discussed in the preceding section. Mansfield and his associates have done thorough studies of the steel, automobile, petroleum, drug, and other industries.[19] They drew on expert appraisals of the main innovations in recent decades in each industry. The innovations were assigned to the firms that did them, and then the patterns were analyzed statistically.

Although the patterns discovered were not uniform, most of them fitted the prediction that small-share firms lead and dominant firms follow. Research continues in this vein. The panel of industries is still rather small, yet it includes important industries with much innovative activity. The research establishes a rebuttable presumption that innovative activity is greatest in firms with roughly 5 to 20 percent market shares. Below that, the firms may be too small to find significant innovations; above 20 percent, they tend increasingly to wait to innovate until forced by other firms.

These studies use sound scientific methods and their results are supported by the common run of experience in concentrated industries. Investment analysts routinely discuss the technical details of how dominant firms (such as Xerox and IBM) prefer to delay new models even after they have been developed, in order to protect the value of their present asset base. The Bell System and certain other "utility" monopolies are seen as naturally controlling the introduction of new technology so as to maximize their security and profits. A large share of innovations comes from lesser firms and outsiders rather than dominant firms.

Dominant firms do innovate, of course, and sometimes they consistently lead. But they usually do less than their proportional share. They tend to explore inventions actively and then to prepare to imitate once their hand is forced. This enables them to avoid "premature" innovations, but also to imitate quickly so as to not lose their market position. Unfortunately, the "fast second" strategy means that many innovations sit on the shelves at dominant firms until competition forces them to act. The social costs of this retarding of innovation may be large. Thus, again, the central importance of competition is confirmed.

More research is needed, using firmer data from a wider variety of industries. The role of entry barriers also needs to be included more fully. A high entry barrier may shift the whole time-cost curve down, or possibly rotate it clockwise.

---

[19] Mansfield, *Industrial Research and Technological Innovation;* and Mansfield and others, *Research and Innovation.* The U.S. steel industry offers a striking instance of retardation, when leading firms avoided the superior new oxygen-furnace technology during the 1950s. See the devastating, and largely unchallenged, analysis by Walter Adams and Joel B. Dirlam, "Big Steel, Invention and Innovation," *Quarterly Journal of Economics* (May 1966), 167–89.

IV. ANALYSIS OF PATENTS

A patent gives its owner exclusive control for seventeen years over the marketing of an invention. Often it does not provide a true economic monopoly in a relevant market because the invention competes closely with other products or production methods. Yet the essence of a patent is (1) to confer a degree of market power upon the owner, and (2) to permit an unrestricted capture of excess profits from the patented idea.[20]

In practice, as we noted earlier, a great many of the 70,000-plus patents granted each year are impractical, valueless, and unused. Many of the others are valuable but have effective lives of only three to seven years before competitors displace them by inventing around them or developing superior ideas. Fewer patents do have full seventeen-year lives and generate large profits. Still others provide a basis for capturing even longer-lasting degrees of monopoly than the seventeen-year term.

The patent system is intensely controversial in that it creates significant monopoly positions in return for uncertain gains from stimulating invention and innovation. It has also become a focus for new industrial organization theory, duopoly modeling, in which alternative settings are posited in order to define the profit inducements for invention and innovation.[21] In these models, it is assumed that inventions and innovations are extremely sensitive to prospective profits: that a higher profit reward always generates more inventive or innovative activity.

That assumption fits the logic of patents, which is to permit the patent holder unlimited capture of all possible profits from the invention or innovation, through a government-conferred monopoly. The resulting profit rewards range from zero (with a loss of the invention's original cost) to very high sums, occasionally hundreds of times larger than the efficient reward.

Yet the logic is not conclusive. Many patented inventions are autonomous: they would occur about as rapidly even in the absence of specific monetary inducements.[22] Even where innovations are accelerated by monetary inducements, the gains are only matters of degree, which may be small (perhaps just weeks or months).

For example, xerography is often cited as a case of major innovation induced by profit hopes (indeed, in the 1960s, there was a spectacular rise in Xerox Company stock prices). Yet xerography was bound to be created sometime in the 1960s by the maturing of technology, perhaps only a few years later than it did emerge. Therefore the colossal gains to the stockholders of the innovating company may have far exceeded the social gains from having xerography available a few months or years earlier.

An important contrasting case is the silicon chip, which was invented almost

---

[20] For a survey of these issues, see Scherer, *Industrial Market Structure,* Chapter 16; also William D. Nordhaus, *Invention, Growth and Welfare* (Cambridge, Mass.: MIT Press, 1969); and Mansfield, *Industrial Research and Technological Innovation.*

[21] See Tirole, *The Theory of Industrial Organization,* Chapter 10; and Kamien and Schwartz, *Market Structure and Innovation.* For a review of "memoryless" patent races, see Jennifer Reinganum, "Practical Implications of Game Theoretic Models of R&D," *American Economic Review,* 74 (May 1984), 61–66; and G. Grossman and C. Shapiro, "Dynamic R&D Competition," *Economic Journal,* 97 (1987), 372–87.

[22] The contrast between induced and autonomous inventions is posed in Jacob Schmookler, *Invention and Economic Growth* (Cambridge, Mass.: Harvard University Press, 1967), as discussed earlier in this chapter.

simultaneously by two people in 1959. Neither of them obtained fame or a large fortune from this important invention. Yet the chip was invented, as it was bound to be soon, by other inventors if not by these two. In short, skepticism is in order about claims for the compelling need to reward innovation.

The patent system is capricious because it confers large rewards that may bear no systematic relation to efficient incentives. By permitting monopoly in return for uncertain social benefits, the system may be socially costly.[23]

In any event, the patent system is based on a fundamental economic error: the belief that invention needs to be stimulated by *indefinite* rewards rather than by finite, *efficient* rewards. As noted earlier, competitive profit rates (as adjusted for risk and other factors) are the correct inducement level. Supra-competitive profits tend to induce lesser amounts of later innovation because the creative activity is voluntary rather than compelled by strict competition.

As a practical matter, it is quite improbable that the system will be revised to align its rewards to the benefits created by innovations. In any event, the system is conceptually detached from an economic basis of efficient incentives.

Duopoly theory has also suggested that patent races can be a powerful incentive to invent and innovate. But the fundamental mechanism is the race to monopolize. The patent itself is only the device, not the goal. Monopoly can be established by other devices, such as secrecy, contracts, or controls over key inputs. Therefore the theories of innovation do not justify patents, at least not in their current form.

The analysis also indicates that patent races can cause excess R&D spending, for two different reasons.[24] First, both duopolists pursue their prospective gains in parallel, even though both cannot win. Therefore the total of R&D spending may exceed the optimum. Second, a "business-stealing" effect occurs when "a firm that introduces a new product does not internalize the loss of profit suffered by its rivals on the product market."[25]

Yet these cases of excess R&D spending are based on strictly short-run and static analysis that treats innovation as a version of product selection among a portfolio of existing alternatives, with randomness in the process of introduction. These assumptions ignore the values that may be created outside the static consumer-surplus framework, in widening the search for new ideas and creating products not yet conceived.

There are many other points of analysis, including the optimum length of patent life and the conditions under which patent owners may use patents to block innovation. The studies typically seek only to clarify, in formal analysis, conditions that have long been known from direct experience: the use of "blocking patents," for example. Many of the "new IO theory" studies are based on Bertrand assumptions of myopic and memoryless duopolists, and therefore their results have little value for complex situations that go beyond maximizing consumer surplus. Yet this is likely to continue as a lively topic for theoretical research.

---

[23] For other criticisms of the patent system, see Scherer, *Industrial Market Structure*, Chapter 16, and the sources noted there.

[24] See Tirole, *The Theory of Industrial Organization*, Chapter 10, pp. 396–404; and S. Bhattacharya and D. Mookerjee, "Portfolio Choice in Research and Development," *Rand Journal of Economics*, 17 (1986), 594–605;

[25] Tirole, *The Theory of Industrial Organization*, p. 399.

V. SUMMARY

The main thread of the subject is the way market power may relate to invention and innovation. Technological opportunity varies among industries. In using these opportunities, firms under competitive pressure are likely to act more rapidly than dominant firms. Economies of scale may work the other way in some industries, so that large R&D groups in dominant firms are superior. Yet large size often breeds X-inefficiency in R&D activities.

The net results of these counterpoised forces are not precisely known. Certain broad patterns have emerged from recent research. The best studies rely on direct evaluations of important inventions and innovations. Cross-section studies of R&D intensity and patents have given rather more ambiguous results. Invention appears to be still primarily a small-scale activity. Innovation appears to be undertaken mostly by firms with small market shares rather than by dominant firms.

Technological change fits well with the findings about pricing, efficiency, and other elements of performance. Monopoly tends to retard it and to levy social costs (though there may be exceptional cases). Competition tends to promote a balanced outcome. Technological progress does not overwhelm the other performance elements in importance.

QUESTIONS FOR REVIEW

1. "Invention follows innovation, but the two processes use quite different resources and may have differing incentives." True?
2. "Patent systems can be worthwhile if induced innovations are important, and if the rewards from patents do speed them up." True?
3. "Positive aspects of technological change are complicated, but normative aspects are quite simple." True?
4. "Technological opportunity must be estimated if one wishes to form normative judgments about technological progress." True?
5. "Under 'normal' conditions of time-cost trade-offs and benefits, the dominant firm will usually lean toward imitating rather than innovating." True?
6. "By analyzing R&D intensity, one can discover which firms are doing the most and the best innovating." True?
7. Discuss three industries with high degrees of technological opportunity, and three industries with very low technological opportunity. What evidence helps you to make these judgments?
8. Why are R&D intensity and patents not good data for testing the influences on innovation?
9. Explain how the "free rider" problem may cause the rate of innovation to be too low. Will it slow down autonomous innovations?
10. "In general, monopoly firms tend to invent adequately but to hold back on innovation." "Monopolies often are able to do innovations that lesser firms cannot manage to finance or carry out."
    Are these both true? Reconcile them, if you can.
11. Explain the "replacement effect," which may cause monopoly firms to innovate less rapidly.
12. Use the "time-cost" analysis to illustrate how a dominant firm may do an innovation more cheaply and slowly, while charging consumers more for it.

7

FAIRNESS IN DISTRIBUTION AND OTHER VALUES

We turn now to broader values. They may be less precisely definable and measurable than efficiency and technological change, but they can be analyzed, and in the ultimate reckoning they may be the most important effects of market power.[1]

Competition is likely to promote fairness, diversity, and a healthy society, in addition to the narrower gains it gives in efficiency. You can reach your own judgment about the relative importance of these elements once you have considered the content of this chapter.

We consider first the value of competition itself, in Section I. Then we look at fairness in distribution: of wealth, income, and opportunity, in Sections II–IV. Section V considers freedom of choice, and security and cultural diversity. Finally, to give a different perspective, Section VI reviews the standard Marxian predictions about monopoly's growth and impacts. These predictions have haunted the debates about competitive capitalism for the last century.

The literature has skimped on these issues. Efficiency (and, to a lesser extent, innovation) have been given center stage, particularly since 1970. Yet the concern about these broader values has never died out.

I. COMPETITION ITSELF: BENEFITS AND COSTS

Competition is not just a neutral means to other ends. It provides value in itself, even beyond the effort, efficiency, innovation, and fairness that it promotes.

1. Benefits

The value of competition lies primarily in providing alternatives for all market participants. Under monopoly, the production of goods is dominated by one firm. Consumers lack alternative sources of, as well as variety in, products. There is no

---

[1] The original Chicago School leader on these issues, Henry C. Simons, was particularly eloquent about the value of the competitive system as a means of controlling power and promoting effective democracy. See his *Economic Policy for a Free Society* (Chicago: University of Chicago Press, 1948).

recourse in economic markets against abusive actions. Citizens have to resort to political action to redress their grievances; that is, they must go outside the market system in order to correct it.

Competition, in contrast, provides an array of choices within the market system, and not just in consumer goods. Workers and other suppliers of inputs are free to try alternative buyers. Managers and investors also benefit because they can form their own firms whenever they wish.

These values add up to more than just "freedom of choice," which is discussed in Section V. Competition is a fundamental social process that expresses (and shapes) basic attitudes. It fosters beliefs in diversity, tolerance, and individual initiative, all of which are blocked by monopoly. Competition promotes independence, self-reliance, and greater mobility among social classes.

When competition is the organizing principle of an economy, it becomes the foundation for an open, flexible society in which merit and personal values take primacy over control from the top. It also permits political democracy to develop, because power and information are dispersed rather than concentrated. The ancient contrast between Athens and Sparta is a striking example: Athens, open, spontaneous, experimental; Sparta, closed, regimented, autocratic.

The contrast can also be seen by imagining an economy composed solely of one colossal conglomerate firm that possesses a monopoly in every market. Suppose that this diversified firm generates good performance in all specific dimensions, including efficiency, innovation, and distribution. This economic organization would still be defective compared to competition because it would be rigid and closed, excluding the crucial process that allows variety and a sharing of power among the populace.

Even if such centralized power is exercised benevolently, it diminishes individual values. Competition is the classic individualistic process, reflecting classical liberal (or libertarian) values. Yet, paradoxically, its value is denied most firmly by recent Chicago-UCLA economists, who profess to favor classical liberalism. They argue that as long as competition's results are obtained (especially static allocative efficiency), it does not matter to a society whether competition or monopoly delivers them.

In their lexicon, *competition* has lost its meaning.[2] If monopoly provides the benefits of competition, they say, then *monopoly really is competition*—or at least the equivalent of, or as good as, competition. This view rejects the core belief of the original Chicago School leaders, Frank H. Knight and Henry C. Simons. It also ignores both common sense and careful technical analysis.

2.   Competition's Limits and Harms

Competition does have certain drawbacks, especially at the level of relentless personal competition *among individuals*. The following five limits and harms can be important:

---

[2] For a fascinating review of the Chicago-UCLA lexicon of "competition," as contrasted with the mainstream usage of terms, see Eleanor M. Fox and Lawrence A. Sullivan, "Antitrust—Retrospective and Prospective: Where Are We Coming From? Where Are We Going?" *New York University Law Review,* 62 (November 1987), 936–88, especially the Appendix, "Rewriting the Lexicon," pp. 969–88.

1. *Shallow and myopic.* Competition sometimes becomes a series of small, intensive, myopic episodes, in which each player tries for specific wins. The pressure for immediate victory and survival can preclude longer-run objectives and larger possibilities. People become stressed, narrow, and limited. Firms adopt a myopic perspective and become tyrannized by short-term financial pressures. U.S. companies have often been criticized for their obsession with quarterly profits in the 1980s.

2. *Anticreative.* The harsh forces of competition can choke off creativity and imagination, as the players are forced to struggle to maximize their current position. Tight competition can set narrow zones for action in the short run, such as cutting costs and responding to immediate conditions. The larger and richer results that creativity makes possible may become an unaffordable luxury.

3. *Divisive.* Competition has an either-or outcome: one competitor triumphs, the other is defeated. Therefore competition requires a strict exclusion of competitors' interests from each player's considerations. One wins by defeating others, eliminating them whenever necessary. Any consideration of the interests of one's competitors reduces one's own chances of success: a boxer wins by knocking out his opponent, not by assisting him. Insofar as it sets *people* against one another, competition can be harmful. Insofar as it sets *firms* against one another, the good effects probably far outweight the bad.

4. *Exhausting.* Because it requires maximum effort and exclusive attention, competition tends to exhaust the players. Since further effort can always enhance one's chances of winning, the demands are ultimately unlimited.

   Intensive sports events are followed by a period of rest and recovery. But market competition permits no such letup. Unrestrained personal competition therefore produces maximum stress. As with divisiveness, though, this problem need not affect enterprises.

5. *Destructive sequences.* Sometimes the results of competition are socially harmful rather than beneficial. With competition driving the destructive process, no one player has responsibility for the outcome. Excess is harder to contain where individual responsibility is lost. Examples are arms races, the destruction of open-access natural resources, and the selling of harmful products.

All these costs can be genuinely harmful in *personal competition.* In *competition among firms,* however, the costs do not generally fall directly on people.[3] Myopia, anticreativity, and destructive sequences *can* be harmful in industrial competition, but these costs seem to be clearly outweighed by the important benefits of competition. Therefore *maximal competition—what Chicago-UCLA economists call "hard competition"—should prevail among enterprises in markets so as to generate the highest levels of corporate performance.* Effective competition matters in its own right, as well as for the good performance it induces. Ordinarily it can be pushed to the limit and held there, without causing major costs to weigh against its important benefits.

II. FAIRNESS IN THE DISTRIBUTION OF WEALTH

Issues.   Market power can cause excess profits, and these are capitalized into the market value of the enterprise (recall Chapter 2). A sharp rise in market power can yield a large, immediate rise in the wealth of the owners. By selling their shares

---

[3] The distinction is not total, of course. Firms are composed of people, and therefore extreme competitive pressures among firms can have some personal impacts. This is especially true of small businesses, which are often little more than extensions of a single owner or a few people. But the distinction is quite important for larger firms, which pose the main problems of market power.

in the firm, the monopolizers can realize this wealth effect soon after the market power is created. The wealth impact becomes vested in the share prices. If the firm's market power is sustained, it will earn excess profit on its assets, at book value. But because the share prices have been bid up, the current owners will earn only a competitive rate of return on their holdings. If the firm's market power declines, the present owners' rate of return will fall below the competitive level.

The original owner-manager of the enterprise can draw off the gains, either directly by taking higher income payments, or in capital gains by selling off shares. In modern corporations, the managers' interests may diverge from the shareholders'. The executives may raise payments to themselves, to employees, and to other input suppliers, absorbing some excess profits. This is one effect of X-inefficiency: it reduces profits and erodes the capital gains of the shareholders. The board of directors—whose members are supposed to control the firm in the shareholders' interests—is expected to prevent such a shift of gains from shareholders to managers or other suppliers of inputs.

In any case, market power shifts wealth away from the many customers to the few owners of the firm. The wealth effects depend on (1) the degree of monopoly held by the firm and (2) the size of the firm. Past wealth effects, therefore, are the summation of many thousands of market positions, ranging from petty local oligopolies to full-blown nationwide monopolies. Other forces have also shaped wealth: luck, inheritance, and taxation, to name the obvious ones.

Market power is often destroyed by a reversion to competition or, as Schumpeter suggests, by a new dominant firm moving in. It is also possible that innovation and superior efficiency will occur in a firm holding market power. Or, instead, the monopoly may become so inefficient or noninnovative that its monopoly profits are curtailed. One needs to factor out these two other influences on profits in order to isolate the true effect of market power.

So the research problem is not simple. Ideally, one could calculate the size and degree of each position of market power since 1890, then allow for relative innovation and efficiency to arrive at the net effect of market power on wealth in each case. These effects could be summed up and compared with the total rise in industrial wealth in order to evaluate the extent of monopoly's impact.

Even were this estimate possible, however, it would still be incomplete, for the social question is whether monopoly wealth adds to rigidity in the class structure. For example, if Rockefeller, Du Pont, and other older family wealth continues to dominate, then monopoly's effect is more socially harmful than if there is flux among the "leading" and lesser families. Such a two-stage evaluation—determining the sequence of new monopoly wealth and then its process of retention or dissipation—is not hard to conceive. In fact, popular discussions repeatedly make crude judgments about the magnitudes (e.g., that the impacts are large and lasting, or small and transient).

Two methods have been used in actual research. One models the process, reaching estimates from various assumptions about the key conditions. The other simply sifts the mass of evidence about actual market power and family wealth. Although the two approaches differ sharply, their findings are in accord.

A Model. There has been only one effort to model the wealth effect. Comanor and Smiley's pathbreaking study posited that the wealth effect reflected several

TABLE 7.1   Estimates of the Effect of Past Market Power on Present Family Wealth, 1962

	ACTUAL WEALTH DISTRIBUTION		ESTIMATED EFFECT ON THE SHARES OF WEALTH FROM THE EFFECT OF MONOPOLY ON WEALTH			
			If Monopoly Profits Were:			
WEALTH CLASSES (FROM POOREST TO RICHEST)	PERCENT OF ALL CONSUMER UNITS IN EACH WEALTH CLASS	ACTUAL WEALTH; SHARE OF THE TOTAL HELD BY EACH WEALTH CLASS IN 1962	2 PERCENT OF GNP		3 PERCENT OF GNP	
			10-YEAR MONOPOLY LIFE	40-YEAR MONOPOLY LIFE	10-YEAR MONOPOLY LIFE	40-YEAR MONOPOLY LIFE
	(%)	(%)	(%)	(%)	(%)	(%)
(1)	(2)	(3)	(4)	(5)	(6)	(7)
1	28.25	0	-0.79	-0.69	-2.00	-1.39
2	17.33	2.41	-2.05	-1.35	-4.86	-2.56
3	14.58	5.26	-3.26	-2.05	-7.65	3.89
4	22.30	17.74	-8.50	-5.21	-9.88	-20.18
5	10.82	19.07	-0.19	-0.32	-0.45	-0.60
6	4.28	14.84	$+4.66$	$+2.71$	$+11.10$	$+5.18$
7	1.22	8.07	$+1.12$	$+0.73$	$+2.68$	$+1.39$
8	0.95	14.09	$+2.51$	$+1.78$	$+5.98$	$+3.39$
9	0.27	18.53	$+6.47$	$+4.40$	$+15.40$	$+8.38$
Groups 7, 8 & 9	2.44	40.69	$+10.10$	$+6.91$	$+24.06$	$+13.16$

SOURCE: Assembled from data in William S. Comanor and Robert H. Smiley, "Monopoly and the Distribution of Wealth," *Quarterly Journal of Economics*, 89 (May 1975), 177–94.

conditions since 1890.[4] First was the degree and duration of market power; this condition generated the estimated flow of monopoly profits. Next was the rate of return on wealth. The third condition was the current dispersal of family holdings: current spending as a share of the wealth, and other forces dissipating wealth (taxes, bequests, etc.). Comanor and Smiley tried reasonable upper- and lower-bound assumptions about these factors in order to derive the range of plausible estimates. The wealth effect would be smaller if: monopoly were slight, the return on assets were small (so they would not build up rapidly), and the rate of dissipation of fortunes were high.

Table 7.1 shows their estimates for several border assumptions about the factors. For example, suppose that monopoly profits were 3 percent of GNP and monopolies lasted forty years. Then 13.16 percent of the 40.69 percent of wealth held by the top three wealth classes would have come from monopoly gains (compare the bottom of columns 3 and 7). Since you have already formed judgments about monopoly's role, you can select the most reasonable assumptions for yourself. Table 7.1 suggests that about one-fourth to one-half of the present highest family wealth traces back

---

[4] William S. Comanor and Robert H. Smiley, "Monopoly and the Distribution of Wealth," *Quarterly Journal of Economics,* 89 (May 1975), 177–94.

to monopoly. The method is comprehensive, but it may contain various biases. The extent of monopoly and its effect on profits are probably both understated, since Comanor and Smiley relied on conventional estimates of the kind discussed in Chapter 5. The rate of return on family wealth is also probably understated, since these fortunes have been managed by leading investment advisers with access to some degree of inside information. You can factor in these and other possible biases in judging how big the true effect has been. You can also try adapting or extending the model, and then using it to derive better estimates.

Other Evidence.   There is much other evidence to sift. One category is the known instances of dominant firms that created flows of excess profits and family fortunes. Those during 1870–1910 are the best known, since they were prominent and widely reported.[5] No complete census of these fortunes has been done, but many of them are still well known. The Rockefeller family drew billions from Standard Oil; Du Pont wealth came from gunpowder and chemicals; American Tobacco created the Duke family fortune; Mellons mined the ALCOA aluminum monopoly; Vanderbilts, Harrimans, Morgans, and others grew rich from dominant positions in railroads and other sectors; Armours and Swifts dominated Chicago society with wealth from meat packing. Nearly every sizable city has had one or more families that created a large newspaper fortune, from Scripps and Pulitzer to Cowles and Chandlers. These are just a small part of the total. Fortunes of the second rank arose from market positions in steel, newspapers, cameras and film, aluminum, soap, razor blades, and scores of other markets, and of course banking. In fact, nearly every dominant firm in finance, utilities, insurance, and retailing has bred at least one family fortune. There are thousands of smaller local wealthy families who drew their fortunes from a bank, hotel, department store, newspaper, lumberyard, or the like. The correlation of family wealth with market power is not tight, for wealth arises from other sources such as luck, effort, and innovation. But some kind of monopoly power seems to be the most frequent source. Even though the wealth is extended via portfolio investment, real estate, or commodity speculation, the original source is often monopoly power. (Try tracing the wealth effect from three dominant firms, national or local. You will need to consult a variety of sources[6] because such connections are usually kept discreetly private.)

Many cases are arguable. Some mingle innovation with monopoly (e.g., Ford's dominance in automobiles during 1910–1925, and Xerox's dominance in copiers after 1960). Others involve trademarks and advertising (e.g., detergents and razor blades). These firms assert that their benefits to society are large, while this monopoly effect is low.

Many cases of wealth-by-monopoly are invisible. Large diversified firms often contain a number of products with high market shares, yet data about them are not

---

[5] See John Moody, *The Truth about the Trusts* (Chicago: Moody Publishing, 1904); and the many sources given in the polemical survey by Ferdinand Lundberg, *The Rich and the Super-Rich* (New York: Lyle Stuart, 1968). Recent surveys are in *Forbes* magazine's annual ''The Forbes 400,'' survey of the richest Americans.

[6] Useful reviews include Lundberg, *The Rich and the Super-Rich*; Cleveland Amory, *Who Killed Society?* (New York: Harper & Row, 1960); A. M. Lewis, ''America's Centimillionaires,'' *Fortune*, May 1968, 152–56; and a variety of company histories and biographies of industrialists. *Forbes* magazine's yearly special issue on ''The 400 Wealthiest Americans'' also includes useful summaries of wealth inherited from powerful enterprises.

available publicly. Even unified single-line firms try to minimize public knowledge of their positions. This problem is doubly true for virtually all family wealth holdings. They are much harder to identify and measure.

Accordingly, only the tip of this iceberg is known. Yet the incomplete facts are consistent with the estimates from modeling the whole process. Market power has created a range of national and local fortunes. The details and precise scope of the wealth effect are not known, and perhaps they never will be. But the main lines are reasonably clear, and there are sound methods for studying them further.

III.   INCOME

Wealth generates income, and thus the wealth effect is paralleled by a redistribution of income toward the owners of new monopolies. The extent of this shift depends on the wealth effect itself, as discussed above.

More visible is the effect on wages, salaries, and bonuses paid to employees. One possibility is that firms with market power pay more to all their employees. The extra payment can be in rates of pay, in various perquisites, or in the form of easier work for given pay. These can all be forms of X-inefficiency (recall Chapter 5).

Evidence about this possibility is mixed. Many dominant firms do give better pay, benefits, and security, and do permit a certain degree of slack in their employees. This pattern, usually described as "paternalism," is often designed to forestall the formation of unions among workers. Yet "paternalistic" pay and benefits may not exceed what union activity would provide. The issue is speculative, and there are no thorough studies of it. Some research has been done on the interactions among concentration, union power, and wage rates,[7] but here, too, the results have been inconclusive. Even if the whole effect were strong, it would not disequalize the distribution of income by very much. It would only alter the benefits between those employees (from top to bottom) who work for monopolists and those who do not.

The other possibility is that pay differentials are sharpened *within* firms holding market power. In particular, the managers' share may be increased, perhaps sharply. Two conditions suggest that market power does enrich top executives. First, the upper managers' pay in large firms is indeed high, with over fifty chief executives receiving more than $1 million annually in recent years. That is about $3,000 or more per working day. Another 220 chief executives received over $600,000. Pay for lower-ranking officers in firms holding market power is commensurate. By contrast, average pay among all workers is about $20,000 per year, in many cases for grueling, skilled, and/or unpleasant work.

Second, these top-executive pay arrangements are often largely self-arranged,

---

[7] See Leonard W. Weiss, "Concentration and Labor Earnings," *American Economic Review,* 56 (March 1966), 96–117, and other sources cited there. See also Lawrence M. Kahn, "Unionism and Relative Wages: Direct and Indirect Effects," *Industrial and Labor Relations Review,* (July 1979), 520–32; Charles T. Haworth and Carol Reuther, "Industry Concentration and Interindustry Wage Determination," *Review of Economics and Statistics,* (February 1978), 85–95; and J. A. Dalton and E. J. Ford, Jr., "Concentration and Labor Earnings in Manufacturing and Utilities," *Industrial and Labor Relations Review,* (October 1977), 45–60.

with no apparent close controls. What *is* a top manager of a lucrative dominant firm worth? Extensive analysis has found no clear patterns among managerial pay.[8] Each situation is different, with some bargaining power held by the chief executive officer, the board, the other officers, and so forth. Company traditions and resources also differ. Even high excess payments to managers will not cut much into the total earnings of really big firms. In short, there are no clear limits on overpayment.

In theory, each employee is paid his or her marginal value product. In practice, this value is not well known and is highly debatable. There is no clear way to test whether managers are overpaid. Their pay arises from personal, market, monopoly, and other obscure factors.

The element of extra pay from market power is probably not small, but it has not been isolated from other influences. Size is probably the major single determinant of managers' pay, but the correlation is not close. Market power's effect is mingled in with others.

Altogether, market power's effects on income distribution have not yet been clearly shown. All we can say for certain is that there is some disequalizing, from larger payments both to wealth holders and to some upper managers.

IV. OPPORTUNITY

Opportunity has long been the alternative criterion to equity, on the theory that even if wealth and income are unfairly distributed now, the opportunities for future gains are open and fair to all. If true, this could make any present inequities more benign, because they would be replaced by fair conditions in the future. The point is controversial. Those holding great wealth stress that (1) they got it by seizing opportunities, but fairly; and (2) in any case, opportunity now is equally open for all to do well in the future. The wise student will note that the very weight one gives to opportunity compared with actual wealth and income is in itself a critical choice. Opportunity may be a key element in fairness, perhaps the dominant one. But then again, it may be minor, obscure, and untestable.

Yet opportunity does appear to be an unequivocal standard. More equality of opportunity is always better than less. Still, there are certain technical problems with the criterion. First, opportunity is virtually impossible to measure. Second, all people do not have equivalent endowments and abilities to strive. Instead, talents and family advantages differ, so that some children have sharply higher opportunities than others.[9] Third, many—perhaps most—people are not temperamentally suited to endless competition. Fourth, the criterion assumes that the rewards to differing talents are equivalent. In fact, some human talents draw great prizes (ruthlessness, calculating, risk taking), while others usually make one *unfit* for commercial success (kindliness, artistic ability, willingness to serve others). Fifth, the argument can be made that people should not have the opportunity to become *markedly* richer than

---

[8] Among many studies, see William A. McEachern, *Managerial Control and Performance* (Lexington, Mass.: D.C. Heath, 1975); Robert T. Masson, "Executive Motivations, Earnings, and Consequent Equity Performance," *Journal of Political Economy,* 79 (December 1971), 1278–92; and Wilbur G. Lewellen, *The Ownership Income of Management* (New York: Columbia University Press, 1971).
[9] Some of the family advantages stem from wealth accrued from *earlier* monopoly power.

others. Fair opportunity would then permit only small prizes to the winners. And sixth, inequalities often seem to have little rational basis.[10] All these problems call into question opportunity's role as an element of fairness. At the least, the subject is so sophisticated that it requires great care to sift out the illogic and rhetoric from the various arguments.

Monopoly power is likely to reduce opportunity and to make it less equal. In extreme cases, it shrinks the number of independent firms to just one. In all cases, it reduces the variety and responsiveness of firms, both as sellers to consumers and as employers choosing among diverse talents. Finally, it may increase discrimination by race, sex, and ethnic origin. (The counterpossibility is that large dominant firms may be neutral arenas in which qualified people have equal opportunities to rise. Yet it is size rather than market power that would provide the neutrality.)

Opportunity is probably more equal in the United States than in any other Western country. This openness reflects many factors: the lack of aristocracy, the ethical traditions, the sheer size and regional variety of the country, the financial markets. Therefore market power has not shut off opportunity. Business opportunities—to set up a firm or to rise within existing firms—are relatively open.

Yet they are abridged by market power in many ways. Dominant firms do reduce or prevent fair competition and entry in a series of national and local markets. Banking connections are tight and widespread enough to limit small firms in many markets (see Chapter 8). Family connections and wealth give many people a head start in business and finance. Finance is especially exclusive: many financial managers come from business families.[11] Undoubtedly, family status strongly affects one's chances for success.[12]

No thorough research on market power's effect has yet been done, but the basic patterns are reasonably well known. Thus for decades most computer experts had had to work for IBM; in copiers, there was mainly Xerox to work for; in telephone equipment and operations, AT&T was virtually the only seller for many decades; in soup, Campbell; and so forth.

Discrimination is of particular interest. It is the use of race, sex, or other extraneous features in evaluating job applicants or promoting employees. The major biases recently have been against women, blacks, and various ethnic groups. Market power may intensify the discrimination, or instead—possibly—alleviate it. The key is white-collar jobs because they represent the higher levels of opportunity and directly reflect the company's hiring policies.

Under perfect competition, firms could not indulge in any irrelevant prejudices, because if they did so, they would incur extra costs and fail to survive. Discrimination, a form of X-inefficiency, would not occur. Indeed, if a group received low wages because of discrimination, competitive firms would hire *more* people in that group. Of course, blue-collar majorities could still pressure firms toward discriminatory hiring policies at their job levels and this has been widely observed in the

---

[10] See Lester Thurow, *Generating Inequality* (New York: Basic Books, 1975).

[11] See W. Lloyd Warner and James Abegglan, *Big Business Leaders in America* (New York: Harper & Row, 1955); and Eugene E. Jennings, *Mobile Managers* (Ann Arbor: Bureau of Industrial Relations, Graduate School of Business, University of Michigan, 1967).

[12] John A. Brittain, *The Inheritance of Economic Status* (Washington, D.C.: Brookings Institution, 1977), is one of many studies that show the role of family advantages. At least half of the wealthiest Americans listed in the "Forbes 400" began with family fortunes and other advantages.

form of union restrictions and other devices—but competitive firms would still be neutral in white-collar jobs.

By contrast, the outcome under market power is not determinate. Since profit maximizing is partially voluntary, managers may maximize among a variety of other objectives. If managers share common prejudices (e.g. against women and blacks), then market power will foster discrimination: white male managers will substitute in favor of other white males, even at some sacrifice in profits. Some managers, of course, may prefer to try for neutrality or even "affirmative action," and that, too, will be possible. The more common and natural effect of market power, however, would be to increase discrimination, for that would reflect widely held attitudes. The benign cases of reverse discrimination would arise from "social motivations," which are usually scarce in private enterprises.

The issue can be tested, indirectly, using data on actual white-collar hiring by firms holding varying degrees of market power. Ideally, one would also allow for skill differences among groups, for they may influence actual hiring. That has not yet been possible, so one needs to evaluate the actual hiring patterns cautiously. Some firms and public agencies do have fairly high proportions of women and even blacks at their upper levels. This casts doubt on the claim that the lack of minority members with adequate skills is the main cause of "apparent discrimination."

To sum up, there are two opposite hypotheses. (1) If monopoly promotes discrimination, then the relation between market power and the minority employment would be *a negatively-sloped curve.* (2) If instead monopoly reduces discrimination, then there would be *a positively-sloped curve.* Statistical tests may be able to give clear choices between these opposite patterns.

One study has compared industry concentration with the share of blacks in upper-level jobs.[13] Figure 7.1 shows one of the comparisons. The data have certain weaknesses. Concentration is not precisely measured, nor does it fully represent market power (recall Chapters 3 and 4). The officials, managers, and professionals categories are not homogeneous. They range from presidents down to executive trainees and assistant plant managers. Yet the patterns for 1966 consistently suggest that open hiring of blacks occurs mainly in competitive industries.

Another study examined the hiring of women and blacks in 300 large firms and banks in 1966 and 1970.[14] The patterns were complex, but the main conditions were clear. Large firms as a group had virtually no women or blacks in upper-level jobs with responsibility. Certain "women's" industries were exceptions (publishing and cosmetics). At the other extreme were the insurance, banking, and computer industries, where small armies of women clerks and programmers were supervised by small groups of white men. Certain other heavy industries (metals, engineering) were almost totally white and male in upper white-collar jobs.

The typical large firm had virtually no women or blacks in upper-level jobs in

[13] W. G. Shepherd, "Market Power and Racial Discrimination in White-Collar Employment," *Antitrust Bulletin,* 14 (Spring 1969), 141–61. See also William S. Comanor, "Racial Discrimination in American Industry," *Economica,* 40 (November 1973), 363–78.

[14] W. G. Shepherd and Sharon G. Levin, "Managerial Discrimination in Large Firms," *Review of Economics and Statistics,* 55 (November 1973), 412–22. See also William A. Luksetich, "Market Power and Sex Discrimination in White-Collar Employment," *Review of Social Economy,* (October 1979), 211–24, and William R. Johnson, "Racial Wage Discrimination and Industrial Structure," *Bell Journal of Economics,* 10 (Spring 1978), 70–81.

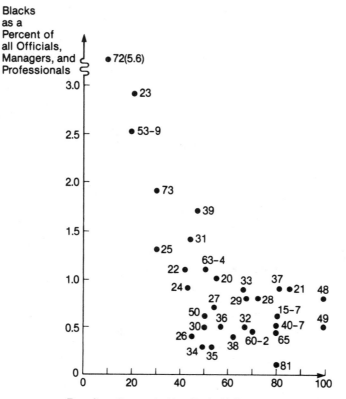

Figure 7.1.   Industry concentration and black employment in upper-level jobs in nine major U.S. cities in 1966.

Note: The number by each observation is the Census Standard Industrial Classification code number for the industry group. (For industry group names, see Appendix 2.)

SOURCE: W. G. Shepherd "Market Power and Racial Discrimination in White-Collar Employment," *Antitrust Bulletin*, 14 (Spring 1969), 156.

1970. Market power intensified this effect slightly, but size was the main factor. Growth and other conditions that might change the patterns played only a small role. Large firms as a group are generally profitable enough to be able to afford to practice discrimination. A few exceptional firms had as much as 5 percent women or 2 percent blacks in the managerial and professional job categories. Yet such apparent "affirmative action" was the exception. Few dominant firms engaged in it.

These patterns are confirmed by widespread commentary in the business press. Moves to include women at upper levels have drawn much attention, but discrimination still exists, particularly in industry, finance, utilities, insurance, and most other sectors of large-scale enterprises. Some blue-collar jobs have been made more open. But the patterns at the upper levels—the real test of firm policies toward opportunity—have only slowly yielded to women's and blacks' incursions.

Large, profitable firms do appear to reduce opportunity for important segments of the population. Further research may alter the details, but the main patterns are likely to hold into the future.

V.   OTHER VALUES

1. Freedom of Choice

Freedom of choice is an important social value. Its simple meaning is clear: freedom to buy what one wants, to change jobs, to set up a business, and so forth. Competition does usually maximize freedom of choice in that sense.

But the concept is more complex. More freedom for some people can mean less freedom for others. Competition may not permit much breadth of choice to large groups of employees and consumers. It disfavors citizens whose temperaments are not suited to the competitive grind and to aggressive, risky behavior. At the least, it fails to provide much choice to the mass of people with low incomes. Competition does not guarantee that freedom will be abundant. It only tends to provide more discretion, and across more areas, than market power does.

Market power does curtail freedom of choice in parts of the U.S. economy. It reduces purchasing power. It narrows the variety of consumer goods. For example, the Bell System offered little variety in user equipment for many decades, until after 1968 competition was gradually introduced. The resulting rise in product variety was large and rapid. Network television tends toward uniformity at mass levels. This is precisely the effect that tight oligopoly gives. It reduces or excludes the scope for competitors in many markets. In short, it enlarges choice for the few owners and managers of dominant firms, while curtailing choice for the many competitors and would-be entrants into the market.

The issue reaches well beyond commercial competition in markets. Political competition is the essence of a democratic process. Concentrated power could destroy this political competition, replacing it with power blocs, syndicalism, and autocratic regimes. That probably occurred in Germany and Japan before World War II.[15] Some degree of this effect already exists in certain states and in the United States as a whole.[16] There is close debate about how far it has gone. The effect is more moderate than in most other countries, and it may have dwindled during the last eight decades, as the power of financiers and major monopolies has been diluted.

Religious competition is also fundamental. Many countries have a single official religion, or a choice between just two organized faiths, and these often control parts of the educational process. The United States' deliberate policy of open entry and no direct support for specific religions is about as procompetitive as possible. The result is even more distinctive for the country than the industrial benefits of antitrust

---

[15] The German and Japanese dictatorships had a complicated and shifting relationship to business power groups during the 1930s and World War II. Yet observers agree that economic concentration facilitated the autocratic regimes and their military ventures. The relationship was symbiotic. See T. A. Bisson, *Zaibatsu Dissolution in Japan* (Berkeley: University of California Press, 1954); and Eleanor T. Hadley, *Antitrust in Japan* (Princeton, N.J.: Princeton University Press, 1971).

[16] The power of copper firms in Montana was long well known. For a detailed claim that Du Pont interests have dominated the state of Delaware, see James Phelan and Robert Pozen, *The Company State* (New York: Grossman, 1973).

policy. The benefits for personal freedom arising from religious competition have been profound.

2. Social Effects

We now consider the social effects of market power more directly. The political process has already been mentioned. Security and cultural diversity will be discussed here.

Economic security means primarily steadiness of employment. Layoffs become a social problem when they are widespread and when no alternative jobs are available. Tight oligopoly does increase the severity of recessions, especially in heavy industries, though the degree of extra instability is a matter of debate. This cost is borne by a wide range of employees, but recessions also impose social costs in the forms of unemployment compensation and general insecurity.

Cultural diversity involves a broader set of issues. Competition can promote and reward diversity, for free market activity can be responsive to the full range of human interests and talents. Yet competition can also shrink and deaden a culture. It may enshrine the cruelty of Gradgrinds and the shallowness of Babbitts. Its participants learn to be selfish, insecure, and anonymous. Universal competition can produce a cultural wasteland. So competition is both good and bad culturally.

Market power, on the other hand, is mostly negative, in several ways. First, it often reduces the civic roles and contributions of company branches in their locales. This has become a major feature of nationally based firms. Because officials are rotated among locations, they have little interest in local affairs. The great majority of them do not participate in, or involve their firms in supporting, local interests. When work is controlled from a great distance, it becomes impersonal and less rewarding for local employees.

The firm's head offices are likely to disregard local interests in making basic decisions about employment and plant locations. Indeed, firms will often exercise economic power to extract special concessions from local officials by playing off localities against one another. Some firms are able to wield great power at the state and national levels, and large multinational firms have done so on an international level.

The social diseconomies of large multiplant firms have become more important in recent decades. As yet, there is no special research method for evaluating them and no thorough analytical study of them has been done. Some appraisals of the effects have been exaggerated. They arise from sheer size and multiplicity of plants, as well as from market power.

Other social effects of market power have been posed from time to time in expert and popular discussion. Like those just mentioned, they are difficult to appraise and to link with market power on a scientific basis. Yet they are likely to be important—perhaps more important ultimately than all the strictly economic costs of monopoly. It takes great skill to judge these kinds of costs.

VI.   MARXIAN PREDICTIONS

This book is about the nature of capitalism and how to evaluate it objectively. To complete the subject, we will consider the Marxian or "radical" section of the literature, if only briefly. Marx observed "finance capitalism" during 1840–1870 in

Western Europe, before its modern forms took shape.[17] His predictions about the evolution of capitalism were clear and dramatic. They have guided the thinking of many later radical economists and, indeed, of much of the world's population outside North America. By reviewing his predictions, we can gain perspective on the whole problem and test our knowledge and methods against the leading alternative approach. This is not a test of Marx's wisdom, since the United States was outside his main focus and a number of policies since 1900 have modified the situation.

1. *Market power would rise until a few giant combines of finance capital controlled the mass of monopolies.* Rises did occur during 1880–1891, 1920–1935, and, less sharply, 1945–1965. Yet finance has been partly separated from industry, and its key role has been diluted. Generally, the rise seems to have slowed down or stopped well short of Marx's prediction. Alternatively: one may hold that concentration is sufficient—in an economy as immense as the United States—to give some of the effects that Marx predicted.

2. *Surplus value (roughly speaking, profits) would rise, supporting a wealthy but shrinking capitalist class.* Profits are about $300 billion per year in the United States and there are many large family fortunes.

3. *Workers would be increasingly pauperized and brutalized.* In fact, average wages have risen, and workdays have become shorter and less burdensome for most people. Those in desperate poverty are a small minority, not the majority. Alternatively: most families have zero or negative net worth. Many are subject to chronic unemployment, layoffs, and other insecurities. Quite a few jobs are still harsh and unpleasant.

4. *Class lines would harden. Workers would increasingly be unable to rise into the capitalist class.* In fact, there is much upward social mobility, at least into white-collar jobs or into proprietorship of small businesses. Alternatively: upward mobility is in fact rather limited. And most new small businesses fail quickly.

5. *Business cycles would grow more severe, until they became intolerable to the workers.* This prediction is why the Depression of the 1930s stirred widespread fears that the revolution was at hand. But cycles are mild now, involving only "recessions." Alternatively: perhaps only government actions prevent severe depressions from recurring. And sharp financial panics still do occur (as in the stock-market crash of October 1987).

6. *Capitalism would become imperialism abroad, exploiting resources and creating wars. Production of weapons would become necessary to maintain capitalist prosperity.* During the late 1960s, this prediction gained added credence, and arms production added to the 1980s prosperity. Yet armaments production is only about 4 percent of national income. Multinational firms do exert some power abroad, but it is not unchecked. Alternatively: U.S. firms do dominate many foreign markets. The United States does promote arms sales abroad, partly to sustain domestic prosperity.

The predictions have been uncannily accurate on some points. But generally, the evolution seems to have stopped well short of the extremes that Marx predicted. Public policies in the twentieth century have modified many of the trends Marx saw in the nineteenth. A crucial question is: Would the predictions have been fulfilled otherwise? Nobody can know the answer, but you should form your own judgment.

QUESTIONS FOR REVIEW

1. "The holders of a monopoly build up their wealth, year by year, from the flow of excess profits." True?

2. "Wealth derived from market power during 1880–1910 is still prominent in the U.S. social structure." True?

---

[17] *Das Kapital* appeared posthumously in 1883. Marx's predictions are summarized in Joseph A. Schumpeter, *History of Economic Analysis* (Oxford: Oxford University Press, 1954).

3. "Dominant firms have discriminated in favor of women and blacks in most cases." True?

4. "Healthy economic competition tends to encourage a healthy democratic process." True?

5. Discuss the values that are provided by competition itself.

6. Which of the harms that competition may cause are the most important, in your view? Do they apply to corporate competition, as well as to personal competition?

7. Discuss three leading families whose wealth arose at least partly from monopoly? Is their wealth still important?

8. Make the case that monopoly firms can provide extra opportunity for women in management. Is it probable that in fact they do? What evidence could clarify that situation?

9. The 1980s have seen extensive competition in the US economy, with little or no business cycle. Has this proven Marx's predictions—and analysis of "monopoly capitalism"—wrong?

8

FINANCE, MERGERS,
AND PUBLIC POLICIES

At each point of time, each market has a structure of some sort. There are numberless varieties of these structures. What are the main conditions shaping them?

Some conditions are largely *exogenous,* working from the outside. For example, there may be large economies of scale in some markets. In other markets, antitrust policies may have large effects. Other conditions are *endogenous,* arising from voluntary choices made by companies already in the market: to merge some firms, to sell off assets, or to undertake certain strategies toward rivals. Still other conditions that alter market structure are *random* and unpredictable.

This chapter and the next one explain the main determinants of market structure and review the evidence about their relative importance. The economies and diseconomies of scale are the traditional core topic. They are reserved for the next chapter, but it can be said immediately that there is a substantial degree of *excess market share* in the U.S. economy's major markets. Technical scale economies do not explain all, or even most, of the actual market shares and concentration (a point disputed, of course, by Chicago-UCLA economists).

This chapter considers the other main causes of market structure. Section I covers financial markets, which are critical to the shape of markets everywhere in the economy. It explains how capital markets influence other markets.

That leads directly to mergers, in Section II. Many mergers are formed in capital markets. Especially during merger booms, such as the one that occurred in the 1980s, they can deeply alter the shapes of markets. As we will see, however, their actual impact on the U.S. economy is open to debate and needs further research.

Section III considers other forces at work: life cycles of products and firms, rapid growth, random processes, and public policies. Section IV concludes the chapter by reviewing the probable main causes of the great rise of competition in the U.S. economy during 1960–1980.

I.   CAPITAL MARKETS

Finance is the controlling sector of the modern economy. It contains two main parts: commercial banking, which deals in credit; and securities markets, which deal in stock ownership and corporate control. These suppliers of capital supervise and influence firms in all the other sectors.

The critical concept here is *perfect capital markets*. It is explained in this section, which also covers the three main roles of banks and securities markets.

1. The Roles of Capital Markets

Capital is the controlling input of capitalism. Each firm's access to funds can be critical to its survival, as well as to its ability to compete effectively. Capital markets allocate funds among firms. The decisions involve the amounts and costs of funds, and the rates of return on them, usually in the presence of risk. In allocating funds, financial markets shape the degree of competition throughout the economy.

Perfect Capital Markets.   Competitive capital markets are the foundation for a competitive economy. Indeed, the assumption that capital markets are perfectly competitive is essential to the Chicago-UCLA doctrine that the economy is effectively competitive and that monopoly reflects only superior efficiency.

A perfectly functioning capital market would provide funds to firms so completely that all projects whose prospective returns exceed the cost of capital would be funded.[1] *All firms (big and small, dominant or tiny competitors) would have equal access to funds on the merits of their efficiency.* This process would reduce market power to the bare technological minimum.[2] Any pecuniary gains or other yields of market power would attract new competition, supplied amply with funds. Any monopoly profit not arising from (1) technical economies of scale or (2) artificial devices for monopoly (patents, franchises) would be eliminated.

A long-established monopolist would have no better access to outside funding than any potential competitor, for the perfect capital market would supply them impartially, in line with their objective efficiency. If capital markets are perfect, or nearly so, the "invisible hand" is more likely to ensure a complete, efficient outcome. Conversely, imperfect capital markets are likely to induce imperfections in other markets. The more faith you have in the private competitive system, the more strictly you must believe that capital markets are perfect, or nearly so.

Are they perfect in the real world? The short answer is no, there are obviously some imperfections. But how large are they? They may be trivial, or at least smaller in the United States than elsewhere. Or they may be large, or even pervasive. A full answer requires us to learn several concepts and review some history and data.

First, there are many types of capital markets, but, as we have said, there are only two main parts of the financial sector: (1) *loans and debt,* which are provided by commercial banks and bond underwriters; and (2) *equity* securities, which are handled by investment bankers and brokers. Dealings in these markets range from close "one-on-one" exchanges by banks and their main clients all the way over to the anonymous masses of market transactions. All financial enterprises share the same basic function: they judge the financial prospects of firms under varying degrees of uncertainty, and they allocate funds among firms. Though centered in "Wall

[1] There is no comprehensive discussion of perfect capital markets. But see F. H. Knight, *Risk, Uncertainty and Profit* (New York: Harper & Row, 1921); and George J. Stigler, *The Organization of Industry* (Homewood, Ill.: Irwin, 1968), Chapter 10.

[2] This is also said to occur in markets that have ultra-free entry (perfect contestability) (see Chapter 11). That conclusion is based on short-term models, which are debatable. Still, free entry could reduce excess market share.

Street,'' these various financial units are spread throughout the United States in the larger cities. They contain some of the sharpest, most energetic minds in the country, playing for very high stakes.

Three functions

Altogether, these financial units play three main kinds of roles: (1) *credit*—that is, the supplying of funds; (2) *counsel,* in the form of advice, connections, and support; and (3) *control,* by enforcing efficiency. We consider these three functions in turn.

Credit: The Supply of Capital.   Capital markets channel savings into investment by firms. The flow of funds is very large, and nearly all firms draw frequently on outside capital of various kinds, especially loans from banks and new issues of bonds and stocks. Firms also have internal funds available: profits plus depreciation from the firm's ''cash flow,'' which can be used for investment (or for dividends). In recent decades, the balance between internal and outside funds has fluctuated, but most firms must obtain substantial amounts of funds directly from capital markets.

Supplying capital funds is probably not the major role of capital markets for the larger mass of established firms. However, that role can be crucial for smaller, fast-growing firms, which need outside capital. The supervision that capital markets provide is also of cardinal importance.

Counsel: Advice, Connections, and Support.   Each firm exists in a set of banking and other relationships that connect the firm with its main advisers and sponsors.[3] This continuity and support provide a degree of direct supervision over company choices and help to determine the firm's future opportunities.

Control: Enforcing Efficiency.   Capital markets enforce efficiency in two ways. First, ''the stock market'' continually evaluates each firm's prospects and performance. Second, a company can be taken over if its behavior is especially deviant.

Capital markets as the control system

Evaluating firms is a continual process. Millions of investors repeatedly judge companies and compare them with other firms as they make numberless investment choices every day. Stock markets are the main locus for this evaluation, but bond markets and rating services also respond to company prospects. These markets are not perfect. They often misjudge the facts, run to fads and herdlike behavior, or even neglect whole industries or classes of firms. Moreover, professional, large-volume specialized traders usually have much better information than do the mass of ordinary investors.

Despite these defects, stock markets do conduct a widespread, rapid, continuing

---

[3] These include the firm's accountants, investment banker, underwriter, outside legal counsel, and advertising agency, as well as its banker.

process of evaluation that, since it reflects choices by investors among the whole array of firms, is comparative and realistic. The "insider" problem does not reduce the long-run efficiency of the outcome. All important information does eventually come out and influence the firm's stock price. Even if the use of inside information distorts the fairness of gains made during the process, the efficiency remains.

A *takeover* is the seizure of one firm by another (Subsection II.3 will give more details about takeovers). Takeovers occur when some outside firm or group believes that it can raise the firm's value well above its present market level. Not all takeovers are resisted by managers, but most are. Therefore the threat of a takeover often scares managers into efficient behavior. If they succeed in getting control, the new owners may make direct changes in behavior or in the officials themselves. Takeovers are the visible tip of the iceberg in the general market for corporate control.

The entire evaluation process is wide, including the infinitude of small trading deals as well as dramatic takeover attempts. The process is also *prospective:* it looks ahead, discounting each firm's future prospects into the current market value of its stock. Finally, it is *comprehensive,* reaching into every corporation to render continuing judgments about the quality of current and expected performance.

The evaluation process puts firms under pressure to perform as well as investors expect. Any serious managerial letup leads to a fall in the firm's stock price, which angers investors because it reduces their assets. And angry investors can threaten managers' jobs.

Capital markets do not perform their taskmaster role perfectly; firms can falter without stirring prompt reactions. But the process operates generally with enormous and comprehensive power, and the result is that capital market supervision enforces efficiency throughout the economy. This is perhaps the most important role of financial markets. Even if they somehow lost their other two roles (credit and counsel), the taskmaster role alone would make them the control system of capitalism.

2. Banking and Equity Markets

History.   The main types of financial units are commercial banks, investment banks, and brokerage firms. They can be combined, as they were in the United States before 1933 and still are in many countries.

Banking had become widespread in the United States by 1850, but mostly on a small local scale. After 1865, capital markets burst forth, on the wave of railroad and industrial expansion. The stock markets were unstable and often rigged, but they provided a growing supply of equity funds.[4] Large-scale financiers such as J. P. Morgan combined direct supervision and financing operations, and often reached in to control company policies in detail. By the 1890s, such operations were restructuring scores of industries via horizontal mergers. Deposit banking was also developing rapidly, often mingling with investment banking and brokerage activities in the same firm.[5]

---

[4] Davis R. Dewey, *Financial History of the United States* (New York: Longmans, Green, 1911).

[5] See Gerald C. Fischer, *American Banking Structure* (New York: Columbia University Press, 1968); and David A. Alhadeff, *Monopoly and Competition in Banking* (Berkeley: University of California Press, 1954). Combining the activities permitted abuses. The bank could use its advantages from inside information to manipulate stock prices and control company policies. The locus of responsibility was unclear, and other investors were often victimized.

Conditions were turbulent and "structure" was fluid. In 1900, a few major financiers (including Morgan and the Rockefellers) were dominant, but their position had begun to recede by 1920. Banks had proliferated to number 30,000; industry was more stable, so investment banking had less scope; and separate stock brokerage firms were developing. The stock craze of the 1920s fed partly on trickery within firms that combined banking, investment banking, and brokerage activities. Therefore the "Great Crash" of 1929 suggested an urgent need to separate these activities.

Under the Glass-Steagall Act of 1935, commercial banking, investment banking, and brokerage were rigidly divided, both from each other and from all nonfinancial operations. Commercial banking was stabilized and insulated in order to avoid bank failures. By the 1930s, half the states had prohibited branch banking; each bank was allowed only one office, in one location. This prevented most competition and new entry among banks.

Investment banking evolved into two main activities: underwriting of new stock and bond issues, and arranging mergers. After 1945, brokerage grew into a major industry because of the spread of stock ownership. Soon, however, "institutional investors"—insurance firms, pension funds, trust departments of banks, foundations—came to dominate trading.

Bank mergers during the 1950s stabilized and tightened structure even further. The 1960s brought a reversal toward more aggressive banking, and the lines between the financial sectors have grown increasingly blurred since then. Still, the basic separation of banks from other markets remains in force, and competition has risen strongly within each sector.

Investment banks and brokerage firms were deeply affected by the "go-go" stock market boom of 1964–1969. Merger activity grew hectic, much of it arranged by the leading investment banking firms. The rise in the volume of stock trading overloaded brokerage firms, many of which were operating by obsolete methods. The boom ended after 1969, but merger activity revived in the middle 1970s with a flow of takeovers, and it surged enormously in the 1980s (see the next section). The New York Stock Exchange was forced to abandon its rigid cartel of set brokers' fees in 1975. The resulting quantum rise in competition among brokers brought the standard benefits of lower rates and greater efficiency—with no clear loss of profitability. Financial markets are now more fluid and competitive than during the 1935–1965 period of rigidity. Yet there are still sizable imperfections in banking relationships.

Banking.   Commercial banks specialize in making loans, transferring money, and supervising clients. The core of banking and its profits is in loans to businesses, especially to the larger, "better" clients. Behind the small-scale "retailing" operations at the cashier's window, the banks mainly deal in large "wholesale" corporate loans and services, nursing along their core of "best" clients. The banks seek to maximize profits by managing a set of assets and liabilities.

All this helps to define that basic unit, "the banking market." The three main levels of the banking market—local, regional, and national—are usually overlapping and hard to separate. Most significant banks operate in two of them; the larger ones are in all three. Defining the "true" market is not easy. (Example: A leading Chicago bank operates in the Chicago "market," the Midwest "market," and the national

TABLE 8.1 Banking Concentration in Selected U.S. Cities, 1979

		PERCENT OF DEPOSITS HELD BY			
METROPOLITAN AREA	TOTAL DEPOSITS ($ BILLION)	LARGEST BANK	SECOND LARGEST BANK	THIRD LARGEST BANK	LARGEST THREE BANKS
Largest Seven					
New York	$132.8	14.1%	14.0%	11.6%	39.7%
Chicago	51.2	19.4	15.8	6.1	41.3
Los Angeles	36.3	27.7	20.0	12.8	60.5
San Francisco	32.5	46.3	19.2	12.1	77.6
Detroit	21.5	26.7	14.2	14.0	54.9
Philadelphia	19.9	18.0	12.7	11.2	41.9
Boston	12.0	30.6	11.1	10.4	52.1
Others					
Phoenix, Arizona	6.2	40.0	26.7	17.4	84.1
Portland, Oregon	5.6	29.9	27.0	8.9	65.8
Columbus, Ohio	4.1	37.0	24.1	21.4	82.5
Hartford, Connecticut	2.9	42.0	37.7	4.7	84.4
Nashville, Tennessee	4.1	25.6	23.4	19.9	68.9

SOURCE: Federal Deposit Insurance Corporation, *Summary of Deposits in All Commercial and Mutual Savings Banks* (Washington, D.C.: Government Printing Office, June 30, 1979).

"market," competing for big clients against New York, San Francisco, and Detroit banks, among others.)

Yet reasonable estimates are often possible because there are fairly complete and accurate data about banking structure. The national shares of all banks are small and need not be listed in detail. Local bank markets, by contrast, tend toward tight oligopoly. Seven large urban banking centers do about 35 percent of the volume of all U.S. banking, but the mass of medium and small firms deal in hundreds of genuinely small local banking markets. The larger banking markets are moderate to tight oligopolies, while most of the smaller markets have tighter structure. Table 8.1 shows some of these patterns.

Barriers to entry in banking markets are high. Entrants must obtain a state and/ or federal charter, and charters for new banks are given sparingly. The entrant must make out a positive case that the area is "underbanked." The established banks, of course, will argue the contrary. Furthermore, in many states, branching into new areas is prohibited or limited.

Banking structure stabilized after the 1930s, though the 1950s bank merger wave raised concentration (the long names of many leading banks reflect their merger history). Since 1960, the average degree of concentration has declined.

Banking Relationships: The Replication Hypothesis.   The ties between banks and their prime clients can be important. Banks prefer secure, lucrative clients to risky, low-profit ones, so their relationships with the "better risks" involve a degree of mutual reliance. In seeking "good risks," banks inevitably offer favorable terms to the more attractive clients.

Yet there is circularity: the favorable terms—longer lines of credit at lower interest rates—themselves improve the security, profitability, and prospects of the client firms. Banking factors can therefore both reinforce and create disparities in market position and profitability. Getting good banker support is often critical to founding or expanding a firm, to entering a market, or to adopting a strategy against rivals; it is equally critical to *preventing* any of these. Moreover, the terms themselves can determine the outcome in advance.

This would be academic if capital markets were perfect. All seekers of funds would be fully evaluated by many alternative suppliers, and capital sources would be irrelevant to market position.

But suppose that banking is a monopoly. The lone banker is a lender to the dominant firm and at the same time, the only source of capital for smaller firms or possible entrants. The bank's support reinforces the monopoly firm's power, so its degree of risk is less. Meanwhile, the monopoly bank will be reluctant to lend funds to any competitor of the dominant firm because if the smaller firm or new entrant should succeed, it will cut into the leading firm's profitability and thereby threaten the bank's own profit-security results on its loans.

Banking monopoly therefore will tend to maintain market power in other markets and to deter lesser firms and entrants. It will also create corresponding gains for bankers from arranging mergers between two or more competing firms. Tight banking market structure would be sufficient to create tight industrial structure even if all other causes were absent.

More precisely: *Banking structure tends to replicate itself throughout other markets.* For competition to increase, additional support must be available from capital suppliers. To analyze industry in isolation from finance is to ignore this basic determinant.

How tight are actual banking relationships? Data and research are scanty because the matter is sensitive to both banks and their clients. Also, banking-client relationships are more a matter of informal usage than of concrete, recorded numbers; facts on them are not collected or published by any official agency. Yet by a variety of indications, we know that banking relationships are usually strong and stable. Leading banks tend to be allied with the leading firms in their markets. Within this general pattern, there are clusters of firms around certain banking groups, such as the descendants of the early Rockefeller and Morgan interests. The normal pattern for firms is a single, enduring banking relationship.[6]

The link is two-sided, with advantages for both the bank and the firm. The firm gets credit in larger amounts and at lower interest costs than it would otherwise. It also gets valuable advice and information from the bank, plus a degree of potential support against future stresses. On its part, the bank minimizes the costs of getting information and making decisions, which would be substantial with new, unfamiliar customers. It also gains continuity and security for its operations. Once formed, a close banking relationship is hard to break into, for the outsider bank must offer much better interest rates and better counsel as well. Such intrusions have become more frequent since the 1960–1965 period, but they still face strong resistance.

[6] This was shown in the Patman hearings, Committee on Banking and Currency, House of Representatives, 90th Congress, 1st Session, *Control of Commercial Banks and Interlocks among Financial Institutions* (Washington, D.C.: U.S. Government Printing Office, 1967).

The Supply of Capital.   Evidently U.S. banking markets differ from the model of "perfect" capital markets, but they are not highly monopolistic. The trend since 1960 is toward more competition, especially in the largest cities. Yet a large share of local and regional banking still occurs under conditions of oligopoly.

How might this affect the supply of capital? Mainly by providing more funds at lower interest rates to firms with the "best" banking relationships. Studies of actual interest rates show that they are inversely related to the size of borrower.[7] Partly this reflects the lower risks and transaction costs of loans to large firms. Yet, again, there is circularity, because the banking relationship itself lowers the risks and transaction costs. Therefore some of the difference in interest rates on loans reflects imperfections in the capital markets. One more cause of the difference is the monopsony power of the larger client firms, which enables them to extract favorable terms from the banks. This result, like the others, could not occur if capital markets were perfect.

International Comparisons.   There are three main points of difference between U.S. and foreign capital markets: (1) banking structure, (2) banking relationships, and (3) stock markets.

1. **Banking structure** is tighter in other industrial economies. In Britain, France, Germany, Switzerland, Japan, Italy, Sweden, and other countries, there are fewer dominant banks, with higher shares.[8] There are usually only three or four truly national banks in each country. Structure has been relatively stable for several decades, with little turnover or decline in concentration. Entry of new banks is generally limited, much as it is in the United States, but behavior is less aggressively competitive than in the United States. In 1992, the move toward greater European integration may increase competition, but that is not assured. Though most leading French and Italian banks are state owned, this appears to make little difference in the cooperative behavior.

2. **Banking relationships** are also tighter abroad. Banks are commonly permitted to hold shares in industrial firms. Alternatively, they often informally assume a degree of control that goes far beyond U.S. patterns. (Example: Deutsche Bank, the largest bank in Germany, owns 25 percent or more of the stock in firms in utility, automobile, shipping, retailing, construction, machinery, and sugar markets. Its officers also hold chairmanships or vice chairmanships in eleven other firms spread among major industries.) Banks frequently perform stock brokerage as well as banking and "merchant banking" functions.

Such direct connections usually exert closer effects than the more informal U.S. relationships. They often put bankers in direct control over company policies and executive selection. They also reduce some competition in industrial markets to little more than extensions of conflicts among the parent banks.

3. **Stock markets** everywhere tend to enforce efficiency through their taskmaster role. Most do less well in providing fairness because "insider" problems tend to bias the gains toward insiders and professional investors. Foreign stock markets

---

[7] See, among others, Donald P. Jacobs, *Business Loan Costs and Bank Market Structure* (New York: National Bureau of Economic Research, 1971).

[8] See David A. Alhadeff, *Competition and Controls in Banking: A Study of the Regulation of Bank Competition in Italy, France and England* (Berkeley: University of California Press, 1968); and R. L. Sayers, ed., *Banking in Western Europe* (London: Macmillan, 1962).

have generally had a higher degree of such abuses and defects, though the massive insider fraud during 1983–1987 in U.S. stock markets was on a comparable scale. Even so, manipulations are more common abroad than in the United States; corners, contrived price movements, fraud, and other abuses are frequent. The use of insider information is routine. There is little public limit on these imperfections, partly because shareholdings are narrower than in the United States.

To sum up, U.S. capital markets are generally competitive, but some parts of them contain significant degrees of market power.

II. MERGERS

Mergers have often been blamed for causing concentration. They certainly did so in the first great merger wave of 1897–1901, and they may have added to concentration during the later merger waves of the 1920s and 1960s. They surely did so again during the immense 1980s merger wave, which outstripped the earlier ones by far.

But the question is one of degree. How large have the effects been compared to the other causes and to the trend in concentration? To assess the research findings, we must start with the basic characteristics of mergers.

In the market for corporate control, whole companies are bought and sold. The main result is mergers, which combine two or more firms into one. The firms may differ in size, with one absorbing the other. The merger may occur amicably, or under hostility, as most takeovers do. And the merger may affect competition.

Mergers occur by the thousands each year, but they are only a small fraction of the endless wheeling and dealing in the market for corporate assets. Perhaps ten mergers are considered and started for every one that is actually accomplished.

Mergers are of three main kinds: horizontal, vertical, and conglomerate, as illustrated in Figure 8.1. Each poses distinctive issues; each may provide greater

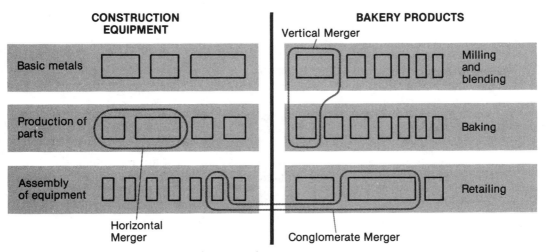

Figure 8.1.   The three main types of mergers.

efficiency and/or reduce competition. Horizontal mergers are the main issue here because they do reduce competition directly.

In covering these issues, we first consider the motives for mergers, and then their actual patterns. Takeovers are discussed next, followed by the "failing firm" problem. Finally, we look at the effects of mergers.

1.   Motives for Mergers

The main underlying motive for mergers is, of course, to gain profits.[9] Firm A believes it can gain more from buying firm B than the price it will have to pay. Mergers may raise profits in several ways. They may also serve other managerial objectives (such as the pursuit of sheer bigness, discussed in Chapter 10). The three main reasons for mergers are market power and profits, technical economies, and pecuniary economies. A particular merger may fit one or all of these categories.

Straight market power and profits

If the firm that results from a merger has more market power, it can achieve higher profitability. **Horizontal** mergers invariably raise market power, for by definition they eliminate side-by-side competition between the two firms. The effect may be small or large, depending on the two firms' market shares and on other conditions of the market. **Vertical** mergers tie together firms in the chain of production. Whether they can increase market power is a matter of debate (to be analyzed in Chapter 15). For now, simply note that any such increase would also raise profitability.

A **conglomerate** merger is a more subtle matter. It joins two unrelated activities, such as bulldozers and books or rugs and steel. It may somehow enlarge the scope of the new combined firm's strategies beyond what the two firms could do before merging. Yet pure conglomerate mergers do not change the structure of either market directly, so a purist can argue that no increase in market power results.

Technical economies

Several kinds of technical economies may be realized by merger. One is **economies of scale,** which horizontal mergers may provide if the merging firms were both below the minimum efficient scale. Economies of scale were introduced in Chapter 2; Chapter 10 goes into details.

A second is **vertical economies,** gained by joining firms at two levels of production. The classic instance is combining iron and steel operations so that pig iron and steel ingots can be sent on to the next processing level directly without losing heat. Chapter 15 treats these issues. A third class, **economies of diversification,** may arise from conglomerate mergers. The whole firm may be stabilized by combining diverse activities, rather than having "all eggs in one basket." The activities' fluctuations will tend to even each other out, making total operations less risky. Also, financial guidance and flows may be more efficient in diversified firms. In addition, it is

---

[9] See David J. Ravenscraft and F. M. Scherer, *Mergers, Sell-offs, and Economic Efficiency* (Washington, D.C.: Brookings Institution, 1987).

claimed that "synergy" results from interactions among different technologies and managers within a conglomerate. (Chapter 10 returns to this.)

The **net gains from merger** are the only relevant point in judging the social contribution of mergers. A merger is but one of three main ways to achieve technical economies. The other two are internal growth and long-term contracts. A firm that chooses **internal growth,** invests its funds to create new capacity rather than buying an existing company. It is true that mergers are quicker than setting up a new unit. It is also true that they tend to reduce competition. Both features can make managers prefer them. Yet nearly any true technical economy available through merger can also be achieved by internal growth (that is, setting up a new firm). In fact, the net technical gain from merger is usually small, zero, or even negative.

Long-term contracts among firms can be, and are, arranged to bring about almost any result, up to extremely close coordination by the contracting firms. Vertical economies, in particular, can often be realized by thorough twenty- or thirty-year supply contracts, which provide for complete security and precision of supplies. In comparison, the net gains from merger may be small or nil.

Pecuniary economies

Pecuniary economies provide money benefits without improving the use of real resources. Mergers result in several main kinds of these economies.

First, the merged firm may be able to enforce lower prices for the inputs it buys. (Example: ITT's rule of thumb in the 1960s was that it could expect to reduce costs by 20 percent just from buying inputs more effectively after acquiring a firm. Whether it always achieved this savings is another matter!)

Second, tax laws and accounting rules may raise the profitability of mergers. Firms are permitted to pool the losses and profits of all their activities; taxes must be paid only on the net total profits. Thus profitable firm X can acquire losing firm Y, pool its original profits on the X activities with the losses on the Y activities, and end up paying no profits tax at all. The losses therefore have a positive value to firm X, even though no technical economies are realized. These and other tax provisions can make mergers profitable even when they yield no technical benefits.

Third, the merger may give "promotional" advantages. (Example: Procter & Gamble bought Clorox in the 1950s, but was forced to divest itself of this company in 1968 after the FTC decided, and the Supreme Court affirmed, that P&G's advertising power would strongly assist Clorox, which had over 50 percent of the bleach market, to hold or increase its market power. The merger would have reduced competition without giving technical benefits.) If marketing power (via advertising, sales networks, and other promotional devices) is transferable, then pecuniary gains result. (This issue is discussed in Chapter 16.)

Besides pure mergers between two freestanding firms, there is much *divestiture* (selling off) of branches by firms. It is a way to dispose of a weak operation or prune back the firm. Sometimes the sold unit is built up by its new owners. Such divestiture is part of the normal functioning of capital markets. Indeed, about half of asset exchanges during 1970–1985 were divestitures. In large part it reflected a disposal of thousands of dubious acquisitions made during the conglomerate wave of 1964–

1969. Yet it also reflected a basic shift toward freer pruning of marginal divisions as the interest in diversification faded.

2.   Actual Merger Patterns

Though mergers are about as ancient as business activity itself, we shall focus on those of the last century. There have been four main waves, the last of which is continuing at this writing.

Many large railroad and industrial firms were formed by mergers between 1850 and 1890. Indeed, the early stock markets from 1870 to 1900 were often dominated by spectacular struggles, alliances, and mergers among the "robber barons" of railroads, steel, shipping, oil, meat, and other companies.

Yet the first mass of large "modern" corporations came out of the "trust movement" that peaked in 1897–1901 (see Figure 8.2). This wave of horizontal mergers, which sometimes united scores of competitors at one stroke, formed near-monopolies in a variety of big and little industries. In 1904, John Moody counted over 300

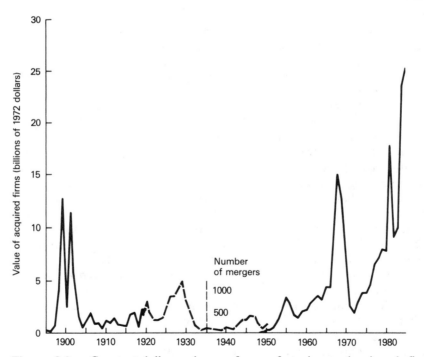

Figure 8.2.   Constant-dollar volume of manufacturing and mineral firm acquisitions, 1895–1985.

Note: Data on the value of manufacturing and mineral company acquisitions are not available for the years 1921–47. The broken line reflects the number of acquisitions in those years.

SOURCE: Ravenscraft and Scherer, *Mergers, Sell-offs, and Economic Efficiency,* The Brookings Institution, Washington, D.C., 1987, p. 21.

such dominant firms.[10] Large aggregate concentration in the economy emerged together with high market shares in individual industries.

Some of this activity reflected the claim that modern industry required the stability that only dominant firms could give. Actually, though, many mergers were instigated by promoters for the purpose of creating high fees and paper gains from "watered" stock. The merger fever was cooled by Theodore Roosevelt's antitrust actions and by a slump in the stock market. Many of the new corporations faded quickly because of internal dissension, inefficiency, or entry by new firms, as Chapter 4 noted.[11] Others persisted in much the same market position for decades or even to the present. Parallel merger waves in Canada, Britain, and elsewhere also created many lasting dominant firms. Yet because collusion was legal in those countries, there was less incentive for firms to merge, so the U.S. wave went further than the others.

There have been three subsequent merger waves in the United States—in the 1920s, the 1960s, and the 1980s. Almost invariably, merger activity rises in a bull market and drops in a bear market. The 1920s wave included a large volume of shaky utility mergers, which made the boom especially unstable. Many horizontal mergers also occurred among secondary firms in industrial markets. This tended to tighten the oligopoly structure of many industries. The shift in industrial structure was not reversed by the subsequent stock market collapse, the Great Depression, or World War II.

Another long rise in mergers reached a peak in the "go-go" boom of 1964–1969. About four-fifths of the mergers in this period were classified as "conglomerate" by the FTC staff. As Table 8.2 shows, these divided further into "product extension," "market extension," and "pure" conglomerate mergers. A product extension merger occurs when firm X adds a product related to its existing product line by buying up firm Y. The concept of a "product line" is not always precise, but in most industries it is fairly clear what a "full line" includes. This type of merger is common in food products and in heavier industry. A market extension merger combines two firms selling the same physical product in different *geographical* markets.

"Pure" conglomerate mergers have—in principle—none of these connections, nor are there any other technical relationships among the activities of the merged firms. They are the "Others" in Table 8.2. In practice, however, there are usually some overlaps among the activities, such as a similar process of production or convergent research trends. Some mergers have large horizontal, vertical, *and* conglomerate elements. The official classifications of mergers should not be trusted too literally. Yet the main patterns are clear enough. Most recent mergers are mainly conglomerate, and this trend is likely to continue.

---

[10] Among the newly merged firms were International Harvester, American Sugar Company, General Electric Company, American Can Company, and U.S. Steel Corporation. Moody's survey is required reading for students of the subject; see his *The Truth about the Trusts* (Chicago: Moody Publishing, 1904); another basic source is Ralph L. Nelson, *Merger Movements in American Industry, 1895–1956* (Princeton, N.J.: Princeton University Press, 1959). For a recent affirmation that this merger wave created the twentieth-century structure of U.S. industry, see Naomi Lamoreaux, *The Great Merger Movement in American Business, 1895–1904* (New York: Cambridge University Press, 1985).

[11] For a lively textbook instance, see Alfred S. Eichner, *The Emergence of Oligopoly: Sugar Refining as a Case Study* (New York: Columbia University Press, 1971); see also William Z. Ripley, ed., *Trusts, Pools and Corporations*, rev. ed. (Boston: Ginn, 1916); and Lamoreaux, *The Great Merger Movement in American Business, 1895–1904.*

TABLE 8.2 Large Acquisitions in Manufacturing and Mining by Type of Acquisition: 1948–1978 and 1967–1978 Compared

TYPE OF ACQUISITION	ASSETS[a] ($ MILLIONS)		PERCENT[b]	
	1948–1978	1967–1978	1948–1978	1967–1978
Horizontal	$ 18,292.0	$12,739.4	16.8%	15.7%
Vertical	10,094.0	5,651.2	9.2	7.0
Conglomerate	80,604.7	62,499.2	74.0	77.3
Product extension	36,729.3	25,731.5	33.7	31.8
Market extension	6,379.9	3,989.5	5.8	5.0
Other	37,495.5	32,778.2	34.4	40.5
Total	108,990.7	80,889.8	100.0	100.0

[a] Acquired firms with assets of $10 million or more.
[b] Sums may not add up to 100 because of rounding.
SOURCE: Bureau of Economics, Federal Trade Commission.
Note: Not included in above tabulations are companies for which data were not publicly available. There were 522 such companies with assets of $13,784.1 million for the period 1948–1978; and 336 companies with assets of $9,488.3 million for the period 1967–1978.

TABLE 8.3 U.S. Merger and Divestiture Activity, 1979–1987 ($1 million or more)

	NUMBER OF TRANSACTIONS	VALUE ($ BILLION)	VALUE IN 1972 DOLLARS ($ BILLION)
1979	1,529	34.2	19.7
1980	1,565	33.0	16.8
1981	2,326	67.3	31.0
1982	2,296	60.4	26.2
1983	2,387	52.6	22.1
1984	3,158	126.0	50.7
1985	3,428	145.4	56.1
1986	4,323	204.4	78.0
1987	3,701	167.5	60.9
1988	3,304	183.0	63.9

Note: A transaction must involve a U.S. company and must be valued at $1 million or more. Partial acquisitions of 5 percent or more of a company's capital stock are included if the payments are $1 million or more. Divestitures of subsidiary units are also included on this basis. Real property sales and transfers are excluded. Where price data of a transaction have not been revealed, the transaction is included if it is believed to meet the price threshold.
SOURCES: From date in *Mergers and Acquisitions,* January–February 1989; and *Statistical Abstract of the United States, 1988* (Washington, D.C.: U.S. Government Printing Office, 1988), p. 450.

The most recent merger boom—the fourth great wave—is outlined in Table 8.3 and Figure 8.2. The totals differ somewhat from those in Figure 8.2 because these 1979–1988 data include leveraged buyouts. The boom peaked in 1986 in real terms, although the volume of activity has remained nearly triple the pre-1984 levels.

Antitrust policies toward mergers explain some of the shift to conglomerate mergers. A merger loophole in the Clayton Act, which remained unclosed until 1950, permitted almost any merger, even if it raised market power. Yet after 1920 most of the leading dominant firms were informally on notice that any horizontal mergers would trigger antitrust action.[12] Therefore the 1920s mergers were mainly by secondary firms, not dominant ones. The Cellar-Kefauver Act of 1950 closed the loophole, but it was gradually applied, beginning only in 1958 and reaching strict limits with the Von's Grocery decision in 1966.[13] Until 1980, most significant horizontal mergers, and many vertical ones as well, were likely to be challenged and prevented in the courts (see Chapter 19).[14] The result was that most merger activity was channeled into the conglomerate category.

Public distrust of horizontal and vertical mergers has been slight in most other countries. In fact, governments frequently promote horizontal mergers to "strengthen" firms against foreign competitors. Accordingly, horizontal mergers are normally a large share of mergers abroad. Generally, foreign governments influence the forms and terms of major mergers among their home companies. Before 1980, U.S. government policies were usually (1) more regular, with definite guidelines about the acceptable range of mergers; and (2) at arm's length rather than closely involved in the design of the merger. Since then, there has been a sharp shift toward minimal U.S. antitrust restrictions on mergers (see Chapter 19).

The volume of mergers abroad has been large, parallel to the U.S. waves in the 1960s and 1980s. From 1956 to 1972, one-fourth of the growth of large British firms was by merger,[15] and French and Japanese patterns were similar. The 1980s have brought a merger boom to Britain.

3. Takeovers

Out of the ongoing stream of mergers and issues, two categories require special analysis: takeovers and mergers that fail.

In a takeover, one firm seizes another against its managers' will. The acquiring

---

[12] These included especially the U.S. Steel Corporation, the Standard Oil successor companies, American Tobacco Company, International Harvester Company, the top meat-packing firms, American Sugar Company, Corn Products Company, and American Can Company—all of which had undergone antitrust action of some kind. Still other dominant firms were also aware of the hazards of horizontal mergers.

[13] The main decisions involved the proposed mergers between Bethlehem Steel and Youngstown Sheet and Tube in 1958; Brown Shoe and Kinney in 1962; and Von's and Shopping Bag grocery firms in Los Angeles in 1966. The cases are *U.S.* v. *Bethlehem Steel Corp.*, 168 F. Supp. 576 (S. D. N.Y. 1958); *Brown Shoe Co.* v. *U.S.*, 370 U.S. 294 (1962); and *U.S.* v. *Von's Grocery Co.*, 384 U.S. 270 (1966).

[14] Horizontal mergers combining over 10 percent of the market were usually challenged during the period 1962–1981. Then Reagan officials relaxed the limits to permit mergers that would give the resulting firm up to 50 percent of the market. Vertical mergers combining approximately 10 percent at both levels were usually challenged during the period 1962–1981, but again, after 1981, the limits were raised sharply, to about 60 percent. The wisdom of these rules depends on the content of the rest of the book.

[15] S. Aaronovitch and Malcolm C. Sawyer, "Mergers, Growth and Concentration," *Oxford Economic Papers,* 27 (March 1975), 136–55.

firm makes a sudden "tender offer" to buy the target firm's stock at a price well above the going price. If it gains at least 51 percent of the stock, the target firm is taken over and absorbed into the acquiring firm.

Takeovers often occur when a firm is thought to be managing its assets so poorly that its stock price is "low" and a new owner could gain better returns and raise the stock price. Frequently, though, a firm's stock is low simply because investors' judgments are too pessimistic. In either case, the firm is seen as a bargain by at least one other firm.

The extent of takeovers cannot be known exactly, for there are all degrees of surprise, stress, and force. Many mergers are partially takeovers. Others that seem amicable are in fact takeovers; the target firm has quietly caved in ahead of time. Even a seemingly "pure" takeover (with a great public struggle) may be mainly a sporting effort by the target firm's managers to make the acquiring firm raise its tender offer.

The Process.   Figure 8.3 illustrates the common sequence of events in a take-over. At first firm B's stock price is "low" for some reason—say, about $20 per share. Firm A may believe that firm B is "really" worth about $40 per share on the basis of the assets it holds, its products and resources, and so on. But it will try to buy firm B at a lower price because paying $40 per share for it would give firm A no room to make capital gains. Large investors will probably have noted any sharp disparity between stock price and company value, and their purchases may have kept the stock price from going even lower. These *arbitragers* tend to close gaps in market values, and they often leap into takeover battles, betting on the likely winners.

Firm A's price offer (the price it bids in its "tender offer") is critical. If it is too low, investors (including the arbitragers) won't pledge their shares, and perhaps

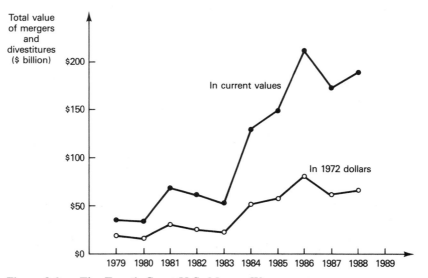

Figure 8.3.   The Fourth Great U.S. Merger Wave

SOURCES: *Mergers and Acquisitions,* January–February, 1989; and *Statistical Abstract of the United States, 1988* (Washington, D.C.: U.S. Government Printing Office, 1988), p. 450.

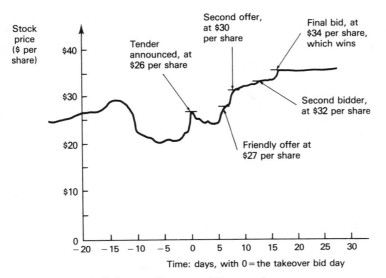

Figure 8.4.   A Takeover Sequence Illustrated

another buyer will appear and succeed with a higher bid. A higher bid will raise the chances of capturing firm B, but will also sacrifice much of the capital gains that firm A hopes to make.

So the bid price is intensively studied and debated within firm A, often up to the last minute. Commonly, the bid price is 20 to 30 percent above the current market price: high enough to induce a strong response, but low enough to allow for gains. Firm A may approach firm B openly and amicably, in hope of a friendly merger, or it may prepare a trap in secrecy.

Assuming secret preparation, the tender offer is sprung, often with great fanfare designed to stir shareholders in firm B to pledge their shares immediately. Firm B typically fights back with its own game plan. The "low" price of its stock will have marked the firm as a takeover candidate, warning its managers of the need to make the company perform better and to prepare for a siege.

A period of battle then ensues. Because firm B's managers fear for their jobs, they will commonly resist the offer by all possible means, including publicity, lawsuits against firm A, inducing politicians to act for them, and directly urging the largest shareholders to hold onto their shares. Firm B will assert that its own plans will soon cause the share price to rise even further, while it portrays firm A as irresponsible, unable to finance the purchase, dangerous to workers' and local interests, and so on. Firm B will also seek to get government agencies to stop the takeover.

The struggle often turns spectacular, and it may force firm A to raise its offer. To that extent, firm B's managers, by counterattacking, have benefited the stockholders as well as themselves. Firm B's managers may seek a "white knight," another, friendlier merger partner. Or one or more other suitors for firm B may emerge and a bidding war may ensue.

Figure 8.4 illustrates the stock price movements. Firm B's stock price jumps up toward the tender offer price of $26, but then sags as the company seems to be staving off the takeover. Firm B's managers arrange a friendly takeover at $27, which stirs firm A to offer $30. Arbitragers bid the price up to that level on the market, but then another bidder enters at $32. Firm A agonizes over whether to raise its offer, and decides to go up to $34. It wins firm B at that price, but it has paid away most of the capital gain it had hoped for.

The Efficiency Effects of Takeovers.   As is so often the case, the market process brings price closer into line with value. Others (arbitragers and investors) share the gains that firm A sought. In fact, firm A's own stock price may dwindle after the merger; that is the common pattern, as Figure 8.5 indicates. The target company often proves less valuable than the acquirer thought and/or the takeover battle turned out to be more expensive. Thus, although takeovers may benefit the economy by helping to enforce corporate efficiency, they often harm the firms that undertake them. As for the target firm, even if it manages to elude being taken over, it often undergoes severe trauma, leading it to tighten its management and improve its innovativeness.

The outcome of each battle depends on many factors, but *the direct effect of takeovers is usually to improve efficiency.* The new management changes officers, recasts policies, and infuses new resources.

Yet there may be large economic and social costs. The target management often adopts self-destructive policies to deter the acquiring firm, such as incurring heavy new debt to make the takeover less attractive. By 1988–1989, such effects had created alarm. The new, victorious owners may also adopt harmful policies, such as attempting to change firm B too rapidly or harshly, or depleting its resources for other purposes. Small shareholders may lose by being stampeded into unwise decisions based on poor information during the battle. And the social effects may be severe if the new absentee owners decide to close whole plants without taking account of local interests.

Finally, the whole takeover process absorbs real resources, both financial and managerial, on both sides of the battle. Lengthy struggles often preoccupy managers for months, while their companies' affairs deteriorate. And during the 1980s, the volume of credit tied up in many simultaneous takeover attempts has often been scores of billions of dollars, possibly crowding out more socially valuable investments.

These costs are not easy to assess and are often exaggerated. They need to be separated out and weighed against the benefits from (1) the direct rise in efficiency from a takeover and (2) the indirect improvements stimulated by the fear of becoming a takeover target.

4.   Mergers That Fail

No merging partners intend to create failure, of course, but many of them do. The business press reports mercilessly on the many mergers that fail. Often these mergers were poorly planned, or were done merely to enlarge the company so as to please top managers' egos. Many times the expected "synergies" do not occur, or worse, the management styles of the two corporate partners conflict.

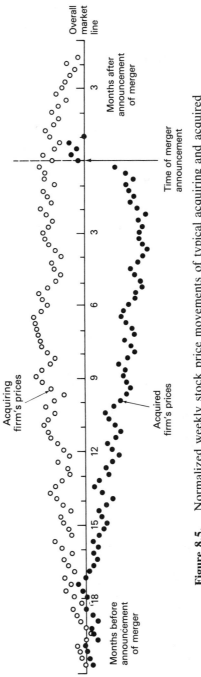

Figure 8.5. Normalized weekly stock price movements of typical acquiring and acquired firms in time period surrounding the merger announcement.

SOURCE: Ravenscraft and Scherer, *Mergers, Sell-offs, and Economic Efficiency.* Washington, D.C., Brookings Institution, 1987, p.4.

The merger of the Pennsylvania and New York Central railroads showed perhaps the most striking confusions and failures of any modern merger. The two sides' officials and workers were involved in virtually open warfare at times, and on one notorious occasion the Penn-Central entirely lost an entire freight train. The Penn-Central bankruptcy in 1970 forced the combining and rebuilding of many eastern railroads in the Conrail Corporation.

Another celebrated instance was the merger of Republic Steel (the third largest U.S. steel company) and Youngstown Sheet & Tube (sixth largest, owned by LTV Corporation) in 1982. Despite promises of $300 million savings in yearly efficiencies from the merger, the actual result was confusion, little coordination, and finally bankruptcy after several years.

Current failed mergers are frequently listed in *Fortune, Business Week,* and the *Wall Street Journal.*

Each merger is, in fact, an experiment, which may fail. Therefore economists read the merger literature with scepticism and amusement.

5.   The Effects of Mergers

What is perhaps the most thorough recent study covers the whole range of merger activity from 1950 to 1977.[16] It found that "operating efficiency fell on average following merger" significantly, though not sharply.[17] Indeed, the purely financial returns to the merging companies were not very good: ". . . the average acquisition, if not downright unprofitable, was not highly profitable."[18]

Moreover, the disciplining effect on management does not show through powerfully.[19] Most acquired firms were already well managed, not sorely in need of improvement. The hoped-for "synergies" typically did not develop, and the improved funding from the "internal capital market" within conglomerate firms did not emerge strongly.

Ravenscraft and Scherer find, in fact, that most of the conventional justifications for mergers did not operate strongly during the 1950–1977 period. Many mergers seemed to reflect "empire-building" urges rather than clear efficiencies. The failure of many of the mergers of the 1960s resulted in the massive divestitures of the 1970s, though some merger partners did manage to consolidate and focus their operations into efficient firms.

The 1980s mergers have involved less conglomerate activity. The horizontal mergers and takeovers of this period may suffer less chaos than befell the 1960s conglomerate mergers. The direct and indirect benefits of takeovers may be rather limited, however, and some of the horizontal mergers have already failed.[20]

---

[16] Ravenscraft and Scherer, *Mergers, Sell-offs, and Economic Efficiency.* Another extensive study is Dennis C. Mueller, *The Determinants and Effects of Mergers,* (Cambridge, Mass.: Oelgeschlager, Gunn & Hain, 1980).

[17] Ravenscraft and Scherer, *Mergers, Sell-offs, and Economic Efficiency,* pp. 195–204.

[18] Ravenscraft and Scherer, *Mergers, Sell-offs, and Economic Efficiency,* pp. 204–207.

[19] Ravenscraft and Scherer, *Mergers, Sell-offs, and Economic Efficiency,* pp. 210–15.

[20] Thus Republic Steel was permitted to merge with Jones and Laughlin in 1983, even though the companies had combined market shares above 40 percent in some specialty steel markets. The merger partners promised $300 million yearly in economies, but the new firm was in bankruptcy within three years.

Leveraged buyouts (LBOs, for short) have become important, as part of the new use of low-quality debt instruments (sometimes called "junk bonds") to finance the takeover of large firms. A group of managers, or an outside firm, issues large volumes of new junk bonds to raise the funds to buy the company. The bought-out company then has high leverage (the ratio of debt to equity capital), and it must cover the high yearly interest costs of those bonds. By 1988–89 there was intense concern about the burden of those costs on the bought-out firms, with the fear that the financial weight would cause them to fail more quickly under business fluctuations.[21]

Are LBOs an economic threat or a boon to efficiency and growth? The net social balance between gains and losses is not yet clear. The losses would be the increased financial risk and possible failures of such burdened companies, which could lead to closures and unemployment. The main possible gains were from the increased efficiency which the threat of an LBO would induce in company managements. As of 1989 the balance of effects was controversial; but the costs were probably not small.[22]

Mergers and Concentration.   There is, unfortunately, little systematic evidence on concentration from the 1980s merger wave. Certain industries have been strongly affected by mergers, notably airlines: a 1985–1987 series of mergers raised the largest eight airlines' combined share of industry traffic from 76 to 91 percent. Furthermore, it created single-firm dominance in many large-city airline markets, where competition used to be centered.

Altogether, the 1980s mergers have probably raised concentration ratios (and equivalent HHI values) by 2 or 3 percentage points. This has not sharply reduced the degree of competition in the entire economy because other forces have been at work, including growth, random processes, and public policies. Some markets even experienced further widening with the rise in imports and other international factors. Still, the merger impact has been significant and, in some cases, strong.

III. OTHER DETERMINANTS OF STRUCTURE

We now turn to several *processes* that may shape market structure.

1. Life Cycles

The most general life cycle involves a decline in market power as the industry evolves. No comprehensive or sophisticated study of this has yet been done, but many—perhaps most—markets do fit this pattern, at least approximately. The cases vary in (1) the original degree of monopoly and (2) the rate of decline in concentration as time passes. Also, odd departures can occur: a public policy that reaches in to

---

[21] With higher leverage, the yearly interest payments are higher. That exposes the firm to greater likelihoods of being unable to cover those payments, with bankruptcy as one result.

[22] A study circulated in 1989 by Kohlberg Kravis Roberts & Co., a leading LBO firm, described the benefits as higher employment, increased research-and-development expenditures, higher tax volumes for the government, higher capital spending, and higher company resistance to instability. KKR's LBO's include Beatrice Companies, Safeway Stores, and the $25 billion purchase of RJR Nabisco in 1989.

increase or reduce monopoly, or a large merger that interrupts the decline in concentration. Finally, some industries trace out the opposite trend (such as the U.S. automobile industry during 1900–1960) or avoid erosion for long periods. The life cycle is more a tendency than a law or a rule.

Among "utilities," though, the life cycle is more definite.[23] Most utilities go through four stages: (1) birth, (2) rapid growth, (3) consolidation, and (4) reversion from "natural monopoly" conditions back toward the possibility of competition. The natural-monopoly conditions hold only during stage 2 and the first part of stage 3, and even then they may cover only part of the activities in "the industry." The utility firm usually tries to extend its monopoly franchise to the whole sector and to hold onto the franchise into stage 4. A few utilities remain in stage 3—examples are city water supply and transit.

Chapter 4, at Table 4.10, showed the stages for many utility industries. The utility life cycle is clearer and more uniform than the cycle in other markets. The cost basis for monopoly is genuine, at least during stage 2 and part of stage 3.

2. Growth

Bain, Penrose, and others have suggested that industry growth tends to reduce concentration and entry barriers. The leading firms are regarded as unlikely to be able to—or want to—keep their shares by maintaining a high growth rate. Growth may also destabilize the market, making it easier for new and smaller firms to rise. This is contrasted with static and shrinking markets, where the leading firms seem more likely to resist inroads and cling to their positions.

Underlying these vague possibilities is a clear analytical hypothesis: demand may rise faster than MES does, reducing the leading firms' possible advantages. This probably happens routinely in the "growth" phase in most industries' life cycle. But even when erosion is possible, it may not occur. The leading firms' long-run optimal strategy may consist of keeping up with rapid growth in order to reap the larger rewards of dominance later on.[24]

In short, growth might dissolve structure, but there are counterinducements at work. The issue invites empirical tests. One approach is to survey actual fast-growing industries to see if dominant firms have declined in most or all cases. This method has yielded mixed evidence. Many dominant firms do fail to keep up, but, as Chapter 4 showed, the average rate of decline is low.

The other approach is to include growth as one variable in regression analyses "explaining" changes in concentration. The first such studies in the 1960s suggested that growth does indeed erode concentration,[25] but further testing has revealed the

---

[23] For more details on the "utility" life cycle, see W. G. Shepherd, *The Treatment of Market Power* (New York: Columbia University Press, 1975), Chapter 9, and Chapter 4, Section IV, above.

[24] For a complex analysis of the conditions affecting the dominant firm's choices, see Darius W. Gaskins, "Dynamic Limit Pricing: Optimal Pricing Under Threat of Entry," *Journal of Economic Theory*, 3 (September 1971), 306–22. See also Chapter 11 of this textbook.

[25] See Ralph L. Nelson, "Market Growth, Company Diversification, and Product Concentration, 1947–54," *Journal of the American Statistical Association* (1960), 640–49; W. G. Shepherd, "Trends of Concentration in American Manufacturing Industries, 1947–58," *Review of Economics and Statistics*, 46 (May 1964), 200–12; and David R. Kamerschen, "Market Growth and Industry Concentration," *Journal of the American Statistical Association*, 63 (March 1968), 228–41.

effect to be statistically faint, with low explanatory power. Also, the coefficient of the growth variable is low, and even a very high rate of growth seems to induce only a tiny reduction in concentration.[26] The findings are much the same for U.S., British, and other industries.

These tests are not definitive, of course, and some experts interpret them as showing *some* effect of growth. It is even possible that a strong effect exists and has just not been measured well. This is a standard type of scientific issue for you to resolve. At any rate, the contention that growth is a determinant of structure has not been affirmed by scientific evidence so far.

3. Random Processes

Several analysts have suggested that a random, or "stochastic," process accounts for much of the existing structure of markets. One version is that the growth rates of firms are independent of their size: any $10 million firm is as likely to grow at 5 percent per year as any $100 million, $1 billion, or $10 billion firm. This hypothesis predicts that firm sizes are lognormally distributed (that is, the logarithms of firm sizes fit a normal, bell-shaped curve). Chance, not specific determinants, is the "explanation" of structure.[27]

Whether or not the hypothesis holds precisely, the random process could be a major force, perhaps swamping the other determinants. "Random" includes all the historical, personal, accidental, and unpredictable events that flow together in shaping a firm's evolution. In short, "random" is everything that is *not* a systematic determinant. A firm may strike oil, hire a genius inventor, suffer an earthquake, happen to have a splendid manager, or make a lucky merger into a new boom industry. Business magazines are full of such surprises. The effects of each may be small or large and long-lasting.[28]

The cumulation of such "luck" may sustain a firm's rise to dominance and profitability. In fact, Scherer has shown that a process involving random disturbances would eventually evolve a set of industries whose structure is similar to the whole array of actual U.S. industries.[29] Williamson has pointed out that dominant firms can emerge by sheer luck and historical oddities, as well as by economies of scale and a direct effort at monopolizing.[30] Once established, they can persist even if there are no economies of scale. (An example is IBM. In 1950–1953, Remington

---

[26] See W. G. Shepherd, "Structure and Behaviour in British Industries, with U.S. Comparisons," *Journal of Industrial Economics*, 21 (November 1972), 35–54. In this and other studies, the coefficient between growth and changes in concentration is frequently not statistically significant. Even where it is significant, it indicates that a doubling of sales would reduce concentration only by one or several points.

[27] For leading discussions in this vein, see P. E. Hart and S. J. Prais, "The Analysis of Business Concentration," *Journal of the Royal Statistical Society*, 110, Part 2 (1956), 159–91; Herbert A. Simon and Charles P. Bonini, "The Size Distribution of Business Firms," *American Economic Review*, 48 (September 1958), 607–17; and Richard E. Quandt, "On the Size Distribution of Firms," *American Economic Review*, 56 (June 1966), 416–32.

[28] See Richard B. Mancke, "Causes of Interfirm Profitability Differences: A New Interpretation of the Evidence," *Quarterly Journal of Economics*, 88 (May 1974), 181–93.

[29] F. M. Scherer, *Industrial Market Structure and Economic Performance* (Skokie, Ill.: Rand McNally, 1970), pp. 125–30.

[30] Oliver E. Williamson, *Markets and Hierarchies* (New York: Free Press, 1975), Chapter 11.

Rand frittered away its lead in the computer market, handing IBM its dominant position on a silver platter.[31])

In theory, runs of luck can explain both dominant shares and high profits;[32] bad luck can quickly take away what good luck has given. But Chapter 4 has already shown that dominance tends to persist, rather than to dissipate quickly. The dominant firm is often able to use pricing, patents, advertising, and other strategies to strengthen its position.

The random element in market structures is undoubtedly large. One sign of it is that our statistical analyses of actual structures "explain" only a small fraction of the actual degree of monopoly. One may assign the still-unmeasured sources of structure to the pursuit of market power, or to randomness, or to some mixture of the two. As research continues, the "explanation" of structure may improve. However, the unexplained—perhaps random—part is likely to remain large.

4. Public Policies

Several kinds of public policies influence market structure in predictable directions. Whether these policies are imposed on the industries or are instead controlled by firms in the industries themselves is often an open question. Frequently both directions of control are mixed together. The following policy "influences" appear to exist in some degree.[33]

Antitrust policies have three main parts (see Chapter 19). They are supposed to act against (1) established high concentration, (2) mergers that may create new market power, and (3) cooperation among firms to reduce competition. All three parts are intended to reduce market power. In practice, it is the balance of strictness among these three directions of policy that affects market structure. Thus U.S. antitrust has been more stringent against collusion, so mergers and established market power may be at higher levels than a neutral policy set would have given. British rules against collusion tightened sharply after 1955. This probably induced a wave of mergers, which raised the degree of concentration in British industry. These broad effects have arisen in a wide range of industrial structures. U.S. antitrust actions have also made direct "trust-busting" changes in quite a few specific industries (see Chapter 19).[34]

Direct controls on structure are also fixed by policy for some industries (see Chapter 20). "Utilities" sectors are given exclusively to one or just a few firms, as in electricity and local telephone service. Entry into many other industries has been

---

[31] See Gerald W. Brock, *The U.S. Computer Industry: A Study of Market Power* (Cambridge, Mass.: Ballinger, 1975), and sources cited there.

[32] Richard B. Mancke, "Causes of Interfirm Profitability Differences: A New Interpretation of the Evidence," 181–93.

[33] For an inclusive survey and analysis of such policies, see William G. Shepherd, *Public Policies Toward Business*, 7th ed. (Homewood, Ill.: Irwin, 1985).

[34] The industries include petroleum (*Standard Oil Co. of N.J. v. U.S.*, 1911), tobacco products (*U.S. v. American Tobacco Co.*, 1911), gunpowder (the Du Pont case, 1913), aluminum (*U.S. v. Aluminum Co. of America*, 1945), shoe machinery (*United Shoe Machinery Corp. v. U.S.*, 1953), and the telephone sector in 1984. There have been indirect effects on a number of others. For evaluations, see Simon Whitney, *Antitrust Policies* (New York: Twentieth Century Fund, 1958), 2 vols.; and W. G. Shepherd, *The Treatment of Market Power* (New York: Columbia University Press, 1975), pp. 304–20.

limited. Such controls range from airtight monopoly franchises to general licensing standards. They are found in a variety of national, state, and local markets.[35]

Public regulation of "utilities" may also indirectly raise the degree of monopoly. Such regulation ordinarily tries to set a "reasonable" profit-rate ceiling (such as 9 percent), which the utility firms are then entitled to earn on all capital permitted in their rate base. This "rate base" method provides an inducement for the utilities to expand their capital investment, either in real installations or by accounting maneuvers. It also dilutes their concern about the prices they pay for capital equipment (and some other types of purchases as well) because higher prices simply increase the rate base. This situation enhances the market power obtainable in the utility *equipment* industries and the profit-risk rewards they may reap. In short, by indirectly encouraging and rewarding collusion or monopolization in the supplying of utility equipment, commission regulation may foster market power in that group of industries.

Patents grant exclusive rights over inventions for seventeen years in the United States and certain other countries. By conferring a monopoly, they can shape a market from its birth. They can also be amassed and used in various legal strategies as a way of gaining and retaining market control. Among the industries strongly influenced by patents are pharmaceuticals, copying equipment, electrical equipment, glass, and photographic supplies. The specific design of patent laws can therefore affect a range of industries where the rate of invention is important.

Purchases and subsidies by public agencies can favor one firm over another. They can also encourage either a tighter or a more competitive structure. Military spending has been a prime instance of this since 1940. The placement of orders is only one part of it; R&D grants are another important flow of military benefits to private firms. Most military spending focuses on a few firms in each market, and thus it has (with some exceptions) tended to make structure tighter. Other public purchases are also important in a range of local and national markets. These include road construction, office and school building, and purchases of equipment of various kinds. The methods of letting these contracts probably influence a wide variety of markets, decisively in some cases.

Tax laws can also influence industrial structure. Tax rules on profit-loss pooling by merged firms may affect the volume and even the patterns of mergers. *Tariffs* are another long-standing device affecting the degree of competition in certain markets. They—and various other physical quotas and import controls—are barriers against entry by foreign competitors.

Other official supports include the Wagner Act of 1935, which permits labor unions to hold and exert monopoly power in labor markets. Many public enterprises—public schools and the U.S. Postal Service, for example—are also given monopoly power in their markets.

Evidently there are quite a few determinants of market structure besides economies of scale. They could account for much or all of the variation in actual structure. One would need to filter out these other determinants in order to define and estimate the true role of scale economies.

---

[35] Utility regulation and other controls are, of course, intensely controversial. For evaluation of the issues, see Shepherd, *Public Policies*, chaps. 10–15; and, at a more advanced level, Alfred E. Kahn, *The Economics of Regulation* (New York: Wiley, 1971), 2 vols., especially vol. II.

IV. CAUSES OF INCREASED COMPETITION DURING 1960–1980

Finally, we return to the recent rise in U.S. competition, in order to estimate its causes.[36] Four causes were present, ranging from internal market forces to outside interventions. The task is to estimate their relative importance.

The four specific causes are: rising import competition, antitrust, deregulation, and reductions in the economies of scale. The first three can be determined with some confidence for many markets, although some of the attributions are tentative. Table 8.4 summarizes the assignments of industries to these causes.

Inevitably, there is some overlap among the causes, especially in numerous industries where antitrust actions were the stimulus for deregulation. Table 8.4 includes some such cases under both headings, rather than pretending that only one cause was present. Overlaps between rising imports and antitrust were fewer. Imports and antitrust are largely substitutable responses to market power, whereas antitrust and deregulation are usually complementary.

Altogether, Table 8.4 includes markets accounting for $234 billion of 1978 national income, when overlapping listings are allowed for. That amount is 16 percent of total national income. It equals 76 percent of the entire rise in the share of effectively competitive markets from 1958 to 1980.[37]

1. Import Competition

The table includes industries that clearly experienced a substantial rise in import competition during the period. They met three criteria: (1) movement to a more competitive category between 1958 and 1980, (2) an import share that was above 15 percent of all U.S. sales in 1980, and (3) imports that were genuinely competitive with U.S. products rather than just brought in by U.S. firms to be marketed under their own brand names.[38]

In general, imports have risen strongly in importance since the mid-1960s, when they were over 10 percent of U.S. sales in relatively few industries. Now the import share exceeds 10 percent in scores of industries, with effects that are widely recognized.

Import competition caused an increase in competition by 1980 in at least thirteen significant industries (see Part 2, Table 8.4), accounting for 3.8 percent of national income. The industries' $59 billion of value added accounts for about one-sixth of the shift toward greater competition between 1958 and 1980. Imports also took larger shares in many markets that were already effectively competitive in 1958.

The imports' inroads may be temporary in some industries. Yet in others—

[36] This section draws on W. G. Shepherd, "Causes of Increased Competition in the U.S. Economy," *Review of Economics and Statistics,* 64 (November 1982), 613–26.

[37] The rise from 56 to 76 percent in competitive markets is a shift of $308 billion of 1980 national income. That amount is the basis of comparison.

[38] The thirteen markets listed in Table 8.4 are only some of the U.S. industries that are affected by imports. Excluded are many markets with high import competition that were already effectively competitive by 1958. Also excluded are many markets where the imports were really semifinished inputs rather than competitive final products.

TABLE 8.4   The Role of Imports, Antitrust, and Deregulation in Increasing Competition, 1958–1980

Industry (Category)	Industry's National Income, 1978 ($ million)[a]	Industry (Category)	Industry's National Income, 1978 ($ million)[a]
1. Antitrust		**2. Increasing Imports**	
Meat packing	$ 2,469	Steel and products (A)	$ 16,269
Baked goods	3,310		
Drugs	4,735	Automobiles	15,844
Aluminum and products	3,754	Aircraft	6,823
		Tires and tubes	3,534
Metal cans	2,521	Shipbuilding	3,287
Shoe machinery	50	Television tubes	3,156
Heavy electrical equipment	6,422	Artificial fibers	2,246
		Television sets	2,090
Telephone equipment (D)	3,416	Cameras	(1,000)
		Copiers (A)	(3,900)
Cable TV equipment	(120)	Vacuum cleaners	361
Photographic equipment and supplies	4,905	Motorcycles	284
		Sewing machines	181
		Total	$ 58,975
Telephone service long distance (D)	17,843	**3. Deregulation**	
		Telephone equipment (A)	$ 3,416
Radio and television broadcasting	4,741	Railroad transportation (A)	14,217
Banking (D)	24,649	Trucking	25,917
Security, commodity brokers (D)	5,428	Air transportation (A)	12,054
		Telephone service, long distance (A)	17,843
Real estate agents	13,677	Banking	24,649
Photofinishing labs	1,435	Security, commodity brokers (A)	5,428
Automotive rentals	2,807	Total	$103,524
Motion pictures and theaters	3,347		
Commercial sports	1,426		
Legal services	16,232		
Total	$123,287		

[a] Figures in parentheses are estimates.
Note: (A) means antitrust was also important; (D) means deregulation was also important.
SOURCES: Adapted from William G. Shepherd, "Causes of Increased Competition in the U.S. Economy, 1939–1980," *Review of Economics and Statistics,* 64 (November 1982), 613–26, Table 3.

automobiles, tires, and steel, for example—the superiority of foreign technology and design appears to be lasting. U.S. firms have found it necessary to study or even to purchase the current technology of the foreign firms in an effort to remedy the cost disadvantages they face. Meanwhile the foreign firms are developing still more advanced techniques, which will prolong the U.S. lag.

Cost superiority has given imports a special force beyond what their market shares alone would indicate. Because these low-cost competitors are able to ignore the incentives for tacit agreement with U.S. producers to establish higher prices, thus causing a shift toward cost-based pricing, they have often forced prices down.

The effects of imports fit the classical analysis of free trade. U.S. firms in certain markets had responded to their tight-oligopoly conditions by developing a degree of inefficiency and slow innovation. These effects were well researched and widely known, but little remedy by public policies seemed possible in the 1960s. Now import competition has provided much of the cure.

Yet there is no guarantee that import competition will continue. It may be vulnerable to political demands for new trade barriers and to a further decline in the dollar's exchange value. Some domestic industries have successfully sought protection from imports, with such results as quotas on steel and automobile imports and the enforcement of "orderly marketing agreements." A new sustained fall in the dollar's value could reduce imports even more quickly and broadly.

2. Antitrust Actions

Antitrust actions are subtler to evaluate for two main reasons. First, formal antitrust cases that proceed to final court decisions are only a small fraction of all antitrust activity. Many other cases are brought formally but settled by compromise. In other cases, the government achieves effects by threats, without having to go into formal litigation. Other cases are started but dropped after the companies yield in order to avoid further litigation. In still other industries, there are indirect effects: firms in industries A through X change their behavior because landmark cases in industries Y and Z set precedents that apply generally.

Also, the two antitrust agencies pursue many actions (both formally and informally) in other public agencies and forums. They intervene with many regulatory agencies to prevent mergers, stop price-fixing, and revoke monopoly franchises. Such actions are often important and widely known in reliable detail, even though they do not take the form of an official antitrust decision.

In all these ways, antitrust's economic effects have gone well beyond the instances reported in the legal casebooks. Moreover, *private* antitrust cases provide added antitrust effects. Rising from several hundred cases yearly before 1960 to over 1,200 yearly since 1970, these actions have had many direct and indirect effects. Though many of the suits have little economic substance or chance of legal victory, others are substantial enough to constitute a significant force.

Second, antitrust's economic effects are hard to estimate accurately. No complete evaluation of individual cases has ever been done. There have been some pioneering efforts to assess various leading cases that led to structural changes, but those few studies have ignored most of the price-fixing and merger cases, as well as the actions leading to deregulation.

An additional question is the duration of antitrust effects. Some actions have only brief impacts, as when price-fixers are penalized with fines but soon resume their collusion. Other actions have effects that develop over the course of many years; examples are the dissolution of the Standard Oil trust in 1913 and the Alcoa case outcome in 1945–1950.

Because of such complexities, there is no complete set of past studies to draw upon. Yet the main task is a focused one, confined to the industries with rising competition between 1958 and 1980. It is possible to assemble the main cases and informal actions that have affected industries, and then to estimate whether those actions have significantly raised competition.

From these estimates, some twenty industries are included in part 1 of Table 8.4. Their $123 billion of national income in 1978 was 40 percent of the rise in effective competition between 1958 and 1980. If industries marked D are assigned solely to deregulation, then the remaining $72.1 billion is 23 percent of the rise in competition. Or, instead, one may include the twenty antitrust-affected industries plus deregulated industries also affected by antitrust. Then the antitrust effects cover $175 billion in national income, which is 57 percent of the rise in competition.

Evidently, antitrust had a substantial influence on the degree of competition in the economy. Yet Table 8.4 may understate antitrust's total influence in three ways. First, it omits all antitrust actions where the industry was already classed as effectively competitive or where the industry was not moved to a more competitive category. Second, it probably overlooks some competition-raising actions that a more complete study would identify. Third, it does not show antitrust's continuing function in maintaining competition throughout the economy at a much higher level than would otherwise exist. If antitrust actions were suddenly to cease, then a large wave of new mergers and collusion would soon raise the degree of market power in a wide range of sectors. By continuing to prevent that rise, antitrust has made possible the overall trend toward a rise in competition.

3.   Deregulation

Deregulation received much publicity during 1975–1985 as a source of new competition. Yet the real impetus behind deregulation has often been the antitrust agencies, especially in the transportation, communications, stock market, and banking sectors. For example, railroad mergers and pricing were the target of vigorous antitrust interventions before the Interstate Commerce Commission (ICC). It was Antitrust Division pressure from 1968 to 1975 that led the Securities and Exchange Commission to abolish the fixing of stockbrokers' fees in 1975. New competition in the telephone sector was largely created by antitrust cases and pressure on the Federal Communication Commission. The deregulation of banking entry and pricing was also advanced by a variety of antitrust actions.

Therefore most of the deregulation cases in Table 8.4 also reflect a large element of antitrust activity. Apart from that, Table 8.4 shows that deregulation has affected seven main sectors, accounting for 4 percent of national income in 1978 and about 20 percent of the 1958–1980 rise in competition. Some of this deregulation is recent and still in progress (airlines since 1975, trucking and railroads since 1976, and banking since 1978), so its ultimate extent is still unknown. Only airlines, air freight, and stock markets can be considered substantially deregulated, and they account for only 1 percent of national income.

Altogether, deregulation's part in the rise of competition has been limited and closely intertwined with antitrust actions. Moreover, some deregulation may be reversed.

4. Economies of Scale

Finally, there is a need to consider whether changes in the economies of scale can explain the change in the degree of competition.

As Chapter 9 will show, scale economies in the 1960s required substantially less industrial concentration than actually existed. The actual market shares of the leading firms probably exceed their minimum efficient scale in many industries with dominant firms or tight oligopoly.

From 1960 to 1980, it is possible but unlikely that MES increased broadly in U.S. industries while the degree of monopoly was declining so markedly. The opposite process—a broad decline of MES in a variety of industries—is much more likely, as Chapter 9 will also indicate. That is further suggested by the fact that it has taken a large volume of mergers to maintain the level of concentration, both in markets and in the aggregate. Furthermore, rapid market growth in new industries (such as computers) creates new competitive opportunities even where MES is constant in physical terms.

The present findings suggest two alternative inferences about the role of scale economies. Competition would have risen as broadly as it has only if (1) MES were already well below actual market shares in many industries; and/or (2) MES declined compared to market size during the period, especially since 1968. It seems probable that both conditions occurred to some degree.

QUESTIONS FOR REVIEW

1. "Capital markets enforce efficiency on firms by continuously rating their performance and prospects." True?

2. "Banking relationships are about as fluid as any other dealings by corporations." True?

3. "The goals of mergers can often be reached by internal growth or long-term contracts." True?

4. "Takeovers can cause increased efficiency even in firms that are not taken over." True?

5. Why is the stock market like a treadmill for managers?

6. Explain the "replication hypothesis"—that banking structure tends to replicate itself in other markets.

7. Pick a merger currently in process. Evaluate its procompetitive and anticompetitive aspects.

8. If firm A is selling its branch to firm B, why is firm A willing to sell it for less than the top price firm B will pay?

9. Why might mergers occur, other than for technical economies?

10. Why is a "failing-firm" condition hard to define in practice?

11. Along with benefits, mergers may impose costs. Those costs may have been large during the 1980s merger boom in the U.S. Which of the costs are most important, in your judgment?

12. Each of four great merger waves is different from the others, in size, motivations, and types of mergers. Compare and contrast them, please.

13. Summarize a recent takeover. Was the target company inefficient? Was the purchase price low, or high? Did the target company damage itself in its efforts to resist?

14. How can many 1960s and 1980s mergers have been unwise, if capital markets operate efficiently?

15. Discuss two U.S. industries where competition rose sharply since 1960. What were the main causes?

9

THE ECONOMIES AND
DISECONOMIES OF SCALE

Now we turn our focus directly to the economies and diseconomies of scale.[1] How much of the actual concentration in U.S. industries is explained (and justified) by economies of scale? How much excess market share is there? Which research methods are best for measuring the economies and diseconomies of scale?

Only *technical* cost conditions are relevant to a social appraisal. *Pecuniary elements* are to be filtered out, for any measures that still contain pecuniary elements are not helpful in answering normative questions. Two main conditions of scale economies are to be measured: the *minimum efficient scale* (MES), and the *cost gradient*. For completeness, possible *diseconomies of scale* also need attention.

Sections I–III present the concepts, carefully distinguishing between *plant-level* and *firm-level* conditions. *Transport costs* and *learning curves* are also presented. Then Section IV reviews the fundamental trends in technology since the Civil War. For decades, technological trends raised the economies of scale, but after the 1930s, they reversed direction and favored smaller scale in many industries. Section V surveys the three most widely used research methods, and Section VI presents their main results.

I. BASIC CONCEPTS

The basic theory is simple and traditional. The average cost curve declines over some range of output until the lowest-cost point is reached. That **minimum efficient scale** may be at a low or high output level, as illustrated in Figure 9.1 by curves 1 and 2. The **cost gradient** (that is, the downslope of the cost curve) may also vary

---

[1] The topic has been discussed in detail since the 1890s. Among the important treatments are Charles J. Bullock, "Trust Literature: A Survey and Criticism," *Quarterly Journal of Economics,* 15 (February 1900–1901), 167–217; J. M. Clark, *Studies in the Theory of Overhead Costs* (New York: Macmillan, 1922); E. A. G. Robinson, *The Structure of Competitive Industry,* rev. ed. (Chicago: University of Chicago Press, 1958); W. A. Lewis, *Overhead Costs* (London: Allen & Unwin, 1948); Joe S. Bain, *Barriers to New Competition* (Cambridge, Mass.: Harvard University Press, 1956); and F. M. Scherer, Alan Beckenstein, Erich Kaufer, and R. Dennis Murphy, *The Economics of Multiplant Operation: An International Comparisons Study* (Cambridge, Mass.: Harvard University Press, 1975).

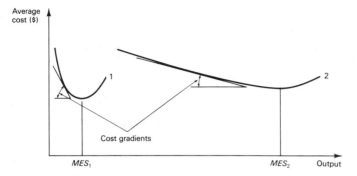

FIGURE 9.1.   Two contrasting average cost curves.

between steep (curve 1) and shallow (curve 2). Firms are not usually at an output level below MES, because that would raise their costs and squeeze their profits.

The economies can arise at the **plant** level in the operation of factories and shops, or at the **multiplant** (or company-wide) level, in the coordination of many plants and in other activities done by the firm as a whole. Above the MES size, there may be diseconomies of scale that cause average cost to slope up. Or there may be a range of constant costs for a space or even at all sizes above MES. The gradient of these diseconomies can be shallow or steep. Figure 9.1 also illustrates these possibilities.

The main contrasts are drawn in Figure 9.2, where total market demand is shown by curve 1. Curve A has steep cost gradients and a distinct low-cost size at q_A. That is the *optimal scale* for the firm. At production much above or below q_A, average cost is much higher, so the firm is confined to that (approximate) size. Curve B has

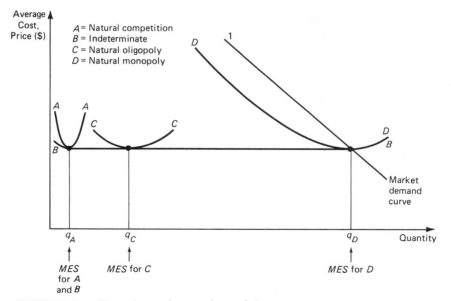

FIGURE 9.2.   Four alternative versions of the average cost curve.

the same MES at q_A, but (1) its cost gradient is lower and (2) its average cost is constant at higher outputs. There is no single level of "best" size. Firms as small as q_A can compete evenly with any and all larger firms, up to size q_D.

Curve C has an optimal scale at q_C, which is a substantial share of the market. Since the cost gradients are rather shallow, the cost penalties from being above or below q_C are not heavy. Finally, curve D has scale economies throughout the size range, up to a size large enough to meet all market demand. Since the cost gradient is steep, any firm below the monopoly share q_D suffers a large cost penalty.

1. Natural Competition and Natural Monopoly

Curve A embodies *natural competition*. All firms must have small market shares, so competition will occur naturally and be intensive. Curve C is *natural oligopoly*. There will tend to evolve four firms, each with 25 percent of the market. Curve D is *natural monopoly*. The first firm to expand can cut its price below any smaller firm's costs and therefore eliminate it. Only one firm will survive. Monopoly is unavoidable and also desirable for its cost efficiency.

Curve B is indeterminate, because any size between q_A and q_D is equally efficient. Costs would not determine market structure. The actual structure would depend on the interplay between competitive pressures and the gains to be secured by monopolizing the market. A full monopoly could occur, or a dominant firm or tight oligopoly. Or market shares could all be driven down to q_A, giving low concentration and effective competition.

For curve B, any size above q_B involves *excess market share:* the market share above MES. Larger size does not provide lower costs, and it usually leads to the costs of monopoly power (X-inefficiency, allocative inefficiency, retarded innovation, unfair distribution, and so on).

Indeed, a firm may seek to hold excess market share even in the range where diseconomies of scale prevail and average cost is rising, so long as the profit gains from the added market power are larger than the cost penalties from the diseconomies. If the cost upslope is shallow and the monopoly gains are steep, the firm may go well into the diseconomies range. Monopoly power and costs will both be substantially larger than the efficient levels.

Excess market share is an important issue because it usually imposes social costs without providing any cost savings to the firm. To measure its extent, we turn to the detailed concepts of scale economies, and then the evidence. First come the basic concepts of technology.

2. Technology

Each firm has a **production function,** which embodies the present state of the art. The simplest function relates two inputs to one output in a one-plant firm. The firm usually has some scope for choice—among the inputs and in the level of output. The optimal choices depend also on the prices of the inputs and the outputs. The firm aligns its *internal* technical choices with the *external* scarcities shown by the market prices of inputs and outputs.

In the short run, at least one input (usually capital) is fixed; in the long run, all are variable. The length of the short run depends on how fixed the "fixed" factor really is. If it can be disposed of quickly (like a rented store or machine), the short run can be a matter of weeks or days. If it is immobile and durable (like a large specialized factory), "short" run may be many years or even decades. This can vary among industries (forest-product firms deal in decades, some clothing firms in months), and even among firms in the same industry.

Production functions may and do reach great complexity, with many inputs and outputs. The underlying technology often evolves, and the production function merely embodies "the state of the art" at that time. The firm's task is dual: (1) static efficiency requires it to maximize profit with a *given* production function (and set of prices), and (2) optimal investment and innovation require it to *change* its own methods as the basic technology shifts. Ultimately the technology does determine the way things are produced. Yet there is usually some room for choice and variation: firms often coexist in a market with different techniques and sizes.

Inputs are of many kinds, and within each category there is further variety. They also vary in degree of "fixity." Capital assets can be "fixed," but so can the trained work force, the land, and the long-term contracts for purchased inputs—at least to some degree. Conversely, capital often is *not* fixed, but instead is on lease or can be quickly sold. Measuring the firm's "fixed costs" therefore requires a subtle analysis of all inputs, not just capital.

Technology defines two levels of operation: (1) in **plants** and (2) in the **firm as a whole.** Scale economies may be gained at either level—plant or multiplant—or both. Each firm reaches and keeps adjusting its "best" choices among sizes and numbers of plants. Good management requires exact *costing* of the firm's activities so that choices can be optimal, prices can be accurate, and performance can be evaluated. Parts of firms are designated as profit centers where cost and revenues are measured so that profits can be assessed.

Specific inputs and costs are easy to assign, but many costs are, instead, **overhead costs.** These are commonly found in firms with any diversity of products.[2] Any input that is shared among products will create overhead costs. Simple examples are management activity and the heating of a whole factory that produces a variety of products. (*Note:* Overhead costs are *not* identical with **fixed costs,** although some overhead costs are fixed costs.) **Joint costs** overlap with overhead costs, but they are usually more specific and more difficult to measure. They commonly arise when one machine produces two products simultaneously. (Examples: A generator turns out electricity both for low-voltage residences and for high-voltage industrial users; a refinery produces both gasoline and heating oil from the same crude petroleum; a railroad track carries both freight and passenger trains.)

There are even more subtle overhead costs, such as an R&D program that creates a full line of ten new computer models *and* trains the personnel who will help customers to program them. Overhead costs are extreme in "public utility" firms (electricity, telephones), but they are also large in some industries we regard as "com-

---

[2] The classic treatment of overhead costs is by John M. Clark, *Economics of Overhead Costs* (New York: Macmillan, 1923). For an excellent test on cost assignments and budgeting, see J. F. Weston and Eugene F. Brigham, *Managerial Finance* (Hinsdale, Ill.: Dryden Press, 1981).

petitive.''[3] Indeed, many or most multiplant activities are overhead costs. High overhead costs widen the room for price discrimination and cyclical price-cutting.

True overhead costs often cannot be assigned by objective economic criteria. Some sort of arbitrary rules can be used, but a fundamentally "correct" allocation of costs cannot be determined. Therefore specific cost assignments to specific products are often debatable.

3.   Technical versus Pecuniary Gains

Before analyzing technical economies of scale, we must distinguish between them and pecuniary gains to scale.

Technical economies of scale are those arising from the actual physical organization of production activities. They reduce the ratio of inputs to outputs, thereby achieving a genuine increase in economic efficiency and a reduction of costs. These are true social gains, whether or not they are captured by the firm as profit or passed on to customers by means of lower prices.

Pecuniary gains are merely a matter of money, not of real efficiency. They occur mainly from lower input prices paid by the firm. The firm's accounting costs are reduced, but not from any change in the real methods of production.

Two points about pecuniary gains need mention. First, the lower prices might reflect technical economies realized *by the supplier* (for example, when GM buys large volumes of tires). If the large firm's orders for inputs are fewer and larger, then the unit costs of producing and handling these larger batches may be lower. Most volume discounts are defended on precisely that ground. Or a large buyer's orders may permit the supplier to grow and realize technical economies of scale for itself. These two effects—of large batches and of pure scale—are distinct in concept, though they may occur together in practical cases and be hard to separate in actual measurements.

Second, the supply of capital may involve especially subtle mixtures of pecuniary and technical gains. Firms often obtain funds at lower costs (in interest rates or dividend payout ratios) because they are genuinely superior: their risks are lower, justifying lower interest rates. Yet circularity may be at work instead: favorable financial connections provide capital in larger amounts and at lower costs, and this in turn lowers the firm's risk. The firm's inherent risk is not less, but the circular process makes it seem so, and therefore provides financial advantages.

Technical and pecuniary gains often occur together, and no easy method for estimating them separately has yet been devised. Yet the conceptual distinction is clear enough and should always be kept in mind. Always ask of any suggested economy of scale: Is it really technical or is it pecuniary? If it is both, what are the proportions of the two parts? How can they be separated?

II.   PLANT-LEVEL ECONOMIES AND DISECONOMIES

We have now finally arrived at the economic core of the topic. We start at the level of the individual plant. What factors may be causing the average cost curve of the plant to decline and then, perhaps, turn up?

---

[3] See A. E. Kahn, *The Economics of Regulation,* Vols. I and II (New York: Wiley, 1971); and for advanced theory of multiplant costs, William J. Baumol, John C. Panzar, and Robert D. Willig, *Contestable Markets and the Theory of Industry Structure* (San Diego, Cal.: Harcourt Brace Jovanovich, 1982).

Average Cost ($)

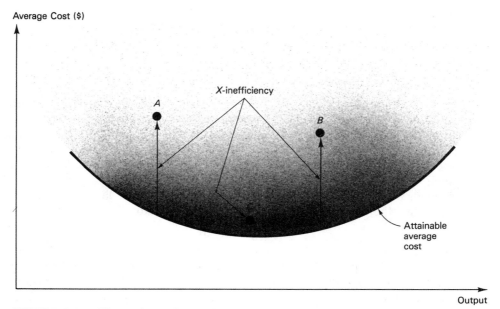

FIGURE 9.3.   Illustrations of X-inefficiency.

Points of Definition   First, consider what a *plant* is. It is a physical facility at a single location. There is usually a building sitting on some land, with machines or other equipment inside. There are transport facilities for bringing in inputs and sending out outputs. These parts are common to a wide variety of plants. Despite their differences, a steel mill, a warehouse, a theater, a barber shop, and a university campus are all plants.

Second, we distinguish between *internal* and *external* factors. Internal factors apply inside the plant. (Example: The technology of an automobile plant reflects the economies of assembly-line methods and inventory controls.) External factors operate from outside. (Example: If the relative costs of transporting cars to market have risen, it becomes more efficient to build many small automobile plants scattered around the country.) We will discuss internal factors first, then external ones.

Third, we keep X-efficiency and economies of scale separate as concepts. The average cost curve is the lower bound to the set of possible average costs, as Figure 9.3 illustrates. Any point above the curve is, of course, available to the firm, but would involve a degree of bad management and unnecessary costs.

Finally, we are concerned here with *long-run* cost curves. They reflect the choices available when all inputs can be varied. Short-run curves, by contrast, are much more steeply U-shaped; once a plant is built for a given optimal level, short-run departures from that level are difficult.

1.   Sources of Economies of Scale

Three main conditions may cause technical economies of scale.

Specialization.   Specialization has long been known as a basic cause of scale economies, and Adam Smith set it at center stage in 1776 in his *Wealth of*

Nations.[4] As a plant's work force expands, it can be put to more specialized tasks. One advantage of specialization is that workers learn to do their specific tasks rapidly and precisely. Another is that it avoids the loss of time and effort from having to shift workers among tasks. Specializing may make jobs more complex (like brain surgery) or, instead, extremely narrow and simple (like turning a bolt).

Machines can also be made more specialized and thereby more efficient. Specialized machines are often complex, expensive, and capable of long production runs. With long runs, the fixed costs of the machine are spread out thinly per unit of output. That gain is a "production-specific" economy: it arises from the setup costs and technology for the given product. It is not strictly coequal with "plant-specific" economies, though the two often go together. The economies of long production runs usually make it more efficient to build plants larger, but not always. It depends on the rate of obsolescence of the product and of the machine, on the costs of holding the output in inventory, and on other factors.[5]

Physical Laws.   **Physical laws** often favor larger size. Volume-surface relationships are one type of law. (Example: As a pipe's size increases, its flow capacity rises more than proportionally to its circumference. Hence long-distance pipelines use one big pipe rather than a bundle of little pipes.) Certain forces operate most efficiently at large scale. (Example: A 20-ton stamping machine rather than 500 hand-held hammers.) High-temperature processes often work more efficiently at large scale. (Example: From 1920 to 1970, ever-larger electric generators were built, using higher heat and pressure.)

Some of these physical laws are intuitively obvious, while others are highly complex. Engineers frequently use a "two-thirds rule." Just as the area of a sphere or of a cylinder of constant proportions varies as the two-thirds power of volume, so the cost of building some process-industry plants rises roughly as the two-thirds power of their capacity—at least within a range. Such a rule of thumb implies sharp economies of scale, at least until complicating factors set in. Other laws cause diseconomies at all levels of production. For any plant, the question is how the many physical laws at work balance out at each size level.

Management.   Management efficiencies are often realized at larger plant sizes. An excellent manager is often capable of supervising hundreds of workers, especially where the technology involves routine tasks. This ability is reinforced by modern methods of processing information, as by computers and telephones. Therefore management gains can often reduce costs up to large sizes of production.

In all this, overhead costs may be important. In a larger plant, they may permit spreading of costs over a range of products. Thus, plants often produce several

---

[4] Adam Smith, *The Wealth of Nations* (New York: Random House, Modern Library, 1937), Book I, Chapters 1–3. Smith used a pin factory as his illustration, but the process can be seen in virtually every modern factory or shop. For example, a restaurant with a cook and waiter instead of two cook-waiters involves specialization; a factory with 20,000 workers will have specialization among assemblers, supervisors, secretaries, janitors, drivers, and scores of other jobs.

[5] For further discussion of the distinction between plant-specific and production-specific economies, see Scherer, et al., *Economics of Multi-plant Operation.* A plant's size is defined in terms of output *per period* (per day or year). A product run is not fixed to a time period. For example, Checker Motors produced the same "taxicab" for more than twenty years after 1955. The plant was small, but the production run was eventually fairly large.

variants of "the" product, using the same machines, workers, and raw materials. This adaptability also permits the larger plant to pool the various risks that exist (such as inputs delivered late, absenteeism of workers, breakdowns of individual machines). Some simple processes have virtually no overhead costs; in some complex cases, overhead costs are as much as half of total costs.

2.   Sources of Diseconomies

The same three sources of economies can become causes of diseconomies of scale for plants if they are pushed too far. If *specialization* becomes excessive, it may breed alienation, careless work, or frequent breakdowns. Work effort may also be reduced, as workers gravitate toward the minimum levels of required effort. Dull jobs in many large factories have bred so much alienation among workers that efficiency and quality have declined. Indeed, a whole movement toward "job enrichment," quality circles, and the sharing of responsibility between workers and managers emerged in the 1970s precisely to reverse these harms of overspecialization.

Also, *physical laws* usually turn against one eventually. (Examples: Too-large pipes will burst; supercritical temperatures can become unstable and dangerous.) As size increases, it usually encounters unfavorable physical laws of some sort, even if some other relationships are still favorable.

Management is the third cause of diseconomies. It often has the effect of a fixed factor, causing average cost to rise as plant size grows. A plant usually does best when there is one manager on the spot, able to catch problems and resolve them decisively. Increasing size dilutes this ability, causing the other inputs to display diminishing marginal productivity. This is evident, for example, in many restaurants and family farms, where close control by a manager seems essential. It also operates generally, in virtually any plant.

Bureaucracy is a related problem. As size increases, the manager must delegate tasks. Committees, staffs, and layers of middle managers arise. Information is passed up, but it is subject to distortion in the process; there is no complete substitute for firsthand contact. Orders are passed down, but that, too, can become an ineffective process. Therefore bureaucracy adds direct costs—of staff, offices, memo writing, groupthink, and so on—and reduces the quality of decision making. For all these reasons, average costs trend higher as size increases.

3.   External Costs and Learning Curves

Now we step outside the conditions internal to the plant, which govern the average cost curve. Two other concepts are important but quite separate from these technical economies and diseconomies. One concept is the external costs of transport. The other is the learning curve. They do *not* affect the shape of the plant's production cost curve.

External Costs, Particularly Transport Costs.   For some goods, transport costs are important, along with production costs. Usually these are "heavy," bulky products whose ratio of value to weight is low. (Obvious examples are bricks, ready-mix cement, and milk, but there are many other, middle-range cases.) When markets

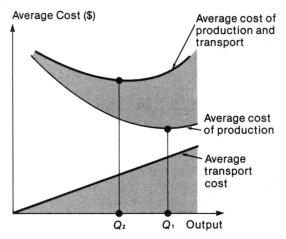

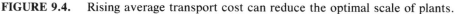

FIGURE 9.4. Rising average transport cost can reduce the optimal scale of plants.

are focused in a small area, transport costs do not much matter. But when the market for a good is spread out geographically, transport cost can influence the total cost curve of the plant.[6] As quantity of production rises, more distant customers must be sought, and the average costs to transport the product to them are a rising proportion of total costs. This reflects plane geometry: as the radius increases, a circle's area increases more than proportionally.

Figure 9.4 illustrates this effect. When high transport costs are added to the production costs set by internal factors, the average total cost curve has a smaller optimal size (at Q_2) and a steeper upslope toward the right. Analogous conditions hold for the transport costs of inputs.

For goods with high transport costs for both inputs and outputs, these external cost conditions can be quite large compared to the internal costs. Generally, the effect arises for (1) outputs—high transport costs per unit and low market density; and (2) inputs—high transport costs per unit and widely spread sources of supply. (Example: Optimal size will tend to be larger in New York City than in Colorado.) So optimal size can depend on external factors as well as internal ones.

The Learning Curve. So far we have presented static analysis, showing the cost levels for a variety of alternative possible output levels at a given time. Time-related conditions can also be important, especially as embodied in the *learning curve*.[7]

When a new product or process is started, a learning process begins. The first units usually involve a degree of trial and error as new methods are established and people are trained. Initial costs per unit are therefore high. As production builds up, people become quicker and smoother at their tasks. Machines are debugged and adjustments are made toward the best possible system of production.

The result is a learning curve, showing a decline in the current average cost of production as *total* production mounts. The phenomenon is an obvious one and has

---

[6] See Scherer, et al., *Economics of Multi-plant Operation,* Chapter 2, for analysis of the transport factor.

[7] See Lee E. Preston and E. C. Keachie, "Cost Functions and Progress Functions: An Integration," *American Economic Review,* 59 (March 1964), 100–106.

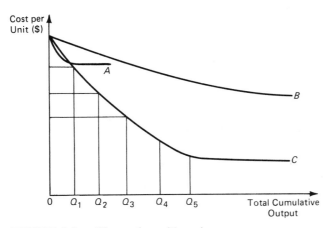

FIGURE 9.5.   Illustration of learning curves.

been known for many centuries. But it was first observed and formulated as an economic concept in the mass production of aircraft during World War II. More recently, economists have stressed that the "first mover" (the first firm to gain substantial size and experience with a product) will have an advantage over late-comers. The latecomers can chase the first mover down the learning curve, as it were, but they may never catch up.

The outcome will depend on the slope of the learning curve for each specific case. Three forms are illustrated in Figure 9.5. Notice that the horizontal axis is the total cumulative amount of production from the first unit on, *not* the level of production to be chosen during one period. A learning curve may have a short, steep slope (curve *A*); a long, shallow slope (*B*); a long, steep slope (*C*); or still other forms. Curve *C* will give the first mover a large advantage over other firms, compared to curve *A*. For example, firm 1 may reach point Q_5 before any rival starts up; its cost advantage will be large. Or it may be only a step ahead of its rivals all the way (it may be at Q_2 when they are Q_1, at Q_3 when they reach Q_2, and so on). Even so, it will always have a cost advantage and therefore be able to make larger profits.

Moreover, that advantage can be extended if the firm is able to develop a series of new products. Then it can move down one learning curve after another, always keeping a cost advantage over its pursuing rivals.

III. MULTIPLANT ECONOMIES AND DISECONOMIES

In the simplest multiplant case, a firm could add one plant after another as it grows. This would yield a virtually flat *firm-level* average cost curve to the right of the MES level of the plant. Figure 9.6 illustrates this situation.

If there are economies of scale in the firm-level activities, the successive plants could be added at decreasing average costs. Or, instead, there may be diseconomies at all levels. Or, perhaps most commonly, a range of declining cost may be followed by an MES for the firm and then a range in which diseconomies prevail.

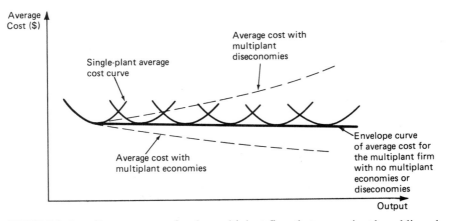

FIGURE 9.6.   Constant costs for the multiplant firm that grows just by adding plants, showing economies and diseconomies.

1.   Technical Conditions

The shape of the multiplant cost curve depends on how the various company-wide activities change with larger size. Extending the firm's scope reduces duplication, but it also causes bureaucracy. For each activity, how do these balance out?

These activities divide into several main types. The most basic category is *management*. Generally, thorough management control requires a hierarchy of officials and reporting activities. Paradoxically, this tends to frustrate its own purpose by diluting information and authority and often sowing confusion. The same problem arises for plants. Such bureaucracy can be mitigated by technical improvements: instant computerized reporting, profit "centers," and so on. Yet bureaucracy will always add layers of administrative costs to the production costs, so the firm must somehow save enough on other activities to offset these extra costs.

Two other activities—*advertising* and *research and development* (R&D)—may also provide economies of scale, but this is debatable. A large-scale R&D program can be bureaucratic and *un*productive rather than fruitful (as Chapter 6 noted). Also, R&D productivity often interacts with market structure rather than operating purely as a determinant of it, "from outside" as it were. As for advertising, it may provide certain economies of scale, but these may be pecuniary rather than technical economies. And advertising also interacts with market structure; it is not a purely external force (see Chapter 6). Roughly speaking, both R&D and advertising may go either way as cost factors.

Various *specialized services* for the firm include purchasing, market research, maintenance, personnel, and marketing. Each of these may display economies or diseconomies as the company's size increases. Purchasing in bulk may achieve technical economies (by avoiding duplication) as well as pecuniary ones. Marketing especially may have low marginal cost once the basic network of sales agents is in place. This factor is independent of production costs; a selling network can even offset diseconomies in production. The "optimal" marketing size, however, is different in each case.

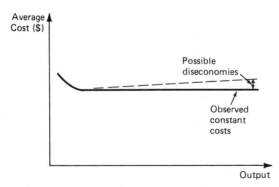

FIGURE 9.7.   Typical cost curve for an industry.

Statistical theory suggests the *pooling of risks* among plants may be a genuine multiplant economy *if* the separate risks are independent *and* the firm can move resources freely among the plants. Then the entire firm needs less total reserve capacity than if the plants were each on their own.

Finance has already been explored (recall Chapter 8). The multiplant firm may be genuinely less risky. It may also be more efficient in obtaining and managing funds, by dealing with large batches at a highly sophisticated level. These economies would be *technical*. Yet there may also be circularity, since the firm's banking support reduces the firm's risk of failure. That lower risk does not really "justify" the lower rate of interest the firm has to pay. Such circular conditions are a *pecuniary* gain—real enough for the firm, but nonetheless not a social gain.

2. Pecuniary Gains

In fact, pecuniary gains are especially likely at the firm level. The firm can often exert bargaining power on behalf of its many plants to force its suppliers to accept lower prices than any single plant could obtain. That is true of many inputs, from labor to ores and chemicals, to semifinished and finished inputs, finance, advertising services, even patents and R&D talent. Price discounts are possible and common on nearly every type of input. So there is virtually a presumption that any observed firm-level cost curve embodies a significant degree of pecuniary economies. The true technical cost curve will lie above it, as Figure 9.7 illustrates. The main question, then, is how large the divergence between observed and technical costs really is.

Note that this pecuniary gain enhances the tendency for firms to capture excess market share. The accounting cost curve, having less upward slope than the technical cost curve, gives a smaller offset to the monopoly gains from market share. Therefore pecuniary gains lead to higher excess market share, higher average costs, and higher market power.

IV. BASIC TRENDS IN TECHNOLOGY

First, consider the larger setting. The Industrial Revolution began in Britain about two centuries ago. In the United States, industrial development boomed after 1850. Then, in the middle of this century, services replaced industry as the majority activity of the modern economy.

Several forces shaped technology during these major periods—primarily power, materials, transportation, and electronics. At first the changes mainly favored bigness in factories and in whole companies. In our terms, they provided technical economies of scale both at the plant level and in multiplant operations. But after the 1930s, this tide appears to have waned or perhaps reversed, as several forces favoring small-scale technology have gained momentum.

Power.   After 1770, the steam engine largely replaced the ancient sources of power—human beings, draft animals, and falling water. Steam was much more powerful, enabling machines to be larger and operate faster than before, by orders of magnitude. Steam power also favored bigger factories where many machines could be run by belts or gears from large steam engines. These "dark satanic mills" typified industrial progress for over a century, and in some industries, large-scale power is still used.

After 1880, electricity provided an increasing counterforce to bigness. Electric motors of all sizes became available, delivering power more flexibly. Electrically powered machines were more adaptable and, in many operations, much smaller and more precise than those powered by steam. Smaller factories became more feasible, in a wider variety of locations.

Materials.   The Industrial Revolution brought an iron age—or rather, a metals age. Metals such as iron, steel, copper, and aluminum were highly exact, homogeneous substances with uniform properties. New metal alloys provided a further range of properties. Unlike leather and wood, metals lent themselves to standardizing and mass production. Chemicals, oil, and other minerals also fitted this trend. So changes in the very materials of industry favored large-scale, uniform processes in place of small-scale crafts and workshops.

Since about 1920, one counterforce to bigness has been the increasing complexity of industrial products and services. Advanced electronics and aircraft, for example, cannot be turned out as simply as tons of steel or bricks. Services, especially, tend to require small scale. Even in the older, simpler industries, the limits of scale have often been fully reached or even overshot. Thus Ford's pre-1920 giant automobile plant at River Rouge was unmanageably oversized as soon as it was built, and the dimensions of most automobile plants today are but a small fraction of that one. In oil, chemicals, metals, meat packing, machine tools, and other industries—even electric generation itself—the trend toward larger plants seems to have faded or reversed, in part because the materials for production are far more refined.

Transportation.   The two great steam-powered transport modes—railroads and steamships—also fostered increases in industrial scale for many decades. Rail lines linked large cities and resource deposits (coal, ores). Along these routes, factories tended to be few, large, and centrally located. Shipping was done in large batches, or even by the trainfull, which, again, favored large-scale factories.

The truck reversed this. Trucks are more flexible for loading, smaller in scale, and able to rove almost everywhere. The rise in truck transportation reopened whole sets of industries and geographic areas to small-scale production. The spread of the interstate highway network since 1950 has deepened this effect. The automobile has furthered the trend by enabling workers to reach a wide range of work places, large and small. Earlier they had to cluster in large cities where the big labor pools favored large-scale factories.

Communications and Computers.   Advances in communications have also shaped technology and optimum size. The telephone network has made possible the close coordination of distant activities. This has favored smaller plants and also large, multiplant firms. The onset of computers since 1950 has made managerial controls deeper and more precise. Computer systems have also replaced whole armies of service workers (such as telephone operators and filing clerks). At first, "giant" computers seemed likely to favor "giantism" in business, but since 1965, the shift toward miniaturized computers and distributed processing has made computer functions available to small firms, plants, and even individual machines (in process controls). The net effect of the computer now appears to favor small-scale plants and firms.

Workers.   Workers, too, have changed. Until the 1960s, they were relatively acquiescent in following orders. The prevalent top-down forms of management favored large plants and firms. Now workers are more individualistic and less willing to suffer the regimentation that goes with large-scale authoritarian controls. This has raised productivity relatively in smaller firms.

All these forces are still at work, and their net effects are changing and unpredictable. You need to approach real industries with an open mind, expecting to find a variety of conditions.

V. METHODS OF RESEARCH

The task is to measure the average cost curve for plants and firms in each market. One would then know the MES, the cost gradient, and the upslope (if any) at higher output levels above MES. *All pecuniary elements would, of course, be filtered out.*

Such a measurement would be a *normative* basis for evaluating *actual* scales of plants in the market: comparing "what is" with "what ought to be." Yet the curves may be blurred rather than sharp, bright lines. The location of MES and the level or range of optimal size may be genuinely indefinite because the underlying technology permits much variety of choice. Still, one must try to estimate what cost curves there may be.

Several concepts about the cost curve that is to be measured need to be defined themselves. One is: the lowest conceivable average cost at each output level, with the best management and technology likely to come available. Line *A* in panel I of Figure 9.8 illustrates this. Another is: the "best current practice," based on present technology and reasonably good (rather than perfect) management. Line *B* in panel I of Figure 9.8 shows this. A third basis is: the "best current practice" at the time the *existing* capacity was put in. In all industries, capacity has been built up over years or decades, under changing cost and engineering conditions. Line *C* in panel II of Figure 9.8 reflects such a "historical" cost curve.

The "best current practice" method (line *B*) is the best all-round definition. It has become the mainstay of the literature.

Again, we are seeking to measure *technical* economies of scale. All *pecuniary*

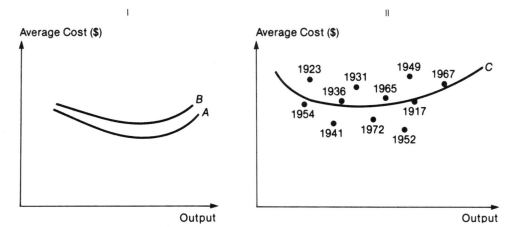

FIGURE 9.8. Alternative definition of "the" average cost curve.

economies must be excluded if the measures are to be valid for normative comparisons. In fact, removing the pecuniary economies is the whole point of the exercise.

Yet it is not easy to factor out pecuniary elements. Several methods for measuring cost curves have been developed since the 1930s. Table 9.1 sums up their features. All leave some degree of pecuniary elements in, though one technique—"engineering" estimates—seems to be better than the others.

One thoroughly unsuitable method is to compare the profitability of different-sized units.[8] Because this method leaves all the pecuniary economies in, the comparisons have no normative value. A firm selling 100 units may be more profitable than one selling 50 solely because of pecuniary gains or monopoly profits, rather than because of true efficiency. Profitability data have their uses, but they cannot help in evaluating efficiency.

We now turn to the research studies and their results. Your main task is to learn the methods and their weaknesses so that you can make your own judgment about actual trends and specific cases. The estimates themselves, which are rather few and doubtful, are mainly a vehicle for mastering the concepts.

Before 1930, there was much debate and loose talk about economies of scale. The "imperatives of modern technology," the need to "consolidate," and so on, in particular industries and in the whole economy, were common fare. Doubts about large-scale technology were also expressed, but there was little objective research to settle the issues. The first efforts, starting in the 1930s, used *average cost data* for cross-section and time-series analysis. Studies of this sort continued through the 1950s. Joe S. Bain introduced the use of *engineering estimates* in 1956, followed up by Pratten's, Scherer's, and Weiss's reports in the 1970s.[9] The *survivor technique*

---

[8] This method was popular from the 1890s through the 1930s. Among a number of studies, no clear pattern emerged: high profitability was registered variously by firms with low and high market shares. Such inconclusive "results" did not, in any case, offer a way to settle the normative issue.

[9] Bain, *Barriers to New Competition;* Scherer et al., *Economics of Multi-plant Operation;* and C. F. Pratten, *Economies of Scale in Manufacturing Industry* (Cambridge: Cambridge University Press, 1971).

TABLE 9.1   The Main Alternative Methods for Measuring Economies and Diseconomies of Scale

AUTHOR AND YEAR OF PUBLICATION	COVERAGE OF INDUSTRIES AND TIME PERIODS	FINDINGS
1. Engineering Estimates. Ask engineers and managers what optimal scale is and what the cost gradients are. Use questionnaires and interviews at several firms in each industry. Research usually focuses on plant rather than multiplant conditions.		
Bain (1956)	U.S. about 1950, 20 selected industries	MES is usually a small share of the industry; multiplant economies are slight.
Pratten (1971)	25 U.K. industries, 1960s	MES is often large relative to U.K. industries
Scherer et al. (1975)	12 industries in U.S., U.K., France, Germany, Italy, and Sweden, about 1965–1967	MES are similar across countries. Most MES are relatively small shares of the U.S. market. Cost gradients are small.
Weiss (1976)	16 selected U.S. industries, late 1960s	MES is usually 1–7 percent of industry output. Cost gradients are small to moderate.
2. Cost Studies. Array actual average cost data to show possible cost curves. Use either cross sections (many firms for one period) or time series (one firm over a series of years).		
Smith (1955)	U.S., 1930s, many industries	A survey article covering cross-section and time series results. Most curves appear to be approximately flat.
Nerlove (1963)	U.S. electricity supply, 1950s	Long-run average cost of generation declines, then tends to rise.
Eads et al. (1969)	U.S. airlines, 1958–1966	No evidence of economies of scale.
3. Survivor Technique. Inspect successive size distributions of plants to see which size classes are "surviving" or increasing their share. Cover many industries briefly *or* study a few industries intensively. The approach is valid mainly for plant-level conditions.		
Stigler (1958)	Several U.S. industries over several decades, firms and plants.	Cost curves are usually dish-shaped, with small MES.
Saving (1961)	83 U.S. industries, 1947–1954, plants only.	MES is small in most cases. Many industries cannot be estimated.

TABLE 9.1   *(continued)*

Author and Year of Publication	Coverage of Industries and Time Periods	Findings
Shepherd (1967)	Over 50 U.S. industries, 1947–1963, plants only	Most industries cannot be estimated. MES is relatively small in the few cases where it can be measured.
Rees (1973)	30 selected U.K. industries, 1954–1968, plants only	MES usually starts at small sizes and does not include the largest sizes of plants.

SOURCES:
Joe S. Bain, *Barriers to New Competition* (Cambridge, Mass.: Harvard University Press, 1956).
George Eads, Marc Nerlove, and William Raduchel, "A Long-run Cost Function for the Local Service Airline Industry," *Review of Economics and Statistics,* 51 (August 1969), 258–70.
Marc Nerlove, "Returns to Scale in Electricity Supply," in Carl Christ, ed., *Measurement in Economics* (Stanford, Cal.: Stanford University Press, 1963).
C. F. Pratten, *Economies of Scale in Manufacturing Industry* (Cambridge: Cambridge University Press, 1971).
R. D. Rees, "Optimum Plant Size in United Kingdom Industries: Some Survivor Estimates," *Econometrica,* 40 (November 1973), 394–401.
Thomas R. Saving, "Estimation of the Optimum Size of Plant by the Survivor Technique," *Quarterly Journal of Economics,* 75 (November 1961), 569–607.
F. M. Scherer et al., *The Economics of Multi-plant Operation: An International Comparisons Study* (Cambridge, Mass.: Harvard University press, 1975).
William G. Shepherd, "What Does the Survivor Technique Show about Economies of Scale?" *Southern Economic Journal,* 34 (July 1967), 113–22.
Caleb J. Smith, "Survey of the Empirical Evidence on Economies of Scale," chapter in George J. Stigler, ed., *Business Concentration and Price Policy* (Princeton, N.J.; Princeton University Press, 1955).
George J. Stigler, "The Economies of Scale," *Journal of Law and Economics,* 1 (October 1958), 54–71.
Leonard W. Weiss, "Optimal Plant Size and the Extent of Suboptimal Capacity," Chapter 7 in Robert T. Masson and P. David Qualls, eds., *Essays on Industrial Organization in Honor of Joe S. Bain* (Cambridge, Mass.: Ballinger, 1976).

was advanced by George J. Stigler in 1958, and has seen several uses since then.[10] Some analysts have also used *existing size distributions* to make a rough approximation of efficient size.

These are the main techniques that have been used so far. None of them gives clear answers, especially for firmwide conditions. Roughly speaking, "engineering estimates" are regarded as the best all-around method. Survivor tests give some useful hints about *plant-based* economies. Existing size distributions are used mainly for crude data to be included in large regression equations. Average cost data have generally been abandoned, being scarce and unreliable.

Each method has serious limitations, and all are expensive and arduous. The wise researcher tries to use at least two of them in any project so that they can

---

[10] Stigler, "The Economies of Scale," *Journal of Law and Economics,* 1 (October 1958), 54–71, presents the merits of the method. Limits are noted in W. G. Shepherd, "What Does the Survivor Technique Show about Economies of Scale?" *Southern Economic Journal,* 36 (July 1967), 113–22; and Joe S. Bain, "Survival-Ability as a Test of Efficiency," *American Economic Review,* 59 (May 1969), 99–104.

supplement and cross-check each other. The issues are changing as further studies are made and the research tools (such as computers, published data, and information from antitrust cases) evolve.

VI. EMPIRICAL FINDINGS

1. Engineering Estimates

Advantages.   In this approach, one assembles "expert" opinions about the shape and position of the cost curves, both for plant and for multiplant activities. The "experts" are engineers and managers in the firms themselves, people who work directly with these issues as they design new plants and operate whole companies. One conducts personal interviews with, and sends questionnaires to, as many well-placed officials as possible. One also searches the specialist trade journals and any other informed sources to triple-check the opinions.[11]

Armed with such direct judgments from at least five inside experts per industry, one estimates the cost curves for the "best current practice" capacity. The method's great strength is that it draws on evidence from professionals who are solving problems on a daily basis, under the pressure of the profit motive. Another strength is that it uses several sources, which are checked against each other to reach the most reasonable estimate.

Problems.   The method is arduous, requiring scores of interviews and much other effort for a study dealing with more than a few industries. To cover a really broad range of industries (say, 80 or 100) would take more expert economists than are now available.

Another weakness is that the experts' opinions are just that—opinions. Each is likely to believe that his or her own firm's size is about right, in which case the estimates would tend to overstate the true range of efficient scale. Or if the experts are swayed by current fashions in technology, their "independent" views will merely reflect the ideas of a few people writing in the journals they all read.

Finally, the method works *least* well when there is only one or a few major firms in the industry, because in that case independent judgments are very difficult to obtain. Yet those are the very industries (near-monopolies and tight oligopolies) where good estimates are most acutely needed for guiding antitrust policy.

Results.   Bain's pioneering study covered twenty industries, as of about 1950. His interviews were heavily supplemented by other, less direct sources, such as trade journals. In most of the industries, "optimal" plant size was a small percentage of total industry size; the cost gradients were small; and multiplant economies were said to be slight. Actual concentration in most of the industries contained a lot of excess market share.

---

[11] Within this approach, there are differing methods. Some researchers use interviews mainly; some use questionnaires; others prefer elaborate analysis of the factors affecting optimal scale; and still others rely heavily on searches of the journals that engineers and other experts read. All four tactics have value, and the best studies use them all to some degree. Still, there is no one rigorous method in the engineering approach.

In 1975, Scherer and several associates provided new estimates of *plant* scale economies in twelve industries, both in the United States and in five other countries (Canada, Germany, France, Sweden, and Britain). Through interviews with 125 companies, plus journal reading, they estimated MES and cost-gradient conditions as of the late 1960s. Since there were seventy-two industry-country cases, they averaged less than two interviews per each one. Still, their project was a major effort. It also explored some features of multi-plant conditions.

The researchers tried to separate the internal production costs of the plant from such external factors as transport costs (recall Section II). They also compared MES with regional markets where those were more relevant than national markets (as in cement and beer). Finally, they tried a number of statistical regressions to test the sources and effects of scale economies. Later, similar studies were done by C. F. Pratten and Leonard W. Weiss.[12]

Their main results, summarized in Table 9.2, are estimates rather than precise cost curves. The broad lessons are similar to those from Bain's study. Scale economies are important in some cases, but in only a few of those cases do they require concentration as high as was found. Pratten's and Weiss's estimates of cost gradients suggest that *the gradients are usually small;* in most cases, a "too-small" plant does not suffer a major disadvantage.

Multiplant economies were said to be generally slight or absent (see columns 2 and 3 in Table 9.3). Only advertising appeared to be a significant source of multiplant "economies," in beer, cigarettes, and refrigerators. In other, smaller countries, scale economies appear to make a degree of concentration more necessary. In roughly half the industries covered so far, the existing concentration abroad—regional or national—did not exceed the estimated MES for the firm.[13]

Though engineering estimates are important, they have been done on only a limited share of the important industries and their results are debatable.[14] For the leading dominant-firm industries (such as computers, newspapers, and soup), no engineering estimates are available, at either the plant or the firm level, for conditions since 1950. The estimates of plant economies are reasonably strong; estimates of multiplant economies are rather weaker and scarcer.

Since 1970, MES levels for both plants and enterprises have probably declined

[12] Weiss relied on interviews or questionnaires covering from three to fourteen sources per industry. See his "Optimal Plant Size and the Extent of Suboptimal Capacity," Chapter 7 in Robert T. Masson and P. David Qualls, eds., *Essays on Industrial Organization in Honor of Joe S. Bain* (Cambridge, Mass.: Ballinger, 1976).

[13] Yet one should keep two provisos in mind. First, the true MES is often much lower abroad, where small-batch technology has been traditionally in line with the smaller size of many national markets. These surveys of expert opinion may have evoked answers based on the latest international journals. This was especially likely during the 1960s, when a cult of bigness was current among industrialists in Europe. Second, trade between countries makes the evaluation more complex. If imports and exports are large, then domestic *production* is a poor index of the level of sales and of genuine competition in the relevant markets. For example, Belgium is only part of a Western European automobile market. Thus, even if high concentration of production seems to be necessary abroad, the true degree of market power may still be lower there than it appears.

[14] For a criticism of the approach, see Bela Gold, "Changing Perspectives on Scale, Size, and Returns: An Interpretive Survey," *Journal of Economic Literature,* 19 (March 1981), 5–33. Gold's own approach deals with plants and attempts to distinguish effects of scale and size, which may involve varieties of products. See Gold, *Productivity, Technology and Capital* (Lexington, Mass.: Heath Lexington Books, 1979).

TABLE 9.2 Estimates of Plant-Level Economies of Scale

Industry	Percentage Elevation of Unit Costs	MES Plant Size as Percentage of 1967 U.S. Consumption
Scherer et al. Estimates	(at one-third MES)	
Beer brewing	5.0%	3.4%
Cigarettes	2.2	6.6
Broad-woven cotton and synthetic fabrics	7.6	0.2
Paints, varnishes, and lacquers	4.4	1.4
Petroleum refining	4.8	1.9
Shoes (other than rubber)	1.5	0.2
Glass containers	11.0	1.5
Cement	26.0	1.7
Integrated wide strip steel works	11.0	2.6
Ball and roller bearings	8.0	1.4
Household refrigerators and freezers	6.5	14.1
Storage batteries	4.6	1.9
Pratten and Weiss Estimates	(at one-half MES)	
Flour mills	3.0	0.7
Soybean mills	2.0	2.4
Bread baking	7.5	0.3
Tufted rugs	10.0	0.7
Printing paper	9.0	4.4
Linerboard	8.0	4.4
Sulphuric acid	1.0	3.7
Synthetic rubber	15.0	4.7
Cellulose synthetic fibers	5.0	11.1
Nylon, acrylic, and polyester fibers	7.0–11.0	6.0
Detergents	2.5	2.4
Passenger auto tires	5.0	3.8
Bricks	25.0	0.3
Iron foundries: large castings	10.0	0.3
Turbogenerators	n.a.	23.0
Diesel engines up to 100 hp	4.0–28.0	21.0–30.0
Machine tools	5.0	0.3
Electronic computers	8.0	15.0
Electric motors	15.0	15.0
Transformers (mix of types)	8.0	4.9
Integrated passenger auto production	6.0	11.0
Commercial transport aircraft	20.0	10.0
Bicycles	n.a.	2.1

SOURCES: See Table 9.1, and F. M. Scherer, *Industrial Market Structure and Economic Performance* (Chicago: Rand McNally, 1980).

TABLE 9.3   Estimates of Firmwide Economies of Scale

INDUSTRY	(1) NUMBER OF MES PLANTS NEEDED TO HAVE NOT MORE THAN "SLIGHT" OVERALL HANDICAP	(2) SHARE OF U.S. MARKET REQUIRED IN 1967	(3) AVERAGE MARKET SHARE PER U.S. BIG THREE MEMBER, 1970
Beer brewing	3–4	10–14%	13%
Cigarettes	1–2	6–12	23
Fabric weaving	3–6	1	10
Paints	1	14	9
Petroleum refining	2–3	4–6	8
Shoes	3–6	1	6
Glass bottles	3–4	4–6	22
Cement	1	2	7
Ordinary steel	1	3	14
Bearings	3–5	4–7	14
Refrigerators	4–8 (incl. other appliances)	14–20	21
Storage batteries	1	2	18

SOURCE: Adapted from F. M. Scherer, *Industrial Market Structure and Economic Performance* (Chicago: Rand McNally, 1980.)

further, as electronic technology has continued to favor smaller scale. Therefore excess market share has probably increased in a number of industries.

2.   Survivor Tests

The survivor technique, current since 1958,[15] relies on actual trends in plant sizes rather than on opinions. The hypothesis is simple: If plants in the size range X are surviving or increasing their share, then they must be "efficient" in all essential activities. One ignores actual costs, expert opinions, and other direct measures of efficiency, and compares instead the size distribution of plants over a series of years, identifying those size groups that are surviving. One can evaluate one industry in depth, over many decades. Or one can compare a few years' shifts in sizes (say, from 1978 to 1986) for many industries. Using data readily available in census reports, one can seemingly make estimates of the "optimal size range" for hundreds of four-digit industries. The technique appears to be both fast and objective.

There are limits to its usefulness, however. The method is worthless for evaluating *firm*-level economies because it automatically includes pecuniary economies. Even some plant estimates may be tainted by pecuniary conditions. This problem is most acute in precisely those problem industries for which good normative mea-

[15] It was used, without fanfare, by Thorp and Crowder in the 1930s, well before Stigler's proposal of the method in 1958. See Willard L. Thorp and Walter F. Crowder, *The Structure of Industry*, Monograph 27, Temporary National Economic Committee (Washington, D.C.: U.S. Government Printing Office, 1941), part I, Chapter 2, pp. 19–57.

sures are most needed. Moreover, the technique does not clarify the *shape* of the cost curve, either outside or inside the estimated range of "optimal scale."[16]

There are also sharp practical problems. The Census Bureau bases its plant data on the number of workers in each plant. If innovation is laborsaving, then all plants may appear to be shrinking faster than their true output levels are. Also, actual survivor tests have been unable to discern coherent shift patterns in most industries. Instead, most shifts appear to be erratic and meaningless.[17]

Accordingly, only a handful of survivor results from Stigler's, Saving's, Weiss's, and the present author's studies can be regarded as reliable. They fit the findings from the "engineering estimates" quite well: MES appears to be less than 2 percent of the industry's total size in most cases. The hopes for doing hundreds of estimates cheaply and reliably have not been borne out. Deeper, careful survivor tests of individual industries can still be valuable, but mainly as a supplement to other methods. These studies require considerable effort. And they cannot—by their very nature—really clarify *technical* economies of scale at the firm level.

Existing Size Distributions.   The present sizes of plants give a possible hint of what the optimal size is. At the extreme: If *all* plants are size *y*, that is likely to be the optimal size. If no plants are size *z*, that is almost certainly not the optimal size. So a careful researcher begins at least by inspecting the actual size distribution of plants for any strong patterns.

Usually, however, the patterns are not strong. The census four-digit industries normally embrace a variety of plants in differing locations and with differing advantages. Plant sizes therefore are usually spread over a wide range (say, from 25 up to 1,000 workers), even when technology might call for a more narrow optimal range (say, from 300 to 500 workers). Actual sizes also reflect differing vintages of plants: "optimal" size may have been different in the past.

Still, some analysts use existing size data as a crude proxy variable for MES in regressions across 50 or 100 industries.[18] The favorite version is to take the average size of existing plants as a rough indicator of the MES. This is not too reckless in a larger analysis, where one needs only some indication of MES, but such estimates would not bear much weight on their own because they are conceptually weak and rest on faulty data.

3. Pecuniary Gains

Now let us consider pecuniary economies in more detail. The main pecuniary gain is the firm's ability to extract excess profits as its market power increases. Chapter 5 evaluated that effect. The other pecuniary gain arises from lower input

---

[16] The method also poses interesting theoretical problems. We can assume that each observed shift is only one in a process moving toward the ultimate state in which plants will only exist inside the "efficient" range. But how far will the shifts go, and in what sort of sequence (asymptotic, rapid, and so on)? Some researchers have assumed a "Markov process," but other bases are also plausible. In short, the conceptual issues are not simple. If really good data were available, these deeper problems would have to be faced and solved more precisely.

[17] To take one example, this author's research on 1947–1958 patterns began with 140 "important" industries. Yet I was able in the end to arrive at reasonably clear "efficient size ranges" for only 10 of those 140 cases. And several of these estimates conflicted with estimates by Weiss and Bain. See Shepherd, "What Does the Survivor Technique Show?"

[18] Examples are William S. Comanor and Thomas Wilson, "Advertising, Market Structure and Economic Performance," *Review of Economics and Statistics*, 49 (November 1967), 423–40; and Scherer et al., *Multi-plant Operations*, especially Chapters 3–6.

prices paid by the firm. There are no advanced research techniques for measuring those possible reductions. One must rely instead on a variety of scattered evidence, only some of which is strong and clear.

Input prices for capital, utility services, advertising, and other purchases are usually lower for larger buyers. Only one main input—labor—is frequently costlier to large firms. Whether the price advantages reflect true reductions in the suppliers' costs or just price discrimination—or both—is not at issue in this section (see Chapter 12 about that). The question here is only how large the discounts are. We will consider the main kinds of inputs one by one.

Capital commonly does offer pecuniary gains. There are two parts to this: the price of funds and their availability. The price of capital is usually lower for larger firms, especially those that hold secure market positions. This is shown by cross-section surveys of loan costs by size of firms, and also by more precise studies.[19] The advantage is often 3 to 5 percentage points and even more (such as between 8 and 12 percent interest rates).

Availability also favors the larger, more secure firms. They have longer lines of credit and other protections against the scarcity of funds common during adverse periods. Credit rationing falls primarily on firms that are smaller and less powerful.

Utility services are usually cheaper to larger users. The price differences are perhaps steepest for electricity and gas, but they are also present to some extent in telephone and railroad rates. (For example, electricity may cost on average at least one-third less to a large user than to a small one.[20]) Transport services usually offer a variety of quantity discounts. Rail freight rates have been highly discriminatory, mainly in favor of larger shippers.

Large-contract discounts are customary also for *advertising* services of many kinds and in many media. Those for television and newspaper advertising have drawn the sharpest comment, but discounts in radio and magazines have probably also been significant. The advantage goes beyond price to include access to prime time and favored pages.

There is naturally great variation in patterns for the many kinds of *raw and semifinished inputs*, but some degree of large-order discounting is common. In some cases, as in tire purchases by major automobile companies, the large-buyer price cuts are deep. In others, they are nominal or absent. In virtually no significant cases do larger buyers pay *more* than smaller ones.

Executive talent may also come cheaper "per unit" to larger firms. Company size inherently offers added scope and rewards to those in charge (or hoping eventually to be). Larger firms within any given industry often attract a superior caliber of executive, at no higher corresponding cost in salary and direct benefits.

The net pecuniary gains to size appear to be significant. In some cases, they may be quite large. The reverse cases, benefiting smaller firms on balance, are probably rare. Pending contrary research findings, one can assume that large firms—and firms with high market shares—do have a degree of pecuniary economies.

---

[19] The Federal Reserve's periodic *Surveys of Bank Loans* are the best basic source of interest rates by sizes of loans and of borrowers.

[20] This can be seen from the Federal Energy Regulatory Commission's *Utility Rate Schedules* (Washington, D.C.: U.S. Government Printing Office, revised frequently), which cover all states. In some cases, the differences are even sharper.

4. The "Antitrust Dilemma"

Altogether, the economies of scale appear to be limited, so that market shares above 10 percent commonly embody mainly excess market share. To round out this issue, we now consider the leading cases of high market shares in U.S. industry. To what extent are their excess profits justified by the scale economies they achieve?[21]

The answer is direct and simple. The research on economies of scale covers eighty-five large U.S. manufacturing firms with market shares above 20 percent during the 1960s. They include such firms as IBM, General Motors, Eastman Kodak, Campbell Soup, and Gillette. Only for a few of these firms was MES greater than a 10 percent market share. And most of the cost curves probably had mild cost gradients.

A 10 percent market share is quite consistent with effective competition. Consequently there was virtually no important "antitrust trade-off" forcing a hard choice between competition and economies of scale. More generally, even in the few cases where excess market share was large, the small cost gradients meant that very little of the excess profits was justified by true scale economies.

In short, technical economies of scale provided little efficiency justification for the market shares above 20 percent held by leading companies in a variety of large U.S. industrial markets in the 1960s. Excess market shares were substantial in that decade, and the underlying trends in the last twenty years have probably increased them. Since scale economies appear to justify very little of the excess profits gained by these firms from their high market shares, the "antitrust dilemma" has been small and is probably getting even smaller.

VII. SUMMARY

The main results of research on the role of scale economies in concentration can be summed up as follows.

Methods.   One will usually need to use "expert" estimates, supplemented by data about existing size distributions and "survival." There is no single quick, clean method. No method is entirely free from bias. It is rarely possible to screen out all pecuniary elements.

There are reasonably reliable estimates of plant scale economies for about thirty industries. At the firm level, fewer than fifteen industries have been reliably estimated more recently than 1960.

General Cost Patterns.   Soft as most of the individual estimates are, when taken together they indicate that most industries have (1) relatively small optimal plant size (MES) and (2) roughly constant costs at the firm level. There is no broad trend toward greater scale economies in industry or other sectors. Cost gradients appear to be relatively flat in most cases, even at levels well below MES.

Pecuniary economies do exist, large ones in some cases. This means that the

---

[21] This section draws on W. G. Shepherd, "Monopoly Profits and Economies of Scale," in John Craven, ed., *Industrial Organization, Antitrust and Public Policy* (Boston: Kluwer Nijhof, 1982).

slopes of observed cost curves probably contain a degree of downward bias, especially at the firm level. The extent of this bias is conjectural. But it does mean that technical diseconomies probably prevail in many industries.

Exceptional Cases.   In most major markets with tight structure, the evidence seems to indicate that technical scale economies do not require the existing structure. The majority of such cases are still open issues that cannot be settled without more intensive scientific study.

Certain ''utility'' markets do have large genuine scale economies. Most such ''natural monopoly'' conditions, however, have not been thoroughly studied. In several important cases (such as railroads), ''natural-monopoly'' conditions have receded in recent decades. In some others (such as electricity and telephones), scale economies are checkered, so that only part of the sector is still a ''natural monopoly.'' (Example: Local telephone, electricity, and postal networks are virtually natural monopolies, but the intercity parts permit some degree of competition.)

Almost all of the true natural monopolies are now at the local level within cities; many of them are now under city ownership (water and sewage systems, for example). Some manufacturing industries verge on monopoly conditions because of the special role of sales forces (IBM and Campbell Soup may be good examples).

There is no clear, fixed line between ''normal'' industries and ''utilities.'' Instead there are shadings and, over time, shifts in the extent of economies of scale. Yesterday's utility has often lost its ''natural-monopoly'' basis and become a ''normal'' industry.

Basic Cost Functions.   Provisionally, research has tended to fit the basic cost diagrams in Figures 9.7 and 9.9. Figure 9.7 is close to the definition of *long-run* costs, while Figure 9.9 is often said to show *short-run* costs. This is roughly correct. Yet the distinction between *industry* conditions and the ongoing *firm* is also important.

The typical ''industry'' cost curve for the firm (see Figure 9.7) is dish-shaped, with MES at 5 percent of the market or less. The constant-cost range may be wide, though presumably average cost rises eventually because of (1) bureaucracy, from absolute size; and/or (2) X-inefficiency, caused by the firm's market power. The

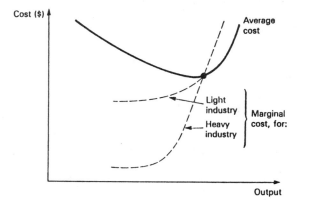

FIGURE 9.9.   Typical cost curve for an ongoing firm.

constant costs may also mask a significant amount of pecuniary gains. If one filters out the pecuniary economies, the typical cost curve may slope upward instead of being flat.

Cost curves for an ongoing firm (Figure 9.9) reflect the firm's capacity. Above that capacity, costs usually rise sharply. Below it, cost levels depend on technology. In "heavy" capital-intensive firms, marginal costs may be quite low. In "light" industry, where labor and other variable costs are more important, marginal costs may be relatively high and constant. The normal or "average" case will lie in between.

Research into economies of scale teaches economists to be modest. The conditions are real and socially urgent in hundreds of important markets. Yet after several decades of research effort, the findings are few and debatable, requiring careful, sophisticated evaluation. This is partly natural: on sensitive issues with high stakes, reliable evidence is likely to be scarce. The need is to select data carefully and use neutral methods on them.

QUESTIONS FOR REVIEW

1. "Many public policies cause structure to differ from what the strictly economic causes would give." True?
2. "Technical economies always occur separately from pecuniary economies." True?
3. "Physical laws always favor larger size." True?
4. "Managerial skill may be a fixed factor that causes diseconomies of scale in the plant or firm." True?
5. "High transport costs usually make the MES of plants larger than it would be from internal factors alone." True?
6. "Since 1880, the use of electric motors has increasingly favored large-scale production." True?
7. "If firms are more efficient, they will be more profitable. Therefore the relative profitability of different-size firms is a good indicator of relative technical efficiency." True?
8. "Engineering estimates are the best all-around method, but they can be supplemented from other sources." True?
9. The survivor test works best for (1) plants, (2) firms, (3) multiplant operations, (4) equally well for all three. Choose one.
10. "A random process could, in theory, account for the actual range of concentration in U.S. industries." True?
11. How does specialization reduce costs?
12. Discuss three physical laws that provide economies of scale.
13. Explain the difference between technical and pecuniary economies of scale.
14. What factors may cause diseconomies of scale in the firm? How can transport costs influence the optimal scale of the plant?
15. Show what is meant by "room for competition" and "excess market share." Try to indicate what those values might be for several real markets.
16. Explain how the learning curve is entirely separate from the average cost curve, no matter how similar they may look.
17. What conditions have probably caused a general decline in MES since the 1950s in US industries?

10 THE FIRM: CONCEPTS AND CONDITIONS

Few human inventions have the vitality and variety of the enterprise. It is the building block of the economy. The decisions of its officials drive the competitive process or—in varying degrees—create and enforce monopoly. The economy and its processes are nothing but the sum total of millions of firms' activities. The dimensions of these activities are suggested by Table 10.1.

This chapter about "the firm" could easily have been placed earlier in the book, to clarify these basic conditions at the outset. But industrial organization is about firms' behavior *in their market settings.* The inner workings of the enterprise are a somewhat different topic, often called *micro-microeconomics,* which is primarily the subject of its own economic field and of business school courses.

The firm is analyzed here mainly to ensure that conditions of motives, profit, risk, and corporate organization—*as they affect competitive and monopoly conditions*—are adequately covered. Therefore this is something of a survey chapter, focusing selectively on organization (Section I), motivations (Section II), and real-world patterns (Section III). Certain related topics of accounting are discussed in more detail in Appendix 3.

I. CONCEPTS OF THE FIRM[1]

The main issue that concerns us is the balance between the *market* process of transactions and interactions and the *internal conditions* of firms, which may organize the allocation of resources just as well. Each market's structure is partly a

---

[1] Among the rich variety of writings on the nature of the firm, see especially Ronald H. Coase, "The Nature of the Firm," *Economica,* 4 (November 1937), 386–405; Kenneth J. Arrow, "Control in Large Organizations," *Management Science,* 10 (April 1963), 397–408; Arrow, *The Limits of Organization* (New York: Norton, 1974); and Alfred D. Chandler, Jr., *The Visible Hand: The Managerial Revolution in American Business* (Cambridge, Mass.: Belknap Press, 1977). For reviews of the literature, see Richard E. Caves, "Corporate Strategy and Structure," *Journal of Economic Literature,* 18 (March 1980), 64–92; Robin Marris and Dennis C. Mueller, "The Corporation, Competition, and the Invisible Hand," *Journal of Economic Literature,* 18 (March 1980), 32–63; and Oliver E. Williamson, "The Modern Corporation: Origins, Evolution, Attributes," *Journal of Economic Literature,* 19 (December 1981), 1537–68.

TABLE 10.1   The Range of US Enterprises, 1984

	NON-FARM PROPRIETOR-SHIPS	PARTNER-SHIPS	CORPORATIONS, WITH REVENUES OF:		
			BELOW $5 MILLION	$5 MILLION TO $50 MILLION	ABOVE $50 MILLION
Total, all sectors					
Number (1000)	11,262	1644	3049	111	10
Revenues ($ billion)	516	318	1314	1321	4312
Agriculture, forestry, fishing					
Number (1000)	322	139	97	2	(2)
Revenues ($ billion)	11	6	76	18	14
Mining					
Number (1000)	153	57	39	2	(2)
Revenues ($ billion)	13	19	16	17	78
Construction					
Number (1000)	1386	64	297	9	(2)
Revenues ($ billion)	66	23	159	105	63
Manufacturing					
Number (1000)	320	29	244	25	3
Revenues ($ billion)	18	18	188	333	2093
Transportation, public utilities					
Number (1000)	572	21	134	4	1
Revenues ($ billion)	29	32	56	47	590
Wholesale, retail trade					
Number (1000)	2381	185	841	52	3
Revenues ($ billion)	196	72	548	667	1036
Finance, insurance, real estate					
Number (1000)	984	791	486	10	2
Revenues ($ billion)	30	55	57	43	331
Services					
Number (1000)	4990	332	891	8	1
Revenues ($ billion)	147	90	261	90	107

SOURCE: US Statistical Abstract, 1988, p. 496.

balance between those two great alternative processes: external market forces and internal firm organization.

The firm is an organization with its own independent life, form, and powers of decision. It is also embedded in a system of (1) market processes, (2) supply and customer relationships, and (3) financial supervision. We start by considering the purely internal conditions.

The firm extends its boundaries to include activities that it can do more efficiently by *internal* controls,than by *external* market transactions. If internal controls were always superior, firms would expand to replace all market activities. Instead, firms do have definite limits within large domains of market processes (except in cases of monopoly).

In theory, the contrast is extreme—internally, control is complete; externally, market choices are free and fluid. In practice, there are shadings. Internal control ranges between being quite complete (in small unified firms) and being very tenuous

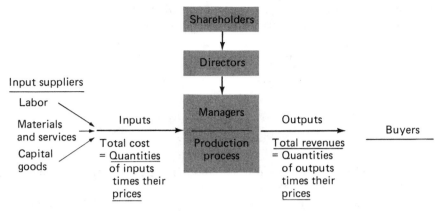

FIGURE 10.1.   The basic economic elements of an enterprise.

(in many large diversified holding companies). External transactions range widely, too—from brief, simple, anonymous exchanges to tight, complicated, long-term commitments that are as binding as direct controls.

The essence of the enterprise is clear and simple: "enterprise" is just a term for any unit where people produce a good or service. The enterprise may consist of one local plant (a factory or an office) or more, or of many hundreds of such plants. The corner drugstore is an enterprise, and so are IBM Corporation, the Chicago White Sox, the hospital where you were born, and your own college.

1.   Choices and Forms

Choices.   The private firm's main purpose is to create profit.[2] It does this by feeding inputs into a production process and then selling the outputs; if the revenues from selling outputs exceed what the firm pays for inputs, there is profit. Profit is the measure of success. It is a vector of the firm's two main activities: (1) *producing* outputs from inputs and then selling them, and (2) *owning* and financing the assets of the firm.

These two functions are performed as *side effects of—or as the means to—the "real," ultimate activity: the pursuit of profit.* The two activities are controlled mainly by the firm's upper managers. They decide policy, and they not only order lower-level employees to carry out their decisions but also supervise the employees' work. A firm's board of directors is legally responsible for its activities, and may have a broad influence, but the top managers usually dominate. Their control is unilateral: information flows up, orders pass down. Figure 10.1 shows the economic essentials of a typical private corporation.

Production is a "flow" concept, a process through time. Its outcome is summarized in the firm's "income statement" of revenues, costs, and profits. There are

---

[2] Other types—public firms, nonprofit enterprises, cooperatives, etc.—are discussed in Subsection III.2. Many of their features—such as accounting, structure, and technology—are identical with those of private firms.

many inputs, at their prices; and outputs, at their prices. The income statement
embodies this basic equation for profit (or net income):

$$\text{Profit} = \text{Total revenue} - \text{Total cost}$$

$$= \sum_{i=1}^{n} (\text{Price}_i) \times (\text{Quantity}_i) \tag{10.1}$$

$$- \sum_{j=1}^{m} (\text{Price}_j) \times (\text{Quantity}_j)$$

where i is one output among all outputs and j is one input among all imputs. Among
the inputs paid for are the executives' own services and the firm's capital, as well
as the routine kinds of raw materials, semifinished goods, and services such as
electricity and advertising. An exception: the "cost" of equity capital is paid out of
profit.

Profit is a margin of revenues over costs. Productivity is shown by the ratio of
total outputs to total inputs. Higher productivity usually yields higher profits. The
firm's actual costs and revenues represent single points on its cost and demand
curves. Good management minimizes the actual costs for the given level (or perhaps
bundle of levels) of outputs.

Ownership is a "stock" concept, involving control of the firm at each point.
The financial values appear in the firm's "balance sheet" of assets and liabilities.
The firm's capital assets embody its "real" production core: physical capital (land,
buildings, equipment), inventories, and working capital. Actually, the firm also exists
in the "human capital" of its workers and in the ongoing organization of the whole
business. But physical capital is the tangible form in which, by legal tradition, private
ownership of the firm exists, bears risk, and draws profit. Profits are earned for,
and transferred to, the owners—from the *income* statement to the *balance* sheet.

The owners are the stockholders; the board of directors supervises in their interests. The pivotal identifying fact of private corporate ownership is the *issuance
of voting stock to private holders*. The shareholders have the direct owner's stake
in the firm's performance. If earnings (net income) rise, dividends will rise and/or
more profit will be plowed back into the firm. Either way—directly by dividends,
or indirectly via retained earnings that raise the earning power and value of the
firm—the shareholders gain.

In this context, profitability becomes a rate of return on the owners' capital:

$$\text{Rate of return} = \frac{\text{Profit}}{\text{Equity capital}} \tag{10.2}$$

For any given level of capital, the rate of return is to be maximized. In the long run,
the level and pattern of investment are to be optimized, so that capital and profits
attain the "best" series of values year by year. Such an optimizing process will
maximize the present value of the firm. This present value in turn is, ideally, reflected
at every moment by the stock market's evaluation of the firm. The company's market
value equals the share price times the number of shares outstanding.

The firm (primarily the top managers, that is) therefore works in two contexts—*production* and *finance*. Production is an activity, a flow. Finance is more closely related to the structure of the firm—its capital and its organization chart. Profit links the two contexts.

Managers also work in two contexts of *time:* (1) they manage the current production process (economists call this "price-output policy"), and (2) they decide whether to change it for the future (investment and innovation choices). Current management is relatively routine. Setting future patterns is creative, difficult, and often risky—the term *entrepreneurship* glorifies it, but the task does require special talent. Investment levels and patterns must be selected. The firm's technology may need changing. Its organization chart may have to be redrawn. Personnel (including managers themselves) may have to be dropped or added. Even sticking with the old patterns often requires positive decisions to reject attractive new ways.

Thus the firm is a complex set of activities going on within a corporate shell, which is itself open to change. Certain forms, techniques, and rules are chosen from among the many possible ones. Profit maximizing is the animating and guiding force, but there is room for choice and debate about all aspects of a firm. Efficient, lively firms do in fact have a continuing process of internal debate and change. The formal, legal conditions of the firm—e.g., owners' "rights" or organization charts and responsibilities—may appear fixed and rigid from the outside, but they only express human efforts and experiments, which are changeable. What happens within the standard business setting is richly human. The marvel of the modern corporation is that it channels the unruly variety of human behavior along relatively consistent and productive lines, which we study here. Those lines evolve, and the degree of efficiency is an open issue, both in the aggregate and from case to case.

Forms. Figure 10.2 depicts the structure of a complex firm. The basic functions in all firms are similar, but in larger firms, they are more specialized and complex. This is the basic dilemma: *Specializing* permits a gain in the efficiency of

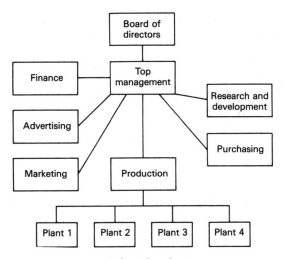

FIGURE 10.2. A functional structure.

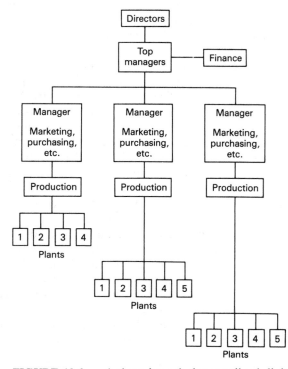

FIGURE 10.3.   A three-branch decentralized divisional firm.

doing the specific task, but *separation of activities* among people and groups makes it more difficult to coordinate and to gain accurate information about what is happening. It also diffuses responsibility. In short, it breeds bureaucracy.

In a one-manager firm, all the activities are done by one person—amateurish, perhaps, but certainly coordinated! Any sizable firm has to divide the activities among tens, hundreds, or thousands of employees. There are two basic ways to delegate the authority over these activities: along (1) *functional* or (2) *divisional* lines. Figure 10.2 shows a functional division. Each subunit is specialized to its task and is the only part of the firm that does it. A three-branch divisional form is depicted in Figure 10.3. Each division (really a separate firm under the holding company) combines many functions and operates in parallel with the others.

Neither the functional nor the divisional form is always "best."[3] It depends on the type and variety of the products, their technical similarity or diversity, the whole firm's size, its geographic spread, and other conditions. Most large firms have both kinds of arrangements: some functional lines in the upper levels, and some divisional separation among product lines. The choices between the two forms are often wide

---

[3] Good surveys and comparisons can be found in Alfred D. Chandler, Jr., *Strategy and Structure* (New York: Doubleday, 1966); and Oliver E. Williamson, *Corporate Control and Business Behavior* (Englewood Cliffs, N.J.: Prentice Hall, 1970). Williamson calls them "U form" for *unified* and "M form" for *multidivisional*.

open and debatable. Yet the underlying—and changing—technology can shape the optimal organization of a firm fairly closely in many cases. Basic changes in management tools (such as daily, comprehensive reports for all units of a large firm, via large computers) can shift the margin of optimal decentralization.

Every firm was new and small at some time. Large ones have simply grown faster and longer. Typically, the firm has a focus in one or a few primary products. As it grows, it may gradually add related items or diversify into whole new ranges of products. But most firms emphasize just one or a few primary lines of business. The firm's position in the markets for these primary products is usually more dominant, secure, and profitable than it is in the markets for its secondary products.

Almost every firm is diversified to some degree.[4] Why? *Technology* may make it easy and profitable to add secondary lines, which use the same basic methods. Research along old lines often leads to new, related products. *Demand* may also spur diversifying. Customers often want a "full line" of products, so sellers must develop them. As consumer preferences shift, the firm may need to shift into new lines. *Risk* may also be reduced by diversifying. The obvious example is pairing a cyclical product with a countercyclical one. More broadly, a mingling of disparate activities brings the central limit theorem into play. The average outcome of all activities will tend to be more stable than each one separately (*if* their individual risks are independent of each other or synchronized in opposition). Subsection II.3 discusses risk further.

These forces help set the degree of diversity in firms (Chapter 15 considers them in more detail). Ad hoc and random conditions also operate, often causing extreme "pure" diversifying that has no "reason." The gains from successful diversity— why, after all, not combine *everything* into one hundred firms, ten firms, or just one big firm?—must offset the costs incurred in trying to control many diverse activities. Delegation works, but within limits.

2. Simple Accounting and Success Criteria

Each firm's actions and conditions are recorded in detail and then summed up in quarterly and annual accounts. The "flow" of production—and the resulting costs and revenues—is shown for the period in an "income statement." The "stock" conditions of ownership are given in a "balance sheet." Samples are given in Table 10.2.

Accounting is far more complex and meaningful than dry lists of items in a ledger. It raises deep and murky issues, and the accounting choices reflected in the actual books are often hotly controversial.[5] Overhead costs are one such issue; the depreciation of capital, the value of inventories, and the treatment of taxes are others.

---

[4] Michael Gort discusses the reasons in his *Diversification and Integration in American Industry* (Princeton, N.J.: Princeton University Press, 1962).

[5] Among the best textbooks for clarifying these issues are Sidney Davidson, James S. Schindler, and Roman L. Weil, *Fundamentals of Accounting,* 5th ed. (Hinsdale, Ill.: Dryden Press, 1975); and Walter B. Meigs, A. N. Monich, and E. John Larsen, *Modern Advanced Accounting* (New York: McGraw-Hill, 1975); Eugene F. Brigham, *Fundamentals of Financial Management,* 4th Edition (Hinsdale, Ill.: Dryden Press, 1986); Charles T. Harngren and Walter T. Harrison, Jr., *Accounting* (Englewood Cliffs, N.J.: Prentice Hall, 1989).

TABLE 10.2   Yearly Accounts for a Typical Firm

($ MILLIONS)

INCOME STATEMENT

	1988	1989		1988	1989
Sales revenues	2,273	2,393	Earnings before taxes	419	433
Costs and expenses	1,854	1,960	Taxes on earnings	186	192
Labor and materials	851	898	Net income after taxes	233	241
Materials	533	561	Dividends	114	116
Services	189	202	Retained earnings	119	125
Depreciation	87	95			
Interest expense	194	204			

BALANCE SHEET

ASSETS	1988	1989	CLAIMS ON ASSETS	1988	1989
Current assets	503	526	Current liabilities	277	298
Financial	417	436	Accounts and rates payable	206	218
Inventories	86	90	Other	71	70
Gross plant and equipment	2,973	3,123	Long-term liabilities: Debt	1,378	1,378
Less depreciation	638	671	Stockholders' equity	1,183	1,302
Net plant and equipment	2,335	2,452	Common stock (when issued)	112	112
			Retained earnings	1,071	1,190
Total assets	2,838	2,978	Total claims on assets	2,838	2,978

Appendix 3 presents several of these technical issues. Here we treat only certain basic points.

The success of subunits of the firm can be gauged by their profitability if all costs and revenues can be correctly allocated among them. Often this is not possible, thanks to overhead costs. Often, too, the branches of the company are designed along functional lines (e.g., advertising, personnel, and finance departments), in which case profit tests for each one are not really appropriate. Other tests are then used—various physical or cost ratios, rates of growth, long-run and yearly targets, and still others. The ideal is to define "profit centers" wherever possible within the firm, and then let profitability serve as their test. Instead, the accounts usually require considerable judgment in adjusting all the activities, rewarding good performance, and steering the whole firm along its maximum profit path.

Profits, as we have said, are the excess of revenues over costs. All of the quantities and some of the prices will be under the firm's influence, if not absolute control. Profits therefore measure the firm's success *as a producer*. They also influence the going price of the firm's stock. That price is an index of the firm's success *as an owner*. The two measures are related but different.

How is the firm's profitability measured (the producing role)? One takes profits as a percentage return on all assets or on equity capital. Equity represents true ownership—the stockholders have the voting rights and assume the main risks of the firm. Return on equity is therefore a standard measure of the degree of profitability. Companies often wish to avoid looking *too* profitable, lest they be accused of overcharging their customers. Accordingly, firms with high turnover (high sales compared with capital) will often point to profits as a percentage of *sales* (e.g., a retail grocer or a restaurant). By contrast, capital-intensive firms will often try to draw attention to their returns on *assets*. The wise student is not fooled. Return on equity or assets is the correct indicator.

Since accounting involves some arbitrary choices, the figures for costs, revenues, and profits need to be evaluated carefully and skeptically (see Appendix 3). In fact, some experts believe accounting profits are so complex and manipulable that they are virtually worthless for evaluating and comparing firms. Special write-offs or tricks, or good luck or disaster from outside, may give strange results. Yet the discerning student will use the figures carefully rather than discard them. One is wise to average several years together, to iron out the odd years. One also inspects carefully for special factors (tax changes, special write-offs, inflation of inventory values, etc.) and is very cautious when comparing firms. Used carefully, accounting data can show both the nature of the firm's activities and the reasons for its success.

One must usually make do with company-wide totals. Firms include subtotals for their main lines of business on the so-called Form 10-K, but overhead costs and other accounting choices often make these details unreliable. Besides, they rarely get down to really detailed figures for products in well-defined markets. The grossing up into totals for the entire firm submerges the true variety of company market positions (in primary and secondary lines) into a bland average. Diversified firms carry this to extremes. As for market shares, barriers, vertical integration, and the like, the published accounting data simply do not, alas, give accurate facts about market positions. On the contrary, firms are always secretive about their market positions, fearing either to expose their best lines to attack or to reveal their weak lines. Certain facts can be obtained, but getting them is an art—and a scramble—as well as a science.

Learn to read company accounts, to ferret out odd items, and to form sound impressions of company performance. Learn also to judge data that differ in coverage and reliability. Rarely can one "just look it up." That is regrettable, but it also reflects the great importance of many of the facts!

3. Interpreting Results

Income Statements.   The top line in an income statement represents the firm's sales revenue, as shown in the sample statement in Table 10.2. The next lines cover the various costs that the firm must pay from its revenues. Most accounts lump the operating or production costs together; they include wages and salaries, materials and services. The wages and salaries paid to labor are usually the largest single cost, averaging about 50 percent of all costs. Materials are generally next in size. After operating costs come two *costs of capital*. The first is *depreciation*, representing the yearly wearing out and obsolescence of machinery and buildings. This decline in the value of the capital is made good by setting aside funds for its replacement. The second cost of capital is *interest* on the company's debt (its bonds and borrowings).

The difference between revenues and costs is earnings (or accounting profit) before tax. From those earnings, the federal tax on profits is paid. The *after-tax profit* is the company's yearly financial payoff for its ownership and production actions. The profit can be large, small, or negative. Since profit usually differs from year to year, it is necessary to take the *average* profit over a period of time to determine the firm's true profitability.

The firm usually pays out some of the accounting profits to shareholders as *dividends*. The paying out of dividends is optional; the firm can omit them, change them, keep them steady, do whatever it thinks best from year to year. The remainder of the profits—about two-thirds on average—is then kept by the firm as *retained earnings*. These funds can be used for expansion or other actions that will increase the value of the firm.

Balance Sheets.   The firm has productive assets, which appear on the lefthand side of its balance sheet. The firm has issued paper securities in the form of stocks and bonds to the people who gave it the money to buy these assets. These paper assets are liabilities to the firm, since they represent claims against its wealth. They appear on the righthand side of the firm's balance sheet. The stocks are the owners' claim on the firm's assets. By accounting methods, the total values in the asset and claims sides of the balance sheet are always equal.

Assets include two categories: current assets and long-term or fixed assets. *Current assets* are mainly cash, accounts receivable, and inventories. *Fixed assets* are the real plant and equipment the firm has built up over the years. They include machinery, buildings, land, and any other valuable and lasting capital that is used in production.

Fixed assets are listed first at their *gross original value,* which is the sum of all the prices paid for the items when they were acquired. Then is listed the sum of *depreciation* accrued (representing the deterioration of the capital). The difference is the net accounting value of the firm's fixed capital, called *net plant and equipment.*

The claims against these assets are of two types. First are *debt liabilities*, amounts of money owed by the firm to its bondholders and to others who have lent money to the firm in loans of varying lengths. These liabilities impose the cost of interest payments, which must be made if the firm is to remain in business. Second is *equity* (or net worth) of the firm: assets minus liabilities equals stockholders' or investors' equity.

The accounting value of stockholders' equity arises from two main sources. One is the money acquired by selling stocks. *Retained earnings* make up the rest of equity. They are simply the sum of all income retained over the years of the firm's existence. Accounting values for equity represent the owners' stake in the business, but only in accounting terms. The actual market value of the firm as judged by investors is determined by the daily buying and selling of the firm's stock in the stock market.

The stock's price may fluctuate widely. Often the firm's market value moves broadly in line with the book value of its assets and stockholder equity, but there is no direct tie. Indeed, the challenge for management is to deploy the firm's assets so that their value in use—in generating excess profits—will be much greater than their cost. The extra value can be created by good management, luck, monopoly power, innovation, or simply by inflation. The accounting values for equity do not show these opportunities. Rather, they merely record the sum of past amounts.

The firm's aim is to have large and growing profits as a return on stockholders' equity, so that it can both pay dividends to the stockholders and build up the business through investment. The stockholders benefit either way: dividends give them an immediate reward, and the plowing back of retained earnings increases the firm's capacity and prospects for future profits, which, in turn, increase the value of the business and cause the firm's stock to be bid up in the stock market. Therefore retained earnings can give the owners a capital gain in their stock prices.

4.   Success Indicators: Profits and Stock Prices

Profitability is the main index of a private firm's economic performance. The company will naturally publicize its other socially attractive activities, such as the number of jobs it creates, the high-quality outputs it produces, its exports, innovations, and so on. But these are all secondary to the firm's main goal: to earn a large and increasing flow of profits for its investors.

Profitability is a matter of degree, not of absolute amounts. The simple total of dollar profits is not enough to show how profitable a firm is. A local lumber company with $1 million in profits in a year may have a higher degree of profitability than the largest oil firm, Exxon, with its yearly total profits of over $3 billion. The reason is that profit as a percentage of capital or *rate of return on equity* is the correct measure of profitability, for that shows how well the firm is managing its owners' capital.

The simple formula for profitability is:

$$\text{Rate of return} = \frac{\text{Net income after taxes}}{\text{Capital}} = \frac{\text{Total revenue} - \text{Total cost and taxes}}{\text{Invested capital}}$$

For total invested capital, the usual accounting figure is stockholders' equity. You can easily calculate the profit rate for the sample firm's 1989 results in Table 10.2:

$$\text{Rate of return} = \frac{\$433 \text{ million}}{\$1,302 \text{ million}}$$

$$= \frac{\$2,393 \text{ million} - \$1,960 \text{ million} - \$192 \text{ million}}{\$1,302 \text{ million}} = 33.3 \text{ percent}$$

This remarkably high rate of return is for one year. To judge the firm carefully, you must consider the average profit over some three to five years, to even out any odd yearly fluctuations.

Each owner and manager seeks profit rates much higher than the 8 to 10 percent that is the average rate of return. Their nightmare is to run losses. Only by managing production well and keeping costs low and revenues high can the firm's officials produce good profits for the owners.

Stock prices are the other main success indicator for the private firm. Each share of stock offers its owners a chance to get future dividends and capital gains (that is, a rise in the price of the share itself). The firm's managers want to satisfy the investor-owners by making the company prosper, so that (1) dividends will grow and/or (2) the stock price will rise and provide capital gains. The share's price depends on demand and supply in the stock market. And both supply and demand, in turn, depend on what investors think of the company's performance.

Since most large-scale investors are pretty well informed, they act quickly (recall

Chapter 8). Therefore stock prices usually move swiftly and sensitively. Accordingly, the market value of a stock largely depends both on the firm's *future* prospects and on its current performance in maximizing profits. *Current stock prices are usually a sensitive, quickly adjusting index of investors' judgments about each firm's whole performance, both present and expected.*

II. MOTIVATION

1. Ownership and Control

In the millions of small businesses, ownership and control are combined in one person, who makes the decisions and also benefits from whatever financial success the firm achieves. But as size increases, *ownership tends to become divorced from control.* The stocks are bought and sold among many investors, while the managers become a more specialized group who draw salaries and may own little of their company's stock.

This divorce of ownership from control evolved after 1890 as large corporations grew and stockholding became diffused. In a landmark book published in 1932, Berle and Means argued that this divorce—a "managerial revolution"—had changed the nature of large corporations.[6] The managers were now free from close control and able to run the firms pretty much as they wished. Since 1932, the trend has continued, so that in many of the largest 1,000 corporations there is no major controlling block of shares.

The board of directors still supervises the executives and has to approve all major decisions. But the board and the executives are often largely independent of stockholder control and can select their own members and set their own guidelines. Indeed, on many boards of directors, the executives themselves hold key positions and dominate the discussions. Single owners or large financial institutions (banks, insurance firms) may hold 2, 5, or even 10 percent of the stock in some of these companies, but control is still firmly in the hands of the managers. Such firms may still perform virtually all their activities and make decisions just as if control and ownership were unified. Indeed, a number of studies have shown that the divorce is not as great, or as influential on behavior, as has been claimed.[7] Table 10.3 compares control of U.S. corporations in 1929 and 1974.

Moreover, the divorce between owning and controlling need not be economically harmful. Instead, it encourages executive continuity and professionalism by replacing the old-style industrial buccaneer with the cool modern manager. This may cause two differences in the manager-controlled corporation. First, actions are usually

---

[6] A. A. Berle and Gardiner C. Means, *The Modern Corporation and Private Property* (New York: Macmillan, 1932; rev. ed., Harcourt, Brace & World, 1968).

[7] See Philip H. Burch, Jr., *The Managerial Revolution Reassessed* (Lexington, Mass.: Heath, 1972). Among the extensive literature on motives in large firms, good surveys can be found in Richard M. Cyert and James G. March, *A Behavioral Theory of the Firm* (Englewood Cliffs, N.J.: Prentice Hall, 1963); and Oliver E. Williamson, *Markets and Hierarchies: Analysis and Antitrust Implications* (New York: Free Press, 1975). For evidence, see William A. McEachern, *Managerial Control and Performance* (Lexington, Mass.: Heath, 1975); and W. Mark Crain, Thomas Deaton, and Robert Tollison, "On the Survival of Corporate Executives," *Southern Economic Journal*, 43 (January 1977), 1372–75.

TABLE 10.3   Varieties of Ultimate Control in the 200 Largest Nonfinancial Corporations in the United States (1929 and 1974)

	NUMBER OF CORPORATIONS		PROPORTION OF COMPANIES	
TYPE OF CONTROL	1929	1974	1929	1974
Management control	81	165	40.5%	82.5%
Minority control	65	29	32.5	14.5
Private or majority ownership	19	3	9.5	1.5
Other (e.g., legal device)	35	3	17.5	1.5
Total	200	200	100 %	100 %

SOURCE: Adapted from Edward S. Herman, *Corporate Control, Corporate Power* (Cambridge: Cambridge University Press, 1981), pp. 58–64.

more predictable and objective, rather than reflecting the personality and whims of a single powerful owner. Second, the managers may focus less on maximizing profits for the owners and more on growth, managerial perquisites, and other social benefits.

2.   Managers' Goals

Managers are not ciphers who make mechanical decisions that maximize profits. Their own personal motivations may influence corporate outcomes, and so these motives need to be examined.[8]

Most managers are rewarded for good performance by extra pay, bonuses, and promotions. Their performance is rated by various criteria, such as personal "efficiency," growth or profits of their unit, or specific actions. At lower levels, there are fairly objective tests and comparisons for finding out who is doing well. The criteria are usually designed to fit the policy goals laid down by the top managers.

At higher management levels the criteria for performance are less precise, and personal differences in style and judgment come to the fore. Upper managers settle complex issues of judgment, which are unique, nonrepeatable, and uncertain. Moreover, the upper manager's pay is a complex matter of bargaining that is not neatly tied to marginal value product.

Agency Theory.   The practical difficulties of judging top management's performance have given rise in recent years to theories about the "principal—agent"

---

[8] Among the large body of literature on motives and large firms, good surveys can be found in Richard M. Cyert and James G. March, *A Behavioral Theory of the Firm* (Englewood Cliffs, N.J.: Prentice-Hall, 1963); and Oliver E. Williamson, *Markets and Hierarchies: Analysis and Antitrust Implications* (New York: Free Press, 1975). and Fritz Machlup, "Theories of the Firm: Marginalist, Behavioral, Managerial," *American Economic Review,* 57 (March 1967), 1–33. Robert F. Lanzillotti, "Pricing Objectives in Big Companies," *American Economic Review,* 48 (December 1959), 921–40, reported authoritatively that large firms' managers expressed a variety of objectives besides pure profit maximizing. Much of that variety may still be common. Another important study is Robert J. Larner, *Managerial Control and the Large Corporation* (New York, Dunellen, 1970).

TABLE 10.4   Directions for Managers' Motivations

DIRECTION OF PREFERENCES	COMMENTS
Profit	This is traditionally the primary criterion.
Time preference	This may vary sharply but still be consistent with long-run profit maximizing.
Risk	Is risk aversion "normal"? Managers differ in attitudes toward risk.
Expense preferences	These are a form of nonpecuniary rewards—"the good life." They may also include simple sloth and slack, or "the quiet life."
Sales maximizing	Or growth maximizing. Sales may just be a rule of thumb for seeking maximum long-run profits.
Social values	These may tip occasional close decisions. "Goodwill" from social actions may increase profits, too.

problem.[9] The basis of "agency theory" is the fact, known since Berle and Means's 1932 book, that managers, though acting as the agents for the stockholders (the principals, or owners, of the firm), may have motives that diverge from those of the principals they are supposed to serve. The theory states that these divergences can be examined under various assumed conditions.

Agency theory assumes that managers vary in their effort levels, and that valid judgments on their performance depend on having access to information about the firm's performance possibilities. In plain English, managers may try to hide the firm's real opportunities so they can ease up in their work. Some of the analysis also uses insurance and risk concepts, in which the owners seek to attain maximum profits, subject to various constraints about the risk of capital losses.

Much of the theory has focused on ways to design management pay so as to align managers' interests with those of the owners. The results have been unsurprising: pay and bonuses should be tied to profits and/or capital gains through profit-sharing or stock option schemes. Those two devices are in fact widely used.

Directions of Managers' Motivations.   Managers' motives may certainly help explain striking differences in performance among real firms. They may also modify the outcomes that monopolists and oligopolists reach. Table 10.4 presents the main points from the growing research on the topic.

"Profit maximizing" by top managers requires using judgment in loose and complex situations. Where the firm is large and dynamic, and its profits are well above minimum competitive levels, the criterion of stock price may be weakened because it is not so directly compelling and precise.

Managers' time preferences will set companies' long-run profit strategies. Re-

---

[9] See Harvey J. Leibenstein, *Beyond Economic Man* (Cambridge, Mass.: Harvard University Press, 1976), for a discussion of managers and workers as agents. See also S. Grossman and O. Hart, "An Analysis of the Principal-Agent Problem," *Econometrica*, 51 (1983), 7–45; and W. Rogerson, "The First-Order Approach to Principal-Agent Problems," *Econometrica*, 53 (1985), 1357–68. Jean Tirole, *The Theory of Industrial Organization* (Cambridge, Mass.: MIT Press, 1988), offers a useful summary of certain pure theoretical issues on pp. 51–55.

placing a "farsighted" president with one who is in a hurry can shift the strategy sharply.

Risk is that part of future uncertainty that is relatively systematic and predictable, but which is still dangerous because it can bring financial ruin. Managers often have strong preferences concerning risk.

Expenses may actually be preferred by managers rather than squeezed to the minimum. Any company has many directions in which a slight increase in inputs can be used to add to the managers' sense of status and affluence. The results can be opulent, especially in things seen and used by the top managers, or subtle and easy to justify as "higher quality," good for the company's "image," necessary to attract good managers, and so forth. "X-inefficiency" and "slack" are concepts that include this effect. In extreme cases, the added expenses can soak up most or all of the available profits. Every lucrative firm faces this problem.

Sales maximizing may also occur.[10] Managers may choose to enlarge their sales as a criterion of success, because (1) large and growing sales enhance their own sense of importance, and/or (2) greater sales may tend to result indirectly in maximum long-run profits. Figure 10.4 illustrates the sales-maximizing choice, using standard curves for total, average and marginal revenue, for costs, and for profits.

The managers may set themselves some floor for a "satisfactory" profit rate, as shown by the slightly up-sloping minimum profit constraint in Figure 10.4. Or they may just choose a level of output that is higher (at point C) than simple profit-maximizing would involve (at point A). Note that point C involves a gap between marginal cost and marginal revenue, in the lower panel of Figure 10.4.

Note also that the vertical gap between A and B in Figure 10.4 involves a sacrifice of profits, and therefore it invites a takeover by other firms eager to achieve those profits. Therefore, the sales-maximizers' sacrificing of profits will rarely be done very openly or clearly! On the contrary, it will be done quietly and only in ways which *don't* look like sacrificing. But if the profit hill is rather flat, then managers would reach much higher sales levels, even if they do not sacrifice very much profit.

In any event, sales-maximizing choices tend to increase the level of output, thereby improving the degree of allocational efficiency. Sales maximizing dilutes the restrictive effects of market power, shifting the monopoly result upward toward the competitive output level.

Does this really happen in any strong degree? Research has been inconclusive. Some moderate sales maximizing may happen in some situations, but the stock-market treadmill (reinforced by the ultimate threat of take-overs) tends to squeeze it out.

Social contributions are often implicit in a company's actions. There are always repercussions on jobs, sales, and prices, which help some and hurt others outside the firm. These effects can enter explicitly into the managers' choices if they temper their private profit-maximizing decisions with social concerns. On occasion, such social stewardship has been said to be important in certain large firms. Indeed, many managers are quite aware of the social impacts of their choices. Often their awareness is sharpened by direct urgings and threats by the outside groups who would be the gainers or losers.

---

[10] William J. Baumol's discussion is perhaps the most realistic: *Business Behavior, Value and Growth,* rev. ed. (Englewood Cliffs, N.J.: Prentice Hall, 1967).

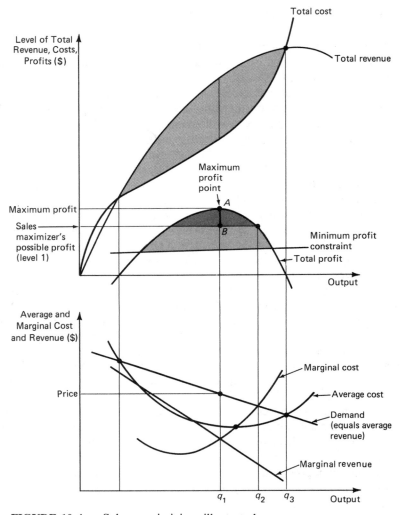

FIGURE 10.4.   Sales maximizing, illustrated.

Normally, profits are reduced when such social aims alter the managers' choice. The classic instance is keeping an unprofitable plant going—or locating a new plant in a distressed region—in order to provide jobs. Others are voluntary avoidance of pollution, "buying American," helping in urban redevelopment, and contributing to education, churches, and other worthy groups. Lucrative firms are, indeed, a prize target for all kinds of requests for benevolence.

Yet the system leans against social motives. The stock market "treadmill" tends to limit them. As for preferences and skills, managers are rarely trained or encouraged to perform "socially" *on* the job. Professionalized management standards leave executives little room for social considerations except as a spare-time hobby. Therefore any corporate philanthropy is usually intended to create goodwill as part of a genuine strategy for long-run profit maximizing. "Social" actions in that sense can often serve a firm's private profit aims. For that reason, the firm will wish to foster the belief that it does make social contributions. But the basic conditions are not favorable for very many of them.

The three main forces militating against social contributions are (1) the stock market treadmill effect (and, ultimately, the threat of takeover), (2) professional standards and methods of management, and (3) the intrafirm competition among managers for pay and promotion. Because of these forces, the company's scope for nonprofit directions of choice may not seem very large to those inside it.

The *insider problem* is one major point about managerial motives that is not listed in Table 10.4. Each firm is, by definition, full of insiders who know their firm's actions and prospects at first hand. Upper-level managers have especially close access to such inside information. It is, in fact, their job to know it and act on it for the firm's (i.e., shareholders') benefit.

Yet inside information is a key to capital gains, for it guides buying and selling stock ahead of the market. The way managers handle the release of information can therefore affect the capital gains that they and others make. Ideally, news of changes that will affect the firm's profitability would be instantly and equally available to all. Instead, it comes out by degrees.

Crude conflicts of interest arise when top insiders trade for their own benefit. In the United States, some of this trading at the expense of shareholders is limited by public rules (so-called insider laws). But subtler, informal methods of using inside information (for friends, relatives, and others) are scarcely limited, even after the insider scandals of 1986–1988. Such actions reduce the fairness of the outcomes. Under certain conditions, insiderism will not harm the efficiency with which companies perform and the capital markets operate, but normally it does cause social costs. Inside information is inherently a widespread problem, which can relate closely to managers' motivation.

3. Profits and Risk

The return to capital contains several distinct economic elements: (1) *the pure interest rate on invested capital,* which would be earned if investment had no risk; (2) a *risk premium,* which is an additional return required to reward investors for risky investment; and (3) any remainder, which is *economic profit* (or "excess" profit). Because risk is a key concept, we consider it first.

When funds are invested, the owner bears some risk about the outcome. Since risk is normally viewed as unpleasant, investors must be rewarded with extra returns. A *risk-return relationship* is, accordingly, a basic feature of investment decisions. To analyze it, we must first define risk.[11]

Risk means a degree of hazard. For the firm, the hazard is financial. Bankruptcy or insolvency are the extreme cases, but there are lesser degrees of distress. If the "bad" result can be defined (e.g., zero profit, or "only" 5 percent profit, or minus 15 percent profit, either briefly or for a certain period), then risk is the probability

---

[11] The classic discussion can be found in Frank H. Knight, *Risk, Uncertainty and Profit* (New York: Harper & Row, 1921), and it is a staple topic in textbooks on corporate finance.

of its occurring. Risk therefore has two components: *severity* and *probability*. Severity is often difficult to define. In practice, managers often deal with a range of technical and financial risks that they do not even attempt to define precisely. Instead, subjective impressions of hazard (severity *plus* probability) influence their choices toward what is "safer."

Many analysts distinguish *risk* from *uncertainty*. *Risk* is that component of dispersion in future events that can be predicted by laws of chance—the "insurable" part. All else is *uncertainty*—unique, unpredictable events for which a probability distribution cannot be derived. We need not adhere rigidly to this distinction because it is often impossible to state just where the line between risk and uncertainty lies. Many firms simply undertake many risks, without trying to insure part or all of them.

Short-Term Risk: Fluctuations.   Most of the analysis in the literature has been about short-term risk. It is usually defined in terms of quarterly or yearly fluctuations (or variance) around a predicted rate of return. This concept can be useful in guiding portfolio choices made by investors, and it also clarifies some choices made by managers. A normal distribution is assumed, and the risks from wide fluctuations in profit rates can be neatly analyzed on an abstract plane. Risk is just the standard deviation of profit rates around their average level.

Actually, true risk would be only the *downward* part of the fluctuations. Also, the variance in rates of return is not the only, or best, way to portray risk. Severity can be defined in terms of cash flow—say, a threshhold volume of cash flow that is regarded as intolerably low. Another reservation about the concept is that a highly precise analysis of risk is grossly unsuited to those many actual risks that can only be guessed at. That instability causes discomfort is obvious; that is the gist of most theories of risk. But risk itself can be complex and hard to measure.

Long-Term Risk.   Long-term risk is often more important. Especially for large and profitable firms, the real risks are that the basic position of the firm will be shaken by big changes in technology, in taste, or in competitive conditions. Such hazards may seem farfetched, and—being subjective—they are hard to measure and analyze. Yet they often haunt, and influence, the major decisions made by managers.

Defining such long-term risks is usually controversial. Even simple comparisons among firms' degrees of long-term risk can be a futile exercise. Yet, even if measurement is difficult, one can still analyze risk-return choices in theory.

The Risk-Return Relationship.   Because risk is unpleasant, people will usually accept it only if they expect compensating rewards. For example, steeplejacks and oil-drilling workers usually get higher pay than comparable workers who have safe jobs. Similarly, in investment choices, the reward for risk bearing is often a higher-than-average level of expected return.

Consequently, economists and financial analysts apply the concept of a *risk-return relationship:* Investments with higher risks must offer higher average returns. Most investors are *risk-averse*—they dislike risk and must be compensated for bearing it. Only the prospect of an unusually high reward will induce them to accept danger. Exceptions can be found, of course, but they *are* exceptions.

Accordingly, there is usually a positive relationship between risk and expected returns. In Figure 10.5, risk is represented on the horizontal axis, from zero to high

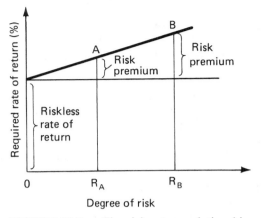

FIGURE 10.5.   The risk-return relationship.

degrees of risk; the required rate of return is represented on the vertical axis. As risk increases, so does the rate of return that the investor will require.

At zero risk, the required rate of return will be 10 percent, the same rate that would be available without appreciable risk to investors in short-term U.S. government securities. At higher risk levels, higher rates of return are required. The difference between these rates of return and the riskless rate of return is the *risk premium:* the reward for bearing risk. In Figure 10.5, a risk level of R_A involves the specific risk premium shown; the higher risk level of R_B requires a risk premium twice as large. These premiums reflect the general preferences of investors between risk and returns, as expressed by their actions in financial markets.

Alternative outcomes along the risk-return relationship are equivalent to one another for the average manager or investor. At each point, the risk premium offsets the disadvantage of the risk. Therefore the riskless return is as attractive as point A with R_A risk or point B with R_B risk.

Risk-return patterns can be observed in actual financial markets. Risk itself is difficult to measure, because it deals with future probabilities that are inherently unknowable with precision, as are all future conditions.

One measure of risk is the ratings of bond quality made by the two major investment analysis companies, Moody's Investors Service and Standard & Poor's Corporation (S&P). These ratings reflect the estimated probability of default on the bonds, which would reduce or eliminate their value. In making the ratings, the two firms assess many features of the companies and governments that issue bonds: their stability, prospects, profitability, and other conditions. They then assign the bonds a rating ranging from "high quality" to "speculative," as follows:

	High Quality		Investment Grade		Substandard		Speculative
Moody's	Aaa	Aa	A	Baa	Ba	B	Caa to D
S&P	AAA	AA	A	BBB	BB	B	CCC to D

The ratings reflect judgments, not mechanical formulas. They are widely accepted as useful practical indexes of risk. They also directly affect the interest rates that must be paid. A B-grade bond of a risky company will have to offer a rate of interest higher than the rate on an Aaa bond, precisely because the B bond carries more risk of loss. U.S. government long-term bonds have the lowest yields because they have the lowest risk.

Diversifying.   One way for investors to reduce risk is to choose a single low-risk investment, such as a U.S. government or an Aaa bond. Another way is to *diversify,* by choosing several investments that, though they individually have risk, will tend as a group to offer stability.

The fundamental principal is the *law of large numbers:* The larger the sample drawn from a random distribution of possible outcomes, the more likely it is that the sample's average value will equal the total distribution's average value. In short, there is safety in numbers. The yield on a diversified selection of investments will tend to be close to the average yield of all assets in the market. It will be higher than the yield on a single risk-free investment.

III.   REAL FIRMS

Now we turn to real enterprises in real markets. This discussion is mainly about corporations, for they handle most of the market activity in Western economies. There are also other kinds of enterprises, as we will see below. By understanding them, you gain a better perspective on the private corporation and its details. The final section presents the shares and trends of the various sizes of firms.

1.   Corporations

Though private corporations are not the most numerous type of firm in the United States, they conduct over three-fourths of the economic activity, as Table 10.1 showed. The corporations' shares dominate manufacturing, utilities, and some other sectors, but not all of them. In farming, retailing, and services, other business types are also common. The corporate shares have been steady for several decades. Partnerships, small proprietorships, cooperatives, nonprofits, public firms, and others are holding their own.

Almost all really large enterprises *are* corporations, for several familiar reasons. The shareholders' liability is limited to the value of their investment. Large volumes of capital can be raised more easily. And the corporation need not be reorganized when mere mortals pass on. Therefore most goods are actually produced in corporations, though consumers may do most of their personal dealings with noncorporate retailing firms.

In the size distribution of all U.S. corporations, the relatively few largest ones do not dominate. Firms below $500 million in assets do 60 percent of sales by all corporations. The patterns are not much different in Britain, France, and other Western countries. We may visualize several kinds of corporations, ranging from "small" to "medium," "large," and "very large." "Small" and "medium" corporations are often managed by the main owner and his or her relatives. Company structure is simple and the product line is usually narrow.

Large Firms.   As size increases, these patterns grow complex. Table 10.5 presents the largest firms in the main sectors of the economy. In such large enterprises, ownership is spread thinly, with few holdings above 5 or 10 percent. Managers are largely free of close shareholder control, and they usually dominate the board of directors. Banking relationships remain strong in all but the few very largest firms.

Much power is delegated. The top executives mainly set basic policy and make a few large decisions (a new plant, reorganizing, "turning around," or merging the firm). Top officers usually hold office briefly; about four years on average. This is normally too short to design and carry out major changes, so larger firms have their own momentum. Since promotion from within is the norm, most top officers share in policymaking over a long period of time.

Therefore policies usually *evolve* through a process of committee decisions. The aggressive individualist—the tycoon, or Schumpeterian type of enterpreneur—is not given much scope in many of the larger firms. These firms tend, instead, to encourage caution and sameness. Management is therefore risk-averse and conservative.

The larger firms usually maintain a reasonable degree of profitability and stability. Even a bad year or two rarely exposes them to threat of bankruptcy or takeover. Among smaller firms, the process of birth, failure, and absorption is much more active. The numbers are large: about 16,000 businesses fail each year in the United States and many others merge, while about 500,000 new corporations are formed. The larger firms stand out as relatively secure exceptions to the flux and risks of ordinary small business.

Real corporations, therefore, differ considerably in size, form, and character. Yet their managers are subject to more stress than is apparent from the outside. And there is uniformity in the pressures for profit and in the racial and sex types of managers.

2.   Other Types of Firms

Much of this chapter's content applies not only to private profit-making firms but also to public, nonprofit, and cooperative firms.

All firms need to make efficient choices about inputs, outputs, and investments, but these other types of firms differ from private enterprises in that profit is not the single motive for their policies and actions. They usually have social goals as well. Some of these firms seek to supply goods to needy people at low prices. Others provide important services that no private firm could supply at a profit. Still others furnish "utility" services (such as municipal electric systems and the U.S. Postal Service) for which private operators, having a monopoly position, might charge too high a price.

Taken together, these nonprivate firms are a diverse and important group of enterprises, covering nearly one-fourth of all U.S. economic activity. Nonetheless, economists have studied them very little, choosing to focus instead on private enterprise.

TABLE 10.5 The Largest US Firms, in Various Sectors

Name	Main Products	Sales ($ Billion)	Assets ($ Billion)	Employees (1,000)	Average Profit Rate on Investors Equity 1985–88[a] (%)
Manufacturing					
General Motors	Cars, trucks	$121.1	$164.1	765.7	12.6
Ford Motor	Cars, trucks	92.4	143.4	358.9	23.4
IBM	Computers	59.7	73.0	388.2	16.3
General Electric	Electric equipment	49.4	110.9	310.0	17.6
Chrysler	Cars	35.5	48.6	130.2	19.8
Du Pont	Chemicals	32.5	30.7	140.5	11.8
Philip Morris	Tobacco products	25.9	37.0	116.5	28.0
Proctor & Gamble	Toiletries	19.3	14.8	75.3	11.2
United Technologies	Aircraft engines, diversified	18.1	12.7	188.4	11.6
Eastman Kodak	Photographic supplies	17.0	23.0	134.9	15.1
Boeing	Aircraft	17.0	12.6	7.5	11.3
RJR Nabisco	Tobacco, food products	16.7	17.8	116.9	21.1
Dow Chemical	Chemicals	16.7	16.2	54.3	19.6
Xerox	Copiers	16.4	26.4	112.8	9.3
USX (US Steel)	Steel products	15.8	19.5	58.8	7.8
McDonnell Douglas	Aircraft	15.1	11.9	116.9	7.6
Pepsico	Soft drinks, diversified	13.0	11.1	230.0	25.8
Westinghouse	Electrical equipment	12.5	16.9	119.6	20.4
Rockwell Intl.	Diversified, military	11.9	9.2	114.2	20.5
Allied Signal	Aerospace	11.9	10.0	112.4	11.8
Oil Firms					
Exxon	Oil and products	79.6	74.3	100.5	15.9
Mobil	Oil and products	48.2	38.8	68.9	9.4
Texaco	Oil and products	33.5	26.3	46.0	8.4
Chevron	Oil and products	25.2	34.0	52.7	9.5
Amoco	Oil and products	21.2	29.9	50.1	14.5

258

Telephone					
AT&T	Telecommunications and equipment	35.2	35.2	303.6	15.0[b]
GTE	Telecommunications and equipment	16.5	31.1	160.0	14.1
Bell South	Local service and related	13.6	28.5	99.5	14.1
Nynex	Local service and related	12.7	25.4	96.4	14.0
Bell Atlantic	Local service and related	10.9	24.7	81.0	14.3
Electric					
Pacific Gas & Electric	Electricity and gas	7.6	21.1	27.0	13.0[b]
Southern Co	Electricity	7.2	22.3	32.6	12.7
S. Cal. Edison	Electricity	6.3	15.8	17.1	15.0
Commonwealth Edison	Electricity	5.6	20.2	17.9	9.0
Transportation					
UAL (United Air Lines)	Airline service	9.0	6.6	66.0	50.0[b]
AMR (Am. Airlines)	Airline service	8.8	9.7	67.9	14.5
Texas Air	Airline service	8.6	8.1	57.5	(−15.0)[b]
CSX	Railroad	7.6	13.0	54.0	4.3
Union Pacific	Railroad	6.1	12.2	47.3	14.4
Norfolk Southern	Railroad	4.5	10.1	35.1	12.3
Banks					
Citicorp	Banking	32.0	207.7	89.5	18.9
Chase Manhattan	Banking	12.4	97.5	42.0	21.9
Bank America	Banking	10.2	94.6	56.6	17.5
Security Pacific	Banking	8.5	77.9	41.9	16.6
JP Morgan	Banking	7.8	83.9	15.5	17.3
Retail					
Sears	Household goods	50.3	78.0	510.5	10.3
K Mart	Household goods	27.7	12.1	342.5	16.0
Wal-Mart	Household goods	20.6	7.0	191.5	27.8
JC Penney	Household goods	15.3	12.3	185.5	20.4
Dayton Hudson	Household goods	12.2	6.5	135.0	15.4

[a] for telephone, electric, transportation, banks and retail firms, profit rates are for 1988.

[b] estimated value, after allowance for a large one-time special charge against earnings or other special conditions.

SOURCES: *Fortune Magazine, The Fortune 500*, April 24, 1989, and earlier annual issues; *Business Week Magazine, The Business Week Top 1000*, Special Issue, May, 1989; and *Forbes Magazine, The Forbes 500s Annual Directory*, May 1, 1989.

Public enterprises are found in all sizes at the national, state, and local levels.[12]

Not-for-profit enterprises also include a great variety of firms "owned" by charitable groups that often have some special social purpose. Examples are many hospitals, private schools and colleges, the Red Cross system, city orchestras and cultural centers, and many day-care centers. Many of these units sell their services, but most rely heavily on contributions. Some struggle along always short of funds; others enjoy ample financing and rapid growth.

Cooperatives are enterprises owned by their customers or suppliers. Millions of farmers sell their crops, livestock, and milk through farm cooperatives, and they buy much of their supplies from them too. In the retail sector, cooperative food stores proliferated in the 1970s. In all cases, the cooperative enterprise tries to cover its costs with sales revenue, and it channels its "profits" back to its owners (customers or suppliers).

There are other types of enterprises even more uncommon, such as worker-owned firms. But virtually all business in the United States is conducted by private firms, public firms, nonprofit enterprises, and cooperatives.

3. Trends and Shares among Corporations

We return to the conditions of large private corporations, the core of industrial capitalism. What is their scope? What causes their position to change? What kind of ties exist between them? Finally, how do U.S. corporations compare to foreign corporations in these respects?

Scope.   Their scope is large, though the precise dimensions are uncertain and are fairly complex to measure. The usual procedure is to seek a single best measure of "aggregate concentration." Yet all such measures available have technical problems. The common measures are shares of assets, value added, employees, and profits; each has a slightly different meaning from the others. Assets may be the best indicator of the corporations' economic power. Value added shows their role in the country's production process. The large firms' share of workers reflects their influence over jobs and, perhaps, votes. And profits show their ability to gain market advantages compared to other types of firms. Figure 10.6 compares several measures, and Chapter 15 analyzes them in more detail.

Ideally, one would like to measure the corporations' role in the entire economy.[13] Yet most studies focus on the manufacturing sector because good, standardized, economy-wide data are not available, and therefore the comprehensive shares and trends cannot be shown precisely.

Even for the manufacturing sector alone, there is a problem in measuring aggregate concentration. Many companies have large foreign operations, which cannot be neatly factored out of their yearly totals. Nobody knows exactly how large this

---

[12] For a review of conditions in public firms, see William G. Shepherd and associates, *Public Enterprise: Economic Analysis of Theory and Practice* (Lexington, Mass.: Heath-Lexington Books, 1976).

[13] The literature on the scope and trends of large firms peaked in the 1960s. Among the best treatments are Berle and Means, *The Modern Corporation and Private Property;* Morris Adelman, "The Measurement of Industrial Concentration," *Review of Economics and Statistics,* 33 (November 1951), 269–96; and A. D. H. Kaplan, *Big Enterprise in a Competitive System,* rev. ed. (Washington, D.C.: Brookings Institution, 1964).

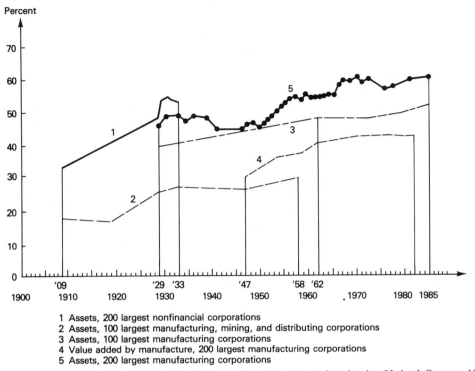

1 Assets, 200 largest nonfinancial corporations
2 Assets, 100 largest manufacturing, mining, and distributing corporations
3 Assets, 100 largest manufacturing corporations
4 Value added by manufacture, 200 largest manufacturing corporations
5 Assets, 200 largest manufacturing corporations

FIGURE 10.6.   Long-term trends of aggregate concentration in the United States, 1909–1982.

SOURCE: Adapted from John M. Blair, *Economic Concentration* (New York: Harcourt Brace Jovanovich, 1972), p. 63; Bureau of the Census, *Concentration Ratios in Manufacturing, 1982*, MC82-S-7 (Washington, D.C.: U.S. Government Printing Office, 1986); and Christian Marfels, "Aggregate Concentration in International Perspective: Canada, Federal Republic of Germany, Japan and the United States," a chapter in R. S. Khemani, D. M. Shapiro, and W. T. Stanbury, eds., *Mergers, Corporate Concentration and Power in Canada* (Halifax: Institute for Research on Public Policy, 1988).

element is or which way it is shifting. The foreign share is probably about 10 to 20 percent of total sales among the one hundred largest firms, and it may be changing.

Finally, which number of large firms is the "best" one for defining the share of large firms? One can slice the large-firm share at any of several levels: the largest 10, 25, 50, 100, 200, 500 firms, and so on. Each has been used. No single one of the measures is best, for each has a slightly different meaning. Also, their trends can go in mildly differing directions. So one tries to look cautiously at several of these measures.

Figure 10.6 presents a selection of the measures. Only a few series go back beyond 1947. The figure shows that the large corporations' share is "large" by any measure. But its rise since 1947 has tapered off, so Berle and Means's 1932 prediction (and Karl Marx's forecast in *Das Kapital*) that the biggest firms' share would keep rising toward total domination by a few firms does not fit recent events. The figure also shows that the shares of assets have continued to rise. However, if foreign activities have been an increasing portion of the total, then the large U.S. firms' share in domestic industry might actually have been decreasing slightly. (By contrast, the top foreign firms' shares in some countries have been rising during the last two decades, as we will see shortly.)

The Largest Firms.   The few really "giant" industrial corporations are a special group. The largest six firms—as we saw in Table 10.5—had well above $20 billion in sales in 1987. These very largest firms do not form an archetype for other enterprises: the sixteen firms with sales between $10 billion and $20 billion are much like the thirty-five firms with sales between $5 billion and $10 billion. "Corporate giantism," or the "megacorp," appears to be a specialized case, often with extensive X-inefficiency and difficulties in innovating.

Causes of Change.   Two kinds of change can occur in the position of large firms: (1) trends in their total share and (2) changes in their rankings. Both changes arise from the same four main causes:

1. *Industry growth rates and price trends differ.* In recent decades, such industries as automobiles, aircraft, electronics, copiers, and computers have enjoyed rapid growth, pulling up firms in these industries. By contrast, slow growth in steel, meat packing, copper, and other industries has exerted a downward pull on their firms. In short, differential industry growth has influenced the rankings of corporations and will probably continue to do so.

2. *Mergers* can cause big shifts in company rankings. Yet mergers have not strongly affected the trends in the shares of the largest firms. During 1909–1947, their role was modest, and during 1947–1980, mergers equaled only about 15 percent of all the asset growth of the 200 largest firms.[14] Even the 1980s merger boom has probably affected the totals only slightly.

3. *Government agencies* pay for much R&D activity, and they are large buyers of output from some industries. Federal funds (mainly through the Defense Department) have covered more than half of *all* industrial R&D. In some industries, they pay for nearly all of it. The effects on growth and size are often mixed, but they can be strong—aircraft and electronics are examples.

4. The *relative efficiency* of large firms may cause the main trends. When the large corporations' share was rising during 1947–1965, that was said to show these firms had superior efficiency. Yet the rise might reflect "pecuniary economies" rather than technical efficiency. At any rate, the steadiness of total shares since 1965 suggests that superior efficiency could not be a big factor.

Informal Ties.   There are several kinds of informal connections among corporations, and they may provide for a degree of control and unity that is greater than the bare company data show. Abroad, such ties often hold together large combines—Japan, Sweden, and Germany offer striking instances. In the United States, the links are usually indirect and incomplete, but they are important in some cases.

Family groups have been important, especially from 1900 to 1940. The Morgan interests reached into many large industries during 1880–1930; J. P. Morgan personally shaped many of these industries. Rockefeller and Du Pont holdings spread during 1890–1930 from oil and explosives to working control of leading firms in

---

[14] See J. Fred Weston, *The Role of Mergers in the Growth of Large Firms* (Berkeley: University of California Press, 1953), for the earlier period; and the Federal Trade Commission's annual reports on corporate mergers (discontinued by Reagan appointees to the FTC after 1979) for more recent decades.

several large industries, including banking, aluminum, automobiles, copper, coal, tires, and chemicals.[15] Other important family groupings also operated then or have arisen more recently, and the earlier ones still exist in diluted form. Much of this is in institutional holdings, by banks, trusts, and insurance firms. Because the holdings are usually less than 20 percent of the firms' shares, the degree of actual control is difficult to estimate.[16]

Interlocking directorates can also tie firms together. The older conventional interlock had one person on the boards of two competing firms. This has been illegal since 1914 under the Clayton Act, and few clear instances of it now exist. *Indirect interlocks*—with officers of the same bank, law firm, or investment bank—are more common.[17] The effect of such parallel seats could be as tight as if the same person occupied them both. Or, if the two people carefully avoid coordinating, the effect could be zero. One cannot measure the actual effects, for they are subtle and secret.

The consensus is that these informal connections (1) have decreased since 1910 and (2) are less important in the United States than in other economies. Yet they are not trivial, and evidence indicates that some groupings do exert influence.

Comparisons with Other Countries.   There are contrasting possibilities.[18] Foreign firms may reflect a smaller-scale technology, and therefore be smaller and less dominant in their own economies. Or, since foreign economies are smaller than the United States, the shares of large firms in them may be larger.

The data are inconclusive on this issue. In fact, there are only a few sets of data, and these deal only with the manufacturing sectors. The clearest basis for comparison is with Britain. Aggregate British concentration matched that of the United States from 1910 to 1955. Between then and the 1970s, British concentration rose sharply, to one-third higher than the U.S. level. Meanwhile, the West German concentration rose to about the U.S. level in the 1970s. Japanese aggregate concentration has long been higher than in the United States, and now is probably about the same as in Britain.[19] (Because many Japanese branches and affiliates are partly owned, one cannot be sure exactly how tight the control is.) On this and other evidence, American concentration emerges as probably comparable to foreign levels.

---

[15] See Peter Collins and David Horowitz, *The Rockefellers: An American Dynasty* (New York: Holt, Rinehart & Winston, 1976); and Alfred D. Chandler, Jr., and Stephen Salsbury, *Pierre S. duPont and the Making of the Modern Corporation* (New York: Harper & Row, 1971).

[16] The ambitious student can browse in the massive collection of data on these patterns in the report by the Committee on Banking and Currency, *Commercial Banks and Their Trust Activities: Emerging Influence on the American Economy,* House of Representatives, 90th Cong., 2nd sess. (Washington, D.C.: Government Printing Office, 1968). See also David Kotz, *Bank Concentration and Economic Power* (Berkeley: University of California Press, 1982).

[17] The student can form an impression of the extent of these connections—and of their possible strength—by reading the report by the Judiciary Committee, *Interlocks in Corporate Management,* House of Representatives, 89th Cong., 1st sess. (Washington, D.C.: U.S. Government Printing Office, 1965); and Peter C. Dooley, "The Interlocking Directorate," *American Economic Review,* 59 (June 1969), 314–23.

[18] See the discussions in Henry W. de Jong and Alex P. Jacquemin, eds., *Markets, Corporate Behavior and the State: International Aspects of Industrial Organization* (The Hague: Martinus Nijhoff, 1976).

[19] For evaluations of these patterns and of their more recent evolution, see Eleanor M. Hadley, *Antitrust in Japan* (Princeton, N.J.: Princeton University Press, 1971); and Richard E. Caves and Masu Uekusa, *Industrial Organization in Japan* (Washington, D.C.: Brookings Institution, 1977).

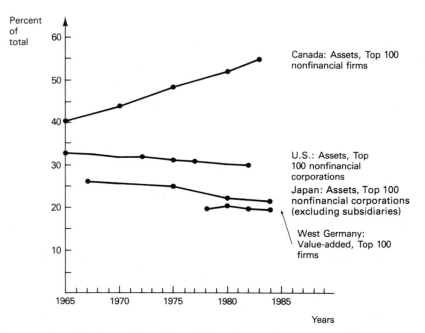

FIGURE 10.7.   Large-firm shares in four countries.

SOURCE: Christian Marfels, ''Aggregate Concentration in International Perspective: Canada, Federal Republic of Germany, Japan and the United States, a chapter in R. S. Khemani, D. M. Shapiro, and W. T. Stanbury, eds., *Mergers, Corporate Concentration and Power in Canada* (Halifax: Institute for Research on Public Policy, 1988).

As for trends, Figure 10.7 shows that large-firm shares have been stable or dwindling in most countries, except Canada.

Informal connections among companies may also affect the true degree of economic power. Ties between firms and bankers—and within family groupings—are less extensive in the United States than in most other countries. Japan, Germany, and Sweden have especially well-developed networks of this sort.

In Japan, the extraordinary *zaibatsu* combines extended by 1940 to all sectors of the economy. The largest seven held one-fourth of all Japanese assets.[20] Facing one another in hundreds of markets, they often adopted diplomatic coexistence as their policy instead of competition (see Chapter 15). The three largest combines (Mitsui, Mitsubishi, and Sumitomo) had been mostly dissolved between 1946 and 1948, but by 1960 they had reassembled. Though somewhat looser than before, these combines still provide a degree of unity and control. German banks hold large blocks of company shares, acting as centers of support and control. In Sweden, there are also important family groupings. The largest are the Wallenberg holdings, which include companies with over $20 billion in annual sales. Based in the Skandinaviska-

---

[20] In addition to Hadley's and Caves and Uekusa's coverages, see Kozo Yamamura, *Economic Policy in Postwar Japan: Growth versus Economic Democracy* (Berkeley: University of California Press, 1967).

Enskilda Bank, these holdings control major positions in a number of Swedish and international markets.

Again, no thorough measures of such connections have been made, so we do not know their precise extent and strength. Yet these factors might well make effective aggregate concentration higher abroad than in the United States.

QUESTIONS FOR REVIEW

1. "Corporations exist to produce; profits are a by-product." True?
2. "The key identifying fact of private ownership is the issuance of voting stock to private holders." True?
3. "Profitability is shown by the rate of return on sales." True?
4. "Even if the firm's profit volume is large, its managers may truly believe they have little room for discretion." True?
5. "The large-firm share has been rising strongly because these firms are more efficient." True?
6. "Most managerial behavior in private firms is in line with the goal of long-run profit maximizing." True?
7. Explain how private corporations differ from cooperative, not-for-profit, and worker-managed enterprises. Aren't they virtually identical in their structure, resources and production activities?
8. What determines the boundary between the firm and the market process?
9. What criteria determine if a 10 percent, 15, or 25, or 45 percent rate of return on capital is "good?"
10. Explain how managers as agents may deviate from the interests of stockowners as principals. Then explain how stock markets tend to squeeze out those deviations.

11

MONOPOLY, DOMINANCE, AND ENTRY

Monopoly and dominance may arise from virtuous, abusive, or neutral types of actions. The market power will have a variety of effects on prices, efficiency, innovation, and the like. Whether the market power persists or fades also involves a complex process of choices and constraints.

This chapter presents the main research findings on those aspects of market dominance. The research has been increasingly active and fruitful since about 1970, after a long hiatus following the earlier peak interest in actual dominant firms (e.g., Standard Oil and American Tobacco) during 1900–1920.

First we look at the main cases and trends of dominance, including the rate of erosion. Then in Section II we explore the origins of dominance. Section III sets out the major theories on the evolution of dominance. Section IV presents concepts of potential competition and entry barriers, while Section V discusses dominant firms' reactions to those barriers. Although the topic of entry is often presented as related to oligopoly, it is clearer when introduced in relation to dominant-firm decisions. Section VI covers the recent theory of ultra-free entry, or "contestability."

Finally, note that Chapter 17 presents five concise case studies of important dominant firms in actual markets: Eastman Kodak, AT&T, Boeing, large-city newspapers, and IBM.

I. LEADING CASES AND TRENDS OF DOMINANCE

1. Leading Cases

In U.S. markets, many leading cases of dominance derived from the great merger wave of 1897–1901. Students who wish to grasp the breadth and sheer audacity of the changes then occurring should consult John Moody's fascinating *The Truth About the Trusts* (1904).[1] He surveys briefly but approvingly the several hundred dominant

---

[1] John Moody, *The Truth About the Trusts* (Chicago: Moody Publishing, 1904).

firms that were rapidly assembled by mergers across the whole range of U.S. industries.[2] Their later evolution was outlined in 1965 by A. D. H. Kaplan.[3]

Most of these dominant firms faded quickly, but some (General Electric, Du
Pont, U.S. Steel [now USX], Westinghouse Electric, Aluminum Company of America) are with us still.

Tables 4.4 and 4.5 sift out the leading dominant firms from this changing as-
sortment, down to the 1970s. Those lists are not complete or precise because the
data on dominance are not fully known. Also, the many newspapers dominating their
citywide markets are too numerous to include. Moreover, some dominant firms are
hidden within large conglomerate enterprises, which do not report them separately.[4]
Yet, even so, these tables do convey much of the core of dominance in leading
industries.

Full monopolies have also been formed and officially approved (and regulated)
in various "utility" sectors, such as electricity, telephones, and railroads.

2.   Trends

The long trend of these groups' share of the economy has been downward, as
Chapter 4 noted. In particular, industrial dominance has faded, especially since the
rise of imports in the 1970s. Many utilities have evolved back toward naturally
competitive technology, and some of them have been deregulated since 1970. Yet
the remaining (and newly emerging) cases are important and interesting.

3.   The Rate of Erosion

The rate of erosion has been slow, as Chapter 4 noted. Before 1970, high market
shares receded at an average rate of about half a percentage point per year, when
not hastened by antitrust or other policy actions. That can be seen in Table 4.4.
Standard Oil, American Tobacco, Corn Products, and Du Pont did decline substantially, but mainly because they lost antitrust cases and were required to divest some
capacity. These cases pulled down market shares a lot faster than the natural rate
of erosion would have, so they probably yielded sizable economic benefits in improved competitive performance.[5] The other firms listed in Table 4.4 generally declined only slowly, or not at all, during the years up to 1968.

Since then, declines in market share have been faster, in both the manufacturing
and the "utility" sectors. The main reason is the new import pressures, often ex-

---

[2] There was also an outpouring of research highly critical of the trusts. Some of it was noted in
Chapter 1. The leaders were Richard T. Ely, *Monopolies and Trusts* (New York: Macmillan, 1900); Charles
J. Bullock, "Trust Literature: A Survey and Criticism," *Quarterly Journal of Economics,* 15 (February
1901), pp. 167–217; and William Z. Ripley, ed., *Trusts, Pools and Corporations* (Boston: Ginn, 1916).

[3] See Kaplan, *Big Business in a Competitive System* (Washington, D.C.: Brooking Institution, 1965).

[4] For example, such diversified food companies as General Foods and General Mills have a number
of products that dominate specific markets. But details on these lines are not published because the firms
regard them as private, sensitive information.

[5] Estimates of the yields are given in William G. Shepherd, *The Treatment of Market Power* (New
York: Columbia University Press, 1975). They fit the general consensus that the cases were beneficial
in economic terms.

acerbated by the inferior performance of the dominant firms. Public policy actions have reduced other important shares, such as AT&T's in telephone service, the U.S. Postal Service's in mail service, and possibly Xerox's in copiers.

Yet numerous important dominant firms remain, including IBM, Eastman Kodak, AT&T, Procter & Gamble, Campbell Soup, Gillette, and scores of local dominant-firm newspapers. The tendency for dominance to persist or to fade only slowly is relevant to the models of dominance presented in Section III.

II.   SOURCES AND SUSTAINING FACTORS OF DOMINANCE

How did these monopolies and dominant firms arise and how do they persist? Chicago-UCLA analysts cite technical scale economies, superior performance, and abuses of state power as the *exclusive* causes. All these factors are undoubtedly important. But mergers, pecuniary economies, sheer luck, anticompetitive actions, and various strategies to exploit market imperfections have also been important in many cases.

Chapters 8 and 9 broadly reviewed the determinants of structure in all market types. Here we focus on specific determinants as they relate to dominance.

1.   Technical Scale Economies

Technical economies of scale have created some natural monopolies in certain utility sectors. But the fundamental pattern emerging in the 1980s is that "natural monopoly" is a shrinking phenomenon, which occurs primarily within city areas, in *urban systems of supply.* Local distribution of electricity, gas, telephone service, cable TV signals, mail, bus and subway service, and ambulance service may be the local remnants of natural monopoly.

This contrasts with the earlier large regional or national monopolies during 1910–1960 in electric power, the Bell Telephone System, the U.S. Post Office, some railroads, and intercity bus lines. Many of these earlier "utility" cases of monopoly were never as "natural" as they seemed.[6] The new competition emerging in bulk electricity markets, for example, could probably have begun decades ago.[7] At any rate, technical economies of scale in utility sectors are now chiefly a local phenomenon.

In other sectors, technical economies of scale are a relatively minor factor for most dominant firms. Where excess market share incurs higher average costs, there may actually be diseconomies of scale.

Pecuniary gains from size may offset such diseconomies. Dominant firms com-

---

[6] See Alfred E. Kahn, *The Economics of Regulation,* 2 vols. (New York: Wiley, 1971); and Richard Schmalensee, *The Control of Natural Monopolies* (Lexington, Mass.: D. C. Heath, 1979); and William G. Shepherd, *Public Policies Toward Business,* 7th ed., Homewood, Ill.: Irwin, 1985, Chapters 12 and 14.

[7] See Paul M. Joskow and Richard Schmalensee, *Markets for Electricity* (Cambridge, Mass.: MIT Press, 1985).

monly obtain volume discounts in price for many inputs, including capital, utility services, advertising, and other tangible inputs. Therefore the recorded average costs are often lower even where true efficiency is not superior. As Chapter 9 noted, because pecuniary gains have been virtually ignored as a research topic, their size is not known. But they have probably been significant for many dominant firms.

2.   Superior Performance

Performance is superior to some degree in many dominant firms. Still, as Chapter 9 noted, there has been little research showing that superiority has been large in any of these cases. Extensive evidence is obtainable from other sources, but gathering it is difficult, and assessing it is inevitably a subjective exercise. Chapter 9 noted the many nonefficiency sources of dominance in several leading firms. Superiority or first-mover advantages were present at the outset in such firms as Polaroid, Ford, and Xerox. But the attainment of dominance has more usually reflected a variety of power tactics that had little to do with superior performance. And since, generally, high profits are a resource for later actions, dominance is cumulative.

In some cases, declines have occurred involuntarily and rapidly. The usual cause is conspicuous errors or slackness. Thus it is generally agreed that General Motors' shrinkage from 55 to 37 percent of U.S. car sales during 1979–1988, and Xerox's abrupt descent from 85 to below 50 percent of copier sales during 1975–1978 both reflected a series of errors and inferior policies by those companies' managements, not extreme pressure by smaller firms.

Overall, superior performance appears to have been a significant (though not exclusive) initial cause of rising market share in a number of cases, but not the major cause of full dominance nor the retention of dominance in most important cases.

3.   Mergers

Though notable during 1897–1901, mergers had by 1950 receded to minor importance as a cause of market dominance (recall Chapter 10). Horizontal mergers were effectively prevented after 1920 in many leading industries, though formal merger constraints were not applied until 1950. The 1960s merger boom also involved few major horizontal mergers; the McDonnell-Douglas aircraft merger and the merger of the National and American football leagues were permitted by special exemptions.

The 1980s merger boom has significantly raised leading market shares in a number of important industries, including airlines, newspapers, and steel. Instead of 4 plus 4 percent, the limits rose to roughly 20 plus 20 percent, and even higher in some cases. But some of these markets were being penetrated by imports, so the broad range of mergers did not markedly increase dominance.

4.   Tactics and Strategies

To maintain or enhance their position, dominant firms use a variety of tactics and strategies. Some of these are strictly anticompetitive, while others are neutral or harmless, depending partly on the setting in which they occur.

Price discrimination has been crucial to the rise, maintenance, and profits of a number of leading dominant firms, notably the old Standard Oil Trust from 1870 to 1890, United Shoe Machinery from 1890 to the 1950s, IBM during the 1930s and 1960s, and Xerox from 1965 to 1975. When carried far enough, price discrimination can become "predatory action" that directly harms competition. These two categories of action are covered in Chapter 12.

In summary, dominance has a mixture of causes that vary from case to case. Superiority is only one, and it fails to account for most instances of dominance.

III. MODELS OF DOMINANT FIRMS

Each dominant firm constantly faces choices about whether to increase, hold, or yield its market share. It weighs the benefits and costs of each alternative, perhaps adopting a long-run strategy. Of course, external events affect these choices, as when a small rival or new entrant suddenly challenges the dominant firm with a major new product.

Interesting models have been developed both for dominant-firm strategies and limit pricing toward new entry. The first is covered in this section, and the second in Section IV.

Dean Worcester noted in 1957 that dominant firms often decline eventually, and he offered an analysis to explain why this may be so.[8] He posited the existence of "fringe" firms, each tiny and all collectively adding up to a minor share of the market. (Note that this ruled out middling-sized firms.) He assumed that the dominant firm is always entirely *passive* to the actions of the fringe firms. (That contradicts the actual behavior of most dominant firms, which are tenacious and forceful in fighting small rivals.)

Then, he noted, *only if* the fringe firms have a cost advantage over the dominant firm, and if the fringe firms keep their prices at the level of their costs, *then* the dominant firm will yield its market share to the ever-expanding fringe firms. The analysis thus generates these seeming implications: dominant firms tend to decline when fringe firms have lower costs. And dominant firms *will decline*.

The implication has been widely asserted, as if the analysis proved it: if dominant firms do not decline, it must be because they are equal or superior to fringe firms in efficiency. Yet that is only an *assumption* of the theory, not a result. There are many strategies and imperfections which permit dominant firms to retain their positions even if they are not as efficient as their competitors.

Therefore the Worcester theory has encouraged a false optimism about dominant firms' supposed superiority and inevitable declines.

---

[8] Dean A. Worcester, "Why 'Dominant' Firms Decline," *Journal of Political Economy,* 65 (August 1957), 338–47. See also the survey in F. M. Scherer, *Industrial Market Structure and Economic Performance,* 2d ed. (Boston: Houghton Mifflin, 1980), Chapter 8.

1. Modelling Optimal Choices Over Time

This led to a more sophisticated analysis, which treats the dominant firms as designing its market-share strategy within a setting of constraints created by small rivals and/or new entrants. The pioneering work in this area was done by Darius Gaskins, but there have been some modifications.[9]

The dominant firm's choices are simplified to this form:

$$\frac{dX}{dt} = k[P(t) - P_0]$$

X is output, t is time, and P is price. The ratio on the lefthand side of the equation is the rate at which the fringe firms will expand their total output in each time period (it is also identically the rate at which the dominant firm's output will contract). $P(t)$ is the dominant firm's price at time t, while P_o is the level of cost (and, equally, price) of the fringe firms.

If the dominant firm sets its price $P(t)$ above the fringe firms' price P_o, then the fringe firms will take away market share from the dominant firm. The bigger the price gap, the faster the shift of market share. The k coefficient governs the general rate at which a given price difference causes a shift of market share.

This process is dynamic—that is, a state variable (the price gap) influences a change over time (the shift of market share)—and the model shows it continuing over time. But it can only be as reliable as the information about k and the degree to which it fits actual market conditions.

Carefully inspected, this general model contains the same biases as the Worcester analysis. It assumes that the dominant firm declines only if the fringe firms have a cost (and price) advantage. Conversely, if the dominant firm persists, it is assumed to be equal or superior in efficiency, rather than exploiting imperfections.

Moreover, the model fails when fringe firms expand by very much, so that the clear contrast between fringe and dominant firms is blurred. Indeed, some users of the model have derived results where the "fringe" firms replace the dominant firm, which shrinks to a "fringe" firm itself! That "result" is absurd, because the two types of firms would presumably adopt identical or reversed policies, as their market shares evolved. But then their market shares would cease to evolve.

In short, the model assumes that there are no interactions, even though they are often the heart of the problem. Many dominant firms follow complex retaliatory strategies which change rapidly and flexibly over time.

Finally, the model follows Worcester in abstracting from any use of price discrimination. Therefore it assumes away much of the rich behavior and impacts which

---

[9] Darius W. Gaskins, Jr., "Dynamic Limit Pricing: Optimal Pricing Under Threat of Entry," *Journal of Economic Theory*, 3 (September 1971), 306–22. Although Gaskins' title seems to limit the analysis to cases involving entry, he is careful in the main body of the discussions to include existing fringe firms as well. More recent analysis is discussed in Scherer, *Industrial Market Structure and Economic Performance*, 236–43, and Jean Tirole, *The Theory of Industrial Organization* (Cambridge, Mass.: MIT Press, 1988).

actual dominant firms impose on their small competitors. Accordingly it neglects much of the heart of the problem.

The Gaskins-type model's strength is in clarifying certain conditions of long-run market-share strategies of dominant firms. But it does rule out much of the interesting content of the problem. Therefore this line of research has not been strongly useful in predicting or explaining the actual processes by which actual dominant firms have persisted or dwindled.

IV. CONCEPTS OF ENTRY AND LIMIT PRICING

The essential idea behind the concepts of entry and limit pricing is simple. New firms can enter a market, but their costs will be higher than those of the existing firms, or their entry will stimulate some degree of retaliation. These conditions create a barrier of some "height" against new entry. Price can be raised up to that height without stirring entry, but above that "limit price," entry will occur. In the extreme case, the entry threat is thought to dominate the industry's pricing: the limit price is all that matters.

As Chapter 1 noted, this theory is controversial, principally because it diverts attention from the market's internal conditions to its periphery, but also because of its technical problems. Still, the concept has become popular, and entry barriers are relevant in some markets. First we will consider the validity of this approach, and then we will work through some of its conventional results.

The topic of entry barriers has frequently been treated as an oligopoly subject, the idea being that the several leading firms adopt a common strategy toward possible entrants. That fitted the interest of the original theorist, Joe S. Bain, who introduced barriers in the 1950s as a factor likely to raise the market power of oligopolists.[10] Barriers would permit oligopolists to achieve firm market control and to increase prices up to the limit price.

Limiting entry is a possible strategy of an oligopoly group, but a more plausible strategy for a single dominant firm. That is why barriers are introduced at this point in the text. Later, in Chapter 13 on oligopoly, you can consider whether several oligopolists are likely to take unified actions and reach similar results. Indeed, those who regard barriers as all-important would say that they govern the market price no matter what the internal structure of the market. That possibility—the case of ultra-free entry (or pure "contestability")—is presented in Section VI.

1. The Nature of Entry

The concepts of entry and barriers have the surface intuitive appeal of a strong metaphor—barriers are dikes holding back the sea of competition. But the technical character of entry and barriers is quite complex and calls for scrutiny.

---

[10] See especially his *Barriers to New Competition* (Cambridge, Mass.: Harvard University Press, 1956). The revised edition of his *Industrial Organization* (New York: John Wiley, 1967) provides a broader framework. See also the surveys in Scherer, *Industrial Market Structure and Economic Performance*, Ch. 8 and pp. 274–80; and Douglas F. Greer, *Industrial Organization and Public Policy*, 2d ed. (New York: Macmillan, 1981), Ch. 8.

The Extent of Entry.   Entry is the addition of one or more new sellers to a market. New capacity is thereby created, adding to the "incumbent" firms' capacity. Entry is therefore partly defined by the extent of new firms' sales. But other firms may exit from a market at the same time that new firms are entering it. Therefore only *net entry*—the entrants' combined new market share *after* subtracting the combined market share of any firms that exited during the period—is relevant.

Yet entry and exit among fringe firms are largely irrelevant to the position of the dominant firm. What matters is the bite which the new entrants take out of the dominant firm's market share. Accordingly, entry is correctly defined not in terms of the entrants' own shares, but rather in terms of the decline of the dominant firm's share of the market. Any other approach misses the true economic impact of entry.

The nature of the entrants is also significant. If twenty tiny fringe firms with 1 percent each are replaced by one entrant with a 20 percent market share, that is likely to affect the competitive situation. And vice versa. Unfortunately, specialists have not addressed this issue in detail nor devised methods for estimating that impact.

The Speed of Entry.   Entry may occur instantly or at a snail's pace. Abrupt entry has greater impact, so the analysis ought to include speed of entry in estimating entry's effects. Yet specialists have not analyzed this element in detail either.

In effect, entry is an intuitive topic whose technical conditions have not been well analyzed. Note that small-scale entry will blend in with the host of small moves by firms already inside the market. Potential competition can therefore be hard to distinguish from actual competition. Indeed, it is merely one of the competitive factors that leading firms will consider in setting their policies.

Discouraging entry is just one aspect of a firm's long-run strategy toward its market share and profitability. Whether one speaks of "entry-limiting" strategies or market share strategies—of actual or potential competition, of barriers or market imperfections—is often just a semantic choice, not an important conceptual one.

2.   Barriers Against Entry

Barriers are the conditions that make entry difficult. Bain emphasized four main sources of barriers, which would influence their "height." Three decades of further analysis have added many other sources, all of them plausible and possibly important. The list now numbers at least fourteen; it is presented in Table 11.1.

The Sources of Barriers.   The sources come in two main categories: *exogenous* and *endogenous*. *Exogenous* sources are embedded in the underlying conditions of the market: the technology, the nature of the products, the need for large-scale capital, and vertical integration, for example. Bain's pioneering discussion stressed these basic factors. Because they exist outside the leading firms' control, they are fundamental causes that cannot be altered.

Endogenous conditions and strategic actions are governed by the dominant firm's own choices. These so-called barrier factors are entirely different from the basic ones, in that they depend strictly on voluntary decisions made by the established firm. The firm can "create barriers" simply by electing to take (or merely threatening to take) a variety of severe actions against an entrant. These "barriers" are virtually

TABLE 11.1   Common Causes of Entry Barriers

I.   **Exogenous: Economic (Intrinsic) Causes of Barriers**
1.   *Capital Requirements* (related to plant and firm size, and to capital intensity)
2.   *Economies of Scale* (from both technical and pecuniary causes)
3.   *Product Differentiation* (occurring naturally among products)
4.   *Absolute Cost Advantages* (from many possible causes, including differential wage rates)
5.   *Diversification* (giving the possibility of massing and redeploying resources among branches)
6.   *Research and Development Intensity*
7.   *High Durability of Firm-Specific Capital* (giving rise to sunk costs, which make entry more risky)
8.   *Vertical Integration* (which may require entry to occur on two or more levels at once)

II. **Endogenous: Voluntary and Strategic Causes of Barriers**
1.   *Retaliation and Preemptive Actions* (by the use of price or other devices; this category is large and varied)
2.   *Excess Capacity* (as a basis for effective retaliation, or for threats of retaliation)
3.   *Selling Expenses, Including Advertising* (to increase the degree of product differentiation)
4.   *Patents* (which provide exclusive control over technology)
5.   *Control Over Other Strategic Resources* (such as ores, locations, specific talents)
6.   *"Packing the Product Space"* (in industries with high product differentiation, as in the U.S. cereals industry)

---

impossible to specify in concrete form because they merely express the (unpredictable) willingness and ingenuity of the firm in taking actions to anticipate and/or retaliate against its small rivals and newcomers.

At a deeper level of meaning, such voluntary "barriers" merely reflect the degree of imperfections inhering in the market, which the dominant firm can exploit *against existing rivals as well as against any possible entrants.* Caves and Porter's concept of "mobility barriers" recognizes this point.[11] If those imperfections are large, then entry barriers will be high.

So once again we come back to the fundamental question of underlying market imperfections: How large are they, and can they be exploited by a leading firm? If they are at all significant, then "barriers" will be substantial strictly because of strategic actions taken by the established firm, apart from any intrinsic, underlying causes of barriers. Since any such market imperfections can also be exploited to inhibit existing small rivals, it may not be meaningful to conceptualize them separately as barriers, but this is a question of semantics.

With these cautions in mind, we can review the main sources of barriers. First are the eight *exogenous* sources.

1.   The most general cost advantage is cheaper and more ample capital, which the established firm may get because of its greater size and security. This "size barrier to entry" especially inhibits entry into large, capital-intensive industries where minimum

---

[11] Richard E. Caves and Michael E. Porter, "From Entry Barriers to Mobility Barriers," *Quarterly Journal of Economics*, 91 (May 1977), 241–61.

efficient scale is large (examples are oil refining and automobiles). Other cost advantages are patented processes, special access to raw materials, and favorable locations.

2.   Scale economies may force an entrant to come in, if at all, at a large market share. This will increase total industry capacity, and therefore the market price is likely to fall. This alone reduces the gain to the entrant. In addition, the established firms are likely to threaten retaliation against such a large entrant in order to prevent its entry. If economies of scale are large, the established firms are likely to have large market shares and be able to inflict sharp penalties on the newcomer.

3.   Product differentiation arises from advertising, marketing strategies, and other conditions. Some advertising is "persuasive," aiming to create preferences for brand names. Once such preferences are formed, the established firm has an advantage over newcomers, so potential entrants may decide not to try to establish their brands. Moreover, an established firm may be able to meet an entrant with selective advertising campaigns that neutralize the newcomer. The newcomer must then advertise so heavily that its costs (including selling costs) are raised well above the established firm's costs. Advertising is only one of several selling expenses; the same reasoning holds for them all. If the large established firm obtains any technical or pecuniary gains from scale in advertising, then the barrier effect is enhanced. Yet advertising and other selling activities may not raise barriers. Many specialists have noted that promotional activity can be a weapon making entry possible, rather than a shield keeping it out. The issues and present status of this debate are presented in Chapter 16.

4.   Absolute cost advantages can arise from differential wage rates, superior talent, random luck, and historical accidents.

5.   Diversified firms may be able to deploy their massed resources at any one branch where needed to prevent entry. These resources may include funds, marketing staff, advertising resources, and R&D capacities.

6.   Large R&D spending may be necessary to get started in a market (examples are advanced electronics, automobiles, and complex chemicals). Moreover, the expenditures may need to be long term in order to build up sufficient R&D capacity.

7.   When entry necessitates incurring large sunk costs, that may discourage entry attempts. Sunk costs may include advertising to create brand loyalty, investment in equipment that has no other uses, and spending to create a marketing network.

8.   When vertical integration is efficient, an entrant must often enter on two or more levels in order to match the existing firms' costs. That requires assembling more capital, R&D, and staff talent, and it often raises the degree of risk.

Next come the six *endogenous* sources of barriers.

1.   Retaliation and preemptive actions embrace a large category of strategic devices, all of which can be applied (or merely threatened) in varying degrees of severity. Prices are only one weapon; others include advertising, targeted innovations of various kinds, actions to "raise rivals' costs," and counteractions in other markets.

2.   By creating and carrying excess capacity, a dominant firm warns other firms that it can block entry easily by expanding its output quickly. This method has been used in prominent cases.[12]

3.   Selling expenses can accentuate the effects of brand loyalties beyond what is intrinsic to the market (exogenous source 3). Firms commonly exercise total discretion over their advertising and marketing activities.

4.   Patents are a voluntary device that firms seek in order to gain exclusive control over

[12] ALCOA consistently carried excess capacity to meet all growing demand and to prevent new entry or competitive growth. Du Pont deliberately built excess capacity in the titanium dioxide industry in the 1970s and 1980s so as to preempt growth and bar entry.

innovations. Strategic patenting (in place of secrecy or other tactics) is important in many industries, such as the drug industry, in preventing new competition.

5.   Many critical resources can be controlled, either through strategic acquisitions or in other ways. Buying the best iron ore, or the best locations, or the best inventors can deter new competition.

6.   In some industries, the product space can be "packed" by a proliferation of branded items, so that new firms have no niches in which to gain a foothold. Although this tactic enhances consumer choice, it also blocks entry (cereals may be such a case: see Chapter 18).

Each of these sources of barriers includes a variety of specific forms and instances. And these fourteen elements operate in many dimensions, such as dollar volumes, types of talent, degrees of product variety, amounts of excess capacity. The whole phenomenon is marked by variety and subtlety.

Attempting to Measure Barriers.   If barriers are important, then scholars should be able to measure and verify them scientifically. To paraphrase Lord Kelvin: If you cannot measure it, it does not really exist.

Today barriers to entry cannot be measured with any reliability, and they probably never will be. The six endogenous, voluntary "barriers" exist only insofar as the established firm has the skill and intention to exploit the imperfections of its market. As for the exogenous, "objective" barriers, they are difficult to specify and measure.

Combining the elements into a total estimate of barriers "height" is more a primitive black art than a well-developed scientific method. Should the elements be added to each other, or is each one independently sufficient to create a high barrier? Do two medium-strong elements create a high barrier? Or should the elements be multiplied by one another in some fashion because they are strongly reinforcing?

More than thirty years after Joe S. Bain's 1956 book, these problems of measurement remain virtually unnoticed in the literature. There are few systematic studies of actual barriers, and those that have been done do not begin to solve the measurement problems.[13] Barriers are still "estimated" as "high," "medium," or "low" largely on the basis of educated judgment. That probably reflects the intrinsic impossibility of reaching precise, systematic measures of barriers.

Internal and External Conditions are Correlated.   High barriers occur mainly where there is also market dominance. Research not only verifies this correlation, but in actual cases has been unable to ascertain whether the causation runs from market shares to barriers, or vice versa, or is mingled.

Can Potential Entrants Be Identified?   The pool of potential entrants is an important determinant of the competitive force exerted by free entry. If there are few candidates in the wings, then entry may exert little pressure even if barriers are low.

---

[13] Two important studies are Bain, *Barriers to Competition;* and H. Michael Mann, "Seller Concentration, Barriers to Entry, and Rates of Return in 30 Industries, 1950–1960," *Review of Economics and Statistics,* 48 (August 1966), 296–307. Both Bain and Mann tried to include several elements in making approximate judgments about barrier heights, but their data were often roughly estimated and they provided no general, objective formula or technique for combining the data on the individual barrier "elements." To recognize this roughness is not to criticize it; the estimates were probably about as good as could be made then, now, or in the future.

Yet virtually no research has been done to develop methods for identifying potential entrants. Most analyses simply assume that there are many powerful potential entrants. But that need not be true, and in many cases it certainly is not.

In short, entry and barriers have been accepted by researchers rather more than warranted. They are complex phenomena, virtually impossible to measure, and intertwined with internal structure. Still, they are an important part of the contemporary debate on competition, so it is necessary to learn about the analysis that has been developed. The next section is devoted to explicating the theory of entry and barriers.

V.   FIRMS' CHOICES IN THE CONTEXT OF POTENTIAL ENTRY

For theory's sake, we assume here that entry and barriers *can* be both defined and measured. Under those assumptions, we can specify the conditions and choices that entry involves for dominant firms.

The entry barrier gives the established firm a chance to raise price above its long-run average cost without attracting new competition from outside (of course, the *existing* rivals may react). *The height of the barrier is shown by this gap between the average cost and the entry-inducing price.* Figure 11.1 illustrates this. For simplicity, average costs are assumed to be constant. When price is set above the entry-inducing level, new competition takes away the firm's customers. Therefore the

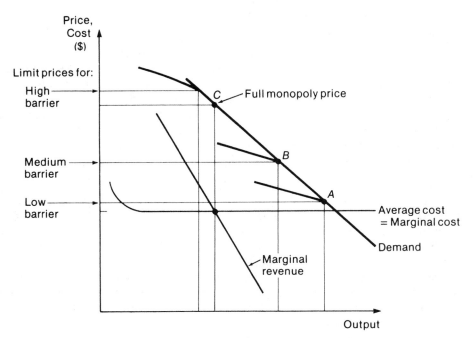

FIGURE 11.1.   General patterns of barriers and the effects of entry.

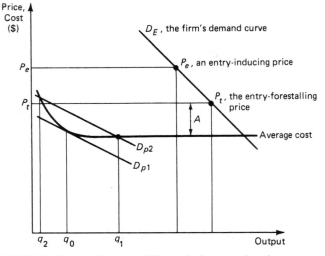

FIGURE 11.2.   Product differentiation as a barrier to entry.

demand curve has a kink at the limit price. The kink will be sharp if entry is quick and full as soon as price rises even a shade above the limit price. In this extreme case, the entry (an external condition) will dominate the market power (an internal condition of the market).

We will now consider three separate forms of barriers: product differentiation, scale economies, and an absolute cost advantage.

Product Differentiation.   If products differ (because of advertising or other selling activities), then their prices can vary. Existing firms can raise price some distance above cost before drawing in new firms. In Figure 11.2, D_E is the demand curve of—in Bain's words—the "most advantaged established firm" (assuming that the oligopolists follow unified pricing). If it charges price P_f, a potential entrant's demand curve is D_{p1}. P_f is just above the entry-forestalling price, since D_{p1} just barely lets the entrant survive. If the established firm raises the price to P_e, the entrant's demand curve rises to D_{p2}. The entrant can now produce any quantity up to q_1. The height of this entry barrier is A.

Scale Economies.   If minimum efficient scale is large, the new entrant may have to be so big that the older firms are bound to retaliate. Also, a large entrant adds to the industry's total capacity, shifting the supply curve down. This will lower price too. The effect is shown by line R in Figure 11.3; its height is the change in price that each level of entry will cause. Add this to the average cost curve itself to get curve E. E is not an average cost curve, but only the curve of the lowest possible prices that will just permit entry at any given scale. Any price below the minimum point on curve E will deter entry. The older firms are able to price in the range B without drawing entrants into the market. B is therefore the height of the barrier caused by economies of scale.

Cost Differences.   Finally, the "absolute cost" barrier, depicted in Figure

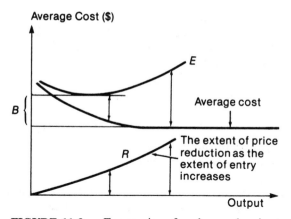

FIGURE 11.3. Economies of scale as a barrier to entry.

11.4, is any cost advantage the established firm has, such as better ores or cheaper capital. These advantages are likely to be sharper at greater sizes. The entrants' and existing firms' cost curves will look like those in Figure 11.4. The interval marked *C* shows the height of this category of barrier.

These three conditions may combine in quite complex ways. They may reinforce or be neutral toward each other. High economies of scale and product differentiation may make for very high barriers, or even "blockaded" entry. But there is no method yet to disentangle these factors. The analysis only permits one to speak broadly of the height of "the" barrier, whatever its parts and sources may be.

A low barrier plus powerful threats of potential entry could force the dominant firm to keep price down close to average cost. That is shown by point *A* in Figure 11.1, just above the competitive level. At the other extreme, a high barrier can permit full monopoly pricing by the firm, at point *C* in Figure 11.1. The firm adopts the

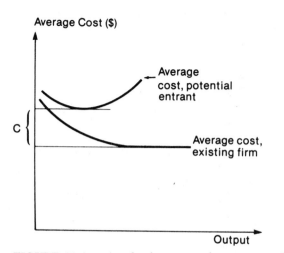

FIGURE 11.4. An absolute cost advantage as a barrier to entry.

price strategy that is best for it. A price just at the entry-limiting level will often be chosen, but sometimes a firm will prefer to take higher profits now and yield up its market share over time. The choice will depend on several conditions, such as the sharpness of the "kink" at the entry-limiting price, the shape of the cost curve, and the dominant firm's particular expectations about other firms' plans and expectations. Also, a higher time discount rate will incline the firm to take profits immediately.

This simple model leads some analysts to the strong conclusion that potential competition can constrain monopolists toward competitive pricing if barriers are low enough. In other words, they argue, *potential competition can substitute for actual competition.* Without barriers to protect them, dominant firms cannot exert monopoly power. With barriers that are high, even a loose oligopoly can reach monopoly levels of pricing and profits. Therefore, they say, high market shares are neither necessary nor sufficient to provide market power. By contrast, entry barriers are. This startling claim is assessed below in Section VI.

One need not choose one extreme or the other on this issue. There are intermediate degrees. Also, the role of barriers probably varies from case to case, being large in some industries and secondary in others. To ignore potential competition entirely would be too narrow. It plays some role; perhaps in some cases, a major role. But, as we have seen, *actual* competition is usually the decisive factor.

Three specific points help to put the role of barriers in perspective.

Several Firms. A single dominant firm with a pricing strategy toward entry is easy to imagine. The idea of several firms practicing a unified limit-pricing policy is less plausible. Such oligopolists naturally face possible competition among themselves as well as from lesser firms in the market. They *may* focus on potential competition from outside, but this would require them to decide that competition among themselves is of little or no importance. If they cannot do that, then the tactics they use against each other as rivals may keep price below the entry-limiting level. An oligopolists' "joint limit-pricing strategy" is therefore rather implausible. The whole issue depends also on the degree of concentration, since a tight oligopoly can be more cohesive than a loose oligopoly.

The Rate of Entry. Entry may range from as slow as molasses to as quick as lightning. The faster the rate of entry, the flatter the firm's demand curve above the entry-limiting price. The slower the rate of entry, the less the entry barriers will matter, in any event. The role of barriers therefore depends not only on their "height" but also on the vigor, resources, and responsiveness of potential entrants.

No clear criteria for measuring or predicting the rate of entry have yet evolved in the literature.[14] The size and profitability of the firms regarded as "potential entrants" are thought to affect how much of a threat they are. Also, some potential entrants are in closely adjacent or similar industries, and such "technological near-

---

[14] Bain stressed two aspects: (1) the *speed* of the entry and (2) the *market share* that it gains. Still other aspects can matter. Thus (3) the degree of *surprise* may also be important (that is, the degree to which entry was by a likely potential entrant rather than by a distant, unforeseen one). Bain gave this whole issue only passing mention in his *Barriers to New Competition.*

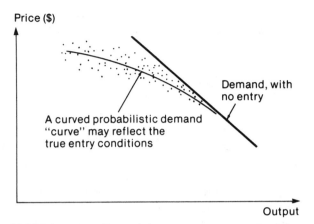

Price ($)

A curved probabilistic demand
"curve" may reflect the
true entry conditions

Demand, with
no entry

Output

FIGURE 11.5.   Potential entry may operate by degrees and with uncertainty.

ness" is thought to make them more likely to move in forcefully.[15] Moreover, one looks to see how many potential entrants there are. A large group can obviously exert more discipline than just one or two.

The height of barriers and the rate of entry are two separate concepts; you must learn to keep them clear and distinct. The degree of constraint that potential competition may exert depends on both.

A Curve Instead of a Kink?   The postulated kink in the demand curve at the limit price is a caricature for most situations. A smooth bend in the demand curve is more valid, since entry would probably happen by degrees rather than on an either-or basis. Figure 11.5 illustrates such a continuous relationship between price and entry.

And remember, entry is often a matter of uncertainty. As price rises, the probability of entry will normally rise. But all the various "real" conditions may not work out. Or, conversely, entry may occur even at lower prices. Strategy toward entry often involves risk and gambling on the odds. This is illustrated in Figure 11.5 by the scatter of possible outcomes around the demand curve.

The conditions may interact in complex ways.[16] For example, imagine there are many potential entrants. This very abundance may deter *all* of them from entering because any entrant would worry that many others would follow it in and thereby intensify competition. By contrast, if there were only one potential entrant, this probability factor would not occur.

Incorporating these two features—a continuous entry-price relationship and the element of probability—into the topic of entry makes it more plausible. They also

[15] Gort and Berry have both shown in detail that most "entry" is done by adjacent firms, who are simply adding to their product lines. See Michael Gort, *Diversification and Integration in American Industry* (Princeton, N.J.: Princeton University Press, 1962); and Charles H. Berry, *Corporate Growth and Diversification* (Princeton, N.J.: Princeton University Press, 1975).

[16] Discussions include Roger Sherman and Thomas D. Willett, "Potential Entrants Discourage Entry," *Journal of Political Economy,* 75 (August 1967), 400–3; and Donald J. Dewey, *The Theory of Imperfect Competition: A Radical Reconstruction* (New York: Columbia University Press, 1969).

make its role less clear-cut, for entry now tends to shade in with other competitive actions that may occur. Indeed, entry is best seen as a modifier of the central conditions in the market.

VI. THE SPECIAL CASE OF ULTRA-FREE ENTRY ("CONTESTABILITY")

An important innovation appeared to occur in 1982 when Baumol, Bailey, Panzer, and Willig (called BBPW here) offered an elaborate theoretical analysis focusing on perfectly free entry and exit. Because it illustrates some important issues of concept and fact, it deserves discussion.

BBPW suggested that the special case of perfectly free, absolute, reversible entry is the best basis for defining efficient allocation. It was, they said, "a new theory of industrial organization," which "will transform the field and render it far more applicable to the real world" and be "extraordinarily helpful in the design of public policy." Since their approach sought to displace the main body of concepts and research about industrial organization, it naturally met sharp criticism. By evaluating the idea, we can see its merits and defects, and in the process we can learn something about the standards used in appraising such ideas.[17]

The BBPW group focuses on several aspects of entry, but their results hold only for the ultra-free case, which involves the following three conditions:

1. *Entry is free and without limit.*   A new firm can do far more than gain a foothold quickly, as conventional free entry envisages. The entrant can immediately duplicate and entirely replace any existing firm, even a complete monopolist. "Entrants can, without restriction, serve the same market demands and use the same productive techniques as those available to the incumbent firms" (BBPW, 1982, p. 5). There are no costs or significant lags in entry, and the entrant can match all dimensions of size, technology, costs, product array, brand loyalties, and other advantages of all existing firms.

2. *Entry is absolute.*   The entrant can establish itself before an existing firm makes any price response. If the entrant obtains an advantage, even a tiny price difference, it will prevail absolutely and displace the existing firm, with no interaction or sequence of moves. This assumption of no response holds even if a pure monopolist faces elimination and would have to abandon its monopoly pricing entirely.

3. *Entry is perfectly reversible.*   Exit is perfectly free, at no sacrifice of any cost. Sunk cost is zero.

These conditions are pure, and the deductive results hold only when they hold.

---

[17] This section draws on W. G. Shepherd, "Contestability versus Competition," *American Economic Review,* 74 (September 1984), 572–87. The main BBPW sources are W. J. Baumol, "Contestable Markets: An Uprising in the Theory of Industry Structure," *American Economic Review* (March 1982), 72, 1–15; W. J. Baumol, C. Panzer, and D. Willig, *Contestable Markets and the Theory of Industry Structure* (San Diego, Cal.: Harcourt Brace Jovanovich, 1982).

See also the contrast between Baumol and Willig, praising the theory, and Marius Schwartz, critiquing it, in William J. Baumol and Robert D. Willig, "Contestability: Developments Since the Book," *Oxford Economic Papers,* November 1986, special supplement; and Marius Schwartz, "The Nature of Contestability Theory," in the same special supplement of *Oxford Economic Papers.* Baumol and Willig maintain that the theory has become widely popular and gives important "insights." Schwartz counters that theory is logically flawed and not robust to real-world conditions.

See also the extensive recent critique by William B. Tye, *The Theory of Contestable Markets: Applications to Regulatory and Antitrust Problems in the Rail Industry* (in process).

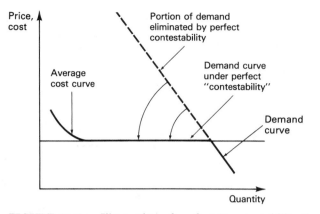

FIGURE 11.6.   Illustration of perfect ''contestability.''

Under any departures from the pure conditions, BBPW's deductive analysis becomes speculative.

For such markets they coined the term *contestable,* but the phrase *ultra-free entry* is preferable for assumptions that, as we have seen, are pure and absolute. Part of the seeming generality of the BBPW conclusions arises from the flexible usage the term *contestable* invites; it is an informal, intuitive term implying inter-actions and imperfections that the ultra-free entry model rules out. The phrase *ultra-free entry* lessens this confusion, by referring to the specific features of the model.

BBPW stress that, under ultra-free entry, the threat of entry will drive prices down and guarantee efficiency even if there is just one monopoly firm in the market. This goes beyond the optimism of the Chicago-UCLA economists, who often expect that two firms are enough to give effective competition. For BBPW, *one* firm is enough. The conditions inside the market are irrelevant. If entry and exit are free, efficiency prevails. If entry or exit barriers exist, some degree of monopoly result will occur, regardless of the market structure. Like Bain's simple free-entry case, ultra-free entry can be seen as a sharp kink or truncation in the demand curve at the price set by the height of entry (and exit) barriers. In this pure case, no lags or probabilities apply. Even a tiny price rise above the limit price will cause a total replacement of the established firm, as shown in Figure 11.6.

Yet the model's assumptions are contradictory. If entry is sufficiently trivial, it may indeed avoid a response. But ultra-free entry also assumes *total* entry. The two assumptions, of trivial entry and total entry, are opposites. If entry is trivial, it has no force. If it is total (or even merely significant), then the no-response assumption is not tenable.

It is easy to reject ultra-free entry because its key elements contradict reality. Also, they are not robust. Note, too, that ultra-free entry can assure efficient results *only if entry dominates all internal conditions of the market.* But that strong as-sumption is not reasonable, as we have seen. Potential competition will almost al-ways have less force than actual competition. Whenever there is more than one incumbent firm, each has to consider its competitor(s) as an immediate threat to its market share. Even if an existing rival is small, it is present. It already exerts in full the pressure a potential entrant may have *if* it chooses to enter. Therefore an actual competitor is more important than a potential entrant of comparable or smaller size. A more tenable assumption is that potential competition is secondary and blends in with other marginal competitive possibilities.

Airlines.   BBPW's one significant industrial example of ultra-free entry has been the airline industry. Each existing or new firm can send aircraft anew into city-pair routes where existing fares are significantly above cost. Exit has low costs, so even a brief entry may be profitable. The threat of such entry may hold price down to cost throughout hundreds of city-pair routes, even those that are seemingly monopolized by one airline. At least, this is the theory.

Under the deregulation carried out from 1975 to 1984, the airline industry *has* displayed rising competition and more flexible pricing. But this does not prove the validity or generality of ultra-free entry theory. One reason is that markets are not well defined, so the roles of barriers, entry, and exit are unclear. The *industry* covers air traffic throughout the United States, along hundreds of city-pair routes. At one extreme, it is possible to define that national industry as the relevant *market*. But at the other extreme, it is possible to instead define *each city-pair route* as a relevant market. That is what the Baumol group does when it claims that each airline's addition of a route is entry into a new market. On this assumption, ultra-free entry may (nearly) exist because the established airlines all act as potential entrants into one another's routes.

Yet most of these hundreds of city-pair routes are not relevant markets by the standard criteria of substitutability. Many are paralleled closely by alternative routes that are close substitutes; many others are merely intermediate stops in longer routes. Moreover, most routes are served as joint products: each flight on each route is only a small element in the airlines' total operations. Therefore most route changes are merely parts of a multipoint competitive strategy in related market segments, not simple entry. Entry into the *industry* by founding a new airline is a much larger and slower task than merely adding routes. That form of entry has been far from total or uncontested. Even simple route addition "entry" has not been ultra-free. Existing carriers have not been displaced at a stroke, and they have usually responded, often effectively. It takes time to establish ground facilities and build up patronage, usually by some kind of interaction involving prices and services. As market shares are gained and lost, the process accords well with mainstream analysis.

Moreover, there are few (if any) documented episodes of brief, profitable entry, as distinct from general impressions. Nor has systematic research established that ultra-free entry has effaced the role of internal structure. There is a significant relation between price-cost ratios and concentration in city-pair routes.[18] High individual market shares are also associated with high price-cost ratios. Though ultra-free entry might enforce uniform price-cost ratios across all submarkets, in fact, market power affects those ratios.[19]

---

[18] See especially D. R. Graham, D. P. Kaplan, and D. S. Sibley, "Efficiency and Competition in the Airline Industry," *Bell Journal*, 14 (Spring 1983), 118–38; and T. E. Keeler, "The Revolution in Airline Regulation," in L. W. Weiss and M. W. Klass, eds., *Case Studies in Regulation* (Boston: Little, Brown, 1981).

[19] These conclusions hold if the measures of cost are valid. It has been said, instead, that unit costs cannot be measured because of the overhead costs in airline operations spanning many routes. If that is so, then *no* tests of price-cost ratios can be made, either to prove or disprove entry's role. In short, airline experience either (1) conflicts with BBPW's interpretation, or (2) cannot be used to support it.

Entry and exit have had some influence on the changes in market shares, but the main effects appear to arise from interactions among the existing airlines. As research on airlines has deepened, its support for ultra-free entry theory has grown weaker and now seems scarcely to exist. Airline competition can be explained well by established concepts of market structure and entry.

Imports.   Finally, consider imports as a type of entry. In recent decades, imports have probably provided the most important form of new competition in industrial markets in advanced economies. They may offer the best chances for applying BBPW's approach, even if the concepts may need adapting.

Import competition is defined by supply functions possessing continuous rather than quantum properties. Therefore imports are probably best analyzed in terms of internal market conditions, not of ultra-free entry. For example, if imports cut General Motors' market share from 55 to 48 percent, that change in *market share* is crucial. Imports are difficult to define as a matter of entry because the outside producer does not fully *enter* the market, even though its products do. No new capacity is created in the market, and "exit" means merely a decline in the amounts shipped in, not a genuine closure. Because import entry reflects basic industry-wide shifts in demand and supply (or in the market's edges), an analysis of strategic choices is largely irrelevant to it. In fact, the conventional entry analysis adds little to research on the comparative costs and demand for imports. Still, this is probably the main research frontier for BBPW's approach.

As often happens, a bright idea has been oversold by a group of enthusiasts. The ensuing debate trims the concept and claims down to reasonable size and fits the approach into the field. Ultra-free entry offers insights, but it is an eccentric case that does not affect the central role of market structure.

QUESTIONS FOR REVIEW

1. Have technical economies of scale in utility sectors tended to shrink or expand in recent decades?

2. Discuss two cases of dominance in which superior performance may have been the main cause, contrasting them with two cases where it wasn't.

3. Are dominant firms likely to adopt a passive stance toward smaller rivals? Explain the resulting decline of dominance, when the firm is passive.

4. Bain suggested that entry barriers would intensify the effects of oligopoly market power, but now entry is said to weaken or eliminate market power. Explain the contrast, please.

5. How is entry to be defined: in terms of numbers of firms, entrants' market shares, "net entry," declines in the incumbent firms' market shares, the speed of entry, or other elements?

6. Contrast exogenous and endogenous sources of entry barriers.

7. How can the endogenous sources of barriers be measured? Once measured, how can they be combined into a single measure of barriers height?

8. Choose two industries and estimate the height of entry barriers into them. Explain your estimates, please.

9. In what kinds of markets is it plausible that a dominant firm is more concerned about newcomers than about its existing rivals?

10. Show with diagrams how scale economies and product differentiation give rise to specific heights of entry barriers. Contrast cases of low and high barriers.

11. What assumptions are required for "perfect contestability?" What actual markets may fit these assumptions exactly? or closely? or at least approximately?

12. Why may "contestability" theory apply mainly to small-scale local industries?

13. Why may imports not be relevant to "contestability" theory?

12 PRICE DISCRIMINATION

What do the following have in common? *Newsweek* costs 72 cents per copy by student subscription, 90 cents by regular subscription, but $2.00 at the newsstand. You pay $5.50 for a movie ticket to see *Frankenstein: A Love Story,* but the urchin sitting next to you pays only $1.50. One hundred bottles of Maalox may cost $124 to the druggist, $64 to hospitals, and only $47 to the Veterans Administration. On a flight from Chicago to New Orleans, your discount ticket cost $79, but the business passenger sitting next to you paid $216, and a standby passenger across the aisle paid only $59.

In all these cases and in millions of others throughout the economy, there are different prices for the same item. Instead of one uniform price, there is a *structure* of prices. That structure will involve price discrimination *if the ratios of price to cost are different among buyers.* For example, if the theater's cost of supplying the movie is $1.50 for all customers, then the ratios of price to cost are 3 to 1 for you and 1 to 1 for that urchin. That difference in ratios is discrimination, and it is quite steep in this case.

Discrimination occurs because firms can make more money by isolating customers (or groups of customers) and charging them "what the traffic will bear." Differences in *demand elasticities* (instead of, or in addition to, cost) then determine prices, with the inelastic-demand customers getting charged the most. In contrast, efficient prices would be in line with cost, as you have seen throughout this book.

Every firm tries to set its prices selectively, giving discounts in line with demand conditions. But its ability to do such discriminating is limited by market conditions. The effects of the discrimination also vary, sometimes promoting competition and sometimes reducing it, as we will see. Price discrimination is a widespread, complex, and important phenomenon. To illustrate the complexity: The standby $59 passenger noted above may be discriminated *against,* as we will shortly see!

This chapter presents the main concepts and real-world versions of price discrimination. The first section gives the basic theory: what discrimination is and why it occurs. The second shows the effects of discrimination on competition, monopoly, and efficiency. The special case of "predatory" actions is presented in Section III, and Section IV reviews a variety of real cases.

I. THE NATURE OF PRICE DISCRIMINATION[1]

1. Preconditions for Discrimination

Price discrimination can occur when three conditions hold:

1. Buyers have sharply differing demand elasticities.
2. The seller knows these differences and can separate the buyers into groups based on these differing elasticities.
3. The seller can keep the buyers from reselling the good to one another.

Under these conditions, the seller will divide the buyers into two or more groups and then charge higher prices to the buyers who have the less elastic demand. Remember that inelastic demand means a higher degree of urgency or need. Those who would pay more *are made* to pay more. Other buyers with more elastic demand— who have good substitutes or simply can't afford to pay more—are charged less.

The classic instance has been the town doctor who treats all comers, rich and poor. For the same appendectomy, the banker is asked to pay $2,500, the poor widow $50. Nineteenth-century railroads were also masters at charging what the traffic would bear: typically, 10 cents per ton-mile out on the plains, and 2 cents per ton-mile alongside rivers with competing barge lines. Perhaps the most familiar instance today is half-price movie, bus, train, and airplane tickets for children. The costs of supply are much the same for both children and adults, yet adults pay a much higher ratio of price to cost.

When discrimination occurs, the elasticity of demand—*not* cost—governs prices. A price discriminator will follow the same basic rule as any other profit-maximizing firm: Set the price and output at the level for which marginal revenue equals marginal cost. A single-price firm will be working with the demand and marginal revenue schedules for the entire market. A price discriminator, however, will set price for each group of customers on the basis of the demand and marginal revenue for that particular group.

To make price discrimination work, the seller must keep the low-price buyers from reselling the product to the high-price buyers, for reselling would pull the high price down toward the low price.

Note that uniform prices can be discriminatory if costs differ. For example, the price is 25 cents to mail a first-class letter anywhere in the United States, across town or from Maine to California. Because that uniform price ignores the greater costs of the more remote locations, it is discriminatory (though not necessarily bad, and possibly quite good). One judges possible discrimination by comparing *price-cost ratios*, not just prices. Cost differences can justify price differences.

2. The Analysis of Price Discrimination

Identical Costs, Differing Prices.   Now consider the simple case where prices differ but costs are uniform. Figure 12.1 illustrates it. Marginal cost is line *MC*. It is constant and identical for the two customer groups; in other words, the product

---

[1] Basic references on the topic include A. C. Pigou, *The Economics of Welfare* (London: Macmillan, 1920); Joan Robinson, *The Economics of Imperfect Competition* (London: Macmillan, 1933); Fritz Machlup, *The Political Economy of Monopoly* (Baltimore, Md.: Johns Hopkins, 1952); and, for "public utility" conditions, Alfred E. Kahn, *The Economics of Regulation* (New York: Wiley, 1971), Vols. I and II.

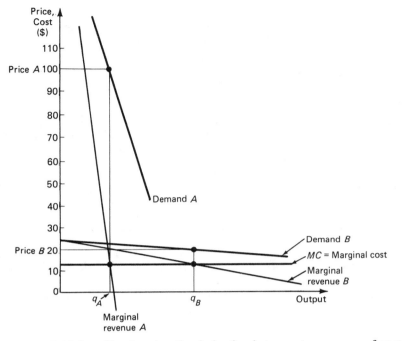

FIGURE 12.1.   Simple price discrimination between two groups of customers.

being sold is precisely uniform in its costs. Group A has relatively inelastic demand, while group B's demand is more highly elastic. Each demand curve has a corresponding marginal revenue curve, marked A and B.

The firm maximizes its total profit by setting output to each group at the level where marginal revenue equals marginal cost. The resulting two prices are sharply different. Group A buyers pay $100, while group B buyers pay only $20 for the same good. Inelastic demand leads to a higher price-cost ratio.

The simple result is:

$$\text{Price } A \ / \text{ Marginal cost}_A > \text{Price } B \ / \text{ Marginal cost}_B$$

This automatically deviates from the marginal conditions of efficient allocation. Even if the Pareto equality of price and marginal cost does not hold closely in the rest of the economy, at least *one* of the two price-cost ratios must be out of line. and here the deviation is sharp.

Figure 12.1 can also illustrate the pricing of a lifesaving drug. The same drug is sold to two groups: (1) to druggists for resale to individuals through doctors' prescriptions; and (2) to large hospitals, for dispensing to patients. The druggists' customers have *low* demand elasticity, for they merely buy what their doctor writes on their prescriptions. By contrast, the hospitals have *elastic* demand. They can bargain shrewdly, playing off the drug companies against one another to get a low price.

Thus the identical drug, costing perhaps $3 per dozen pills to make, might sell for $16 per dozen to retail druggists and $5 per dozen to hospitals. (In practice, the

TABLE 12.1   Conditions Influencing Demand Elasticities

1. *Customer conditions*	a.	Preferences.
	b.	Income and wealth.
	c.	Knowledge.
2. *Technical limits*	a.	Physical connections and apparatus usually make demand less elastic.
	b.	Ability to shop around.
3. *Competition*	a.	Extent of competition. Intense competition causes the firm's demand curve to be highly elastic for that specific product; lack of competition will permit demand to be inelastic.
	b.	Threat of entry.
4. *Vertical conditions*	a.	Monopsony power causes demand to be more elastic.
	b.	Ability to self-supply lets buyers have more choice, so demand is more elastic.

ratios of price to cost often differ even more sharply.) The inelastic demand results in a higher price to one group, which in this case is retail druggists.

Many other familiar situations give rise to price discrimination, some of which are listed in Table 12.1. The critical fact is the differing price-cost ratios among customers. In the drug instance:

$$\frac{\text{Price}_1}{\text{Cost}_1} = \frac{\$16}{\$3} = 5.33 \text{ which does not equal } 1.67 = \frac{\$5}{\$3} = \frac{\text{Price}_2}{\text{Cost}_2}$$

Prices Differing LESS Than Costs.   Now consider a much more complicated case, as illustrated in Figure 12.2. Costs differ sharply. Suppose that Marginal Cost C (MC_C) is for regular provision of airline passenger service on a reserved, guaranteed-seat basis. Marginal Cost D (MC_D) is for standby service, for people (students, backpackers) who are willing to take a chance that there will be an empty seat.

MC_C is high, at $75, because it involves the provision of guaranteed service on a plane, even if the demand for that plane on that day is low. The cost includes all of the expenditures for capital, maintenance, staffing, and fuel that are required to provide this guaranteed-seat airline service. MC_D is lower, at $10, because the airline incurs little extra cost from letting someone fill a seat that would otherwise have been unoccupied. The marginal cost involves hardly more than the extra fuel to carry one more body.

In deciding on its prices, the airline seeks to maximize its profits from each of the two groups; it sets output for each where marginal revenue equals marginal cost. That results in a fare of $100 for regular passengers and $50 for standby passengers, as shown in Figure 12.2. A regular passenger might be irritated to see a standby rider pay only half fare, but in fact *the discrimination runs the other way*. It is the standby passengers in group D who are being discriminated against, because the ratio of price to cost for that group is higher than group C's ratio. The price-cost ratios are exactly 4 to 3 for group C and 5 to 1 for group D.

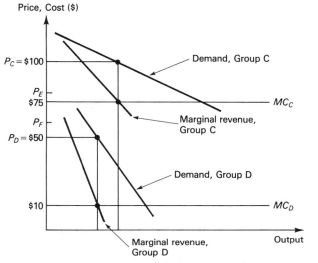

Price, Cost ($)

$P_C = \$100$ — Demand, Group C

P_E \$75 — MC_C

P_F

$P_D = \$50$ — Marginal revenue, Group C

— Demand, Group D

\$10 — MC_D

Marginal revenue, Group D   Output $\left(\dfrac{P_C}{MC_C} = 100/75,\ \dfrac{P_D}{MC_D} = 5/1\right)$

FIGURE 12.2.   Price discrimination with differing costs.

If the firm instead chose a single price for both groups in Figure 12.2, that, too, would be discrimination. Price P_E is such a single discriminatory price. (The price-cost ratios would be about 1.1 for the buyers in group C and 5.0 for those in group D.) Price P_F is another. (The ratios are now 0.9 and 4.0.) P_F is especially discriminatory because group C buyers now pay even less than the cost of supplying them. Both P_E and P_F are irrational as shown, for they do not maximize the firm's profits. Marginal revenue is not in line with marginal cost for both groups. But there may be occasions when a firm will indeed set price below cost; such "predatory" pricing will be discussed shortly.

Discrimination is intensive when (1) demand elasticities vary sharply among customers, and (2) the barriers to reselling by customers are high. Elasticities vary for a number of reasons, which Table 12.1 summarizes. Customers differ in psychology, knowledge, and affluence. Some people urgently need the product for convenience, safety, or health; others are virtually indifferent toward it. Some are wealthy, others poor. Some are ignorant of alternatives; others are informed and quick to change. Technical conditions also vary. Some buyers have facilities for shifting among products or shopping around; other buyers have simple and limited facilities.

Competition can vary sharply among the parts of a market. For some products and customers, the firm may face many competitors; for others, it may be the only supplier. The threat of entry may also vary across a large market.

Finally, vertical conditions can cause differences in elasticity. A monopsony buyer—or set of oligopsony buyers—can play sellers off against one another. They can also threaten to integrate back into producing for their own needs.

All these conditions can combine to form sharp differences in elasticity. The differences can be stable and long-lasting, or rapidly shifting. (Examples: Stable variations are found in electricity demand, by time of day, day of the week, and seasons. Fashion clothing and toys often have unstable—but still sharp—variations in elasticity.)

3.   Types of Price Discrimination

Discrimination is not limited to the simple case of a single product sold to two groups of buyers. The number of products and of buyer groups can both range up to high levels. The products can be parts of a "full line"; or they can be components that fit together in "systems" being marketed (parts of computers or electrical supply systems are an example). What matters is that the firm may sell related products at differing price-cost ratios. This happens frequently, for most firms do sell a variety of related products.

Buyer groups can be ever more finely divided, until at the extreme the seller reaches perfect discrimination among every unit sold to every one of its customers. This is shown in Figure 12.3. The seller somehow knows just what each customer will pay, sets that price for each one, and no reselling occurs. The prices fit the market demand curve itself, so that all consumer surplus is taken by the seller.

In his classic analysis of price discrimination, A. C. Pigou called this "first-degree" price discrimination. Examples of it are the small-town doctor who neatly sets each bill for each item in line with each patient's ability to pay. Also a rug merchant who haggles the maximum price from each rug sold, one by one. "Second-degree" discrimination is simply a cruder version, in which the seller can only array the prices by descending price groups (in Figure 12.3, the "sawteeth" would be larger and fewer). "Third-degree" discrimination involves "functional" groupings of customers (such as residential versus industrial customers, or by separate geo-

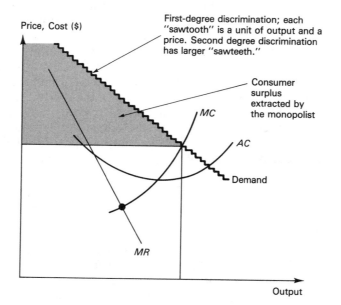

FIGURE 12.3.   "First-degree" discrimination.

Table 12.2   Some Types of Price Discrimination

PERSONAL DISCRIMINATION

Haggle-every-time.   Common in bazaars and private deals.
Give-in-if-you-must.   Shading off list prices.
Size-up-his-income.   Fit the price to the customers. Doctors, lawyers, and other professionals have long done this.
Measure-the-use.   Even if marginal costs are low, charge heavy users more. Xerox and IBM have used this strategy.

GROUP DISCRIMINATION

Kill-the-rival.   Predatory price-cutting to drive out a competitor. Said to have been commonly done by American Tobacco and Standard Oil before 1900.
Dump-the-surplus.   Selling at lower prices in foreign markets (where demand is more elastic) has occurred for drugs, steel, TV sets, and other goods. But complaints about dumping are often inaccurate.
Promote-new-customers.   Common with magazine subscriptions, this lures in new customers.
Favor-the-big-ones.   Volume discounts are steeper than cost differences. Endemic in many markets.
Divide-them-by-elasticity.   The general result, common in utility services.

PRODUCT DISCRIMINATION

Pay-for-the-label.   The fancy (premium) label gets a higher price, even if the good is the same as a common brand.
Clear-the-stock.   "Sales" are used to stabilize inventory. Any college town has scores each year.
Peak–off-peak differences.   Prices may differ by more or less than costs do, between peak-hour congested times and slack off-periods. Nearly universal in utilities.

SOURCE: Adapted from Fritz Machlup, *The Political Economy of Monopoly* (Baltimore, Md.: Johns Hopkins, 1952).

graphical areas). Figure 12.1 gave the simplest two-group "third-degree" case. There could be many groups.

In short, price discrimination can arise under a wide range of conditions, from simple groupings to comprehensive, highly refined systems. It has many sources—the seller may impose it, or the buyers may impose it on the seller, or a mixture of both may occur. It can be a stable, deep system, or it can be a series of responses to changing conditions.

This variety of conditions has given rise to a number of common names for price discrimination, including *price discounting, demand-based pricing, selective pricing, value-of-service pricing, loss leaders, price sharpshooting,* and, of course, *charging what the traffic will bear.* The ordinary SALE! often involves price discrimination. All the phrases usually refer to the same basic fact: a variation among the price-cost ratios for a seller's related goods.

The sheer variety of price discrimination is reflected in an amusing classification made by Fritz Machlup and summarized in Table 12.2. You probably know examples of each category. Even more familiar instances are presented in Table 12.3.

Table 12.3   Instances of Price Discrimination—and Nondiscrimination

Good or Service	Consumer Groups	Costs and Prices	How Reselling Is Prevented	How Does This Affect Competition?
1. Prices differ more than costs: DISCRIMINATION				
Movies, airplane trips, train trips	Adults, children	Costs are about the same for all customers, but children pay much less than adults	By letting only children use children's tickets	Usually not much at all
Magazines	Newsstand sales, regular subscriptions, special subscriptions, (to new subscribers, students, etc.)	Costs are about the same, but prices differ sharply among customers	Magazines are bulky and easily damaged; subscriber lists are kept separate	Often it promotes competition; rarely does one magazine dominate the market
2. Costs differ more than prices: DISCRIMINATION				
Bus trips in town	People taking various-length trips	There are uniform fares, but costs differ for different lengths	Tickets are issued only for the ride	Not much for the most part because competition is already excluded by the bus franchise
Electricity	Various times of day and week	Prices per kilowatt-hour do not vary by the time of use, but peak-time costs sharply exceed off-peak costs	Storing electric energy is difficult; reselling is illegal	Not much because competition is already excluded by the utility's franchise

II.   PRICE DISCRIMINATION'S EFFECTS

By setting prices selectively, each firm tries to do two main things: (1) maximize its profit from whatever market position it holds, and (2) raise or defend that market position against other firms. You already know how the first aim is pursued. Now we focus on the second part—using discrimination as a weapon to increase market share and/or entry barriers.

1.   The Competitive Weapon

Each firm (large or small) tries to take customers from its competitors. Selective pricing is a crucial device for that, much superior to broad price cuts. *Any price cut reduces the revenue on the preexisting sales,* so it is painful to the firm. Selective

Table 12.3   (*continued*)

GOOD OR SERVICE	CONSUMER GROUPS	COSTS AND PRICES	HOW RESELLING IS PREVENTED	HOW DOES THIS AFFECT COMPETITION?
3. Prices and costs differ proportionally: NOT DISCRIMINATION				
Long-distance phone calls	Daytime callers, night and weekend callers	There are higher prices for calls made at peak times; costs at peak times are also higher	Timing cannot be switched	Not much, for the telephone company has an exclusive franchise
Clothing sales	Regular sales, bargain sales	There are low sales prices; the true costs of the clothes are also low, because clothes are excess (recall opportunity costs)	Sales are held only after clothes have lost their popularity	It promotes competition, for the firms rarely have large market shares
Restaurant meals	Luncheon customers, supper and evening customers	At peak-capacity times, costs are higher, even though food costs are uniform; dinner prices are well above luncheon prices	By time of day; meals cannot be stored or resold by those who buy them	It promotes competition by filling restaurant tables at flexible prices; rarely do restaurants dominate their markets

price cuts (that is, discrimination) minimize that sacrifice. They let the firm offer lower prices only to those buyers who require them.

In panel I of Figure 12.4, the firm sells q_1 at price P_1 to begin with, making profit in areas A and B. It will have to offer the reduced price P_2 to draw the buyers in the q_1–q_2 range. If it can do that while not cutting to P_2 for the original sales (0–q_1), it will keep the shaded profit area A, while adding profit area C. But if selective pricing is impossible, it will lose the A profit amount in trying to raise sales to q_2.

Meanwhile, its rival (in panel II) may have inelastic customers for a related good, whom it is charging a price of P_3. Its elastic customers are charged the lower price, P_4. Our firm will attack the inelastic segment first, because it is more lucrative. Its price will be P_5, which will take all the rival's sales from that segment of the market. The rival will try to respond selectively, cutting price only for the q_3–q_5 customers and trying to keep the 0–q_3 customers at price P_3. If that fails, other selective price cuts or a broad price-cutting counterattack may be tried.

In short, each firm uses selective price discounts to the hilt in trying to get market share or defend it. Selective sharpshooting can also be used to fight off (or scare off) an entrant. In every case, the firm limits the price cuts to minimize its sacrifice.

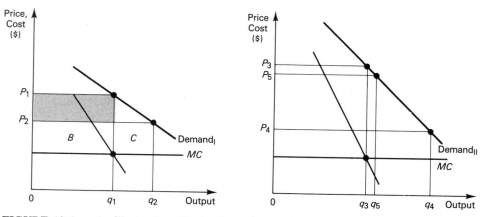

FIGURE 12.4.   An illustration of selective price tactics between firms.

As all these efforts proceed in the thick of complex pricing battles, the firms limit one another's success. Ideally, the whole process tears away at the higher price-cost margins and forces all prices broadly down to cost. But where that fails to happen, the firms with high market shares can milk higher profits by means of price discrimination.

2.   Promoting or Reducing Competition

Price discrimination evidently can promote or reduce competition, depending on the situation. The two critical features are (1) the *market position* of the firm doing the discriminating and (2) how *systematic* and complete the discrimination is. The higher the firm's market share is, the more likely it is that competition will be reduced. As we saw, high market shares often cover a wide variety of demand elasticities, which can be known and separated. Small-share firms, in contrast, can rarely know or divide their customers effectively by differences in elasticity. Systematic discrimination involves more market control and excess profits.

These two criteria are applied in Figure 12.5. Price discrimination can occur in any combination of those conditions. But it is clearly procompetitive in zone *A*—sporadic discrimination by firms with small market shares. In fact, many small-share firms—which hold no market power—compete by selective price-cutting. Such price cuts, often called "loss leaders," are common in grocery, drug, clothing, and camera stores.

Several items are temporarily offered at discounts, to draw customers in. Once there, the customers may buy other goods that have higher profit margins. Newspaper ads for grocery and clothing sales are often full of such "loss leaders."

At the other extreme is the utility firm, holding a complete monopoly and selling to many different buyers. It is always tempted to apply deep price discrimination. That is one reason why utilities in electricity, gas, and telephones need to be regulated by public agencies.

Discrimination can be the lifeblood of competition when it is *sporadic* and/or

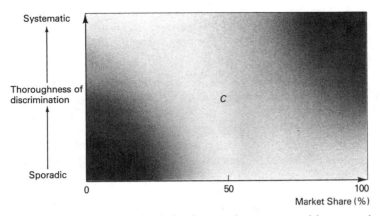

FIGURE 12.5. Price discrimination can be procompetitive or anticompetitive.

done by *smaller* firms, as in zone *A*. But when it is done forcefully and systematically by dominant firms, as in zone *B*, price discrimination is usually anticompetitive. Indeed, if firms with small market shares try to keep prices systematically out of line with costs, they will lose money and may go out of business.

Zone *B* discrimination can forestall new competition. A dominant firm will often cover a full line of products in a market, while its smaller rivals tend to specialize in a narrower range. The dominant firm naturally meets competition where it arises; it sets low price-cost ratios where its rivals are strongest. The dominant firm can therefore hold comparably efficient competitors (or new entrants) to little or no profit in those parts of the market.

By contrast, effective competition attacks the most lucrative markets, forces lower price-cost ratios, spreads to all submarkets, and drives prices down toward costs evenly throughout the whole market. Systematic discrimination (which prevents that process) is a prime indicator of market power.

In the middle range (zone *C*), the effects are mixed. Here one must assess each case carefully, looking at the setting and the pricing actions.

Effects on efficiency

Type *A* discrimination is part of the competitive process, which yields efficient allocation and X-efficiency. Type *B* discrimination will usually be part of the monopolist's restrictions, which distort allocation and may breed X-inefficiency.

There is one possible exception—the "natural monopoly." If scale economies are very large and if they could not be achieved were a single price charged, then some degree of *B* discrimination may improve allocative efficiency. In this case, the firm's cost and demand curves cannot yield profits with a single price. But if differing prices are set for groups I and II, then the firm can make a profit. In this special case, discrimination makes it impossible for the firm to exist at all as a private enterprise. Group I, though "overcharged," is better off than with no supply whatever. This "utility" case is a limited one. Few markets really have such scale economies combined with special demand conditions that require discrimination if the firm is to survive. And for those that do, the socially justified degree of discrimination (that which is just necessary to let the firm exist) may be much less than the firm will wish to practice. In fact, "utility" firms can usually practice sharp discrimination.[2] Good policy sees to it that "natural-monopoly" conditions do not become the excuse for a blank check for discrimination.

"Ramsey Prices" (the "Inverse-Elasticity Rule").   An opposite view is offered by William J. Baumol, John C. Panzar, and Robert D. Willig.[3] They have relabeled discriminatory prices "Ramsey prices," after an obscure economist of the 1920s, Frank Ramsey. Ramsey's short 1927 paper on taxation provided a simple (and obvious) rule for minimizing the impact of taxes on consumer surplus: vary tax rates inversely with elasticity.[4]

Often called the "inverse-elasticity rule," Ramsey pricing applies only to natural-monopoly firms that produce multiple products. The rule calls for setting price–marginal-cost ratios that vary inversely with demand elasticity. Thus price-cost ratios would be highest where elasticity is lowest. That, in fact, is a definition of price discrimination.

Inverse-elasticity (or Ramsey) pricing does maximize static consumer surplus (that is, it minimizes the reduction of consumer surplus incurred in raising any given amount of revenue, so as to cover the firm's total costs). But it is valid only when the enterprise would otherwise suffer a financial deficit because of its declining-cost nature (that is, a natural monopoly with multiple products facing differing demand elasticities). Also, the discriminating enterprise must be constrained so that its profits do not exceed bare-minimum levels. *Then,* and only then, are Ramsey prices efficient.

Ramsey prices are conceivably applicable in assessing actual discrimination. But this criterion is hazardous in four main ways:[5]

1.   The efficiency properties occur only when the multiproduct natural-monopoly enterprise does face a financial deficit. Such cases are rare and difficult to verify.

2.   The enterprise will seek to earn excess profits, and constraining them to minimum levels will usually be virtually impossible.

3.   The static-efficiency properties omit all other economic goals, including X-inefficiency, innovation, and the rest (recall Chapters 2 and 5–7). Monopoly enterprises are likely to violate these other criteria, as we have noted, and therefore any static-efficiency gains from Ramsey prices may be exceeded by social costs.

4.   Discrimination can serve as a device for reducing competition when it is employed

---

[2] The customer is often physically connected (by a wire or pipe, as in the cases of electricity, telephone service, gas, and water), and reselling is impossible or illegal. Customers cover the whole spectrum of households, businesses, and public agencies, so demands differ sharply. The "utility" service is a "vital necessity" for many, even most, customers (that is, demand is highly elastic for many customers), so there is an opportunity and incentive for steep overcharging.

[3] See their *Contestable Markets and the Theory of Industry Structure* (San Diego, Cal.: Harcourt Brace Jovanovich, 1982).

[4] See his "A Contribution to the Theory of Taxation," *Economic Journal,* 37 (1927), 47–61. Ramsey died shortly after this paper was published, having written little else.

[5] See William G. Shepherd, "Competition and Sustainability," a chapter in Thomas G. Gies and Werner Sichel, eds., *Deregulation: Appraisal Before the Fact* (Ann Arbor: Bureau of Business Research, School of Business, University of Michigan, 1982). For favorable treatment, see Jean Tirole, *The Theory of Industrial Organization* (Cambridge, Mass.: MIT Press, 1988).

by a monopoly or dominant firm, as noted in Section I. The firm may therefore use discriminatory pricing to extend its monopoly or to retain it after the natural-monopoly conditions that gave rise to it have ceased to exist.

Altogether, Ramsey prices (and other such variants of price discrimination) offer only limited possible gains, in limited settings, while risking large social costs. Despite the relabeling, they remain price discrimination.

Primary and secondary line effects

Efficiency effects can be on two levels: (1) *Among sellers.* These first-level effects (often called "primary line" effects) are on the competitive status of the discriminator and its rivals. (2) *Among buyers.* Second-level effects (often called "secondary-line effects") are on the competitive positions of buyers. An example: The electric company discriminates, so Apex, Inc., gets electricity cheaper than its rivals, cuts its prices, and takes market share away from its rivals. They are unable to respond evenly because the higher electricity price they pay has made competition unbalanced.

3.   Problems of Cost

Cost is the critical element in judging price discrimination. Marginal cost is the correct criterion, for it is the true measure of opportunity cost. In long-run equilibrium, a competitive firm's marginal and average costs will be equal. Also, average cost is often much easier to measure than marginal cost. Therefore it is sometimes roughly permissible to use average costs in evaluating whether discrimination has occurred. But they should not be used in complicated cases, and most of the interesting cases are complicated.

Marginal cost is what matters, but it is hard to measure. *Fluctuations are one problem.* As a firm's demand fluctuates, its level of marginal costs will change. This can occur regularly, as in peak and off-peak times for electric and telephone service. Fluctuations also occur over the business cycle.

Marginal costs are low in slack times and high during booms. If prices shift in response to these changes, they may or may not involve discrimination. If capacity is idle, then a price cut down to the low marginal cost level might not be discriminatory (depending on what is done with other products and time periods). Yet if the price cut causes sales to rise, then marginal cost may soon be above the price level.

Joint costs are another problem. Many products share overhead or joint costs with other products.[6] Management, research and development, and many other companywide activities are often pooled over a range of products. Often the same machine makes two or more products, and dividing the cost among them is difficult. Some processes yield by-products (petroleum refineries produce airplane and au-

---

[6] Classic books on this crucial topic include J. M. Clark, *Studies in the Economics of Overhead Costs* (Chicago: University of Chicago Press, 1923); and W. Arthur Lewis, *Overhead Costs* (London: Allen & Unwin, 1948). The Baumol-Panzar-Willig analysis in *Contestable Markets* does offer interesting insights on defining multiproduct costs and efficiency conditions.

tomobile fuel, kerosene, fuel oil, and tar products from one common process). All these conditions make cost allocation arbitrary and debatable.

In short, marginal costs may be hard to measure in precisely those complex situations where price discrimination is likely to be sharp. You should grasp the concepts clearly, but expect trouble in applying them. Often one must use rough measures of average or variable costs as a first approximation for marginal costs.

4. Tie-ins

A tie-in requires you to buy good B, which you don't want, in order to get good A, which you do want. The tying product (good A) is often a patented product of some kind or a popular branded item. The tied item is often a new product, an inferior one, or simply a complement. The firm holds more market power for good A than for good B. Tying B to A therefore gives B some of the selling power (or market control) of A. Even though this tactic causes less of A to be sold, it often permits the firm to raise its combined profits on the two goods.

Tying is an ancient custom, though a rather specialized one that crops up only in certain situations. Market processes usually undermine tie-ins, as new firms offer the tied goods separately. While it lasts, tying can (1) extend market power from the tying product into the tied product, and/or (2) as a form of price discrimination, serve to extract more profit. Many economists deny that market power can be levered in this way from product A to B, but there is agreement that discrimination can occur from tie-ins.

Tying by dominant firms (especially those with patents or some other special advantage in good A) can reduce competition in good B's market. Even if such leverage is not strong, the tie can raise entry barriers by forcing any new entrants to offer both products, not just one.[7] Some benefits are possible, though less likely. The joint purchase might realize cost savings in ordering, shipping, or servicing. Also, tying makes it hard to identify the separate prices of the tied goods, so an oligopolist might use it as a device for quietly offering concealed price cuts.

Antitrust Cases Involving Tie-ins. Generally, policy has treated the social costs of tie-ins as overwhelming where market shares are large. In contrast, small competitors and sporadic ties are often regarded as harmless to competition. For example, the early **IBM** made its customers use only IBM cards (which were set at a high price), and it had overwhelming dominance (over 90 percent) of both markets. In 1936, the Supreme Court rejected IBM's claim that other computer cards would jam the machines or cause errors.[8]

International Salt required users of its patented salt-processing machines to use only its salt in the machines. It claimed that was the sole way to protect the machines from malfunctioning. Though there were competitive machines, and the effect of foreclosure was only "creeping" rather than "at a full gallop," the Court convicted International in 1947.[9]

---

[7] See also John S. McGee, "Compound Pricing," *Economic Inquiry*, 125 (April 1987), 315–40.
[8] *International Business Machines Corp.* v. *U.S.*, 298 U.S. 131 (1936). By 1956, IBM still had over 90 percent of the card business.
[9] *International Salt Co.* v. *U.S.*, 332 U.S. 392 (1947).

American Can required buyers of its patented can-closing machines to use only its cans in them. When a major monopolization case against it and Continental Can was settled in 1949, a central clause was the prohibition of this tie-in.[10] In 1954, an Antitrust Division action challenging **Eastman Kodak**'s dominance and its tying of film processing to film purchasers was settled.[11] The tie was broken, and henceforth film buyers could have a choice of processors.

By 1951, a small firm named **Jerrold Electronics** had begun marketing equipment for the embryonic cable TV industry. A cable system receives distant TV signals at one big antenna and then feeds them by a wire network to households. Such systems began in small, remote towns. By 1960, they had spread to larger towns, and cable equipment had become an established growth industry.

From the start, Jerrold required its customers to use whole Jerrold systems rather than let them patch in non-Jerrold parts.[12] They were also required to have a service contract with Jerrold. The firm claimed that this enabled it to protect the quality of its working systems. This point had merit, especially for smaller customers not well able to design and manage cable systems.

At first, Jerrold's practices helped develop the industry, in competition with other services. But by 1957, Jerrold was no longer a firm in an "infant" industry, but rather a dominant firm practicing tie-in sales. The Antitrust Division sued, and in 1961 the courts declared that Jerrold could no longer price in that way. Tie-ins permitted to a firm in a formative industry had become anticompetitive for a dominant firm in an established market.

For many decades before 1956, **United Shoe Machinery Corporation** dominated its industry and used tie-ins. USM would only lease machinery, not sell it. Customers (that is, shoe manufacturers) were required to use *only* USM machinery if they wanted to use any USM equipment. Only USM supplies could be used with USM machines.[13] Consequently, USM tied together (1) various machines, (2) maintenance services, and (3) supplies. These provisions clearly did reduce competition in all these areas and in the industry generally. Because USM was dominant, the tie-ins were among the practices forbidden when USM was convicted under the Sherman Act in 1956.

The **Loew's** decision in 1962 again involved movies.[14] The owners of a large library of old films had required the TV networks to take packages of films rather

[10] The case is *U.S.* v. *American Can Co.*, 87 F. Supp. 18 (N. D. Cal. 1949); see also James W. McKie, *Tin Cans and Tin Plate* (Cambridge, Mass.: Harvard University Press, 1959). American and Continental together held 86 percent of both levels (machines and cans).

[11] A complaint had been prepared in July 1954, whereupon Kodak negotiated to settle the suit before it was filed. The settlement and suit were both filed in December 1954. See *Trade Cases,* para. 67,920, and the case study of Kodak in Chapter 17 of this textbook.

Kodak had held a complete monopoly of processing of Kodacolor and Kodachrome film by selling the film only at a price that included the processing charge. The settlement ended this. Kodak also agreed to license its processing patents to others, at reasonable royalties. Within seven years, Kodak promised to divest facilities if its share of processing had not gone below 50 percent.

[12] The matter became a landmark antitrust case, *U.S.* v. *Jerrold Electronics Corp.*, 187 F. Supp. 545 (E.D. Penna. 1960), aff'd per curiam 365 U.S. 567 (1961).

[13] In all, there were seven separate types of tie-ins, forming a tight web of limits and exclusions. The discussion here brings out their essential effects. They are discussed fully in Judge Wyzanski's opinion (*U.S.* v. *United Shoe Machinery Corp.* 10 F. Supp. 295, 1953); and in Carl Kaysen's excellent treatise, *The United Shoe Machinery Case* (Cambridge, Mass.: Harvard University Press, 1959).

[14] *U.S.* v. *Loew's, Inc.*, 371 U.S. 38 (1962).

than let them select among separately priced films. (Thus *The Man Who Came to Dinner* was tied to *Gorilla Man* and *Tugboat Annie Sails Again*.) Loew's claimed that old movies were less than 8 percent of all TV offerings, and therefore a minor competitive factor. The device was primarily aimed at maximizing profits rather than extending the firm's market power. Yet it was held to be illegal per se. Note that Loew's was a large factor in the old-movie sector of the entertainment industry.

These cases fit the general economic rule relating the harm of tie-ins to the market share of the firm. Tie-ins are considered innocuous only when market shares are low.

III. "PREDATORY ACTIONS," INCLUDING PRICING

Small firms frequently complain that they have been unfairly treated by larger competitors, who go "too far" in some sense. A lawyers' phrase, "predatory actions," has evolved in antitrust cases to denote such excessive competition. Economists have tried to give that phrase some economic meaning, especially since 1972, in what has become a wordy, uneven, and inconclusive debate.[15] Though the term *predatory* has little economic content, the issue focuses on selective, discriminatory actions. Such actions can hurt or promote competition, *depending on the setting in which they occur.* The proper lessons can be summed up as follows, in a series of points.[16]

1. Testing for Unfair Competition

1. Each firm can use many specific devices (or weapons) to compete. Price is one; its levels and structure can be changed. Alterations in product quality and design are another category of actions. The many other types of specific actions include

---

[15] The main writings are John S. McGee, "Predatory Pricing: The Standard Oil Case," *Journal of Law and Economics*, 1 (October 1958), 137–69; Ronald H. Koller II, "The Myth of Predatory Pricing," *Antitrust Law and Economics Review*, 4 (Summer 1971), 105–23; Basil S. Yamey, "Predatory Price Cutting: Notes and Comments," *Journal of Law and Economics*, 15 (April 1972), 137–47; Philip Areeda and Donald F. Turner, *Antitrust Law* (Boston: Little, Brown, 1978); Frederic M. Scherer, *Industrial Market Structure and Economic Performance*, 2nd ed. (Chicago: Rand McNally 1980), pp. 335–40; Oliver E. Williamson, "Predatory Pricing: A Strategic and Welfare Analysis," *Yale Law Journal*, 87 (1977), 284–340; Paul L. Joskow and Alvin K. Klevorick, "A Framework for Analyzing Predatory Pricing Policy," *Yale Law Journal*, 89 (1979), 213–47; Joel B. Dirlam, "Predatory Pricing and Antitrust Policy: Economic Theory and the Quest for Certainty," in Kenneth D. Boyer and William G. Shepherd, eds., *Economic Regulation: Essays in Honor of James R. Nelson* (East Lansing: Institute of Public Utilities, Michigan State University, 1981); Steven C. Salop, ed., *Strategy, Predation and Antitrust Analysis*, conference volume (Washington, D.C.: Federal Trade Commission, Bureau of Economics and Competition, September 1981); and Steven Salop and David T. Scheffman, "Raising Rivals' Costs," *American Economic Review*, 73 (May 1983), 267–71.

See also M. R. Burns, "Predatory Pricing and the Acquisition Cost of Competitors," *Journal of Political Economy*, 94 (1986), 266–96; D. Fudenberg and Jean Tirole, "A 'Signal-Jamming' Theory of Predation," *Rand Journal of Economics*, 17 (1986), 366–76; P. Milgrom and D. J. Roberts, "Predation, Reputation and Entry Deterrence," *Journal of Economic Theory*, 27 (1982), 280–312; Janusz A. Ordover and Garth Saloner, "Predation, Monopolization, and Antitrust," in Richard Schmalensee and Robert D. Willig, eds., *Handbook of Industrial Organization*, New York: North-Holland, 1987; D. J. Roberts, "A Signalling Model of Predatory Pricing," *Oxford Economic Papers*, Supplement, 38 (November 1986), 75–93; and Garth Saloner, "Predation, Mergers, and Incomplete Information," *Rand Journal of Economics*, 18 (Summer 1987), 165–86.

[16] This section draws on my "Assessing 'Predatory' Actions by Market Shares and Selectivity," *Antitrust Bulletin*, 31 (Spring 1986), 1–28.

advertising and other promotional programs. All of these can either be carried out concretely or merely threatened persuasively enough to affect rivals' choices.

2. Some of these competitive devices are selective; others are applied uniformly. Selective actions include price discounts to specific buyers or groups, product changes aimed at specific rivals, and promotional campaigns fitted precisely against one or several competitors in an area. Uniform actions include across-the-board price cuts and broad-scale advertising campaigns. Selectivity is a matter of degree; often there is no sharp break between selective and uniform actions. But selectivity is a condition that can be evaluated.

The economic task is to determine the conditions, if any, under which selective actions have anticompetitive effects. All selective actions can be procompetitive; only in certain settings do they reduce competition.

3. All firms, all of the time, use any or all of these weapons (selective and uniform) in their efforts to defeat competitors and to gain market control and the resulting excess profits. Competition itself comprises the totality of such actions, in the on-going give and take of the struggle. When competition is effective, the competing firms have access to the same weapons, and their use of these devices is mutually constraining among all participants.

4. Yet some firms—in some situations—are able to harm competition by going "too far" in certain of their actions, and they may do so repeatedly and systematically (rather than only in the odd irrational case) and successfully. Dominant firms with high market shares (in the range of 50 to 95 percent) dealing with much smaller competitors are usually in this category. They can damage or eliminate efficient small competitors if they choose to do so, because they have sufficiently larger financial and other resources. They are like adult boxers facing child boxers, or teams with fifteen players facing teams with five.

5. Such firms will indeed often choose to go "too far," for two reasons. First, the firm may have a comprehensive strategy in which this first (money-losing) action is only one step toward a larger total profit. For example, a monopoly newspaper may give away its Sunday editions free if it faces a new paper that is trying to get started with a Sunday edition. By stopping the newcomer in this "money-losing" way, the monopolist may protect its total seven-day monopoly and gain larger profits. Many other such strategies are tried routinely, in many markets: loss leaders, deep discounts, two-for-one sales, and so on often involve small sacrifices for big gains.

Second, the action may be intended as a signal to other firms for the future. By treating one competitor severely, a firm may deter others from entering or intimidate other small rivals into passive behavior. The sacrifice therefore has a multiple payoff. For example, suppose it cost the early Standard Oil $1 million to cut its price in one region to drive out its small rival, and it could only make $900,000 in profits there later by raising its price. If ten other rivals in other regions were frightened by this display of ferocity, Standard Oil might be able to buy them all out at lower prices, and that would save it many millions.

These two reasons conflict with the Chicago-UCLA belief that anticompetitive actions will not occur because the profits recouped later cannot exceed the costs of the actions. In fact, the recoupment by the larger firm (in the related strategies or in other markets receiving its signals) can systematically exceed the actions' initial costs.

6. Therefore actions that harm the competitive process are not self-averting. Dominant firms have inducements to intimidate or eliminate smaller competitors. They will presumably do so by using the least costly method. That method involves selective actions, which aim precisely to compel the lesser firm's surrender (that is, closure or merger into the larger firm at the least price) with the least cost to the larger firm. For example, selective price cuts will, if they discriminate perfectly, take the small firm's customers while minimizing the larger firm's revenue loss from reducing its prices. Put in general terms, selective actions are the dominant firm's ideal device for adding market share profitably.

Selective actions are not equally available to the smaller firms, because those firms face more complete competitive pressures than do dominant firms. Any selective actions they may take are doomed to have only minor effects because the competitive pressures on them are so pervasive and restrictive. On the other hand, a dominant firm can often use those selective actions sharply and effectively. Selective action is anticompetitive (some would also say unfair) when it gives to dominant firms a category of effective weapons unavailable to lesser competitors.

In short, selective actions are anticompetitive when they are taken by a firm whose market share is high *and* higher than the share of the target firm. The task is to design a policy confined precisely to those conditions. An efficient policy will, of course, not prevent firms from vigorously competing. Only the specific category of *selective tactics done by firms with high market shares* is anticompetitive. Restraining those actions will equalize competition, giving all firms access to a comparable array of effective competitive tactics.

2. Alternative Criteria

Using this basic criterion, one can evaluate three specific tests that have been proposed for judging if an action is anticompetitive.

Price and cost

First is a method based on *prices* only. Areeda and Turner argued in 1975 that actions might reduce competition only if the firm set price below cost (that is, incurred a definite financial loss). If no loss is suffered, they said, the action has not gone "too far." This would be a special, extreme form of discrimination in which the price-cost ratio goes below 1.0. The discrimination could be both (1) *chronological,* between the price-cutting period and the later monopoly pricing; and (2) *simultaneous,* among various goods the firm sells.

Using this approach, one compares the prices with the "true" costs, which are usually marginal costs. If the pricing is being done by a dominant firm, one usually takes its *long-run* marginal costs as the test, since the firm obviously expects to remain in the market in the long run. Pricing below long-run marginal cost is presumptively predatory, unless specific conditions (such as an inventory backlog) clearly exonerate it. In practice, one often finds that average costs are the best available estimator of long-run marginal cost.

One problem with this approach is that it ignores the many other competitive devices available to firms. Another is that there are large complexities in measuring costs and in setting the correct limits on prices in actual cases. The seeming objectivity of the price-costs tests is mostly illusory (as Areeda-Turner and many other writers recognize). In short, the Areeda-Turner approach ignores many of the relevant anticompetitive devices; the tests often founder on unclear measures of costs; and the crucial competitive setting of the actions is omitted.

Effects

Second, the effects of the larger firm's actions might be used as the test of anticompetitiveness. But that approach will face impossible difficulties. As noted, *all* successful competitive actions by all firms will inherently harm their rivals' capital values. Any economist who tries to measure those effects and to separate the "excessive" ones from (1) the endless variety of impacts from "fair" competition and (2) differences in the firms' efficiency will face a virtually hopeless task. Also futile would be an effort to set threshold levels for the severity of the permitted effects. For example, if the smaller firm is only crippled but not killed, would the action be rated not excessive?

One would need to estimate not only each action's effects, as distinct from the effects of all the other actions taking place, but also the relative efficiency and innovativeness of the two firms. Only then could one judge if the affected firm's difficulties were caused by the larger firm's tactics rather than by the smaller firm's incompetence. Such judgments are not only complex, but bound to be debated as matters of controversial "expert" opinion about managerial quality, specific decisions, and the companies' surroundings. Therefore the judgment would inevitably be inconclusive.

For example, suppose a dominant firm takes certain selective price cuts and advertising actions against its very small but efficient rival. In extremity, the smaller firm resorts to desperate cost cutting and gambles on long-shot innovative actions. Despite the trauma, it is lucky enough to survive, but barely. How can the separate effects of the larger firm's two actions be weighed? Were they excessive in some sense? Even if that could be decided, does the smaller firm's bare survival render the larger firm's actions innocuous? It should not if the smaller firm is unable to match the larger firm's tactics.

Intent

Third, policies might conceivably be based on judgments about the firm's intent. But that approach is neither logical nor feasible. All firms naturally intend to defeat their rivals, and the actions they take to do so are usually part of healthy competition. Trying to determine when that intent goes "too far" is like trying to judge when an athlete is trying "too hard." What matters is the setting of the action and the weapons used by the rivals. If the setting and weapons are equivalent, then intent is irrelevant. If the setting and weapons are imbalanced, intent is *also* irrelevant. In any event, intent is usually a complex mixture of attitudes that are virtually impossible to discover and to measure against an objective scale.

To summarize, effective competition requires that the rivals be able to use comparable competitive actions against one another. Otherwise a large market share for one firm will lead cumulatively to further imbalance, which makes competition increasingly one-sided and ineffective. Dominant firms can use selective tactics small rivals cannot effectively employ. For effective competition, the larger firm must be prevented from employing selective actions that are unavailable to its competitors.

The basic criterion

The basic economic criterion is therefore simple. It proscribes (1) *selective actions* by firms (2) whose *market shares* are sharply larger than their rivals'. That is all: no price-cost tests are needed, no measures of effects or intent, no evaluations of relative efficiency. Though there are some complexities, they will usually be smaller than those of the other tests.[17]

The proper test is based on the market positions of the two firms. It is those different positions that govern the ability, if any, of the attacking firm to harm competition. Only selective tactics—both price and nonprice—are anticompetitive. One simple criterion is applied: the disparity between the market shares of the attacking firm and the affected firm. If the attacking firm is smaller or only a little larger than the other, then its actions can only be part of fair competition. But if its market share is, say, 30 points higher than the other firm's, selective actions can clearly be unfair. For example, IBM with 60 percent of the market can take many selective actions that Unisys and Control Data (with 5 to 8 percent each) cannot match.

Economists can therefore define anticompetitive actions by market share differences and selectivity. The other tests are usually too narrow, too hard to apply, and/or irrelevant to the real problem.

Specific instances and rules

Creating the American Tobacco Monopoly.   Some early U.S. cases have been thoroughly mined for lessons. McGee argued that Standard Oil's actions were not "predatory," but Scherer and others have noted strong contrary evidence. Malcolm Burns has studied the creation of the American Tobacco monopoly during 1890–1900.[18] He finds that the monopolizing actions had the predictable effect of driving down the value of the competitors' assets so that they could be acquired cheaply. This fits our general analysis, in which impacts show up in asset values, permitting monopolization and excess profits.

The "Stay-Low" Pricing Rule.   Baumol has noted that a simple rule can frustrate attempts to price low with the intent of eliminating competitors, in hopes of

---

[17] Comparisons of prices and costs can still be a helpful supplement, but they are often difficult to measure. This is true also of the tactic of "raising rivals' costs," which Salop and Scheffman have analyzed in several articles, including the one cited in footnote 15 above. By forcing up its rivals' costs, a dominant firm can supress competition.

But proof of that will require data on the rival's actual prices, actual costs, and hypothetical undistorted costs. Those data may be hard to obtain in reliable forms. In any event, the root cause of the anticompetitive problem is the dominant firm's dominance.

[18] Malcolm R. Burns, "Outside Intervention in Monopolistic Price Warfare: The Case of the 'Plug War' and the Union Tobacco Company," *Business History Review,* 56 (Spring 1982), 33–53; Burns, "Economies of Scale in Tobacco Manufacture, 1897–1910," *Journal of Economic History,* 43 (June 1983), 461–74; and Burns, "Predatory Pricing and the Acquisition Cost of Competitors," *Journal of Political Economy,* 94 (April 1986), 266–96.

reaping later profits large enough to justify the initial sacrifice.[19] If the price-cutter can be forced to keep down the newly-cut price, then the payoff will be prevented. Knowing that this will happen, firms will avoid such actions when they are anticompetitive.

The rule is simple and correct, but it suffers from practical problems. First, it is valid only when the setting involves sharp market share differences, as noted above. Therefore, applying the rule requires careful study of the market setting.

Second, pricing is often arcane where there are multiple versions of products, variability of quality, and other complexities. These may permit the offender to circumvent any constraint on a specific price.

Third, the rule covers only pricing. All other selective actions are ignored. If prices are strictly constrained, then firms may develop nonprice methods to accomplish much the same results.

Predatory Innovation.   Innovations can have anticompetitive effects in certain situations. A leading case occurred in 1969–1971, when IBM redesigned certain computer components in ways that reduced the ability of rivals to make compatible equipment.[20] These small rivals were virtually eliminated from the market, and their lawsuits against IBM alleged that the innovation was predatory.

IBM was the dominant firm, with over 70 percent of the market. Although IBM won the cases (on this and other issues), the possibility that product changes can harm competition is genuine and interesting. Another such instance involved Berkey Photo's accusation that Eastman Kodak deliberately designed and introduced its new Instamatic Camera in ways that would remove Berkey as a competitor in film processing (see Chapter 17).

Janusz Ordover and Robert D. Willig have suggested a test for such cases.[21] If the innovation would be profitable even if no rivals were forced from the market, then it is not anticompetitive (or predatory). But if the innovation would be profitable only if at least one competitor leaves the market, then it has to be considered anticompetitive (or predatory).

This rule suffers from the same problems as the others: (1) It ignores the setting of relative market shares. (2) It ignores impacts that are less than fatal (though still destructive to competition). (3) It requires facts (about profits and rivals' actions) that are usually impossible to ascertain. The problem remains unresolved.[22]

IV. CASES OF PRICE DISCRIMINATION

Practical cases can convey the variety of price discrimination and illustrate how to evaluate it. But before we turn to cases, several practical lessons can be drawn.

First, perfect ("first-degree") discrimination is rare. Usually, even the purest

---

[19] William J. Baumol, "Quasi-Permanence of Price Reductions: A Policy for Prevention of Predatory Pricing," *Yale Law Journal,* 89 (November 1979), 1–26.

[20] *California Computer Products, Inc., et al.* v. *International Business Machines Corp.,* 613 F. 2d 727 (9th Cir. 1979).

[21] Ordover and Willig, "An Economic Definition of Predation: Pricing and Product Innovation," *Yale Law Journal,* 91 (November 1981), 1–31.

[22] For further criticism of the rule, see Joseph G. Sidak, "Debunking Predatory Innovation," *Columbia Law Review,* 83 (June 1983), 1121–49. Sidak's view is that innovations rarely have anticompetitive effects and that any protective rule would discourage future innovation. But his points are speculative; he gives no economic or practical basis on which to make such judgments.

monopolists can only manage to reach third-degree discrimination, with perhaps four to twelve groupings.

Second, there has been little evidence that discrimination is necessary for the firm to be viable. Some of the "utilities" *are* "natural monopolies" (at least in part), but price discrimination has scarcely ever been shown to be strictly necessary. Discrimination is usually enjoyed by the monopolists as an extra benefit, not as an essential.

Third, discrimination does not always clash diametrically with cost-based pricing. Supply to elastic-demand customers often happens to be at low cost, and therefore the demand-based and cost-based prices turn out to be roughly in line. The problem is to determine costs and then judge how far prices depart from them. Yet costs are often so hard to measure, especially for utilities with their large joint costs, that one's judgment about discrimination must often be imprecise.

The following cases will proceed roughly from pure monopoly to low market shares.

Telephone service

"Value-of-service pricing" has permeated telephone pricing for many decades. One aspect is the variation in telephone rentals among cities of different sizes. The Bell System recognized that costs were about the same for cities of all sizes. Yet big-city users typically were charged much more than small-town users.

Figure 12.6 illustrates another discriminatory facet of traditional telephone pricing. The familiar flat-rate monthly rental makes individual calls free, no matter how many they are, nor when they occur, nor how long they last. One can make an hour-long (or two-hour!) local call during the business-hour peak period for no charge. Yet costs are normally high for such calls, since peak loads involve relatively high capacity costs.[23] The telephone companies have preferred such promotional pricing in order to build up use. Figure 12.6 shows how strongly discriminatory the pricing might be: the peak-time cost level is over ten times as high as the off-peak cost level.

In contrast, long-distance telephone rates have traditionally fitted some of these cost differences. Experimental plans to set local-exchange prices along similar time-of-day lines have had little success. Metering costs discourage any widespread shift to time-of-day pricing of local calls. Still, the present system does contain discrimination.

Many users in large cities must now pay "message rates," such as 10 cents per call above 70 calls per month. This is also shown in Figure 12.6. The message rate also discriminates against off-peak callers. Only when calls are charged accurately by duration and time of occurrence can discrimination be eliminated.

Electricity

Most electricity systems have long had five to ten different rate schedules for their main customer groups. Residences, small businesses, "general" (medium-large) users, and large industrial users are the main traditional categories. Their

---

[23] Studies have estimated that peak costs per three-minute call are at least five times the level of off-peak costs; see S. C. Littlechild, "Peak-Load Pricing of Telephone Calls," *Bell Journal of Economics*, 1 (Autumn 1970), 171–210. These are averages across broad periods. More exact studies would be likely to find higher ratios.

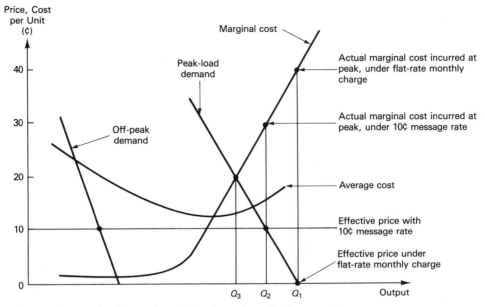

FIGURE 12.6.   An illustration of local-service telephone pricing.

Users pay a flat monthly fee (such as $15 per month) and get unlimited free calls. At that zero price per call, they use service out to level Q_1. At Q_1, the marginal cost of service is high, and the inefficiency is shown by the gap between price and marginal cost.

The efficient peak-load price is where demand intersects marginal cost, giving output level Q_3. A "message rate" may be set, such as 10 cents per call. But it still ignores peak–off-peak cost differences. It would give the output Q_2, with still a large gap between price and marginal cost.

average prices often differ by a factor of 2 or more; for example, businesses may pay about 2 cents per kilowatt-hour and residents about 6 cents. Yet costs can also differ because industrial customers take power at higher voltages, with smaller connection costs, and often on a more predictable basis. The utilities say these factors reduce costs enough to justify the price differences. Most experts judge instead that there is some discrimination against smaller residential customers.

The patterns by time of day involve clearer discrimination, as in the case of telephones. Many electricity price schedules have had a "declining block form," as shown in Figure 12.7. Yet the top power amounts are often taken at peak-load times, when costs are very high. Therefore peak-load power is often priced sharply below its cost, while off-peak prices are well above cost.[24] The whole issue has grown acute since 1970 as energy costs have risen. Some utilities have adopted peak-load

---

[24] The issue has been intensively discussed since the 1890s. Important analyses include Hendrik S. Houthakker, "Electricity Tariffs in Theory and Practice," *Economic Journal,* 61 (March 1951), 1–25; Ralph K. Davidson, *Price Discrimination in Selling Gas and Electricity* (Baltimore, Md.: Johns Hopkins, 1955); James R. Nelson, ed., *Marginal Cost Pricing in Practice* (Englewood Cliffs, N.J.: Prentice Hall, 1964); and Kahn, *Economics of Regulation.* Recent decades have seen a surge in discussion and experiments with marginal cost pricing of electricity, but the changes so far have only been modest. Incidentally, reversing the tilt—so that the blocks "rise"—would not solve the problem of discrimination. Or would it?

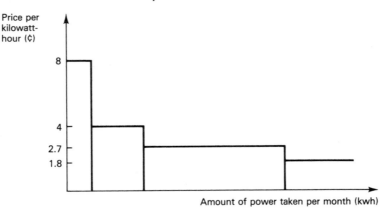

FIGURE 12.7.   Illustration of a "declining block" electricity tariff.

pricing, but the old discriminatory patterns tend to persist. Public regulation has, incidentally, applied only moderate pressure toward these revisions.

Drugs

Patented drugs typically are produced by the patent-holding firm, plus one or two other licensed firms. The prices are arranged to maximize profits during the seventeen-year patent life. As we noted earlier, large, bulk-volume buyers—such as the Veterans Administration—are able to obtain low prices. Prices shade upward from this level to the retail prices for individual buyers, who have highly inelastic demand.

The selection of drug pricing patterns in Table 12.4 shows that the prices can differ by high multiples. The drug firms claim that costs of packaging and distribution account for some of the differences, but these costs are usually quite modest, so most of the price differences can be laid to discrimination. Patents protect most such discrimination from legal challenges by giving the patentor virtually a free hand in exploiting the monopoly.

Computers

Until 1956, IBM offered equipment only on rental, not for sale. For years after that, IBM used relative rental-sale price ratios to help keep rental the main pattern.[25] This raised entry barriers by (1) requiring competitors to build up an expensive stock of machines for leasing, and (2) making the sales and support network more important (thereby forestalling the rise of large discounters, who might have exerted monop-

---

[25] The antitrust consent decree in 1956 compelled IBM to put sales on parity with rental. But until 1968, only about 20 percent of these machines were sold. Since then the share has risen moderately. See Gerald W. Brock, *The U.S. Computer Industry* (Cambridge, Mass.: Ballinger 1975); and W. G. Shepherd, *Market Power and Economic Welfare* (New York: Random House, 1970), Chapter 15. For an extensive study of IBM's price discrimination, see Richard T. DeLamarter, *Big Blue* (New York: Dodd, Mead, 1986).

TABLE 12.4 A Selection of Drug Pricing Patterns

	Price to the Veterans Administration (Fiscal 1969)	Price Quoted to Other Federal Agencies (1970)	Price to Druggists (1970)
Ritalin (Ciba) 10 mg 1,000's	$ 17.34	$ 44.97	$ 54.51
Doriden (Ciba) 0.5 gm. 1,000's	18.04	32.01	40.01
Placidyl (Abbott) 500 mg. 100's	2.09	4.84	5.00
Compazine (SKF) 10 mg. 5,000's	180.16	229.50	576.00
Griseofulvin (Ayerst) 250 mg. 500's	11.06	40.10	52.00
Furadantin (Eaton) 100 mg. 1,000's	75.537	199.992	270.00
Macrodantin (Eaton) 50 mg. 1,000's	38.115	84.996	114.76
Maalox Susp. (Rorer) 6 oz.	0.0934	0.20	0.59
Gelusil (Warner) 1,000's	7.60	12.04	14.50
Rio-Pan (Ayerst) 400 mg. 12 fl. oz.	0.20	0.88	1.02
Diuril (Merck) 0.5 gm. 1,000's	20.90	44.69	48.45

SOURCE: Subcommittee on Monopoly, *Report on Competitive Problems in the Drug Industry*, U.S. Senate Select Committee on Small Business (Washington, D.C.: U.S. Government Printing Office, 1971), Part 20, p. 8181.

sony power). Therefore rental-sale price ratios are one direction of probable discrimination.

IBM's other main discrimination has been among its computer systems and components. Cost and demand conditions both favor systematic discrimination. IBM's overhead costs are only about 25 percent of all costs—the rest are development, sales and support, and other types. These costs are partly mingled in the development of new products, so that IBM has much latitude in assigning "costs" to each system or component.

Also, demand for computers sharply varies among users. Most large users are well informed and sophisticated, whereas smaller ones tend to be more dependent and have fewer choices. Competitors have also been stronger in larger computers; IBM's "heartland" has been the medium-size computer systems, where competition has been less.

Conditions have shifted occasionally; thus new competition arose for "peripheral" equipment in 1967–1971, and minicomputers ate into the smaller-scale systems market. But the main cost and demand patterns have been relatively clear and stable since the mid-1950s.

IBM has naturally varied its price-cost margins in response to the differences in competition (differences in demand elasticity), as noted in Chapter 17 below. The broad "third-generation" 360 set of systems (from the small 360/20 line to the large 360/90 line) was announced in 1964. The price-cost ratios were deliberately set to shade from high margins on the smaller systems down to virtually zero on the largest systems. Two specific systems (the 360/44 and 360/67) were added later, with actual losses, in response to better models that competitors had brought out. Then, in 1971–1973, IBM cut prices deeply on certain peripheral equipment that had drawn new competition, and it altered its machines to make them incompatible with competitors' equipment.

The whole pattern is one of selective pricing in line with demand conditions. Price cuts were sharp where needed, and as conditions evolved, IBM blocked each new inroad by narrow-line firms with price cuts. Whether the pricing was "predatory" in one or many directions is still being debated. At any rate, systematic discrimination did occur. It was natural, even inevitable, that such a dominant firm would do it. Still, the effect was severe on competitors in many submarkets. The whole pattern and its effects fit closely with what theory predicts.

Standard Oil

From 1870 to 1890, the Standard Oil Company's monopolizing of the new oil industry involved two main kinds of discrimination. One was selective price-cutting in various regions, some of which may well have gone below costs. John S. McGee asserts that little predation occurred, but others disagree.[26] Regardless, there was extensive, flexible discrimination, which aided in the absorption of competitors.

The second discrimination was by the railroads. Standard Oil pressured the railroads to give it cheap freight rates for oil and to pay Standard a rebate for each barrel of *competitors'* oil carried! This was perhaps the main single source of Standard's monopoly.

Airline fares

The industry consists of a mass of city-pair routes in the United States and abroad, served by a group of major and minor airlines (see Chapter 18). Demand elasticities vary sharply among expense account business customers, vacationers, and various other travelers. Most business travelers and certain vacationers have low elasticity of demand; some tourists have very high elasticity.

Since the deregulation of the airlines in 1978, price discrimination has become extremely widespread and thorough.[27] At first the airlines merely developed a com-

---

[26] See McGee, "Predatory Pricing: The Standard Oil (N.J.) Case." F. M. Scherer rejects his conclusions in *Industrial Market Structure and Economic Performance*, pp. 274–76.

[27] See Alfred E. Kahn, "Surprises of Airline Deregulation," *American Economic Review*, 78 (May 1988), 316–22; Elizabeth E. Bailey, David R. Graham, and Daniel P. Kaplan, *Deregulating the Airlines* (Cambridge, Mass.: MIT Press, 1985); John R. Meyer and Clinton V. Oster, Jr., *Deregulation and the Future of Intercity Passenger Travel* (Cambridge, Mass.: MIT Press, 1987); and my "The Airline Industry," a chapter in Walter Adams, ed., *The Structure of American Industry*, 8th ed. (New York: Macmillan, 1990).

plex and flexible array of fares, attuned to the variations among demand elasticities of customer groups. But soon fare-cutting was forced to extremes by the newer maverick airlines such as Peoples Express, World Airways, and Air Florida, often along with "no-frills" service. The larger airlines fought back by matching or undercutting those discount fares. These "fare wars" involved deep discrimination by the large airlines, which tried to pinpoint their discounts without undermining their standard fares. They weakened and eventually eliminated the maverick low-fare airlines.

As computer reservations systems became more sophisticated, the airlines' ability to discriminate advanced, so that by 1985, the larger airlines were ready to make the discounting more systematic. American Airlines led the way, freezing the discounting in "Super-saver" and other fare categories, each of which had firm limits on availability. Discounts were now available only if one stayed over Saturday night and bought the ticket in advance, and the degree of discounting tended to be uniform among the airlines. The tickets were often not refundable or adjustable.

By 1987, discrimination had become systematic rather than flexible. Large airlines employed hundreds of staff in "yield management," whose job was to continually juggle the number of discount seats on each flight so as to extract the maximum revenue from passengers. Officials candidly expressed their delight that discounting had been controlled to the point where price was no longer a sharp, aggressive weapon. Competition reverted toward the pre-1978 patterns, in which conditions of service (meals, decor, scheduling of flights, etc.) were the main methods of competing.

Discounting is still prevalent in the airline industry, affecting some 90 percent of tickets sold. But the explosive competitive impacts of unrestrained discrimination have been contained. Moreover, the discounts closely fit the degrees of monopoly on individual routes. Altogether, much airline price discrimination corresponds to the anticompetitive conditions of selective pricing by dominant firms.

Magazines

Magazine selling is packed with differential pricing, as Table 12.3 notes. Each term, students are offered various "special" discount rates, and most magazines routinely offer a variety of discounts to new subscribers and various classes of renewal subscribers. Is this discrimination? Does it affect competition?

Consider two points. First, subscription prices usually differ sharply from newsstand prices. But so may costs. Subscription requires addressing and mailing costs; newsstand sales involve wholesale and retail markups. The publisher's net price per copy may be the same. Only a full cost comparison will tell.

Second, consider student discounts versus "regular" subscription rates. These usually *do* involve discrimination, because costs probably are about equal. The publishers' reasons for giving you special bargains are understandable. First, you are on a low budget, and you can easily borrow copies or use library copies; therefore your demand elasticity is relatively high. Also, they want you to become loyal readers, willing to pay the regular subscription rates for the rest of your life, as your income rises.

Indeed, pricing involves a great variety of discounts, changing flexibly. Moreover, most magazines have modest or small market shares. Therefore discrimination is mostly type A, tending to promote competition.

Sales

Retailers often stage a *Sale!* to clear their inventory and/or to draw customers who might buy other items at regular prices. Clothing, groceries, furniture, automobiles—virtually every retail market has a stream of such sales. Two kinds of discrimination might be present. One is between the sale items and the others not on sale. The second is chronological, between the sale items before and during the sale. If the sale prices are cut 50, 60, or 70 percent below standard levels, the discrimination might even seem to go below cost.

Yet actual discrimination may be much smaller, or not present at all. The key is the true level of cost. If the goods in stock are definitely surplus, the retailer will reappraise their true cost at a much lower level than if they were selling well and needed to be replaced. Indeed, if the good is really a glut on the market (as vast stocks of Bicentennial souvenirs were after 1976), their marginal cost may be nearly negative.[28] The ratio of the sale price to such costs may actually still be higher than the price-cost ratios of (1) the good at a time before the sale or (2) other, "regular" goods.

All sellers face this recurrent problem of balancing inventory. As long as it is sporadic rather than systematically planned, it is part of the competitive process by which the outcomes of risky decisions are adjusted. You can judge every local sale in your town from this perspective.

Entry: Eastman Kodak

A dominant firm may use loss leaders to build up a share in an adjacent or a new market. It can add new competition in this way, but it may also crowd out other efficient firms that do not have a dominant base in another market. Therefore the whole effect on competition and performance may be ambiguous.

In 1976, Eastman Kodak mounted major efforts to enter the instant camera and copying machine markets. Both were extensions of Kodak's product line in photographic supplies, where Kodak had long been the dominant firm. To launch its "EK-6" instant camera in 1976, Kodak apparently "spent $45 to manufacture each one and $11 to promote it, bringing the total cost per camera to $56. Yet the cameras were sold to retailers for $46, for a loss of $10 each." As for the "Ektaprint" copier machines, estimates were that Kodak would take at least five years to show a profit. Kodak's selling below cost would seem to be "predatory," by the cost criterion. But Kodak was a new firm in the market, facing an established virtual monopoly. Therefore its pricing tactic really increased competition, allowing it to become a competitor.

---

[28] That is, a warehouse full of unwanted goods is a burden, which one might even pay to have hauled away.

V. SUMMARY

This chapter has outlined the main directions of price discrimination and given a few examples from its endless variety. Discrimination is prevalent, and in markets with tight structure, it can be a major factor in market power and excess profits. Look for it where demand elasticities vary and reselling by customers can be prevented. Customers may be dealt with as individuals or as groups.

The effects depend mainly on the market position of the firm and on whether the discrimination is systematic or sporadic. Discrimination can help create, maintain, and enrich dominant firms. Or it can be central to healthy competitive pricing when it is done by firms with small market shares. "Predatory pricing" is an extreme case of discrimination. It is one among many actions that can affect competition. Only when done against firms with much smaller market shares is it anticompetitive.

One approaches discrimination carefully, using these few concepts in trying to judge individual cases objectively. As you gain experience, you will notice more and more discrimination of all types around you.

QUESTIONS FOR REVIEW

1.   "Discrimination occurs when prices vary in line with costs." True?
2.   "Discrimination can occur even if the prices for two goods are the same." True?
3.   Suppose demand elasticities vary sharply, but customers can resell the good freely among themselves. Can price discrimination occur?
4.   Which of the types of discrimination in Table 12.2 are always procompetitive? Which are always anticompetitive?
5.   "Marginal cost can vary with the level of operations of the firm." True?
6.   "Demand-based pricing always moves in opposite directions from cost-based pricing." True?
7.   "Systematic discrimination is the natural, rational behavior of a dominant firm. Therefore any anticompetitive effects do not really occur." True?
8.   "Tie-ins are an indirect form of discrimination. Therefore they always tend to reduce competition." True?
9.   How would you judge whether the following involve price discrimination? (1) Magazine subscriptions are half price for students. (2) First-class fares are 50 percent higher than coach fares on the same plane. (3) Householders pay 3 cents per kilowatt-hour for electricity, while industrial firms pay 1 cent. (4) Pencils cost 10 cents apiece singly, or 89 cents per dozen.
10.   Give three examples of procompetitive price discrimination.
11.   Does the phrase "predatory pricing" have any economic meaning? What is that meaning?
12.   Discuss how Ramsey prices do maximize static consumer surplus, for any given array of demand elasticities. Now let competition increase for some goods and diminish for others; will the Ramsey prices now change?
13.   If the firm does not face an overall financial deficit, because its marginal costs are not below average costs, then are Ramsey prices relevant?
14.   Explain the strengths and limits of the "stay-low" price rule against predatory pricing.
15.   Explain how uniform prices for local telephone use probably involve price discrimination by time.

13

THEORIES OF
OLIGOPOLY

Oligopoly continues to baffle and fascinate economists. When a market contains only a few main rivals, the outcome is usually quite indeterminate. The rivals are interdependent, with a kaleidoscopic variety of possible changing strategies. The action can easily become more complex than a chess game among three players who are simultaneously playing in a three-dimensional space, thinking at least three moves ahead, and constantly forming or breaking coalitions.

Or, to change the image, every oligopolist is like a general on the battlefields of commerce, trying to outwit, bluff, and bludgeon its rivals. Yet, since oligopoly rewards team play, the generals are constantly tempted to form alliances with their "adversaries." Then the warfare gives way to collusion among some or all of the combatants.

Many economists have felt challenged to capture oligopoly's variety in a single, all-powerful theory or, failing that, in several theories. The effort has waxed and waned in several waves of oligopoly theorizing, the first beginning as far back as 1838 with Augustin Cournot. Oligopoly theory and strategy have been particularly active topics since 1975.[1] Yet the power of the models remains limited, as we will see.

The actual extent of tight oligopoly in the U.S. economy has dropped sharply in recent decades, from about 35 percent to about 18 percent, as we saw in Chapters 1 and 4. And oligopoly variations may be a secondary matter. In essence, oligopoly is simply *a range of variation around the basic patterns caused by market shares* as they affect profits, efficiency, and innovation. That was illustrated in Figure 3.3.

Predicting oligopoly is much like predicting the weather. Rough averages and ranges can be guessed at, but reliable and precise answers are virtually impossible. Yet the theorizing goes on, and this chapter conveys several favorite models that have been developed. The next chapter will survey the varieties of real-world oligopoly collusion.

---

[1] Useful summaries of recent oligopoly theory can be found in Jean Tirole, *The Theory of Industrial Organization* (Cambridge, Mass.: MIT Press, 1988); Michael Waterson, *Economic Theory of Industry* (Cambridge: Cambridge University Press, 1984); Lester Telser, *Theories of Competition* (Amsterdam: North Holland, 1988); Joseph E. Stiglitz and C. Frank Mathewson, *New Developments in the Analysis of Market Structure* (Cambridge, Mass.: MIT Press, 1986); and Alexis Jacquemin, *The New Industrial Organization* (Cambridge, Mass.: MIT Press, 1987).

I. BASIC THEORIES OF INTERDEPENDENCE

Oligopoly involves *interdependence* among several firms (actually from two to about ten). Members of the group can either coordinate or adopt intensely competitive behavior.

Oligopoly therefore involves *indeterminacy,* because it provides a wide range of possible outcomes.[2] That diversity of outcomes is great, because there are infinite varieties of (1) oligopoly structures, which differ in concentration, inequality among the leaders, and other elements; and (2) attitudes and motives among the rival firms.

The shining hope of theorists has been to find *determinate* solutions to the innate indeterminacy of "the oligopoly problem." Augustin Cournot was the pioneer, writing lucidly about *quantity-setting* duopolists as early as 1838. His analysis was unread by economists until discovered in the 1880s by J. Bertrand, a Frenchman, who suggested in a brief paper that each duopolist might instead take action by setting its *price* rather than its output.[3]

The subject then lay largely neglected again until 1932, when Edwin Chamberlin placed it at the center of the newly discovered "Oligopoly Problem," and then John von Neumann and Oskar Morgenstern offered their formidable *Theory of Games and Economic Behavior* in 1944. Active research attempts followed, but by 1960 it was realized that oligopoly theory was of little use in explaining or predicting real market behavior, such as in the automobile or steel industry.

In 1959, Carl Kaysen and Donald F. Turner devoted a whole book to the tight-oligopoly riddle, which U.S. antitrust policy could not seem to treat effectively. Oligopoly remained stubbornly unsolved, except in abstract blackboard games. By 1970, oligopoly was a passé topic, while tight oligopoly was a shrinking phenomenon in actual markets.

Surprisingly, oligopoly modelling revived after 1975, as a popular topic for theorists, and oligopoly is now often treated as a topic in business strategy. There is little pretense of providing full solutions fitted to real markets. Rather, the assumptions are admitted to be extremely narrow, in hopes that some suggestive "insights" about business choices may result.

Most of the results of oligopoly merely confirm larger, intuitively obvious truths. For example, basic Cournot analysis indicates that (under certain assumptions) an increase in the number of equal rivals will move the outcome closer toward the competitive level of prices. That could be concluded from intuition, wider experi-

---

[2] Important references on oligopoly behavior include the following: Edward H. Chamberlin, *The Theory of Monopolistic Competition,* 6th ed. (Cambridge, Mass.: Harvard University Press, 1962); John von Neumann and Oskar Morgenstern, *Theory of Games and Economic Behavior* (Princeton, N.J.: Princeton University Press, 1944); William J. Fellner, *Competition Among the Few* (New York: Knopf, 1949); Joe S. Bain, *Barriers to New Competition* (Cambridge, Mass.: Harvard University Press, 1956); A. D. H. Kaplan, Joel B. Dirlam, and Robert F. Lanzillotti, *Pricing in Big Business* (Washington, D.C.: Brookings Institution, 1958); Carl Kaysen and Donald F. Turner, Jr., *Antitrust Policy* (Cambridge, Mass.: Harvard University Press, 1959); Paolo Sylos-Labini, *Oligopoly and Technical Progress* (Cambridge, Mass.: Harvard University Press, 1962); Lawrence E. Fouraker and Sidney Siegel, *Bargaining Behavior* (New York: McGraw-Hill, 1963); and George J. Stigler, "The Theory of Oligopoly," *Journal of Political Economy,* 72 (February, 1964), 44–61.

[3] See Augustin Cournot, *Researches into the Mathematical Principles of the Theory of Wealth* (Homewood, Ill.: Irwin, 1963); and J. Bertrand, review of Cournot's book in the *Journal des Savants,* September 1883, pp. 499–508.

ence, or simpler theory, but the analysis satisfies the urge of theorists to "prove" something, even if only in a rarefied model.

The value of oligopoly theorizing lies in subjecting "obvious" truths to deductive reasoning. Occasionally, there are counterintuitive results, and certain original findings have also been reached. The hazard is that duopoly modelers will think that their narrow models are yielding general conclusions that cover all important conditions. Instead, as you will see, they merely analyze cases that can be framed in short-run, quasi-static models, usually containing only two duopolists (or one incumbent and one potential entrant). Often it is like "explaining" an entire baseball game in the manner of primitive video games: the pitcher chooses to deliver a strike or a ball, while the batter decides to swing or not. That can be an interesting exercise, but it omits most of the two teams, the rich varieties of action that can take place in a real ball game, and the underlying process of complex managerial strategies.

Despite these limits, oligopoly theorists are often excited, ambitious, and skilled in theoretical techniques. Their enthusiasm is easy to catch. They regard their work as the cutting edge of the entire field. Their profusion of models has suggested that possible collusion and interactions are more important than direct dominance. Once you have learned the following tools, you will be in a position to begin judging for yourself how important they—and the oligopoly problem—really are.

1. The Central Tendency Under Oligopoly

A central tendency in oligopolistic markets is for firms to converge on identical prices and product features. Collusive prices under tight oligopoly are just one part of this tendency. We now explain it in broader terms, using Hotelling's analysis.[4]

The customers in a market are often distributed along a range of geographical areas, of product types, or of time periods. Typically, the distribution has a central cluster with two tails, as shown in Figure 13.1. For example, a country town is spread along the main road, with a clustering of population at the center.

If there are just two competitors ("duopolists"), they will locate at the exact center of the distribution. Thus two gasoline stations, restaurants, bookstores, department stores, or banks will usually be found close to each other at the middle of town. In practical terms, they will both locate at the main intersection, downtown.

Just so, two sellers will tend to offer identical products at the middle of the range of product types. Thus two television networks tend to produce the same sort of mass programming, aimed at the center of the distribution of program preferences, and the two political parties, Republicans and Democrats, tend to offer similar programs to voters, rather than take radically opposed positions. Duopolists always tend to adopt uniform product types at the center of the market.

This tendency continues even when there are three or more oligopolists, though

---

[4] The classic statements of the analysis are in Harold Hotelling, "Stability in Competition," *Economic Journal,* 39 (March 1929), 41–57; and Arthur Smithies, "Optimum Location in Spatial Competition," *Journal of Political Economy,* 49 (June 1941), 423–39.

These claims are disputed by William Long and David Ravenscraft, in a Brookings Institution study which found that LBO's *reduced* all of those conditions. See Thomas E. Ricks, "Two Scholars Blast KKR Buy-Out Study That Reached Pro-Takeover Conclusions," *Wall Street Journal,* May 10, 1989, pp. A2, A8.

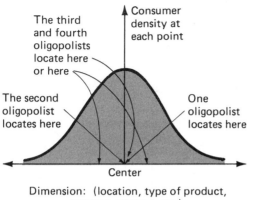

Dimension: (location, type of product,
                program content, etc.)

FIGURE 13.1.   Under tight oligopoly, the firms cluster at the center of the market.

it weakens as the group gets bigger. Consider what happens when other firms enter the market. A third oligopolist would also move to the middle of the market, for that is where it can hope to attract the most demand. Additional firms, however, might begin to locate away from dead center, in order to seek out special customer groups.

For example, a fifth TV network might specialize in the arts, popular sports, or news. That is, indeed, what has happened since 1978: specialized cable and satellite networks have emerged, offering all-day sports and news coverage, religion, old movies, and advertising channels. Radio stations have also specialized as the old network dominance has been diluted. Every city has several types of popular music stations, each specializing in one "sound," rather than all offering the same music.

Even if customers are distributed evenly, with constant density along the spectrum, the oligopolists will cluster toward the middle. Two firms will still locate at the midpoint, back to back. Only if there are four or more will some firms leave the middle range. This clustering is a deficient outcome, because it poorly serves the customers toward the two ends. For a social optimum, firms would locate evenly throughout the range. Oligopolies of two or three firms fail to give that result.

The same is true of price decisions. If consumer demand permits firms to choose among a range of prices, then two or three firms will tend to choose identical prices at the "middle" of the distribution (if their cost and other conditions are similar). Each maximizes its individual profits in that way, by avoiding being relegated to a low-density range of demand. If they initially locate away from this middle range, then each will gain profits by moving toward it.

Therefore the Hotelling type of spatial analysis tends to affirm the result indicated both by common sense and by Chamberlin's and Stigler's theories of oligopoly.

2.   Conflicting Incentives: Cooperation versus Cheating

The basic question about cooperation is: Can it stick? If it succeeds, the group of colluders raises prices and gains excess profits. But paradoxically, by succeeding, it automatically rewards each member for cheating on the group and therefore de-

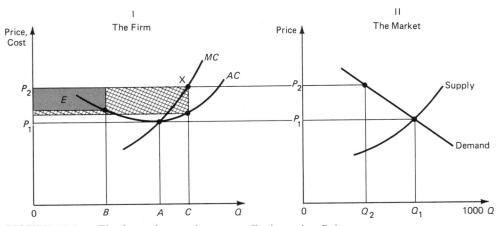

FIGURE 13.2.   The incentive to cheat on collusive price-fixing.

stroying the collusion. The ideal is to be in an industry where collusion is keeping price high but you are holding your price just a little lower, getting large profits as you draw off the other firms' customers.

To some Chicago-UCLA economists, every price-fixing ring is self-destructive, likely to collapse quickly amid mutual cheating. At the other extreme, some experts regard price-fixing as inherently stable and powerful, even in unfavorable circumstances. The realistic view is that the success will vary with the conditions.

Incentives to Cheat.   It is easy to show the incentives to cheat. Figure 13.2 illustrates a typical firm (panel I) in a market (panel II). Under competition, price is P_1 and total market output is Q_1 (in panel II). Our typical firm's output is at A in panel I. A price-fixing ring now raises the price to P_2. That requires cutting total output to Q_2; the firm is assigned to cut back its own production to output B. If all firms hold at B, the collusion works and they each make profits shown by the shaded rectangle E.

But this firm's maximum profit point is instead at X, where its marginal cost equals the fixed price (which therefore is its marginal revenue). If it cheats on its assignment and sells the amount C, its profits are E plus the crosshatched area. Even if it doesn't go as far as point X, it gains by every extra unit it sells. Every little bit of cheating has a high payoff.

3.   Concentration and Information

The obvious tendency of higher concentration to breed more collusion is clarified by Stigler's analysis of concentration and information.

Collusion is stronger when cheaters are exposed quickly. Quick exposure is more likely when (1) firms are fewer, so that the numbers of possible cheaters are low and their actions more readily detectable; and (2) information about cheating is transmitted rapidly. So the two conditions that enhance collusion are high concentration and reliable systems for transmitting information about pricing and output.

Low concentration—as in loose oligopoly—undercuts collusion. So does any device for hiding price cuts.

If the oligopolists are of equal size, then an increase in their number will reduce their concentration. (If they are *not* of equal size, then concentration and the number of firms may not be related at all.) Because lower concentration involves more sellers, each with a smaller share, it is more difficult for any one (or several) of the firms to detect price-cutting and who is doing it.

For collusion to be effective, cheaters must be identified and punished. Lower concentration reduces and slows the ability to punish effectively. Information is also critical. Anything that increases information lags will reduce the effectiveness of collusion. Two main bars to information are (1) secret contracts and (2) diversity among products. Secret contracts mean that rivals do not know directly and immediately what prices and quantities have been set. They must find out informally or wait for their own sales to be affected. Even then, they may not know precisely who has cut prices, so it is impossible to inflict an exact, effective penalty. Diversity means that products are not exactly comparable. Products with differing characteristics will often need different prices. But many times the ''correct'' price is too complex to pinpoint, so once again, it is hard to identify price cheating and inflict efficient penalties.

So concentration and information are critical to collusion. Tight oligopoly promotes collusion for clear, explicit reasons. Prices rise toward pure-monopoly levels even if the oligopolists make independent decisions. Markets with lesser concentration among sellers are usually more competitive in behavior. And, broadly, randomness and uncertainty breed competition; while instant knowledge among sellers favors collusion. Likewise, a cartel can organize more completely if its members' costs are known exactly. Then prices, market sharing, and payoffs can be fine-tuned. By contrast, ignorance about costs makes coordination unstable. If costs are uncertain, then the system of controls must be ill fitted, which encourages the members to chisel.

Asymmetry of Information. In both cases—cuts and costs—the key issue is whether sellers know more than buyers. Only if sellers' information is better than buyers' can the seeming paradox—that better information encourages collusion rather than competition—hold.

One lesson is that the cure for oligopoly collusion is not to reduce information among sellers. Instead, the *buyers'* knowledge should be improved, for when the buyers have better information than the sellers, collusion does not hold. That fits the general rule that informed consumers are a key to effective competition and efficient allocation.

4. A Stair-Step Pattern?

Is there a distinct break in behavior at some degree of concentration? Chamberlin, Bain, and others have believed so, placing it at the level where each firm becomes aware of its own impact on prices. For equal-size oligopolists with similar costs and demands, this has been thought by many to be in the range of 60 percent four-firm concentration (approximately a 1,000 HHI). At that point prices would show a stair-step rise from roughly competitive levels to near-monopoly levels. If market shares or costs varied, then the firms' preferred prices would usually be more diverse, making price agreements harder to reach. The critical concentration value would rise, perhaps to 70 or 80 percent. Conversely, if conditions of similarity and mutual knowledge made binding price agreements easier to enforce, then the stair-step might move down to 50 or even 40 percent.

In fact, not all oligopoly structures have equal-size firms; they come in many gradations, as Chapter 4 noted. Costs and demands differ, too. If there is a critical value, it probably differs among industries, for each set of conditions. A wide range of statistical research has found a smoothly sloped relation between concentration and price-cost margins (recall Chapter 5), not a stair-step.[5]

These findings do not settle the issue. There may be stair steps in some, most, or all markets, but at varying levels. Or some or all industries may have only a slope rather than a critical concentration level. But there is a consistent lack of evidence confirming a stair step pattern.

II. MODELS OF NONCOLLUSIVE DUOPOLY

If the setting is narrowed down to two rivals, it is possible to reach determinate results under certain assumptions about costs, demands, and the rivals' decision rules. That is what recent oligopoly theorists have done: modeled duopolies to gain a variety of insights. The results are usually compared with intuition, for "confirmation." Since 1975, theorists have written many scores of papers on duopoly models, the gist of which can only be noted briefly here.

These determinate models have three main weaknesses (apart from requiring mathematical skills to read them). They are short-run. They assume that each firm is myopic, incapable of learning when its assumptions are falsified in practice. And they further assume that firms are strictly noncollusive.

The two contrasting approaches most commonly used are: (1) *Cournot models,* where each firm sets only its quantity; and (2) *Bertrand models,* where price is the only decision variable. In each case, there are just two firms, of equal size and industrial conditions. Average costs are constant, and therefore equal to marginal cost. Consequently, each firm has no specific capacity: it can produce just one unit or all of the industry's output, at the same cost per unit.

1. Cournot Output-Setting Models

Cournot analysis is similar to the passive dominant-firm analysis in Chapter 11. After we give the simple duopoly case, we will adapt it to get some results for unequal firms with differing conditions.

We begin with the market demand curve and horizontal cost curves, as shown in Figure 13.3. Each firm is assumed to maximize its profit by accepting the other firm's existing output level and then choosing its own best output level. Suppose that firm 2 has chosen the output level Q_2, as shown. Firm 1 then has a residual

---

[5] Recall Chapter 5's review of the evidence. Also see Stephen Martin, *Industrial Economics* (New York: Macmillan, 1988), Chapter 7.

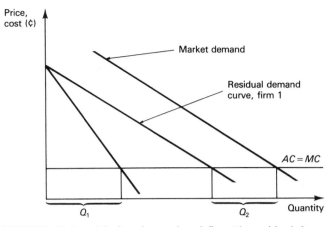

FIGURE 13.3.   Market demand and firm 1's residual demand curve.

demand curve, which is to the left of the market demand curve by the Q_2 amount. Firm 1's demand curve also defines a marginal revenue curve, as shown in Figure 13.3. In this case, firm 1's maximum profit point, where its marginal revenue is equal to its marginal cost, is at output Q_1.

The same exercise can be done for every other level of output that firm 2 may choose. As Q_2 rises, firm 1's demand curve is shifted further left, and its chosen Q_1 value is lower. At one extreme, firm 2 may choose to supply all the market output, as shown in Figure 13.4. Firm 1 is then left with a residual demand curve so far left that it supplies nothing. At the other extreme, firm 2 may choose to supply zero. Firm 1 then has the whole market demand to itself, and it will set output at Q_1, as shown in Figure 13.5.

Generally, firm 2 must set its output at the competitive level—where price equals marginal cost—in order to drive its rival from the market (as in Figure 13.4). But if

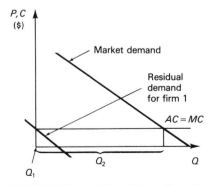

FIGURE 13.4.   Firm 2 supplies all output.

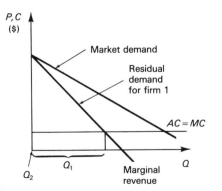

FIGURE 13.5.   Firm 2 supplies zero output.

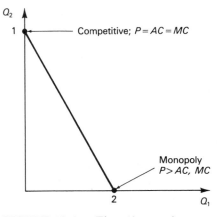

FIGURE 13.6.   Firm 1's reaction curve.

firm 2 chooses instead to withdraw from the market (as in Figure 13.5), then firm 1 can set the monopoly output, with the monopoly price.

The result is a *reaction curve* for firm 1, which relates the output it chooses to firm 2's prior output level. This curve is shown in Figure 13.6, with the extreme cases as we just derived them. When firm 2's output is at the maximum level (consistent with a price that covers costs), then firm 1 produces zero, as shown by point 1. That is the competitive level for the market. When firm 2 produces zero, then firm 2 is able to set the monopoly level of output (at point 2). It is just half of the competitive level, because average costs are constant.

Between these two extreme cases, we can interpolate the intermediate points. For a straight-line demand curve, they lie along the straight-line reaction curve shown in Figure 13.6.

Because the situation is assumed to be symmetrical to both firms, firm 2 will have a reaction curve that is the mirror image of firm 1's reaction curve. It is derived by the same steps we went through for firm 1. Both reaction curves are shown in Figure 13.7. Each has a competitive and monopoly extreme, but in reversed locations.

These two curves define the possible outcomes. At all points except where they cross, they involve a conflict between what the two firms expect of each other.

That can be seen by considering a sequence of moves, as illustrated in Figure 13.8. For example, suppose that firm 1 produces zero because firm 2 has been producing the competitive market output at point 1. Now that firm 1 is producing zero, firm 2 will react by cutting its output in half, to the monopoly level Q_m. Firm 1 now reacts in turn, by moving to point 3 on its reaction curve; firm 2 reacts by moving to point 4; and the process converges on the point common to both curves. That is where "Cournot equilibrium" exists, with the two rivals dividing the market equally. Because each firm sells the level expected by the other, no change occurs in this stable equilibrium.

The result is in the middle of the range between pure monopoly and pure competition. The pure-monopoly output Q_m could be sold by one firm or the other, or divided between the two along the dashed line between Q_{m1} and Q_{m2}, as shown in

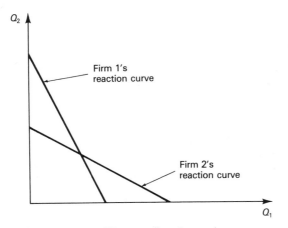

FIGURE 13.7.   The two firms' reaction curves.

Figure 13.9. But to move onto that line, the two firms would have to coordinate their actions, carefully and deliberately. Conversely, the pure-competitive output could be provided by any combination lying along the dashed line between Q_{c1} and Q_{c2}.

Compared to these extremes, the combined equilibrium output (Q_1 plus Q_2) is below the competitive level, toward the pure-monopoly level. Indeed, it is closer to monopoly than competition; in this case, Cournot behavior tends to give a degree of monopoly pricing, albeit monopoly pricing reached by strictly independent choices.

This result fits intuition, of course. We expect high concentration to yield a degree of monopoly behavior, even if not by direct collusion. But the assumptions underlying the model are certainly exotic. Firms are always independent but passive, never challenging each other. Neither do they cooperate with each other. This pas-

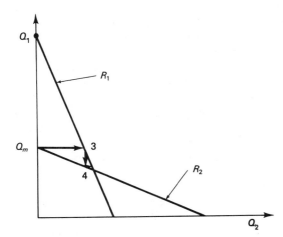

FIGURE 13.8.   Convergence on the equilibrium point.

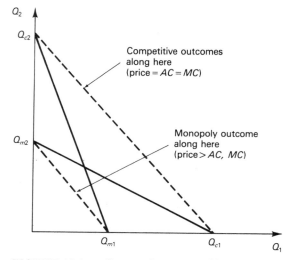

FIGURE 13.9.   Contrasting competitive and monopoly outcomes.

sivity is the underlying assumption that makes it possible to derive a result that includes a degree of monopoly effect.

More oddly, these firms are strictly myopic, never looking beyond each period, even though any normal firm in a situation of rivalry would quickly learn to anticipate future adjustments. That is, after all, the essence of the interdependency.

Thus the sequence shown in Figure 13.8 involves dimwitted behavior in which the same error is repeated over and over again. For that matter, the whole approach assumes the two firms are operated by dimwits, because they obviously could quickly coordinate to reach full monopoly results.

Also, the meaning of identical size is peculiar when, by assumption, costs are constant. When that is true, any firm can freely produce any amount of output at the same cost. Accordingly, the firm has no well-defined capacity or size. These firms are really not producers so much as jobbers who can get any amount of output to sell at the going cost level. Such firms have little to do with real enterprises producing with specific capacity and costs in real markets.

Still, the model gives an interesting insight: a degree of monopoly can occur even when there is no direct collusion. Some theorists take comfort that sensible conclusions can be derived rigorously, even if in a surreal model. Moreover, one can add more firms to the situation. *If* they are assumed to be of equal size, then each firm is passive toward a larger total output set by all its rivals. Under these conditions, each firm sets a smaller quantity for itself, but the summed total of all firms' output is larger than when there were only two firms. As the number of (equal-size) firms rises, the equilibrium approaches more closely to the competitive output.

The analysis can also cover two *unequal*-size firms, but only by a further restrictive method—that is, by assuming different cost levels for the two firms. Returning to Figure 13.3, suppose that firm 1 is able to adopt a superior method of production, which reduces its costs to cost *B*, well below the original level at Cost *A*. This is shown in Figure 13.10, where firm 2 remains stuck with the old, higher-cost method, cost *A*.

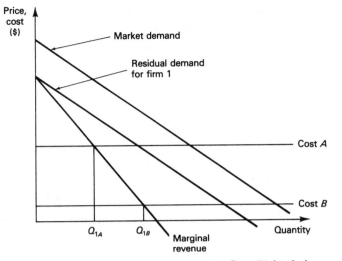

FIGURE 13.10.   Firm 1's lower cost (at Cost B) leads it to set a higher output.

Firm 2's reaction curve will remain unchanged, but firm 1's will not. For any output level chosen by firm 2, firm 1 will now choose a higher output level for itself: Q_{1B} rather than Q_{1A}, in Figure 13.10. Therefore firm 1's reaction curve will shift to the right by these amounts, using the same approach as before.

As shown in Figure 13.11, the equilibrium now will have firm 1 producing more than before, while firm 2 produces less. Firm 1's cost advantage has led it to take a larger market share, while firm 2 accepts a smaller share. Whether price is proportionally closer to the monopoly levels than before is not determined.

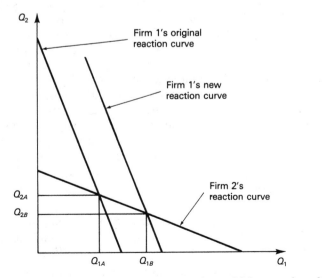

FIGURE 13.11.   Lower costs lead to a higher market share.

In analytical terms, the cost drop has given firm 1 a higher degree of market power. Recall that the Lerner Index of Monopoly is

$$(P\text{-Marginal cost})/\text{Price}$$

It can be shown that

$$\frac{P - MC}{P} = \frac{\text{Market share}}{\text{Demand elasticity}} = \frac{MS}{E_D}$$

for each firm. A lower cost gives a higher Lerner Index, which is expressed by the role of market share in the right-hand side of the equation. This can be extended to the whole market, using an industry-wide average of firms' marginal cost (MC_{AV}) and the HHI. It can be shown that

$$\frac{\text{Price} - MC_{AV}}{\text{Price}} = \frac{\text{HHI}}{E_D}$$

for the market. Such results make the HHI more attractive to theorists to adopt as the measure of concentration, for the results seem to show rigorously that the HHI is valid and can be directly linked to other market conditions.

Yet these insights should be interpreted cautiously. The "market power" is derived solely from cost superiority; therefore the analysis is narrowly limited to market power that stems solely from lower costs. It excludes the many other possible sources of market power. Indeed, this analysis instills the bias that monopoly power really does arise only from cost superiority. And that is certainly not true.

Moreover, to get large market share differences, there must be very large differences in costs indeed. A degree of market dominance involving market shares of 60 percent for one firm and 10 percent for four others would require that the lesser firms' costs be six times as high as the dominant firm's. Such extreme differences might occur in odd cases, but they are generally quite implausible, except when the dominant firm excludes rivals from technology by monopolistic means (e.g., patents). Dominance would then *not* arise strictly from market forces and superior efficiency. Rather, the cost "superiority" would reflect imperfections and monopoly controls.

So, once again, you need to evaluate cautiously the insight provided by the analysis. The Cournot models assume narrow and dimwitted decisions, in a strange setting of cost and demand. Even at its best, the analysis merely confirms a few obvious points more easily arrived at through intuition and experience.[6]

2.   Bertrand Price-Setting Duopolists

Assume that the duopolists continue to be myopic and dimwitted, but that they now set *prices* rather than outputs. This may be a somewhat more realistic model, because it involves the possibility of differences between the two firms' products.

---

[6] The next level of analysis involves "conjectural variations." They can be found in the textbooks noted in footnote 1, of this chapter.

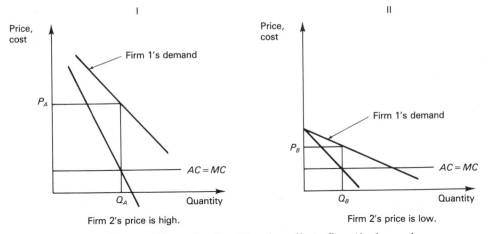

FIGURE 13.12.   Bertrand Duopoly: firm 2's price affects firm 1's demand.

But it, too, assumes that the two firms accept each other's price as a given when setting their own price, never learning to anticipate or to design strategies. As before, this artifice is adopted because it yields definite answers, not because it has much to do with real markets.

Price-setting duopolists require a somewhat different technique of analysis, but it will also lead to reaction curves for the two duopolists. We begin by assuming that the two firms' outputs are differentiated and there is some brand loyalty, so that a price difference will lead some buyers to shift to the cheaper seller. The two sellers are assumed to maximize their profits by choosing their best price, while expecting that the other firm's price will stay where it is.

How differentiated the two products are is the key condition governing each firm's residual demand curve. If they are highly differentiated (e.g., two goods with strong brand loyalties), then each firm's demand will be relatively close to the market demand curve. At the other extreme, similar products will have much higher elasticities of demand, because buyers will shift drastically even if only small price differences occur.

Firm 1 will have a different residual demand curve for every given price already chosen by firm 2. Figure 13.12 illustrates two such curves, one if firm 2's price is high (panel I), and another if firm 2's price is low (panel II). Firm 1's profit-maximizing choices then follow routinely, as shown by the *MC—MR* points in each diagram. Generally, a higher price by firm 2 elicits from firm 1 a price that adjusts in that direction; and vice versa when firm 2's price is low. Intuitively, if firm 2 prices monopolistically, firm 1 will have more scope to do so also. But a low firm 2 price will put pressure on firm 1 not to raise its price very far out of line.

Now watch carefully. *If* the demand curves are straight lines, and *if* they shift strictly in parallel (rather than rotating or twisting in some other way), then firm 1's reaction curve can be derived. It is in terms of the two firms' *prices,* as shown in Figure 13.13. The same is done in deriving firm 2's reaction curve, which is a mirror

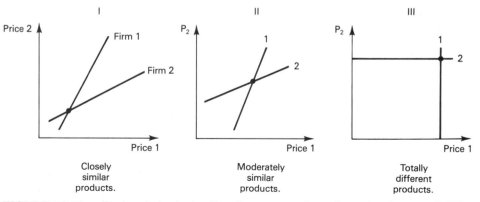

FIGURE 13.13.   Bertrand Analysis: Reaction curves depend on the degree of difference between the firms' goods.

image of firm I's curve. Figure 13.13 shows three sets of reaction curves, for rising degrees of differentiation between the two products. The curves in panel I illustrate slight differentiation. *Both are upsloping, because the two prices tend to move together, not in reverse to each other, as in the Cournot output-setting model.*

As the degree of differentiation between the products increases (panel II), firm 2's curve rises and becomes flatter, while firm 1's curve moves to the right and becomes steeper (they are still mirror images of each other). The extreme case of complete differentiation is shown in panel III. Of course, in that case, the two goods are not really in the same market because (by assumption) they are not mutually substitutable. To that extent, what we really have here is a pair of monopolists, not duopolists competing in the same market. Whether this really analyzes oligopoly or monopoly is doubtful.

In any event, the crossing point of the two reaction curves defines the equilibrium result for each case. When the products are closely similar (that is, more directly competitive), the outcome is near the competitive price level. At the other extreme, total differentiation permits each firm to price as if it were a pure monopolist, which indeed it is. In the middle range, greater degrees of differentiation will move the result closer to the monopoly pricing levels.

This Bertrand price-setting analysis provides a nice contrast to the Cournot model. Product differentiation is now included, at least as a matter of degree, and the logic differs in certain respects. The reaction curves take contrasting, positive slopes, and the outcome depends on product differentiation rather than on the numbers of (equal-size) firms.

But the intellectual limits of this modeling are still very narrow. The two firms' myopia is complete. The assumption of product differentiation violates the requirement that products in the same market be close substitutes. And in the end, both analyses are merely roundabout, artificial ways of illustrating what is already known from intuition and mainstream experience: namely, that fewness, cost advantages, and product differentiation tend to breed monopoly behavior.

III. GAME THEORY AND PAYOFF MATRIXES

The early excitement over game theory has yielded since 1970 to Cournot-type modeling, but games analysis can still be useful and illustrative. It is usually carried out by assuming that the players make independent choices. That is a severe limit, because in fact all duopolists constantly consider whether to collude with their rivals. Even so, games analysis neatly illustrates the broader problem of trying to arrange joint-maximizing outcomes in the face of price-cutting motives.

The main lessons about joint maximizing, interdependence, and stability can be conveyed by simple game situations, such as those that I have concocted for Figure 13.14. In this typical games matrix, there are two firms or "players." (To model three rivals would require a three-dimensional cube; that would be highly confusing, and not much more instructive.) Their prices can differ briefly, we assume, but they will have to be equal in any equilibrium.

1. Interpreting a Matrix

Prices are ranged along the two price axes, from low prices (top left) to high (bottom right). Suppose that the two firms are Nike and Reebok, which are actually the current leaders in the athletic shoe market. The resulting payoff matrix has one

Prices that Nike can choose ($)

Each cell gives Nike's profit (top) and Reebok's profit (bottom).

Prices that Reebok can choose ($)	10	20	30	40	50	60	70	80	90	100
10	-300 / -300	-200 / 0	-10 / 2	-20 / 4	-30 / 7	-42 / 11	-55 / 16	-70 / 22	-90 / 30	-120 / 38
20	0 / -200	-5 / -5	-1 / 6	-5 / 9	-11 / 15	-18 / 20	-26 / 25	-50 / 31	-65 / 38	-80 / 46
30	2 / -10	6 / -1	10 / 10	8 / 25	6 / 29	0 / 33	-10 / 37	-23 / 41	-37 / 45	-50 / 55
40	4 / -20	9 / -5	25 / 8	22 / 22	20 / 38	17 / 42	10 / 46	4 / 50	-5 / 55	-15 / 70
50	7 / -30	15 / -11	29 / 6	38 / 20	33 / 33	31 / 55	28 / 60	24 / 65	19 / 70	15 / 80
60	11 / -42	20 / -18	35 / 0	42 / 17	55 / 31	48 / 48	35 / 70	31 / 75	28 / 80	25 / 90
70	16 / -55	25 / -26	37 / -10	46 / 10	60 / 28	70 / 35	61 / 61	55 / 80	48 / 90	38 / 100
80	22 / -70	31 / -50	41 / -23	50 / 4	65 / 24	75 / 31	80 / 55	75 / 75	62 / 97	40 / 105
90	30 / -90	38 / -65	45 / -37	55 / -5	70 / 19	80 / 28	90 / 48	97 / 62	88 / 88	78 / 93
100	38 / -120	46 / -80	55 / -50	70 / -15	80 / 15	90 / 25	100 / 38	105 / 40	93 / 78	77 / 77

FIGURE 13.14.   An illustrative payoff matrix for duopolists Nike and Reebok.
Each cell gives the profits for Nike and Reebok at the given pair of prices. Thus, if Nike's price is $80 while Reebok's price is $60, the cell is 75/31. Nike gets $31 million and Reebok gets $75 million.

cell for each pair of prices for the two firms. Thus, with Nike shoes at $80 and Reebok shoes at $60, the numbers are 75\31 in the corresponding cell. The numbers mean that Nike gets $31 million in profits, while Reebok gets $75 million. That comparison is plausible: the lower-price firm gets higher profits.

The numbers in Figure 13.14 are merely illustrative, but they do fit common sense. Thus, for any given price for Nike, Reebok's payoffs rise for a while as Reebok raises its price, but then they decline. Together the two firms can raise their combined payoff by raising their prices simultaneously. But this is true *only* up to a point.

Now let's examine the basic nature of this matrix. It is a *variable-sum, symmetrical* matrix, as shown by the following properties. First, as with any matrix, you can best interpret it by focusing on the *diagonal* going from low to high price values; in figure 13.14, that is from the upper left to the lower right corner. Along the diagonal, market equilibrium is possible, because the two firms' prices are equal.

The matrix is not *zero-sum,* because the total amounts of the two firms' profits do vary throughout it. You can verify this by comparing cells around the matrix. The matrix is *symmetrical,* as you can test by comparing corresponding cells on its opposite sides. The matrix is, of course, strictly artificial, made up merely to illustrate games. It is also imaginary, rather than fitted to some real industry. In fact, efforts to fit matrix values to real industries have had little success.

2. Solutions

Now look along the diagonal to identify the two interesting solutions: (1) the joint-maximizing prices and (2) the competitive-equilibrium outcome. They are the two shaded cells.

First, the joint maximum. If both Nike and Reebok set a price of $90 per pair, then each makes $88 million, and the jointly maximized profit is $176 million. No other cell gives a combined total profit that large (the next largest is $169 million, when prices of $90 and $100 are simultaneously chosen: 78\93 or 93\78).

This joint-maximum result is an equilibrium at the full monopoly price, but, unfortunately for the firms and fortunately for consumers, it is an unstable equilibrium. It has to be arranged by deliberate cooperation of Nike and Reebok, and it must be enforced by trust and/or penalties. It would not emerge by independent voluntary choices. You can verify that by starting at any low price on the diagonal. If either firm raises its price, it makes *less* profits while its rival makes more. So neither firm would move first.

The joint-maximum result at $90 illustrates the general truth that two duopolists (or, more generally, all oligopolists) can attain the same monopoly results that complete merger would yield. But the monopoly outcome may not be maintained. As Section II explored in detail, each firm can instead gain higher profit for itself by cutting price a little, as long as the other firm does not also cut its price (recall Figure 13.2). In the matrix, each firm makes $97 million if it cuts price from $90 to $80 while the other stays at $90.

In the matrix, Nike is shown as the price-cutter, getting the circled $97 million profit by cutting its price to $80. Then Reebok reconsiders its choices; while Nike is at $80, Reebok can raise its profit from $62 million to $80 million by cutting price to $70, as shown by the arrow. Naturally, Reebok decides to cut its price to $70.

Now it is Nike that must reconsider and respond; by cutting to $60, it can get its profit up from $55 million to $70 million.

And so this price war goes on, ratcheting down to the competitive equilibrium price of $30 per pair. There the two rivals will stay, because neither can gain by raising its price while the other does not. The matrix illustrates that noncollusive actions can yield competitive results, whereas a higher equilibrium price might come about only by direct collusion. And the collusive price will be subject to instability from cheating.

But the degree of instability cannot be told from the matrix alone. It is a much more complex matter, depending on the duration of the short-run taking of profits and the severity of retaliation by the rival. Finally, bear in mind that the instability is strictly made up; other payoff values could easily be written in that would make it stable. (Indeed, it is a good review exercise for the reader to do so.)

This matrix neatly shows the contrast between the low-price and high-price outcomes. It displays both the oligopolists' dream (of joint maximizing) and their nightmare (of a spiraling price war). It does not show how strong the forces for collusion or collapse are; that depends on the length of time that a price-cutter can make extra gains. Thus, if price-cutting is quickly discoverable, the gains from it may be so small that both sides know it will not be worth trying. Discoverability depends, in turn, on the concentration and secrecy conditions treated by Chamberlin, Stigler, and Bain (recall Section I.3).

The matrix also helps convey another point. The players could adopt a larger strategy against price-cutting. Each could threaten to cut price immediately to the $30 competitive level as a swift punishment for any price-cutting at all. This could eliminate any prospect of gains from price-cutting, thereby making the joint-maximum equilibrium more stable.[7] In effect, such threats—provided they are credible—revise downward the obtainable short-run profits in the cells of the matrix.

These points flow from this particular matrix. Matrixes can be composed to illustrate virtually any variety of patterns. You could, for example, prepare one with a stable joint-maximizing equilibrium and an unstable competitive-price equilibrium.

At any rate, games matrixes can nicely illustrate interdependence. The specific conditions of the game situation can favor joint maximizing, or make it fragile, or encourage a continual oscillation between the extremes. The greater the number of firms, the more unstable a joint maximum will usually be.

Games analysis can illustrate these lessons well. It has also been applied in some experiments in which students or other volunteers play games by preset rules.[8] These tests have borne out the same lessons. The "student oligopolists" do try to collude, frequently with remarkable success. But often the games quickly degenerate into

---

[7] See Tirole, *The Theory of Industrial Organization,* Chapters 6 and 9, and the sources noted there. Also see Steven C. Salop, ed., *Strategy, Predation, and Antitrust Analysis,* (Washington D.C.: Bureau of Competition, Federal Trade Commission, September 1981); and Donald Hay and John Vickers, eds., *The Economics of Market Dominance* (Oxford: Basil Blackwell, 1987), Chapter 1.

[8] Quite a few experiments were run with groups of students acting as oligopolists. Specific rules and payoffs were set for the players of these games. Then the speed, direction, and stability of adjustments were studied. Martin Shubik also attempted to apply games analysis to actual industries, but without much success; see his *Strategy and Market Structure* (New York: Wiley, 1959). See also Anatol Rapaport, *Fights, Games and Debates* (Ann Arbor: University of Michigan Press, 1960); Lester G. Telser, *Competition, Collusion and Game Theory* (Chicago: Aldine-Atherton, 1972); and James W. Friedman, *Oligopoly and the Theory of Games* (Amsterdam: North-Holland, 1977).

price wars, at least for a while. Your own experience in a four-person Monopoly game would attest to the variety of outcomes and shifts, as the players repeatedly form alliances and change them.

Remember, though, games analysis is almost strictly illustrative. Someday it might be possible to apply it to major real industries, modeling their principal conditions and deriving important new lessons, but this has not been possible so far. Actual oligopoly is so complex, and so sensitive to "personal" factors, that formal games models have not been able to improve upon expert judgment.

IV.   KINKED DEMAND CURVES, TO ILLUSTRATE RIGID PRICES

Oligopoly tends toward rigid prices, changed relatively infrequently. For example, steel and automobile prices in the 1950s and 1960s followed a distinct stair-step pattern: constant for 12 months, and then raised uniformly by all firms in August of each year. Airline fares have moved in that direction since tight oligopoly was reestablished in 1986–1987.

An ingenious analysis to explain this rigidity—which economists call the *kinked demand curve,* because the curve, indeed, has a kink in it—was developed in the 1930s and is still a widely accepted model of oligopoly.[9] It is particularly valuable for showing the kind of pricing dilemma that oligopolists face, once an industrywide price has been established.

Its general form is illustrated in Figure 13.15. Suppose you run an oligopolistic firm and are trying to determine the results of changing your price. As in a chess game, your strategy depends on the reactions of the other players, or firms in the industry. In fact, the demand curve for your firm depends on your rivals' responses. Figure 13.15 illustrates one possible set of such assumptions. It shows what is expected, not necessarily what will happen on each occasion.

For example, if your rivals adopt a *no-response* strategy, then you will lose a lot of sales to them if you raise your price, and gain a lot of sales if you lower it. Your demand curve will be relatively *elastic,* as illustrated by curve Demand$_N$ (N is for nonresponse) in Figure 13.15. Alternatively, suppose that your rivals adopt a strict strategy of *full response,* meaning they match your price changes exactly and immediately. Then your demand will be relatively *inelastic,* as illustrated by curve Demand$_R$ (with R for response).[10]

1.   Timid Attitudes

Which assumption is logical, or common in practice, or most interesting—or all three? Sweezy's classic analysis simply began with the firm at the market price. That firm then adopts the most timid, pessimistic approach: the worst is expected

---

[9] The original source is Paul M. Sweezy, "Demand under Conditions of Oligopoly," *Journal of Political Economy,* 47 (August 1939), 568–73. For an attack on the theory, see George J. Stigler, "The Kinky Oligopoly Demand Curve and Rigid Prices," *Journal of Political Economy,* 55 (October 1947), 432–49. The analysis has its limits, but it has great value for clarifying the results of specific expectations.

[10] This complete response or nonresponse pair is not the most extreme set of assumptions. Rivals could overreact, going the opposite way or making an even larger change than you do. The two standard assumptions merely give a natural set of opposites, for passive and exact-response behavior.

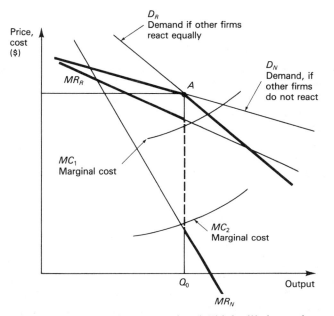

FIGURE 13.15.   The conventional "kinked" demand curve for a timid, pessimistic oligopolist.

in each direction. The firm expects its rivals to match its price cuts (thereby holding its sales gains to a minimum), while not responding at all to its price increases (thereby maximizing this firm's loss of sales).

That dual pessimism gives the demand curve an actual kink, as shown in Figure 13.15, at the initial price-output point. This kink causes an actual discontinuity in the composite marginal revenue curve, at the original output level. Each half of the kinked demand curve has a corresponding half-length marginal revenue curve. For Demand$_R$, the marginal revenue half-curve is labeled MR_R; for Demand$_N$, the marginal revenue half-curve is MR_N. The discontinuity occurs where one moves from MR_R to MR_N, going rightward. This kink may be quite large, if the two demand curves differ sharply in elasticity. That is illustrated in Figure 13.15.

The firm, as always, sets output where its marginal revenue equals its marginal cost. As illustrated, that may occur in the discontinuity, even if the marginal cost curve rises as high as MC_1 or falls as low as MC_2. Thus the firm holds its price steady, even if costs shift over a wide range: that gives the rigid-prices property of oligopoly. Note, too, that price will also exceed marginal cost, possibly by a lot (as in the case of MC_2).

This "normal" kink explains the long periods of rigid prices that occur in some tight oligopolies. It also suggests why oligopolists often maintain constant market shares over long periods—even decades, as in the case of the four leading U.S. meat packers' during much of 1880–1920 (see Chapter 14).

2. Aggressive Attitudes

But the analysis is more versatile than this. Suppose the firm's attitude changes abruptly from pessimism to optimism. Perhaps an old, cautious president is replaced by a brash new top manager. The new aggressive president expects the *best* in either direction: price rises will be matched by rivals, but not price cuts. That will cause a kink in the demand curve, as shown in Figure 13.16, that is the reverse of the conventional kink in Figure 13.15. Accordingly, the opposite halves of the two marginal revenue curves will also be reversed.

The new, aggressive manager will definitely change price, for marginal cost now equals marginal revenue at two points, *A* and *B*, both of which are away from the original output level. Either *A* or *B* will be chosen (we cannot tell which), so price behavior will be active, not rigid.

Of course, the new manager may encounter sobering responses that differ from the optimistic expectations. Indeed, industries often go through a period of aggressive action that is succeeded by a settling down into timidity and rigidity. Stable equilibrium will occur only when all the oligopolists have a "normal" pessimistic kinked demand curve. These kinks may be mild or sharp, and they may (and presumably will) vary among the rivals. In any event, the contrasting attitudes, and their effects on price rigidity, can be visualized with Figures 13.15 and 13.16.

It is important not to take the theory of the kinked demand curve *too* literally. The managers of oligopolistic firms do not spend their time staring at diagrams of discontinuous marginal revenue schedules. But their choices may seem *as if* they

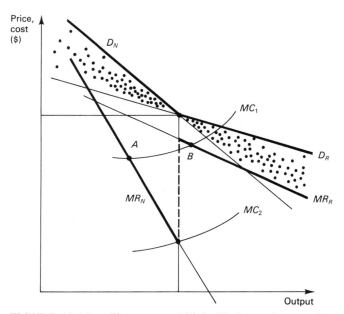

FIGURE 13.16.   The reverse "kinked" demand curve for an aggressive, optimistic oligopolist.

did this sort of analysis. The theory's value derives from the fact that it illustrates the kind of interdependence oligopolists face. The effects of future price changes can never be anticipated with certainty, since rivals' reactions are often unpredictable. By illustrating this interdependence and uncertainty, the kinked demand curve is useful for understanding oligopoly.

V. TACIT COLLUSION AND PRICE LEADERSHIP

Oligopolists have a joint interest in fixing prices, in behaving as a "shared monopoly." To keep one another in line, they may rely on binding contracts, elaborate organizations, or other tangible controls.[11] In countries where such explicit schemes are illegal (as in the United States), "tacit" collusion may evolve instead. Though it is rarely as forceful as full-blown price agreements, it can make a significant difference.

Tacit Collusion.   Tacit (or "implicit") collusion requires that the oligopolists build up a degree of shared knowledge and trust. The coordination is precarious, for the firms do not apply a system of explicit controls and penalties. The controls and penalties must be present, however, if only in the shadowy form of shared expectations about what will be done to price-cutters. The main penalty is some form of retaliation, to match or undercut the price-cutter. It must be applied often enough to be believed and feared. Such "price wars" are costly to the enforcers. In each industry, the lengths to which enforcement by retaliation will proceed reflect a balance between the gains from collusion, the individual rewards to price-cutters, and the profits lost by enforcing penalties on price-cutters.

Obviously, **concentration** favors effective tacit collusion. In loose oligopoly, on the other hand, little or no enforcement may be worthwhile. Tacit collusion is therefore usually endemic in tight oligopoly and scarcely possible in loose oligopoly.

Homogeneity of products also favors tacit collusion. Uniform products make for clear, simple prices, that can be easily understood and accepted. If, instead, products are varied and complicated, the prices themselves become complex and ambiguous. The firms will then have difficulty in coordinating what they expect and accept from one another.

Stable industry conditions also make tacit collusion more effective. Shifts in cost and demand require frequent adjustments in the precarious balance. Disagreements and misunderstandings are then more likely to occur.

Long industry experience helps build and maintain the shared understanding that makes tacit collusion easier. In older industries with settled structure, the participants come to know one another and to accept one another's positions. Each firm's actions are then more predictable by the others.

All in all, tacit collusion is likely to be most common in older, stable industries with standardized products and high concentration. Chapter 14 will show that experience does fit this pattern.

---

[11] See Paul W. MacAvoy and Daniel Orr, "Price Strategies to Promote Cartel Stability," *Economica*, 32 (May 1965), 186–97; Almarin Phillips, *Market Structure, Organization and Performance* (Cambridge, Mass.: Harvard University Press, 1962); Tirole, *The Theory of Industrial Organization*, chapters 5–7; and Scherer, *Industrial Market Structure and Economic Performance*, chapters 5–8.

Price Leadership.   "Price leadership" is one form that tacit collusion may take. [12] The phrase is merely a loose intuitive one. It refers to the process by which one firm "leads" a price increase, with the other firms following. Each follower would gain by *not* following; this was shown by Figure 13.15 for the timid oligopolist. Why, then, would the leader boldly raise price, unless it were reasonably confident that the rest would follow? This implies tacit collusion.

During 1890–1940, especially, many concentrated industries did seem to display collusive price leadership. Prices would be stable for a period. Then one firm would raise price sharply. The others would quickly match the rise, often in exact detail. The new price would hold for a long period, until the next round, which was often led by the same firm. The meat-packing industry from 1890 to 1920, and the cigarette and steel industries during the 1930s, showed such patterns strikingly. Early analysts of oligopoly in the 1930s took it for granted that such price leadership was tacit collusion at work. Later, in the 1950–1970 period, steel and autos also followed this stair-step pattern. Again, collusion seemed to be at work.

Yet the process may instead be "barometric" price leadership.[13]. The firms themselves will routinely claim at the time that the price rises are required in order to cover rising costs, investment requirements, and so forth. They may be right. If so, the process itself matters little. Indeed, firms may hold back "timidly" (recall Figure 15.13) even after price increases are warranted, until one firm breaks the logjam. If prices are not held at monopolistic levels above cost, then "barometric" price leadership is consistent with competition and its results.

"Collusive" and "barometric" elements are often hard to identify in actual cases. One looks first at the *sharpness* of the price change (its speed and height). Is it a large, rapid rise, coming after a long period of constant prices? The degree of complexity of the prices can also be a hint. If a complex schedule of individual prices is matched exactly by others in a short time, that is suspicious; detailed cost conditions are unlikely to be so exactly similar. A third test is whether or not the same firm leads all the time. A random process of leadership is more likely to be barometric.

"Price leadership" is an imprecise phrase, and the two types of leadership are not clearly distinct. Actual cases are likely to mix some attributes of both collusive and barometric price leadership.

VI.   COST AND DEMAND CONDITIONS

Costs.   When oligopolists' costs differ, agreement on prices becomes more difficult. That is natural and obvious. Figure 13.17 illustrates it for a simple case. The demand and average cost curves are assumed to be identical for the two firms. Only the marginal costs differ between them (as shown by MC_1 and MC_2). The firms will want different prices, as shown by P_1 and P_2. How can they pick "the" price?

---

[12] Basic discussions are in Jesse W. Markham, "The Nature and Significance of Price Leadership," *American Economic Review,* 41 (December 1951), 891–905; and Joe S. Bain, "Price Leaders, Barometers and Kinks," *Journal of Business,* 33 (July 1960), 193–203. See also the survey by Scherer, *Industrial Market Power and Economic Performance,* 176–84.

[13] The "barometric" aspect was stressed by Markham. Actually, "thermometric" would have been more exact; the price changes merely reflect present cost conditions rather than predict future ones.

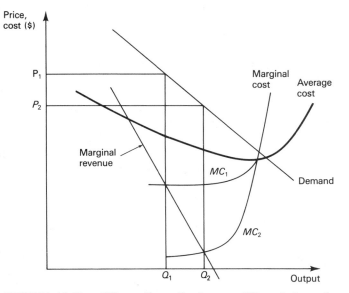

FIGURE 13.17. When oligopolists' costs differ, their preferred prices are likely to differ also.

Only by negotiation, mixed perhaps with sharp price-cutting or other tactics to penalize each other. The resulting price will not be a stable equilibrium.

Such cost differences can arise from many causes. The firms may differ in their locations, in their access to cheap inputs, or in their quality of management. They may have built plants of differing sizes, at differing times. They may have chosen different factor combinations (e.g., one is labor-intensive, the other capital-intensive). These and other variations have always plagued the efforts of firms to fix prices, and they will continue to do so.

Demand.   The same holds for demand differences. When demand curves differ, the preferred prices will usually differ, even if costs are identical.

When both costs and demand vary, the chance that the firms will prefer the same price is remote. Oligopoly pricing therefore tends to be unstable, and agreement is difficult except in odd cases. Oligopolists have a mutual interest in reducing such variations, by whatever means. A classic example is OPEC, the worldwide cartel of oil-producing countries. The members' costs differ, from about 50 cents a barrel in Saudi Arabia to $10 a barrel and more in Venezuela and other countries. Their pricing debates have been intense and permeated with clashing interests. Only strong loyalties among the Arab members—especially the Saudis—have kept the cost variations from causing the agreements to collapse.

The shifting of demand over the business cycle is an important special case. As demand falls during a recession, price warfare often breaks out among oligopolists. Why don't they instead maintain prices, or perhaps reduce them only gradually? The main reason is cost differences. Some firms are capital-intensive, with low marginal costs. Other firms have less machinery, relying more on labor; this gives them a higher marginal cost at below-capacity levels of output. Those with lower marginal costs will wish to cut prices more deeply.

This helps to clarify the instability of oligopoly pricing over the course of the business cycle. It suggests that oligopoly pricing is likely to be especially fluid during recessions as differences in costs come into play. Conversely, any stable and uniform pricing by oligopolists during recessions stands out as unusual. If that happens, then either (1) costs and demand are neatly aligned—which is unlikely—or (2) some other basis for agreement exists. More generally, the shifting of demand tends to destabilize pricing by requiring changes and by exposing differences in preferred prices.

Altogether, differences in cost and demand are potent forces making oligopoly pricing unstable. They keep the payoffs in the game matrix from being symmetrical. They make them less definite, and this breeds efforts to chisel. And they pose direct conflicts among oligopolists in their preferred prices.

"Destructive Competition."   When overhead costs are high and marginal costs are low, firms often complain that "destructive competition" will occur.[14] The idea is an old one; during the 1890–1910 era, it was used to justify mergers or price-fixing in order to keep markets "orderly" and "rational." It still crops up frequently; and in some oligopolies, it is part of the rationale for public regulation.

The concept is simple. If demand falls below full-capacity levels for a firm, that firm will be willing to cut price sharply, since marginal cost is low. The industry's competitive price equilibrium is precarious, and destructive price wars will be chronic. This will keep profits below the "normal" level and deter investment.

There are two main cases of possible "destructive competition": cyclical shifts and long-term "sick" industries. Cyclical shifts are focused in heavy durable-goods industries where the accelerator effect causes demand to change sharply. The industries are often capital-intensive, with a high proportion of overhead (or "fixed") costs. Often, too, their products are relatively uniform, so that price differences can cause quick shifts by customers.

These conditions breed a fear of price competition, especially during recessions. Is such competition really "destructive," by social criteria? Or is it, rather, healthy and effective? The correct broad answer is that no social harm occurs in *most* cases.

True damage could occur for just two main reasons. First, the price-cutting may kill efficient smaller firms purely because they lack strong banking connections to tide them over the recession. In fact, lesser firms do complain the loudest and usually go out of business in larger numbers during recessions. Yet if a recession does hit them proportionally harder because of their lack of banking support, then financial markets rather than price-fixing would be the proper focus for a cure.

Second, price wars may cause firms to fail and withdraw capacity below the efficient long-run level for the industry. The boom-bust-boom-bust sequence may keep investment too low and cause extra costs of adjustment. The extra risk from the fluctuations may also deter investors, so that investment stays below the efficient margin.

---

[14] Synonyms are "ruinous" and "cutthroat." All these terms are loose and intuitive. See John M. Clark, *Studies in the Economics of Overhead Costs* (Chicago: University of Chicago Press, 1923); and Lloyd G. Reynolds, "Cutthroat Competition," *American Economic Review,* 30 (December 1940), 736–47, among many discussions.

This second line of reasoning rests mainly on the presumption of irrationality in producers and investors. Rational decisions will not be drawn away from long-run efficient patterns merely by transient, predictable shifts. Instead, the ups and downs will tend to balance out. Investors will base their long-run decisions on the true fundamental conditions, undeterred by predictable short-term variations. Even where irrationality is great, the net social cost may be slight and brief.

"Sick" industries pose similar issues. The problem here is that because demand is "permanently" below capacity, the industry must shrink. Depleting the capital may take a long while (decades in some cases), so there may be some social gain from averting deep price slashing during the structural adjustment. Examples include railroads in the eastern United States since 1930, U.S. coal mining in the 1930s, New England textile firms during 1910–1950, and British coal mining from about 1925 to 1965. Many industries that are said to be "sick" are in reality tolerably healthy.

Here again, much or all of the price-cutting is healthy. An overbuilt industry needs to shrink, and financial losses are the correct signal for *dis*investment. The equality of price and marginal cost is still the basic rule for efficient allocation (recall Chapter 2). It permits the best social use of the capacity during the transition to smaller capacity. The financial losses are painful to the shareholders, but keeping prices up above long-run marginal cost will usually cause a social loss. The idle capacity should be priced at or near its low marginal cost. If public assistance is really needed, it would be better to apply it directly to the shareholders instead of keeping prices too high. At any rate, price-raising is often self-defeating in the end if demand is at all elastic. The volume of purchases simply declines further.[15]

"Destructive competition" is a recurring complaint. It raises interesting issues, and often it influences policies. Yet it has little economic substance in most cases.

VII.   RULES OF THUMB, INCLUDING SALES MAXIMIZING

Oligopolists have a range of choice. Many of them settle these choices by rules of thumb. Despite the many possible reactions of rivals, they plow ahead according to these simple rules. Such behavior is especially common in retailing and in other situations where many prices have to be decided quickly. Simple rules of thumb as an alternative to complicated games-type strategies imply that the interreactions are not very big or important.

From about 1940 to 1965, many scholars suggested that these rules of thumb were outside traditional price behavior. Others said that they were an alternative to oligopoly pricing; that they bypassed the action-reaction problem.[16] However, they are actually quite compatible with "normal" pricing behavior, as we will soon see.

---

[15] A prominent instance of this has been railroad passenger service during the 1950s and 1960s. Fares were set at high levels, in the hope of covering costs (including sunk costs). While passenger capacity was largely idle and therefore at relatively low cost levels, the high fares helped to shrink rail passenger travel even further.

[16] Among the most prominent were R. L. Hall and Charles J. Hitch, "Price Theory and Business Behavior," *Oxford Economic Papers,* 2 (May 1939), 12–45; and William J. Baumol, "On the Theory of Oligopoly," *Economica,* 25 (August 1958), 187–98.

In fact, they are usually just practical methods for achieving maximum profits in various competitive situations. They pose no deep conflict between "theory" and "reality."

1. Markup Pricing

Sellers often take their average cost, add a standard markup, and set price at that "cost plus markup" level. (Example: Clean Foods buys canned fruits at 50 cents per can, adds a 20 percent standard markup, and sells them for 60 cents each. Box Company figures its average costs for cardboard boxes at $200 per thousand, adds a 50 percent markup, and sets price at 30 cents per box). Indeed, rare is the seller who does not calculate, know, and evaluate results on the basis of his markups. They give quick answers to pricing needs.

Markups are more flexible than they seem. The percentage markup can be varied with the size of order or the type of good. It can be adjusted to fit differing degrees of competition. Thus industrial firms often set different margins on various parts of their product lines, to reflect "market realities" (translation: "degrees of competition"). A department store often has a wide variety of markups among its sections (e.g., toys, jewelry, shoes, and rugs) and even within sections. Sellers often give discounts or hold a *Sale!* departing from standard markups. Some sellers almost always negotiate special deals below the formal, markup-based price. New-car sales by dealers are a fine example of this. (*Never* pay the sticker price for a new car. Instead, offer $150 over the dealer's cost and bargain from there.)

In short, markups are a rubbery but useful rule of thumb. They can be adjusted, varied, or simply departed from, wherever conditions warrant. They are one simple tool for maximizing profits.

2. Sales Maximizing

Firms often seem to base their decisions on a simple rule: Grow. Another related version is: Hold (or increase) market share. These guidelines can give the oligopolists a definite outcome by ignoring their interdependence. The guidelines seem to demote profits in favor of the firm's mere physical or dollar size. And they ignore rivals' reactions. The firm looks just at its own role—its size, growth, market share, whatever, as discussed in Chapter 10.

Such rules may lead some firms well above the output level at which their profits are maximized. This is especially true when the profit hill has a blunt top. The lesson for social welfare can be favorable. Sales maximizing may cause price to be lower and output higher than market power would give; at the extreme, the outcome is close to the competitive result.

But once again, the outcome may be quite conventional.[17] Sales maximizing can be consistent with long-run profit maximizing. Indeed, that is precisely what managers may expect in the end from a series of growth-oriented choices. As for oli-

---

[17] This is concluded by William J. Baumol, even though his theory of "satisficing" by sales maximizers was one of the most distinct departures from the traditional profit-maximizing assumption. See his *Business Behavior, Value and Growth*, rev. ed. (Englewood Cliffs, N.J.: Prentice Hall, 1967).

gopoly, the interdependence can be inserted by giving the profit hill a kink. This corresponds to the kink in the demand curve as seen by a timid oligopolist. If the kink is sharp, then the sales-maximizing price may be only slightly above the profit-maximizing price.

Sales maximizing is inevitably related to maximizing market share; having bigger sales usually means having a larger market share. Many firms appear to use some mixture or version of sales and/or market share as a rough guide for pricing and investment policy. Especially in large, complex firms, such practical guides for managers can be of value.

QUESTIONS FOR REVIEW

1. "Oligopoly outcomes are usually determinate." True?
2. "Oligopolists will usually converge on the 'center' of the market and set nearly identical prices." True?
3. "Real-world oligopolies are always instances of fixed-sum games." True?
4. "Sellers will usually prefer that their degree of mutual information be greater than what the buyers have." True?
5. "The 'reverse kink' demand curve reflects an oligopolist with aggressive, optimistic attitudes." True?
6. "A stable, homogeneous-good oligopoly is likely to be relatively unsuccessful at tacit collusion." True?
7. "If new entry is rapid and large, the existing firms will have relatively sharp kinks in their demand curves at the entry-inducing price." True?
8. "Limit pricing by a dominant firm is less plausible than limit pricing by a tight-oligopoly group." True?
9. "If costs differ, cooperation is harder to attain." True?
10. "Destructive competition arises particularly when overhead costs are low and demand is inelastic." True?
11. Why don't oligopolists always engage in complete joint maximizing of profits?
12. How does access to information affect the ability of oligopolists to coordinate on prices?
13. Show kinked demand curves for an aggressive firm and then for a timid one.
14. Cournot analysis is brittle and unrealistic, because of its narrow assumptions. But make the case in its favor, pointing out its value.
15. Explain why higher concentration provides more information to enforce collusion.
16. Derive the Cournot quantity-setting reaction curves for two firms, one with two-thirds of the market and one with one-third.
17. Is it meaningful to specify the outputs when output is what the firms *will* be setting?
18. Show how the HHI is related to the Lerner Index, in a Cournot setting.
19. In a Cournot analysis, can market shares differ when the firms do *not* have costs which differ in (inverse) proportion to those market shares?
20. Prepare your own pay-off matrix, for a non-zero sum, *asymmetrical* duopoly, with (a) a stable joint maximum, and then (b) an unstable joint maximum. For (b), show step-by-step how the outcome degenerates to a competitive outcome. Do your matrixes fit actual industries?

14 COLLUSION IN REAL MARKETS

Among the 2,500 industrial cartels that flourished in Britain from the 1930s to the 1950s, many were formalized in elaborate contracts that spelled out in minute detail exactly how the price-fixing was to be done and enforced. In fact, open collusion was common throughout Western Europe during that period because governments tolerated what the market participants wanted to do.

Price-fixing has been illegal in the United States since 1899, under enforcement of Section 1 of the Sherman Antitrust Act. Therefore it is not practiced openly, and hidden efforts to collude are often weak and transient. The great electrical equipment price conspiracy among U.S. companies during 1930–1960 was a patchwork of devices and meetings that tried, and sometimes failed, to enforce higher prices. Executives in many industries will confide that price-fixing is "a way of life," but it must be done furtively and cannot be strictly enforced.

As Chapter 13 noted, the urge to collude is universal in oligopoly, even though duopoly models may rule it out by their assumptions. When collusion succeeds, it can be powerful and extensive. This chapter presents a selection of the types of collusion that occur, especially in U.S. markets, in order to give you practice in interpreting the patterns in actual markets.

Section I notes the conditions that favor collusion, and Section II considers the extent of cooperation. Section III reviews the various types of pricing behavior, from formal cartels and softer controls and agreements to the mysteries of tacit collusion. Section IV surveys the various trade associations and joint ventures that may enhance cooperation.

I. CONDITIONS FAVORING COLLUSION

What market conditions favor collusion? Concentration and a similarity among the sellers' costs and demand conditions were noted in Chapter 13. Here they are treated in greater depth, along with several other conditions favorable to collusion.

Concentration and Fewness. High concentration means there are few major sellers. Hence they will learn quickly of others' cheating and be able to apply heavy punishments. Full cartel organizations can be formed more easily. Fewness means tighter control, moving toward a complete monopoly outcome.

Costs.   There are two main, contrasting points. The first is that similar costs make for easier coordination, as we noted in Chapter 13. The second is that high overhead costs make coordination more difficult because they result in low marginal costs, which give stronger rewards to price-cutting.

Low marginal costs make deep price-cutting more possible and likely during times of low demand. Even in "normal" times, when the whole industry is in equilibrium, some sellers may occasionally be short of orders. They will be tempted to make sharp price cuts to maintain their operations. This destabilizing effect limits the ability of the group to hold prices above long-run cost levels. Therefore, prices may be more flexible and volatile in industries with low marginal costs.

Demand.   Here, too, similarity favors coordination. So does stability of demand. Demand shifts may be random or systematic (for example, the business "cycle" is partly predictable), or sometimes one and sometimes the other. Random shifts of demand are a routine threat to price-fixing, for they erode the oligopolists' ability to control events and to focus their expectations on the same price levels. Systematic shifts could in principle be anticipated and neutralized.

But in industries making durable producer goods—"heavy" industries, generally—the shifts are often very sharp because of the "accelerator" effect.[1] Their timing and severity are often not entirely predictable. Such sellers have special incentives to contain price-cutting. They will come to regard price competition as "destructive" or "cutthroat" or "ruinous." Schemes to "stabilize" prices to make competition "orderly" will be common in these cases.

Focal Points.   These can be an important basis for making cooperation stick. A focal point is any prominent price or location that competitors can easily identify and agree on. Round numbers are a prime example. If several firms are considering charging $89, $93, and $97 for their leaf-blowers, it is easy and natural for them to settle on $100 and stick to it. Standard markups are another example. If all firms set price at cost plus 25 percent, cooperation will be more effective than if they all use differing markup ratios.

Location is another example. Geographic lines and boundaries are often a basis for dividing up markets. The divisions can be fitted to natural focal points such as rivers or state lines. Coordination and market splitting are easier when focal points are available.

Nonprice Competition.   This can be a substitute for price competition. Many markets combine a variety of nonprice interactions (in product design, advertising, and so on) with effective cooperation on prices. Competition is thus rechanneled in "safer" directions. The room for this secondary competition varies among indus-

---

[1] The "accelerator" works in industries with derived demand, such as the capital goods used to produce "final" consumer goods. If final consumer sales fall off 10 percent in a recession, new orders for the equipment to produce them will fall more sharply, perhaps to zero for a year or two. This accelerator effect is a basic Keynesian concept from the 1930s. See Paul A. Samuelson, "A Synthesis of the Principle of Acceleration and the Multiplier," *Journal of Political Economy,* 47 (December 1939), 786–97, or any good macroeconomics text.

tries. Some industries are rich in nonprice dimensions, or at least the nonprice features can be cultivated. Others are bare of the nonprice frills; simple, homogeneous products are the obvious instance.

Airlines before 1978 were an important example of nonprice competition. Fares were set largely at uniform levels by the airlines and the regulatory agency (the Civil Aeronautics Board). Efforts to compete for passengers were transferred to decor, food, convenience, and frequent scheduling of flights. The main result was an excessive frequency of half-empty flights offering expensive frills, rather than the efficient scheduling, price flexibility, and varied service conditions that competition provides.[2]

One needs to judge nonprice competition carefully. It is often trivial, but it can be substantial. It can also be integrated with, and reinforce, price strategies.

Information.   Information can make cooperation easier. To the degree that sellers are better informed than buyers, they can detect price-cutting more quickly and penalize it more fully. This puts a chill on price-cutting and shifts the range of likely prices upward. If information is tilted the other way, then buyers can induce more price-cutting, since detection and retaliation by sellers will be slower.

The tilt toward buyers is likely to occur in markets for simple and uniform products, where buyers can easily comparison-shop. By contrast, more complex products where special-order contracts are the rule give sellers the advantage on key information. Colluding sellers will set up systems to force quick disclosure among themselves (*not* to buyers) of the prices being set in the market.

By 1960, economists had roughly agreed on two types of oligopoly: (1) Loose oligopoly was seen as largely a hopeless setting for collusion. (2) Tight oligopoly was seen as relying on implicit collusion; explicit agreements were thought to be unnecessary. The intermediate range of oligopoly (roughly, four-firm concentration of 40 to 60 percent) was seen as the main arena for formal price-fixing schemes.

Since 1960, the issues have become more complex. Some analysts have added entry barriers as a controlling factor on oligopoly cooperation (recall Chapters 3 and 13). If barriers are high, cooperation (or some form of joint pricing policy) might be possible even for loose oligopolies.

New evidence about actual price-fixing, however, leans the other way. Hay and Kelley found that formal price-fixing is frequent even in very tight oligopolies.[3] The strategies for successful cartels have also been clarified. Generally, the cartel that can threaten an "excessive" penalty for price-cutters will be effective. As we have seen, the ability to apply such sharp punishments will vary with industry conditions.

Therefore one cannot apply any simple rule. One expects a variety of cooperative systems to emerge, corresponding to the differences in industry conditions. Some will provide full monopoly control; others will have no real effect.

---

[2] See Daniel P. Kaplan, "The Changing Airline Industry," a chapter in Leonard W. Weiss and Michael W. Klass, eds., *Regulatory Reform: What Actually Happened,* Boston: Little, Brown, 1986, and sources noted there; and Chapter 18 of this text.

[3] See George A. Hay and Daniel Kelley, "An Empirical Survey of Price Fixing Conspiracies," *Journal of Law and Economics,* 17 (April 1974), 13–38.

II. THE EXTENT OF COOPERATION

There are two main questions: How extensive are cooperative efforts? What specific forms do they take? The first question can be answered briefly and broadly. The second involves details, that occupy the rest of this chapter.

Cooperation in price-setting *is* extensive. Most forms of price-fixing are illegal in the mainstream U.S. industries, under the antitrust laws.[4] And yet the phenomenon is endemic. As one experienced executive put it in 1975: "The overwhelming majority of businessmen discuss pricing with their competitors." Said another: "Price-fixing has always been done in this business, and there's no real way of ever being able to stop it—not through Congress, not the Justice Department. It may slow down for a few years. But it will always be there." And still another: "It's just the way you do business. There's an unwritten law that you don't compete. It's been that way for 50 years."[5]

In many industries, price-fixing is simply a way of life. Many local markets normally have some degree of price-fixing (bread, milk, and construction are common instances), and the phenomenon is often found in larger national industries as well. Formal schemes are most common in concentrated, homogeneous-product markets.

Table 14.1 indicates some recent patterns of industrial price-fixing in U.S. markets. Few price-fixing systems in the United States have full formal controls of price, output, and profits, but many have combined some formal controls with ingrained habits to achieve a high degree of "shared-monopoly" power.

In some other countries, where such cooperation has been legal, the degree of control and detail is greater than in the United States. From 1930 to 1956, some 2,500 schemes for price-fixing and market sharing emerged in British industries.[6] Numbers are comparable for other Western European countries.[7] New laws have reduced the formal schemes in some countries, perhaps shifting the industries toward informal agreements. The true degree of price-fixing abroad may still be nearly as high as it was from 1930 to 1960.

Generally the cooperative tendencies are strong and common in many types of markets. Outlawing them merely shifts down their margin of effectiveness and

---

[4] *Some* cooperation is useful and inevitable—on engineering standards and terms, for example. The main U.S. law against price-fixing and other anticompetitive collusion is the Sherman Antitrust Act of 1890, first applied strictly to price-fixing in 1899. Many industries have been exempted from the antitrust laws, and much local and intrastate trade is also outside the Sherman Act's jurisdiction.

[5] These quotations are among many in this vein from an excellent survey article, "Price-fixing: Crackdown Under Way," *Business Week,* June 2, 1975, pp. 42–48. See also, Simon N. Whitney, *Antitrust Policies* (New York: Twentieth Century Fund, 1958), 2 vols., for extensive accounts of price-fixing activities in twenty major industries in the years before 1958.

[6] Most of them were abandoned by 1962, under the Restrictive Trade Practices Act of 1956. See R. B. Stevens and B. Yamey, *The Restrictive Practices Court* (London: Weidenfeld and Nicolson, 1965); and annual *Reports* of Registar of Restrictive Practices (London: Her Majesty's Stationery Office).

[7] See Corwin D. Edwards, *Cartelization in Western Europe* (Washington, D.C.: Department of State, 1964); and J. P. Miller, ed., *Competition, Cartels and Their Regulation* (Amsterdam: North-Holland, 1962), especially Chapters 4 and 5. The European cartel craze peaked in the 1930s under the stress of economic stagnation. The changes since 1950 simply restore much of the competitive conditions that had existed earlier. The corresponding U.S. version of cartels—the National Recovery Administration (the NRA)—lasted only a few years in the 1930s.

TABLE 14.1   Selected Price-Fixing Conspiracies in U.S. Industries, 1961–1970

MARKET	GEOGRAPHICAL SCOPE	FOUR-FIRM CONCENTRATION IN THE MARKET	NUMBER OF CONSPIRATORS (AND THEIR SHARE OF SALES)	NUMBER OF FIRMS IN THE MARKET
		(%)	(%)	
Wrought steel wheels	National	85	5 (100)	5
Bedsprings	National	<61	10	20
Metal library shelving	National	60	7 (78)	9
Self-locking nuts	National	97	4 (97)	6
Refuse collection	Local		86	102
Women's swimsuits	National	<69	9	
Steel products (wholesale)	Regional	66	5 (72)	
Gasoline	Regional	>49	12	
Milk	Local	>90	11 (>80)	13
Concrete pipe	Regional	100	4 (100)	4
Drill jig bushings	National	56	9 (82)	13
Linen supplies	Local	49	31 (90)	
Plumbing fixtures	National	76	7 (98)	15
Class rings	Regional	<100	3 (90)	5
Tickets	Regional	<78	9 (<91)	10
Baked goods (wholesale)	Regional	46	7	8
Athletic equipment	Local	>90	6 (100)	6
Dairy products	Regional	>95	3 (95)	13
Vending machines	Local	93	6 (100)	6
Ready-mix concrete	Local	86	9 (100)	9
Carbon steel sheets	National	59	10	
Liquid asphalt	Regional	56	20 (95)	

The omitted figures are not available.
SOURCE: Adapted from George A. Hay and Daniel Kelley, "An Empirical Survey of Price Fixing Conspiracies," *Journal of Law and Economics,* 17 (April 1974). Adapted from the Appendix table.

changes their course of direction. The downshift depends on (1) the *probability* of being caught and convicted (in other words, the strictness of policing by public agencies), and (2) the *severity* of the penalties (in fines, jail terms, and/or damage claims). Some laws—such as most state antitrust statutes—are not enforced at all, and others only trivially.[8]

III.   TYPES OF COLLUSION

The main categories (from the strongest to weakest) are: cartels, controls on entry and market areas, price-fixing agreements, and tacit collusion. All are found in the United States as well as abroad. There is space here only to describe and then illustrate each type with several examples.

---

[8] On the content and force of antitrust policies, see William G. Shepherd, *Public Policies Toward Business,* 7th ed. (Homewood, Ill.: Irwin, 1985), Chaps. 4–9.

1. Cartels

Cartels come in many varieties. The standard cartel has written rules and penalties that the parties have agreed to, plus a staffed organization to see that the rules
are followed. Almost every conceivable device has been tried at some time and
place, and many of these devices still persist—by the thousands. Some cartels are
arranged and enforced by the state itself; others are supported by the courts as an
enforceable contract. In other settings, the courts may be neutral and government
agencies may also be neutral or even hostile.

Full cartels control all aspects—pricing, output, product mix, investment, and
profit pooling—much as a genuine unified monopoly firm would. This requires large
staffs and complete information. Even such thorough cartels may break down or
need revising, but while in existence, they usually exert strong control.

Among less complete cartels, the marketing cartel—called a *syndicate* in Germany—is a common type. It handles all its members' sales and manages their revenues. Thus it controls every aspect but profit pooling and investment (and those it
influences indirectly). Some cartels can close down "excess" or "uneconomic"
plants. Others control only prices and output, in varying degrees. The latter have
smaller staffs and less power to penalize mavericks. Weaker cartels shade down into
price agreements and trade associations (see Subsection III.3 and Section IV). The
test of a "cartel" is whether there are contractual controls, with a staff and powers
to apply known penalties.

OPEC.   One prominent international cartel; the Organization of Petroleum
Exporting Countries, has a membership consisting mainly of the oil-rich Middle East
Arab countries.[9] It achieved startling success, first in 1973–1974 by raising the world
price of oil from about $3 to $11 in the space of six months, and then in 1979 by
raising it to about $30. Few cartels in history have matched OPEC's extent of price
multiple, which reached 10 in 1979 and was nearly sustained until in 1985 the price
fell from $28 to below $15. It has stayed in the $12 to $19 range since then. As noted
in Chapter 5, this cartel has transferred many hundreds of billions of dollars of
windfall profits to the OPEC nations. No cartel in history has remotely approached
the colossal volume of OPEC's profits and total economic impact.

Yet OPEC is not actually a tightly knit, unified cartel, because there are deep
divisions among its members. Some members have vast reserves of cheap oil: Saudi
Arabia in particular produces oil at little more than $3 per barrel and it does not
need to maximize short-run returns. At the other extreme, several high-cost producers (such as Nigeria) need high prices, and they also need the funds more urgently.
Other producers range in between, with varying mixes of costs and short-run needs
for funds.

OPEC meetings to set quotas usually involve clashes, reflecting these differences. Saudia Arabia and the small Persian Gulf states usually seek restrained production, but at prices which do not strain relations with western importing countries
such as the US. The high cost, short-run oriented nations instead seek high prices
and maximum quotas for themselves, which they routinely violate in practice by

---

[9] See John M. Blair, *The Control of Oil* (New York: Pantheon Books, Random House, 1976).

over-producing. In addition, Iran and Iraq, as deadly enemies, have each demanded to have a quota larger than the other.

There are large producing nations outside of OPEC, so that OPEC is not only internally divided but also not even a majority of world oil production. Even so, OPEC's 16 years of varying success have been astonishing, helped in part by the lack of any countervailing power exerted by the oil-importing nations.

It is largely the Arab states' (partly) shared beliefs and willingness to sacrifice that holds this "cartel" together. They are helped by the fact that the buyers are many and diverse, so there is no firm basis for exerting monopsony power. OPEC's future impact depends on the balance between Arab solidarity on the one hand and (1) the possibility that the new oil exporters (Britain or Mexico) will become price-cutters and (2) possible monopsony action by buyers on the other.

Transport.   This industry has had many forms of cartels. Before deregulation began in 1975, airline, railroad, and waterborne shipping rates were generally proposed by the shippers themselves and then, after some evaluation, approved and enforced by public agencies. In the United States, the Civil Aeronautics Board (for airlines, including some international routes), the ICC (for domestic railroads and waterways), and the Maritime Commission (for other water traffic) functioned in effect as key parts of cartel systems.

Milk.   This familiar local product is under a thorough cartel system.[10] The U.S. Department of Agriculture authorizes milk marketing boards in some sixty-one urban areas including over 150 million people. Using formulas and various administrative procedures, the boards fix the prices paid to producers for their milk. Many states also control milk prices, including at the retail level. These cartels are less than complete, but they do control most aspects of milk marketing, and they do raise milk prices above competitive levels.

2. Controls

We come next to specialized controls, which may be firm but are incomplete. The most common type in the United States is control on entry. Definite standards are set, which all sellers in the market must meet. The number of sellers may also be explicitly limited by setting overall totals or by giving scarce franchises or charters to existing firms. In addition, sellers may be limited to one submarket within the whole market. These controls can be applied by the sellers on their own or by involving the powers of a public "regulatory" agency. They have resulted in restricted supply and higher prices.

There are many examples of specialized controls in the United States. One is commercial banking. Entry has been restricted for over sixty years by chartering; new entrants must make a positive case that more banking services are needed and that they meet high standards of probity. Over twenty states prohibit branching by

---

[10] See Shepherd, *Public Policies Toward Business*, Chap. 19; and Geoffrey S. Shepherd, *Marketing Farm Products*, 5th ed. (Ames: Iowa State University Press, 1984). See also Richard A. Ippolito and Robert T. Masson, "The Social Cost of Government Regulation of Milk," *Journal of Law and Economics*, 21 (April 1978), 56–69, and Anthony J. Greco, "State Fluid Milk Regulation: Antitrust and Price Controls," *Antitrust Bulletin*, 32 (Spring 1987), 165–88.

a bank into more than one physical location. There have been restrictions on pricing; interest rates on savings were limited; and interest could not be paid on demand deposits until recent years. Despite some loosening since 1970, banking controls are still powerful.

Various "professions"—medicine, law, and accounting, for example—have entry restrictions of some kind. Others—beauticians, barbers, and morticians, for example—are controlled by state licensing laws. The restrictions often underpin effective price-fixing by the professionals' associations.

Even where public agencies apply them, this does not change the nature of the controls. They are market controls, and they replace competition with a degree of cooperation.

3.   Agreements

Next is the large realm of price-fixing agreements, ranging all the way from tight pacts to loose, wishful efforts. They are a common occurrence, even where illegal.

One can only guess at the thousands of price-fixing schemes now existing in the U.S. economy. Many of them claim some praiseworthy goal, such as stable prices, standardization, orderly contraction, reducing uncertainty. All of them attempt to raise prices and increase members' profits. The most effective and durable agreements are, almost by definition, the least known. Table 14.1 gives a sample of this variety.

Price is the key element controlled. Price agreements may be reinforced by market divisions and other controls. But elaborate systems are vulnerable in the United States because antitrust laws condemn all price-fixing, and price discussions and schemes are the key targets of the laws. They occur in producer-goods as well as consumer-goods markets.

Some price schemes multiply the price manyfold; OPEC and the 1960s quinine "cartel" are prime examples. The "normal" price agreement raises price by 10 to 30 percent, with occasional collapses.[11] Such a margin looks moderate, but of course it can sharply increase the rate of return on investment to 30 percent and more. Among many hundreds of instances, we will consider four examples.

Meat Packing.   From at least 1885 to 1902, five leading meat-packing firms operated a "pool" that assigned quotas to each firm every week. Market shares were kept almost perfectly constant, prices were stabilized, and profits were raised. Heavy penalties were applied to any packer that exceeded its quota.

Electrical Equipment.   In 1960, an extensive price-fixing ring among U.S. producers of heavy electrical equipment was discovered and penalized.[12] In many

---

[11] Yet not all of them succeed in doing so. One study suggests that firms actually convicted of colluding are less profitable than other firms, on average. This could reflect either of two things: firms that get caught are less efficient, or less profitable firms are desperate enough to break the law trying to become more profitable. See Peter A. Asch and Joseph J. Seneca, "Is Collusion Profitable?" *Review of Economics and Statistics,* 58 (February 1976), 1–12.

[12] For an excellent summary, see Richard A. Smith, *Corporations in Crisis* (Garden City, N.Y.: Doubleday, 1962), Chapters 5 and 6; and Ralph G. M. Sultan, *Pricing in the Electrical Oligopoly,* 2 vols. (Boston: Harvard Business School Division of Research, 1974). This case provoked 1,900 damage suits by utility firms that had bought electrical equipment. There were conspiracies in seven related markets, covering billions of dollars in sales over many years.

TABLE 14.2   Extent and Coverage of Price-Fixing Conspiracies in the Nine Largest
Electrical Equipment Product Lines

PRODUCT	ANNUAL (1959) DOLLAR SALES ($ MILLIONS)	NUMBER OF FIRMS INDICTED	SHARE OF MARKET (%)
Turbine generators	$400*	3 (6)*	95 (100)
Industrial control equipment	262*	9*	75*
Power transformers	210	6	100
Power switchgear assemblies	125	5 (8)*	100
Circuit breakers	75	5	100
Distribution transformers	220	8	96
Low-voltage distribution equipment	200*	6 (10)*	95*
Meters	71	3	100
Insulators	28	8	100

* Includes companies named as co-conspirators but not indicted.
SOURCE: Adapted from Clarence C. Walton and Frederick W. Cleveland, Jr., *Corporations on Trial: The Electrical Cases* (Belmont, Cal.: Wadsworth Publishing Company, Inc., 1964.)

tight oligopoly submarkets, elaborate mechanisms had evolved as a way of life over at least several decades. Table 14.2 shows the main patterns. The methods of fixing the prices were designed to preserve market shares, usually with the sellers rotating by "phases of the moon" and other devices. At the industry's trade association meetings there would be private sessions upstairs to keep the price arrangements going.

Despite much stress, frequent acrimony, and occasional breakdowns, the schemes variously raised prices by 10 to 30 percent over long periods of time. They were apparently undetected and unchallenged for decades, perhaps because the buyers were mainly regulated utilities that included the value of the equipment in their rate bases. Yet these buyers were "knowledgeable," and in principle they should easily have detected the price-fixing. After 1960, some cooperation continued, in the form of tacit collusion (which is discussed in Subsection III.4).

Steel-Reinforcing Bars.   This small but successful conspiracy began in 1969 at meetings of the Concrete Reinforcing Steel Institute. Large buyers were playing off the sellers against one another. Under this pressure, the sellers found common ground. They agreed upon prices, and arranged ahead of time who would be the low bidder on construction jobs. An antitrust suit stopped the scheme after five years.

Cast-Iron Pipe.   The six leading producers divided the market into several regions and established a price-fixing committee. They controlled two-thirds of sales outside the eastern seaboard. Prices were raised, and an "auction pool" was run to settle who would be the lowest bidder at public lettings. The conspiracy ran for many years until the late 1890s, when it was the target of the first landmark antitrust opinion, which in 1899 declared price-fixing to be flatly illegal.[13]

---

[13] The case was *Addyston Pipe and Steel Co.* v. *United States,* 175 U.S. 211 (1899). Old as it is, the conspiracy was preceded by many others in other industries in many earlier decades.

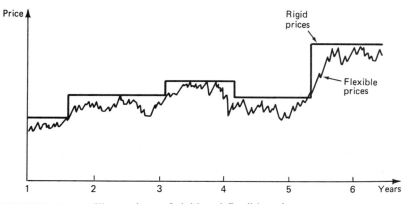

FIGURE 14.1.   Illustrations of rigid and flexible prices.

4. Tacit Collusion[14]

The only way tight oligopolists in the United States can adopt common prices legally is to do it tacitly. They can give indirect signals, such as a series of public statements about "the need to raise prices," which form a consensus for an actual rise. Or the firms may simply learn to coexist and to follow one another's moves to support "orderly" pricing—this is often called "price leadership."

The common pattern is for the oligopolists' prices to be steady for long periods, even when costs and other factors are changing. Then prices change all at once, by a substantial amount. There follows another period of constant prices, and then another jump. The resulting stair-step pattern of prices is illustrated in Figure 14.1.

Such rigidity contrasts with the flexibility and frequent adjustments of genuinely competitive prices, which are also illustrated in Figure 14.1. Either tacit or direct collusion is strongly suggested by the stair-step pattern.

The defense of such prices has been that while the formal (or "book") prices are rigid, they are *not* the prices at which transactions actually occur, but merely a starting point for haggling to get special discounts. Thus real prices are often flexible despite the rigidity of book prices.[15] This may be true of some markets—which is why one always checks carefully to find the true transactions prices—but there are many instances in which stair-step prices have ruled and reflected collusion. The following examples show varying degrees of direct or indirect collusion.

Cigarettes.   In a classic instance, the three main cigarette sellers kept virtually identical prices from 1923 to 1941 and stuck to a tight pattern of price leadership. Prices held steady for long periods—despite large shifts in costs—and then changed suddenly, usually within a day's time. The firms earned an 18 percent return on investment. After 1946, the structure of the industry became somewhat less concentrated and cigarette pricing became less rigid.

---

[14] Other terms for the same behavior are *shared monopoly, conscious parallelism, price signaling, indirect collusion, administered prices,* and, in the U.K., *parallel pricing.*

[15] A full discussion of the role of "actual" versus "list" prices can be found in George J. Stigler and James K. Kindahl, *The Behavior of Industrial Prices* (New York: National Bureau of Economic Research, 1970).

Metals.   Many metals prices have followed stair-step patterns in recent decades: periods of constant, uniform prices, with brief shifts in between. Prices have often stayed stable, or even risen, during periods of slack demand.

These are "list" prices; actual "transactions" prices are occasionally more flexible, as sellers offer various special deals or extras during off-years or add special charges during booms. Nevertheless, the price level stays up, or even rises, during recessions.

Since metals markets differ in structure and technology, the price patterns do not reflect a uniform pricing approach. Yet the pricing is not as freely flexible as a fully competitive structure would provide. Generally the largest firm is the price leader. Thus, for example, the steel industry engaged in formal collusion between 1900 and 1920; from 1920 on into the 1960s, U.S. Steel was usually the price leader, but now leadership rotates and pricing is more flexible.

Turbine Generators.   After the 1960 convictions of electrical equipment firms for price-fixing, sharp competition prevailed in the industry for three years. Then, in May 1963, General Electric announced a new system of pricing with four parts. (1) It greatly simplified the formulas for setting prices and published its method in detail. (2) It added a simple multiplier (.76, to be precise) for converting book prices to actual bids. (3) It promised to put a "price protection" clause into all sales contracts, whereby if GE lowered price for any customer, it was bound to extend the discount—retroactively—to all sales made during the preceding six months. This self-penalty assured Westinghouse that GE would not give selective discounts. (4) All orders and price offers were to be published, so Westinghouse would not fear secret price cuts.[16]

This ingenious plan surrendered all the secret methods and strategies of price competition that make oligopoly competition work for a system of open coordination.

To see this, imagine that GE and Westinghouse have both sold fifteen turbines in six months for $20 million each. But GE wishes to get a major new contract for five turbines by bidding only $18 million each. The retroactive price cut (to $18 million each on the fifteen earlier turbines) would cost it $30 million, besides the $10 million on the five new turbines. That extra $30 million penalty will discourage GE from making the price cut. Moreover, since Westinghouse would know exactly what GE would do, the chances for avoiding competition would be high.

Westinghouse immediately copied GE's plan, even down to the precise numbers in it. Each firm now could coordinate confidently with the other. From 1964, the firms used the same multiplier applied to identical book price levels. There was no price-cutting, no flexibility. The system went beyond simple parallel pricing, but stopped a little short of explicit price-fixing. That GE intended the system to make collusion work is shown by internal company documents.

The parallel pricing was therefore strongly reinforced by advance assurances that price-cutting would not occur, and that if it did, it would be easily detectable. The firms abandoned the system in 1976 after one large buyer sued (American Electric Power, in 1971) and the Antitrust Division threatened to sue.

---

[16] As the Antitrust Division memorandum in support of the consent decree in December 1976 pointed out, customers were even permitted to audit the two sellers' own sales books in order to ensure that no secret price-cutting was occurring. The memorandum is in *U.S.* v. *General Electric Co. and Westinghouse Electric Corp.,* U.S. Dist. Ct., Eastern Dist. of Penna., Civil No. 28228.

Tetracycline Drugs.   In the 1950s, the U.S. makers of tetracycline (a broad-spectrum antibiotic) drugs achieved remarkable identity of prices at levels that yielded very high profits. An antitrust charge of direct conspiracy was not upheld by the Supreme Court. Scherer has suggested that, instead, the firms used obvious "focal points," which led them to identical prices and excess profits.

If focal points were involved, the sellers would still be successful tacit colluders. By sticking to the focal-point prices, they all avoided selective price cutting in the face of strong pressure from some large buyers. The question is how did they manage to agree to stay with the focal points without discussing and agreeing on them directly?

5.   Delivered Pricing (Basing-Point Pricing)

Many goods are sold at delivered prices: the nominal factory price plus a shipping markup equals the actual delivered price. The resulting configuration of prices is like a contour map. Competition may obviously be reduced by delivered pricing if (1) the buyer has no option to buy at the factory instead and ship it himself, and (2) several or all firms adopt the same set of delivered prices. Moreover, delivered pricing distorts the location of industry.

Such schemes and effects were important from the 1880s to 1948 in the steel and cement industries and several others. Since 1948, the practice has been diluted, yet some of its earlier effects live on, and delivered pricing deserves a brief analysis.

Analysis

Delivered pricing matters when output is (1) *uniform* (for example, steel, cement, corn oil), (2) *bulky,* so that transport costs are large, and (3) *centralized* around special inputs (for example, ores, farm products). Consider the simplest system—say, a steel industry whose dominant firm is located at Pittsburgh. That firm (call it U.S. Steel) sets prices at $50 per ton at Pittsburgh plus freight (as shown in Figure 14.2 and publishes a detailed price book listing delivered prices for every city in the country. This is a "Pittsburgh-plus" system, with Pittsburgh as the "basing point."

All other producers reprint the price book as *their* price lists. Result: Buyers at each location face identical prices. A seller (1) whose full cost is below $50, or (2) who has idle capacity, or (3) who wishes to break in and get new clientele does not cut price to do so. *First effect:* Rigid, identical delivered-pricing schemes prevent competition. The identical prices reflect cooperation, not the free play of market forces.[17] This causes the usual losses in efficiency and equity.

---

[17] The degree of identity in prices was often astonishing. During the 1930s, when the purchasing agent for the Fort Peck Dam opened ten sealed bids for reinforcing bars, each of them was for $253,633.80. When the Navy Department opened fifty-nine bids for steel pipe, each of them was for $6,001.83. And when the Army Engineers opened eleven bids for cement at Tucumcari, New Mexico, each of them was for $3.286854 a barrel, identity being carried to the sixth decimal place. Again in 1947, when the Illinois Department of Highways asked for bids on cement to be delivered in each of the 102 counties in the state, those submitted by eight companies were identical for each of the 102 deliveries.

On the anticompetitive effects of delivered pricing, see F. A. Fetter, *The Masquerade of Monopoly* (New York: Harcourt, Brace 1931); "Exit Basing Point Pricing," *American Economic Review,* 38 (1948), 815; and Fritz Machlup, *The Basing Point System* (Philadelphia: Blakiston, 1949).

Arguments on behalf of delivered pricing include J. M. Clark, "The Law and Economics of Basing Points," *American Economic Review,* 39 (1949), 430; and Arthur Smithies, "Aspects of the Basing Point Problem," *American Economic Review,* 32 (1942), 705.

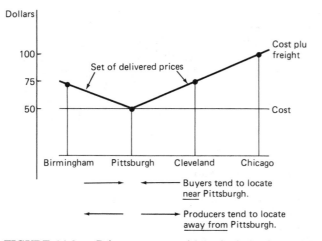

FIGURE 14.2. Price contours with a single basing point.

Location of industry is soon affected in two ways. New steel *makers* may locate away from Pittsburgh, selling at "Pittsburgh-plus" and pocketing the plus as "phantom freight." But they may be punished by being made (perhaps temporarily) a basing point themselves. If so, they will choose to locate at Pittsburgh instead. The net effect may go either way, toward overcentralizing or toward spreading the industry out more thinly than the underlying costs prescribe. Only by a fluke will location happen to be efficient. Meanwhile, steel *users* are induced to locate more closely around Pittsburgh than is efficient. *Second effect:* The location of producers and users may be strongly distorted.

Also, buyers have no incentive to minimize transport costs by buying from a nearby producer. *Third effect:* Transport resources are wasted.

Several basing points may develop. In that case, the locational and transport-wasting effects will be less severe, but they will still exist. Even if every plant is a basing point, new steel plant choices may be affected. And even with universal basing points, the collusive role remains.

Actual systems and treatments

The practice began in steel in 1880, grew slowly until 1890, and by 1900 embraced nearly every steel firm and product. In 1901, the United States Steel Corporation was organized, and from then on, the level of prices was effectively controlled, first through open agreements, later through the Gary dinners, and finally through price leadership. From 1901 to 1903, most steel was sold on a zone price basis. But thereafter all products but rails were priced at Pittsburgh-plus levels.

The system gradually evolved toward multiple basing points after 1920, but it still was a device for collusive pricing in 1946. The cement industry followed a similar pattern from 1902 to 1946, under a trade association. After trying since 1924, the

FTC finally won Supreme Court decisions in 1948–1949 making rigid basing-point pricing illegal.[18]

Delivered pricing has persisted in some industries, usually with multiple basing points. An exceptionally strong recent instance is plywood, which before 1963 was produced in the Northwest but then expanded to the South. More than twenty plywood firms kept prices at the old levels of Northwest-plus-freight, as if the southern mills were all in Portland, Oregon! Buyers near the South therefore paid large amounts of "phantom freight" on $600 million per year of southern plywood. Purchasers were prohibited from buying directly from the mill and using their own trucks for delivery. The system was rigid, universal, and effective.

IV.   OTHER DEVICES: TRADE ASSOCIATIONS AND JOINT VENTURES

1.   Trade Associations

Trade associations and related "technical" cooperative activities also promote cooperation in many cases, but they are too diverse to permit simple judgments. Trade associations are numerous; virtually every industry has at least one. There are aout 2,000 national associations, 3,000 state and regional ones, and 8,000 local ones. Some 70 of these associations have full-time staffs of over 400.[19] Many of them have extensive operations that are bound to increase cooperation.

Trade associations are focused in certain industries—particularly lumber products, electrical equipment, textiles, aerospace industries, and alcoholic beverages. The largest ones are in utilities, various branches of transport, and, above all, the many lines of insurance. Most local trades (such as laundries, real estate, and construction) have frequent meetings and other mutual customs. Generally, trade associations are minimal in very tight oligopolies and merely nominal in very loose oligopolies and atomistic markets.

Trade associations have frequently increased cooperation among sellers. At their regular meetings, members have often gone upstairs to fix prices (as in the electrical equipment conspiracies). And the associations' programs can affect the amount of information disseminated among sellers as a basis for limiting price-cutting.[20]

Some procompetitive effects can occur. The associations' information reporting can help buyers, though it is usually tipped in favor of sellers. Some associations are among lesser firms, aiming to strengthen them against the dominant firms. Others try to exert countervailing power on behalf of their many small members (for example, the purchasing associations of small grocers).

---

[18] Other efforts had been made against basing-point pricing in cement, corn products, malt, milk cans, crepe paper, rigid steel conduits and bottle caps, among others.

[19] See U. S. Department of Commerce, *Directory of National Associations of Businessmen* (Washington, D.C.: Government Printing Office, issued occasionally).

[20] A celebrated antitrust decision held that such a price information system among sellers of cardboard boxes would chill price-cutting. Each seller could call up competitors and demand instant disclosure of the latest price offered. Buyers were not included in this privilege. By shortening the time before price cuts were disclosed to competitors, the scheme did discourage price-cutting. See *U.S.* v. *Container Corp. of America*, 393 U.S. 333 (1969).

Though many trade associations may have trivial effects, and a few may be procompetitive, the general effect has probably been to raise the degree of cooperation in pricing. Since each case is a little different, one needs to judge individually and carefully.

2. Joint Ventures

Many *joint ventures* have been created by competing firms, usually for some laudable purpose, such as to perform research or operate mines. They are extensive in many industries, especially steel, copper, oil, and chemicals. The usual claim is that the resources of two firms (or more in some cases) are needed to support the activity. This may be true in some situations, so that net increases in production or innovation do result, yet it is perfectly clear that joint ventures can coalesce interests and inhibit competition.

The desired effect would be a balance between these two directions. Most joint ventures are rather small units held by large firms,[21] which suggests that the concentrative effect is relatively strong compared to the possible increase in production and innovation.

In the U.S. oil industry, over sixty joint-venture pipelines for oil and oil products knit together all large oil firms shipping to virtually all significant markets.[22] The lines are built to fit their owners' locations and needs. Also, the partners have to coordinate their flows in each pipeline. This ensures that the firms cannot take sharp competitive moves against one another, and that outsiders cannot use the pipelines to enter the market.

The joint scheduling systems have a variety of exclusive and collaborative features unnecessary to the pipelines' financing and operation. The pipelines could instead be financed, built, and operated as independent units, open to all comers. As it is, they increase the degree of cooperation in the oil industry at the refining and marketing levels.

In 1982, a major joint venture was announced by General Motors and Toyota Motors of Japan involving a West Coast plant that Toyota would operate to produce cars to be sold by General Motors. Thereby the leading U.S. producer allied itself with its leading foreign competitor. The tie clearly would reduce competition between these major competitors and give them jointly more influence over the market. Ford and Chrysler both challenged the venture, but it was approved (after intense debate) by the Federal Trade Commission. Whatever net technical benefits it might provide are small, because each firm separately could achieve them. Therefore the anticompetitive effect is not offset by efficiencies. Even if one redefined the automobile market to include all worldwide production, the two partners would still hold nearly

[21] Stanley E. Boyle, "An Estimate of the Number and Size Distribution of Domestic Joint Subsidiaries," *Antitrust Law and Economics Review*, 2 (Spring 1968), 81–92. But see also Sanford V. Berg and Philip Friedman, "Causes and Effects of Joint Venture Activity: Knowledge Acquisition versus Parent Horizontality," *Antitrust Bulletin*, 25 (Spring 1980), 143–68; and Berg and Friedman, "Impacts of Domestic Joint Ventures on Industrial Rates of Return: A Pooled Cross-Section Analysis, 1964–1975," *Review of Economics and Statistics*, 63 (May 1981), 293–98.

[22] The biggest two are the Colonial and Plantation pipelines, which connect the Texas and the New Jersey areas. Colonial is owned jointly by eight of the eleven largest U.S. oil firms; Plantation by the other three largest.

50 percent of it. This case therefore illustrates the anticompetitive possibilities of small joint ventures between firms with large market shares.

QUESTIONS FOR REVIEW

1. "A cartel must control price, output, investment, and profits in order to have much effect on competition." True.
2. "Focal points make it more difficult for explicit or tacit collusion to succeed." True?
3. "Price-fixing is least likely to be found in tight oligopolies." True?
4. "OPEC is a complete cartel." True?
5. "Price-fixing usually adds only about 3 percent to the level of price." True?
6. "Unless the conspiring firms control all sales in the market, they cannot hope to raise price appreciably." True?
7. "A system in which a firm pledges not to offer discounts will generally discourage price cooperation." True?
8. "Trade associations always reduce competition." True?
9. Which conditions favor the coordination of prices?
10. Does overt cooperation occur mainly in loose and medium oligopolies? Explain.
11. What items of behavior does a complete cartel control?
12. How might joint ventures decrease competition? Increase it?
13. A group of bidders for highway paving contracts never submits identical bids. Yet somehow they spread the work evenly among all of them, in a regular rotation. Could there be bid-rigging?
14. Explain why tangible price-fixing may be unusual in tight oligopolies, even though the pay-offs for it may be high.
15. Suppose that in the 1960s, General Electric had sold $100 million of generators every month. It considers cutting price by $20 million. Show how much its six-month "price protection" policy would cost it from such a price cut. Would that discourage price-cutting?
16. Explain why basing-point pricing biases location decisions, by encouraging customers to locate near plants and competitors to locate away from them.
17. When General Motors and Toyota set up a joint-venture to make cars in California, why might that have had anticompetitive effects?

15

VERTICAL CONDITIONS, SIZE, AND DIVERSIFICATION

Vertical and conglomerate issues have always been a sideline to the main horizontal conditions of markets. They can be important in some cases, and they pose intriguing problems. But they are tricky to measure and to evaluate. And it may be, as some analysts claim, that vertical and conglomerate conditions do not affect competition at all, or at least not very much.

This chapter presents the main issues that have drawn sharp debate. Monopsony (or countervailing power) is the exertion backward of buyers' market power against sellers. Its role is covered in the first section. Vertical integration may permit economies *and* anticompetitive effects, including "squeezes." Vertical mergers and vertical restrictions on markets (including resale price maintenance) also pose competitive issues. Sections II and III cover them.

Next we turn to large size and diversification, which have been common conditions for more than a century. Both are secondary elements in judging the degree of market power and its effects, yet in extreme cases they can influence the market outcome sharply. The debate about them has often run to excess, with extravagant claims and criticisms. Indeed, firms that are "giant" and/or "conglomerate" may deeply affect society, but the directions and force of their influences are debatable. The core of knowledge about the *economic* roles of size and diversification is small and tentative.

Size is analyzed in the fourth section: How does one define it, and what are its likely effects? Section V appraises four specific ways in which diversification may restrict competition: by cross-subsidizing, reciprocal buying, reducing potential competition, and spheres of influence.

I. BILATERAL MONOPOLY

Pure monopsony consists of one buyer for an entire market. We usually assume the opposite condition: atomistic buyers, none holding any monopsony power. Yet many combinations are possible, as Figure 15.1 shows. The oligopoly-oligopsony middle ranges can become very complex. Only the three shaded areas give a de-

Buyers: Degree of Monopoly (Concentration)

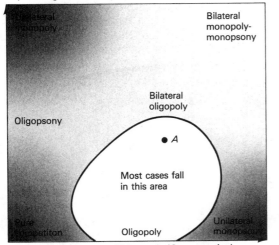

Sellers: Degree of Monopoly (Concentration)
FIGURE 15.1.   There are many varieties of vertical structure.

terminate result. At each point in the rest of the figure, the outcomes are not definite; they depend on the bargaining struggle between sellers and buyers.[1]

1. Pricing Within a Range

In fact, most markets probably lie in the round area drawn onto Figure 15.1; that is, they have some degree of oligopoly facing a lesser degree of oligopsony. The products of most industries fan out among many different user industries.[2] Buyer concentration is probably much lower than seller concentration, on the whole.[3] Few important monopsony shares over 40 percent are known (apart from some small local instances). Even tight oligopsony is uncommon except for some narrowly defined products. Monopsony power is a problem focused on a narrow range of cases. Most analysis ignores it, assuming it is minor.

Theory suggests that monopsony can promote good social performance *if* certain conditions are favorable.[4] Consider the bilateral monopoly illustrated in Figure 15.2.

[1] Moreover, each point in the middle range of Figure 15.1 can represent an array of different oligopoly and oligopsony structures. Thus point *A* may represent a 60 percent oligopoly with four 15 percent firms, or one firm with 54 percent and three with 2 percent each, or many other variations. The 40 percent oligopsony at point *A* may be four 10 percent firms, or many other sharply different patterns.

[2] This can be seen most clearly in the input-output tables of the U.S. economy prepared for various years. Each industry commonly sells the bulk of its output to more than five industrial and retailing sectors.

[3] Yet there are no reliable, comprehensive data. No data corresponding to the census concentration ratios for sellers are prepared. And informal information about prominent cases is much less extensive than it is for dominant-firm sellers (recall Chapter 10). Some evidence is given in Ralph L. Nelson, *Concentration in the Manufacturing Industries of the United States: A Mid-century Report* (New Haven, Conn.: Yale University Press, 1963).

[4] The leading discussions in the literature include A. L. Bowley, "Bilateral Monopoly," *Economic Journal,* 38 (December 1928), 651–59; James N. Morgan, "Bilateral Monopoly and the Competitive Output," *Quarterly Journal of Economics,* 63 (August 1949), 371–91; and James W. McKie, *Tin Cans and Tin Plate* (Cambridge, Mass.: Harvard University Press, 1959).

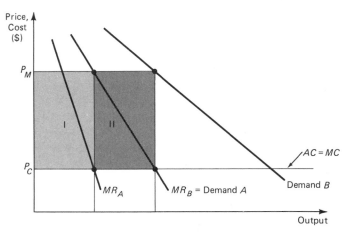

FIGURE 15.2.   Bilateral monopoly illustrated.

Firm A sells its product to firm B, which simply resells it to final consumers. D_B is the final demand curve faced by firm B. It has a marginal revenue curve MR_B, but that curve is also the effective *demand* curve (D_A) for firm A's output. It has a corresponding marginal revenue curve MR_A. To simplify the analysis, firm A's cost of supply is assumed to be constant, so that average and marginal cost are identical at that constant level.

The monopsonist firm B prefers to buy from firm A at the competitive price P_C. Then it can resell the output at the higher (monopoly) price P_M. But this clashes with firm A's choice. Firm A wants to collect the price P_M in selling to firm B so *its* profits will be maximized. If firm A prevails, it gains the excess profits shown by area I. If firm B wins (and buys at price P_C rather than P_M), its excess profits are areas I and II.

The price paid to firm A by firm B is not determinate; firm A prefers price P_M, while the monopsonist firm B prefers to pay as little as possible, at price P_C. The matter is strictly a private struggle between them. The final price and output levels are given; the firms simply fight over the spoils.

If monopsonist firm B faces effective competition as a *seller,* then it may neutralize firm A's monopoly power. Suppose that firm B's competitors can sell at price P_C (drawing their supplies from other sources). Then firms A and B must meet price P_C if they are to survive. So firm B's status as a *seller* can be crucial. Though it may seem improbable that a monopsonist could sell under competitive conditions, a little thought should satisfy you that it is quite possible. Sears, Roebuck or big discounting chains could be good examples. It is from the final level that pressure may be exerted backward to hold the bilateral monopoly to competitive results.

Bilateral oligopoly follows much the same lines as bilateral monopoly, though, of course, the effects are not as sharp or clear. Powerful buyers will now play off the sellers against each other, extracting low input prices. Some will threaten to integrate vertically. The sellers will be charging "what the traffic will bear," in line with demand elasticities.

The whole process breeds price discrimination, along the lines covered in the last chapter. The net tendency toward restrictive or competitive results will still depend on the oligopsonists' status as *sellers*. Given the endless variety of oligopoly structures at each level, the subject is a jungle of theoretical possibilities. But the possibility of "countervailing power" is a major feature.

2.   Countervailing Power

Note that monopsony is an attractive position. Locate a monopolist, interpose yourself as a monopsonist retailer, and then you can cream off some or all of the monopolist's profit for yourself. J. K. Galbraith urged in 1952 that precisely this would happen to most oligopolies: "As a common rule, we can rely on countervailing power to appear as a curb on economic power."[5] The result could be ideal—oligopolies would achieve economies of scale and pursue innovation, but their market power would be neutralized. Strong retailers were among the units of "countervailing power" that Galbraith cited.

Later debate has shrunk the scope of such spontaneous countervailing power. Many dominant firms are able to prevent monopsony power by elaborate sales networks (computers, drugs, and copiers), passive dealer systems (automobiles), and other marketing policies. Some other monopolies (such as most "utilities") have technology that automatically excludes new monopsonists.

Yet the process of countervailing power is at work. Where technical conditions permit, it can be important, as the spread of discount chains attests. An example is private-label brands. Many food items (such as soup, coffee, and flour mixes) are sold by dominant firms under their own brand names, at premium prices. These firms often supply the same products with the chain grocers' own brand labels pasted on, at much lower prices. Chains are always trying to force suppliers to a private-label basis. Where they succeed, price is usually lower than under the original brands. (Conspicuous failures include most cereals, soda pop, beer, and razors.) Monopsony *plus* competitive selling at retail gives a good social result.

Monopoly-monopsony power blocs can, instead, retain the monopoly effects if conditions permit. One possible example is large-scale union power in major tight oligopoly and monopoly industries. The effect may be (1) to transfer some of the oligopolists' profits to workers and (2) to strengthen the pair of units as a whole power bloc. This has been a structural source of inflation in the last three decades, which frustrated macroeconomic policies from 1946 to 1953 and from 1966 to 1982.

II.   VERTICAL INTEGRATION

1.   Defining and Measuring Integration[6]

Definition.   The production of any good usually involves a series of stages in which raw materials are first extracted, then processed into intermediate goods, assembled, finished, and eventually distributed as final products. For example, steel

---

[5] John Kenneth Galbraith, *American Capitalism: The Theory of Countervailing Power* (Boston: Houghton Mifflin, 1952).

[6] Among the leading treatments of this topic, see Morris A. Adelman's chapter on integration in George J. Stigler, ed., *Business Concentration and Price Policy,* (Princeton, N.J.: Princeton University Press, 1955); Michael Gort, *Integration and Diversification in American Industry* (Princeton, N.J.: Princeton University Press, 1962); Frederick R. Warren-Boulton, *Vertical Control of Markets: Business and Labor Practice* (Cambridge, Mass.: Ballinger Publishing, 1978), and Robert D. Blair and David L. Kaserman, *Antitrust Economics* (Homewood, Ill.: Irwin, 1985).

products begin with the mining and shipping of ores, and they emerge at the end after smelting, fabricating, and finishing. When a local baker bakes loaves in the back and sells them in the front of the store, there at least two stages of production. The baker may also keep the accounts and clean the premises, both of which could also be done by hired outside services.

Vertical integration is the joinder of two or more of these successive stages of production. In theory, the integration can be total, from the raw ore to the distribution of final products to consumers. All transfers of goods at each stage would then be internal, occurring among the branches of the vertically integrated firm. Or, if the firms at each stage were separately owned, production could occur with no vertical integration at all. Each stage's outputs would then be sold to the next by transactions on open markets.

In practice, virtually all firms have intermediate degrees of integration. That is, they combine some successive operations, but they also buy inputs from other firms and their own outputs are sold to others for further processing or distribution. In the stream of production, firms can do upstream—or "backward"—integration, and downstream—or "forward"—integration.

Between nonintegrated firms, goods pass from one stage to the next by arm's-length market transactions, at the going market prices. In contrast, integrated firms transfer the goods by internal shifts, valuing them at internal transfer prices. Those prices need not equal the current market prices; they can be arbitrarily set according to the firm's internal motives and systems.

It is important to recognize at the outset that integration can be a matter of degrees and shadings rather than strict yes-no conditions. The market transactions can be tight long-term contracts that provide nearly as much control as direct ownership. And the controls actually applied under integration can be on a highly delegated basis, with little actual exertion of authority.

There are many reasons to integrate, as we will shortly see, but many firms remain independent. Markets often contain firms with widely differing degrees of vertical integration. The determinants of the scope of vertical integration are a complex matter, and there is often much blurring.

Whether integration can affect monopoly power is a hotly disputed issue. Chicago-UCLA economists argue that integration cannot transfer (or "lever") monopoly power from one level to another, nor create more market power than exists from horizontal conditions. The opposite view is that integration, in displacing open transactions, forecloses the market and therefore can exclude rivals from access to market supply or sales.

To examine this problem, we first note how integration can be defined and measured, and next the reasons why firms adopt it. Then we consider its likely effects and the policies that have been applied to vertical mergers.

Measurement. Though the meaning of vertical integration is intuitively simple, it is surprisingly hard to measure. One method is to count "stages of production"; the greater the number of stages embraced, the greater the integration. But defining the stages is often a matter of judgment and debate. A "stage" can include many individual steps. Alternatively, one can take the ratio of a firm's value added to its final sales revenue as an index of its degree of integration. An integrated producer adds value by processing at many stages, so its ratio would be high. A retailer, by contrast, adds little value, so its ratio would be low. Yet this method also has its faults. Some one-stage industries have high value added (that is, the processing is extensive, though simple)—bricks are an example. Other industries have many stages, each of which adds little value. Moreover, the ratio of value added to sales tends to be smaller for industries that are further along in the chain of production, so comparisons of industries using this simple ratio are subject to systematic bias.

Therefore there is no perfect measure, nor even a very good one. Since no official indexes of integration are published, the research lessons about its existence and effects are not clear.

A widespread but elusive phenomenon, integration poses important riddles that may never be answered precisely. It appears to close out the market and permit anticompetitive actions. For decades, the U.S. Supreme Court treated it as dangerous to competition, barring vertical mergers with as little as 5 percent of market sales. Since 1970, vertical conditions have stirred extensive writing and litigation.

2.   Reasons for Vertical Integration

There are three categories of reasons why firms adopt vertical integration: (1) to achieve efficiencies, (2) to avoid government burdens, and (3) to take advantage of monopoly-related conditions. We consider them in turn.

Efficiencies

These divide further into two main types: technical conditions and savings on transactions costs.

Technical Savings.   Some efficiencies are *physical*. Heat and transport resources can be saved by, for instance, smelting iron in blast furnaces adjacent to the steel mills. Pig iron can be fed in immediately, rather than having to be shipped over distances and reheated. Other metals may also be combined more efficiently.

Other savings come from better *organization*. Operations at the two (or more) stages may be coordinated more smoothly. Scheduling can be directly planned, among all operations, without risk of default or external failures.

Transactions Costs.   Williamson has stressed the value of reducing transactions costs. By owning and directly controlling their own operations, integrated firms can avoid the costs of searching for the best and cheapest suppliers, negotiating the complex terms of contracts, monitoring the flows and qualities of inputs, and enforcing contractual provisions on less-than-reliable suppliers. Williamson cites several basic conditions that favor integration.[7]

One is "bounded rationality," which means the limits on knowing what is happening in markets. Human beings cannot process and interpret unlimited details

---

[7] Oliver E. Williamson, "The Economics of Antitrust: Transaction Cost Considerations," *University of Pennsylvania Law Review,* 122 (May 1974), 1439–96.

about market conditions, while at the same time seeking to make rational profit-maximizing decisions. Integration offers a way to reduce that burden.

Another condition favoring integration is "opportunism," which means the wayward tendencies of suppliers to mislead, cheat, and generally underperform. An integrated firm minimizes these hazards by owning and directly controlling its own suppliers.

Avoiding government restrictions

Taxes.   When taxes are levied on the sale of raw materials or intermediate goods, there is an incentive to integrate because the internal transfer of the goods escapes the tax. Thus the downstream unit has lower costs than its nonintegrated competitors.

A separate tax incentive arises if the tax rates on the various stages of production differ. The firm will gain by integrating to the lower-taxed stage and then using transfer pricing to minimize the total tax. This has been important in the oil industry, where extracting oil is taxed at lower rates than refining it. By integrating and using adroit transfer pricing, the larger oil firms have reduced their taxes, in some cases to zero.

Utility Regulation.   The traditional U.S. form of regulating natural monopolies has set limits on their profit rates (see Chapter 20). The firms are permitted to obtain an adequate rate of return on their invested assets, after all costs are covered. This indirectly rewards a firm for integrating backward into supplying its inputs, including its capital equipment.

The integrated utility seeks to charge itself high transfer prices on its inputs, as much as it can get the regulators to accept. At the extreme, if the regulators permit unrestricted raising of the inputs' prices, the monopoly firm is able to exploit its utility monopoly as fully as if it were entirely unregulated.

This motive probably partly explains AT&T's fierce defense of the vertical integration of Western Electric into it from 1881 to 1984. Western Electric supplied virtually all of the old Bell System's capital inputs. Though AT&T asserted that this system produced only economies and no overcharging, the issue was hotly debated. Eventually it was a strong reason for the vertical divestiture forced upon AT&T by the government in 1984 (see Chapter 19).

Price Controls.   Suppose that an input is put under price controls. This happened to oil in the United States during the 1970s, and governments have done it on many other occasions. Backward integration by the users of the input will remove it from open-market transactions and therefore from the price control. If all users of the input integrate backward, the price control can be nullified completely.

Monopoly-related incentives to integrate

Over six specific types of monopoly-related incentives have been identified. They either raise the firm's ability to charge monopoly prices, or they strengthen its ability to avoid paying monopoly prices for its inputs. Here we will consider only three of the most important incentives.

Raising Barriers to Entry.   If most or all of a market's supply is contained within integrated firms, then independent and new firms may find it necessary to have capacity at both levels, fearing that otherwise they will be unable to obtain sufficiently secure and reasonably priced supplies. That double-level necessity may impose increased costs, so that entry barriers are raised.

The clearest form of this increased cost is the greater capital that is required to set up new capacity at both levels. Unless capital markets are perfect (recall Chapter 10), the resulting rise in barriers can be important. There may also be additional risk from creating two new production entities rather than just one. Capital markets may then impose a risk premium on the cost of capital.

Crucial inputs may also be controlled, which would, again, raise barriers. Many industries use inputs that are in limited supply or that have distinct differences in quality. Ores are one example; some lodes are superior to others, and the total supply is limited. Oil, specialized locations, rights to inventions, and copyrights are further examples; owning these can give a firm a cost advantage over rivals, or even exclude competitors altogether.

Vertical integration into those levels can reduce competition at the downstream levels. In addition, firms may take strategic actions that "raise rivals' costs."[8] Only if all market processes are perfect will the previous owners of the assets extract all profits from the assets in advance. So again, the monopoly-creating effects of integration hinge on the degree of imperfections in markets.

Vertical "Squeezes."[9]   Nonintegrated firms complain chronically about being "squeezed." Table 15.1 illustrates such an episode. Firm A supplies ingots to itself and others at $1,000 per ton. The ingots are then processed into pots and pans and sold by all parties at $2,000 per ton. Firm A's ingot price to itself is a "shadow" price. It now raises the ingot price to $1,490. This changes its total accounting costs of pots and pans to $1,990, but it now makes $490 more profit per ton on ingots. The other firms, however, have no such accounting balance. Their profits are actually "squeezed" down to $10 per ton for pots and pans, which may be below their cost of capital. They are certainly less profitable; they may even go out of business. Yet firm A's total profit is unchanged.

Such "squeezes" are possible wherever "tapered" integration occurs (that is, integrated firms sell both to themselves and to independents). But are "squeezes" rational? Perhaps firm A's ability to manipulate price arises just from its monopoly of ingots. That, and not the integration, would make the "squeeze" possible.

But integration can be a factor, again because market conditions are not perfect. If uncertainty and barriers are present, the threat of squeezes can make small independents more passive and keep new entrants out. Without the integration, these reductions in competition at the second level could not be so great.

---

[8] See Steven C. Salop and David Scheffman, "Raising Rivals' Costs," *American Economic Review,* 73 (May 1983), 263–71; and Thomas G. Krattenmaker and Steven C. Salop, "Competition and Cooperation in the Market for Exclusionary Rights," *American Economic Review,* 76 (May 1986), 109–13.

[9] There are no classic discussions of the "squeeze" phenomenon. Rather, there have been analyses and complaints concerning a series of specific industries, such as steel and aluminum. On aluminum, see the Alcoa decision, *U.S.* v. *Aluminum Company of America,* et al., 148 F.2d 416 (2d Cir. 1945); and Merton J. Peck, *Competition in the Aluminum Industry* (Cambridge, Mass.: Harvard University Press, 1961).

TABLE 15.1   Illustration of a "Squeeze"

	INTEGRATED DOMINANT FIRM		OTHER FIRMS NOT INTEGRATED	
	First Price ($/ton)	Second Price ($/ton)	First Price ($/ton)	Second Price ($/ton)
First Level:				
Aluminum ingot				
Cost	$ 800	$ 800	$—	$—
Price	1,000	1,490	—	—
Profit	200	690	—	—
Second Level:				
Aluminum products				
Cost (ingot price plus fabricating)	1,500	1,990	1,500	1,990
Price	2,000	2,000	2,000	2,000
Profit	500	10	500	10
Total profit	$ 700	$ 700	$ 500	$ 10

Generally, market imperfections of all kinds make some degree of squeeze a true possibility and link it with integration. Note, too, that integration prevents the rise of monopsony, which could neutralize the market power at earlier levels. That issue was stressed in Section I as an important point in evaluating vertical structure. This indirect effect alone could give integration a major role in reducing competitive performance below what it might be.

Neutralizing Upstream Monopoly.   When a firm at level B, holding some monopoly power, faces a supplier from level A, exerting monopoly power, backward integration can raise the B-level firm's profits by assuring supplies at lower prices. Otherwise the B-level firm is prey to strategic actions and threats by its supplier, which raise its input cost.

The problem is likely to grow worse over time because of "asset specificity."[10] The B-level firm will inevitably invest in capacity that is specific to its suppliers, and that will reduce its choice among alternative suppliers. As a result, entry or competition by other suppliers will be more difficult and costly.

To escape the price-raising impacts of this, the B-level firm may integrate backward into level A. This kind of integration occurs not for the sake of efficiency, but to offset monopoly. Yet the outcome is an even more powerful two-level monopoly whose ability to exploit its position by raising its prices will not be less than what it was before, and may be more.

Against all these possibilities that integration may increase monopoly power rather than just achieve efficiencies there has stood for forty years an uncompromising counterhypothesis: *that integration does not raise monopoly power at all.*

---

[10] Michael H. Riordan and Oliver E. Williamson, "Asset Specificity and Economic Organization," *International Journal of Industrial Organization,* 3 (December 1985), 365–78; and Oliver E. Williamson, "Vertical Integration and Related Variations on Transaction-Cost Economies Themes," in Joseph E. Stiglitz and G. Frank Mathewson, eds., *New Developments in the Analysis of Market Structure* (Cambridge, Mass.: MIT Press, 1986).

We shall examine this Chicago-UCLA hypothesis against the effects of integration in the market.

In a frictionless, well-functioning market system, integration would be done only when it gives technical economies.[11] Integration could not serve as a lever to extend monopoly power from one level to another. Monopoly may exist at one or more levels and have its usual effects, but that horizontal condition is the only proper focus for concern.

At each level, production occurs and a profit margin is added, whether or not integration exists. The final price charged by the integrated firm will contain the cumulative production costs and no greater total profit margin. If there are economies of integration, the final price can be lower.

Imperfections.   This view of integration has been a fixture in the literature, and it does have a large kernel of truth. Yet the issues are not so pure. Under some conditions, integration can raise market power, as we have seen. Markets are not pure and frictionless, with perfect certainty and free entry.[12] When market shares are substantial and imperfections are significant, some monopoly-raising effects are likely. The real question is: At what market share are the effects likely to become important: 10 percent, 25 percent, 40 percent?

The answer depends on concepts and facts that came up in earlier chapters: (1) the degree of competition in capital markets, (2) the role of entry barriers, and (3) the extent of uncertainty and market imperfections generally. It would depend also on a thorough analysis of actual behavior in industries with vertical integration. No such study has yet been done. Most recent research has been on a hypothetical level, with fairly simple models.

One case does show that vertical factors can govern price decisions. Steel pricing in the United States after 1955 was designed to preserve the vertical structure of oligopoly prices.[13] When the prices of imported steel dropped to 40 percent below U.S. prices for wire rods and wire products, U.S. integrated firms chose not to meet the new price. Doing so would have forced revisions over a wide range of steel products, at various vertical stages of production, and this would have risked a collapse of oligopoly-pricing discipline at several levels.

By contrast, the nonintegrated oligopolists did cut prices to meet the import competition. Integration therefore led the larger firms to accept a drastic loss in sales to imports (and a corresponding loss of jobs). This was not a classical "squeeze"; here the oligopolists endured damage because of vertical conditions. Still, vertical integration clearly affected pricing decisions.

---

[11] Original statements of the hypothesis are by Morris A. Adelman, in "Integration and Antitrust Policy," *Harvard Law Review,* 63 (November 1949), 27–77; and Joseph J. Spengler, "Vertical Integration and Antitrust Policy," *Journal of Political Economy,* 58 (August 1950), 347–52. Robert H. Bork restated the ideas in "Vertical Integration and the Sherman Act: The Legal History of an Economic Misconception," *University of Chicago Law Review,* 22 (Autumn 1954), 157–201.

[12] See Joe S. Bain's discussion in *Industrial Organization,* rev. ed. (New York: Wiley, 1968). Arrow notes that vertical integration to reduce uncertainty of supply may commonly eliminate competition, even if no other vertical economies exist. See Kenneth J. Arrow, "Vertical Integration and Communication," *Bell Journal of Economics,* 6 (Spring 1975), 173–83.

[13] See the analysis by Walter Adams and Joel B. Dirlam, "Steel Imports and Vertical Oligopoly Power," *American Economic Review,* 54 (June 1964), 626–55.

3.   Vertical Mergers

Mergers for integration have posed the issues with special clarity. Antitrust decisions have stopped some vertical mergers and shed some light on their role.

Net Economies, Compared to The Alternatives.   Mergers are only one of several ways to achieve the benefits of vertical integration. Internal growth can provide the integration, though it takes longer. Such internal growth also adds new capacity and new competition. Long-term contracts often reduce risk and provide coordination as fully as integration would. (An iron-clad thirty-year ore-supply contract from firm X can be virtually as binding and reassuring to a metals producer as owning firm X would be.) There are many such "captive suppliers" operating on that basis.

The net effects of vertical mergers are therefore a balance between two things:

1.   Those *net economies* gained by merger that could *not* be obtained by direct growth or long-term contracts.
2.   The possible *anticompetitive effects,* such as from raising barriers to entry.

The anticompetitive effects are not likely to be large, as we saw in the section just above. Yet the net economies from merger are also likely to be small, because other ways (direct growth and contracts) are also available. In extreme cases, of course, a vertical merger's costs or benefits (or both) could be large. Large costs could arise if the two merging firms are both heavily dominant at their levels, and capital barriers are high at one level.

In fact, high market shares raise a presumption that the social costs of a vertical merger exceed the benefits. The imbalance is not usually large, and some exceptional cases will lean the other way. No clear research measures have yet emerged so the threshold levels of market shares can only be guessed at. The consensus among experts would probably be in the range of 15 to 30 percent market shares for the two firms. Before 1980, the antitrust limits were set at about 10 to 20 percent.[14] A vertical merger between two 10 percent firms would probably not be challenged, but a vertical merger between two 20 percent firms would probably be resisted and, in the end, not permitted.

After 1980, Reagan officials applied Chicago-UCLA doctrine and stopped all resistance to vertical mergers (see Chapter 19). The correct policy margin remains an open issue. The following landmark antitrust cases offer a basis for judgment.

Du Pont–General Motors.   Since the 1920s, E. I. Du Pont de Nemours, the chemical company, had held a large percentage of General Motors stock.[15] General Motors had long bought much of its paint and fabric from Du Pont. During 1946–1947, Du Pont's share was 67 percent of GM's paint purchases, and over 40 percent of GM's fabric supplies. These shares were above Du Pont's market shares in the

---

[14] See William G. Shepherd, *Public Policies Toward Business,* 7th ed. (Homewood, Ill.: Irwin, 1985), Chap. 7.

[15] The share was 23 percent of all GM stock. Du Pont's purchase of the stock was made during 1917–1919, with funds from divestiture of a Du Pont factory and from large war profits on gunpowder. Pierre S. Du Pont became GM's chairman during the crucial period before 1926. Details of the Du Pont–GM relationship were brought out by the Antitrust Division's suit; the eventual decision is *U.S.* v. *E. I. Du Pont de Nemours & Co.,* 353 U.S. 586 (1957).

whole markets. Deciding a suit filed in 1949, the Supreme Court in 1957 held the shareholding to be illegal because it reduced competition in the two specific markets.

The matter may seem trivial compared to the large scale of the two firms. But the burden from severing this link was also small, since no direct loss or managerial disruption was involved. The Court was willing to lean toward strictness where no technical benefit was threatened.

Brown Shoe.   Brown Shoe Co., which held about 4 to 10 percent in various U.S. shoe markets in 1955, planned to merge with Kinney, a shoe producer and retailing chain with 2 percent of U.S. retail shoe sales. Since Brown also retailed shoes in competition with Kinney (and Kinney also produced some shoes), the merger raised both horizontal and vertical issues. It was prohibited in 1962, partly on horizontal grounds, though the vertical feature was also cited by the Supreme Court. The vertical joinder would have given Brown the chance to tip Kinney's purchases toward Brown shoes, to the exclusion of other shoe makers.[16] Though the horizontal shares seemed very low on a national basis, some of the urban and regional shares were in the 20 to 30 percent range. Therefore the vertical foreclosure could have significantly affected the outcome in some markets.

Thus the Court again leaned toward strictness. Direct growth or other means were available as alternatives to the merger. Though the costs and benefits were not precisely measured, this case set the precedent for policy. As of 1989, Kinney and Brown are still independent shoe firms, and whatever gain or loss in efficiency that occurred because of the Court's decision has probably been minor. Yet it was a precedent-setting case, and it stirred an almost hysterical Chicago-UCLA opposition to the tight new merger policy.[17]

III.   VERTICAL RESTRICTIONS

Vertical restrictions have drawn increasing debate since 1960, as antitrust cases have proliferated. Moreover, Chicago-UCLA economists have made them a battleground to prove that vertical restraints are usually beneficial rather than harmful. The discussions include mainly (1) territorial restrictions and (2) resale price maintenance.

1.   Territorial Restrictions

Manufacturers often limit their dealers to specific areas. For example, Coca-Cola, Pepsi-Cola, and the other soft drink companies set exact local areas in which each of their bottlers is permitted to deliver. Any delivery outside the area (that is,

---

[16] "Vertical foreclosure" was more likely because Brown had consistently followed that kind of behavior in the past, requiring newly acquired retail chains to shift their purchasing to Brown. Brown's president had also made a number of statements favoring such foreclosure.

[17] For polemics, see Robert H. Bork, "The Crash of Merger Policy: The *Brown Shoe* Decision", Chapter 9 in his *The Antitrust Paradox*, (New York: Basic Books, 1978). A more reasoned critique is given in John L. Peterman, "The Brown Shoe Case," *Journal of Law and Economics,* 18 (April 1975), 81–146. Also see the sober appraisal in Philip Areeda and Donald F. Turner, Jr., *Antitrust Policy,* (Boston: Little, Brown, 1978). The case itself is *Brown Shoe Co. v. United States,* 370 U.S. 294 (1962).

any competition with another bottler) can cost the bottler the franchise. With territorial restrictions, the producer reaches forward to prevent competition among its sellers at the retail level. That clearly reduces competition.

The local distributors usually prefer to be given large, *exclusive* franchise areas. In fact, they press the national suppliers to set such franchises. Yet all of them are prey to conflicting incentives. If only they could invade their neighbors' areas, they could raise profits; but counterinvasions by those neighbors would hurt profits. So, as a group, distributors and dealers usually prevail upon the supplier to rigidly divide up the markets to prevent them from competing. In addition, they fear the many local dealers aspiring to new franchises, for if they were to succeed, that would shrink and weaken the existing dealers.

The national supplier normally prefers to have a maximum of competition at the wholesale and retail levels, because that expands the level of output that it can sell at its profit-maximizing price. When franchises are restricted, the added degree of monopoly reduces competition and output. This shrinkage in volume shrinks the supplier's profits. The question then, is: Why do suppliers set such exclusive franchises, since they seem to be against their own interests?

The literature has identified two classes of reasons for these vertical restraints: those creating market power and those promoting efficiency.

CREATING MARKET POWER. The *market power* reasons simply note that the restraints eliminate competition, often by direct price-fixing enforced by specific contracts. Market power is created and exercised, with all the usual harms (recall Chapter 2).

PROMOTING EFFICIENCY. The *efficiency* reasons cite either transactions costs or the support of high-quality dealer networks. Williamson has stressed that supply contracts often involve high costs in searching out good dealers and assuring their performance in promoting the good.[18] The restraints permit organizing and enforcing dealer networks to avoid many of these costs.

The dealer-quality reasons are essentially two.

BUILDING UP A SMALL FIRM. The supplier may be trying to develop a new market position. To attract retailers, it may reward them with protected market areas and extra profits. If this strategy succeeds in helping the supplier build up its market share and challenge the existing market leaders, then the restrictions will promote competition at both levels. But that would hold only during the buildup phase. As with price discrimination, actions that would reduce competition when taken by dominant firms can promote competition when done by small or new firms.

SUPPORTING QUALITY SERVICE AGAINST "FREE RIDERS". The supplier may seek to have its products carried by "high-quality" dealers (as in bookstores, automobiles, cameras and supplies, and stereo equipment). Quality involves extra advice and service for customers, stocking more models and parts, and reliability and trustworthiness in backing the products. These extra-quality services are costly, and it may not be possible to price them out separately so as to charge customers for them.

Hence the "free rider" problem: customers rely on the good dealers for some

---

[18] See Williamson, "Vertical Integration and Related Variations on a Transaction-Cost Economies Theme."

of the extra services (e.g., advice), but buy the actual products (cameras, stereos, books, etc.) from discounters because they offer lower prices. Thus the discounters are "free riders," taking free advantage of the costly services maintained by the "good" dealers.

Eventually this will drive the "good" dealers out of the market, leaving only discounters and other less responsible, transient dealers. The product's reputation and sales will suffer from lack of the necessary support services.

The free rider problem is the Chicago-UCLA explanation for vertical restraints.[19] In this view, the restrictions don't create market power; they merely respond to the free rider problem, helping to give customers better service. Therefore the restraints are to be welcomed, not condemned.

The matter is one of degree, requiring a cautious appraisal of facts. Only if free rider problems are large, with large impacts, could vertical restraints yield benefits substantial enough to offset the inevitable monopoly harms.

The free rider problem arises only when the extra services cannot be separately priced out for specific sale to customers. This kind of unbundling occurs routinely for many products, in the form of specific warranties and service contracts. Also, many dealers do manage to confine their extra services to their own customers. Furthermore, many customers remain loyal to "good" dealers over the course of many purchases and repurchases. Finally, suppliers often can pay directly to subsidize the extra services if they believe them necessary.

Restricting competition to make dealers more profitable is therefore only one way to support high-quality service, and its monopoly costs may exceed whatever gains are obtained by taking care of the free rider problem. As yet, little reliable research has been done to show that free riders cause extensive economic harm in actual markets.

That hasn't stopped the Chicago-UCLA economists from asserting that the free rider problem is large enough to justify permitting all vertical restrictions on territories and pricing (see resale price maintenance below). The case is strongest for complex goods requiring high dealer expertese and trust from customers, who really need the extra service and cannot get it by alternative means. If a free market for the services would not easily develop, then some restrictions may benefit society to some degree, by protecting high-quality dealers. The Chicago-UCLA position on this issue is inconsistent with the school's more general view that free markets will develop for any valuable service, and that monopoly restrictions are harmful.

Returning to the territorial restrictions in the soft drinks industry, the FTC investigated those of Coca-Cola and PepsiCola in the 1970s. Their market shares range between 30 and 45 percent, high enough so that the restriction on *intrabrand* com-

---

[19] See especially Lester Telser, "Why Should Manufacturers Want Fair Trade?" *Journal of Law and Economics,* 3 (October 1960), 86–105; Ward S. Bowman, Jr., "The Prerequisites and Effects of Resale Price Maintenance," *University of Chicago Law Review,* 22 (Summer 1955), 825–73; and the summary in Thomas R. Overstreet, Jr., *Resale Price Maintenance: Economic Theories and Empirical Evidence* (Washington, D.C.: Bureau of Economics, Federal Trade Commission, November 1983). The same logic applies to a variety of vertical restraints, including territorial restrictions and resale price maintenance.

For balanced evaluations, see William S. Comanor, "Vertical Price Fixing and Market Restrictions in the New Antitrust Policy," *Harvard Law Review,* 98 (March 1985), 983–1102; and F. M. Scherer, "The Economics of Vertical Restraints," *Antitrust Law Journal,* 52 (September 1983), 687–718.

petition (i.e., among Coca-Cola bottlers) would substantially reduce competition in the market as a whole. In 1978, the FTC adopted that reasoning in holding the territorial restrictions illegal under the antitrust laws. The soft drink companies immediately obtained an antitrust exemption from Congress, which is why the restrictions are still in full force. Leading beer companies place similar restrictions on their wholesalers in many states, as noted in Chapter 18.

You undoubtedly know of many franchised dealers (try listing ten of them, each in a different line, *other* than hamburger stands). One case is automobile dealerships. The three large producers have fostered a system of many thousands of dealers, who combine sales and service. The product is complex, and many customers are easy victims of fraud and exploitation. The dealers are mostly kept in a dependent role; their credit and "authorized" parts supply are controlled by the producers, and their franchises can be canceled. Until the 1970s, they were usually prohibited from carrying other car lines. Their local sales areas are mainly protected from proliferation of new dealerships.

In short, the dealer networks are a compromise among the divergent interests. Customers can go to any dealer they choose, though of course they cannot go very far if they expect to rely on the dealer for service.

2. Resale Price Maintenance

RPM (often called by the euphemism "fair trade") is the setting of *retail* prices by the original *manufacturer*. Many familiar items have been fair-traded, including books, cameras, appliances, and toiletries. In fact, manufacturers print "suggested" prices on the labels, or circulate them privately to retailers, for just about every kind of consumer product.

Often the suggested prices have no force; automobile "sticker" prices, for example, are just a starting point for you to negotiate a lower price. Yet fair trade laws were in force in many states from 1937 to 1976, prohibiting retailers from selling below the RPM price. Thus was price-fixing backed up by the power of the courts.[20]

RPM is basically an agreement among retailers, enforced by the producer, not to compete on price. Although the manufacturer selects the actual price, it often has no real interest in RPM. Indeed, producers usually prefer full competition in retailing their products. On the other side, RPM might strengthen their retailers' loyalties, and this can be valuable for some types of goods and for firms building up a dealer network (just as with territorial restrictions, discussed earlier).

RPM was often pressed upon reluctant suppliers by dealers' associations and then used to penalize or exclude maverick dealers. It frequently maintained prices 20 percent or more above competitive levels, and eventually it helped induce the spread of discount chains during the 1960s. Though fair trade laws were voided in 1976, the practice of "suggesting" prices is still widespread.

Why do manufacturers accept RPM? After all, it cuts the level of retail sales by raising retail prices, and that should reduce the manufacturer's profits. There are

---

[20] Some RPM laws extended the enforcement to retailers that had not signed as participants in the "fair trade" schemes. The price-fixing therefore reached out to include all retailers, not just those actively joining in the scheme.

three main possible reasons. Two are the desire to build up a new dealer network and the need to support "high-quality" dealers, (as just explained for territorial restrictions).

The third reason is to maintain a quality brand image. Manufacturers often seek to prevent the discounting and rack jobbing of their branded products, which undermines the quality of those products by equating them with leftovers. For example, Levi Strauss & Company enforced high resale prices of their blue jeans for decades in an attempt to maintain their brand image for quality. Distributors who sold Levi's to discounters were cut off by the manufacturer.

These three justifications are matters of degree. They could be large enough offset the monopoly harms in specific cases. Chicago-UCLA economists have argued emphatically that the benefits are large. RPM deserves a case-by-case evaluation, they say, which would weigh social costs against social benefits. That ideal treatment would require large judicial resources and time to weigh scores of expert witnesses' assertions about largely unmeasurable effects. Instead, the antitrust laws treat RPM essentially as straightforward price-fixing, which is illegal "per se" (without further detailed evaluations).

As part of their campaign to apply Chicago-UCLA doctrines, Reagan officials sought to use the "Spray-Rite" case in 1983 to establish the principle that RPM could be beneficial.[21] For decades up to 1968, the Spray-Rite company was a retailer of Monsanto's herbicides to farmers, and it was known as an energetic price discounter. Monsanto had a program of RPM for its products, which it enforced.

In 1968, Monsanto terminated Spray-Rite as a dealer, which forced the company out of business (by 1972). This action helped Monsanto to successfully pressure other dealers to maintain resale prices. Eventually, in 1984, the Supreme Court upheld the conviction of Monsanto for cutting off Stray-Rite, though it left open the possibility that some RPM situations might be legal.

Most economists believe the strict policy line against vertical price-fixing is still valid. Moreover, they regard RPM as only a small corner of the nation's monopoly problem. But to the lawyers and experts involved, RPM is a big issue, and it matters to them that there is now room to defend specific cases of RPM. So far, however, the Chicago-UCLA effort to reverse the presumption against RPM has made little progress in the courts and virtually no impact on real markets.

IV. THE EFFECTS OF BIGNESS

Now we turn to conditions that have stirred more popular discontent: bigness and conglomerates. Both are denied to cause monopoly effects by Chicago-UCLA analysts. In each case, we must first define the condition—not a simple task—and then consider its social benefits and costs.

Absolute size—or "size per se"—is distinct from *relative* size—the firm's share of the market. Size means bulk or sheer mass. Economic mass means the ability to influence economic results. There are at least several indexes of size. Capital, em-

[21] The case was *Monsanto Co.* v. *Spray-Rite Service Corp.*, 104 S.Ct. 1464 (1984).

TABLE 15.2   The Proper Index of Size Depends Partly on the Context

Indexes of Size	Context: What the Index Shows
1. *Financial*	
a. Real investment	Staying power; ability to apply financial resources.
b. Portfolio assets	Banking assets; ability to select among paper assets.
c. Profits	Ability to gain profits and reward investors.
2. *Economic Activity*	
a. Sales	Extent of the firm's role in market transactions.
b. Value added	Scope of economic activity and total production.
3. *Power Over Jobs and Votes*	
a. Employment	Dependence of citizens on the firm for jobs and security.
b. Geographic extent	Power and involvement in local and national affairs.
c. Number of stockholders	Breadth of citizen's dependence on the firms for investment success.

ployment, sales, value added, and profits are frequently used; recall Chapter 10.[22] Which index to use depends partly on the context, as Table 15.2 indicates. If the firm's "financial power" is in question, then the size of its capital or profits would be decisive rather than the number of jobs or volume of sales.

In principle, there is no best all-purpose index. In practice, sales and assets are the most commonly used measures of size, as Chapter 10 noted. For many purposes, either measure of size is good enough, and of course the two measures are closely related for the normal run of firms. Yet each measure has its own limits and technical problems. Table 10.5 shows how these two indexes and employment can diverge for a selection of large U.S. industrial firms. A firm may have "giant-sized" assets but a pigmy-sized volume of employees (oil firms and banks lean that way), or high sales and low assets (as most retailers do).

What effects might size have? Several possible effects have been advanced during the last one hundred years.

Market Power.   Ever since the first period of criticism of nationwide monopoly in the United States, from 1885 to 1920, bigness has been said to provide market power. A strong counterargument was mounted after 1945, urging that size per se is irrelevant to market power.[23] This in turn was countered by Bain's stress on entry barriers.[24] A "capital barrier" can be caused by sheer size if a new entrant must assemble large-scale financing (recall Chapters 3, 4, and 11). Therefore a big firm gains some market power from its size per se.

---

[22] The measures have been judged and used by many writers, including A. D. H. Kaplan, *Big Enterprise in a Competitive System,* rev. ed. (Washington, D.C.: Brookings Institution, 1965); and John M. Blair, *Economic Concentration* (New York: Harcourt, Brace & Jovanovich, 1972). For an early landmark discussion, see A. A. Berle and Gardiner Means, *The Modern Corporation and Private Property* (New York: Macmillan, 1932).

[23] See Morris A. Adelman, "The Measurement of Industrial Concentration," *Review of Economics and Statistics,* 33 (November 1951), 269–96; and the debate stirred by Adelman's article in that *Review,* May 1952.

[24] Joe S. Bain, *Barriers to New Competition* (Cambridge, Mass.: Harvard University Press, 1956).

This fits common sense—General Motors *is* a more formidable competitor than an otherwise identical but tiny firm producing toy cars. Yet how much added power does size give? The effect of size is probably small, especially if barriers are only a minor element of structure (again, recall Chapters 3, 4, and 11). The issue is open, with some analysts seeing a large effect and others regarding it as minor.

Control and Ownership.   Berle and Means's thesis was noted in Chapter 10: that the control of large corporations is divorced from ownership. This could give large scope for managerial choice, toward such nonprofit directions as growth or X-inefficiency. For three decades, the Berle-Means concept was accepted, and there was much discussion of "new" corporations, "managerial elites," and "unconstrained power." The rethinking since 1965 has stressed that many large firms really are owner-controlled and that the stock price "taskmaster" and financial supervisors do force managers to hew mainly to profit maximizing (recall Chapter 10). Also, research has not shown big differences between the profitability of manager- and owner-controlled firms, as Chapter 10 noted.

These points help us to judge the role of size per se. Managers have complete control of many firms, and they stray far from strict profit maximizing in some cases. But in the mass of large firms, managerial autonomy may not be very large, nor do the managers perceive it as large. On the whole, large size has probably not altered the basic nature of control in enterprises. Yet the research has not given strong conclusions either way.

X-Efficiency and Economies of Scale.   Size *has* made it harder to avoid internal inefficiency. In small firms, the manager sees everything and can directly enforce efficient operations. Large enterprises always involve a degree of bureaucracy, with layers of control. Although valid information is crucial for managers, the process instead often sends up false information and unreliable proposals. Size per se encounters diminishing returns because of the fixed factor, which is a single locus of effective management. Size breeds mistakes, and it weakens controls on costs. It also tends to weaken employees' identification with their firms and therefore to undermine their efficiency.

There may be some opposing factors that favor efficiency even in very large firms. Large firms may use superior methods of management. They may also be more likely to use advanced technology for managing, such as computerized processes for inventories, coordination, and supervision of performance. Therefore the degree of X-efficiency of each large firm will reflect the balance between such gains and the general deadening effect of bureaucracy. And, of course, size often provides *pecuniary* gains, from lower input prices.

The lessons of Chapters 6 and 9 apply in this context. Technical economies are not likely to extend into the very large size range, except possibly for firms in a few unusual industries. Pecuniary economies, by contrast, are likely to be gained up to indefinite sizes. Yet they are not true social economies.

Stability and Planning.   Size may increase the stability of the firm and permit it to do better long-range planning. Galbraith sees large firms as having great security and "control of the market."[25] Their planning process has come to dominate their markets. Others note that many large firms have fluctuated sharply in recent years, though few of the largest 200 have failed. They also note that large-firm planning is not always of superior quality or successful. Size does give greater stability; the profit rates of larger firms fluctuate less than do those of smaller firms. But how great the planning benefits are is an open question. And the stability may encourage a loss of X-efficiency.

Job Conditions Within the Firm.   The quality of work and social activity within the firm can be reduced by size. The bureaucratic tendencies are toward impersonal, narrow jobs, with orders flowing down from above. Large firms tend to separate the worker from both managers and customers. There is enough evidence that worker satisfaction is reduced by size to make this a general rule.[26] Some large firms are able to offset this by higher pay and specific alterations in job conditions. Much of the new management approach toward sharing power in the 1980s is meant to ease these problems, but ultimately, basic changes in the power structure within large firms might be necessary.[27]

Political Power.   Large size can also yield political power, for two main reasons. First, large firms hold large-scale financial resources, which can be quickly mobilized and deployed effectively. Second, their large employment rolls give them some influence over voting patterns. In this, large firms are not unique. Trade associations among smaller firms (such as druggists or grocers) can also assemble sizable funds and voting influence. But their actions are fragmented and cumbersome compared to the direct actions of large firms.

This power is commonly stronger at the local level, where large firms can often apply leverage and play off small cities against each other in order to secure tax rebates and other advantages.[28] At the national level, many large firms have modest influence. Yet some (such as banks, oil, and insurance firms) have exerted strong control over congressional and regulatory policies toward them.

Much more research is needed to factor out these mixed effects. Size seems to raise market power, and it also causes X-inefficiency. Large firms gain stability, but at the cost of some sluggishness. Size also yields political power. Great size alone does not create market power; that arises mainly from dominance and barriers in a market. But size is not irrelevant.

---

[25] J. K. Galbraith, *The New Industrial State* (Boston: Houghton Mifflin, 1967).

[26] See F. M. Scherer's chapter, "Industrial Structure, Scale Economies, and Worker Alienation," in Robert T. Masson and P. David Qualls, eds., *Essays on Industrial Organization in Honor of Joe S. Bain* (Cambridge, Mass.: Ballinger, 1976), pp. 105–21, and sources that Scherer cites. Harvey J. Leibenstein, *Beyond Economic Man* (Cambridge, Mass.: Harvard University Press, 1976), explores the ways that company conditions influence effort.

[27] "Worker participation" and "codetermination" have been steps in that direction in several Western European countries. Yugoslavian "worker-managed" enterprises go further; see Jaroslav Vanek, *A General Theory of Labor-Managed Market Economies* (Ithaca, N.Y.: Cornell University Press, 1970).

[28] See the classic discussion in Carl Kaysen, "The Corporation: How Much Power? What Scope?" in Edward S. Mason, ed., *The Corporation in Modern Society* (Cambridge, Mass.: Harvard University Press, 1959).

V. DIVERSIFICATION

1. Possible Benefits

Nearly all sizable firms produce a group or "line" of products, and many go beyond that to cover an array of unrelated products. By 1950, many diversified firms had long been well established. The East India Company from 1700 to 1850 was the prototypical conglomerate, and some late-nineteenth-century enterprises spread into many sectors and regions. The merger wave of the 1960s created many new conglomerates, some of them by lively takeover battles (recall Chapter 10). As is ever the case, new conglomerates were resisted by old conglomerates and unified firms. But the motives for diversification, and the effects of it, are universally the same.

Diversification can be (1) *product* extension (as in adding to a line of products), (2) *geographic* extension (same product, different area), or (3) *pure* (no relation to the firm's existing products). Since diversification is neither horizontal nor vertical, some doubt that it affects competition and performance in the market at all. That is the Chicago-UCLA hypothesis. Most diversification is not pure. The typical firm tends to diversify by creeping into adjacent markets rather than leaping randomly into new sectors.[29] The diversified firm usually has two or three main market positions plus a clustering in several nearby areas, with a number of other holdings scattered out in "distant" markets.

The degree of diversification has probably been rising in the United States since 1950.[30] Yet the increase during the 1960s merger wave was largely reversed by the dismantling of many conglomerates after 1969 (as Chapter 10 noted). The absolute amount of diversification is surely rising as large firms grow and spread their activities, yet the *relative degree* of diversification might be steady or declining.

Since diversification is so prominent in modern industry, one must evaluate its possible effects. The simplest hypothesis is the Chicago-UCLA view that (1) it does not reduce competition, by leverage or any other device; and (2) it can provide true economies.[31] This parallels the Chicago-UCLA thesis about vertical integration. A counterhypothesis, led by Corwin Edwards and John Blair, is that diversification can increase market power while impairing efficiency.[32] The literature has tended toward polemics, but there are clearly several possible benefits from diversification and several possible social costs. We will consider the benefits first, and then the costs.[33]

---

[29] See Gort, *Integration and Diversification in American Industry;* and Charles H. Berry, *Corporate Growth and Diversification* (Princeton, N.J.: Princeton University Press, 1975).

[30] This is clear from two fairly recent studies: Berry, *Corporate Growth;* and T. Crawford Honeycutt and Donald L. Zimmerman, "The Measurement of Corporate Diversification: 1950–1967," *Antitrust Bulletin,* 21 (Fall 1976), 509–35.

[31] Although they deal with mergers, the following two discussions treat the general issues well from that viewpoint: Peter O. Steiner, *Mergers: Motives, Effects, Policies* (Ann Arbor: University of Michigan Press, 1975); and Donald F. Turner, "Conglomerate Mergers and Section 7 of the Clayton Act," *Harvard Law Review* (May 1965), 1313–95.

[32] Corwin D. Edwards, "Conglomerate Bigness as a Source of Power," in G. J. Stigler, ed., *Business Concentration and Price Policy* (Princeton, N.J.: Princeton University Press, 1955); and Blair, *Economic Concentration.*

[33] We consider here only the effects relating to competition and monopoly. Mergers creating diversification may have other costs, as the United States's 1980s merger boom showed (recall Chapter 10)—chiefly the tying up of huge volumes of capital and the distraction of managers.

For each benefit, one asks how much more of it the diversified firm provides than could have been supplied by a separate firm or firms via market processes. For example, diversified firms allocate capital to their branches. But so does the capital market, perhaps as well or even better. Size is so closely mingled with diversification that a clear dissection of diversification's role may be impossible.

Transfer of Technology.   The firm may extend its proven technology into new markets. The direct transfer may be stronger and quicker than market processes could give. The firm may see the opportunities more clearly and be geared up to experiment and develop the new technology more fruitfully. Since most diversification is into technologically related processes, the transfer process may be important.

Allocating Capital.   The managers of a diversified firm allocate capital among its branches. Besides internal cash flows, the firm raises funds from external sources. This control over investment policy is often the main power and role of top-level managers. Pure conglomerates, in fact, often approximate a purely financial allocative process, much like the portfolio and controlling operations of an investment bank. But even when top management reaches down to control operations closely, it still allocates capital.

By knowing its branches well, top management may allocate capital better than the market process could. Especially in building up branches in new markets and in entering markets against dominant firms, the conglomerate may go further than capital markets would. Indeed, some new 1960s conglomerates claimed precisely that: they were filling the gaps caused by imperfect capital markets by supplying new competition and funding new ventures.

Pooling Risk.   If the branches' risks are randomly distributed—or follow offsetting cycles—then their combined risks are lower.[34] Thus the whole diversified firm would tend to have stable total profits. This is analogous to an individual investor reducing risk by buying at least five stocks rather than just one. But these gains are finite: above five branches, the risk-pooling gain is slight. Also, the branches may all suffer from the same basic cyclical reverses—a recession, after all, is adverse for most industries at once.

Takeover Discipline.   Takeovers can exert direct pressures toward X-efficiency in target firms (recall Chapter 10). The effect also spreads out to other potential target firms: by increasing X-efficiency, they reduce the likelihood of being targeted in a takeover attempt. This benefit arises strictly from *mergers* (and merger threats) rather than from internal diversification. The effect can be strict and widespread, and is therefore an important economic benefit.

Not only do takeovers often raise X-efficiency in particular firms. They are also part of the broader process of renewal and growth whereby new entrepreneurial talent enters the scene and challenges older pockets of control. Protecting this access can improve the performance of the whole market system.

---

[34] By the central limit theorem, in which the mean values of several random processes will converge on a stable mean for the whole group.

These four classes of social benefits can be important in total. Some types of diversification give almost no benefits; other types give large benefits. The degree of *market dominance* of the parent firm and the branch can affect the competitive result. Linking two dominant firms is sharply different from linking two lesser firms. The dominant firms may mutually entrench each other, whereas a "toehold" merger with a small firm may help it to intensify competition.

Since diversification includes so much variety, no general rule about its effects makes sense. The next section presents the four main ways in which diversification may reduce competition.

2.   Possible Harms to Competition

Cross-Subsidizing.   Cross-subsidizing is often said to permit using profits from branch A to support deep, "unfair" price cuts by branch B. This is a special case of "predatory" pricing; recall Chapter 12. Such pricing may be unlikely; after all, the price cuts are costly, and other ways to achieve the same gains for branch B will usually be cheaper and easier. Yet deep price cuts may be done, or threatened, to intimidate other firms, perhaps frequently and effectively.

If cross-subsidizing is taken to mean merely general support of a diversified firm for competitive ventures by branch B, then it clearly does occur. This support rarely goes much beyond the levels of venture capital that open capital markets would supply to branch B. Yet such backing of a branch is a natural and important function of a diversified firm, and is surely widespread and frequent. However, the conglomerate's "deep pocket" may not be very deep in reality. Moreover, the financial support may not be as important as other resources provided to the branch (managerial, scientific, advertising).

The competitive effect of such support depends mainly on the market position of branch B. If branch B is dominant, the support will tend to entrench it further. But if branch B has a small market share, the support will increase the competition it is able to apply to the other, more dominant firms. For example, in the 1970s and early 1980s, Phillip Morris injected funds for major advertising blitzes by its "Seven-Up" subsidiary. That was procompetitive on balance, because it raised competition with the larger Coca-Cola and PepsiCo firms. If all branches of a diversified firm are dominant in their markets, however, their pooled resources are likely to increase their dominance through greater price discrimination, threats of punitive actions, and so forth.[35] By contrast, a firm holding small-share branches is more likely to promote competition than to reduce it—that is, if it can help its members at all.

In fact, many conglomerates have much less ability to "cross-subsidize"—to apply economic power to assist one part of the firm—than unified firms have. One determines this by looking at the basic market position, degree of security, and flow of funds the firm has. An insecure, widely stretched conglomerate with no strong market base and thin profit margins can affect competition far less than an established, lucrative, dominant firm.

---

[35] ITT became a prime instance of a conglomerate holding a string of firms with leading positions in their markets; see James S. Campbell and William G. Shepherd, "Leading-Firm Conglomerate Mergers," *Antitrust Bulletin,* 13 (Winter 1968), 1361–82. Of course, many older firms also hold a series of leading positions—General Motors, Du Pont, General Electric, and Procter & Gamble are examples.

Reciprocal Buying.   *Reciprocity* is an exchange of favors. Reciprocal buying is one form of it. At its simplest, firm A buys from firm B because of some purchase that B makes from A. (Examples: A railroad buys its locomotives from General Motors because GM ships its cars over that railroad. Or Bethlehem Steel provides its purchasing agents with records of its steel sales so that these agents can tilt their purchases toward those firms that bought any steel they needed from Bethlehem.)

For diversified firms, the possible impacts are more varied. Branch O might alter its purchases toward firm S if the latter buys its supplies from branch P. Such reciprocity might come at many points in a really diverse firm.

Reciprocity is common in many heavy industries, and it is a constant temptation for diversified firms.[36] Customers will normally try to induce the firm to make reciprocal deals. Yet such favors are usually departures from strict rational choices. The Chicago-UCLA view is that reciprocity is irrational, and therefore cannot be extensive or harmful to anyone but the firms themselves. This is largely true. Both sides have to give up a favor in order to get the extra sale. The net economic gain is often small or even negative.

Since reciprocity has such shallow roots, it is likely to reduce competition only where both branches are dominant.[37] A conglomerate with only minor market positions can scarcely reduce competition by reciprocity, and it might increase it.

Mergers Reducing Potential Competition.   Potential competition may be important for some markets, as earlier chapters noted. If a potential entrant merges with a firm already inside the market, the ranks of actual plus potential competitors are reduced by one. That decreases the total degree of competitive constraint, even if only slightly.

There are two special reservations to this point.

1.   Potential entrants are hard to identify. Potential entry has been easy to theorize about, but practical applications of it are mainly guesswork.

2.   The position of the acquired firm in the market can be decisive. If a dominant firm is acquired, its new parent's resources may entrench it further. But if a minor firm is taken over, the resources to build it up will increase competition. Conglomerate mergers that give "toeholds" in the market can improve competition.

The "ideal" conglomerate merger is an unexpected entrant acquiring a minor firm. By contrast, if an important potential entrant buys up a dominant firm (or vice versa), competition will be doubly reduced. Even so, the total effect may not be sharp. It will depend on the degree of actual and potential competition that remains, as well as on the market power of the parent firm.

Spheres of Influence.   Now we consider the big picture, rather than market-by-market effects. Imagine an extreme situation, with five big diversified firms extending into all major sectors. They coexist in parallel, touching one another within hundreds of markets. Whatever their effects on each market might be, they pose a larger problem of spheres of interest, of diplomatic behavior replacing competition.

---

[36] Steiner's discussion in *Mergers,* pp. 218–54, is helpful.

[37] Reciprocity may even promote competition, if (1) it permits price shading that would not occur otherwise and (2) it is done by lesser firms. See Bruce T. Allen, "Industrial Reciprocity: A Statistical Analysis," *Journal of Law and Economics,* 18 (October 1975), 507–20.

Each firm would weigh any action in one market against the possible retaliations by the other firms in that market *and* in other markets. The indeterminacy of oligopoly would be compounded many times over. Most observers have predicted that coexistence would replace competition.[38] Each firm would know more about its rivals' behavior and have more dimensions in which to react effectively.

Japan and Germany approached such extreme conditions between 1920 and 1945. After some postwar structural changes by the Allied forces, the combines were reassembled, but they are now less close-knit, so the processes of retaliation and interaction are weaker.

U.S. industry is well below this degree of diversification, so far. But within some industry groups, there are sets of diversified firms mingling in scores or hundreds of individual markets. Chemicals firms are one instance; large electrical-electronic firms are another; food products and publishing are still others.[39] A degree of mutual restraint is likely in such cases.

Local Effects.   We still have to consider the impacts of absentee ownership upon localities. Though these social effects are less technically proven, they may ultimately be important.

One impact occurs through plant closures decided by distant officials who are unaware of, or insensitive to, local strengths. Conglomerate mergers are frequently followed by abrupt decisions to dismiss workers or close whole factories. Often these decisions ignore the true values offered by the work force and the locale.

The other category of impacts is more subtle. Local firms are normally knit into their communities, with the companies' officials contributing and participating in local affairs, such as fund drives, schools, and city government. When taken over by large firms, the companies typically stop their local involvement. Indeed, there is often a shift toward pressuring the city for tax reductions and other favors.

VI. SUMMARY

Vertical patterns are a luxuriant field for study. They are usually a secondary element of market structure, but they can be decisive in certain market situations. Buyer concentration is generally lower than seller concentration, but good measures of either are scarce. Bilateral market power usually gives indeterminate results, as the seller and buyer strain for advantage. Bilateral oligopoly—a common situation—is particularly indeterminate.

Competition in final consumer markets can force the previous levels toward competitive outcomes. Countervailing power is not an automatic corrective device for sellers' market power.

Vertical integration could be irrelevant to market power if markets were perfect and frictionless. In actual markets, integration tends to raise entry barriers and re-

[38] Including Edwards, "Conglomerate Bigness"; Blair, *Economic Concentration,* pp. 48–50; and F. M. Scherer, *Industrial Market Structure and Economic Performance,* 2d ed. (Chicago: Rand McNally, 1980), 340–43.

[39] On chemicals, see A. E. Kahn, "The Chemical Industry," in Walter Adams, ed., *The Structure of American Industry,* 3d ed. (New York: Macmillan, 1961). On other patterns, see Blair, *Economic Concentration,* Chapters 3 and 12.

duce competition. Where vertical integration reinforces dominant positions at both levels, the negative effects are clear. Vertical mergers are only one way to achieve the economic benefits of integration; internal growth and long-term contracts are others. The net effects of vertical mergers are therefore a balance between moderate anticompetitive effects and moderate *net* technical economies.

Vertical restrictions include limits on franchises and resale price maintenance. Both often reduce competition without providing social benefits. Size and diversification are marginal issues in market structure and performance. They probably have little effect in most markets, though fairly sharp impacts in some. Much of their influence can be translated into conventional concepts, such as entry barriers and price discrimination. One can identify some categories of each that are more likely to harm competition—or, in some cases, improve it.

Conglomerate mergers' effects (both costs and benefits) are generally small. Therefore, apart from the general takeover benefits, there is usually little reason to prevent *or* encourage them.

QUESTIONS FOR REVIEW

1. "Pure bilateral monopoly gives a definite final price and output; only the price paid to the supplier is indeterminate." True?

2. "In the typical market, buyer concentration is usually higher than seller concentration." True?

3. "Bilateral monopoly and oligopoly always result in twice the monopoly effect of the seller monopoly alone." True?

4. "Private-label" brands are usually a good indicator that countervailing power is absent." True?

5. "Vertical integration helps to extend monopoly power from one level to another except where uncertainty and market frictions exist." True?

6. "Vertical integration is easily measured by using the ratio of sales to value added." True?

7. "Vertical price squeezes cannot occur, for they are irrational." True?

8. "Vertical mergers may give small net benefits, compared with internal growth or long-term contracts." True?

9. "Vertical restrictions only benefit society when the manufacturer has a large market share." True?

10. "Resale price maintenance is always initiated by dealers rather than producers." True?

11. "Size per se can be measured by (1) assets, (2) sales, (3) profit rate, (4) employees, (5) leverage." Which?

12. "Large size can cause entry barriers to be high." True?

13. "Berle and Means showed that ownership is combined with control in the modern large corporation." True?

14. "Large firms encounter problems of bureaucracy, but some of them manage to avoid X-inefficiency." True?

15. "Large firms are, on average, less profitable and less stable than small firms." True?

16. "Diversification usually grows by moves into wholly different innovative areas." True?

17. "Conglomerates may allocate capital, transfer technology, and pool risks better than market processes do." True?

18. "Reciprocal buying arises only in conglomerate firms." True?

19. "Conglomerate mergers on a toehold basis are better for competition than mergers with dominant firms." True?

20. Which conditions of bilateral monopoly will yield competitive prices?

21. Show that vertical integration will not affect competition in perfectly functioning markets.

22. Then discuss three conditions under which vertical integration will reduce competition.

23. Compose your own numerical example of a price "squeeze."

24. You have been asked to judge whether a merger will foreclose potential competition. What data would you try to use, both about the firms and about the market?

25. What is the best measure of "size"?

26. What main social benefits may diversification give?

27. Explain the "free rider" justification for RPM. Which industry conditions favor it? Discuss three actual industries for which it may be valid and important.

28. Explain why market shares are important in judging the inter-brand and intra-brand effects of vertical territorial restrictions.

16 PRODUCT DIFFERENTIATION, ESPECIALLY ADVERTISING

Competition is most rigorous when products are identical. Then buyers can compare goods precisely and switch freely among them. When goods are "differentiated," competition may be less effective. Comparisons are harder to make, and buyers get attached to specific goods. The whole flood of advertising seeks to tie people to their "favorite" brands, so that sales (and profits) on each one can be higher. Advertising, in short, may reduce competition.

Since 1965, product differentiation (especially as accentuated by advertising) has been a hot topic, attracting scores of articles and a number of books. Advertising interests and some industrial groups have praised advertising's procompetitive role, and many economists have agreed; numerous other economists have called it a source of monopoly. *Does* advertising reduce competition, or possibly increase it? Although the debate has often been heated, the research answers have been inconclusive.

Since the problem is confined to a relatively few consumer-goods industries, it has been saved for this later chapter. We begin with the motives and types of selling expenses, viewed abstractly. Then Section III presents the case that product differentiation can be a barrier to entry, as well as the opposite possibility: that advertising promotes competition. Section IV discusses the research lessons about advertising and competition.

I. SELLING EXPENSES

There are many ways to promote sales. *Advertising* is the most visible device, and it is often important. *Sales forces* are another major technique. A third form of selling effort is the use of *promotional discounts, samples,* and *special pricing.* Such methods do not alter the product. They try instead to change demand conditions. These methods are substitutable to varying degrees. Many firms use all three of them all of the time. Here advertising will be the main focus, but the analysis applies to the other forms of selling expenses as well.

1. Effects of Advertising

The simple concept is this: Selling expenses add to costs in order to add to demand.[1] They are an alternative to price-cutting as a competitive tactic. They are "softer" and safer than price-cutting. Since they usually run into diminishing returns for any given product, they are not likely to cause as much mutual harm among rivals as price-cutting would.

Advertising is an input to the firm. Optimal advertising choices by the firm are similar to those governing other inputs.[2] Selling effort is slightly different; it does influence demand, while other inputs are strictly matters of the supply side. That does not change the firm's basic choice.

The motivation and effects of selling effort for the firm are analyzed in Figure 16.1. Selling costs are added to production costs. They may alter demand, in some degree. There are two critical issues: (1) How is demand changed? (2) Does the selling effort achieve economies of scale? If economies of scale do occur, then the optimal size of the firm is increased.

There are counterpoised effects. Sales effort may produce a saturation or threshold effect. Thus a nationwide sales force or advertising campaign may be necessary, but once it is accomplished, further spending is unnecessary. This gives scale economies once the minimum scale is reached. Against this, sales effort typically faces diminishing marginal effectiveness in altering consumer demand for any one product. Additional messages, facts, or sales visits may have little effect.

Figure 16.1 reflects one possible balance of these conditions. The result of selling effort in this case is the shift from point A to point B, with higher price and profit. Whether the level of output rises will depend on (1) the conditions for this firm (in this case, output is increased); and (2) whether this firm takes sales away from other firms, which is likely. The whole effect of sales effort is the net increase of welfare above the cost of the sales effort. This net effect need not be positive. For example, the rise in demand may be tiny, while advertising costs are high.

---

[1] To dig into the literature, the student could begin with Joe S. Bain, *Barriers to New Competition* (Cambridge, Mass.: Harvard University Press, 1956), Chapter 4 and Appendix D; P. Doyle, "Economic Aspects of Advertising: A Survey," *Economic Journal,* 78 (September 1968), 570–602; William S. Comanor and Thomas Wilson, *Advertising and Market Power* (Cambridge, Mass.: Harvard University Press, 1975); Julian L. Simon, *Issues in the Economics of Advertising* (Champaign: University of Illinois Press, 1970); and, in a more polemical vein, Jules Backman, *Advertising and Competition* (New York: Aspects of Advertising," *Review of Economic Studies,* 18 (1950), 1–27. An excellent survey of all arguments is provided in William S. Comanor and Thomas A. Wilson, "The Effect of Advertising on Competition: A Survey," *Journal of Economic Literature,* 17 (June 1979), 453–76.

See also Richard E. Caves and Peter J. Williamson, "What Is Product Differentiation, Really?" *Journal of Industrial Economics,* 34 (December 1985), 113–32; and the survey and sources cited in Douglas F. Greer, *Industrial Organization and Public Policy,* 2d ed. (New York: Macmillan, 1984), Chapters 4, 5, and 11.

[2] See Robert Dorfman and Peter O. Steiner, "Optimal Advertising and Optimal Quality," *American Economic Review,* 44 (December 1954), 826–36.

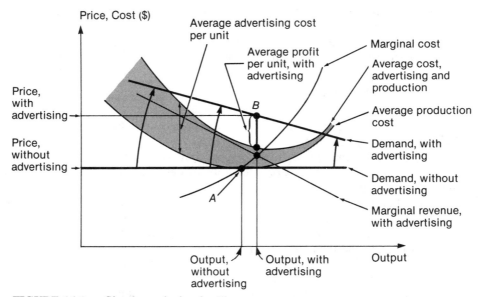

FIGURE 16.1.   Simple analysis of selling expenses.

A simpler view is that if consumers are willing to pay for advertising (in the price of the good), they must want it. This assumes that consumer preferences *after* being shaped by sales effort are more valid than the preferences that existed in the absence of sales effort. That is a tenable position, but its premise—that prior preferences are necessarily inferior—is a stronger one than most analysts are willing to accept. A stickier problem is that the customer often cannot buy the good without paying for the advertising. That is, advertising is "tied" to the good. If customers cannot buy just the good, then little can be said about the value of advertising to them.

2.   Optimal Levels of Advertising

Advertising expenses are both the *effects* of decisions made by each firm and the *causes* of other patterns, such as market shares and profits. We first consider advertising as an effect.

There is a simple theory defining the profit-maximizing level of advertising for a firm.[3] In 1954, Dorfman and Steiner analyzed the firm whose quantity sales depend on price and advertising, with an inverse demand function $P(q, a)$, where a is the total expenses for advertising. Advertising is assumed to affect consumer choices, although consumers do not enjoy advertising per se.

The Dorfman-Steiner model is based on the following restrictive assumptions: no lags in advertising's effects, constant product quality, no advertising or price responses by rival firms, and complete knowledge of the relevant elasticities. When

---

[3] Dorfman and Steiner, "Optimal Advertising and Optimal Quality."

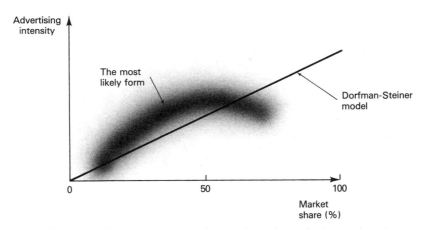

FIGURE 16.2.   The relationship of advertising intensity to market shares.

these hold, the firm's advertising intensity, shown by the ratios of advertising expenditure to sales revenue (labeled A/S), will be:

$$\text{A/S} = \frac{\text{Elasticity of demand with respect to advertising}}{\text{Elasticity of demand with respect to price}}$$

or

$$\text{A/S} = \frac{\%\ \text{Change in quantity}/\%\ \text{Change in advertising}}{\%\ \text{Change in quantity}/\%\ \text{Change in price}}$$

In this narrow case, advertising intensity will vary with the *inelasticity* of demand. Market shares are positively related to inelasticity: as market share rises toward 100 percent, the firm's demand curve tends toward the market's demand curve. There is decreasing substitutability with the products of other firms, so higher market shares give lower elasticity of demand.

Accordingly, higher degrees of monopoly would tend to cause higher advertising intensity. Conversely, firms with very low market shares would find it best to advertise very little. This pattern generally fits reality: advertising is heaviest in markets with high concentration. But the theory is too rigid. It implies that the effect carries right up to pure monopolies, which would advertise most heavily of all. Yet it is obvious that pure monopolies—with no rivals—would not need to advertise.

The general pattern is illustrated in Figure 16.2 as a fuzzy band that peaks in the middle ranges of market share. Each setting is likely to generate its own specific, and different, function. Its shape and position will depend on the market shares and response functions of this firm's rivals, the nature of the good, and the lags in advertising's impacts. The Dorfman-Steiner result is illustrated by the straight line in Figure 16.2, which is implausible.

In short, theory merely suggests what is known generally: that tight oligopoly tends to breed intensive advertising. This will hold true even when firms do not respond specifically to one another's actions. The effect is even sharper when they do respond, so as to generate standoff advertising (as discussed in Chapter 5.)

3. Defining Advertising Intensity

The advertising/sales ratio is commonly used to indicate advertising intensity. This is generally a good index, but it can be deceptive.[4] For example, the U.S. automobile industry is very large, and it advertises heavily. Its frequency of messages per potential customer is high because of its large absolute spending on advertising (some $1.5 billion per year). Yet the total sales revenue of the industry is so very high that the advertising/sales ratio is actually rather low; it is around 1 percent, compared with over 10 percent for cereals, beer, and other advertising-intensive industries.

One alternative index is expenditure per customer or per capita of the population. Another is the number of messages received by buyers. But these, too, have problems of measurement and interpretation. So the advertising/sales ratio is likely to continue to be the workhorse index of advertising intensity.

4. The Social Contribution of Advertising

This chapter focuses on advertising's relation to competition and monopoly. There are plenty of other issues, but they extend into different fields. Yet one does warrant mention here: the possibility that there will be "too much" advertising according to social criteria. This possibility was noted in Chapter 5, when we assessed the inefficiencies traceable to market power. All persuasive advertising may be regarded as a subtraction from the goods flowing to consumers in line with their preferences. But if a certain amount of advertising is necessary to induce consumers to buy the goods, then advertising costs may be regarded as a necessary part of production.

Here one rigorous theoretical conclusion may be noted. Dixit and Norman have analyzed the contribution of advertising to consumer welfare.[5] They posit an advertising-induced rise in the firm's demand that is determined by the firm as it equates its private marginal revenue with its private marginal cost. The added advertising cost adds to the price of all the units of the product that are sold. To those buyers who would not have bought in the absence of advertising, the result is in balance: the good costs more, but the advertising has induced them to be willing to pay the price. Extra cost, then, is offset by extra value (that is, as perceived by consumers after being exposed to advertising).

But some customers would buy the good even if it were not advertised. Since they are forced to pay the higher price that includes advertising costs, they suffer a loss in welfare. For them, advertising has been strictly excessive and wasteful,

[4] See also F. M. Scherer, *Industrial Market Structure and Economic Performance,* 2d ed. (Boston: Houghton Mifflin, 1980), Chapter 14.
[5] See A. Dixit and V. Norman, "Advertising and Welfare," *Bell Journal of Economics,* 9 (Spring 1978), 1–17. See also F. M. Fisher and J. J. McGowan, "Advertising and Welfare: A Comment," *Bell Journal of Economics,* 10 (Autumn 1979), 726–27; and Dixit and Norman, "Advertising and Welfare: A Reply," *Bell Journal of Economics,* 10 (Autumn 1979), 728–29.

and it subtracts from their incomes. They could choose not to buy the product at all at the higher price, but that subtraction from their range of choice is just another way of defining the welfare loss they have suffered.

The magnitude of this loss depends on (1) the extent of the customers within the whole class of buyers, and (2) the extent of the advertising as it raises cost and price per unit. If both components are large, then the welfare loss may be quite large. You can introspectively assess this effect for familiar goods that you buy. Try to envision how much of them you would have bought if there were no advertising. That volume, times the advertising-caused increment to price, is the welfare loss that advertising has inflicted on you.

5.   The Market Setting

In pure competition, selling expenses are irrelevant. Price is simply given by the market, and the firm's selling effort cannot alter the flat demand curve. In pure monopoly, selling expenses play a limited role. They can be used to reduce demand elasticity to raise the amount of profit taken in. Advertising may also sharpen any differences in demand elasticity among customer groups. This raises the scope for price discrimination and further profits. Yet, on the whole, a monopolist need not make much selling effort. Some regard this as one benefit of monopoly—that it avoids "excess" selling expenditures.

It is in the intermediate range—especially with dominant firms and oligopoly—that selling expenses flourish. They are valuable to the sellers as a "safer" method of competition than price-cutting. Demand can be altered, and a firm can hope to raise its market share and profits sharply by many kinds of promotional blitzes. Defensive advertising often becomes routine for oligopolists. Even if they plan no aggressive promotional campaigns, they find it wise to nourish their customers' brand loyalties against the possibility that other firms might attack them.

Since all oligopolists in a market will share these incentives, the result is widely believed to be "standoff" advertising, in which oligopolists engage in very little price competition but are responsible for a large flow of parallel advertising. The advertising largely cancels itself out among the firms. Each is willing to stop advertising, but is too afraid to do so because the others might not. In the end, all are engaging in partly functionless expenditures.[6]

Oddly, tight oligopoly also tends to minimize the variety of product offerings (recall Chapter 13). Selling effort substitutes for true variety by trying to make the similar products *seem* different. Therefore tight oligopoly tends to raise the level of selling costs while reducing the degree of true product variety. The waste can occur even if all the selling effort purveys accurate, valuable information rather than just jingles and images.

---

[6] See Bain, *Barriers;* Comanor and Wilson, *Advertising and Market Power;* William J. Fellner, *Competition Among the Few* (New York: Knopf, 1949), pp. 183–91; and J. M. Clark, *Competition as a Dynamic Process* (Washington, D.C.: Brookings Institution, 1961), pp. 245–63. For further analysis of excess advertising, see Dixit and Norman, "Advertising and Welfare," pp. 1–17.

6.   Informational and Persuasive Advertising

This brings us to the basic point that some selling effort is (1) *informational,* while some is (2) *persuasive.* The consensus is that the informational part is socially beneficial, up to the point at which its marginal social benefits equal its costs. Informational advertising genuinely adds to consumers' knowledge of what is available; it improves competition and consumer choice. Examples are classified advertisements in newspapers and the factual material offered to a customer by a sales representative.

Persuasive advertising, by contrast, merely tries to change consumer preferences or to divert attention from facts to images. It occurs most obviously in "image" advertising, as when a cigarette ad shows a person glowering and saying, "I smoke because I like to!" Most persuasive advertising either impairs consumer choice or is irrelevant to it. If it helps a new competitor enter the market, it might have social value. But that would occur only because the other firms were already using persuasive selling. And if they weren't, it might have the socially bad effect of forcing them to switch from informative to persuasive advertising.

Since their values and impacts are different, the distinction between information and persuasion is important. Most sales efforts mix the two, however, so it is hard to factor out the components in practice. (Even a classified ad often contains a sales pitch; and even cigarette ad copy includes the tar content.) Try estimating the percentage of information and persuasion in samples from six different media: television, newspapers, magazines, trade journals, mailings, and store window displays.

7.   Search and Experience Goods

A further distinction is between "search goods" and "experience goods."

Search goods have objective features. Therefore they can be described accurately so that consumers can understand them well *before* choosing which ones to buy. Consumers need only search for adequate information in order to make correct decisions. Examples are paper, paint, gasoline, and many industrial products such as chemicals, steel, and cloth.

Experience goods, in contrast, have (at least some) features that are complex and difficult to describe. They can be judged only by direct, personal experience. Examples are automobiles, restaurant meals, movies, and computer programs.

The two categories are often mingled in actual goods, of course, but the conceptual distinction is helpful in pinpointing the reasons and effects of advertising. *Informative advertising* fits search goods; it provides objective data about conditions that can be verified. Experience goods tend to be promoted by *persuasive advertising,* which attempts to shape buyers' preferences so that they will not only buy the good, but also tend to like owning and experiencing it. To put it succinctly, informative advertising helps buyers to purchase what they prefer, whereas persuasive advertising helps them to prefer what they have bought.

The search-experience distinction also clarifies the difference between *industrial* and *personal* goods. Industrial purchasers are usually tough, expert, and well informed; they need only to be helped with information. Final consumers, in contrast, often have weakly formed preferences, little basis for judging technical details, and a tendency to impulse buying. They frequently rely on brand names as a proxy for quality. That helps to explain why persuasive advertising focuses on personal products, seeking to instill brand images and preferences, while virtually all advertising of industrial products is of the informative variety.

II. ACTUAL PATTERNS OF ADVERTISING

Advertising as we know it is a relatively new activity. It emerged on a large scale in the 1920s, with the advent of the radio and mass magazines. It then boomed in the 1945–1955 period, and has grown rapidly ever since. It is now an important cultural fact.

As Table 16.1 shows, advertising expenditures in 1986 were about $102 billion,

TABLE 16.1   Estimated Advertising Expenditures in the United States, 1970–1986

	Expenditures ($ million)			Percent		
Medium	1970	1980	1986	1970	1980	1986
Total	**19,550**	**53,550**	**102,140**	**100.0**	**100.0**	**100.0**
National	11,350	29,815	56,850	58.1	55.7	55.7
Local	8,200	23,735	45,290	41.9	44.3	44.3
Newspapers	5,704	14,794	26,990	29.2	27.6	26.4
National	891	1,963	3,376	4.6	3.7	3.3
Local	4,813	12,831	23,614	24.6	24.0	23.1
Magazines	1,292	3,149	5,317	6.6	5.9	5.2
Weeklies	617	1,418	2,327	3.2	2.6	2.3
Women's	301	782	1,376	1.5	1.5	1.3
Monthlies	374	949	1,614	1.9	1.8	1.6
Farm publications	62	130	192	.3	.2	.2
Television	3,596	11,424	22,585	18.4	21.3	22.1
Network	1,658	5,130	8,570	8.5	9.6	8.4
Spot	1,234	3,269	6,570	6.3	6.1	6.4
Cable (National)	(NA)	50	752	(NA)	.1	.7
Local	704	2,967	6,514	3.6	5.5	6.4
Cable (Local)	(NA)	8	179	(NA)	(Z)	.2
Radio	1,308	3,702	6,949	6.7	6.9	6.8
Network	56	183	423	.3	.3	.4
Spot	371	779	1,348	1.9	1.5	1.3
Local	881	2,740	5,178	4.5	5.1	5.1
Direct mail	2,766	7,596	17,145	14.1	14.2	16.8
Business papers	740	1,674	2,382	3.8	3.1	2.3
Outdoor	234	578	985	1.2	1.1	1.0
Miscellaneous	3,848	10,503	19,595	19.7	19.6	19.2

NA = not available. Z = less than .05.
SOURCE: *Statistical Abstract of the United States, 1988*, p. 530.

after rapid growth since 1970. Television advertising was $23 billion, newspapers carried $27 billion, and all other advertising was $52 billion.[7]

Sales networks are the other main selling expense. Their size is hard to estimate because they mingle with service, delivery, and other retailing operations. Probably they total about $175 billion yearly.[8] The economic magnitudes, as you can see, are large.

These selling expenses are highly focused in certain industries. Table 16.2 indicates that only a handful of industries have advertising intensity above 5 percent (patterns have changed little since Comanor and Wilson's 1954–1957 data). There is not much advertising in producer-goods industries, of course, because most industrial buyers have clear needs and sophisticated buying skills. Some big consumer-goods industries have large advertising levels, even if the ratios to sales are small; the automobile industry is a good example.

Table 16.3 shows that selling *other* than advertising reaches high levels in a number of industries. One-fourth or more of revenues are absorbed by total selling efforts in seven of these industries.

Table 16.4 lists the firms spending the largest dollar volumes on advertising. These amounts do not include other selling costs, such as those in Table 16.3.

For completeness, Table 16.5 shows advertising spending by city areas. Note the high intensity of the advertising in these cities, at over $500 per household.

There are no accurate measures of how sales efforts divide between informational and persuasive types. Some analysts regard television ads as mainly persuasive and newspaper ads as mainly informational. You can try to make your own rough estimate. If half and half would be a reasonable first approximation for all sales effort, then the persuasive part would be about 3 percent of net national income.[9]

III. ANALYSIS OF ADVERTISING'S ROLE

1. Is Advertising a Barrier to Entry?

Since 1965, research has crystallized on the possibility that advertising raises entry barriers. Bain had stressed "product differentiation" in the 1950s. Comanor and Wilson focused on advertising, with the analysis summarized in Figure 16.3.

To enter a market of advertised goods, a new firm must meet "penetration costs." These are shown rising in Figure 16.3, because gaining a larger market share requires sharply rising advertising efforts. (The analysis holds also for the other forms of selling expenses.) Total costs for an entrant (production plus normal advertising costs plus penetration costs) are higher than those for an established firm with established brand images. As Figure 16.3 indicates, this opens up a barrier, whose

---

[7] Good sources of information on advertising include *Advertising Age* magazine, *Printer's Ink* magazine, and U.S. Bureau of the Census, *Statistical Abstract of the United States* (Washington, D.C.: Superintendent of Documents, annual).

[8] Thus there are about 4.3 million sales workers other than salesclerks in stores. Their median earnings are about $25,500, and related costs are probably at least $8,000. This suggests a total cost of some $175 billion. See Census Bureau, *Statistical Abstract, 1982–3*, pp. 386, 404.

[9] Scherer adopts the half-and-half estimate and regards it as a rough consensus in the literature; see his *Industrial Market Structure*, pp. 324–32.

TABLE 16.2   Advertising Intensity in Various Consumer-Goods
Industries, 1954–1957

INDUSTRIES	PROFIT RATE[a] (%)	ADVERTISING EXPENDITURE[b] (%)
Hats	1.6	2.2
Carpets	4.5	2.0
Costume jewelry	1.4	4.0
Jewelry	5.3	3.2
Wines	7.3	5.2
Watches and clocks	1.9	5.6
Cigars	5.3	2.6
Cereals	14.8	10.3
Hand tools	11.4	4.2
Perfumes	13.5	15.3
Distilled liquor	5.0	2.1
Electrical appliances	10.3	3.5
Books	10.1	2.4
Soaps	11.7	9.2
Confectioneries	10.6	3.5
Soft drinks	10.0	6.2
Cigarettes	11.5	4.8
Drugs	14.0	9.9
Instruments	12.0	2.0
Malt liquors	7.2	6.8
Radio, television, and audio equipment	8.8	2.2
Bakery products	9.3	2.9
Canning	6.4	2.9
Dairy products	7.9	2.2
Meat packing	4.6	0.6

[a] Profit rate is profit as a percentage of equity capital.
[b] Advertising as a percentage of sales. Only industries with a ratio of 2.0 percent or higher are included.
SOURCE: Adapted from William S. Comanor and Thomas Wilson, *Advertising and Market Power* (Cambridge, Mass.: Harvard University Press, 1975).

height is as shown. It also reduces slightly the optimal scale for the entrant, from q_2 to q_3. If no advertising were required, optimal scale would be much smaller, at q_1. If penetration costs should instead have economies of scale (that is, if APC sloped down instead of up), the effect on optimum scale would change. Yet the barrier effect would still occur.

Among established firms, advertising has a further effect. Average advertising costs (line AAC) show economies of scale, which increase the optimal firm size from q_1 to q_2. This tightens the oligopoly and places smaller firms at a cost disadvantage.

The whole effect is to let established firms raise price up to the "limit price" level of P_3. Without selling costs, price would instead be at P_1. The increase from P_1 to P_3 is advertising's effect. The degree of market power is higher, entry is

TABLE 16.3   All Selling Expenditures of 10 Most Advertising-Intensive Industries, 1975

	ADVERTISING SALES (%)	OTHER SELLING EXPENDITURES SALES (%)	TOTAL (%)
Proprietary drugs	20.1	15.0	35.1
Toiletries	13.8	14.8	28.6
Bread, cake, etc.	2.0	26.3	28.3
Cutlery (including razors)	12.8	12.8	25.6
Chewing gum	12.3	13.1	25.4
Distilled liquors	11.9	13.4	25.3
Household vacuum cleaners	3.0	22.2	25.2
Typewriters	1.2	22.5	23.7
Hosiery	9.4	14.1	22.5
Calculating, accounting machines	2.8	19.3	22.1

SOURCE: Adapted from Leonard W. Weiss, George Pascoe, and Stephen Martin, "The Size of Selling Costs," *Review of Economics and Statistics*, 65, (November 1983), 669.

TABLE 16.4   U.S. Firms Spending the Largest Amounts on Advertising, 1987

			AMOUNTS:	
RANK	NAME	MAIN PRODUCT AREA	$ MILLIONS	AS A % OF SALES
1	Philip Morris	Tobacco, beer	$1,558	7.0
2	Procter & Gamble	Soaps, personal	1,387	8.2
3	General Motors	Automobiles	1,025	1.0
4	Sears, Roebuck	Retailing	887	2.0
5	RJR Nabisco	Food, tobacco	840	5.3
6	Pepsico	Soft drinks	704	6.1
7	Eastman Kodak	Photographic goods	658	4.9
8	McDonald's	Fast food	649	13.5
9	Ford Motor	Automobiles	640	0.9
10	Anheuser-Busch	Beer	635	7.7
11	K Mart	Retailing	632	2.5
12	Unilever	Personal products	581	13.4
13	General Mills	Foods	572	11.0
14	Chrysler	Automobiles	569	2.2
15	Warner-Lambert	Personal products	558	16.0
16	AT&T	Telecommunications	531	1.7
17	Kellogg	Cereals	525	13.8
18	J.C. Penney	Retailing	513	3.7
19	Pillsbury	Foods	474	7.7
20	Johnson & Johnson	Medical supplies	459	5.7

SOURCES: For advertising amounts, *Advertising Age Magazine*, "Power Charts," December 26, 1988, Special Section, pp. 1–4. For sales data, *Fortune Magazine*, "The Fortune 500," April 25, 1988, pp. D11–D12.

TABLE 16.5 Ten U.S. Cities with the Highest
Intensity of Advertising per Household, 1987

RANK	CITY	ADVERTISING REVENUES PER HOUSEHOLD
1	Miami	$598
2	San Diego	585
3	Dallas-Ft. Worth	589
4	Washington, D.C.	560
5	Los Angeles	557
6	Houston	545
7	San Francisco	542
8	Atlanta	541
9	Denver	528
10	Boston	526

SOURCE: Data are from *Advertising Age Magazine*, "Power Charts," December 26, 1988, Special Section, pp. 1–4.

impeded, and of course the customers pay a higher price. With the tighter oligopoly, product variety will be less.

Two patterns of advertising intensity will occur: *within* industries and *among* industries. The question is how advertising intensity will vary with market power.

Within an industry, advertising intensity will often decline as market share rises. This reflects the "threshold" condition: One national sales network, or saturation advertising campaign, may be enough; further pitches would be largely ignored. The dominant firm—say, with a 50 percent market share—spreads this cost over a larger volume. Its smaller rivals (say, with 25 and 10 percent market shares) will have

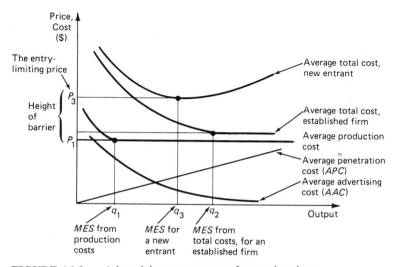

FIGURE 16.3. Advertising as a cause of entry barriers.

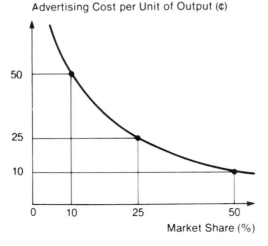

FIGURE 16.4.   Within an industry, advertising intensity and market share may be inversely related.

average advertising costs per unit of output that are, respectively, two and one-half times as large and five times as large as the dominant firm's.

Figure 16.4 illustrates this result. The dominant firm will gain higher profits per unit because of advertising. The detergent industry actually fits these conditions; Procter & Gamble (50 percent market share) has a much lower advertising cost per box of detergent than does Lever Brothers (a 10 percent share).

Figure 16.4 seems to show economies of scale in advertising. Are they technical or pecuniary? The dominant firm does use less advertising resources per unit of output than do the smaller firms, but, remember, their advertising may have been forced on them by the dominant firm's advertising! Very likely they would prefer to advertise much less or not at all. Looked at another way, the advertising may be persuasive rather than informational.

Both factors would make the pattern in Figure 16.4 pecuniary rather than socially beneficial. Generally, the seeming scale economies in selling efforts are not regarded as being on the same footing with technical scale economies in production. The burden of proof can only be overcome by showing that the advertising is informational and is not imposed on the lesser firms.

Among industries, advertising intensity is likely to be related positively to concentration. Higher concentration—that is, tight oligopoly—tends to breed greater sales effort, as was noted earlier. Sales effort becomes an important substitute for price strategies.

Moreover, the causation can run the other way, from advertising to concentration. The intraindustry effect graphed in Figure 16.4 will help the dominant firms to thrive and grow relative to lesser firms. This would tighten market structure and reduce the necessary advertising-sales ratios in highly concentrated industries.

If the Dorfman-Steiner analysis holds, then a linear pattern may be observed, as shown in Figure 16.5. But the scale economies effect and other departures (lags,

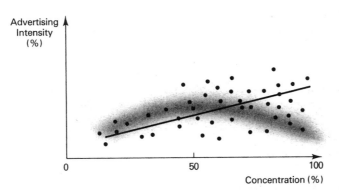

FIGURE 16.5.   Among consumer-goods markets, concentration and advertising intensity may be directly correlated, in either linear or curved fashion.

responses by rivals, and the lesser need for monopolists to advertise) would tend to give the curved pattern also shown in Figure 16.5.

In fact, the pattern *is* probably curved, according to recent research. Weiss, Pascoe, and Martin regressed the intensity of sales expenditure (for both advertising and other types of sales efforts) on the degree of concentration and the type of goods (producer or final goods).[10] Their main results for 92 U.S. industries in 1975 are summarized in Table 16.6. Concentration is included twice, both by itself and squared. The $CR4^2$ term is a test for curvature. If it is negative and significant, then it offsets the linear rising effect of the simple CR4 term, at higher levels of concentration. In fact, the coefficient of $CR4^2$ is significant and negative, as shown in Table 16.6.

Therefore the inverted U shape is confirmed, for these data. The relationship with advertising intensity appears to peak at a concentration ratio of 56 percent. For other selling expenses, the relationship peaks at 50 percent. In both cases, sales effort is correlated with the degree of industry sales to final consumers, as expected.

TABLE 16.6   The Inverted-U-Shaped Correlation of Advertising

MEDIA ADVERTISING
Advertising Sales $= -0.054 + 0.040^{c}\text{FC} + 0.229^{a}\text{CR4} - 0.205^{b}\text{CR4}^2 \quad R^2 = 0.0856$
OTHER SALES EFFORTS
Other Sales Expenses Sales $= -0.022 + 0.061^{b}\text{FC} + 0.372^{a}\text{CR4} - 0.372^{a}\text{CR4}^2 \quad R^2 = 0.555$

Note: For a sample of 92 consumer-goods industries. Certain explanatory variables have been suppressed for compactness. CR4 = four-firm seller concentration ratio. FC = fraction of industry sales going to final consumers.
[a] Statistical significance at the 1 percent level.
[b] Statistical significance at the 5 percent level.
[c] Statistical significance at the 10 percent level.
SOURCE: Adapted from Leonard W. Weiss, George Pascoe, and Stephen Martin, "The Size of Selling Costs," *Review of Economics and Statistics*, 65 (November 1983), 671.

[10] Leonard W. Weiss, George Pascoe, and Stephen Martin, "The Size of Selling Costs," *Review of Economics and Statistics,* 65 (November 1983), 668–72.

This test is suggestive rather than definitive, but it does fit sound theory.

The larger effect of advertising is to raise entry barriers. This, in turn, leads to excess profits, which will vary closely with market shares. The question is how strong the effect is. The process—from advertising to excess profits—might be separable from other influences on profits, such as economies of scale and growth. If so, it could be isolated and measured. Yet it operates through market share, so it may be impossible to separate out advertising's role from the general role of market share.

2. Advertising May Be Procompetitive or Neutral

There are two main suggestions that advertising does *not* increase market power.

First, advertising can be a powerful device by which new or small firms succeed. This obvious point could hold even if the barriers effect existed. Some real cases fit this suggestion, as Section IV will note. Conceivably they could more than offset the barriers effect. Backman urges that they do, giving several examples.[11] Dial soap is a good example; it was Armour & Company's entry into the soap industry in the 1950s, by means of heavy advertising. Yet a full appraisal presumably requires a census of all such cases, and that has not remotely been done.

Second, advertising may just be a process of investing in customer loyalty.[12] That investment is costly. It cumulates, like any other capital good: each year's spending on advertising offsets the natural "depreciation" of the "investment" (by refreshing customers' brand images and contacting new consumers). It may also add to the "investment." Such a valuable stock would need to yield a normal stream of profits. These returns to advertising investment might just account for the excess profits that advertising's barrier effect seems to cause.

If this is true, advertising would be neutral toward market power and profits. Even so, the social value of the investment in advertising would still be in question. But at least advertising would not be anticompetitive.

IV. EVIDENCE ON ADVERTISING'S ROLE

We now turn to research on the impact of sales effort. Since 1960, most of it has focused on advertising. It has drawn the patterns fairly clearly, but there is still room for debate.

Barriers Effects.   Comanor and Wilson's study of advertising and profit rates is the main focus. These two authors tested whether profit rates are "explained" statistically by advertising intensity. Their test covered 41 consumer-goods industries where advertising intensity ranged from 15 down to less than 1 percent (see Table 16.2). A consistent positive association did emerge between profit rates and advertising intensity (as illustrated in Figure 16.5). They regarded this as confirming the barrier effect.

---

[11] Backman, *Advertising and Competition.*
[12] Lester G. Telser, "Some Aspects of the Economics of Advertising," *Journal of Business,* 41 (April 1968), 166–73; and Backman, *Advertising and Competition.*

Some evidence also confirms the effect shown in Figure 16.4. Advertising intensity fits that pattern in the automobile, toiletries, cereals, beer, and detergents industries, among others. (You can make your own appraisal, using *Advertising Age* and *Printer's Ink* trade journals.) These industries include the most highly advertising-intensive cases.

Further tests have consistently, if not uniformly, confirmed the Comanor-Wilson findings.[13] "Inconsistent" findings occur mainly when the tests are applied to *all* industries, or to odd time periods.[14] Certain questions of interpretation do remain. For example: Is advertising *the* causal factor? Or does it interact with market share, so that market share is really the cause of higher profit rates? There is room for much research beyond Comanor-Wilson's pioneering study and the more recent work, although the odds are low that further study will reverse the present consensus.

Procompetitive Advertising Cases.   Cases of procompetitive advertising blitzes by small and new firms are fairly numerous. They are hard to document and appraise. Usually, other factors besides advertising were involved: a new product, mistakes by the leading firm, changes in tastes. And often the blitz served only to establish a new brand of the leading firm, which does not necessarily increase competition. There is no census of all cases of entry via advertising because such a complete census is not really possible. Therefore one must approach these cases carefully, remembering to ask whether the advertising blitz would have been necessary if the dominant firm had not already been a heavy advertiser.

Were all cases known and properly evaluated, there would still be no direct quantitative test to determine whether procompetitive effects offset the barriers effect of advertising. Most discussions rely on tiny samples of the phenomenon and offer little more than guesswork.

Advertising as an Investment.   This concept is logical, and the issue turns on practical evidence. Weiss's research is the major study of the matter so far.[15] It suggests that the investment feature accounts for little, if any, of the profits arising from advertising. The tax treatment of current costs (advertising is one such tax-deductible expenditure) is part of the problem, as is the tax treatment of returns to capital. (Thus, if advertising were treated as a flow of investment, it would be taxed differently and would appear to offer different profit yields). Subsequent challenges have left Weiss's results largely intact.[16] The burden of proof is against the investment concept of advertising as a substitute for the barriers effect.

Case Studies.   Three cases can serve to illustrate advertising's tendency to

---

[13] These include Simon, *Issues;* Roger Sherman, *Oligopoly: An Empirical Approach* (Cambridge, Mass.: Ballinger, 1972), and sources cited there. A recent study suggests that "advertising leads to greater concentration," but that "the product differentiation barrier to entry is not very great." See Allyn D. Strickland and Leonard W. Weiss, "Advertising, Concentration and Price-Cost Margins," *Journal of Political Economy,* 84 (September–October 1976), 1109–21.

[14] See Lester G. Telser and others, "Symposium on Advertising," *Journal of Industrial Economics,* 18 (November 1969), 76–94; Richard Schmalansee, *The Economics of Advertising* (Amsterdam: North-Holland, 1972); and Backman, *Advertising and Competition.*

[15] Leonard W. Weiss, "Advertising, Profits and Corporate Taxes," *Review of Economics and Statistics,* 51 (November 1969), 421–30.

[16] See Robert Ayanian, "Advertising and Rate of Return," *Journal of Law and Economics,* 18 (October 1975); and Harry Bloch, "Advertising and Profitability: A Reappraisal," *Journal of Political Economy,* 82 (March/April 1974), 267–86.

reduce competition. The cigarette industry has led the way in intensive advertising for over fifty years. The several major sellers are locked in classic conditions of standoff advertising, most of it of a persuasive kind. That may be costly, but it discourages entrants. Few firms have, in fact, entered this market since 1920.

In the bleach market, Clorox has been dominant for decades, with a market share above 50 percent. The company uses intensive advertising to build strong brand loyalties, even though bleaches are chemically uniform. Despite the attracting power of Clorox's high profit rates, new firms have found it difficult to enter the market in the face of Clorox's advertising power. Clorox's main rival, Purex (with about a 15 percent market share), has also been limited by advertising. In one episode, Purex attempted to raise its share by regional sales promotion, whereupon Clorox mounted its own promotional blitzes in the same regions, blocking Purex and deterring it from further efforts.

The cereals industry presents a more subtle version of sales effort, on two levels.[17] First, the three major cereals firms (Kellogg, General Mills, and General Foods) advertise heavily, raising the familiar barrier to new entrants. Entry has in fact been minor in the last four decades. Second, they have joined in a practice of "packing the product space." As explained in detail in Chapter 18, advertising has helped to bar new competition by supporting a proliferation of brands. The result has been high profit rates for the Big Three.

The Big Three reject this view, stressing their innovativeness in offering a great diversity of choices to consumers. The "packing" was merely a full response to consumer preference, they say. That interpretation doesn't alter the observation that advertising appears to limit competition and promote high profits.

In short, the research consensus so far is that much advertising is beneficial and neutral to competition, especially informative advertising of search goods. Some of it is procompetitive. But advertising does tend—with certain exceptions—to raise market power and monopoly profits, especially persuasive advertising of experience goods. And persuasive advertising is a fairly large share of the total.

Advertising's effect in raising entry barriers has not proved to be overwhelming. Also, the effect clusters in relatively few consumer-goods markets rather than spreading across the whole economy. Selling expenses are a rather specialized problem, and their effects are often mixed.

QUESTIONS FOR REVIEW

1. Selling expenses include (1) advertising, (2) promotional campaigns, (3) sales networks, (4) X-inefficiency. Which?

2. "Advertising and sales networks are always substitutable for each other." True?

---

[17] See Richard L. Schmalansee, "Entry Deterrence in the Ready-to-Eat Cereal Industry," *Bell Journal of Economics,* 9 (Autumn 1978), 305–27; and F. M. Scherer, "The Welfare Economies of Product Variety: An Application to the Ready-to-Eat Cereals Industry," *Journal of Industrial Economics,* 28 (1969). See also Chapter 18 of this text.

A major FTC case attacked the leading cereals firms for "shared monopoly," using these points. But the case was finally dropped in 1982 by the FTC, so there is little policy action or guidelines toward tight-oligopoly behavior. See FTC: *In the Matter of Kellogg Co. et al.,* Docket No. 8883, Complaint, April 26, 1972, decision January 1982.

3. "Advertising is strictly identical to other inputs to the firm." True?
4. "A single firm with 90 percent of the market is likely to spend less on advertising than would four equal-sized firms totaling 90 percent of the market." True?
5. "Standoff advertising means informational rather than persuasive advertising." True?
6. "Oligopoly may result in a maximum of advertising expenditure and a minimum of true product diversity." True?
7. "Persuasive advertising can promote competition." True?
8. Advertising often encounters (1) diminishing returns, (2) economies of scale. Which, or both?
9. "Advertising is an investment. Its normal returns could explain the high profits of firms that advertise intensively." Is this (1) logical, or (2) borne out by factual evidence, or (3) both, or (4) neither?
10. Does advertising generally raise barriers to new entry?
11. Explain why tight oligopoly is likely to develop heavy selling expenses.
12. Make the case that all advertising is valuable and procompetitive.
13. Derive the optimal levels of advertising when demand elasticity is 1.2 or 2.0, under Dorfman-Steiner conditions. Is that kind of analysis reliable?
14. Discuss the likely social impacts of advertising, in light of Dixit and Norman's approach.
15. Discuss two examples of "experience" and "search" goods. Does their advertising generally fit the predictions about persuasive and informative advertising?

17

DOMINANT FIRMS: EASTMAN KODAK, AT&T, BOEING, NEWSPAPERS, AND IBM

These two chapters turn the spotlight on nine cases where market power appears to be high. The opposite kind of examples, where competition is effective, could also easily be added, but their main conditions are familiar enough. By focusing on market power under dominance and tight oligopoly, these chapters bring out the lesser-known—and relatively uncommon—problems of monopoly.

The five cases of dominant firms summarized here—Eastman Kodak, AT&T, Boeing, leading city newspapers, and IBM—have been fascinating and prominent in the economy for many years. Each of them presents standard dominant-firm characteristics, which are duly reviewed and assessed. Each case also presents certain special issues of its own, which will be emphasized. Together these five cases nicely sample much of the variety in the dominant-firm phenomenon in U.S. industry (recall Chapters 4 and 11).

I. EASTMAN KODAK IN PHOTOGRAPHIC SUPPLIES[1]

Kodak has dominated the amateur photographic film industry since its formation and rise in the 1890s. Its founder, George Eastman, led the way in creating the popular market for photography by adopting a crucial market strategy: the early box

---

[1] Helpful sources include William L. Baldwin, "The Feedback Effect of Conduct on Industry Structure," *Journal of Law and Economics,* 12 (April 1969), 123–53; Don E. Waldman, *Antitrust Action and Market Structure* (Lexington, Mass.: Lexington Books, 1978) Chapter 7; James W. Brock, "Structural Monopoly, Technological Performance, and Predatory Innovation: Relevant Standards Under Section 2 of the Sherman Act," *American Business Law Journal,* 21 (1983), 291–306; and Brock, "Persistent Monopoly and the Charade of Antitrust: The Durability of Kodak's Market Power," *University of Toledo Law Review,* 14 (Spring 1983), 653–83.

camera was merely a low-price vehicle for selling profitable film.[2] That is still Kodak's basic approach: those little yellow boxes yield Kodak's main profit.

Kodak has brought out new films as time has passed and, until the mid-1950s, it also dominated the film-developing market. Kodak is also the main seller of simple snapshot cameras. But it is Kodak's dominance of film which provides the pivot for exerting control over the entire photographic supplies industry.

1.   The Market

There are three related markets in the industry: (1) film, (2) cameras, and (3) photo-finishing.[3] Amateur photographic film has long been widely agreed to be the most important relevant market in this industry. Professional films are different in nature, in marketing channels, and in pricing. Other photographic supplies (cameras, photo-finishing) are complements rather than substitutes for film.

Yet mutual entry among the three markets might matter. The other producers of related products (mainly the Japanese, who have largely taken over the 35-mm. camera market, and Polaroid, which dominates the instant-photograph market) might be thought to be capable of entering the film market if Kodak raises its prices too far. And Kodak has tried to venture into instant cameras (unsuccessfully, in the 1970s), and sells snapshot cameras such as Instamatics.

The connections among the three markets are indeed important. Control over film products provides Kodak with influence over equipment and finishing, by setting the technical standards (for spool sizes, film characteristics, etc.). Because Kodak is dominant in film, it largely controls the standards, and it has been able to affect competition in all three markets. Therefore the markets have been closely related, not only because of technical conditions but also because of the policies followed by Kodak.

2.   Structure

Kodak's market share of the dollar sales of film has been close to 90 percent since before 1910. Table 17.1 shows its share during 1955–1976; there has been little change since then. Its next rival is Fuji Film, at about 10–15 percent.

This 80-plus percent market share gives an unusually high degree of dominance. If all three markets for photographic supplies are grouped together, Kodak's share of total revenues is below 50 percent, and there are substantial other competitors, including Polaroid and the Japanese camera makers. But that is too broad a grouping to be the true market.

Concentration has little additional meaning in the film market, given the presence of Kodak's near-monopoly. The broader film-and-camera market would be a tight oligopoly, but with areas of dominance within it.

Entry barriers into the film market are probably very high because of Kodak's

---

[2] As a small footnote, Eastman's descendants, all possessing wealth from Eastman Kodak's market success, include Linda Eastman, who is married to Paul McCartney, the former Beatle.

[3] For a lucid assessment of Kodak's control in these three markets, see James W. Brock, "Industry Structure and Market Power: The Relevance of the 'Relevant Market,'" *Antitrust Bulletin,* 29 (Fall 1984), 535–60.

TABLE 17.1 Amateur Conventional Film: Kodak Share, 1955–1976

	DOLLARS ($ MILLIONS)		ROLLS (MILLIONS)	
YEAR	TOTAL	% KODAK	TOTAL	% KODAK
1955	90.5	91	166	84
1960	137.6	92	190	86
1965	186.1	90	224	85
1970	292.6	89	281	87
1972	338.5	90	324	88
1976	—	—	408	85

SOURCE: Adapted from James W. Brock, "Industry Structure and Market Power: The Relevance of the 'Relevant Market,'" *Antitrust Bulletin*, 29 (Fall 1984), 546; based on Kodak Appeal Brief at addendum A, table 4, *Berkey Photo, Inc.* v. *Eastman Kodak Co.* (Jan. 30, 1979); Berkey Petition for a Writ of Certiorari to the United States Court of Appeals for the Second Circuit at chart 2, *Berkey Photo, Inc.* v. *Eastman Kodak Co.* (Oct. Term, 1979).

history of heavy advertising to build brand loyalty. Moreover, Kodak's control over industry standards makes entry even more difficult. New firms would need to comply with Kodak's design standards. But Kodak can change these standards so as to make the entrants' products noncompatible.

Capital requirements to enter are also large, partly to overcome the strong retaliation that Kodak would inevitably seek to inflict. An entrant's spending for R&D would need to be substantial, and some provision for entering the film-*developing* market might also be needed, in order to assure good-quality final photographs.

In contrast to this appraisal, one can assess the industry from Kodak's viewpoint; the barriers might not be very high, if the larger high-technology firms in cameras actually determine to diversify by entering the film market. Large capital requirements might not be a major problem for them, and they might be able to withstand Kodak's retaliation. Yet, in fact there has been no entry by these firms.

3. Determinants

Kodak's growth has mainly been by internal sources during the decades since it gained dominance, rather than by mergers. Advertising is intensive, and it is an important element favoring continued dominance by Kodak. Although Kodak has done creditable innovations from time to time, its record is not so good that rapid innovation can be credited entirely for its continuing dominance. Thus its 1980s disk camera, with tiny film windows set in a disk, was a commercial failure, because it provided mediocre picture quality.

The technology of film production and marketing probably gives a Minimum Efficient Scale that is not greater than 20 percent of the market, so that Kodak probably has excess market share of about 60 percent.

Kodak's view, instead, is that superiority and scale economies explain its near-monopoly position entirely. Kodak also suggests that scale economies are actually large, and that its control over industry standards has not added to its market power.

4.   Behavior

Kodak's behavior has largely followed dominant-firm lines, in being unilateral rather than cooperative. It has used the links to its film-market dominance to strengthen its position in all three markets in the industry.

Kodak has not been purely aggressive. It has coexisted with Polaroid (as the supplier of virtually all of Polaroid's film) and since 1955 with other film finishers.[4] But it has applied its control steadily so to maximize its market share and profits. In an episode that provoked a major antitrust case, Kodak attempted to eliminate Berkey as a rival in film-finishing in the 1970s.[5] In the 1980s Kodak was convicted of infringing major patents of Polaroid, when it entered the instant camera market in 1976. Generally Kodak has adopted rough unilateral tactics from time to time.

But these can be regarded as merely "hard competition." Kodak was eventually acquitted in the Berkey case, and the patent infringement is likely to cost it a large penalty payment. In this view, Kodak may be just a strict competitor facing tough actual and potential rivals.

5.   Performance

The Berkey case brought out evidence that Kodak had set high price-cost margins and high rates of return on investment. These were sustained over decades. Kodak's own lawyers admitted in the Berkey case that film was "a market where there has not been price competition and where Kodak has been able to price its products pretty much without regard to the products of competitors."[6]

As for X-efficiency, the 1980s brought a rising recognition in the business press that Kodak had become slow, conservative, and burdened with excess employees. Kodak turned out to be able to cut costs by over 10 percent while maintaining production levels. This suggests that its profit-maximizing prices were at even higher levels above minimum *attainable* costs. Therefore both allocative efficiency and X-efficiency may have been significantly reduced.

Kodak's record of innovation in film itself has been mixed and moderate. Kodak has brought out new films, with an emphasis on quality and reliability rather than a rapid pace of introducing new film products. In two recent film-related innovations (instant-picture cameras in the middle 1970s and the disk camera and film in the 1980s), Kodak's innovations have failed and the products have been abandoned.

Viewed more broadly, Kodak has blocked some innovations that other firms sought to make.[7] Kodak has refused to market any film not compatible with its own cameras, either in still or motion-picture photography. That has narrowed the range of possible innovation in the sector, by excluding other types of cameras, such as

---

[4] In settling an antitrust suit, Kodak in 1954 agreed to stop tying the processing of its color films to their sale. That ended its near-monopoly on processing but not its ability to control the industry's standards.

[5] See *Berkey Photo, Inc. v. Eastman Kodak Co.* (the "Berkey Photo" case) 457 F. Supp. 404 (A.D.N.Y. 1978). *modified*, 603 F.2d 263 (2d Circ. 1979), *cert.* dismissed, 444 U.S. 1093 (1980).

[6] *Berkey Photo,* 603 F.2d at 270.

[7] Brock has been particularly persuasive that Kodak's record on innovation has been inferior and obstructive, in "an industry structure that stultifies and chokes technological progress"; see Brock, *American Business Law Journal,* 1983, quoted at page 305.

the sub-miniature cartridge-loading cameras.[8] In fact, Kodak appears to have been a slow, mistake-prone and often obstructive innovator.

More favorably, one might say that Kodak's pricing and profits were a reward for its long superiority in quality and bringing out new products, plus its undertaking the risks of new competition and new-product failures. Those risks are demonstrated by Kodak's two recent new-camera failures. As for X-inefficiency, perhaps Kodak was a benevolent employer, planning for growth that did not materialize. Its excess levels of employees and resources might have been merely reserves for assuring higher quality and growth.

6. In Summary

One can draw contrasting versions. Kodak may have been a classic dominant firm, tenaciously preserving a large degree of excess market share by a series of actions which suppressed its rivals in all three markets within the industry. Its pricing and profits were high, its costs higher than necessary, and its innovations ranged from reasonable ones, to failures, and even to the deliberate obstruction of innovations by other firms. This version has largely been supported by academic research, by widespread business press accounts, and by the weight of expert testimony in antitrust cases.

The alternative, more favorable view is consistent with a number of plausible facts. Kodak has provided generally a high quality of film and service, while facing possible new competition. Its profitability may be seen as a reward for many decades of innovations in film.

II.   AT&T IN THE LONG-DISTANCE TELEPHONE SERVICE MARKET

Until it was divided up in the spectacular divestiture of the Bell System in January, 1984, the American Telephone & Telegraph Company was the world's largest private enterprise.[9] It was also the century-old firm which had controlled nearly all of the telephone sector in the U.S. for over seven decades. In that divestiture, forced by a successful antitrust action by the U.S. government, AT&T kept (1) its virtual monopoly of U.S. long-distance telephone traffic in the U.S., plus (2) its research arm (Bell Laboratories), and (3) Western Electric Co., its firm which had monopolized the supply of telecommunications equipment to the Bell operating systems.

---

[8] This blocking of innovation was conceded by Kodak's own expert in the Berkey case, and Judge Kaufman in that case concluded that Kodak's denial ". . . drastically reduced the ability of rival manufacturers to compete by introducing new camera formats." See *Berkey Photo,* 603 F.2d at 284.

[9] Among numerous books on the AT&T divestiture, see Peter Temin, *The Fall of the Bell System* (New York: Cambridge University Press, 1987); Alvin von Auw, *Heritage and Destiny: Reflections on the Bell System in Transition* (New York: Praeger Publishers, 1983); and David S. Evans, ed., *Breaking Up Bell* (New York: North-Holland, 1983). See also Paul W. MacAvoy and Kenneth Robinson, "Winning by Losing: The AT&T Settlement and Its Impact on Telecommunications," *Yale Journal on Regulation* 1 (1983), pp. 1-42. An earlier analysis is W. G. Shepherd, "The Competitive Margin in Communications," a chapter in William M. Capron, ed., *Technological Change in Regulated Industries* (Washington, D.C.: Brooking Institution, 1971). Even earlier is John Sheahan, "Integration and Exclusion in the Telephone Equipment Industry," *Quarterly Journal of Economics* 70 (May 1956), pp. 249-69.

The long-distance telephone market is our topic here, because AT&T's continued dominance of it provides one of the leading U.S. examples of dominance in a large, rapidly-growing market. It is also a leading policy question: is competition now effective enough to permit a full deregulation of AT&T?

Not only is AT&T still one of the largest U.S. firms, but long-distance telephone service is also an unusually important market. It touches nearly every household and enterprise in the country, often crucially for their well-being and profits. The technology is complex, vulnerable and rapidly changing.

AT&T's total (but regulated) monopoly in long-distance service was subjected to new competition in the 1970s, as MCI, GTE-Sprint (now U.S. Sprint) and a few others forced their way in under new regulatory policies. But AT&T has fiercely resisted the gradually growing competition, and in 1989 it still held over 70 percent of total traffic. As is customary with dominant firms, AT&T claims to be under severe pressure and risk from its little rivals. In contrast, the little rivals claim to be small and vulnerable compared to AT&T's power and controls over the market.

This case study offers the drama of small newcomers challenging a mighty enterprise. AT&T has been demanding freedom from regulation so that it can compete freely in every dimension of pricing and service. By 1989 U.S. regulators had greatly loosened the restraints and were considering taking off the remaining restraints. Should they? Is competition already effective? Will it stay vigorous? Events are unfolding, and the answers are hotly debated.

1.   The Market

There is sharp debate about the extent of this market. At its broadest, it would be a single market, embracing all long-distance traffic, of all categories of users and types of messages transmitted. The customers include not only residences but also all sizes and types of businesses. The business customers range from millions of small ones to a few hundred very large ones, with a variety of needs and patterns of use. The types of messages include voice conversations as well as business information and large-scale data transmission.

Narrower market definitions are possible by types of users, types of messages, and geographic regions. The divisions are reinforced by the pressures applied by larger customers to obtain special discounts and services, under threat of changing suppliers or creating their own communications systems. Large hotel chains, for example, have demanded lower prices, and the pressures and temptations to price discriminate are very high.

The market is segmented to some degree, because large-scale business traffic does have different properties from small-scale residential use. And 800-line service (free to those calling in) has still further differences. Whether or not these are genuinely distinct markets is debatable. All of the significant firms (AT&T, MCI, Sprint, and others) compete across the range of customers, message types, and regions. Therefore, all of the parts of the market are linked by the firms' larger strategies, as they vie across the full range of customers and traffic categories.

Moreover, all customers of each company share basically the same capacity, as they use the system. Technically, this pooling of the use of capacity causes the parts of the market to mingle, as if they were all part of a single market. There are some distinctions between night and day traffic, because most conversations are during the waking hours, while data transmission can be heavy during the night.

Altogether, it is safest to proceed as if there were one broad market for long-distance service. That approach captures the main zone of consumer choice and competitive strategies.

2.   Structure

AT&T's share of all long-distance revenue has evolved from 100 percent before 1970, down to about 90 percent by 1980, to about 70-75 percent in 1989. MCI and U.S. Sprint are the next largest firms, with about 10 and 8 percent, respectively. The next tier of firms is very small, with none above 2 percent. AT&T continues to hold clear dominance, though its share has been slipping while the little rivals are enlarging their shares. AT&T predicts a rapid dwindling of its share, and it has demanded to be freed of regulatory constraints so that it can offer price discounting against its small rivals.

The little rivals portray themselves as vulnerable to AT&T and to outside events. Their profits have been unstable, with U.S. Sprint still running losses in most recent years. The technology makes it possible for larger customers to switch rapidly among suppliers, so that MCI and U.S. Sprint may be sharply affected by AT&T's pricing tactics.

In short, there is still a high degree of dominance, which has receded gradually. MCI and U.S. Sprint are established but of minor size. The next five years may be critical for them and especially for the smaller rivals to gain strength. The further dwindling of AT&T's dominance is not assured.

3.   Determinants

Long-distance service involves several components: (1) city-based systems connecting individual customers, (2) inter-city transmission, by wires, satellites, optical fibers, lasers, or other means, and (3) coordinated switching to complete and hold the connections. Traditionally, all of these were believed to be parts of a necessary natural monopoly, providing a single, coordinated national network in the Bell System. Bell System officials fostered that view, in capturing exclusive control of the new micro-wave transmission technology in the late 1940s and in resisting the rising efforts in the 1960s to inject competition.

By 1968 the Federal Communications Commission recognized that the market could be made to be competitive. Other companies could develop inter-city facilities and handle traffic at costs below AT&T's costs, but they needed access to local Bell systems so as to connect individual customers. The Bell System prohibited this crucial "interconnection" until the FCC (and ultimately the U.S. Supreme Court) forced it to give access in the 1970s.

It appeared at first that the entrants were merely exploiting the efficiencies created by the unified Bell System. But in the 1980s the small competitors have demonstrated that they can establish their own nation-wide networks in parallel with AT&T's capacity. Indeed, they have invested in extremely efficient fiber-optic capacity more rapidly than has AT&T.

In short, the market is naturally competitive, as long as city-based interconnection is open and fair. That crucial link was assisted by dividing up the Bell System in 1984, which separated the local Bell monopolies from AT&T. Those newly-independent local firms (the "baby Bells") no longer serve AT&T's old interest in blocking competition. In contrast, they have now sought to enter the lucrative long-distance market themselves, in direct competition with AT&T. But so far the judge supervising the divestiture has prevented that. The baby Bells would have incentives to control interconnection and block MCI, Sprint, etc., to their own advantage. Therefore, the baby Bells might exclude every other supplier, including even AT&T.

Yet this risk might be worth taking. The baby Bells would be a powerful source of new competition, able to compete strongly with AT&T's dominance. If one regards MCI, Sprint, and the other existing rivals as too small and weak to provide effective competition against AT&T, then the baby Bells may be the only true source of effective competition. The question then is whether the technology would permit them too much control over the gateways to local interconnection. That matter is still open to debate, and of course the technology could be adjusted or managed so as to assure fair interconnection by all.

It would be better to rely instead on the rise of MCI, Sprint, and other smaller competitors to become strong challengers to AT&T. Once five or six such rivals become well established and profitable, then competition could be effective without risking the special problems posed by the baby Bells. But it will take many years for the smaller firms to reach adequate market shares and strength. Their rise will need to be protected by the F.C.C., with continuing restraints on selective pricing by AT&T. AT&T would need to sink below a 50 percent market share, so that market dominance gives way to strong competition on a more even playing field.

4.   Behavior

The small entrants have set prices below AT&T's rates, initially by 30 to 50 percent. Until 1989, AT&T continued to be regulated by the FCC, which kept AT&T from fully matching the rivals' discounts. The price gap permitted MCI, Sprint, and others to get started, and their rising quality of service enabled them to narrow the discounts while still growing. AT&T has priced largely on a standardized basis and relied on its reputation, customer loyalty and advertising to retain its dominance.

But since 1987 AT&T has urged that competition is now fully effective, so that it should be permitted to offer specific price discounts like any other competitor. Such price discrimination would enable AT&T to pinpoint the most lucrative customers and try to obtain them, without cutting prices to others. In 1988 it sought FCC approval to offer a volume discount to Holiday Inns, the largest U.S. hotel chain. Holiday Inns had threatened to drop AT&T for a rival unless it were given a large enough price discount. If the FCC approved, AT&T could adopt the classic behavior of dominant firms, with systematic price discrimination which tends to suppress competition (recall Chapter 12).

The FCC did move in late 1988 to unleash AT&T, with a new "price cap" approach which would give AT&T wide discretion over individual prices. If competition were fully effective already, this could be harmless. But if AT&T's market share really were 75 percent, compared to 10 percent or less for its next-largest rivals, then price discrimination could reverse the rise of competition and solidify AT&T's dominance.

By late 1989, AT&T was using the new ''price cap'' freedom aggressively to offer deep selective discounts so as to win crucial customers such as Holiday Inns and Marriott Hotels. The F.C.C. appeared to have given AT&T wide latitude, nearly to the point of full deregulation. AT&T seemed to be regaining market share rather than losing it. The underlying natural-competitive conditions would then be thwarted as AT&T hardened its dominance.

5. Performance

Because AT&T has been regulated (though rather gently, on the whole), it is difficult to assess its performance. The Bell System's past innovation is widely recognized to have been slow, in line with its monopoly incentives (recall Chapter 6). Bell Laboratories may have performed invention and patenting actively, but practical innovations of those ideas were often restricted and delayed. Notable examples include rotary dialling (to replace live operators), microwave transmission, and computerized electronic switching of calls.[10]

In the long-distance market, AT&T has followed rather than led the development of fiber-optics capacity. Before 1984, AT&T also set high prices on long-distance service, where competition and regulation were weakest, so as to pool them with its other finances in the politically most advantageous pattern.

That high profitability on long-distance service is what attracted new competition so strongly to the long-distance market, and that competition has indeed forced down prices and costs in line with the classical predictions. The quality of service has not suffered substantially from the competition and divestiture. Service quality is still high, but customers also have a wider choice among types and price/quality varieties of service. The big question is whether competition will continue to develop, so as to sustain the gains of the last two decades.

That competition itself has been a substantial gain, as customers who want freedom of choice among alternatives can have it. Some residential and small-business customers may miss the cozy maternalism of the old Ma Bell monopoly. But large-business users and many others find great value in the freedom of choice to select among, and play off, competitors.

6. In Summary

New competition has had the classic effects: reducing costs and prices, increasing innovation, and widening freedom of choice. A seeming natural monopoly has turned out to be naturally competitive. But dominance has remained, receding only gradually. In 1989, the market is in a delicate phase, partly competitive but still subject to anti-competitive actions by AT&T if it is freed to apply them.

Normally, the dominant firm's market share would need to fall below 50 percent, with at least five strong rivals in place, before there could be confidence that competition is effective. The second tier of small firms will need to expand markedly,

---

[10] See Shepherd, 1971, *op. cit.*, and sources cited there.

in order to provide that balanced, competitive structure. Only if AT&T's customer base is vulnerable to rapid shifts will competition become fully effective. The next five years are likely to show if that is true.

III. BOEING AIRCRAFT

The Boeing Aircraft Company, located in the state of Washington, has been the dominant U.S. aircraft producer during most of the period since World War II. From many competitors in 1945, the industry narrowed down to just three main rivals by 1967 (Boeing, McDonnell-Douglas, and Lockheed). By the 1970s, Boeing stood alone among U.S. firms, with McDonnell-Douglas a distant second.

Boeing's biggest rise came with the jet age, beginning in 1959. Its planes were generally superior, and Boeing was also aided by resources and technology developed under favorable contracts for military aircraft. Boeing continued to develop high-quality aircraft (its 747 jumbo jet, the 737, and mid-size late-1970s craft), but in the 1980s it faltered. New competition from the European consortium Airbus Industrie challenged its dominance, and Boeing's share of the now-global jet airliner market was in serious danger.[11] While blaming unfair foreign government maneuverings for its troubles, Boeing adopted a severe internal reshaping program to recover efficiency.

In 1989 Boeing's position had strengthened, largely because new fears about disintegration of older aircraft stirred a rush of replacement orders. But the company continued to face the classic performance problems of dominant firms.

1. The Market

The product is full-size civilian passenger aircraft, for use by airlines. This is distinct from military aircraft, small aircraft (100 seats or less), helicopters and other such equipment. Since 1959, the main aircraft in this market have been jets, but some turbo-props have also been sold and newer hybrids of them may be produced in the 1990s.

Geographically, the market expanded during 1965-75 from a national to a worldwide basis, as all airlines became largely free to buy from any producer. Even so, political and nationalist aspects often are deeply involved in airplane sales. Although aircraft are the tangible product, sales often also involve vastly complex financing deals negotiated between the airlines and the producers, often with intimate involvement by the governments on both sides.[12]

This market definition is virtually universally agreed.

2. Structure

Boeing's market share was in the range of 50-65 percent in the 1960s and 1970s, even as the market widened. Other firms faded, though Airbus Industrie was formed. By 1980, Boeing's share of current sales was nearly 80 percent. But as of 1986-87,

---

[11] For example, see "Boeing Now Gears Up to Block the Inroads of Airbus in Plane Sales," *Wall Street Journal,* September 2, 1987, pp. 1, 12.

[12] Many foreign airlines are owned by their governments, in contrast to the U.S. where all civilian airlines are privately owned. But even private foreign airlines often are closely affected by their governments in working out deals to purchase aircraft.

Boeing's share was in the 50 percent range and under pressure from Airbus. Airbus's share appeared likely to go over 50 percent.[13]

But in 1988 a series of accidents appeared to demonstrate that the fleets of existing planes were aging more rapidly and dangerously than had been thought. Many airlines scrambled to order replacements, turning mainly to Boeing as the established leader. By 1989, the surge in demand appeared to have rescued Boeing from Airbus's challenge, with an order backlog that indicated continued dominance in the range of 60 to 70 percent. McDonnell-Douglas continued to subsist on a 10-15 percent market share.

Three-firm concentration is at virtually 100 percent, a fact which adds little knowledge to the market shares.

Entry barriers appear to be extremely high. Reputation is important, including a full back-up of personnel, technical capacity, and finances for fixing any problems that arise. The capital requirements for entry are very high, because of scale economies, industry size, and R&D needs. Connections with governments are important, for three reasons. U.S. military contracts have provided important profits and product spin-offs. U.S. officials' support can help sway plane purchases. And foreign governments are also often involved in purchase decisions by foreign airlines, because the large financial and job impacts can affect national economic performance.

From Boeing's point of view, the barriers seem more moderate. After all, Airbus has been able to enter. To that extent, scale economies would remain as the main barrier source, and entry would not seem to be blocked.

3. Determinants

Much the same factors have shaped the structure. Scale economies are important, though the MES level for firms is probably not more than 20 percent of the market. That would leave room for about five comparable competitors. The U.S. military's decisions have probably shaped the industry, by allocating important contracts among the aircraft producers.

Airlines also prefer to standardize and unify their fleets, so as to reduce the costs of servicing and repairs. Still another determinant is reputation. Airlines lean toward suppliers which can assure them of airdraft safety, so as to minimize the apparent risk of crashes. That leads them toward the larger, established suppliers such as Boeing.

Moreover, this industry appears to face unusually high degrees of risk. The technology is subject to major changes, such as in the possible turn to turbo-prop aircraft in the 1990s. Demand is also difficult to predict, as airlines juggle decisions about ordering large numbers of planes. Demand is also subject to volatile factors: thus, the aging of the 1960s fleet of jets may—or may not—require a very large scale wave of replacements in the 1990s. Economic recessions, oil price shocks, and other random factors may also continue to make aircraft purchasing unstable. Such risks favor the dominant firm, by making entry or small-firm rises much more difficult to plan and finance.

---

[13] For instance, see "Aircraft Boom May be Only Beginning," *Wall Street Journal*, September 26, 1988, page 6.

4. Behavior

Boeing's actions have been largely unilateral, in its continual battle to obtain plane sales. Most of the action occurs out of public view, and there have been no charges of unfair tactics directed specifically at Boeing (as distinct from accusations that U.S. officials have taken actions to promote Boeing's international sales). Little cooperative behavior is found in this market, possibly because the products are not standardized and the customers each differ in their needs and financing possibilities.

In fact the financing of sales has become nearly as important as innovation and efficient production. Producers are often forced deeply into packaging special financing for sales, often with complex leasing and quasi-leasing conditions.

5. Performance

Here is the distinctive part of this case study. After over 25 years of dominance (punctuated by panic cut-backs in 1969 over a fall-off in orders), Boeing appeared to develop some standard dominant-firm performance defects in the 1980s. They appeared mainly as X-inefficiency and slowed innovation. Boeing's pricing and profits had reflected some monopoly power, but not to great excess.

But profits did fall in the later 1980s, and the firm came under new pressure from an innovative, aggressive Airbus. Boeing candidly discussed the need to reform its production operations, aiming for cost reductions of 25 percent (apart from volume changes). That high percentage may overstate the true levels of X-inefficiency, but even 10 percent reductions would reflect unusually high X-inefficiency.

As for innovations, Boeing seemed to adopt a slower pace in the late 1980s, not anticipating the pressure and innovativeness from Airbus. This matter is debatable, since the new aircraft technology is experimental. Boeing may turn out to be intelligently conservative, rather than slow to innovate. But the negative impact on its position and profits in the 1990s may be large.

6. In Summary

This case involves an unusually clear market definition and a high degree of dominance. Boeing may be following the long-term path of many dominant firms, rising in part from its own innovations and good luck, staying for decades, and then fading under the weight of X-inefficiency, slowed innovation, and new competition. Or the late-1980s boom in demand may refresh the dominance, even if Boeing slows its innovation.

These are matters of degree and judgment. Boeing's rise may have involved more than superior new plane types, and its continued dominance may be affected by other factors, such as random luck and foreign-government interventions.

IV. NEWSPAPERS

The newspaper industry contains a large number of dominant firms, which have emerged in scores of urban markets in the U.S. Each major city is a distinct market for newspapers, within the nation-wide newspaper industry. Some city markets have been dominated by just one paper for decades, but all of the rest have been under increasing tendencies toward dominance. Few cities have more than two substantial papers left, and in many cities one newspaper dominates with little real challenge. The *Los Angeles Times, Washington Post* and *Baltimore Sun* are just a few examples drawn from Table 1.

The march toward newspaper monopoly raises problems not only of economic monopoly but also of media control.[14] Some cities have cross-media monopolies, with local newspapers and television stations under the same owners. In addition, when city-based newspaper monopolies are linked together in large chains, the combined resources and interests may provide a degree of control and influence, which pose a danger to the freedom of the press. The tendency toward newspaper monopoly seems likely to continue, and so the hazards for media quality and competitiveness will persist.

This industry's most interesting questions focus on market definition, economics of scale, and the meaning of good performance.

1.   The Market

Newspapers have traditionally posed only moderate difficulties in defining the true markets. The main product type is newspapers. They may range between "serious" newspapers such as *The New York Times* and the "sensational" or "gutter" press such as the *New York Post* ("Cops Blast Killer" or "Gorby Goes for It"). It is indeed arguable whether those two papers do compete in the same market.[15] But most newspapers, as illustrated in Table 17.2 by figures for the largest twenty U.S. cities, are in the middle range.

One may also treat morning and evening papers as in distinct markets. But that difference may have faded in importance in recent decades, as most papers are now issued in the morning, and some "evening" papers often have "morning" editions. Table 2 treats all daily papers as one market and Sunday papers as a separate market.

The local scope of nearly all newspaper markets is also obvious, though the exact edges are often debatable. Do the Boston *Globe* and *Herald* compete mainly in Boston, in eastern Massachusetts, or throughout Massachusetts? Is the *Des Moines Register,* a morning paper oriented to state and national news, in competition with the afternoon, local-oriented *Ames Daily Tribune* and dozens of other local Iowa papers? Also, there are suburban newspapers in many city edges. They provide some competition with the city-wide newspapers, but often that competition is limited and indirect.

There are some overlaps, often important ones, but the general patterns are well agreed: major cities are recognized to be meaningful markets.

A more sophisticated question arises in considering an alternative dimension for the market: competition may be for *local media advertising,* rather than for *newspaper readership.* The "real" competition may be between newspapers and radio

---

[14] See Ben H. Bagdikian, *The Media Monopoly,* 2nd Edition, (Boston: Beacon Press, 1987), and sources there.

[15] For that matter, much of the New York Times's circulation is outside New York city. Therefore its share of the total New York market for newspapers is lower than Table 1 suggests. But, in another twist, the Times is still virtually the only "serious" newspaper in New York, holding a virtual monopoly.

TABLE 17.2   Newspaper Shares of Metropolitan Circulation, 1988: Daily and Sunday Editions

Newspapers[a]		Circulation (1,000)	Share of Category[b] (%)
1. New York			
New York News	Morning	1,286	60[c]
	Sunday	1,615	100[c]
The New York Times	Morning	1,057	(100)[d]
	Sunday	1,645	(100)[d]
New York Post	Evening	765	35[c]
People's Daily World	Morning	60	3[c]
New York City Tribune	Morning	50	2[c]
2. Los Angeles			
Los Angeles Times	Morning	1,104	81
	Sunday	1,368	88
Los Angeles Herald Examiner	Morning	240	18
	Sunday	190	12
Los Angeles Daily Journal	Morning	21	1
3. Chicago			
Chicago Tribune	Morning	765	52
	Sunday	1,117	61
Chicago Sun-Times	Morning	637	43
	Sunday	646	36
Chicago Defender	Morning	35	2
Southtown Economist	Evening	44	3
	Sunday	57	3
4. Houston			
Houston Chronicle	Evening	406	56
	Sunday	532	59
Houston Post	Morning	316	43
	Sunday	374	41
The Citizen	Evening	8	1
5. Philadelphia			
Philadelphia Inquirer	Morning	500	67
	Sunday	1,000	100
Philadelphia Daily News	Evening	250	33
6. Detroit			
Detroit News	Morning	687	52
	Sunday	838	53
Detroit Free Press	Morning	645	48
	Sunday	744	47
7. Dallas			
Dallas Morning News	Morning	390	61
	Sunday	522	61
Dallas Times Herald	Evening	246	39
	Sunday	246	39

TABLE 17.2   (*continued*)

NEWSPAPERS[a]		CIRCULATION (1,000)	SHARE OF CATEGORY[b] (%)
8. San Diego			
San Diego Union	Morning	255	66
	Sunday	415	100
The Tribune	Evening	125	32
San Diego Transcript	Morning	9	2
9. Phoenix			
The Arizona Republican	Morning	307 ⎫	78
	Evening	100 ⎭	
	Sunday	480	100
Phoenix Gazette	Evening	115	22
10. San Antonio			
Express-News	Morning	147 ⎫	100
	Evening	49 ⎭	
	Sunday	277	55
San Antonio Light	Sunday	224	45
11. Honolulu			
Honolulu Advertiser	Morning	99	50
	Sunday	210	51
Honolulu Star Bulletin	Evening	99	50
	Sunday	205	49
12. Baltimore			
Baltimore Sun	Morning	227 ⎫	100
	Evening	180 ⎭	
	Sunday	481	100
13. San Francisco			
San Francisco Chronicle	Morning	560	78
	Sunday	715	50
San Francisco Examiner	Evening	155	22
	Sunday	710	50
14. Indianapolis			
Indianapolis Star	Morning	231	65
	Sunday	404	100
Indianapolis News	Evening	125	35
15. San Jose			
San Jose Mercury News	Sunday	315	100
16. Memphis			
The Commercial Appeal	Morning	226	100
	Sunday	295	100
17. Washington, D.C.			
Washington Post	Morning	797	89
	Sunday	1,113	100
The Washington Times	Morning	100	11

TABLE 17.2   (*continued*)

NEWSPAPERS[a]		CIRCULATION (1,000)	SHARE OF CATEGORY[b] (%)
18. Milwaukee			
The Milwaukee Journal	Evening	294	78
	Sunday	518	100
Milwaukee Sentinel	Morning	85	22
19. Jacksonville			
The Florida Times-Union	Morning	159	80
	Sunday	518	100
Jacksonville Journal	Evening	41	20
20. Boston			
The Boston Globe	Morning	516	60
	Sunday	805	63
Boston Herald	Morning	346	40
	Sunday	482	37

[a] English-language newspapers only.
[b] There are two categories: daily newspapers (combining morning and evening editions) and Sunday newspapers. This may understate market shares if morning and evening newspapers actually comprise distinct markets.
[c] Percent of daily New York popular newspapers (excluding *The New York Times*).
[d] Estimated percent of "serious" New York papers (*The Wall Street Journal*, a national newspaper, is probably the *Times*'s main rival).
SOURCE: Calculated from data in "The Working Press of the Nation," Vol. I, *Newspaper Directory*, 1989 edition.

and television broadcasting, as they seek advertisers. The customer then is the advertiser rather than—or as well as—the reader. This advertising market is still local, but it is wider. A seeming newpaper "monopoly" may be in competition with one, two or more broadcasters (unless the newspaper and broadcasters are under the same owners, as they are in some cities because of "cross-media ownership").

Most analysts regard "local newspaper markets" as true relevant markets, measured by circulation or total revenues. But the alternative "local media advertising market" can also be meaningful for some purposes.

2. Structure

Table 17.2 indicates the high degree of dominance. It combines both morning and evening daily papers: if they were considered to be distinct products, then dominance would be even tighter. Cities smaller than these 20 cases have even higher degrees of dominance, because there is less room for competition.

Yet there are exceptions. Little Rock, Arkansas, has two comparable, vigorously competing newspapers, as do some cities in Table 17.2. The case for natural dominance in newspaper markets is not yet established.

Among the 100 largest cities, most have one dominant paper and some have two. In 20 of these largest cities, the two newspapers have actually been partially merged; they have one owner and one printing system, but they maintain two separate editorial staffs. Therefore monopoly, or single-firm dominance, has become common, with a few duopolies also still in being. There is also a fringe of suburban papers and weekly advertisers, but they are not very important in most cities.

The trend toward dominance has been especially strong since about 1960. In the 1950's, many cities had at least three papers. But mergers have been widespread, often as papers faced (or merely claimed to face) financial failure.

In local advertising markets, dominance has not necessarily risen. Television (including cable TV) has moved into local markets since 1948. Perhaps not coincidentally, newspaper failures have been paralleled by increasing newspaper-broadcasting competition. It may be that true monopoly has not increased, although newspaper readers may think it has.

The same points hold for concentration. Either concentration is virtually irrelevant because of the widespread newspaper dominance; or tight oligopoly newspapers have been replaced by tight-oligopoly inter-media rivalry.

As for barriers to entry into newspaper production, they are extremely high. There may be exceptions for small market niches such as suburban papers or advertising-based weeklies. But even these are largely filled and blocked by existing papers.

3.   Determinants

The news function of the newspaper appears to involve relatively small economies of scale. Most cities would probably support four or five newspapers if only the news reporting and features were needed. That is partly because wire services and other sources are so ample and accessible.

The scale economies (and pressure toward monopoly) instead appear to come mainly from the (1) production and distribution activities, and (2) advertising. It is generally cheaper to have just one large printing press, and the delivery trucks and personnel also involve economies of scale. But the cost gradients on these may not be steep, so that the cost penalties of having several newspapers per city might be rather small.

Advertising is commonly cited as the main cause of newspaper monopoly. Advertisers are said to apply a continual pressure for one newspaper to emerge as victor, because some advertisers inherently prefer the vehicle with the largest circulation. Newspaper officials say that advertisers will abandon the weaker of four, three or two newspapers, so that monopoly becomes inevitable.

The claim is debatable. Smaller-circulation papers can offer lower rates to attract advertisers. If newspapers can survive handily in cities of 100,000 population and less, there seems no strong reason why they cannot do so in larger cities just as well. Therefore the advertising-based argument for dominance may be merely a self-interested claim advanced by newspapers seeking approval for mergers which will create dominance.

The main direct determinant of newspaper-market structure has been mergers, which have eliminated competition in scores of cities. Whether they reflect technical economies of scale is at the heart of the debate.

4. Behavior

Collusion has not been the main pattern of newspaper behavior in recent decades. Instead, unilateral efforts to defeat rival papers have been common. A full range of pricing, advertising and other strategies has been typical, but when the papers have been of comparable size, no serious anti-competitive effects have occurred. But when one has gained the upper hand, then there have probably been significant cases of competition-reducing actions. Some of them have involved collusion with advertisers to reduce their spending in the smaller rival newspaper.

Curiously, an unusual form of collusion between two newspapers may also have occurred in some cases. If both newspapers can seem to be losing money, and facing closure, then pressure can be put on government officials to approve a merger or quasi-merger. The "failing firm" would seemingly cease to be a rival anyway. This apparently happened in Detroit in the 1980s, as the *News* and *Free Press* engaged in a circulation battle that predictably put them in current losses. Their pleas for a quasi-merger, to rescue them from this self-inflicted difficulty, were finally granted in August, 1988, by a lame-duck Attorney General.

5. Performance

Newspapers have commonly raised their advertising rates and copy prices substantially, upon attaining dominance (or after making quasi-mergers). Their profit rates also rise, commonly to rates of return which are in line with their dominant market positions. Many leading newspapers have been among the most secure and profitable enterprises in the economy.

No general information is available about actual X-efficiency, rates of innovation, or the quality of news coverage. They are all likely to be reduced, but thorough research is yet to be done. There has been a narrowing of news and editorial coverage, as the number of alternative papers has dwindled to one or two in each city. Bagdikian also shows that the extension of chain ownership has brought standardization and central editorial control, in place of the previous variety and independence of local papers.

The current structure provides little basis for press scrutiny—either in deeper reporting or editorials—of the interests of corporate advertisers. As the large media "conglomerates" have merged further in the 1980s, newspapers have become more subordinate to complex corporate interests, especially those of the newspaper owners themselves.

Performance in this sector involves serious impacts on societal welfare.

6. In Summary

If local newspapers are the correct markets, then dominance has become much greater than in any other important unregulated industry in the entire U.S. economy. Virtually pure monopolies are not rare in this industry, while few of the city markets have more than two direct competitors.

The mergers creating this situation may have reflected major underlying technical economies of scale. More probably, the scale economies are moderate, and the dynamics of advertising may be the stronger cause.

The effects of dominance on prices and profits have usually been substantial. The effects on larger social dimensions, particularly on the quality of news coverage, may eventually be larger.

V. INTERNATIONAL BUSINESS MACHINES

This company first held 90 percent of the tabulating-equipment market from the 1930s into the 1950s, and it has had 60 to 80 percent of the main-frame computer market since 1955. As advances in computer technology have come thick and fast, IBM has seemed to embody technological leadership. But it has also used controversial pricing tactics and apparently been a slow innovator.

Without question, "Big Blue" is one of the most powerful, profitable, and controversial companies in American industrial history. A major antitrust case during 1969-1982 brought many of its inner conditions out into full view, and so the brief summary here has more than the usual array of facts to rely on.[16]

1. The Market

During roughly 1955 to 1975, the new computer industry consisted primarily of mainframe computers. They involved large, central memory and processing capacities, with access by peripheral equipment such as tape drives and terminals. Then distributed processing also developed in the 1970s, along with minicomputers and, in the 1980s, the personal computer. Yet the mainframe computer has remained as the industry's core product, sold to a wide range of business users. While smaller units and complex processing networks have become important, especially for word processing and specialized tasks, the mainframe computer is still the workhorse processor of information, accounts, payrolls and the like for many companies.

Whether mainframe computers comprise a distinct market is debatable. Minicomputers and personal computers can perform many functions of mainframe computers, and so a plausible case can be made that all forms of computers are parts of one comprehensive market for data processing equipment. Yet mainframe computer systems are distinct from the others for many large-scale uses. Many companies treat the different types as *complementary* for many uses, rather than as *substitutes*. On the whole, it is still meaningful to treat mainframes as a market that is largely separate from the markets for minicomputers and personal computers.

---

[16] The case was *U.S. v. International Business Machines Corp.*, 69 CIV 200, So. Dist. of N.Y., filed in 1969, litigated from 1975 to 1982, and dropped by the government's Antitrust Division in 1982. Other sources include Gerald Brock, *The U.S. Computer Industry,* Cambridge, Mass.: Ballinger Publishers, 1975; Richard Thomas DeLamarter, *Big Blue: IBM's Use and Abuse of Power,* New York: Dodd, Mead, 1986, which gives thorough coverage to IBM's pricing and product strategies; and William G. Shepherd, *Market Power and Economic Welfare,* New York: Random House, 1970, Chapter 15.

For statements of IBM's views by economists hired to defend it in antitrust cases, see Franklin A. Fisher et al, *Folded, Spindled and Mutilated: Economic Analysis and U.S. v. IBM,* Cambridge, Mass.: MIT Press, 1983, and Fisher et al, *IBM and the U.S. Data Processing Industry: An Economic History,* New York: Praeger, 1983.

The matter is not simple, because there are a variety of mainframe equipment types and combinations, to fit a variety of processing needs and sizes of users. IBM now has a range of mainframe systems, in vintages ranging from the 360 family of the 1960s and 370 systems of the 1970s on into the 1980s. Their components can be varied, and other firms' equipment can often be combined with them. Therefore there is not a bright line around "the mainframe computer market." Even so, the general lines are reasonably clear.

2.   Structure

IBM's market share in mainframes has been generally in the 60 to 70 percent range, but it has gone as high as 80 percent.

In the early 1980s, mainframes were about 50 percent of IBM's revenues and about 70 percent of its profits. By 1989 those ratios were 45 and 50 percent.

IBM has been able to gain only a minor role in minicomputers, and its share of personal computers has dwindled during the 1980s from a high of 25 percent to 13 percent in 1989. Its entry into the new "workstation" product category has been "a highly visible failure."[17] But its dominance of mainframe computers remains steady.

Moreover, IBM is taking measures to strengthen its mainframe position, extending the technical standards for its systems to embrace a wide range of computer equipment. By blocking combined usage with rivals' machines, that would enlarge the range of users who find it necessary to use IBM equipment.[18] If IBM succeeds in this strategy, its mainframe position will remain the core of a growing share of total computer-industry revenues.

Other mainframe producers have market shares less than 10 percent, and so IBM's dominance is extreme. The lesser rivals have banded together with some major users to promote alternative technical standards, which involve "open architecture" that accomodates all systems. But they have had only moderate influence. IBM's ability to set industry standards is still substantial.

3.   Determinants

IBM was able to move from its dominance of tabulating equipment into dominating computers in the 1950s, because the same powerful IBM sales force simply added the new equipment to its widespread selling across the whole business community. Two main determinants have continued to shape the industry's structure.

The first is that sales force, which has been IBM's main strength since the company began in the 1920s. It is a unified, comprehensive system of sellers, able to mobilize large resources in order to win contracts. It not only blankets the ranks of customers, offering generous assistance to customers on the margin. It has also

---

[17] *Business Week Magazine,* "A Bold Move in Mainframes," May 29, 1989, pp. 72-78, at p. 77.

[18] The standards are called "Systems Application Architecture," or SAA. According to a recent article, "We would like to see SAA accepted as an official standard," says Earl F. Wheeler, head of IBM's Programming Systems Group. If this happens, IBM's mainframe sales should boom. SAA "will require more mainframe power and more storage," Wheeler adds. Beyond that, the company would begin to leverage its strength in large systems into sales of computers that would be attached to its mainframes." See "A Bold Move Into Mainframes," *Business Week Magazine, op. cit.*

discouraged the rise of powerful computer leasing companies, which otherwise would have emerged and exerted countervailing pressure on IBM. Some leasing companies have developed, but they are vulnerable to IBM's continuing product changes.

The second influence is production economies of scale, in supplying individual computer models and whole families of systems. But these do not explain IBM's dominance. There is great creativity in this industry among small firms. IBM itself has recognized this by decentralizing much of its development work so as to avoid stifling bureaucracy. "Smaller is better" throughout most activities in much of the sector, except possibly in sheer marketing muscle.

The production economies are rather limited, and indeed much production is farmed out to relatively small firms in Asia. The development of families of systems involves large scale, but it too does not require IBM's scale. The best recent estimates are that MES is probably below 20 percent of the market in all branches of the computer industry, from mainframes down to personal computers.

Therefore, IBM probably has a large degree of excess market share in mainframe computers. That is attested by the continuing ability of very small rivals—such as Unisys, Cray, and Honeywell—to compete.

4. Behavior

Two patterns of IBM behavior stand out.[19] (1) One is the raising of prices to yield high rates of return. Until 1986, IBM consistently earned profit rates above 18 percent on invested capital; during 1977-85, the rate of return was between 21 and 26 percent. For two decades, IBM stabilized its profitability by pricing strategies which encouraged customers to lease machines rather than buy them outright. The flow of lease revenues from IBM's large fleet of equipment provided its main profits, and the policy encouraged customers to stick with IBM. It also forced competitors to match the strategy, and so they had to build up large inventories of equipment for leasing. That imposed extra costs of entry, and made it more costly for small rivals to add market share. IBM eventually shifted toward a higher ratio of sales to leases, after which its profit rose strongly until 1986.

(2) IBM also adopted extensive price discrimination among its products.[20] Among computer models, IBM set prices to attain different profit rates, reflecting the differing degrees of demand elasticity. The 360 family of computers in the 1960s is a good example.[21] For smaller models, where buyers are less expert and more likely to pay more to get the IBM name, IBM set prices about 40 percent above costs. On larger models, where buyers are sharper and rivals had better machines than IBM, prices were set just barely above or even below costs. And when IBM desperately fought back against two kinds of superior machines during 1967-70, they lost money heavily on the so-called "fighting ships."

Further, IBM set much higher price-cost ratios on peripheral equipment (where

---

[19] See Shepherd, *Market Power and Economic Welfare, op. cit.*; and DeLamarter, *Big Blue, op. cit.*. For an opposite view, see Fisher et al, *Folded, Spindled and Mutilated, op. cit.*.

[20] See Shepherd, *Market Power and Economic Welfare, op. cit.*; and DeLamarter, *Big Blue, op. cit.*.

[21] See Shepherd, *Market Power and Economic Welfare, op. cit.*. As DeLamarter shows (*op. cit.*, Chapter 6), IBM also set highly discriminatory prices among the components of each of the systems!

competition was expected to be weak) than on central units. Moreover, IBM has offered different special deals to individual customers (such as free programming and other assistance) in order to get specific contracts. And finally, IBM has virtually given away computers to many universities and colleges in order to get students habituated to their products.

Such saturation price discrimination is *pro-competitive* when done sporadically by small-share firms (recall Chapter 12). But it has been largely *anti-competitive* in the mainframe computer market, where IBM dominates and has done the discrimination systematically. In the other computer markets, where IBM has small shares, the effects have been harmless or pro-competitive.

5.   Performance

Despite its endless assertions of technological superiority, IBM has had a mixed record of efficiency and innovation. Chapter 5 noted briefly that IBM tried in 1987-89 to reorganize in order to reverse cure decades of bureaucracy. It cut its work force by 4 percent, mothballed 5 of its 19 U.S. plants, and planned a further 5 percent cut in employees. It cut out an entire layer of management, cut the product-development cycle in half, and closed down 36 in-house publications. Yet knowledgeable observers describe IBM as "still too bloated." During 1986-1989, IBM's sales expenses rose 60 percent even as its total revenues declined.

Such X-inefficiency flourished because IBM could afford it, as a profitable dominant firm. The higher competition it faces in the smaller-computer markets is forcing IBM to trim the fat.

Company-wide profits were steadily above 18 percent on investors' capital until 1986. Until 1985, mainframe computers provided about 70 percent of IBM's profits, though they are only about 50 percent of its sales. That reflects the high profits IBM can attain from its dominant position in mainframe computers.

IBM's innovation has fitted the dominant-firm preditictions. On most innovations, IBM has followed its smaller rivals. For example, its 360 line was launched in haste and under the pressure of superior systems being marketed by rivals. Then IBM stuck with its System/370 through the 1970s even though it was, by IBM's own admission, outdated (having been designed to handle batches of punched cards). More recently IBM has been unable to keep up in several kinds of computers, including personal computers (against Compaq and Apple). For another example, "IBM's workstation, the three-year-old RT-PC, has been a highly visible failure . . ." And IBM's diversification into telephone equipment (by buying Rolm Corp.) also "failed."[22] Although IBM has scored many successes, its general record of innovation is mixed.

6.   In Summary

IBM has been a complex enterprise with an ambiguous economic history. Its dominance is in a shrinking market within the entire computer industry. Though IBM has been marked by X-inefficiency and slow innovation, it has maintained high

---

[22] *Business Week, op. cit.,* p. 77.

growth and profitability in this turbulent industry for over 35 years. IBM's great strength has been in marketing, with a powerful sales network and complex pricing patterns.

QUESTIONS FOR REVIEW

1. Explain how the three inter-related markets in the photographic supplies industry tend to accentuate Eastman Kodak's market control.

2. What conditions shape the entry barriers into the three markets?

3. "Eastman Kodak used its control over film specifications to extend its market power in the film-processing market." Evaluate this claim, please.

4. Is "the market" for long-distance telephone service a single broad one or a set of segments within the total?

5. If AT&T does sink to a 40 percent market share, and MCI and Sprint each have 30 percent, will competition be fully effective?

6. Is competition effective enough now to justify full deregulation?

7. Is the aircraft market a simple case of a single, well-defined world-wide market? What products are at the edges, possibly in or out?

8. What "natural monopoly" or "natural dominance" conditions does the aircraft market have? Are they overwhelming?

9. In defining newspaper markets, are they possibly really local multi-media markets? Discuss the conditions in at least one city you know about.

10. Using two cases from Table 2, discuss the degree of monopoly in two actual newspaper (or multi-media) markets.

11. If some smaller cities (e.g., Little Rock, Arkansas) continue to have two vigorously competing newspapers, does that indicate that the economies of scale are really small?

12. Explain the main lines of IBM's price discrimination.

13. Make the best case that competition in the computer market is *effective*.

18

TIGHT OLIGOPOLIES: CEREALS, SPORTS, BEER, AND AIRLINES

The classic tight oligopoly involves a standardized industrial product, like steel or cement, on which the several leading firms try to set collusive prices. Those struggles may appeal to oligopoly modelers, but the products are—let us face it—rather dull, and the outcomes tend to be one-dimensional (along a price continuum).

This chapter considers several industries that have more colorful conditions: breakfast cereals, sports, beer, and airlines. These oligopolies are certainly tight, with high concentration and entry barriers. But the products are complex and interesting rather than uniform, and the action involves a number of dimensions.

Moreover, the products and companies will be familiar to many readers: who does not know Cheerios and Count Chocula, Babe Ruth and Magic Johnson, Heineken and Bud Light, MaxSaver fares and a missed plane connection? You can therefore draw on direct experience in making judgments.

I. BREAKFAST CEREALS[1]

Crisp cereals first challenged the old tradition of hot porridge in the 1890s, with the advent of shredded wheat and grape nuts. By 1905, corn flakes, puffed wheat, and puffed rice had also been brought to market, and the industry has grown steadily ever since. Note that four of the five main production methods (extrusion was introduced in 1941, with Cheerios) have existed for at least eighty-five years.

In the 1950s, sugared cereals were marketed in a variety of forms, reinforced by increasingly intensive advertising to children. The addition of small candy bits and fruits, plus further advertising intensity, followed in the 1960s. The rise of "nat-

---

[1] For helpful summaries, see F. M. Scherer, "The Breakfast Cereal Industry," a chapter in Walter Adams, ed., *The Structure of American Industry*, 6th ed. (New York: Macmillan, 1982), pp. 191–217; and Richard Schmalensee, "Entry Deterrence in the Ready-to-Eat Cereal Industry," *Bell Journal of Economics*, 9 (Autumn 1978), 305–27. This section of the chapter relies on Scherer's coverage for a number of details.

These two writings grew out of a massive Federal Trade Commission case involving the leading cereal makers during 1972–1981. Energetic readers may wish to explore that case, whose specific source reference is FTC: *In re Kellogg Company et al.*, Docket No. 8883, filed 1972.

ural'' cereals in the mid-1970s was succeeded in the 1980s by a variety of brands claiming to be more healthful (with bran, for example).

Altogether, the industry's basic products and technology have altered remarkably little since 1910. The ranks of competitors changed during the early days, but they, too, have remained quite stable since the 1930s. Kellogg's took the lead in the 1930s, and has held it ever since. Its two main rivals, General Mills and General Foods, have joined Kellogg in forming one of the tightest, most stable, and most profitable oligopolies in the U.S. economy.

This industry's special features are intensive advertising (frequently directed at children), brand proliferation, limited scale economies, and sustained high profit rates. In an experimental antitrust case that ran a rocky course during 1972–1981, the Federal Trade Commission sought to test whether the oligopoly was really a ''shared monopoly'' whose tacit collusion (recall Chapters 13 and 14) approximated the essential outcomes of monopoly. Eventually the case was dropped under extreme political pressure, but it developed information that clarifies many of the industry's conditions.

1.   The Market

There is wide agreement that dry ''ready to eat'' breakfast cereals sold in the United States are the correct market definition. Hot cooked cereals are quite distinct, and so are pop-tarts, diet bars (with or without chocolate coverings), and, of course, toast, ham, eggs, and pancakes. Whether granola-type cereals should be included was a significant question at their peak popularity in the mid-1970s, but they are a relatively minor factor now. Though there is much product variety, the best-selling products have changed little since 1950, or even since 1910.

2.   Structure

The early firms in the market included Quaker Oats, Post (later part of General Foods), and Kellogg; they were later joined by General Mills (which bought the maker of Wheaties in 1928). Each specialized in its original product and then added other forms of cereals. Since the 1950s, Kellogg's has maintained about a 45 percent share, with General Mills at approximately 20 percent and General Foods at about 15 percent. Ralston Purina (''Chex'') and Quaker Oats are significant but smaller rivals.

Three-firm concentration is in the 80–90 percent range, where it has been for many decades. The four-firm ratio has been between 83 and 90 since 1954. Few U.S. markets have displayed such stable and enduring high concentration.

Entry barriers are generally regarded as high, owing mainly to the importance of brand names and intensive advertising. Any significant entrant (or attempt by the smaller sellers to increase market share) would face sharp retaliation in the forms of advertising and deep, selective price cuts. Moreover, the incumbents have filled virtually all market niches in the product space (see Subsection I.4). New competitors offering new types of cereals would have to go up against not only the numerous existing brands but also still more new types that the incumbents could quickly put on the market.

A more optimistic view of conditions in this market is possible, and indeed the cereals companies have urged it. They say that since the minimum efficient scale (MES) is rather low, small entry could be successful if backed up by strong selling efforts.

3. Determinants

Economies of scale in production are known to be limited, with MES reached at about a mere 5 percent market share.[2] That scale provides for several production and packaging lines, to give sufficient flexibility. Indeed, the producers build their plants at about that size rather than larger ones. Therefore, judged by scale economies in production, Kellogg and the other leading producers have large amounts of excess market share.

Advertising is a stronger determinant of the existing tight-oligopoly structure. It is directed largely at very young children, often on Saturday morning television cartoon shows, with potent effects. Although a Federal Trade Commission investigation of this process in the 1970s was eventually curtailed by outside pressure without reaching conclusions or taking action, the power of the advertising is generally admitted. It has probably hardened the tight-oligopoly structure since 1950, by favoring existing firms which held large market shares (recall the logic of Chapter 16).

That structure has also been shaped by the critical role of the distribution system in interaction with the scarcity of grocery shelf space. The major sellers maintain extensive delivery systems, which give them direct influence over the use of shelf space in groceries. Shelf space acts as a bottleneck in reaching final customers because new access to it is restricted by the need to accommodate the leading cereals firms. These firms are also able to obtain the more favorable positions most of the time because they have their own delivery staffs placing their boxes on the retailers' shelves. Thus the leading sellers are able to continue crowding out smaller, or new, producers into inferior locations.

4. Behavior

The main behavior, packing of the product space by proliferating brands, appears to have been implicitly collusive. The extent of brand proliferation has indeed been great: in 1973, the six leading producers had a total of eighty brands, and many brands have been added since then.[3]

The effects of this process on competition are illustrated by Figure 18.1. Imagine that each product characteristic (shape of cereal, type or mix of grain, sugar content, bran, etc.) exists along the horizontal axis, varying by degrees. Existing products are at points *A, B* and *C,* each selling at $1.00 per box.

If an existing or new rival tries to offer an identical product, it will be forced by competitive pressure to keep its price at $1.00. The most profitable products will

---

[2] Louis W. Stern, Technical Study Number 6, *Studies of Organization and Competition in Grocery Manufacturing* (Washington, D.C.: National Commission on Food Marketing, 1966); and see the testimony of Michael Glassman in the FTC Cereals case: *In re Kellogg et al.,* Docket No. 8883, filed 1972, transcript at pp. 26319–72.

[3] FTC, *In re Kellogg et al.,* CX-409.

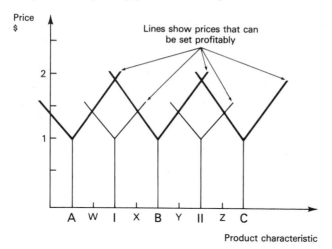

FIGURE 18.1.   Brand proliferation in product space.

be those positioned midway between existing products, shown as points *I* and *II* in Figure 18.1. There a higher price can be charged because consumers will be willing to pay more for a noticeably different new product.

If existing firms fill those points with their own products, then the new entrants will be confined to less attractive market niches, at points *X*, *Y*, and *Z*. If the existing firms are really thorough about it, they will fill those points X, Y and Z too, leaving virtually no product space for newcomers to enter profitably. Because newcomers and small rivals are forced to incur extra advertising costs in order to enter with new brands or raise market share, it follows that competition from either can be averted by packing the product space in advance.

Of course, the existing firms will portray their actions as being innovative and responsive to consumer demand. To an extent, that is true. Nonetheless, the effect of the brand proliferation in excluding competition is powerful, and it is fully known to the main cereals companies.

This effect, plus the reliance upon brand advertising, has kept the big three cereal firms from having to resort to the more dangerous form of direct price competition in their internecine rivalry. Indeed, from 1957 to 1972, the leaders jointly refrained (perhaps after direct agreement) from offering special premiums in their cereal boxes.

Therefore brand proliferation does tend to reduce competition, although it can be portrayed instead as lively competition arising from independent decisions. Though very little direct price competition has occurred, a variety of nonprice methods of rivalry (including rebate coupons in the boxes) might provide significant competition in this market.

5. Performance

The three firms' profitability has been high and sustained, with rates of return on investment averaging about 20 percent since the 1940s.[4] Price effects are suggested by the price increases that occurred when the FTC's shared-monopoly case

---

[4] During 1958–1970, the average returns on cereal division assets were: Kellogg, 18.9 percent; General Mills, 29.5 percent; and General Foods (Post), 15.1 percent, for a combined weighted average of 19.8 percent. See *In re Kellogg et al.*, CX-701A.

against the three oligopolists was ended in 1981. Retail prices of cereals quickly rose by approximately 20 percent, as if a restraint on prices had suddenly been removed.

There has been no general lapse of X-efficiency, although General Foods' "acknowledged inefficiencies" were large and sustained in the 1960s.[5] The advertising of cereals absorbs from 10 to 15 percent of sales and is almost exclusively of the persuasive type. If that spending is regarded as a welfare loss, then this oligopoly causes a waste of several hundreds of millions of dollars per year.

Innovation has consisted mainly of creating new combinations of grains and sugars in differing shapes, with brand names and images. This innovation is partly a response to changing consumer demand, as when bran and "whole grain" cereals were added to take advantage of the health and fitness boom that began in the 1970s. Yet much demand is induced by advertising aimed at children, and much brand innovation has been partly aimed at blocking competition from new and smaller firms.

The nutritional value of the cereals came under severe attack in 1970.[6] Critics asserted that the companies' products had little nutritional content and the heavy use of sugar was damaging children's teeth. Though "nutritional" brands have been added in the 1980s, the companies still rely heavily on sugared cereals eaten by children.

On balance, the misallocation effects and waste of advertising resources have probably been substantial.

6.   In Summary

Although the "shared-monopoly" antitrust action was withdrawn, the big three cereal makers continue to exemplify tight oligopoly, with strong differentiation and an ability to influence buyers by advertising.

II.   SPORTS

For many Americans, sports are the economy's most important industry of all. They play, watch, debate, gamble, and generally dote on sports.

The populace engages in an astonishing variety of sporting activities, ranging from duck hunting, rock climbing and yachting to bowling, drag racing, hang gliding, synchronized swimming, baseball, motocross, rooster fighting, archery, and tractor pulls. Sports are so profuse in this country that they compete with one another for attention and for fans' spending.

Sports are also big business. The economics include the costs of putting on games, ticket sales, advertising and broadcasting of games, as well as support services such as arenas. There are also large ancillary activities, such as gambling, insignia clothing and other loyalty items sold to fans, and the whole sportswriting culture spawned by newspaper sports sections and sports magazines. Though per-

---

[5] The quote is from Scherer, "The Breakfast Cereal Industry," p. 211.

[6] A detailed analysis of sixty cereals' content was given in U.S. Senate, Committee on Commerce, Subcommittee for Consumers, Hearings, *Dry Cereals* (Washington, D.C.: U.S. Government Printing Office, 1970), pp. 2–43.

TABLE 18.1   Patterns of Professional Sports, U.S.A., 1970–86

SPORT	UNIT	1970	1975	1980	1984	1986
Baseball, major leagues:						
Attendance	1,000	29,191	30,373	43,746	45,262	48,452
Regular season	1,000	28,747	29,789	43,014	44,742	47,506
National League	1,000	16,662	16,600	21,124	20,781	22,333
American League	1,000	12,085	13,189	21,890	23,961	25,173
Playoffs	1,000	191	276	407	248	624
World Series	1,000	325	308	325	272	322
Players' average salaries	$1,000	29	45	144	329	413
Basketball:						
Teams	Number	14	18	22	23	23
Attendance, total	1,000	4,912	7,591	10,697	11,110	11,491
Regular season	1,000	4,341	6,892	9,938	10,015	11,215
Average per game	Number	7,563	9,339	11,017	10,620	11,893
Playoffs	1,000	556	685	740	1,096	979
Players' average salaries	$1,000	(NA)	(NA)	170	275	375
National Football League:						
Teams	Number	26	26	28	28	28
Attendance, total	1,000	10,071	10,769	14,092	14,053	17,304
Regular season	1,000	9,533	10,213	13,392	13,398	13,582
Average per game	Number	52,381	56,116	59,787	59,813	60,635
Postseason games	1,000	538	556	700	655	734
Players' average salaries	$1,000	23	40	79	158	202
National Hockey League:						
Regular season attendance	1,000	5,992	9,522	10,534	11,359	11,621
Playoffs attendance	1,000	462	784	977	1,107	1,152
Players' average salaries	$1,000	(NA)	(NA)	108	145	158

SOURCE: *Statistical Abstract of the United States, 1988*, p. 218.

sonal participation is the only form of sports that promotes health, and amateur games (high school and college) are often more exciting, it is the major professional sports that have long posed the main questions of market power.

This section follows the literature, by focusing on the four leading professional sports in this country: baseball, football, basketball, and hockey.[7] Their main economic dimensions are shown in Table 18.1. Though they are the backbone of commercial sports, their total yearly ticket sales (just under 90 million in 1986) are lower than those for horse racing and dog racing (about 95 million). A hidden economic role of the four sports is gambling: total annual betting on these four league sports (all illegal) has been estimated at over $50 billion.

The four sports share the phenomenon of *leagues,* which function as private cartels. They organize their sports under common rules, excluding all direct competition (that is, rival leagues). Do the leagues abuse their market power? The main issues are player drafts, rights, and salaries; the large flows of television funds; and

---

[7] They are the main focus of the large body of literature on the economics of sports. See especially Roger C. Noll, ed., *Government and the Sports Business,* 2d ed. (Washington, D.C.: Brookings Institution, 1985), and sources listed there. This is not to deny that the major intercollegiate sports also pose some of the same issues, in lesser forms.

the controls over any moves of teams among cities. Ultimately the problem is the stranglehold that these team owners have upon the nation's principal spectator sports. Is it benevolently and efficiently managed? Or is it classical monopoly: narrow, restrictive, inefficient, and slow to innovate?

1. The Markets

The basic product is the *game*. It has three elements: a display of talent, an entertainment, and a suspenseful event whose outcome is in doubt. The game is part of an ongoing yearly season, which climaxes in a championship playoff.

The basic producer is the *team*, although, alternatively, the *league* can be considered the true decision group. No clear answer is possible between these alternative views of "The firm." Teams are partly independent firms making their own decisions, and partly mere units of the league. In any event, the league can be considered a natural monopoly within its sport's market.[8]

Defining the markets for these sports is a complex task. The four professional sports can be considered four distinct markets, because they are separately organized, involve contrasting types of games, operate in (partly) separate seasons, and are generally regarded as distinct. Moreover, the leagues carefully minimize their overlaps with college and other sports.[9]

Yet their seasons do overlap during parts of the year, so that TV viewers can substitute among them. Moreover, advertisers often deploy their advertising among them in ways that suggest the sports are competing with one another for broadcasting revenue. Indeed, at the viewing level, sports "compete" in a broad sense with all other entertainment.

Conceivably each city with a team can be considered a market because that is the zone of the local team's loyal customers *for tickets*. Yet that definition is probably too narrow. At the other extreme, "all professional sports" is generally agreed to be too broad a market definition. All in all, "each professional sport" is the most meaningful market definition.

2. Structure

Each league holds a monopoly of its sport, operating as a very tight cartel. There is potential competition from lower leagues in the sport (e.g., "minor" leagues in baseball and hockey), but these are generally kept in a peripheral role. Indeed, baseball's minor league teams are usually owned by the major league teams.

The leagues have enforced insuperable barriers against any new teams or leagues that might try to enter.[10] The sports arenas in major cities are owned or exclusively contracted for by the teams. If new teams did emerge outside the established leagues,

[8] See the entertaining article by Walter C. Neale, "The Peculiar Economics of Professional Sport," *Quarterly Journal of Economics,* 78 (February 1964); as well as chapters by Noll, James Quirk and Mohamed El Hodiri, Benjamin A. Okner, Lance E. Davis, and Steven R. Rivkin in Noll, *Government and the Sports Business.*

[9] Thus football times are neatly segregated: high school on Friday nights, college on Saturday afternoons, and professional mainly on Sundays and Monday evenings.

[10] That is illustrated by the sorry fate of the World Football League in the early 1970s and the United States Football League during 1983–1986. The leagues have also been helped by their ability to sign exclusive contracts with the major television networks.

the latter would exclude or boycott them, and probably threaten to leave any city that permitted such a new team to start.

There are some countervailing sources of vertical pressure on the league monopolies. Players are organized in unions, some of which are quite strong, and "stars" are able to bargain for maximum pay for themselves. The resulting battles (with hold-outs, disputes, even player strikes) often create more drama than some of the games on the field. The leagues also face powerful broadcasting groups (especially the networks and cable sports systems) in hard bargaining over TV payments and exclusive rights.

In addition, the owners have to deal with their host cities over stadium provisions and costs and other forms of support. But the cities are usually mild negotiators because they fear any pressure would cause their local teams to decamp. So, generally speaking, the vertical pressures do not threaten the leagues' control over their sports.

3. Determinants

The market structure is partly shaped by inherent forces, such as the owners' overwhelming incentives to organize each sport into just one unified system. That permits them to control the players' entry to the sport as well as their moves among teams. Such control helps the leagues to keep players' salaries down, which they did quite successfully before the 1970s. With two leagues, the players' bargaining position is far stronger, as during the two-league NFL-AFL situation in 1960–1967 and the NFL versus U.S. Football League episode in the early and mid-1980s.

Yet the monopoly structure is largely an artifact of the owners' making, to suit their interest in minimizing players' salaries. There could well be two or more leagues in each sport, as indeed there are in Europe, where soccer and basketball players move freely among soccer and basketball teams in Britain, France, Italy, West Germany, Spain, and so on. There could also be several tiers of leagues, from the top leagues on down to minor ones, so that teams could rise to higher leagues as their quality improves. That is the case in British soccer's "relegation" system (more about it later). A mix of private and city-owned teams is also possible. Moreover, the structure and rules have evolved and changed by deliberate choices. The current patterns do not reflect perpetual determinants in any sense.

This self-created league structure is carefully managed by elaborate rules that each league follows in order to maintain competitive parity among the teams. The first draft choices of players go to last year's lowest-ranking teams. Some leagues set limits on the teams' salary budgets. Television revenues and home game ticket revenues are (usually) divided in ways that tend to equalize team quality. By renewing parity, the leagues attempt to assure that games are suspenseful.

Altogether, professional sports' structures are consciously designed and adjusted rather than governed by exogenous determinants.

4. Behavior

Behavior mainly concerns the controls on players' choices in joining and changing teams, and the division of revenues. There is vast variety among the leagues, with changes over time as well. The main trend has been toward greater player freedom to choose, but within controls that are still pretty tight.

The teams' owners obtain new players by a yearly "draft," in which choices are in reverse order of last year's degree of success. This tends to provide competitive balance within the league, which is crucially important in every market as we have seen. But it also clashes with players' freedom of choice in selecting employers, a fundamental right in a non-slave society. This conscription removes much of the players' ability to negotiate for a maximum salary and signing bonus, and so this unified management behavior strongly affects the pay levels of new players.

Players are further required to stay with the teams that conscripted them, again preventing freedom of choice. But under pressure, the various leagues have reluctantly adopted various schemes for players to seek "free agent" status, usually by playing without a contract for a year and then taking their chances on getting suitable offers. This permits the better players to seek salaries up to their marginal revenue product (that is, their commercial value to the teams).

But owners can gain by conspiring to avoid a full bidding process for the free agents, as they did in baseball during the 1985–86 and 1986–87 seasons. Kirk Gibson, a Detroit Tigers star, along with 66 other players, was unable to obtain even one bid from any of the other 25 baseball teams. All players, thus chastened, were forced to stay with their teams or give up baseball entirely. The owners' 1985–86 conspiracy was judged and penalized by an arbitrator during 1988–89, and it presumably will not recur in such a complete fashion. But mutual restraint is still in the owners' collective interest, and some degree of it may be endemic.

Generally, basketball has had the least degree of market control by the owners, while football and baseball (which has had an explicit exemption from most antitrust enforcement since 1922) have had the most. But each is subject to change, under almost monthly pressures and new legal challenges.

5. Performance

Teams' financial success is influenced by several standard factors, especially their win-loss record, their signing of stars, and the population and income level of the cities they play in.[11] Regression analyses have commonly shown that the following variables most strongly affect attendance:

$$\text{Attendance} = f \begin{pmatrix} \text{win-loss ratio, population,} \\ \text{per capita income, number of star players,} \\ \text{ticket prices, advertising, etc.} \end{pmatrix}$$

Star athletes often raise team revenues (attendance times ticket price) by $1 million or more per year. Therefore the stars are seeking to capture their marginal revenue product when they bargain for high salaries. Presumably, the owners do not pay them more than that marginal revenue product (that is, their commercial value to the team).

Winning records can also be crucial. Teams that had been playing to near-empty stadiums suddenly find the seats crowded when they become playoff contenders.

---

[11] See especially the regression analyses of the sports' attendance patterns by Roger C. Noll in Chapter 4 of Noll, *Government and the Sports Business.*

The levels of population and income have the expected effects. Teams in New York and Los Angeles are often the most profitable, simply because their pools of potential customers are so large. Television revenue reflects the winning and star effects, because national viewers want to watch winning teams and the most famous players, and advertisers respond to these mass viewership patterns.

Are teams highly profitable? Team accounts are mostly kept secret and, in any event, usually reflect arcane accounting processes of manipulation and tax minimization. But it is safe to say that teams in such large cities as New York and Los Angeles are usually highly profitable, and most of the other teams probably do turn solid profits. Even teams based in smaller cities that regularly lose on the playing field have recently obtained record prices when sold to new owners.

Pricing behavior in sports fits many monopoly predictions. Many football stadiums are small and the games are relatively few (16 regular-season football games compared to nearly 100 basketball and 162 baseball games). The football team owners use this advantage to set high prices and tight conditions for season tickets.

The pricing of players also fits monopoly predictions. In sports with looser controls on players (especially basketball), salaries have risen much faster than in the more tightly controlled sports (especially football). Bilateral monopoly therefore has differing effects, depending on the owners' relative power.

Of course the competitive equilibrium salaries of each sport may differ according to skills, talent pools, length of career, injury risks, and other nonmonopoly factors.[12] But the sharp relative rise in basketball salaries when controls eased in the 1970s shows how important vertical power is. Indeed, the salary rise in all four sports reflects the rise in players' bargaining power.

X-inefficiency is impossible to judge scientifically, but many sports buffs have strong views about the varying quality of the management by team and league officials. As for innovation, the leagues have made continuing adjustments in rules and format to sustain spectator interest. They are helped by the extensive sector of sports journalism, whose thousands of writers, in thousands of daily sports pages, stimulate and sustain the fans' interest in even the smallest minutiae of each sport.

The one major failure of supply and innovation is seen in the relative fewness of teams. As Table 18.2 shows, over thirty-five cities with populations above 500,000 lack any significant team in baseball, football, *and* basketball. Only twelve cities have teams in all three of those sports. The lack of baseball teams in Washington, D.C., and Dallas are only the most remarkable instances.

The leagues restrict supply not only by limiting the numbers of their own teams and controlling their locations, but also by blocking the creation of other leagues and teams. The reservoir of sports demand in nearly all cities below 1.5 million in population is probably very large, and it will continue to be unmet as long as the current leagues maintain their exclusive control.

---

[12] Thus players' ''high'' salaries are usually earned only for a few years and are highly taxed. The players constantly risk injuries that can terminate their careers. After retirement, their remaining years are usually spent at relatively modest-paying activities.

In addition, multiyear contracts usually have current values much below their face values. Thus a star may have a ten-year contract at $1 million per year. Discounted at 10 percent and taxed at 33 percent, that stream of earnings has a present capitalized value after taxes of just $4.4 million, even ignoring the dilution caused by future price inflation. Discounted at 15 percent, the present value after taxes is only $2.9 million.

TABLE 18.2   Teams in Large Cities

Metropolitan Area		Population 1986, total (1,000)	Base-ball	Basket-ball	Foot-ball	Hockey
New York–Northern New Jersey-Long Island, NY-NJ-CT	CMSA	17,968	2	2	2	2
Los Angeles-Anaheim-Riverside, CA	CMSA	13,075	2	2	2	1
Chicago-Gary-Lake County (IL), IL-IN-WI	CMSA	8,116	2	1	1	1
San Francisco-Oakland-San Jose, CA	CMSA	5,878	2	1	2	
Philadelphia-Wilmington-Trenton, PA-NJ-DE-MD	CMSA	5,833	1	1	1	1
Detroit-Ann Arbor, MI	CMSA	4,601	1	1	1	1
Boston-Lawrence-Salem-Lowell-Brockton, MA	NECMA	3,705	1	1	1	1
Dallas-Fort Worth, TX	CMSA	3,655	1	1	1	
Houston-Galveston-Brazoria, TX	CMSA	3,634	1	1	1	
Washington, DC-MD-VA	MSA	3,563		1	1	1
Miami-Fort Lauderdale, FL	CMSA	2,912		1	1	
Cleveland-Akron-Lorain, OH	CMSA	2,766	1	1	1	
Atlanta, GA	MSA	2,561	1	1	1	
St. Louis, MO-IL	MSA	2,438	1		1	1
Pittsburgh-Beaver Valley, PA	CMSA	2,316	1		1	1
Minneapolis-St. Paul, MN-WI	MSA	2,295	1	1	1	1
Seattle-Tacoma, WA	CMSA	2,285	1	1	1	1
Baltimore, MD	MSA	2,280	1			
San Diego, CA	MSA	2,201	1		1	
Tampa-St. Petersburg-Clearwater, FL	MSA	1,914			1	
Phoenix, AZ	MSA	1,900		1		
Denver-Boulder, CO	CMSA	1,847		1	1	
Cincinnati-Hamilton, OH-KY-IN	CMSA	1,690	1		1	
Milwaukee-Racine, WI	CMSA	1,552	1	1		
Kansas City, MO-KS	MSA	1,518	1		1	
Portland-Vancouver, OR-WA	CMSA	1,364		1		
New Orleans, LA	MSA	1,334			1	
Norfolk-Virginia Beach-Newport News, VA	MSA	1,310				
Columbus, OH	MSA	1,299				
Sacramento, CA	MSA	1,291		1		
San Antonio, TX	MSA	1,276		1		
Indianapolis, IN	MSA	1,213		1	1	
Buffalo-Niagara Falls, NY	CMSA	1,182			1	1
Hartford-New Britain-Middletown-Bristol, CT	NECMA	1,083				1
Charlotte-Gastonia-Rock Hill, NC-SC	MSA	1,065		1		
Salt Lake City-Ogden, UT	MSA	1,041		1		
Oklahoma City, OK	MSA	983				
Rochester, NY	MSA	980				
Louisville, KY-IN	MSA	963				
Memphis, TN-AR-MS	MSA	960				
Dayton-Springfield, OH	MSA	934				
Nashville, TN	MSA	931				
Birmingham, AL	MSA	911				
Greensboro-Winston Salem-High Point, NC	MSA	900				
Orlando, FL	MSA	898		1		
Providence-Pawtucket-Woonsocket, RI	NECMA	890				
Jacksonville, FL	MSA	853				
Albany-Schenectady-Troy, NY	MSA	844				
Bridgeport-Stamford-Norwalk-Danbury, CT	NECMA	821				
Honolulu, HI	MSA	817				
Richmond-Petersburg, VA	MSA	810				
New Haven-Waterbury-Meriden, CT	NECMA	779				
West Palm Beach-Boca Raton-Delray Beach, FL	MSA	756				
Tulsa, OK	MSA	734				
Austin, TX	MSA	726				
Scranton-Wilkes-Barre, PA	MSA	726				
Worcester-Fitchburg-Leominster, MA	NECMA	661				
Allentown-Bethlehem, PA-NJ	MSA	657				
Raleigh-Durham, NC	MSA	651				
Syracuse, NY	MSA	649				
Grand Rapids, MI	MSA	649				
Omaha, NE-IA	MSA	614				
Toledo, OH	MSA	611				
Greenville-Spartanburg, SC	MSA	606				
Tucson, AZ	MSA	602				
Knoxville, TN	MSA	591				
Fresno, CA	MSA	588				
Springfield, MA	NECMA	586				
Harrisburg-Lebanon-Carlisle, PA	MSA	577				
Las Vegas, NV	MSA	570				
El Paso, TX	MSA	562				
Baton Rouge, LA	MSA	546				
Youngstown-Warren, OH	MSA	510				
Little Rock-North Little Rock, AR	MSA	506				
Bakersfield, CA	MSA	494				
Green Bay, WI	MSA	88			1	

An effective solution is readily available, but it would loosen the stranglehold of the current leagues. Its model is the British soccer "relegation" system based on four league levels. Any town or group can form a team in the low-level county leagues, build it up gradually, and seek to boost it to the higher leagues. Each year the two top teams in each league rise to the next league up, while the two lowest teams are relegated to the next league below.

Small-town teams can and do rise to the very top league, by skill and resources. Many of these top-quality teams are from towns much smaller than the cities listed in Table 18.2 that lack teams in any of our four top professional sports. The biggest-city teams sink down to lower leagues when they perform poorly. Moreover, suspense is intense throughout the system, as losing teams fight desperately to avoid relegation. By contrast, losing teams in U.S. leagues play out the end—or even the majority—of their seasons in dull, meaningless games.

The relegation system is more efficient in generating sports interest with given resources. If adopted in the United States, it would be open, fluid, and far more responsive to both demand and supply than the current tight, limited monopolies. It could provide hundreds of cities with a chance to form strong teams that aspire to the top leagues. Seasons could be exciting throughout for nearly all teams.

Instead, the major league teams have throttled the lower leagues, especially by limiting their access to television coverage. Cities' and fans' freedom of choice is limited to a relatively few teams playing in partly meaningless seasons.

The contrast shows how strong and costly the U.S. leagues' controls are. Monopoly continues to exact a high toll on performance in this sector.

6. In Summary

These markets are controlled by tight, profit-maximizing cartels that have many features of monopoly firms. The results appear to fit predictions from the theories of collusion, exclusion, and unequal bilateral monopoly. Though each league maintains its balance and continuity pretty well, a larger perspective suggests that performance falls far short of the results that an open, flexible, genuinely *competitive* structure would give.

III. BEER[13]

Beer is a thoroughly traditional product, widely used since at least the earliest ancient Egyptian kingdoms. Nowadays in the United States, beer drinking is centered in a youngish male group, aged about twenty-one to thirty-five, sometimes referred to as "Harry Six-Packs." Though producers try to instill strong brand loyalties, most beers cannot be distinguished reliably in a blind taste test and every brewer can duplicate any other brewer's flavor.

Brewing was an extensive local-regional industry, with hundreds of companies, before the 1918–1933 Prohibition era. Since 1933, the industry ranks have thinned

[13] For a helpful introduction to this industry, see Kenneth G. Elzinga, "The Beer Industry," a chapter in Walter Adams, ed., *The Structure of American Industry*, 7th ed. (New York: Macmillan, 1986), and the sources there.

down to a few major national brewers plus a fringe of regional and local ones. Despite the emergence of chic micro-breweries in many locales over the last decade, the market is dominated by the heavily advertised national brands such as Budweiser and Miller. Have the mergers reduced competition? Is competition effective in national and/or regional markets?

Also, the leading brewers enforce exclusive distribution territories in many states, just as Coca-Cola and PepsiCola do in soft drinks. Is that anticompetitive?

1. The Market

The product is largely standardized: a pale gold fermented drink, sold mainly in small bottles or cans, as well as in kegs. Ales, lagers, and beers are largely substitutable to many buyers, although the darker, strong-tasting versions may be a (much smaller) separate market. Possibly the higher-priced brands and imported beers are distinct from the mass brands, but the physical differences are generally minor and there is extensive substitution among them.

Geography poses the harder questions. Are beer markets local, regional, or national in scope? Transport factors suggest regional markets: shipping costs are important relative to total costs, and actual shipping is mostly within 300 miles. Yet since the major standard brands are produced in multiple plants across the country, the interactions among the main corporate producers are often national in scope.

An equivocal answer seems unavoidable. Some competitive conditions occur within regional markets, or when a national brewer adopts strategies against one or several strictly regional sellers, such as Samuel Adams, Rolling Rock, or Olympia. But the main market is a national one, in the struggle for sales among Anheuser-Busch Miller, Stroh, and Coors.

Distribution.   A second market level is in the retail distribution of beer. Beer is delivered by truck to retail outlets such as package and grocery stores. These delivery-market areas range between roughly the largest urban areas and middle-size states. The deliveries can range as far as 150 miles or so, though ordinarily they are within 50-mile areas that trucks can easily reach in a day's run.

2. Structure

The earlier local markets were tight oligopolies among the local leaders, but they have been replaced by the set of leading national companies led by Anheuser-Busch and joined by Miller and Stroh. Since 1954, four-firm concentration in the industry has risen strongly and steadily toward 80 percent, as Table 18.3 shows. This sustained rise is highly unusual in U.S. markets, and has largely reflected the success of intensive advertising. Some once-famous brands have disappeared (e.g., Rheingold, Ruppert) as many companies faded or were bought out. Anheuser-Busch rose by internal growth and has been close to market dominance, while Stroh and Miller gained by important mergers.

Entry barriers are high, mainly because of the intensive advertising that is necessary to become viable. Newcomers can find local market niches, but they are crowded and subjected to pressure by the national companies. To go national at all,

TABLE 18.3   Concentration in the U.S. Beer Industry, 1954–1982

Year	Value of Shipments ($ million)	4-Firm Concentration Ratio (%)
1982	11,105.6	78
1977	6,612.9	65
1972	4,038.6	52
1967	2,900.3	40
1963	2,282.0	34
1958	1,972.1	29
1954	1,854.8	27

SOURCE: U.S. Bureau of the Census, *Concentration Ratios in Manufacturing, 1982*, MC82-S-7 (Washington, D.C.: U.S. Government Printing Office, 1986), pp. 7–61.

a firm must mount a major advertising campaign against the inevitable retaliation of the leading firms. Like the cereal market, the beer market illustrates the theory of advertising as an entry barrier discussed in Chapter 16. Yet, as Chapter 16 also noted, a sufficiently large market blitz can probably establish a new product.

3. Determinants

Scale economies in brewing are not small, with MES probably at about 1 to 1.5 million barrels per year.[14] That is some 5 percent of national output and, of course, large compared to MES in most local-regional markets. Advertising is the other main factor; it provides "economies of scale" possibly up to 20 percent of the national market. Yet these are partly just pecuniary economies, as noted in Chapters 9 and 16.

Mergers were important from the 1950s to the 1970s (though not to Anheuser-Busch), stirring strong debate whether they reflected monopolizing or efficiency. In fact, many of them mainly reflected advertising's effects, as noted, and therefore may have been inevitable.

At the distribution level, the technology is simple and leaves large scope for competition. There can be many overlapping delivery firms in any area, and these can freely move into adjoining areas by adjusting their central shipping points.

4. Behavior

Classic tight-oligopoly behavior is evident in the firms' general avoidance of direct price competition. Advertising, the devising of "new" brands, and the use of special promotions are softer methods, which skirt the mutual dangers of price wars. There is some price discounting by all firms, but price stability is the general pattern.

[14] See F. M. Scherer et al., *The Economics of Multi-plant Operations* (Cambridge, Mass: Harvard University Press, 1975); and the sources noted in Elzinga, "The Beer Industry."

This tight oligopoly displays more discord than the cereal firms, partly because the mix of geographical markets is more complex.

As for unilateral anticompetitive actions, Anheuser-Busch was charged in the 1950s with price discrimination in the Missouri area market, which allowed it to increase its market share from 17 to 39 percent.[15] Anheuser-Busch has continued to take selective actions, even though its share of the market today is much larger. Price discrimination may not be critical to its continued leadership, but it has probably been significant.

At the distribution level, the larger brewers have set rigid territorial limits on their distributors in many states. Any sales to adjoining areas are forbidden, on pain of terminating the franchise. This blocks *intra*brand competition. As noted in Chapter 15, this type of action is neutral or procompetitive when market shares are small. But when done by Anheuser-Busch and other firms with substantial shares, it prevents a large amount of intrabrand competition.[16] The FTC held Coca-Cola's and PepsiCola's similar systems to be illegal in 1970 (as noted in Chapter 15), but those firms obtained a special exemption from Congress. The brewers' vertical restrictions are under challenge by officials in some states, but during the Reagan Administration, antitrust officials showed no concern.

5.   Performance

Prices have probably been held significantly above competitive levels, but not markedly so. The leading firms' profits have been high, with Anheuser-Busch averaging 18 percent returns on equity capital since 1970.

Beer advertising is virtually all of the image-forming, persuasive type, so it is largely an economic waste (recall Chapters 5 and 16). Most of it is also mutually canceling among the oligopolists. The resources amount to over $1 billion per year.

As for innovation, this industry has had limited technological opportunity. Lower-calorie beers caught on in the 1970s, on the second try. Aluminum cans were developed from the outside by the container industry. Little other innovation has been done for forty years, except for "new" brands. That may seem natural for a product that originated thousands of years ago, and technological opportunity in this industry is probably limited. Even so, the rate of innovation has been quite slow by any reasonable standard.

In distribution, the limits on intrabrand competition have probably raised prices significantly. That conclusion is disputed by industry sources, who say that free competition would eliminate smaller dealers, permitting the few survivors to raise prices further. Though doubtful, this outcome can not be ruled out for every area.

6.   In Summary

The beer industry is not simple. It mixes tight oligopoly with a degree of dominance by Anheuser-Busch, and regional markets with a national-brand market. Heavy advertising has shaped its structure toward higher concentration, and it pro-

---

[15] Details are in *Federal Trade Commission* v. *Anheuser-Busch*, 363 U.S. 536, an antitrust case that dealt with the episode.

[16] For further detail, see W. John Jordan and Bruce L. Jaffee, "The Use of Exclusive Territories in the Distribution of Beer: Theoretical and Empirical Observations," *Antitrust Bulletin*, 32 (Spring 1987), 137–64.

vides the oligopolists with a way of minimizing direct price competition. It also accounts for the main monopoly loss in the industry. Tight territorial restrictions on beer distribution in many states also probably cause significant monopoly effects.

More effective competition might not increase innovation by very much in this ancient industry. Nor is it clear how advertising could be reduced. Yet the technology would permit much lower concentration. Tight-oligopoly conditions could yield to a looser structure and a more efficient, flexible process of competition.

IV. AIRLINES[17]

Among the array of American industries, the airline industry stands out as a very special case. It is fast-growing and important to the economy, as well as a leading, sharply debated experiment in deregulation.

From 1938 to 1977, the airline industry was controlled by about eight major airlines, whose power was protected and gently regulated by the Civil Aeronautics Board. During 1977–1981, the CAB's controls were removed, and effective competition set in. But then U.S. policies went lax, permitting market power to be reasserted. By 1983, the airlines were beginning to quell price competition, and after 1985, several of the largest airlines were permitted to merge with others, creating even higher concentration than had existed before deregulation.

This outcome has generated strong controversy. Some optimistic observers see strong competition, efficiency, and innovation, whereas others see market power and anticompetitive pricing.[18]

In fact, the industry combines strong competition on some routes with high degrees of monopoly on many others. The hub-and-spoke system involves high dominance of many large-city markets. And price discrimination is anticompetitive on many routes and areas. The airline oligopoly poses major problems, which do not have easy solutions.

1. Brief History

A brief historical survey may help. Through the 1920s and most of the 1930s, air travel grew from a small business run by a group of hedge-hopping daredevils into a new industry dominated by about six trunk airlines.[19]

---

[17] This section has benefited from research done for a chapter by the author on "The Airline Industry," in Walter Adams, ed., *The Structure of American Industry*, 8th ed., New York: Macmillan, 1990.

[18] Among the optimists, see especially Alfred E. Kahn, "Surprises of Airline Deregulation," *American Economic Review*, 78 (May 1988), 316–22; and Elizabeth E. Bailey, David R. Graham, and Daniel P. Kaplan, *Deregulating the Airlines* (Cambridge, Mass.: MIT Press, 1985).

For critics, see Melvin A. Brenner's "Airline Deregulation—A Case Study in Public Policy Failure," *Transportation Law Journal*, 16 (1988), 179–228, and his "Rejoinder to Comments by Alfred Kahn," in the same issue, pp. 253–62; and "The Big Trouble with Air Travel," *Consumer Reports*, June 1988, pp. 362–67.

[19] See Richard E. Caves, *Air Transport and Its Regulators* (Cambridge, Mass.: Harvard University Press, 1962); William A. Jordan, *Airline Regulation in America: Effects and Imperfections*, (Baltimore, Md.: Johns Hopkins University Press, 1970); and Bailey, Graham, and Kaplan, *Deregulating the Airlines*, which covers the deregulation process thoroughly.

By 1938, the biggest airlines were seeking friendly "regulation" as a way to minimize competition. They got it in the form of the Civil Aeronautics Board. From 1938 until 1975, the CAB permitted virtually no entry into the scheduled airlines part of the industry, while the number of airlines shrank from sixteen to eleven. Structure was monopolistic: 90 percent of city-pair routes, with 59 percent of all passenger miles, were monopolies. The airlines behaved like a market-rigging cartel, agreeing on fares among themselves and then obtaining CAB approval and enforcement. In this way, they managed to prevent price-cutting.

The airlines did compete indirectly, on amenities (such as decor and meals) and by scheduling more frequent flights, even though planes flew half empty on average. Pay rates for workers were also generous. CAB regulation therefore tended to raise costs, possibly by 30 to 50 percent over efficient levels.[20]

Economists documented these costs, and by 1975, a momentum had developed for change. Actually, airline deregulation was part of a larger deregulation "movement" in the 1970s that challenged regulation in a number of sectors, such as telephones, railroads, stock markets, and natural gas.

Deregulation of the airlines began in 1977 and was virtually complete by 1981. The airlines' response was immediate and strong, breaking the old patterns. Some regionals expanded into nationwide routes, while the larger airlines shifted their routes actively. Hub-and-spoke patterns developed, with each airline routing most of its traffic through one or two airports. New maverick airlines, such as People Express and World Airways, entered the market rapidly, cutting fares steeply while offering "few frills" service.

The older airlines responded sharply to the new discount airlines. Fare discounts spread to over 75 percent of tickets by 1983. Competition became widely effective, especially on the high-density routes such as New York–Chicago.

Deregulation brought several economic gains. Productivity increased and lower fares were introduced. Choices were more diverse, and the whole industry showed the flexibility and variety of effective competition. Yet the lower costs derived partly from "union bashing" that allowed the airlines to cut work forces and pay rates.

In 1984–1986, the industry reverted to monopolistic patterns. The leading airlines adopted rigid rules for most ticket discounting, and they were permitted to make a series of mergers that increased their dominance over their hubs. National concentration rose. Table 18.4 suggests how the mergers affected concentration. The dominance of "fortress hubs" is indicated in Table 18.5.

The Sector Now.   Figure 18.2 shows the main parts of the sector. The airports and flight controllers constitute the infrastructure; the reservations systems are the medium for selecting and ticketing most flights; and the airlines move aircraft and people.

Most of the largest airports shown in Table 18.5 are heavily congested. The loading gates and time slots are overcrowded, especially during preferred travel times. Congestion has spread in the 1980s because traffic has doubled while airport capacity has stayed about the same.

---

[20] See Caves, *Air Transport and Its Regulators;* Jordan, *Airline Regulation in America;* and Theodore E. Keeler, "Airline Regulation and Market Performance," *Bell Journal of Economics,* 3 (Autumn 1972), 399–424.

TABLE 18.4   Structure of the Domestic Airline Industry

1978		1983		1987	
CARRIER	% OF REVENUE PASSENGER MILES	CARRIER	% OF REVENUE PASSENGER MILES	CARRIER	% OF REVENUE PASSENGER MILES
1. United	21.1	1. United	18.7	1. Texas Air[a]	20.3
2. American	13.5	2. American	13.8	Continental	10.2
3. Delta	12.0	3. Eastern	11.1	Eastern	10.1
4. Eastern	11.1	4. Delta	11.1	2. United	17.3
5. TWA	9.4	5. TWA	7.1	3. American	15.4
6. Western	5.0	6. Republic	4.2	4. Delta[b]	13.0
7. Continental	4.5	7. Northwest	4.2	5. USAir	8.9
8. Braniff	3.8	8. Western	3.9	USAir	4.0
9. National	3.6	9. Continental	3.5	Piedmont	3.5
10. Northwest	2.6	10. Pan Am	3.3	PSA	1.4
11. USAir	2.2	11. Southwest	1.7	6. Northwest and Republic	7.9
12. Frontier	2.0	12. Frontier	1.7	7. TWA[c]	6.4
				8. Southwest	2.5
				9. American West	1.8
				10. Pan Am	1.6
				11. Braniff (New)	1.0
				12. Alaska	0.9
Top Four	57.7	Top Four	54.7	Top Four	66.0
Top Eight	80.4	Top Eight	74.1	Top Eight	91.7
Top Twelve	90.8	Top Twelve	84.3	Top Twelve	97.0

SOURCE: Congressional Budget Office, *Policies for the Deregulated Airline Industry* (Washington, D.C.: U.S. Government Printing Office, July 1988), p. 15.

Note: Northwest's workers were on strike for part of 1978. Data for 1987 reflect mergers of American with Air California and USAir with Piedmont and PSA, even though operations were not affected for the entire year.

[a] Continental acquired → People Express, Frontier, and New York Air, all discount airlines.
[b] Delta acquired → Western.
[c] TWA acquired Ozark.

TABLE 18.5   Dominance at Selected Airports, 1988

AIRPORTS	AIRLINE SHARES OF PASSENGERS
Atlanta	Delta, 58%, Eastern 35%
Chicago	United 50%, American 30%
Denver	United 44%. Continental 41%
St. Louis	TWA 82%
Detroit	Northwest 60%
Pittsburgh	US Air 85%
Dallas-Ft. Worth	American 64%, Delta 26%
Minneapolis	Northwest 78%
Charlotte, N.C.	US Air 92%
Salt Lake City	Delta 80%

SOURCE: U.S. General Accounting Office, *Report on Airline Competition*, June 1989.

Among the major airlines listed in Tables 18.4, the main development has been the rise of Texas Air by buying Continental, Eastern, Frontier, and People Express during 1984–1987. Each airline centers its flights on its hub airports, and the control over gates and slots makes them into fortress hubs.

These are the survivors from the old airlines and the sixty or so newcomers that

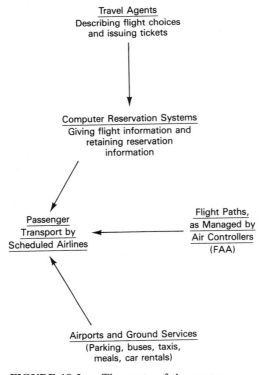

FIGURE 18.2.   The parts of the sector.

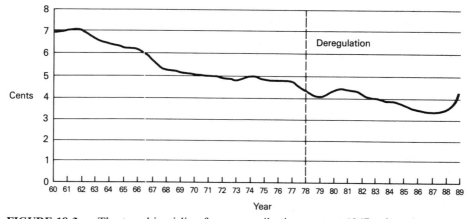

FIGURE 18.3.   The trend in airline fares per mile, in constant 1967 values (cents per mile).
SOURCE: Congressional Budget Office, *Policies for the Deregulated Airline Industry* (Washington, D.C.: U.S. Government Printing Office, July 1988), p. 6.

emerged during 1978–1985. The carnage has been severe, with some fifty airlines disappearing. Most of the scores of regional feeder lines have either been absorbed or subordinated to large airlines.

Traffic varies from huge volumes among the largest cities to thin trickles among the hundreds of smaller cities. The map is dominated by the *hub-and-spoke* pattern: most flights go to a hub city, and most long flights are broken in the middle by a transfer at a hub.

These parts combine in a vast set of operations. Several thousand flights take place in the United States each day, for a total of over 400 million passenger trips a year.

It has been estimated that deregulation has reduced fares sharply below their likely levels under regulation: savings of $6 billion to $12 billion a year have been claimed. Figure 18.3 shows the basic trend of fares per passenger mile, adjusted for inflation. On the other side is the fact that fares had been declining since 1960. Many factors besides deregulation have been at work, including new aircraft types and changing fuel prices.

By 1986, there were rising complaints that deregulation had been subverted, with the result that we now have an unconstrained cartel. How competitive is the sector? Do its behavior and performance fit monopoly patterns?

2. Defining the Markets

Product features are relatively simple in the airline sector, while geographic features are complex and debatable.

Product Substitutability.   Airline travel is highly distinct from alternative forms of travel. It is so much faster than bus, train, or automobile travel over distances above about 150 miles that these cannot be said to be substitutes; that is, they are not "in the market" with airline services. For some short-range travelers the choice may be close (e.g., driving or taking the Amtrak shuttle between New York and Washington takes about as long as flying, in total). And a few executives can choose between their company jets and scheduled airlines. But these are small exceptions to the general rule: There is no close (or even remote) substitute for air travel.

Geographic Substitutability.   This is a more complicated matter. The whole area of the United States is clearly not one big "market." For instance, if you need to go from Miami to New York, a flight from Seattle to Chicago is of no use to you, and even a closely parallel flight from Tampa to Philadelphia is virtually valueless.

Some observers go to the other extreme, saying that *each* city-pair route is a separate market. Since there are hundreds of cities, that would mean that there are thousands of individual-route "markets" within the whole airline industry. But that goes too far, because some city-pair routes overlap others quite closely.

Consider the New York–Denver route as an example. It is overlapped by the New York–Chicago–Denver, New York–Pittsburgh–Denver, and New York–St. Louis–Denver routes, and even the New York–Dallas/Ft. Worth–Denver route. Your travel agent's screen may in fact display such alternative flights as taking about the same time and having similar ticket prices. Despite their physical differences, these flights may be quite close economic substitutes in service (getting from New York to Denver) and price.

The same is true of scores of other overlapping routes. City-pairs are often only parts of larger regional or multicity area travel markets. Yet there is no simple pattern to this. Many of the "spokes" on the airline "hubs" are true individual markets.

In general, some of the main trunk routes have a degree of substitution by alternative routes, but most of the lesser city-pair routes do not. One can also think of major hub airports as being local markets of their own in some degree, because they control access along their spoke routes, into and out of the hub airport. But those hub markets too are not simple or rigid because some of the spoke routes are paralleled by the spoke routes of *other* hubs.

Economic experts have therefore come to rather complicated conclusions in defining markets within the industry. There are many shadings of market edges, and for some parts of the sector no clear markets can be agreed on. But many city-pairs are pretty clear markets. And many hub cities can be regarded as meaningful markets or as cores of regional air travel markets. Each case needs to be inspected on its merits, in terms of the availability of other flights that (1) take about as long, (2) are at similarly convenient times, and (3) involve similar ticket prices.

3.   Structures and Degrees of Competition

Shares of Traffic.   In this complex industry, conditions are mixed. Some "markets" are dominated by one airline, as Table 18.5 shows for some major hub cities. Trunk routes tend to have low concentration, especially if parallel routings are considered. Lesser routes often show high concentration, and many spoke routes are virtual monopolies.

Does the total concentration of all U.S. air travel under the main airlines reveal the true degree of market power? No: it grossly understates that power because there is a honeycomb of many markets rather than just one big national "market." The airlines are well aware that they are spread across a complex sector where any fare-cutting that breaks out in one part is liable to catch fire and hurt them all. High national concentration has increased the incentives to avoid price-cutting.

Conditions of Entry.   Some experts have urged that entry into all of the individual markets is easy, even ultra-free. During 1978–1983, Kahn, Bailey, and Baumol and others urged that airplanes are "capital with wings," meaning airlines can send them instantly into any route where a dominant airline is making excess profit. High market shares could not matter where potential entry was so severe a threat.

This idea of "contestable" markets with "ultra-free entry" was the driving force behind deregulation and government permission for the mergers of 1986–1987.[21] But were airline markets really open to ultra-free entry? The answer has turned out to be no. First of all, it takes huge funds and considerable skills to create a new airline company, and a long time to build reputation and attract staff. Virtually none of the entrants of 1978–1985 has survived, and entry into the sector has been virtually closed since about 1984.

But what about city-pair entry? Can't existing airlines fly new routes to undercut monopoly pricing on specific routes? Usually they cannot, for several reasons. First, boarding gates and time slots are extremely scarce at many airports, and they are controlled by the dominant airlines (which is one of the major reasons for their dominance). Airport expansion is extremely costly and slow, and little of it is now in prospect.

Second, new entry is usually met by sharp retaliation. Generally, it takes months to develop profitable repeat-business clientele for new routes, but rivals can cut fares in minutes, to levels below the entrant's prices. Thus do footholds disappear almost before they are gained.

Third, American and United Airlines own computer reservations systems, which have helped them steer travel agents and passengers their way.[22]

Taken together, the industry's concentration, hubbing, entry barriers, and reservations systems have limited competition immeasurably. There is tight oligopoly, with high dominance in many markets, but mingled with competition on some routes. Much of the industry now appears to be effectively noncompetitive.

[21] Recall from Chapter 11 William J. Baumol, John C. Panzar, and Robert D. Willig, *Contestable Markets and the Theory of Industry Structure* (San Diego, Cal.: Harcourt Brace Jovanovich, 1982); and see Elizabeth E. Bailey and William J. Baumol, "Deregulation and the Theory of Contestable Markets," *Yale Journal on Regulation,* 1 (1984), 111–37, for admissions that airlines are not contestable after all. Also, for a critique of the concept and its relevance to airline markets, recall William G. Shepherd, " 'Contestability' versus Competition," *American Economic Review,* 74 (September 1984), 572–87.

[22] Bias is possible because the flight desirability hinges on departure times, the number of plane changes, the fare charged, the time interval between departure and arrival, and other features. It is easy to set the computer's priorities for listings so that they favor one airline over another. See the CAB's analysis of the problem in its *Report to Congress on Computer Reservations Systems* (Washington, D.C., U.S. Government Printing Office, 1983). See also the criticism of bias in Bailey, Graham and Kaplan, *Deregulating the Airlines,* pp. 187–90.

As Meyer and Oster note, "A bias that diverts only one passenger per month with a $200 round-trip flight for each SABRE computer terminal would gain American Airlines, and cost American's competitors, $120 million per year." Since marginal costs per passenger are low, the shifted revenues are virtually all net profit.

4. Determinants

Before 1978, airlines were often said to be unsuitable for open competition. It was assumed that competition would be unstable and destructive because the large airlines would be able to exploit economies of scale to drive out others.

Economies of Scale.   By 1970, however, research had showed that economies of scale in the industry were pretty much exhausted at a relatively small scale: there was no technological advantage to large size. Indeed, the emergence of many smaller regional "commuter" airlines after 1977 proved that great variety can exist in the industry. These new airlines offered service in various regions and at several levels, ranging from no-frills to luxurious executive-class travel. The diversity would have gone much further had the large airlines not moved so effectively to eliminate or dominate the upstarts.

The industry was and is naturally competitive. Flexible, complex, effective competition is possible without sacrificing economies of scale.

Economies of Scope.   There are significant *economies of scope,* which is a recent term for the familiar "network effects." Once an airline has established a hub with a number of routes extending out, it can often add new routes at relatively low cost. That enables it to generate large profits on those routes while standing ready to use deep price cuts to prevent others from entering. When airport capacity is filled, entry is blocked in any case.

Mergers and Affiliations.   Mergers have strongly shaped industry structure since 1980. First the large carriers either bought or subordinated most of the smaller airlines. Then, after 1985, they proceeded to merge among themselves, as noted in Table 18.4. Some of these mergers created severe management problems rather than efficiency.[23]

5. Behavior

Oligopoly-plus-dominance permits a wide range of behavior, from sustained "fare wars" to collusion to a set of local monopolies. The reality of the airline industry today involves all three, although the trend is from open warfare to controlled competition.

Pricing has largely fitted tight-oligopoly patterns. The airlines tend to match one another's prices quickly, keep them for long intervals, and then change them quickly—the object being to hold flexibility and uncertainty to a minimum.

Since 1985, the leading airlines have adopted the same structure of fare discounts (the "supersavers" and "maxsavers"), with similar restrictions about advance payments, Saturday night stayovers, and nonrefundability. No airline offers fare discounts on any one-way flights. With all the maverick airlines (World Airways, People Express, Florida Air, etc.) eliminated, active price-cutting is over.

[23] Thus in 1988 Northwest Airlines was "still struggling to solve its service problems," caused by its merger with Republic Airlines in 1986. And Texas Air, after its buyouts of Eastern Airlines, Continental, Frontier, and People Express, was still "struggling to integrate all of its parts into a smooth-running whole." *The New York Times*, "How to Beat the Mega-Carriers," April 12, 1988, p. D1.

In 1987, Continental Airlines, which had been the low-cost lower-fare airline, explicitly shifted to a policy of leadership in fare increases. In March and November of 1988, Continental again led the fare increases. *The New York Times* noted that "In general, the major airlines have decided to compete not by cutting fares but by increasing service. They now promote convenient departure times and frequency of service, as well as improvements in food and a better handling of baggage."[24]

That precisely describes the indirect, largely ineffective competition that occurred under the CAB *before* deregulation. Only now the concentration is even greater.

Price Discrimination Under "Yield Management."   Fare discounts have become common, involving over 80 percent of tickets. But the structure of discounts now tightly segments the market, rather than giving free play for flexible price-cutting. Discounting is so deep that the same flight contains passengers who have paid sharply different prices (e.g., $123 and $489) for comparable service.

Discounting has become a complex process by which each airline strives to maximize the revenue it extracts from its customers. Every large airline has hundreds of pricing staff working on "yield management." Their sole objective is to maximize the revenue from each flight by repeatedly adjusting the number of seats offered on discount.[25] As the day of the flight approaches, choices may change hourly because staff are trying to fill every seat, but still charge each customer the maximum he or she is willing to pay.

Yield management approaches the extreme result of perfect price discrimination, in which the seller extracts all of each buyer's consumer surplus.[26] Airline pricing is, in fact, a vast process of price discrimination in which virtually all seats are sold at varying ratios of prices to costs.

It is also heavily anticompetitive, for reasons explained in Chapter 12. The leading airlines have jointly established a uniform structure of discounts and restrictions. Within that fixed pricing structure, the system milks customers for maximum revenue, and makes entry difficult. The behavior may not be totally equal to that of a single all-controlling monopolist, but the basic pattern is much the same.

"Predatory" Actions.   In addition, there have been anticompetitive pricing actions directed against specific airlines. During 1980–1985, large airlines eliminated some small rivals from the market by setting extremely low prices on key routes.[27]

---

[24] *The New York Times,* "Air Fares Rise for Many Travelers as Big Carriers Dominate Market," March 15, 1988, pp. A1 and D8.

[25] For example, American's yield managers "monitor and adjust the fare mixes on 1,600 daily flights as well as 538,000 future flights involving nearly 50 million passengers. Their work is hectic: a fare's average life span is two weeks, and industrywide about 200,000 fares change daily." *The New York Times,* "The Art of Devising Air Fares," March 4, 1987, p. D1.

[26] As an American Airline official noted, "You don't want to sell a seat to a guy for $69 when he's willing to pay $400." See *The New York Times,* March 4, 1987, p. D1.

[27] For example, in June 1984, People Express entered the Newark-Minneapolis route, at fares of $99 on weekdays and $79 on evenings and weekends. Previously, the lowest fare had been $149, and the standard coach fare was $263. Northwest, the dominant firm, promptly cut its fares to $95 and $75, for service that was much better (in seating, meals, baggage handling, etc.). Therefore Northwest was undercutting People's fare.

Desperately, People cut its fares further, to $79 and $59; Northwest matched those cuts. Unable to survive such deep cuts, People Express eventually was bought by Texas Air. After merging with Republic, Northwest had over 80 percent of the traffic into Minneapolis. It then increased its fares sharply.

Other Strategic Actions.   The handling of computer reservations systems by United and American is behavior that has reduced competition and continues to weaken it.

The development of hub-and-spoke patterns has also reduced competition, on balance. It has created a series of local dominant firms or duopolies at most of the important airports, and fares have gone up in line with market positions. Against this, there have been some gains. To an extent, hubbing permits smoother connections between on-line flights in the airport than if passengers had to change between airlines. Gates are closer, and baggage is handled directly. But the monopoly effects are strong, including the forcing of split flights on most long routes.

Moreover, each airline knows that if it cuts prices to invade another airline's hub, it can expect selective retaliation at its own hub. Accordingly, there is reluctance to initiate price-cutting. The airlines prefer to protect their spheres of influence instead.

6. Performance

The effective competition of 1978–1985 brought significant gains. Airline load factors went up, from 56 percent in 1977 to 62 percent in the mid-1980s. Ticket prices rose less rapidly, saving passengers perhaps $6 billion to $12 billion annually.[28] The volume of air travel rose far more rapidly, since more people could now afford to fly.

Accordingly, deregulation's initial benefits are often said to have been large. But *net* benefits may have been small, and market power since 1984 may have erased them.

Prices and Service Quality.   Morrison and Winston attribute to deregulation a 30 percent cut in ticket prices. Fuel prices rose sharply during 1979–1981, reflecting the jump in oil prices from about $14 to over $30 per barrel. Other input prices rose too, including average wages and aircraft. Allowing statistically for these rises, relative fares appear to show a fall.

But Figure 18.3 suggests no such large impact. Several factors were at work in the downward trend, so deregulation's effect is not clear. Indeed, the severe decline in oil prices during 1986–1987 did not cause a reduction in ticket prices: rather, they rose.

Moreover, the quality of service has fallen, perhaps even proportionally more than fares. Service quality includes such elements as the time taken by the flight (including that spent at the airport checking in), the risk of missing flights or connections, the risk of delay or loss of baggage, the crowding in lines and in the plane itself, and the general quality of the experience.

All of these have deteriorated markedly since 1978. Hubbing causes most long flights to be broken into two legs. That lengthens the time of the flight, doubles the

---

[28] The figure is controversial because it compares actual prices with those that might have occurred under certain assumed conditions. See Morrison and Winston; Melvin A. Brenner, "Airline Deregulation—A Case Study in Public Policy Failure," *Transportation Law Journal*, 16 (1988), 179–228, and his "Rejoinder to Comments by Alfred Kahn," in the same journal issue, pp. 253–62.

Steven A. Morrison and Clifford Winston, *The Economics of Airline Deregulation*, (Washington, D.C.: Brookings Institution, 1986).

number of landings and takeoffs (which causes anxiety for some travelers), and increases the effort and risk in making connections. The risk of missing connections is raised, as is the risk that baggage will not make the connection. Check-in times and lines are longer, and crowding is commonplace.

Flying is now much like bus travel, thanks to a sharp loss of quality that may more than offset any fare decreases. Moreover, the cost reductions have come mainly from cutting employees' pay rates. That merely transfers money from workers to passengers, without reducing the real resources used.

Innovation.   Before 1978, airline innovations in both services and discounting were reasonably rapid. Deregulation brought a burst of new innovation in services, such as no-frills flights at low prices, led by People Express, World Airways, and Air Florida. Computer reservations systems were improved rapidly. New fare discounts were developed, from extremely low "peanuts" fares to off-peak discounts.

Service quality was degraded. But small commuter-type aircraft were introduced on many new small-city routes, filling the gap left when large airlines withdrew large aircraft from those routes. Staffing was streamlined, and the hub-and-spoke system was a major innovation.

Since 1983, however, innovation has slowed, perhaps because of market power as well as other conditions. Recent innovations have tended toward price discrimination and the further extension of hubbing.

Small-Airport Service.   Deregulation always raises fears that small cities will lose service. In the event, full-size jet aircraft were withdrawn from many smaller airports. But new, small-craft commuter lines emerged to maintain or increase service in most cases. Still, fares are higher; those on small-city routes have risen roughly 30 to 50 percent compared to those on the major routes.

Safety.   During 1978–1988, the fatality rates per volume of flying declined moderately, but "near-misses" increased. Deregulation is accused of inducing airlines to skimp on maintenance, under financial pressures. Yet the main causes of risk lie outside the airlines. One is the firing of all striking air controllers in 1981 and then rigidly refusing to rehire any of them later. Another is the FAA's meager budgets.

A general summary of airline performance since 1977 is: Price-quality levels have little improved or actually worsened. Efficiency is up, but partly from simple wage cutting. Innovation rose during the strong competitive period but declined again. Safety has not worsened.

7.   In Summary

The behavior and performance of the airline industry have reflected its changing structure, just as basic theory would predict. Unless concentration and barriers are reduced, performance is likely to stay well below its potential.

QUESTIONS FOR REVIEW

1. Is the ready-to-eat cereals market a tight oligopoly or dominant-firm case? Does the distinction matter much in this case?

2. If competition is vigorous and effective, how can the leaders' market positions have remained so stable for so long?

3. If scale economies in producing cereals are low, what explains the high degree of concentration?

4. Explain the meaning of "packing the product space." In your view, was it a process which maximized market power, consumer choice, or both in some degree?

5. How is Kellogg's sustained 20-plus percent rate of return to be explained: market power, innovation, efficiency, or what?

6. Define the markets inhabited by the four main professional sports. Are they overlapping with each other? with collegiate and high-school sports? or divided among local monopolies, by teams?

7. Evaluate how strong the countervailing forces are: Players? Cities? Television networks? Do they differ markedly among the sports?

8. Are these sports really natural monopolies, which must have league monopolies? Discuss the effects of organizing new leagues to vie with the existing ones.

9. In the effort to reach the most efficient economic results, should players be free to move among teams, as part of effective competition?

10. Discuss one of the main professional sports: has it been X-efficient and innovative, in your judgment?

11. What is the true market (or markets) for beer? Discuss especially the factors that might give local or regional markets.

12. Is beer just another industry where advertising has created concentration much higher than production and marketing economies would justify?

13. Discuss the definition of air travel markets. Is there one national oligopoly, a series of large-city dominant firms, or some mix? If a mix, what is it mostly?

14. Explain how scarce gates and slots affect the degree of "contestability" of many airline markets. Explain how airline mergers and the channeling of fare discounting into standard patterns have reduced competition.

15. If service quality has deteriorated by 30 percent since 1977, does that nullify the gains from deregulation?

Part VII   *PUBLIC POLICIES*

19   ANTITRUST POLICIES

When European economists discuss what is special about the United States economy, they frequently mention its large size and abundant natural resources. But even more distinctive than these, they often say, is "your touching faith in competition, as shown by your antitrust policies." They also point to our treatment of the main public utility industries, where we regulate private companies rather than convert them to public ownership. Indeed, antitrust and regulation are unique American experiments, and they are the country's main defenses against monopoly power.

Yet the 1980s brought a massive cutback in U.S. antitrust enforcement, under Chicago-UCLA and "contestability" doctrines. The correct degrees of antitrust and regulation are controversial, because the lessons of industrial organization research are not conclusive.

Antitrust is the great, fundamental industrial policy of the United States, driven deep into the bedrock of the American economy.[1] It reaches into most sectors, seeking to make competition so effective that other, more intrusive types of controls on monopoly will not be needed. Antitrust policies are designed to punish price-fixers and to prevent anticompetitive mergers. Regulation attempts to set limits on utility prices in order to obtain the efficiencies of natural monopoly while preventing monopoly pricing.

These policies attract intense debate because they deal with urgent, complex issues where the stakes often run into many billions of dollars. Thus the loosening

---

[1] A review and analysis of the policies is given in William G. Shepherd, *Public Policies Toward Business,* 7th ed., Homewood, Ill.: Irwin, 1985. For more extended coverage, see the monumental coverage in the policies provided in Philip Areeda and Donald F. Turner, *Antitrust Law,* 4 vol. (Boston: Little, Brown, 1978 et seq.); and A. D. Neale and D. G. Goyder, *The Antitrust Laws of the United States of America,* 3d ed. (Cambridge: Cambridge University Press, 1980). The summary by F. M. Scherer, *Industrial Market Structure and Economic Performance,* 2d ed. (Boston: Houghton Mifflin, 1980), Chapters 18–21, is also helpful. For a Chicago-UCLA view of many antitrust points, see John S. McGee, *Industrial Organization* (Englewood Cliffs, N.J.: Prentice Hall, 1988). To assess the current flavor of the debates between the mainstream approach and the newer schools, see the superb discussion by Eleanor M. Fox and Lawrence A. Sullivan, "Antitrust—Retrospective and Prospective: Where Are We Coming From? Where Are We Going?" *New York University Law Review,* 62 (November 1987), 936–88. Excellent journals specializing in antitrust include *The Antitrust Bulletin* and *The Antitrust Law & Economics Review.*

of merger restraints in the 1980s helped unleash a vast merger boom (recall Chapter 10) involving over $600 billion in assets. Antitrust and regulation are energetically denounced, not only by their natural targets, but also by the Chicago-UCLA School and the more recent "contestability" group of economic theorists.[2]

These groups claim—on the free market doctrines that have become familiar throughout this book—that most mainstream antitrust policies are unnecessary and harmful, because markets are already competitive enough. These doctrines were adopted wholesale during the 1980s by Reagan Administration officials, who deregulated some sectors, withdrew most antitrust actions, and shrank the agencies responsible for enforcement.

This chapter will first present the mainstream antitrust policies that have evolved since the enactment of the Sherman Act in 1890, and then note the severe 1980s cutbacks. In 1989 the Bush Administration appeared to be shifting antitrust slightly back toward established lines summarized in this chapter. Readers can judge for themselves if the shift involves more than rhetoric.

Section I shows concisely how antitrust and regulation originated and evolved for a century. It also defines the economic guidelines for efficient policy choices. Section II presents the settled main lines of actual, pre-1980 antitrust policies, and notes the extent of the Reagan era reductions. Sections III to V give details on the three specific parts of antitrust: toward existing market domination, toward mergers, and toward price-fixing.

This chapter's coverage of antitrust must be brief, but it should suffice since several points about antitrust and significant cases were noted in earlier chapters.

I. ORIGINS AND STANDARDS OF U.S. ANTITRUST POLICIES

Since 1890, U.S. antitrust policies have been hammered out amid turbulent political action, and they remain the focus of intense battles. With such origins and continuing pressures, the three policies—antitrust, regulation, and public enter-

---

[2] The leading Chicago-UCLA critic has been Robert H. Bork, who taught first at the University of Chicago, then became a law professor at Yale and a federal appeals court judge, before being rejected in 1987 as a Supreme Court nominee. His *The Antitrust Paradox: A Policy at War with Itself* (New York: Basic Books, 1978), denounces virtually all antitrust actions. Dominick T. Armentano goes even further. He recommends terminating all U.S. antitrust enforcement; see his *Antitrust and Monopoly: Anatomy of a Policy Failure* (New York: Wiley, 1982). A more gently phrased, but often even more nihilistic view of antitrust, is Donald J. Dewey, "The Antitrust Experiment, 1890–1990: A Judgment," *Antitrust Bulletin,* Special Commemorative Issue for the Sherman Act, 1990, in process.

Perhaps the most sophisticated Chicago-UCLA critic has been Richard A. Posner, law professor at the University of Chicago, later an Appeals Court judge. See particularly his *Antitrust Law* (Chicago: University of Chicago Press, 1976).

William J. Baumol has not only led the attack on regulation with his group's "contestability" theory (recall Chapter 13), but has also severely criticized antitrust policies. See William J. Baumol and Janusz Ordover, "Use of Antitrust to Subvert Competition," *Journal of Law and Economics,* 28 (May 1985), 247–65. (Note that a large share of the papers attacking both antitrust and regulation have appeared in the University of Chicago's own local journal, the *Journal of Law and Economics.*)

The attack on regulation has been led by George J. Stigler, who started and fostered a series of studies at the University of Chicago that attempted to show that regulation has had nil or negative effects. See his *The Organization of Industry* (Homewood, Ill.: Irwin, 1968). Many of these studies have also reached print through the *Journal of Law and Economics.*

prise—are naturally imperfect rather than ideal. The task is to discover what these policies are really doing to the economy.

1.   Three Waves

There have been three major waves of policies. The first came in 1885–1915, when antitrust policies and regulatory agencies began. Then, from 1933 to 1950, a second wave occurred, especially as airlines, telephones, and electricity came under regulation. Finally, between 1965 and 1975, the third wave created a battery of agencies regulating safety and health. Figure 19.1 includes some of the main antitrust and regulatory parts of these waves.

Each wave reflected the public's discontent with recent business performance and its belief that government action was needed. Many of the actions were inadequate, went too far, or applied the wrong incentives. Some of the faults were corrected after each wave, when efforts were made to trim back the policies.

The crucial formative period for policies was 1890–1910. Before 1890, there had been a scattering of rules and laws dealing with the early forms of business, mostly at the local and state level. In cities, the gas and water utilities were controlled in various ways, often under city ownership. The charges for using turnpikes and canals presented problems of monopoly pricing, met in diverse ways by the various states.

Upon this localized scene the U.S. industrial revolution burst with great force from 1865 to 1900. The railroads spread across the country, forming monopolies in some regions and charging discriminatory prices. Stirred by the Civil War and the railroad boom, heavy industries expanded rapidly. Gold rushes, land rushes, the invention of electric light systems and telephones, the dramatic growth of the oil industry from 1870 to 1890—these and other new developments created an industrial transformation of the country. Moreover, after 1890, the great financiers—especially J. P. Morgan—were busy forming "trusts" in many industries by merging scores of little firms into big ones.

Regulation.   The 1880s saw rising public agitation against these changes. Farmers organized to fight price gouging by the railroad monopolies. They and other

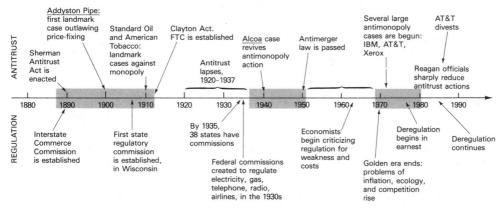

FIGURE 19.1.   Main events in antitrust and regulation.

citizens increasingly denounced the new industrial trusts. Amid sharp political debates, two kinds of policy action were initiated. First, *regulation* was established, starting with the Interstate Commerce Commission in 1887 to regulate the railroads. Then state regulatory commissions were created from 1907 on to regulate electricity, telephones, and railroad traffic within the states. These steps accepted the *private* ownership of the basic utility operations, in contrast to the public ownership of the railroads and city utilities that was already common in other countries.

The regulatory commissions were supposed to control the private utilities strictly, permitting only "fair" rates of return and "just and reasonable" prices (without too much price discrimination). By the 1930s, most of the states had their own regulatory commissions, and new federal commissions had been created to cover *interstate* operations in the main utility sectors.

Antitrust.   Second, *antitrust policy* was created in 1890 to reduce monopoly in the rest of the economy. It was called "antitrust" because it was aimed against the creation of industrial trusts (which were combinations of independent firms). The Sherman Act of 1890 outlawed both monopolizing by one firm and collusion among competitors. After some delay, the law was applied firmly to price-fixing in 1899 and to some dominant firms in 1911. As further enlarged in 1914 and 1950, the U.S. antitrust laws became a uniquely thorough method for curing industrial monopoly and price-fixing.

Yet antitrust and regulation have had checkered careers since 1920, reflecting the larger economic trends and political swings. Antitrust has veered between great waves of action (1938–1952 and 1968–1980) and relatively inactive periods (the 1920s and 1952–1968). Regulation took a long time to get established, with full coverage and powers being reached only in the 1950s. At most times, both antitrust and regulation have been sharply criticized, by business for being too harsh and "antibusiness," and by others for being too weak and "probusiness."

The selections of people to run the agencies are made under political pressure, which often results in mediocre appointments. The agencies' budgets are also politically limited. Frequently, the strongest lobbying is done by the very companies the policies are supposed to control. In these and other ways, the companies may influence policy as much as policy influences the companies' actions.

Since actual policies evolve in a rugged political setting, often under intense pressures from many sides, one must expect antitrust, regulation, and public enterprise to be imperfect and limited. We will also show where they have often come close to sound economic results.

Public enterprise has not been eclipsed. It has continued in the U.S. Postal Service, many hundreds of city electric and transit systems, thousands of city water works, and still other cases to be noted in Chapter 20. Yet it has scarcely been tried in manufacturing and finance. This is a sharp difference between the United States and many other countries. Since 1945, foreign experience with public enterprise has included all economic sectors, though since 1980 a privatization movement has shifted some enterprises to private hands.

2. Standards of Efficient Policies

Economists commonly judge policies by "cost-benefit analysis." It merely adopts the familiar comparison of marginal costs and benefits. Recall that each economic action provides benefits, usually a good that people will pay for. The same action also incurs costs—the effort and resources needed to produce the good. Efficient economic decisions carry production until the marginal benefits just equal marginal costs, as we stressed in Chapter 2. The marginal unit is just worth its cost.

The Cost-Benefit Margin.   Public policy choices face the same criterion of efficiency: *Each action should be carried up to the level where its marginal benefits just equal its costs.* The *public's* benefits arise when monopoly's effects are prevented; then there is greater efficiency, lower prices, more rapid innovation, and other desirable goals. If the action is wise, the public reaps these benefits through the improved performance of the economy.

But there are also policy costs. They are mainly incurred by the public in paying for the agency to take the action. Agencies use resources (in staff members' salaries and other costs) in applying their policies. For example, the antitrust chief considers whether to prosecute five bakers in St. Louis for fixing the prices of their bread. It is a marginal case among forty other small price-fixing cases. This case will cost $10,000 to carry out (in working time, travel, and so on), and it will only improve conditions in one small market.

Ideally, the official weighs the benefits and costs, at least approximately, in such marginal cases and decides to pursue those that have the larger yield. In practice, the judgments may be faulty or the agencies may be given either too many or too few resources. Moreover, the logic applies only when the same people bear the costs as reap the benefits. If, instead, some pay costs while others draw gains, then the analysis gives weak guidance.

The choice is illustrated in Figure 19.2. At point A, the marginal benefits of added degrees of competition will just equal their costs. Any level below A is too little; at A_1, for example, the marginal benefits of doing more are well above the marginal cost. Therefore, doing more is "worth it" at the margin. That holds for successive levels up to A. Beyond A, action is not worth it. At A_2, for instance, the marginal cost of greater competition is well above the marginal benefits.

This kind of cost-benefit comparison is the correct basis for appraising antitrust and regulation. The economic task is to judge which policies have been carried too far or not far enough, in light of their probable costs and benefits. The specific sums are rarely easy to measure, so careful judgments have to rely on reasonable likelihoods rather than on actual numbers. For example, was the large antitrust case against AT&T (which resulted in dividing up the Bell System) worth its cost? Should the regulation of long-distance telephone service, banking, even of electric service, be withdrawn? In these and scores of other cases, you can practice the kind of cost-benefit thinking that is the test for rational policies.

Design and Amount.   The choices have two main elements: *design* and *amount.* Each policy's *design* is to be as close to ideal as possible, attaining a maximum of benefits for a given amount of cost. It will apply a correct set of incentives

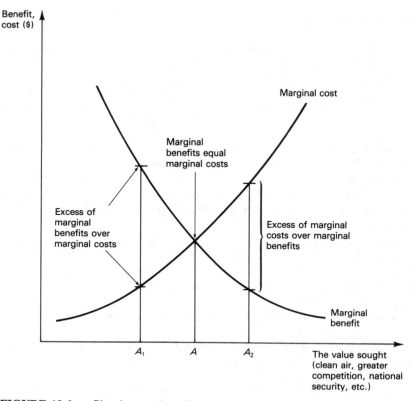

FIGURE 19.2.   Simple cost-benefit analysis.

to the firm to induce its behavior to fit optimal lines. For example, an antitrust treatment of a monopolist might deftly negotiate compliance at little cost, rather than launch a vast, costly court battle that may eventually achieve little.

The best-designed policy is then to be carried out to the efficient *amount,* just up to the efficient margin—or, in plainer terms, to the point where it is just strict enough.

These concepts are rarely applied precisely in practice. For one thing, data for making such careful judgments are often lacking. For another, these terms are not even familiar to most officials. The choice often appears, as in Figure 19.3, with wide bands of estimated possible values for costs and benefits. A person who estimates benefits low and costs high will choose point *B,* with little policy effort. But one who rates benefits high and costs low will urge level *C,* which is far more ambitious. In general, Chicago-UCLA analysts lean to point *B* results, with minimum action, while others would go higher. There may be intense debate between advocates of *B* and *C* because both can appear to be correct.

Intelligent decisions proceed *as if* they were fitting these logical concepts, using the best evidence at hand. They informally weigh the main good effects against the likely costs and try to go as far as seems "reasonable." If done consistently, such

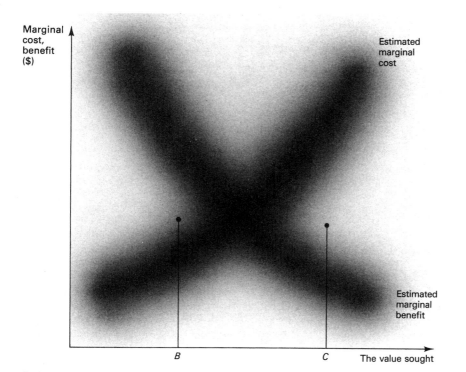

FIGURE 19.3.   Cost-benefit choices can be uncertain when the amounts are uncertain.

rough judgments will in most cases come close to the patterns given by complete analysis.

Costs of Policies.   Now we need to consider the costs of policies in more detail. Broadly speaking, there are two types: direct and indirect.

Direct costs are the dollar budgets spent for public agencies. These can be substantial, but some agencies have tiny budgets compared to the interests they supervise. For example, the two U.S. antitrust agencies spend less than $80 million yearly in dealing with markets totaling at least $4.8 trillion of gross national product.

Indirect costs are of several kinds. One is **private-firm response costs.** These are spent by firms in resisting or influencing the public actions, or both. For example, a firm may spend $10 million in defending against an antitrust case that the FTC spends $1 million on. Or a utility may spend $2 million on a rate hearing that costs the regulatory commission $300,000 to hold.

Another indirect cost is **public supervision:** the scarce ability of the political process to evaluate and to exert control in the public interest. Information is costly, and the ability of citizens to acquire it, weigh it, and act upon it has high opportunity costs.

Costs of interference are the third type of indirect cost. Policies set limits, preventing some private firms from taking actions they would prefer to take. Firms may also lose efficiency when profits are restrained. The result can be a loss of productivity. Of course, a well-designed policy can also cause *increases* in the efficiency of firms.

These effects vary from case to case. Often, too, they are hard to measure and predict, which is why they are highly debatable.

Benefits of Policies.   These also require careful weighing. They include the full range of benefits that competition provides, from technical efficiency and innovation to broad values of fairness, freedom, and the others noted throughout this book.

3.   Bias in Policies

In the ideal public agency, the officials would seek and apply optimal policies. But real agencies depart from the ideal. Several theories have been offered to explain the defects of "real" regulation.

Compromise.   Agencies' policies are really a form of compromise among the interests involved in each market: companies, consumers, workers, suppliers, and the like. These groups could thrash the matter out in Congress or in the courts by a pluralistic bargaining process. But an agency is usually more efficient in striking the balance.

Generally, the officials give other reasons for their choices, claiming that they have been determined by clear logical criteria. But economists looking for the real effects beneath the surface verbiage often find a mere attempt to split the difference or to minimize political trouble.

Compromise need not be "wrong," either as an approach or as a result. However, compromise is a different conceptual basis from ideal, unilateral control by authorities.

Capture.   Agencies can come under the control of the firms they supposedly control. The degree of capture can vary, but some observers believe that it is usually nearly complete. A captured agency acts like a tool of the firms. It is one-sided, rather than responsive to many influences.

The capture concept is consistent with both right-wing and left-wing views: with Chicago-UCLA opinions and with Marxian theories that the state is merely the arm of capitalist interests. A capture theory is also consistent with a third, more cynical, view: that many officials are simply corrupted by the firms. Actually, corruption is not necessary for capture; the managers of captured agencies often have high personal standards of integrity.

Inefficiency and Lags.   Another theory is that agencies develop as much bureaucratic fat and slowness as is permitted. Officials seek to build empires, to minimize their own risks, and to prolong their careers. Accordingly, the agencies may make mistakes and operate poorly because of sheer ineptitude and bureaucracy. Policies are slow or wrong then because of bureaucratic incompetence, rather than (or as well as) because of compromise or capture.

Altogether, the underlying realities influencing the policy agencies can lead to sharp distortions from ideal results. Yet some agencies have performed close to the ideal patterns during some periods, so distortions are not inevitable or universal.

Specific causes of bias

Yet policies are subject to certain specific biases, as follows.

Spending What Is at Stake.   The firm being treated by a policy will consider how much money it should spend to resist (that is, to bend the policy to its own interests). As a general rule: *The rational firm will ultimately be willing to spend as much as the profits at stake, in order to protect those profits.* The resulting spending may be quite large. For example, a firm making $20 million a year in monopoly profits would, as a sound, routine business decision, be willing to spend up to that amount in legal and other costs in defending against antitrust policies that would remove the monopoly power. Usually, it is not necessary to spend the full amount, but the firm's incentives make it ready to do so.

Taxes.   Accentuating this effect are taxes. The firm's resistance costs are usually tax-deductible business expenses, so the firm's opportunity cost of spending on resistance is less than the accounting expense. For example, a firm that has $20 million per year in after-tax monopoly profits at stake will have an incentive to spend much more than that to protect those profits from policy actions. The tax rate makes resistance dollars "cheaper" to the firm, so it is willing to spend them more freely.

The resulting spending can dissipate in advance the very benefits that the policy is intended to gain for consumers and the public. Moreover, the firm can *threaten* to eliminate all of those benefits by overspending on its resistance. If that threat deters the agency from acting, then it frustrates the policy action in advance! Thus the firm's spending, or the threat of it, can effectively discourage the public agency from trying to enforce the policy.

Time Bias.   Two biases related to time are frequently important. *First:* Often one side (the agency or the firm) can impose delay on the proceedings and gain benefits from doing so. The stalling thus distorts the outcome.

Second: The time bias is strengthened by the brevity of most policymakers' tenure. New policies often require at least three years to prepare and ten years for benefits to be fully harvested. Yet most top antitrust and regulatory decision makers are in office less than four years. Inexperience often neutralizes them for the first year or two, and after that they are eager to show results. Therefore they tend to take quick, visible, and shallow actions rather than thoughtful, effective ones.

Probability Bias.   An uneven burden of proof can bias the outcome sharply. Thus the laws and traditions of private property rights normally set the burden of proof against changes in the status quo. This basis often departs from an even choice among alternatives. An even burden of proof presumes, of course, that there is equal access to the critical data. Without such equality of access, the actual burden of proof may be tilted. In fact, the burden of proof is decisive in a wide range of cases.

Information Bias.   Public agencies need complete and timely information on sensitive variables (market shares, prices, costs, innovation choices, competitive tactics, and alternative treatments), both past and future. But they often lack it. Such information is known intimately by firms, and when it endangers their profits, it will naturally be secreted. Because firms also try to influence public fact-gathering policies, the data put out in the public realm are often scanty. This can cause a bias in specific policy choices, as well as in the general evaluation of policy needs and urgency.

Taken together, these biases have three effects. First, industrial policies are less complete than they would otherwise be, because the problems and potential yields are underestimated. Second, whole problems, areas, and cases are probably slighted, because of ignorance. Third, more agency resources have to be spent on mere fact-gathering than a neutral information state would require. These biases may cumulate to large distortions.

Some observers, therefore, regard virtually all policy actions as harmful, on balance; that is, their benefits are smaller than their costs. That is the standard Chicago-UCLA view. Alternatively, if the biases all tend to suppress policies, then the correct lesson is to *enlarge* the policy efforts and thus offset the biases.

Benefits and costs of actions

Each case aims to restore full competition more quickly than natural market forces would. In Figure 19.4, the gain is the shaded area, where competition is greater than it otherwise would be. If natural decline is slow and the case acts rapidly, then the net gain may be large. But if the natural decline is fast, then the case may not speed it up much at all, so its benefits would be small.

Figure 19.5 illustrates the benefits and costs of an antitrust action. The costs of litigation and transition occur first. The resulting flow of benefits, it is hoped, will be large enough to justify the costs. Discounting the values for time will usually shrink the benefit-cost ratio, because the benefits come later, often after many years.

The benefit-cost results of these cases are usually debatable. Chicago-UCLA economists theorize that monopoly power declines rapidly and cases are so slow that antitrust action brings little net gain in competition. Moreover, because they

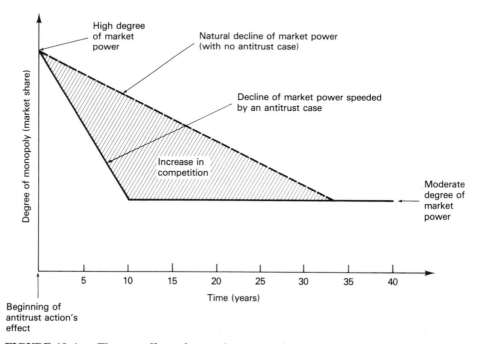

FIGURE 19.4.   The net effect of an antitrust case in raising competition.

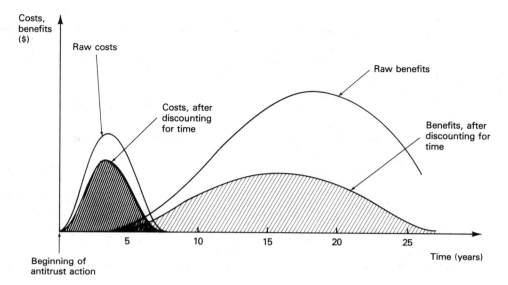

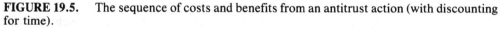

FIGURE 19.5.   The sequence of costs and benefits from an antitrust action (with discounting for time).

regard monopoly as weak, they regard the flow of benefits (in Figure 19.5) as small. Therefore they favor little or no Section 2 cases.

Other experts theorize that natural declines are so slow that antitrust cases can effect large net gains in competition. Since they also think that the benefit flows will be large, they favor extensive Section 2 actions.

II. U.S. ANTITRUST POLICIES: FORMS AND COVERAGE

There is no single "best" set of laws, agencies, or procedures to bring about the "optimal" patterns of competition. There are many possible tools, which can be combined in various ways and degrees of strictness. American antitrust is one specific set of techniques, developed since 1890 and altered frequently.

1. The Laws and Agencies

Laws.   The Sherman Act of 1890 is the basic antitrust law, prohibiting monopoly and collaboration in broad terms. In 1914, the Clayton Act made certain specific actions illegal. It was amended in 1936 to limit certain kinds of price-cutting, in 1937 to permit "fair trade" (the Miller-Tydings Act), and in 1950 to limit mergers (the Celler-Kefauver Act). Table 19.1 codifies the main laws.

The Sherman Act has two main sections:

Section 1. Every contract, combination in the form of a trust or otherwise, or conspiracy, in restraint of trade or commerce among the several states, or with foreign nations, is

TABLE 19.1   The Basic U.S. Antitrust Laws

1. *Restraint of Trade* (Sherman Act, Section 1)
   Collusive actions, such as price-fixing, market rigging, and sales-allocating schemes and other restrictive actions, are all forbidden.

2. *Monopolizing* (Sherman Act, Section 2)
   Both monopolizing and *attempting to monopolize* a market are illegal.

3. *Mergers* (Clayton Act, Section 7, amended in 1950)
   Any merger that may substantially reduce competition in any market is illegal.

4. *Other Actions That Are Prohibited:*
   a.   Interlocking directorates (one person serving on the boards of two competing companies).
   b.   Price discrimination that harms competition (Robinson-Patman Act of 1936).
   c.   Exclusive and tying contracts (Clayton, Section 3). (If good A can only be bought by also buying good B, the two goods are "tied.")
   d.   "Unfair" methods of competition (FTC Act, Section 5). These are unspecified in the law, but would include abusive or extreme actions.

hereby declared to be illegal. Every person who shall make any such contract or engage in any such combination or conspiracy, shall be deemed guilty of a misdemeanor. . . .
   Section 2. Every person who shall monopolize, or attempt to monopolize, or combine or conspire with any other person or persons, to monopolize any part of the trade or commerce among the several states, or with foreign nations, shall be deemed guilty of a misdemeanor. . . .

Section 1 is against cooperation. The key words are "Every . . . conspiracy, in restraint of trade . . . is . . . a misdemeanor." The classic Section 1 target is price-fixing. Section 2 makes market dominance illegal: "Every" monopolization or "attempt" is a misdemeanor.
   The Clayton Act of 1914 outlawed four specific practices, and added a general rule against unfair methods of competition. The particular devices that were outlawed by the Clayton Act were discrimination in prices, exclusive and tying contracts, intercorporate stockholdings, and interlocking directorates.

   Section 2 of the act forbade sellers "to discriminate in price between different purchasers of commodities" but permitted such discrimination where there were "differences in the grade, quality, or quantity of the commodity sold," where the lower prices made "only due allowance for differences in the cost of selling or transportation," and where they were offered "in good faith to meet competition."
   Section 3 forbade sellers to "lease or make a sale or contract for sale of . . . commodities . . . on the condition that the lessee or purchaser thereof shall not use or deal in the . . . commodity . . . of a competitor. . . ."
   Section 7 forbade any corporation engaged in commerce to acquire the shares of a competing corporation or to purchase the stocks of two or more corporations that were competitors.

None of these prohibitions was absolute; the three practices were forbidden only where their effect, in the words of the law, "may be to substantially lessen competition or tend to create a monopoly. . . ."

> Section 8 prohibited interlocking directorates between corporations engaged in commerce where one of them had a capital and surplus of more than $1 million and where "the elimination of competition . . . between them would constitute a violation of any of the provisions of the antitrust laws."

To sum up, the Sherman Act is the basic law, while the Clayton Act (as further amended) has refined it. Many states have some form of antitrust law (often called "baby Sherman Acts"), but most of these laws are weak or dormant.

Scope. Despite their broad language, the laws have a limited reach. Many sectors are exempt by law, including much *intra*state commerce, patent monopolies, agriculture and fishing, milk, labor unions, baseball, and—in part—a variety of regulated industries. Others are exempt by custom: education, health services, urban services, national defense suppliers, and so forth. The borders of antitrust are blurred and shifting. (For example, antitrust agencies have some influence over mergers and behavior in "regulated" industries [banking, electricity, etc.] and much intrastate commerce has some effects across state lines: federal agencies have been able to reach down into some city markets. But the "correct" limits of interstate commerce are debatable, and so are most other borders of antitrust.)

The "rule of reason" is another limit on antitrust. The laws are flat and complete: they proscribe every monopoly or attempt to monopolize, and every conspiracy to restrain trade. But in 1911, a rule of reason was added to Section 2 by the Supreme Court in the *Standard Oil* case. Monopolies that were not abusive were exempted. This limit was formally removed in 1945 in the *Alcoa* decision. But other limits evolved, and they continue to apply a *de facto* rule of reason, as we will see.

Agencies. U.S. antitrust policy consists of (1) agencies, which enforce (2) laws. There are two federal enforcement agencies: (1) the Antitrust Division within the Department of Justice; and (2) the Federal Trade Commission, an independent agency created in 1914.

Both were small until the late 1930s: a "corporal's guard," as one expert put it.[3] They grew to about 300 lawyers by 1950, stabilized, and then expanded again after 1970. Their budgets for antitrust enforcement were about $4 million each in 1950, and were still below $12 million in 1970. In 1980, the budgets were less than $40 million each, still tiny compared to an economy of $4.8 trillion and a federal budget of over $600 billion.

Reagan Administration officials cut the agencies' resources after 1980 by about 30 percent. As of 1989, the agencies still have potentially strong legal powers, but their practical resources are small.

These resources are thinly spread.[4] Major industries are dealt with by perhaps

---

[3] Walton Hamilton and Irene Till, *Antitrust in Action*, Volume 26 of Temporary National Economic Committee, Investigation of Economic Power (Washington, D.C.: U.S. Government Printing Office, 1940).
[4] The FTC spends about half its resources on non-antitrust matters, such as consumer complaints, fur labeling, and fraud.

four or five equivalent full-time lawyers and economists. Many other sectors, especially new industries, are given, at best, only passing attention. A single big case can engross a sizable share of the whole agency's resources. At the top, the agencies are run by political appointees, who are usually in office for only three years or less. Most significant actions take between five and fifteen years to run their course. Lacking sustained guidance, policies often back and fill.

The agencies are run by lawyers, applying "the" law. Economists are often called in to give some guidance, and of course the officials are guided by what they believe to be "correct" economic standards. But the main actions reflect legal tests and goals.

The Antitrust Division takes firms to court, seeking to get convictions and remedies. It also does much bargaining behind the scenes, and it settles many cases with "consent decrees" before a final judgment is reached. The FTC staff takes firms before the commission itself for rulings (often with a first-round decision by an FTC administrative law judge, which the commission then affirms, overrules, or modifies).

The two agencies operate in harmony. They overlap in authority, and often one agency takes up a matter that the other has declined. The Division focuses on "heavy" industries; the FTC specializes in lighter, consumer-oriented industries. But both roam over the whole spectrum of markets.

Because they are so small, the two antitrust agencies mainly try to develop a series of precedent-setting cases, rather than to pursue and catch every firm that might be breaking the antitrust laws. We will present some of those landmark cases in the third section of this chapter.

The Setting.   The setting for the agencies includes (1) the rest of the government and (2) private antitrust resources. Though they are nominally free from outside interference, in actuality, the agencies are subject to various pressures. Their budgets are set by the executive branch and Congress. Firms try to use officials (in the White House, Defense Department, and elsewhere) and congressional members to influence the agencies. Actions can be appealed to the appellate courts and the Supreme Court, either to reverse decisions or merely to delay the process.

On the private side, the large defendant firms often have large resources to resist or manipulate the policy efforts. The private antitrust bar employs about 10,000 lawyers. Large firms routinely apply five, ten, or twenty times as many lawyers and experts to a case as the agencies do. This fits their large stakes in the outcomes, often running into hundreds of millions of dollars. Their interests will induce them to spend up to the total amount of profit that is at stake in order to win, as Section I explained. Of course, small firms have small resources, so the agencies routinely have the upper hand against them.

Private antitrust suits—by one firm against another—often trigger or supplement actions by the public agencies. Each year there are over a thousand such cases, in a great variety of markets. In theory, they could neatly fill in any gaps in public policies. In practice, private cases are often lacking precisely where they are most needed.

Sanctions.   The agencies' powers boil down to several kinds of economic penalties that they can inflict:

1. *Investigation:* The study process can be large, long, and costly to the firm, by choice either of the agencies *or* of the firms themselves (if they choose to mount a win-at-any-cost defense).

2. *Suit:* A case inflicts

   a. Direct costs of litigation. These can run up to $10 million and more, even in medium-size cases.

   b. Diversion of executive attention. Chief officers often spend a large share of their time on major cases.

   c. Bad publicity. This can affect a company's image and goodwill.

3. *Stoppage of company action:* The contested action is often stopped as soon as it is challenged, though it may be eventually exonerated.

4. *Conviction:* This is only a decision on the legal outcome. Its power lies solely in leading to these possible penalties:

   a. Fines and other civil or criminal penalties.

   b. Remedies, which are of two main sorts:

   (1) constraints on behavior ("injunctive relief")

   (2) changes in company structure (perhaps by divestiture).

   c. Private damage suits. They often claim over $100 million but settle for $5 million or so.

Fines have been so unimportant for most large defendants that experts now recommend raising their ceilings. The $5,000 limit set in the Sherman Act was raised to $50,000 in 1955, and raised again in 1974 to $500,000 for individuals and $1 million for firms. Most fines are far below the limits and are minor expenses for large firms. Since 1976, officials have applied criminal penalties more severely, with jail sentences in some price-fixing cases.

In short, the agencies operate in a large and complicated domain, with modest resources. They are under many pressures and limits, but they can apply various penalties. The outcomes may or may not fit the ideal balance between competitive benefits and possible true economies of scale. Both the general force of antitrust and the inner balance among its various parts are open to question. Experienced observers expect only that antitrust approximate the main lines of correct policies, at least for some periods of time. Some experts regard antitrust as radically mistaken; almost none believe that it is steadily close to ideal.

2. Development of Antitrust

After a shaky start, the Sherman Act was applied firmly against price-fixing in 1897 in the *Addyston Pipe* case (the case is summarized in the third main section of this chapter). That strict prohibition of price-fixing is still enforced. No longer able to collude with one another after 1897 because of this new precedent, many firms simply merged. Figure 19.6 charts the waves of mergers and antitrust actions since 1890. The pattern of action and response is clear. Each new wave of mergers stirred anxiety in the populace that corporate power was being enlarged. Antitrust officials then renewed their efforts.

First came Theodore Roosevelt's "trust-busting" campaign, actually carried through mainly during William H. Taft's presidency in 1909–1913. The Standard Oil

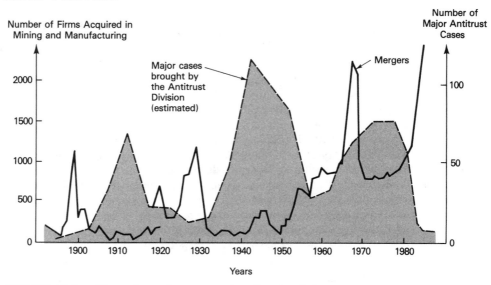

FIGURE 19.6.   The pulses of merger and antitrust activity.

The four merger waves—of 1897–1901, the 1920s, the 1960s, and the 1980s—have been dramatic and turbulent. Antitrust actions have come in three distinct waves, as shown by the number of cases (weighted for importance). To some extent, the actions have been a response to the mergers and other industrial events.

SOURCE: Adapted from Richard A. Posner, "A Statistical Study of Antitrust Enforcement," *Journal of Law and Economics,* 13 (October 1970), 374–81.

Company and the American Tobacco Company were each divided into several companies, and several other firms were required to sell off a plant. For example, Standard Oil was separated back into its original regional monopolies, while American Tobacco was forced to divest some capacity, so that three firms came to exist in 1913 (they are still operating—American Tobacco, Liggett and Myers, and P. Lorillard).

Because the Sherman Act is so terse and broad, business interests soon demanded more details about exactly which actions were illegal. Under Woodrow Wilson's "progressive" approach, the Clayton Act in 1914 was written to try to cover those details, though only a few specific offenses were spelled out. The Federal Trade Commission was also created at that time to enforce the law.

Antitrust was then cut back deeply during the Roaring Twenties, even as the second great merger boom mounted to its peak in 1929. The balance of antitrust actions actually favored mergers and cooperation among firms. But the Crash of 1929 and the Great Depression of the 1930s renewed pressure to act against what was seen as rising corporate power.

The second antitrust wave, from 1938 to 1952, touched many dominant firms. Thus the aluminum monopoly (Alcoa: the *Al*uminum *Co*mpany of *A*merica) was challenged in 1937, and two new competitors were finally added in 1950. The duopoly in metal cans (American Can Company and National Can Company) was subjected to restraints by a court decree in 1950. The dominant National Broadcasting Company (NBC) was required to sell one of its two radio networks in 1943, thereby creating the American Broadcasting Company (ABC). Movie companies were forced by the Paramount Pictures decision in 1948 to sell their theater chains. There were also major cases against some tight oligopolies, including the leading cigarette companies.

The pace of antitrust slowed again from 1953 to 1968. The only exception was the application in 1962 (the *Brown Shoe* case—recall Chapters 8 and 15) of strict new limits against mergers among competitors. On other antitrust fronts, little was done to reduce market power or to stem conglomerate mergers during the "go-go" merger boom of the 1960s.

During 1968–1974, the antitrust pulse quickened, especially with several large cases alleging that IBM, Xerox, AT&T, and the big cereal companies had monopolized their markets. Then, during 1981–88, the Reagan Administration sharply reduced the reach of both antitrust agencies. Efforts to lessen market dominance were stopped; the AT&T case was settled and the IBM case was dropped. Merger rules were relaxed, price-fixing cases were cut back to petty offenders, and cases against vertical and strategic actions ceased to be brought.

3. Antitrust Criteria

Economists try to see through the legal details of antitrust to discern its (1) economic criteria and (2) economic effects. Table 19.2 presents the main antitrust criteria that have evolved in the courts since 1890, in hundreds of precedent-making cases and decisions.

The wording of the statutes sounds broad and conclusive, but the laws have come to be applied only within "reasonable" limits—following what the lawyers call a "rule of reason." In practice, "reasonable" means what the courts will accept, and the limits of enforcement often shift as the courts and the country's political complexion changes. For example, the Supreme Court under Earl Warren in the 1960s tightened the criteria against mergers and dominant firms. The Burger Court of the 1970s and 1980s drew back the margin of antitrust enforcement toward lenient treatment of mergers and of the pricing tactics used by dominant firms.

Defining the Market.   Throughout, one pivotal issue has emerged: the definition of the market. *The two sides usually offer sharply differing definitions of the true extent of the market.* The plaintiff (an agency or a private company claiming to be a victim of monopoly) urges a narrow definition, which gives the defendant firm a high market share. The defendant claims instead that the market is much larger, so that its share of that market is small. The Court's decision on this point often governs the outcome of the case, for if it accepts a large market, then harmful market power could not exist. Generally the Warren Court defined markets narrowly, whereas the Burger Court accepted broad market definitions.

4. Precedents

Policy is applied by bringing individual cases, which the agency lawyers develop, to trial and trying to win. Some of the cases become vast, involving scores of lawyers, years of preparation, and millions of documents, as we will soon show. Many others

TABLE 19.2   The Main Economic Patterns of Antitrust Policy

---

1. *Toward Existing Structure* (mainly Sherman Act, Section 2).

Firms with market shares above 60 percent, high barriers to entry, and high rates of profit may be sued. If market power is high and seems to have economic costs, the court weighs possible economies of scale and the danger that an antitrust conviction will harm a broad range of the company's stockholders. Although its decision on the case will usually reflect all these factors, the court's formal opinion will generally cite only the market power and any abusive actions by the firm. If the firm is convicted, the remedies and penalties applied to it will usually be only moderate, such as levying fines or setting limits on the firm's future actions, rather than requiring the firm to sell part of its capacity.

Since 1980, no new Section 2 cases have been brought.

2. *Toward Mergers* (Clayton Act, Section 7).

Horizontal mergers of firms with a combined share above 15 percent of the market were usually challenged. If the degree of concentration in the industry was rising, and if the merger would not give demonstrable economies of scale, the courts would usually stop the merger. *Vertical mergers* of firms with more than 20 percent each at their stage of the industry were usually stopped. *Conglomerate mergers* were usually permitted unless they united two firms that were dominant in their own markets.

Since 1980, horizontal mergers combining as much as 45 percent of the market have not been resisted. No vertical or conglomerate mergers have been resisted.

3. *Toward Price-Fixing and Other Such Actions* (Sherman Act, Section 1).

All efforts to fix prices will be prosecuted if they are discovered. This is true even if the firms have only a small share of the market. Most firms will be convicted if there is tangible proof of the collusion. Most firms involved in market splitting (dividing up the sales in the market) and other explicit collusion will also be sued and convicted. Tacit collusion is exempt from prosecution, unless it becomes very thorough and obvious.

Since 1980, prosecutions have been confined to small firms, mainly in highway construction.

---

are compact and clear, taking only a year or two from the violation to the final decision. The courts' decisions in these cases set precedents, which then govern subsequent cases. The precedents all reduce to fairly simple patterns, as shown in Table 19.2.

Toward Existing Structure.   The threshold criterion for prosecution was (1) a 60 percent market share, (2) *plus* some evidence that the firm intended to gain dominance or acted unfairly. Since any firm with a market share under 60 percent will almost certainly be acquitted, traditionally no cases are brought against firms below that threshold. Since 1980, the threshold value seems to have risen to about 80 percent.

Even with a market share above the threshold value, a firm can argue that its position arose from "superior skill, foresight, and industry" (that is the usual legal phrase), so that it deserves its dominance. Judges are often persuaded by that argument. IBM had particular success with it, winning a series of cases since 1968. Market shares above 60 percent often go untouched for decades because the antitrust officials expect that any suit against the firm would fail in the courts.

Mergers.   During 1966–1980, horizontal mergers were usually stopped if the resulting firm would have more than 15 percent of the market. Thus a merger between Ford and Chrysler automobile companies (with market shares of 20 and 10 percent) would almost certainly have been prevented. A merger of two 8 percent firms would be permitted if they could prove that they would thereby achieve economies of scale. Since 1980, the margin has fluctuated in the 25–45 percent range.

Vertical mergers were usually stopped if the firms had more than 20 percent each of their markets. For example, Ford was stopped from buying Autolite, a firm that sold 25 percent of automobile spark plugs. Such a merger would have excluded other battery companies from a fair chance to sell to Ford. However, Ford would be permitted to build up its own company, if it wished, by creating new capacity. Since 1980, all cases against vertical mergers have been stopped.

Conglomerate mergers were left mostly untouched, especially if they involved small firms and small market shares. Thus a tire company might buy a bakery, and then a railroad might buy the tire company. Since no market shares are increased in any market, an antitrust challenge to the merger would probably not occur. Only if each of the firms had a large share of its market *might* the merger be challenged. Since 1980, even that possibility has ended.

Price-Fixing.   Price-fixing is treated most strictly. The courts will not permit a defense based on the claim that it was "reasonable." The agency merely needs to show at trial that the price-fixing occurred, even without proof that its effects were strong. The courts will then usually convict per se (that is, guilty "in itself"). Since 1980, cases have been fewer and smaller. Officials have tried to legalize some forms of vertical price-fixing (recall Chapter 15).

5. Economic Effects

The economic effects of these policies are debatable, but they probably have been as follows. Some major dominant firms have been reduced in size, mainly through actions taken before 1950; but the AT&T divestiture in 1984 brought massive changes. Tight oligopoly has scarcely been touched. Many horizontal mergers were forestalled during 1958–1980, though hundreds of mergers from 1890 to 1962 had already led to substantial concentration in many industries. Price-fixing has mostly been driven underground, which has probably eliminated a good deal of it. Yet secret collusion does continue routinely in many industries and in a variety of tight oligopolies.

Altogether, antitrust policies have probably kept U.S. industrial concentration and the extent of price-fixing much lower than they would otherwise have been. If antitrust were abolished, an immense merger boom would immediately occur, raising concentration sharply in many industries. Formal price-fixing cartels, with official staffs and binding contracts preventing price competition, would be created in thousands of markets. Therefore antitrust has created important economic benefits, which continue quietly because antitrust itself continues.

Yet the economic effects of antitrust have also caused some imbalance. Dominant firms are now largely free to set prices internally over large shares of the market. But the smaller rivals of dominant firms can neither meet to fix their prices nor merge with each other.

In cases like this, the law is gentle to the big and strict toward the small. Once a firm has gained dominance, it is largely immune from antitrust actions, free to do things internally that lesser firms cannot do among themselves. Ideally, antitrust would be equally strict toward dominant and little firms.

Antitrust's ultimate effects are *debatable,* then, perhaps promoting efficiency on the whole, but perhaps also lacking balance. The effects are also *limited,* for antitrust reaches only part of the economy. As Table 19.3 shows, most local markets, newspapers, all labor unions, all patents, much weapons production, and most public enterprises are exempt from antitrust.

The antitrust domain is, therefore, the core of national manufacturing industries and trade, altogether less than half of the U.S. economy. Meanwhile, various other policies directly reduce competition in many markets. They are summarized in part 2 of Table 19.3. On the whole, antitrust's reach is far from complete. And even where it does reach, its resources are usually stretched thin.

Think of antitrust as *interacting with industry,* not standing above it exercising lordly powers. Like any other policing agents, antitrust officials are influenced by industry, by Congress, by the executive branch, and by swings in popular attitudes. Policy choices are often political, mistaken, rash, or too cautious—in short, thoroughly human, fallible, and changeable. Yet the basic economic effects—against price-fixing and mergers—remain relatively steady.

TABLE 19.3   Departures from Antitrust: Exemptions and Policies That Reduce Competition

---

1. *Exemptions*
   Much local and statewide activity: construction, shops, repairs, services.
   Labor unions at all levels.
   Local utilities and urban services: electricity, gas, telephone.
   Social services and health services: schools, hospitals.
   Public enterprises: many electric, transit, and water systems at the local and regional levels.
   Farm and fishery cooperatives: dairy cooperatives.
   Many military suppliers: aircraft, missile systems, tanks, ships, ammunition.
   Baseball and, to a lesser degree, other professional sports.
   Newspapers' joint publishing arrangements in many cities

2. *Policies That Reduce Competition*
   Tariffs and other barriers to international trade, such as quotas and agreements to limit imports.
   Patents: They provide a monopoly for seventeen years.
   Banking regulation that prevents new entry in many banking markets.
   Price raising for certain farm products (milk, tobacco) is enforced by the U.S. Department of Agriculture.
   Shipbuilding and shipping: Price-fixing is permitted by the Federal Maritime Commission.

III.   TOWARD EXISTING DOMINANCE

The first wave of Section 2 actions from 1902 to 1916 did make changes in several prominent industries. The second wave from 1940 to 1952 had a smaller reach and less effect. The third wave since 1968 touched a few conspicuous firms, but only one case (AT&T) had strong effects.

Elements

The standard case now has two parts: (1) proof of a high market share *plus* (2) some other evidence of intent to monopolize or of abusive actions. The firm's market share has to be at least 60 percent (that is, a clear dominant-firm position) if the case is to be brought at all. The case therefore begins with a definition of "the relevant market." The agency usually urges a rather narrow version of "the market." The firm responds with some very wide "market." The adversaries often use the right terms, such as "cross-elasticity of demand" and "interchangeability" (recall Chapter 3). The main criteria are *product* features and *geographic* areas, much as in professional discussion. "Line of commerce" is the technical term used in trying to define distinct products. "Section of the country" is any geographic area—region, state, or city—that may fit the true, "relevant" market.

Usually measures of the critical variables are not available (as Chapter 4 noted). The court must then make a "reasonable" judgment about the "true" market. Recently, claims about barriers have become important; the agency will allege them to be high, while the firm will say that they are low or absent.

If the true market is small enough to show that the firm has a share above 60–80 percent, the next question is the "plus." It may be a specific memorandum, or a course of action, or a pricing strategy. Price discrimination is often used to show that the firm deliberately set out to get and keep its dominance. Whatever it is, the "plus" must show intent. Some sort of abuse is an especially convincing "plus."

The firm commonly defends itself by saying that its market position merely reflects its own excellence; the standard phrase is now "superior skill, foresight, and industry." The firm usually claims as well that it achieves economies of scale, and that conviction and remedy would "penalize success" and "sacrifice efficiency." The firm also stresses how innovative it has been, and asserts that tampering with it would stop its progress and growth.

The process is usually lengthy. Preparing the suit often takes several years. Then pretrial preparation can take two to four years more; the trial itself may last a year; and further appeals, remands, and opinions average about three to five years more. At that point, remedy may *begin*. From start to finish, it may take ten to fifteen years or more to identify dominance, process the case, and get a cure started.

To be successful, a Section 2 case must meet several other tests that have come to be included informally. (1) Economies of scale must be absent or small. (2) The firm must have been earning excess, "monopoly" profits. (3) The technology must be relatively simple, so that the courts are not afraid to consider changes in the firm. In short, the agency has to make a positive case that a major shift toward competition is needed and will give large benefits. This burden of proof is a heavy one. At the

TABLE 19.4   Leading Section 2 Cases

	Market Position First Formed	Policy Action Begun	Final Decision	Outcome
First Wave				
Standard Oil (N.J.)	1870–1875	1907	1911	Dissolution into the regional Standard Oil firms
American Tobacco	1890	1908	1911	Dissolution into three main firms
U.S. Steel	1901	1909	1920	Acquitted; informal limits on future mergers
Second Wave				
Aluminum Co. of America (Alcoa)	1890s	1938	1945	War plants sold to new entrants rather than to Alcoa
United Shoe Machinery	1890s	1947	1954	Share finally reduced by direct actions after 1968 rehearing
Du Pont "Cellophane"	~1925	1949	1956	Acquitted
Third Wave				
IBM	1920s	1969	1982	Case withdrawn by the Division
Cereals firms	~1980–1910	1971	1981	Decided for the firms
Xerox	1961–1963	1972	1975	Partial opening of some Xerox patents to other firms
AT&T	1881	1974	1983–1984	A settlement dividing the Bell system into AT&T plus seven regional holding companies

least, it requires much research, which takes time and can be resisted point by point. The firm has strong incentives to stall.

Section 2 cases came to be seen as long, complex ordeals, with uncertain outcomes. Since 1980, no new ones have been brought. Yet the AT&T case shows that large complex changes can be achieved.

Cases

The leading cases are grouped in Table 19.4. The **Standard Oil Company** (N.J.) and the **American Tobacco Company** convictions were obtained expeditiously, and by 1913, the remedies had been achieved.[5] This peak of "trust-busting" had sharp limits. Chief Justice White's opinion in *Standard Oil* inserted the "rule of reason"; only "bad" trusts violated the true meaning of Section 2. The two firms were only divided back into their earlier parts; in Standard's case, into a set of regional mo-

---

[5] *Standard Oil Co. of N.J. v. U.S.*, 221 U.S. 1; and *U.S. v. American Tobacco Co.*, 221 U.S. 106.

nopolies. More modest changes were achieved with Du Pont and AT&T, but a series of other cases were stopped by World War I and its aftermath. In 1920, the Supreme Court acquitted the U.S. Steel Corporation by a four-to-three vote, saying that it had been a "good trust."[6] In 1927, it acquitted the International Harvester Company on similar grounds.[7] Section 2 action then largely ceased.

Alcoa.   In the revival of the Antitrust Division after 1937, the Alcoa case became the centerprice.[8] After a long process of preparation and trial, it was decided in 1945 with an opinion by Judge Learned Hand. Judge Hand rejected the rule of reason, saying that the Sherman Act forbade all monopolies, not just bad ones. Among several ways of defining the market, Judge Hand chose the use of new aluminum ingot as the relevant market, leaving Alcoa with a share of over 90 percent. He also noted that 60 percent might be a monopoly and that 30 percent surely was not. That brief incidental remark has become the rule of thumb for enforcement, ruling out cases below 60 percent. (Note that it does not fit the continuous nature of market power.)

Alcoa claimed that monopoly was "thrust upon it" by its excellence. Judge Hand said that such defenses were irrelevant, and he also refuted them in detail with arguments that Alcoa's pattern of behavior showed clear efforts to monopolize. The doctrine was clear, but the actual remedy was moderate. New World War II aluminum plants were sold off in 1950 to Kaiser and Reynolds rather than to Alcoa, creating a tight oligopoly that has continued with little change.

1945 to 1952.   Then came Section 2 cases against AT&T, IBM, Du Pont "Cellophane," United Shoe Machinery, and others. USM was convicted. Its market share was high and the "plus" included extensive systems of price discrimination. Yet the remedy only limited certain exclusionary actions (and in 1968 further direct action to reduce USM's market share below 50 percent was found to be necessary).

After 1952, Section 2 actions again languished. In the "Cellophane" case, the Supreme Court by a vote of five to four defined a broad market for all packaging materials, and Du Pont's share was held to be only 18 percent.[9] Though the Court soon shifted to drawing markets narrowly (in the Du Pont–General Motors case and in merger cases, see below), the agencies virtually stopped Section 2 actions. The IBM and AT&T cases were settled in 1955–56 with little effect.

After 1968, **IBM** was one main case. The Antitrust Division's handling of it was dubious and slow. The trial bogged down in a morass of issues and opinions, rather than being focused on the key legal and economic elements. The suit alleged a 60 to 70 percent market share after 1955, plus anticompetitive pricing and production actions during the 1960s. IBM's defenses included a claim that it held only a 35 percent share of the "office equipment" market, and that it had achieved good efficiency and innovation.

As the lengthy trial was drawing to a close in 1981, observers expected the judge to convict IBM. But the new conservative antitrust head withdrew the suit in January 1982, arguing that the case was actually weak and that years of appeals would make

[6] *U.S.* v. *U.S. Steel Corp.*, 251 U.S. 417.
[7] *U.S.* v. *International Harvester Co.*, 274 U.S. 693, 708.
[8] *U.S.* v. *Aluminum Co. of America*, 148 F.2d 416.
[9] *U.S.* v. *Du Pont*, 118 F. Supp. 41.

the result obsolete. His key assessment was that the "fighting ships" had not been genuinely predatory, by the Areeda-Turner standard. This case completed IBM's series of triumphal victories in all its antitrust battles. By exonerating IBM, these results widened the range of permissible "hard" competition.

The **Xerox** case was settled quickly by the FTC, with a slight remedy (giving access to a few Xerox patents). But, partly in response to Xerox's errors and sluggishness, new Japanese competition soon eroded Xerox's position, from 90 percent in 1974 to less than 50 percent in 1980.

AT&T.   After the 1913 agreement and the 1949–1955 case, the issue of Western Electric was reopened in 1974 with a new suit by the Division. As a fifty-man FCC task force report (of 1,500 pages) had recently recommended, the Division sought to separate Western Electric and possibly divide it into several competing firms within the whole market for telecommunications equipment. The new suit also contemplated separating out the Long Lines Department, "some or all" of the Bell operating companies, and Bell Laboratories. True natural monopoly could remain intact, but the Bell System would be prevented from using that advantage to capture other, naturally competitive markets. Because this case succeeded in 1982 in securing the most extensive (even astounding) divestiture ever attained, it requires a detailed discussion.[10]

It carried forward changes that had been developing for several decades—in new technology, in FCC actions, and in private antitrust suits. Table 19.5 shows the main events. Bell had frequently reached out to enter adjacent markets, ranging from telephone equipment, movies, and microwave transmission to copper scrap recycling. But it had come under increasing pressure to let competition into its own domain, especially by FCC actions in 1968–1969 and 1977, and by the Supreme Court in 1979. Technology now permitted competition in all but the local telephone calling market, where one set of wires and switches was still most efficient. The case simply forced AT&T into a new structure reflecting that reality.

Figure 19.7 shows the Bell System as challenged in 1974–1981. The case lay largely dormant for three years, but then a new judge (Harold Greene) sped it forward. The two sides were forced to agree on simple points, and thus to identify the main issues for trial. By preventing delay and excessive discovery procedures, Judge Greene forced the trial ahead briskly. After the Division's side was presented, he announced that AT&T had probably committed violations. When the rebuttal case went poorly, AT&T decided that settlement was preferable to conviction (and the resulting flood of treble damage claims). A settlement was reached and announced (together with the *IBM* case withdrawal) in January 1982. After full hearings and some modifications by Judge Greene, divestiture occurred on January 1, 1984.

[10] Among many sources on the topic, see David S. Evans, ed., *Breaking up Bell: Essays on Industrial Organization and Regulation,* (New York: North Holland, 1983), for lucid analysis supporting the Antitrust Division's case. On the other side, see William W. Sharkey, *The Theory of Natural Monopoly* (Cambridge: Cambridge University Press, 1982).

On the rationale for the divestiture, see Timothy J. Brennan, "Why Regulated Firms Should be Kept Out of Regulated Markets: Understanding the Divestiture in *United States v. AT&T,*" *Antitrust Bulletin,* 32 (Fall 1987), 741–91. Other books include Peter Temin, *The Fall of the Bell System* (New York: Cambridge University Press, 1987); Alvin von Auw, *Heritage and Destiny: Reflections on the Bell System in Transition* (New York: Praeger Publishers, 1983); and David S. Evans, ed., *Breaking Up Bell* (New York: North-Holland, 1983).

TABLE 19.5   Events in the AT&T Policy Sequence

1881	Western Electric added as supplier.
1890s	AT&T grows, adds most cities and states.
1910–1913	Antitrust case prepared. AT&T agrees to divest Western Union and to stop acquiring phone companies.
1920–1940	AT&T enters radio, movie, sound, and copper recycling markets. Vertical integration with Western Electric is investigated by FCC.
1949–1955	Antitrust Division sues to separate Western Electric. The case is largely dropped in 1955.
1962	Arguments grow against market capture by Bell.
1968–1975	FCC decisions open possible competition in equipment (*Carterfone*) and long-distance service (MCI). AT&T yields slowly.
1969	Widespread service failures undercut Bell's reputation for quality, permit challenges to its monopoly.
1970s	Bell moves into numerous markets for electronic equipment.
1974	Antitrust Division case against AT&T is filed.
1975–1988	Bell seeks congressional approval of monopoly throughout the sector.
1977	FCC orders competition in buying of equipment.
1979	Supreme Court requires FCC to permit competition in long-distance service.
1981	MCI wins $1.8 billion verdict against AT&T for preventing competition.
1981–1984	Antitrust Division case tried; compromise announced January 1982; modified after hearings during 1982–1983, divestiture occurs at beginning of 1984.

The main change was to detach the Bell Operating Companies (BOCs) from AT&T. (The twenty-one BOCs are shown in Figure 19.7). The basic concept of the settlement identified two parts of the Bell System that needed to be separated: (1) *natural monopolies* (the local operations); and (2) the rest, which were regarded as *naturally competitive,* or likely to become so. Dividing them would prevent the abuses of the past, in which the monopolies were used as the base for capturing and controlling other markets.

The twenty-one BOCs were grouped into seven regional firms (Nynex, US West, Bell South, Ameritech, Bell Atlantic, Pacific Telesis, and Southwestern Bell). They operate in the 164 LATAs ("local access and transport areas"), which cover all metropolitan areas. The regionals are also permitted to sell (but not produce) new equipment to customers, in competition with AT&T and others. That maximizes competition in equipment sales. To avoid letting the regionals use their monopoly position to gain advantages in equipment sales, they must sell through separate subsidiaries.

AT&T today has two main parts: regulated long-distance service (by AT&T Communications), and unregulated activities, including equipment production and marketing and foreign activities (by AT&T Technologies). The old Western Electric was dissolved and merged into four new units under AT&T Technologies. Long-distance service by AT&T covers all transmission among LATAs, so the coverage now extends to a lot of *intra*state calling. AT&T faces competition from MCI, Sprint, and others on long-distance service, but still has 75 percent of sales (as of early 1989).

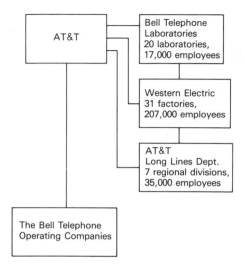

FIGURE 19.7.   The AT&T structure before 1984.

There are two main competitive issues. First, on long-distance service, is competition effective? Not yet, because the newcomers are still small and vulnerable. Chapter 17 covers that issue in detail. Only when AT&T's market share recedes below 50 percent may competition be fully robust and effective.

Second, is competition in equipment effective? Has vertical monopoly (between Western Electric and the BOCs and Long Lines) ended? The answer is yes. The seven regionals have taken independent stances toward AT&T and are buying equipment from a variety of sources, on competitive terms.

In both areas (long-distance service and equipment buying), the case only added to changes already in process. But the difference is large, and the changes are now irreversible. The antitrust effort has worked well, yielding classical benefits of increased competition, especially innovation. The old defenses of the Bell monopolies, such as the extravagent claims of vertical economies and "systematic integrity," are now recognized to have been mistaken. The new patterns fit well the true emerging technology and scope for competition.

The case also disposes of fears that Section 2 actions have grown too large and complex to manage. Instead, a brisk judge proved that perhaps the most complicated sector of all could be assessed clearly at trial and reorganized efficiently by means of massive divestiture. Section 2 and the divestiture remedy have both been restored as effective tools.

IV. TOWARD MERGERS

Economic analysis suggests that policy should be strict on horizontal mergers, liberal toward vertical mergers, and largely neutral toward conglomerate mergers. U.S. policies during 1960–1980 roughly fit that pattern.

TABLE 19.6   A Selection of Leading Antitrust Cases against Mergers and Price Fixing

CASE	YEAR OF MERGER OR PRICE-FIXING	YEAR OF DECISION	MARKET SHARE HELD BY THE MERGING OR PRICE-FIXING FIRMS (%)	ACTION TAKEN
Horizontal Merger				
Brown Shoe–Kinney Shoe (shoes and shoe retailing)	1957	1962	20	The merger was prevented.
Von's Grocery–Shopping Bag (grocery stores in Los Angeles)	1959	1966	8	The merger was prevented.
Vertical Merger				
Du Pont–General Motors (paints and fabrics)	1920	1957	30	Du Pont was required to sell its shareholding in General Motors.
Conglomerate Merger				
Procter & Gamble–Clorox (bleach)	1958	1967	55	Clorox was restored as a separate firm.
ITT and various firms (hotels, baking, car rental, insurance)	1960s	1971	"leading"	ITT chose to retain Hartford Fire Insurance and to sell several other firms.
Price-Fixing Cases				
U.S. v. *Addyston Pipe & Steel Co.* (cast-iron pipe)	1890s	1899	30	Conviction and fines.
U.S. v. *Socony-Vacuum* (gasoline)	1930s	1940	35	Conviction and fines.
Electrical Equipment Cases (heavy electrical equipment)	1930s– 1950s	1960	over 90	No defense: fines and several brief jail terms.
U.S. v. *General Electric and Westinghouse* (turbine generators)	1963–1975	1976	over 90	Compromise. The scheme for tacit collusion was renounced.

These policies developed slowly. After 1914, Section 7 of the Clayton Act forbade mergers that would reduce competition. There was, however, a substantial technical loophole, which permitted many large horizontal mergers. But some dominant firms wisely avoided big horizontal mergers anyway. Much later, the Celler-Kefauver Act of 1950 plugged the loophole, and a strict policy was established by a series of dramatic cases from 1958 to 1966. Certain major cases are shown in Table 19.6.

1. Horizontal Mergers

Bethlehem-Youngstown. Bethlehem Steel Corporation, the second-largest steel company, proposed in 1956 to merge with Youngstown Sheet and Tube Company, the sixth largest. Bethlehem was mainly an East Coast firm, while Youngstown operated mainly in the Middle West. Bethlehem portrayed the proposed merger as a "geographic extension" merger between two regionally separate firms that were not actual competitors. Besides, it claimed, the merged firm would be better able to compete against the leading firm, U.S. Steel.

Yet the Antitrust Division was able to show that in many regional product markets the two merger partners were already direct competitors. The merger was held to be in violation of Clayton Section 7, and the decision was not appealed.[11]

Brown Shoe. This 1962 decision firmly drew tight horizontal and vertical merger policy lines.[12] Brown and Kinney were both small in the national market as a whole, but they had sizable stores in many urban shoe markets. In addition, the Supreme Court majority noted a trend toward concentration in the industry, which it wished to halt in its incipiency. Vertical aspects were also involved, since Brown was mainly a producer and Kinney was mainly a retail chain. The shares at each level were not large, but Brown appeared likely to make Kinney carry Brown shoes and exclude others. The Court held that these vertical effects were also illegal. A vigorous dissent by the minority urged that, instead, the markets would still be thoroughly competitive with the merger.

Von's Grocery. This 1966 decision set the seal on horizontal limits. It involved the merger of two retail food chains in Los Angeles. Von's Grocery, the third-largest food chain in the area, had acquired Shopping Bag, the sixth largest, thereby moving into second place. But Von's share of the market after the merger was only 8 percent. The share of all the market leaders was declining, and there was no barrier to the entry of new concerns. Still, the Court noted that the number of stores operated by individual owners had fallen. And it found the merger to be unlawful on the ground that it was the purpose of the law "to prevent concentration in the American economy by keeping a large number of small competitors in business."[13]

General Dynamics. Here a merger among firms producing coal in Illinois and vicinity raised the concentration of production in that region (in the top four firms from 43 to 63 percent during 1957–1967). The Supreme Court's decision in 1973 acquitted, on two grounds.[14] First, the relevant market was held to be much broader than the Division alleged. This loosened the precedent that "any" significant market would demonstrate a violation. Second, the Court declared that other facts about the industry must also be considered in judging the competitive effect. Thus the clear simplicity of the 1960s precedents was diluted with flexibility, and the standard of

---

[11] *U.S.* v. *Bethlehem Steel Corp.*, 168 F. Supp. 756.

[12] *Brown Shoe Co.* v. *U.S.*, 370 U.S. 294.

[13] *U.S.* v. *Von's Grocery Co.*, 384 U.S. 280 (1966). As in the *Brown Shoe* case, a sharp minority dissent argued that the effect of the merger would be trivial or procompetitive. The Court's minority was basically setting a higher burden of proof on the government.

[14] *U.S.* v. *General Dynamics Corp.*, 341 F. Supp. 534 (N. D. Ill. 1972), *affirmed*, 415 U.S. 486 (1973).

proof for conviction was raised. The shift in policy was not sharp, since the changes were of degree rather than of kind.

The strict treatment of horizontal mergers was perforated by various exceptional cases.[15] Some "failing-firm" mergers were also permitted. RCA and General Electric sold their large computer operations to competitors in 1970–1972 without official opposition. In 1975–1978, more than ten sizable mergers took place among brokerage firms, directly raising concentration. This reflected the new competition unleashed by the ending of brokerage fee-fixing.

Since 1980.   Reagan officials in 1981 announced more liberal attitudes toward mergers—specifically, they raised the 4-plus-4 percent line to 7-plus-7 percent. That would probably have prevented most of the leading cases (*Brown Shoe, Von's, General Dynamics*) from being brought, even thought the policy limit was still nearly as tight.[16] A number of mergers quickly tested their policies. Stroh's acquired Schlitz, which was a declining formerly major brewer. The combined market shares were above the old limits but still moderate, and Schlitz was perhaps on the brink of failure. The merger was not challenged.

General Motors and Toyota proposed in 1983 a joint venture to produce cars in California. Though the link was far short of a full merger, it was likely to affect competition. The two firms could be regarded as the two largest competitors in the combined Japanese-American market; or, for that matter, in a worldwide market. Or Toyota was the largest importer *and* potential entrant in the U.S. market. In any case, a significant reduction of direct competition was likely. Ford and Chrysler both opposed the joint venture vigorously. Yet the FTC permitted the link, on grounds that it would create added capacity and strengthen GM's ability to compete. In fact, the benefits have been moderate, and in 1989 the plant was reduced to part-time operations.

In 1983–1984, two steel mergers tested the limits still further. First, fourth-ranked Republic Steel proposed merging with third-ranked Jones & Laughlin. Their combined share of total U.S. production would be 15.8 percent in 1983, just under U.S. Steel's 16.7 percent; their shares would be as high as 50 percent in specific steel products. Then U.S. Steel offered to buy National Steel, giving a combined share of 22.7 percent. Actual shares, after allowing for imports at about 15 percent of all sales in the United States, would be 14 percent for Republic-J&L and 20 percent for U.S. Steel–National.

The steel industry had long been ailing, so a failing-firm basis might exempt them. Also, one could broaden the market to include all world steel because imports, even though partially restrained by quotas, had become substantial. In such a large market, the merged firms would have small market shares.

Yet the industry's ills reflected past inefficiencies and mistakes encouraged by market power, and the mergers might perpetuate the problems rather than cure them. The world market was not free, since restrictions on sales to the United States had been in place since the 1960s.

---

[15] These include the merger between the McDonnell and Douglas aircraft firms in 1967 and the Penn-Central merger in 1968.

[16] Eleanor M. Fox, "The New Merger Guidelines—A Blueprint for Microeconomic Analysis," *Antitrust Bulletin,* 27 (Fall 1982), 519–91.

Nonetheless, the Republic-J&L merger was permitted, though U.S. Steel-National merger was called off. Then the rosy promises were belied, as the merged firm soon sank into bankruptcy!

These cases show how intricate the issues had become. Market shares are a more complicated matter when imports are substantial. And the other factors—the effects of the mergers, the degree of "failing," and the reason for the failing—give no clear guides. The new approach appears to apply a zone (30 to 45 percent?) rather than a clear threshold and to involve a weighing of complex issues. Officials are now more receptive to claims of economies and the need to make exceptions.

2. Vertical Mergers

The current economic consensus is that vertical mergers will reduce competition only when market shares are substantial. (Chicago-UCLA economists deny that *any* reduction will occur). Court decisions have reached down to very small shares, but Reagan officials, again, raised the thresholds for bringing cases.

Vertical merger policy has not had a steady evolution or rich set of precedents. Most cases present unique features, and claimed economies are often provable. The *Yellow Cab* decision in 1947, *Paramount* in 1948, and *A&P* in 1949 established that vertical integration could not be used to foreclose competition at either level. But specific practices had been adduced in these cases; no general rule against vertical integration per se was applied. Subsequently, the Court drew closer limits, nearly accepting that a large rise in vertical integration is per se likely to have the effect of foreclosing competition and raising entry barriers.

Du Pont–General Motors.   The case was filed in 1949, alleging that Du Pont's holding of GM stock gave it preference in the market for automobile fabrics and finishes (recall Chapter 10).

GM's purchases were over half of the fabrics and finishes markets; Du Pont's sales to GM were about 30 percent of the market, a "substantial share." The vertical tie had controlled GM's purchases, limiting Du Pont's competitors' ability to compete.[17] Vertical integration had only been partial, and the decision set a moderate limit on the market shares held by the firms.

Brown Shoe.   The *Brown* case had vertical aspects, too. Brown made shoes and Kinney sold shoes. The Court looked less at the small market shares than at Brown's likely policy of requiring Kinney to carry Brown shoes. This would foreclose competition in a market that already had rising concentration. Before the merger, Kinney bought no shoes from Brown. Soon after, Brown had become Kinney's largest outside supplier, with 8 percent of Kinney's purchases. An incipiency test was applied.

The 1982 and 1984 merger guidelines, as enforced, involve a virtual end to restraints on vertical mergers. Mergers that raise barriers, promote collusion, or eliminate a disruptive buyer might be opposed, if either market is a tight oligopoly. But no cases have been brought, and the practical thresholds now appear to be very high.

---

[17] *U.S.* v. *Du Pont*, 353 U.S. 586 (1957).

3. Conglomerate Mergers

The backdrop of policy toward conglomerate mergers includes many well-established diversified firms in major markets. The new conglomerates have often been corporate raiders (or trivial houses of cards). An efficient policy will reap the efficiency-inducing effects of conglomerate mergers while filtering out the possible reductions in competition. Those gains arise mainly from (1) improved allocation of capital, (2) rises in competition from "toehold" mergers, and (3) pressure for efficiency as caused by takeovers.

Conglomerate Firms.   The share of *new* conglomerate firms in the 1960s wave was large but still less than half the total of conglomerates. Their leaders included:

International Telephone and Telegraph, (ITT) was, before 1960, the foreign twin of AT&T, operating many telephone systems abroad. After 1960, it shifted to takeovers of a string of dominant firms in middle-size industries. It acted when cost savings of at least 20 percent could be foreseen. It tended to redirect old managers rather than sack them.

Litton Industries, an early and respectable science-based conglomerate, began in the 1950s. It acquired second-echelon firms and added scientific capabilities. *Ling-Temco-Vought* (LTV) took over a series of improvable and ever-larger firms during 1960–1968, ending with Jones & Laughlin (the sixth-largest company in steel). *Gulf and Western Industries* grew from auto parts and sugar to a wide variety of products, including movies, paper, and metals.

Policy Criteria.   There were sharp turns in policy as the wave of mergers mounted in the 1960s. In 1969, the Division made a broad-scale attack on conglomerate mergers, with LTV and ITT the main targets. This helped to stop the merger wave, but the attack was compromised before reaching the Supreme Court for a clear decision on the merits.

There are several possible grounds upon which a conglomerate merger might be challenged. The agencies focused on the danger of reciprocity, on potential entry, on size disparity and the unfair advantages that a branch might acquire, and on the "toehold" doctrine.

FTC v. Procter & Gamble (1967).   When Procter & Gamble bought Clorox Chemical Company in 1958, P&G was the largest household products firm. It did not sell bleach, but it had been planning to enter the bleach business. Some of its products were related to bleach, and P&G management had considered making a direct entry—by building a new factory to produce bleach—before deciding to enter the market by buying out the Clorox Company instead. Clorox itself was the dominant bleach firm, with a long-established share of 49 percent of the national market. Clorox's share in the Midatlantic region was as high as 71 percent, compared to 15 percent for Purex, the next-largest bleach producer.

The merger would clearly have subtracted a leading new "potential entrant" from the bleach market: P&G itself. That would have reduced competition and, by itself, should have been enough to lead the FTC to stop the merger. Yet the FTC (later affirmed by the Supreme Court) instead cited P&G's advertising advantages as the main grounds for preventing the merger.

The FTC and the Court stressed that P&G would be able to give Clorox overwhelming advantages in advertising and distributing its bleach. P&G was the nation's largest advertiser (spending over $175 million on advertising in 1967), and its discounts and market power were likely to entrench Clorox further as the dominant bleach firm.

A "toehold" acquisition by P&G of a small bleach company (say, Purex or smaller) would not have encountered this objection and would likely have been allowed. The loss of a potential competitor would have been more than offset by the increase in the small firm's ability to compete vigorously.

ITT's Conglomerate Mergers.   During the 1960s, the International Telephone and Telegraph Corporation bought up a series of large firms that were leaders in their markets: Continental Baking (Wonder Bread), Avis (car rentals), Levitt (house builders), Sheraton Hotels, and Canteen Corporation (dispensing machines), among them. The Antitrust Division sued ITT in 1969, saying that ITT's large financial resources would help to further entrench these leading firms, thus reducing competition. By contrast, smaller "toehold" mergers—in which ITT bought firms with 10 percent market shares or less—would have promoted competition by building up little firms to compete more effectively with the market leaders.

ITT settled the case in 1972 by selling off some of the firms. Because the case was not tried and brought to a decision, it did not set any clear precedents for other conglomerate mergers. But policy seemed to have settled into reasonably clear lines. If one firm was clearly a potential entrant to the market, by any strong evidence, the merger might be challenged. "Toehold" mergers were more acceptable than leading-firm mergers.

But by 1980, the Chicago-UCLA doctrines exonerating conglomerate mergers had prevailed. Since 1980, no cases against conglomerate mergers have been filed.

V.   TOWARD PRICE-FIXING AND OTHER ACTIONS

1.   Price-Fixing

The agencies may catch only a small part of the price-fixing that goes on in oligopoly markets. Even so, the range of cases and convictions is remarkably wide (recall Chapter 14). In one six-month period, cases in the biweekly *Antitrust and Trade Regulation Report* (which your college library may have) included: Korean wigs, ready-mix concrete, Hawaii package tours, paper labels, timber, Utah egg dealers, steel products, construction firms, bakeries in El Paso, liquid asphalt, plumbing supplies, and scores of others.

U.S. v. Addyston Pipe and Steel Company (1899).[18]   In this first landmark case, six producers of cast-iron pipe in the region including Ohio and Pennsylvania had divided up their markets and operated a bidding ring. To prevent competition, they arranged to rotate the contracts among themselves, designating who would make the lowest bid on each contract. Such a bidding ring ensures cooperation among

---

[18] *Addyston Pipe & Steel Co. v. U.S.*, 175 U.S. 211.

sellers and gives buyers no real choice. Though the six firms held less than half of the markets, their price-fixing was convicted as illegal per se by William H. Taft, then an Ohio judge. Thereupon the firms soon merged with one another and began to fix their prices internally, and legally!

The flat prohibition of price-fixing was followed for twenty years, with decisions against collusive bidding by purchasers of livestock, exclusion of competing railways from a terminal, the use of patent licenses to fix the prices of bathtubs, and the operation of a boycott by retail lumber dealers.

Other Landmark Cases.   In 1927, the *Trenton Potteries* decision reaffirmed the per se rule.[19] Firms producing 80 percent of vitreous enamel bathroom fixtures (bathtubs, sinks) had agreed to fix prices and to sell exclusively through jobbers. The Court refused to accept the defendant's claims that the prices fixed were reasonable.

The final landmark decision came in 1940 in the *Socony-Vacuum* case.[20] The major oil firms in ten midwestern states had arranged a scheme for avoiding periodic price cuts on "excess" oil. They did not control prices completely, and they urged in their defense that stabilizing prices was socially beneficial. Justice Douglas's opinion put the per se rule clearly:

> Any combination which tampers with price structures is engaged in an unlawful activity. Even though the members of the price-fixing group were in no position to control the market, to the extent that they raised, lowered, or stabilized prices they would be directly interfering with the free play of market forces. The Act places all such schemes beyond the pale.

The ruling of the Court was sweeping. Any such agreement, even if affecting only a minor portion of the market, was forbidden; any manipulation of prices, whatever its purpose, was against the law.

In 1960, sixty-one years after *Addyston* made price-fixing flatly illegal, the Electrical Equipment conspiracy case showed that price-fixing had been a way of life for decades in seven major markets for heavy electrical equipment (generators, transformers, switch gear). Producers of heavy electrical equipment had run secret bidding rings, using formulas based on phases of the moon to rotate orders among themselves. Some twenty-nine companies, including General Electric and Westinghouse, and scores of their officers were involved. There were fines and damage suits by customers, and some officials served brief jail sentences.

These cases illustrate two features of policy toward price-fixing. First, the agency simply had to show that price-fixing occurred, not that its effects were bad. A normative evaluation would have required endless rummaging among debatable opinions. Second, the treble damage claims triggered by the cases provided the real economic punishment. This is still true for many cases.

The flat rule against price-fixing and related devices is probably efficient. It avoids normative evaluations of each situation. Conceivably, this victimizes a few price-fixing schemes that do provide more social benefits than costs. Yet—as we

---

[19] *U.S.* v. *Trenton Potteries Co.,* 273 U.S. 392.
[20] *U.S.* v. *Socony-Vacuum Oil Co.,* 310 U.S. 150.

have seen—such instances are probably rare in the common run of markets the antitrust agencies deal with. Moreover, many industries have managed to get themselves exempted from antitrust, as we have also seen. Such a process of exemption may nicely take care of any cases where price-fixing has net "good" effects.

Tacit Collusion.   Policy is not so clear-cut toward other kinds of cooperative activities that are less explicit and tangible. Tacit collusion among tight oligopolists has proved especially hard to resolve. It could come under Section 1, as an indirect form of conspiracy, or under Section 2, as a "shared monopoly." So long as it is strictly tacit, it is now virtually exempt from treatment.

From 1939 to 1946, the Court moved to define "conscious parallelism" as being equivalent to explicit collusion, where the effect was the same. The landmark case was *American Tobacco* (1946), in which the three leading cigarette firms were convicted under Section 1.[21] In delivered pricing systems (1948)[22] and booking of movies (1950),[23] the Court drew the line against tacit collusion even more tightly. These convictions, however, were not followed by basic remedies. The structure and habits remained. After 1952, the Court and the FTC changed tack and rejected parallelism as a proof of conspiracy.

The area has lain fallow, despite various proposals for action under Section 2. Only extreme degrees of tacit collusion will stir action; the one recent case is General Electric–Westinghouse (1976), which was presented in Chapter 14. But in that case, there was no trial, conviction, penalties, or precedent.

2. Single-Firm Actions

The main issue here is price discrimination. It can be a device to gain or retain dominance or to promote competition (recall Chapter 12). Roughly speaking, the pre-1980 policies fit the economic criteria noted in that chapter. Systematic discrimination by dominant firms was often held to be illegal, either by itself or as a count in a Section 2 case. Sporadic price discrimination by firms with small shares was rarely challenged.

The leading case in which discrimination by dominant firms has been held by the courts to reduce competition is *United Shoe Machinery* (1953).[24] The United Shoes Machinery Corporation developed extensive discrimination among customer groups. This behavior was held to be "monopolizing." After 1968, actions against IBM and Xerox cited price discrimination—which is even more thorough—as a main indicator of monopoly.

A number of private cases challenged "predatory actions" by IBM and a wide variety of other firms. But virtually all of them failed because many judges adopted the Areeda-Turner price-cost basis for assessing the actions. The agencies have ceased bringing predatory cases because no significant instances meet the strict Areeda-Turner standard.

---

[21] *American Tobacco Co.* v. *U.S.,* 328 U.S. 781, 810.

[22] *FTC* v. *Cement Institute,* 333 U.S. 683.

[23] *Milgram* v. *Loew's, Inc.,* 94 F. Supp. 416.

[24] *U.S.* v. *United Shoe Machinery Corp.,* 110 F. Supp. 295.

VI.   POLICY BALANCE

Antitrust policy is now rather strict toward price-fixing, lenient toward horizontal mergers, but nil toward existing concentration. Thus a firm with an 80 percent market share is permitted to continue untouched, fixing prices pretty much as it pleases over the 80 percent of the market it controls. Meanwhile, other firms usually are not permitted to merge to acquire more than 40 percent of the market. Nor may they cooperate to fix prices in *any* part of the market. This gap between 80 percent dominance by evolution and 40 percent by merger does not appear to fit the scientific analysis in the rest of this volume. The imbalance tends to preserve the industrial structures that have evolved through the decades, so that once formed, much market power is safe from public action, if not from market pressures.

The whole set of antitrust policies probably does keep concentration and price-fixing lower than they would otherwise be. Many experts, however, favor a revival of antitrust. And the differing strictness in the three parts suggests a need to redress the balance.

QUESTIONS FOR REVIEW

1.   "There is only one proper form of antitrust policy, and the United States has it." True?
2.   "Antitrust covers only a part of the American economy, especially industrial and whole-sale markets." True?
3.   "Antitrust agencies can apply various real sanctions in addition to fines." True?
4.   "U.S. antitrust has fluctuated rather than evolved smoothly." True?
5.   "Price-fixing is per se illegal under U.S. law, even if the price-fixers have less than half of the market." True?
6.   "Tacit collusion has always been safe from antitrust attack." True?
7.   "Section 2 cases must not only show a high market share and a 'plus,' they must also meet other informal tests." True?
8.   "In Section 2 cases, the agency adopts a broad market, while the firm claims a narrow market in order to show that its share is small." True?
9.   "The present tight policy toward conglomerate mergers evolved in the 1940s." True?
10.   "A firm can now hold a 70 percent market share, but two firms with 25 percent each cannot merge to acquire 50 percent." True?
11.   How has antitrust policy probably affected market structures in the United States?
12.   Is a per se rule against price-fixing a sound policy?
13.   Since antitrust enforcement has evolved and fluctuated during some ten decades, is it crucial now to know exactly what Congress in 1889 intended it to accomplish? Should it seek static efficiency or broader goals as well?
14.   If the costs and benefits of antitrust actions aren't clear in each case, does the cost-benefit logic still apply in reaching sound enforcement decisions?
15.   Does the "capture" theory of public agencies always apply? Discuss an agency that seems to have been captured.
16.   Explain three biases that may cause antitrust actions to be too strict or too lenient.
17.   Section 2 of the Sherman Act prohibits "monopoly." Does this mean only pure mo-

nopoly? If not, how far down the scale of market share should Section 2 be applied: 70 percent, 55 percent, 40 percent?

18. The Reagan Administration stopped bringing new Section 2 actions in the 1980s. Was this wise, in your view? If not, which cases are good candidates?

19. Describe the varying standards for bringing Section 2, Section 1 and horizontal merger cases. Is there a gap among these standards, which makes antitrust imbalanced?

20. If there is a gap, does it merely reflect the uncertainties in knowledge about market power's effects?

21. Was the AT&T case largely a success, or failure, or a mixture? Explain your criteria, please.

20

REGULATION, DEREGULATION, PUBLIC ENTERPRISE, AND PRIVATIZATION

When you switch on a light or mail a letter, you are dealing with the subject matter of this chapter. Electricity is a classic case of a natural monopoly placed under public regulation. The U.S. Postal Service is a public enterprise, but it too is regulated.

In these cases and others, competition is not efficient. Instead, the public lets the supplier have a monopoly and then regulates its prices. The supplier may also be put under public ownership. These approaches rest on several clear economic concepts, which we present in this chapter. But in practice, the problems are often complex and the results debatable. We present some of those issues, too.

In the first section, we discuss the economic regulation of natural monopolies. Then, in Section II, we present the problems of deregulation. Section III covers public enterprise briefly, and the chapter ends with Section IV on the privatization of public enterprises.

I. REGULATION OF NATURAL MONOPOLY[1]

In some markets, one or several firms are given an exclusive franchise and then supervised by a regulatory commission. The commission has powers to scrutinize the firm and to control its prices. Such price regulation has covered a series of public utilities and several oligopolies (such as airlines). It is a distinctively American approach, combining a maximum of private ownership with some degree of public control. It is supposed to achieve economies of scale in cases of natural monopoly, while keeping the monopolist's prices down toward costs.

The economic objective of regulation is shown in Figure 20.1, for electricity

---

[1] There is a large literature on the economics of regulation. One can begin with William G. Shepherd, *Public Policies Toward Business,* 7th ed. (Homewood, Ill.: Irwin, 1985), chaps. 12–14; and, for more advanced analysis, Alfred E. Kahn, *The Economics of Regulation* (New York: Wiley, 1971), Vols. I and II; and James C. Bonbright, *Principles of Public Utility Rates* (New York: Columbia University Press, 1962).

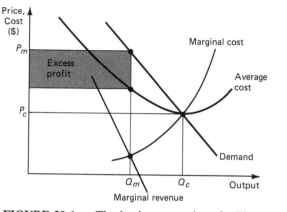

FIGURE 20.1.   The basic economics of utility regulation.

service. There are large economies of scale, with the average cost of electricity declining to the output level Q_c. The demand curve for electricity intersects the average cost curve at that same output level, if capacity has been well planned to coincide with demand. The regulators now set the price of electricity at P_c, so consumers demand—and receive—the output level Q_c. In this ideal case, no excess profits are earned by the firm, capacity is fully used, and electricity is supplied at the lowest possible cost. The economies of scale are achieved, while price is held down to the level of cost.

At its best, regulation does apply such controls, briskly and fairly. The economic task has two parts. One is to set price levels so that the firm does not earn excess profit and exploit its customers. The other part is to set a price structure among the variety of customers that is "just and reasonable." The monopoly will try instead to set discriminatory prices, along the lines discussed in Chapter 12. Economic efficiency requires aligning prices with marginal costs instead. Remember that the alignment of price and marginal cost brings value into line with sacrifice at the margin.

Ideally, the commission does these two tasks with a minimum of cost and delay. And when natural monopoly conditions fade away, the regulation and the franchise are withdrawn, so that competition can take over the job.

Yet regulation may, instead, go wrong. It may become a captive of the industry. It may be applied where natural monopoly conditions do not exist. It may be slow, ineffective, and costly, and it can have inefficient side effects.

Regulation now covers industries with small fractions of national income and total investment. Yet it raises important and complicated issues. And regulation is highly controversial: Is it a charade, as some experts suggest? Sluggish? Highly effective? A captive? A cause of waste? Since 1960, criticism of regulation has been rising. In fact, in the 1970s, several major sectors were deregulated.

1.   Patterns of Regulation

What is to be regulated?

Ideally, regulation is applied to natural monopoly, as shown by the downsloping average cost curve. The firm's resulting monopoly power could be enhanced if (1) the good is a "necessity," with highly inelastic demand (such as electricity, water, and telephone service); and (2) users are physically connected to the supplier (as by wires or pipes). In those cases, consumers would be especially vulnerable to exploitation and harmful price discrimination.

These conditions are all matters of degree, however. Economies of scale are often moderate rather than extreme, as we saw in Chapter 9. Industries do not divide neatly into natural-competition and natural-monopoly boxes. Moreover, technology often changes, so that the economies of scale grow or recede. Today's natural monopoly may be tomorrow's naturally competitive industry. Therefore the proper scope of regulation is often uncertain and changing, rather than clear.

Commissions

There are three main federal regulatory commissions and nearly fifty state regulatory bodies. They are summarized in Table 20.1. Most commissions have three to seven commissioners, who hear and decide issues brought before them by the regulated firms, customers, the commission staff, or other parties. Commission resources vary from scant to large. Housekeeping and peripheral tasks (such as safety at railroad crossings and the licensing of small operators) absorb much of the resources of some commissions.

Commissioners are political appointees. Usually they are politically active lawyers, either ambitious young ones or older ones on the way out. Since the more talented commissioners generally rise to higher positions elsewhere, they are usually in regulatory office less than three years, with little time to develop or change basic policies. Staffs tend to be bureaucratic, cautiously adjusting among the conflicting interests of firms, customers, and other groups. Like antitrust, the process is run by lawyers, who use adversary procedures to turn out decisions meeting legal criteria. The formal legal powers of the commissions are usually large, but the duties and criteria are vague ("fair," "just and reasonable," the "public interest," and so on).

Background.   The concept of the "independent regulatory commission" was developed between 1885 and 1910 in the hope of applying expert, honest, nonpolitical control to the problems of natural monopoly. The "utility" firms themselves often lobbied to be put under regulation, since it gave them a monopoly franchise and might be manipulated to serve their own interests.

The Interstate Commerce Commission (ICC) was the first federal commission, established in 1888, though it did not gain real powers until after 1910. Wisconsin Progressives started the first state-level commission in 1907. Other state commissions followed, and by the 1930s, most states had regulatory bodies of some sort. The other federal commissions date mainly from the 1930s. Their coverage and activities have evolved with practice and do not fit a uniform pattern.

Until 1944, most commissions were ineffective, stalled by debates over the value of company assets. The firms claimed that the *current* value of assets must be used in setting "fair" profits; but that would have mired regulation in endless, obscure controversies over what the current values really were. In 1944, a landmark Supreme Court decision made the original accounting cost of assets the standard basis for setting profits. This has provided a relatively firm footing for commissions to set strict controls on profits.

TABLE 20.1   The Main Federal Commissions and Five Selected State Commissions

COMMISSION (YEAR ESTABLISHED)	NUMBER OF MEMBERS	NUMBER OF STAFF MEMBERS	BUDGET, 1983 ($ MILLION)	JURISDICTION
Federal				
Interstate Commerce Commission (1888)	5	1652	$29.4	Partial regulation of railroads, water shipping, oil pipelines
Federal Energy Regulatory Commission (1920, 1935)	5	1191	22.8	Electricity, gas, gas pipelines, oil pipelines, water power sites
Federal Communications Commission (1934)	7	1785	32.8	Long-distance telephone service, CB radios, ham operators, etc.
State				
California	5	522	12.2	Electricity, gas, telephones, railroads, water supply, warehouses, sewage, etc.
Colorado	3	72	1.0	Electricity, gas, telephones, railroads, oil pipelines, water supply
Georgia	5	57	0.8	Electricity, gas, telephones, railroads
New York	5	343	12.8	Electricity, gas, telephones, oil pipelines, water supply
Wisconsin	3	140	3.2	Electricity, gas, telephones, railroads, buses, taxis, oil pipelines, water, sewage

SOURCE: Federal Energy Regulatory Commission, *Federal and State Commission Jurisdiction and Regulation* (Washington, D.C.: Federal Power Commission, 1986).

A few commissions have applied strict regulation, during some periods. Others have been passive or vigorously procompany. Only in the 1960s did the Federal Energy Regulatory Commission, Federal Communications Commission, and the Civil Aeronautics Board begin to assert firm control over rate levels, rate structures, and the scope of the monopoly held by individual firms.

From 1940 to 1968 was something of a golden age for most regulated sectors (except railroads). Growth was achieving economies of scale, costs were steady or falling, and the problems to be solved were rather simple. Since 1968, however, severe problems have battered both firms and regulators. These include rapid inflation, ecological impacts, multiplying fuel prices, consumer activism, nuclear power, and antitrust challenges. Regulation has come under great stress, and some commissions have been forced to go deeply into price structure and competitive issues.

The 1970s and 1980s were a watershed, with Congress removing most regulatory controls over airlines, air freight, railroads, trucking, telephones, cable television, banking, and natural gas. This wave of deregulation was a major event, as part of the general rise of competition (recall Chapters 1 and 4).

Evolution.   Most utility sectors evolve through a four-stage process, as was shown in Chapter 4. Stage 1 is the birth of the industry. Stage 2 is rapid growth. Stage 3 brings stability, and the industry matures. Stage 4 is a reversion to natural competition, when regulation is no longer needed. These utilities are natural monopolies only during the first three stages, when there are large economies of scale. The economies then shrink, which allows competition to develop. Therefore natural-monopoly conditions will usually justify regulation only for a finite period.

Regulation itself evolves. It is usually promotional at first, to boost the industry's growth and penetration of the market. Then, in stages 3 and 4, it often tries to protect the firm from new competition. Deregulating is frequently a difficult process, resisted by the commission *and* by the regulated firms.

But since 1975 there have been radical cutbacks by regulators, particularly by Reagan appointees at the F.C.C.. Also, officials at the Department of Transportation chose not to apply controls over airline mergers (recall Chapter 18). Altogether, deregulation may fall short or overshoot in specific cases.

Also, the real scope of effective regulation frequently differs from the area that, by the legal definitions, is supposed to be under control. Even when a commission reaches the right fit, the conditions may soon change so that regulation is again out of alignment.

Process.   Commissions hold open hearings on issues put before them and then render decisions. In the typical rate case, the firm announces a new, higher set of prices and asks the commission to approve them. Hearings are scheduled at which the company makes a detailed case for its request, often using expert witnesses as well as company officials. The commission staff or ''public rate counsel'' then presents a rebuttal, presumably representing the consumers' interests. The staff usually urges setting a lower rate of return and price level, and perhaps a different structure of prices. Other parties may also join in.

The hearings often take months, and the ensuing decision may come as much as a year after the original request. The commission customarily grants a fraction of the request (half and half is the most common division) on the basis of its collective judgment.

The procedures provide ''due process,'' with an open forum for all interested parties. Each cites criteria and facts that favor it. The outcome is usually a compromise among the conflicting interests, stated in terms of some criterion or mix of criteria (fairness, efficiency, and so on).

2.   Decisions on Price Levels and Structures

Commissions deal with three main kinds of economic issues: price level, price structure, and the scope of competition.

Price level is the conventional topic, refined by decades of practice to a traditional litany of issues. The elements are summed up in the following equations, which will be familiar to you. They represent the rate of return of the firm.

$$\text{Rate of return} = \frac{\text{Total revenue} - \text{Total cost}}{\text{Invested capital}}$$

$$\text{Rate of return} = \pi = \frac{\Sigma(X_i \cdot p_i) - \Sigma(x_j \cdot p_j)}{\Sigma(A_k \cdot p_k)}$$

where X_i is an output and p_i is the price of that output; x_j is an input and p_j is its price; and A_k is an asset and p_k is its price at the time it was acquired.

The commission decides what the firm's "rate base" is (its amount of capital invested in the business). Next, it decides what rate of return is "fair," (this is usually in the range of 7–13 percent). Then the firm is allowed to set price levels that will generate enough sales revenue to provide the fair rate of profit on the rate base. Hence this approach is often called *rate-base regulation*.

If the commission permits higher output prices, that will raise total revenue, increase profits, and raise the rate of return. The company wants maximum profits, while the commission tries to hold profits (and prices) down to much lower levels.

The basic choice is shown in Figure 20.1, again for the ideal case. The utility firm is assumed to have built the right level of capacity; the demand curve cuts both the average and marginal cost curves as close as possible to the minimum of average cost. Therefore a price set at marginal cost will give economic efficiency. Marginal cost pricing will also avoid excess profits and will achieve the lowest possible average cost.

The utility would prefer a higher price, at P_m, with large excess profits. But the regulators try to set price at P_c, which gives the utility enough total revenue to cover its total costs. The utility is required to produce Q_c, which is the amount that people want to buy at the regulated price P_c.

Economic criteria

Price Level. Some ceiling or "permitted" rate of return is to be set by the commission, but its level is controversial. The laws usually require a "fair" rate of return, neither too high (unfair to customers) nor too low (unfair to the firm's shareholders). It should also be efficient, by several possible criteria: (1) it should equal the cost to the firm of its capital (the "cost-of-capital" criterion); and/or (2) it should be high enough to attract just the optimal amount of new investment (the "capital attraction" criterion); and/or (3) it should be in line with the risk-return conditions in other industries (the "comparable returns" criterion).

These three criteria all relate to the same basic concept of efficient allocation of capital. But they are not precise guides to real conditions. "Fair" rates of return usually lie between 7 and 13 percent, but the correct level for each case can be debated endlessly without arriving at a definitive answer. The commission simply applies its judgment and picks a figure or range, such as 10.25 percent or 9.5–11.0 percent.

Then the value of the rate base is fixed by the commission. The firm's invested capital includes (1) fixed capital, at various possible depreciation rates; and (2) other assets, including a range of short-term and liquid assets. Some or all of this is allowed in the rate base, in what can be a complicated judgment by the commission.

Total costs may also be reviewed, to make sure that they are necessary and not inflated—in our terms, to assure that they are X-efficient. The specific price level then follows fairly directly, since it is the price change needed to let the firm's profit rate go up to the permitted ceiling rate.

These price decisions usually ignore two complications. First, demand may be elastic. Since price changes will alter the amounts consumed, the net revenue change may not be a simple matter at all. Second, future conditions may change, so that the new price schedule turns out to yield profits either above or below the permitted rate of return. Indeed, actual profit rates often do rise above the permitted ceilings.

The decisions are usually only a prediction about the price level that will actually result in the optimal or reasonable profit. Moreover, despite arcane debates about criteria, the rough-and-ready decisions made are really just a compromise. Even so, the regulatory outcomes often turn out to be reasonably close to the ideal solutions.

Price structure.   It is supposed to be "just and reasonable," in the standard legal wording. Price discrimination by these firms is likely to be very sharp; after all, they have a complete monopoly, and they sell to a wide variety of customers (in homes, in shops and factories of all sizes) who have very different demand elasticities. Some degree of discrimination may be efficient; but that is a very complex issue, beyond the scope of this chapter. Generally, optimal pricing would contain much less price discrimination than the firm would prefer.

Instead, the proper criterion for prices is cost—specifically, marginal cost. For each specific customer group, price should be set as close to marginal cost as possible. That will bring the utility into line with efficient allocation in the rest of the economy.

The structure of costs may be quite complicated. The regulatory task is to bring prices at least roughly into line with that cost structure, while avoiding discriminatory patterns. Overhead and joint costs (costs incurred supplying all customers) often make marginal costs unclear. Also, most regulated utilities have marked fluctuations in demand, such as the peak loads for electric and telephone service during business hours, and off-peak levels during nights and weekends. These fluctuations cause marginal costs to vary sharply.

Therefore the efficient price structure will also need to have marked differences—by seasons, by day, and by time of day, as we will analyze shortly. The topic can grow difficult, obscure, and frustrating in actual hearings.

Until the 1960s, most commissions allowed firms to decide the bulk of their price structures. The firms, in turn, tended toward (1) discrimination or (2) flat across-the-board price changes that, being uniform, minimized complaints among customer groups. Since about 1965, price structure has received closer attention from some commissions.

3.   Four Economic Issues of Regulation

Four specific economic issues of regulation are: setting the correct boundaries of regulation, setting prices in line with marginal costs, the inefficiencies that regulation may cause, and "cream skimming" and competition.

The boundaries of regulation

The early tradition was that only "public utilities" should be regulated: such "economic infrastructure" as railroads, electric power, water, and sewage. This standard was broadened in 1877 by the *Munn* v. *Illinois* decision, which held that any business "affected with the public interest" could be regulated.[2] In 1934, *Nebbia* established that regulation could be applied to virtually any market.[3]

Yet regulation does not, and probably should not, extend to all markets. Today it mainly covers certain "utilities." Some are monopolies, others are oligopolies.

Natural monopolies are not a distinct group. Most regulated sectors contain a mix of "natural monopoly" and naturally competitive parts. These conditions often shift or evolve. The firm, of course, wishes to put the whole sector under its exclusive control. Other firms usually contest this, wishing to stay in the market or expand in it. The commission's task is to trim the franchise to the conditions, preventing any "excess" monopoly.

In fact, several criteria could single out markets where regulation is appropriate. They have been used frequently in debates over the "proper" scope of regulation. They include:

1.   There are large economies of scale, which create "natural-monopoly" conditions.
2.   Demand elasticities vary sharply among customers, with some very inelastic.
3.   Output fluctuates steeply and regularly, so that costs and demands vary widely by time of use.
4.   Users are connected physically to suppliers by wires, pipes, or other means. Users cannot easily change suppliers, and suppliers can control use and prevent reselling by customers.
5.   The output from the supplier is "vital" in some sense (a "necessity").
6.   The industry has high fixed capital.

Criteria 5 and 6 are no longer accepted as good normative guidelines. The other four boil down to *scale economies plus price discrimination*. They are matters of degree and are often hard to measure. Moreover, many markets have one or two of the conditions but not the others. The hard-core "utilities" have all of them, at least for some period of years. The intermediate cases are more numerous and difficult to judge.

In practice, regulation covers some of these conditions and not others. Airlines, railroads, barge lines, and natural gas producers are oligopolies that have been regulated; of course, nearly all oligopolies, some with much tighter structure, are not regulated. Even the true utility sectors usually contain parts that are not at all natural monopolies.

There is no easy way to define the correct boundaries of regulation, nor to apply them to complicated and changing industries. In principle, it could be done, with new sectors being added in (hospitals? sports?) and older ones being dropped (airlines, trucking, natural gas production). The actual process is much looser and more dubious. You should inspect each regulated sector and then judge for yourself.

---

[2] *Munn* v. *Illinois*, 94 U.S. 113.
[3] *Nebbia* v. *New York*, 291 U.S. 502.

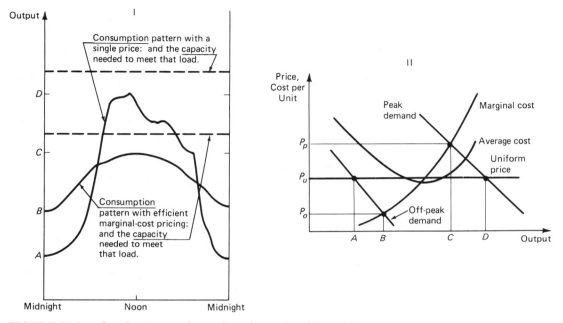

FIGURE 20.2.   Load patterns, demand, and cost in utility pricing.

The letters A through D are aligned between the two diagrams. The load fluctuates sharply between levels A and D if a uniform price is charged at all times. That uniform price is P_u in panel II. It results in the black-line load curve in panel I. But if prices are set equal to marginal cost during the peak and off-peak times (P_p and P_o), then the load pattern will be smoothed. It is reduced to C at peak times and raised to B at off-peak times, as shown by the blue-line load curve.

Marginal cost pricing

Regulated firms usually have a variety of outputs, differing by physical features (size, weight, design) or by conditions of supply. Seemingly uniform products can vary sharply in costs. For example, the cost of a kilowatt-hour of electricity at midnight will differ from that of one at noon. More generally, off-peak production is usually cheaper than production at peak-load times. That is shown by the typical daily load curve in panel I of Figure 20.2.

Output peaks during the day, and then falls to low levels during the off-peak nighttime hours. The best equipment is run continuously, giving low costs at off-peak times. That corresponds to low marginal cost in panel II. But at peak times, costly extra capacity must be started up and used, at high marginal costs. Therefore peak-load marginal costs are commonly a multiple of off-peak costs.

But remember that *price should equal marginal cost*. If price diverges sharply from marginal cost, then allocation is inefficient. Therefore utility regulators should strive to get utility price structures into line with marginal costs. That calls for *peak-load pricing,* with prices set much higher at peak times than at off-peak times. In panel II of Figure 2, the efficient prices are P_o and P_p, with outputs at B and C. A single uniform price, P_u, would instead lead to too much quantity demanded at D, while cutting off-peak outputs to level A.

Such marginal cost pricing is socially efficient, and often the regulated firm would gain greatly from adopting it. For example, setting prices too low for peak outputs could encourage too much load at peak times and threaten the whole utility system with collapse. Indeed, marginal cost pricing often lies in the same direction as price discrimination, at least for parts of the utility's output. For example, low-cost bulk power may go to large users who have high elasticity of demand. Both cost and demand would then call for a low price.

Yet cost and demand conditions often diverge, so that the regulators must force the firm to follow efficient, marginal cost pricing. Setting high prices at peak-load times is especially important. But it is often hard to enforce because it usually requires higher prices for the periods when the system seems to be "most urgently needed." Also, rate-base regulation may encourage the regulated firm to add more capacity than is efficient. In the great mass of regulated outputs, marginal cost pricing is both correct and reasonably practical to accomplish.

Nevertheless, before 1968, these lessons were largely ignored, for utilities were eager to raise their growth by means of promotional pricing, which is often discriminatory. Peak-load output was usually priced low, at average costs or even at zero (for local telephone calls, for example). The new scarcities and stresses that have arisen since 1965 have made marginal cost pricing seem wise, even urgent, both to many regulators and to the firms themselves.

Practical cases

Electricity prices used to ignore high peak-load costs almost entirely, thereby encouraging people to use electricity out to level *D* of Figure 20.2. This, in turn, required the companies to build too much capacity to meet those overstimulated peak-load levels. Local telephone pricing has been even worse. By charging a *zero* price for local calls, the firms have encouraged too high a level of use. That was shown in Chapter 12. Calls made at peak times have a true marginal cost that is very high. Thus, when you call a friend at 4 P.M. and chat for a half hour, the true cost may be a dollar or more, although the call's value is low, as shown by the demand curve. But since you pay nothing extra, you (and millions of others) make the calls, and the system absorbs those extra costs.

Long-distance prices reflect marginal costs more closely than do local-service prices. The price differences are familiar and can be obtained from the front pages of any telephone directory. Prices during business hours are often double or triple the off-peak (nighttime and weekend) prices. Therefore marginal cost pricing has been routine in certain utility services, even though it has been avoided in most others.

In the 1970s, there were new efforts to shift toward marginal cost pricing. In electricity, perhaps a third of the companies adopted time-of-day pricing. A typical time-of-day price schedule is shown in Table 20.2 for Wisconsin Electric Power Company. Peak times are defined rather roughly as 7 A.M. to 7 P.M. Monday to Friday during the seasonal hot weather peak in July–October, when the heavy use of air conditioners strains the whole electric system's capacities and makes marginal cost very high. Off-peak hours are 7 P.M. to 7 A.M. and weekends. From November

TABLE 20.2 A Time-of-Day Price Structure for Electricity (Wisconsin Electric Power Company)

CLASS OF SERVICE	RESIDENTIAL—TIME-OF-USE	
Effective in	All Areas Served	
Availability		
To residential customers contracting for electric service for domestic purposes for a period of one year or more.		
Rate		
Customer charge, including one meter	$7.00 per month Billing periods	
Energy charge per kWh	July–October	November–June
On-peak energy[a]	12.20¢	8.20¢
Off-peak energy[b]	1.30	1.30
Meter charge		
The monthly meter charge for each meter in excess of one shall be $2.50.		

[a] Residential on-peak energy usage is the energy in kilowatt-hours delivered between 7 A.M. and 7 P.M. Central Standard Time, Monday through Friday, including holidays.
[b] Residential off-peak energy usage is the energy in kilowatt-hours delivered during all hours other than during on-peak hours.

to June, the 7 A.M. to 7 P.M. hours are an in-between category, neither peak nor off-peak.

Notice that peak-load prices of 8.2 cents per kilowatt-hour are set far above the off-peak price of 1.3 cents per kilowatt-hour. The in-between period has an intermediate price—5.2 cents per kilowatt-hour. These prices fit the cost patterns shown in Figure 20.2. Even if they are not fine-tuned to fit marginal cost closely, these peak-load prices do at least fit the main patterns of cost. Therefore they give a practical instance of efficient pricing under regulation.

Despite some progress in this direction, much pricing of electricity, gas, and telephone service is still in the old uniform-price patterns that ignore marginal costs. Many economists continue to criticize those policies. They have also studied the cost and demand conditions intensively and have developed detailed proposals for revised prices.

The effects of regulation on costs

Standard regulation lets the firm charge prices that will cover its costs plus a "fair" profit. This "cost-plus" approach may permit or even encourage X-inefficiency in the firm. If its monopoly power is sufficient, the firm can raise prices enough to cover its costs even if they are greatly inflated.

This tendency is reinforced by the firm's interest in providing high-quality, reliable service, which usually entails extra costs. It is difficult to set the socially efficient level of quality and reliability, and the cost-plus-profit basis of regulation may induce the firm to choose too high a level of quality and cost.

In the total cost part of the basic regulatory equation, both the prices (p_j) and the amounts (q_j) of the inputs may be raised because of regulation. That is because the firm gets the profits whether it keeps input costs down or not.

This problem of "cost-plus" inefficiency has long been familiar in military weapons buying by governments. Under regulation, it is more subtle but still chronic. There are two main limits on it: (1) the professional standards of the industry (managers and engineers presumably apply good sense and technical criteria to what is needed in their system); and (2) scrutiny by the commission (from the start, regulators and courts have recognized the need to guard against possibly extravagant or unnecessary costs). In practice, the controls have usually been weak. The firm's expenses are often listed and looked over in some detail, but little can be done to challenge or rectify dubious cases.

Investment may also be too large under regulation. The conventional method of rate-base regulation encourages the firm to increase the value of the rate base itself. Normally, the permitted rate of return is set a little above the cost of capital. The firm's shareholders, therefore, gain a little (or a lot) of profit from each extra bit of capital included in the rate base.[4] The process probably works subconsciously, but it encourages the firm to use more capital than is economically efficient.

The rise could come about in two ways: (1) Actual investment could be higher. In choosing new technology, the firm would lean toward more capital-intensive methods. Capacity to meet peak loads might also be higher because of the rate-base effect. This would give the firm more protection against embarrassing breakdowns at peak times. (2) Accounting choices would be made to maximize the recorded value of assets. Depreciation methods would be the main item to be adjusted, toward writing down the assets' value slowly. The firm might permit overcharging in the prices of the equipment it buys.

The whole rate-base effect has never been accurately measured and, of course, the firms deny that it occurs at all. It probably does shift the margin of choice by some degree in most regulated utilities.

"Cream skimming" and competition

All utility industries have some markets that can be supplied competitively. The regulated firm, however, naturally wishes to encompass them in its exclusive franchise. Indeed, the rate-base effect encourages it; the firm wants to add to its rate base the capital in the adjacent market. Meanwhile, other firms want to get in to compete against the utility.

The key point is that the newcomers are often naturally attracted to the most lucrative parts of the regulated firm's market, where the price-cost ratios are highest. Since there is price discrimination, the entrants usually fasten first onto the "creamy" markets. This "cream skimming" (the British call it "picking the eyes out of the market") is regarded as an acute threat by the regulated firm.

The firm will claim that cream skimming strikes at the "system integrity" of the utility, for the creamy parts are necessary to support the skim parts. With the cream gone, either (1) the whole system will go bankrupt, or at least (2) prices for most consumers will have to rise. That, at any rate, is the claim.

---

[4] Suppose that the cost of capital is 7 percent and the permitted rate of return is 9 percent. Then every additional $100 million in the rate base will increase net profits by $2 million (that is, $9 million return minus $7 million cost of capital). Capitalized at a 10:1 ratio, that $2 million might equal $20 million in added stock value to the shareowners.

The regulated firm therefore resists any and all competition. If competition is permitted, the original firm demands the right to meet the competition by selective price-cutting. But if that is permitted, the price cuts may be deep and predatory enough to keep out competition, while still maintaining a discriminatory price structure. The commission thus gets drawn into setting *floors* on specific prices as well as *ceilings* on the firm's whole price and profit levels. And to do this it must usually rely on cost figures prepared by the regulated firm itself.

This baffling problem stems from the basic sources of natural monopoly: overhead costs and economies of scale. These conditions make the regulation necessary, and yet the natural monopoly basis does not extend throughout the system. Competition can, and probably should, enter into some parts. But which parts, how far, and on what competitive terms?

Often the conditions are highly complex and changing, and the pressures are intense. Moreover, since commissions are usually imperfect and short of resources, their treatments tend to be inefficient. They may give the utility firm too wide a franchise or be slow to allow new competition.

The difficulties have been widespread in postal service, airlines, railroads, telephones, banking, electricity—anywhere that a commission has had to supervise a firm with an exclusive franchise. Cost and competitive conditions vary by gradations, rarely fitting into neat boxes. Regulators are forced to cope with these problems as best they can.

4. The Proposal for "Price Caps"

Dominant firms have recently begun requesting to be regulated under "price caps" in place of the traditional rate-base method. "Old regulation," it is said, is obsolete and discredited as causing inefficiency. "Price caps" are said to be more effective and less harmful, and the F.C.C. applied them to AT&T's long-distance services in 1989.

The idea is taken from a theory advanced in the early 1980s in the U.K. as a way to constrain newly privatized utility firms, such as British Telecom (the telephone system).[5] The virtue of price caps is their simplicity: they merely limit the average of the firm's price increases to the rise in the consumer price index, minus a factor to reflect productivity gains. The formula is as follows:

$$\text{Permitted rate of price rise} = \text{Rate of rise of consumer price index} - X$$

or

$$\Delta \text{Price} = \Delta CPI - X$$

where X is some percent designed to squeeze the firm a little to encourage efficiency.

---

[5] The influential version of the proposal is in Stephen C. Littlechild, *Regulation of British Telecommunications' Profitability* (London: Her Majesty's Stationery Officer, 1983); see also Michael Beesley and Stephen Littlechild, "Privatisation: Principles, Problems, and Priorities," *Lloyds Bank Review*, 149 (July 1983) 1–20.

Ironically, this method has been largely discredited in Britain, for reasons I will go into shortly.[6] Nonetheless, in the late 1980s, U.S. regulators were urged to accept it. Several states did so, and the FCC adopted the "new" method in 1989 for AT&T in long-distance service.

The fundamental fault is that "price caps" permit the dominant firm to take any selective actions it wishes. Those actions, as we have noted, can be critical in enhancing dominance. In other words, "price caps" can be a license for unlimited anticompetitive actions.

More specifically, the formula's basis is unreliable. First, it accepts the current prices as valid, seeking to constrain only additional rises. Yet some or all of the utility's prices may be at inefficient levels to begin with. There may be elements of X-inefficiency in the firm's costs, or the utility's overall profits may be too high or too low. If there are such errors, the "price cap" will build them in as permanent conditions.

Second, each specific element of the formula is defective. The permitted average price rise ignores individual price changes. Therefore it is appropriate only when there is just one output price to be constrained. That simple condition holds for few significant regulatory cases.

Third, the CPI is the wrong index to use. An index based on the utility's *costs* would be far more appropriate, though great technical care would have to be exercised in constructing and adapting such an index because the weights among inputs usually change over time. If the "price cap" is to apply only to some of the utility's outputs, the task would become virtually impossible. Overhead costs cannot usually be assigned by clear economic criteria, and the utility firm could move its accounting costs in a manner that frustrated the constraints. These problems are at the core of "the utility problem," and the resort to "price caps" will not make them go away.

Finally, the third element in the formula—the "X factor"—poses intractable problems. Settling on a percent to subtract from the rate of increase in the index in order to ensure efficiency requires a judgment about the technological opportunity of the industry and a forecast of coming trends. How much would autonomous technological progress be likely to reduce costs as innovations emerge? The answer involves sophisticated, complex judgments about multidimensional trends of technology. Moreover, correct judgments may produce unexpected results, such as an X level high enough to require price *reductions* rather than rises.

In short, "price caps" will probably require as much detailed attention to costs as established regulation has been forced to provide. In addition, it demands judgments about technological trends that the old system of regulation has largely been able to avoid. These problems appear to make "price caps" at least as difficult as traditional regulation.

If "price caps" are attempted, economic analysis suggests that they should take the following dual form. First, the formula should be:

$$\begin{array}{ccc} \Delta \text{ Price} & \Delta \text{ Cost} & \text{Savings} \\ \text{of} & = \text{ of} & - \text{ from} \quad - X \text{ (Squeeze factor)} \\ \text{outputs} & \text{inputs} & \text{autonomous} \\ & & \text{progress} \end{array}$$

---

[6] See also Cento Veljanovski, *Selling the State* (London: Weidenfeld and Nicolson, 1987), especially Chapter 7; *Annals of Public and Co-operative Economy,* Special Issue, "The Privatization of Public Enterprises—A European Debate," April–June 1986, especially the paper by Heidrun Abromeit.

The input cost index must be correctly weighted and adjusted for shifts. The savings from autonomous progress must be decided after thorough evaluations of the industry's technological opportunities; it may also need frequent adjustment as new opportunities develop. The squeeze factor is needed in order to apply incentives to utilities to maintain tightness in costs and innovation. How large X should be is a matter of delicate judgment for which there are no simple criteria.

This applied formula is not enough. A second level of constraint is needed, on individual prices. Because selective actions will inevitably be tried by the dominant firm under the "price caps" system, regulators must be alert to prevent them. That requires constraints comparable to the traditional price-structure restraints that the "old" regulation is supposed to apply.

Altogether, "price caps" are an illusory attempt to escape regulatory reality. They will probably prove not only more indirect and ineffective than conventional regulation, with all its faults, but also more onerous. "Price caps" are appropriate only under near-impossible conditions: when (1) the outputs are very few, (2) the rivals are already near parity, (3) reliable input cost indexes can easily be constructed (with little or no overhead costs shared between "capped" and "uncapped" outputs), (4) technological opportunities are accurately known and widely agreed upon, and (5) a correct "squeeze factor" can be applied.

The "price cap" literature and British policies have understated these problems and implied that solutions are direct and simple. Instead, "price cap" regulation is likely to increase staffing, the complexity of regulatory tasks, and the intensity of public complaints.

II. DEREGULATION

The years 1975–1985 could be called the Decade of Deregulation. Controls were removed from a range of industries, including airlines, banks, trucking firms, railroads, buses, broadcasters, telephone systems, and stockbrokers.

The sheer variety of the changes has made for confusion about what has been done and how large the benefits are. In fact, *deregulation* has been used to denote so many changes that its very meaning is unsure. The clearest definition is *the replacement of government controls with effective competition*. And the most difficult type of deregulation is shifting a franchised, price-regulated, pure-monopoly utility all the way over to being an unregulated competitor in an effectively competitive market.

None of the deregulations undertaken so far has done this. Most have been "easy" cases that merely opened up an officially protected oligopoly cartel (such as among the airlines, banks, trucking firms, and stockbrokers) to a greater degree of competition, by reducing procartel and antientry restrictions. The core cases— local telephones and electricity and gas distribution—are still traditionally regulated.

Yet if the deregulatory movement continues, even the hard-core regulated industries may soon be stripped of controls over prices. One critical question is: Will the resulting competition be effective, or will removing regulation unleash monopoly power? A second, related question is: Can antitrust constraints be applied to prevent monopoly from reemerging? In short, effective deregulation depends strictly on the creation of effective competition.

1.   Criteria for Effective Deregulation

Therefore the analysis reviewed in this book helps to set the standards for effective deregulation. The focus is on the dominant firm as it evolves from monopoly to competition. Normally, market dominance is not effective competition, as Chapter 11 indicated. That leads to the first economic criterion:

Market Share Below 50 Percent.   The dominant firm's market share must sink below 50 percent, and there must be at least four or five comparable competitors, before competition is effective.

Dominant firms are not eligible for full deregulation. A market share over 50 percent indicates the need to retain price constraints, both against too-high monopoly prices and against selective price cuts designed to eliminate smaller rivals. The firm will condemn the restraints as unfair and crippling. It will demand the right to compete fully. But a dominant market share makes that unwise, because competition is not yet effective.

Bottleneck Controls.   Competition cannot survive independently in the presence of bottleneck controls through which one or several firms exclude others or overcharge them for access to the market. Either such bottlenecks must be removed or placed in outside hands, or regulation must be retained to ensure that access is open and fairly priced.

Once effective competition has evolved or is imminent, then regulatory controls on the formerly dominant firm can be withdrawn. Hence the third criterion:

Deregulation After Competition.   Regulatory controls are to be removed *after* effective competition is established. Premature deregulation is the cardinal error of deregulation policy.

After deregulation, the market is usually a tight oligopoly, which can easily move back to dominance. Therefore there is a strong need to apply strict antitrust policies to mergers and strategic behavior.

Strict Antitrust.   Mergers must be carefully screened, and selective pricing tactics must be limited, so as to prevent a reversion to dominance. Entry barriers need to be kept low. These criteria would fit the established, pre-1980 lines of U.S. antitrust policies.

2.   The Threat to Local Service

Deregulation commonly stirs the complaints that it will cause service to small-town users to close down. For instance, when the telephone, bus, truck, railroad, and airline industries were deregulated, there were aggressive claims in each case, that small-town services would disappear.

The incumbent sellers contend that they have been "cross-subsidizing" the costly small-town services with profits from their profitable, high-density main routes. New competition will fasten upon the profitable denser routes, they say, and skim that cream, so that the unprofitable small-town routes will either have to be closed down or priced much higher. Thus is competition portrayed as a threat to

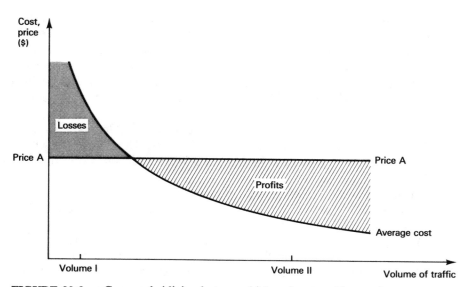

FIGURE 20.3.   Cross-subsidizing between high-volume and low-volume routes.

the Jeffersonian values of a democratic small-town America. In political terms, the thousands of smaller towns in rural regions throughout the country that feel threatened by deregulation often wield disproportionate influence in elections and legislatures.

The danger has some analytical validity. As shown in simplified form in Figure 20.3, the average cost of service may decline with the size of the route. Thus on high-density truck and telephone routes, average costs per unit are often much lower than on the sparsely used peripheral routes to (and among) small towns out in the countryside.

Suppose that the price per unit of service is kept largely uniform in order to be "fair," as is illustrated by price A in Figure 20.3. That has often been done simply to avoid accusations of favoring one group of customers over others. Then big losses will occur on small routes (volume I) and big profits will be gained on the high-traffic routes (volume II). If all routes are part of a monopolist's single system, then a pooling of the losses and profits can maintain the whole system at zero excess profits while assuring "universal" service. Letting competition enter the dense markets will take away the profits that maintain the whole system's "integrity." Small-volume routes will be closed, or else prices for them will have to be raised prohibitively high to cover the true costs, as shown in Figure 20.3.

This problem of vulnerable cross-subsidization has been used to resist deregulation in virtually every instance so far. Often the services to small towns do dry up, unless regulators forbid abandonment, as was done with railroads from the 1930s to the 1970s.

Yet the real threat is frequently much smaller than is claimed. The costs of small-town service may not be as high as the monopolists assert, and often are debatable because of joint and overhead costs. And many times the "rural" groups turn out to be well-to-do gentry living in affluent suburbs rather than poor farmers or artisans.

Moreover, the technology of supply often adjusts to maintain service at lower costs and prices. In air travel, for example, the main airlines have cut back their flights by full-size jet aircraft to smaller airports, but smaller "commuter" planes have emerged to take their place on many thin routes, at costs lower than those for partly filled large jets. Therefore the actual costs have been much lower for small-town traffic than the curve in Figure 20.3 suggests. Much the same may be possible in other industries.

Where small-town service does involve some financial losses, they may be measurable and compensable by direct public payments. Those payments will probably be small compared to the benefits of X-efficiency and innovation that competition will deliver.

The issues are not simple, but experience so far suggests that this supposed danger is frequently an illusion invoked by incumbent firms to defend their monopolies.

The best regulatory approach has two parts. The first carries out independent studies of the actual costs on thin routes, covering alternative technologies where possible. (Do not rely on the monopolist's cost estimates, for they reflect not only self-interest but also narrow technological choices based on a monopoly-oriented system.) The second part weighs any provable small-route losses against the benefits competition is likely to provide. Small losses in a few locales can often be covered in order to realize the large gains from competition throughout the industry.

3. Diversifying

As deregulation proceeds, firms often make ambitious moves to diversify, even into markets wholly unrelated to the original utility services. Regulators often resist this, for several important reasons. First, diversification can divert managerial attention and commitment from the established activities. Also, it adds financial risks to the whole enterprise and may cause the firm's cost of capital to rise. And if a financial crisis does occur, it may undercut the firm's ability to meet its utility responsibilities. This problem is aggravated if the pooling of finances between the old and new activities makes it hard for the regulators to assess the firm's actual financial soundness in its utility operations. Moreover, the firm may be able to use its market power in the utility lines so as to gain unfair advantages in the new lines. Prudent regulators therefore tend to resist all diversifying.

The correct criterion, though, is more specific, following directly on the earlier analysis of dominant firms. *Only dominant firms may raise problems by diversifying. Fully competitive firms can be left free to diversify as they choose.* Diversifying by dominant firms may indeed endanger the basic service responsibility and frustrate regulation, as well as threaten effective competition in the new markets. Regulators may therefore properly require that risky, unrelated lines not be added by a dominant firm and that the finances of utility and other operations be kept separate. As in other matters, the firm will gain freedom from these limits only when it loses its dominance.

4. Relying on Antitrust Agencies

One often hears that the problems can be left to the antitrust authorities (the Antitrust Division in the U.S. Department of Justice and the Federal Trade Commission) to solve. It is true that the criteria do deal with monopoly and competition, as do the two agencies. Yet the agencies will not usually be adequate to the task, for the following reasons.

First, the antitrust agencies are very small units compared to their awesome responsibilities covering most of the U.S. economy. Their resources are tiny and stretched as it is. Adding major utility sectors to their burdens is asking for weak handling.

Second, their methods of enforcement are narrow. The agencies can only bring lawsuits to stop specific anticompetitive conditions or actions. They cannot exercise continuing formal or informal control over complex conditions.

Third, the dominant-firm case is precisely the one that the antitrust agencies are least fit to handle. Effective deregulation requires sustained attention to move the monopolist down below 40 percent of the market, to prevent anticompetitive actions, and to enforce service responsibilities along the way. The agencies have repeatedly shown in large lawsuits that they cannot persuade the courts to deal effectively with dominant-firm conditions, even in much simpler cases. And in the 1980s, Reagan antitrust officials simply refused to bring Section 2 cases. Regulation was created precisely to fill the gaps left by these agencies.

Fourth, the agencies go through sharp changes in quality and political direction. Until 1980, these changes were usually only moderate. Since then, however, antitrust was sharply reduced. Antitrust is no longer a steady policy to rely on.

5. Cases of Deregulation

Two particularly interesting cases of deregulation have already been discussed in some detail: AT&T in long-distance telephone service (Chapter 17), and airlines (Chapter 18). The criteria just discussed (market shares, selective pricing, etc.) are very much involved in those cases.

Some further discussion of AT&T will be helpful, along with a treatment of the bulk supply of electricity.

Long-Distance Telephone Service

As Chapter 17 noted, AT&T held a complete monopoly in this industry before 1975. But decisions by the Federal Communications Commission in 1968 and later, as well as actions by the Supreme Court, gradually opened up long-distance telephone service to entry by "specialized common carriers" such as MCI and US Sprint. By 1984, when the Bell System was divided up under the antitrust settlement, the entrants had gained some 10 percent of long-distance traffic, and by 1988, AT&T's share may have receded to about 75 percent.

There are some interesting questions of market definition (choosing between total traffic, or large-business customers, etc., as the relevant markets), but AT&T is still clearly the dominant firm. Moreover, MCI and Sprint have been enduring financial losses in some recent years, so they may not be powerful enough to apply great pressure to AT&T.

In the late 1970s, the Bailey-Baumol-Panzar-Willig group was employed by AT&T to develop concepts that would be relevant to AT&T's interest in protecting its monopoly and reducing the limits on its freedom of action. The main new concepts this group came up with were "sustainability" and "contestability."

Sustainability refers to the ability of a multiproduct utility firm to "sustain" a set of prices (a price vector) that is as efficient as possible, given the need to practice some price discrimination in order to avoid financial deficits. To put it in more technical terms, decreasing costs required Ramsey pricing, in line with the inverse-elasticity rule. Although a violation of sustainability would merely alter the price vector to a new set of Ramsey prices, the Baumol group's term *sustainability* and their usage of it suggested instead that the utility firm's own existence was threatened by the entry of a single-output firm. Therefore their analysis wrongly implied that utility firms such as AT&T should be protected from new competition (a lesson that fitted AT&T's corporate point of view).

Contestability also seemed to identify a vulnerability of AT&T to new competition. As Chapter 11 noted, the theory holds where a new entrant can replace the incumbent firm entirely, at a stroke, by offering only a small price advantage. Long-distance service seems to present such a case: AT&T provides the network, and a newcomer could (in theory) simply offer lower prices and suddenly evict AT&T from its own system! Since MCI and Sprint did offer lower prices, the contestability concept seemed to justify letting AT&T make whatever pricing changes were appropriate to keep from being totally eliminated.

In fact, as noted earlier, MCI, Sprint, and AT&T's other competitors have only made modest inroads on AT&T's dominance, even after ten years of setting prices 20 percent or more below AT&T's, this despite the fact that the FCC (over AT&T's protests) has adopted policies that give customers an unbiased set of choices among suppliers. Contestability theory would have led one to expect the newcomers to cut deeply into AT&T's market share within a year or two, if not within months.

What went wrong with contestability in this case? Mainly customer loyalty, based on decades of previous experience. Technically, a customer's change from AT&T to a rival was trivially easy, and often economically sound. But price has not proved a decisive factor for most users, even those who stood to gain the most. By advertising, direct contact, and general reputation, AT&T had created customer loyalty, and it enhanced that loyalty after competitors were allowed into the market by intensifying its advertising and direct marketing.

So a physical feature (ease of switching between telephone companies) was erroneously thought to provide easy economic entry when the real barriers lay elsewhere—in other bottlenecks and in customers' reluctance to change. Ordinarily, changes occur by degree, taking extended periods and often halting after only moderate degrees of transfer. Nonetheless, the FCC chose to regard long-distance competition as already strong and the dangers of selective pricing as weak. Therefore it removed regulation in 1989, replacing it with "price caps."

Bulk Supply of Electricity

Another important deregulation case is bulk electricity supply. It is now well recognized that meaningful bulk electricity markets exist in various regions and could be opened up for competition.[7] Many of them are capable of effective competition, with relatively low concentration and a variety of comparable cost sources of supply. Moreover, there would be a variety of buyers of power, many large enough to exert strong pressure against any tendencies to collusion among the sellers.

But vertical integration between the transmission and retail-distribution levels currently blocks the emergence of effective competition. The integrated private companies are both (1) the major suppliers of bulk power at the transmission level and (2) powerful rivals of publicly owned systems at the retail level. This permits the private systems to control their retail rivals' access to bulk supplies and to set or manipulate the prices they charge those rivals for their key input. Accordingly, the playing field is not level.

Only if integration were dissolved would bulk supply markets have a chance to become effectively competitive. Some initial steps in that direction may be emerging in areas involving Chicago, Virginia, and New York. Moreover, there have been experiments in bulk supply marketing in the Southwest, and monopsony pressure is being developed by public system pooled buying in other regions. But it will take added changes, such as divestiture, to set the basis for fully effective competition.

Even if that happens, regulators will still need to define markets and retain controls on firms that hold dominant positions. Electric markets may be difficult to define sharply, because power can be transmitted over long distances at graduated cost differences. Therefore dominance may be hard to identify and control.

It may be necessary, instead, to treat transmission as a core service, dividing it out to be coordinated in a separate nationwide transmission entity, or possibly in several regional systems. Access could then be open and fair, and dominance in bulk supply would cease to be a problem.

Dominance in retail distribution of power would remain, however, and the standard criteria would apply. Price constraints would still be needed, and service responsibility and obligations to serve peripheral areas would continue to apply. Diversification would be restricted, including takeovers by firms located in other markets.

Since competition in both bulk and retail electricity is still limited, the practical criteria for deregulating either level have to be imprecise at this point. But if competition does develop, the basic criteria will provide useful guidelines for the eventual deregulation.

---

[7] The classic articles are by James E. Meeks, "Concentration in the Electric Power Industry: The Impact of Antitrust Policy," *Columbia Law Review* January 1972, pp. 64–130; and Leonard W. Weiss, "Antitrust in the Electric Power Industry," in Almarin Phillips, ed., *Promoting Competition in Regulated Markets* (Washington, D.C.: Brookings Institution, 1975). See also Paul Joskow and Richard Schmalensee, *Electric Power Markets* (Cambridge, Mass.: MIT Press, 1984).

III. PUBLIC ENTERPRISE[8]

A public enterprise is owned by the state, on behalf of the citizenry. It can be identical to private firms in every respect, other than having private stockholders. It uses inputs to produce outputs, and it keeps thorough accounts of costs, revenues, and profits. But despite these parallels, the public firm need not maximize its profits as a private firm does. It may pursue other goals, and so its economic performance may differ sharply from that of a private firm. Therein lies the fascination of public enterprise, for it offers a wide variety of possibilities and outcomes.

1. Coverage and Purposes

The United States differs from other Western economies chiefly in the low share of public enterprise in its utilities, industry, and finance. The typical pattern in Western economies is (1) *utilities,* entirely or mainly publicly owned; (2) *finance,* one or several public banks; (3) *insurance,* large social insurance programs; (4) *industry,* several major industries under partial public ownership; (5) *social services,* mainly under public ownership; and (6) *distribution,* with little public enterprise.

Public enterprise exists in many parts of the U.S. economy. There is a great variety of forms and behavior, ranging from conventional utility cases, such as the Tennessee Valley Authority, to industrial and service areas, over into certain subsidy programs, and into important *social* enterprises such as public schools and universities, mental hospitals, the courts, and prisons. Yet these public enterprises tend to be a phantom presence in the United States, not recognized for what they really are.

There are many reasons for creating public firms, but the most valid normative reason is that the enterprise can serve some social purpose a private firm would ignore or violate. This social purpose usually falls under the following headings:

1. *Social preference.* A society (city, state, or country) may simply prefer public to private control, especially for certain prominent sectors. Such cultural preferences seem to explain much of the great variation among countries.

2. *Inadequate private supply.* A new industry or project may seem too large and risky for private firms to invest in. They will demand government guarantees, grants, or other subsidies. It may seem wiser to put the unit under direct public ownership.

3. *Salvaging firms.* The public often "rescues" failing firms by buying out their capital and supporting their rehabilitation. There are always new candidates for such salvage operations. Some are valid. But they tend to burden the public with sick industries that absorb large subsidies.

4. *External impacts.* Public firms may allow for outside social harms or benefits that private firms ignore. In the extreme, the service may be a pure public good calling for a full subsidy.

5. *Sovereignty.* A country may take over the local branches of large international firms in order to neutralize their power.

The typical public firm, therefore, has a *social element* to serve, which is apart

---

[8] For a survey of economic issues relating to public enterprise, see W. G. Shepherd and associates, *Public Enterprise: Economic Analysis of Theory and Practice* (Lexington, Mass.: Heath, 1976); and Shepherd, *Public Policies Toward Business.*

from its usual commercial goals of producing its services efficiently and selling them at prices that fit cost and demand conditions. For example, a local bus line is supposed to provide reliable service throughout the city, on a more extensive schedule than a strictly commercial bus line would provide.

The social element is usually debated intensely, both its nature and its extent. What social element is provided by the Postal Service, for instance? And does it require daily deliveries, including Saturday? Should "junk mail" be subsidized? If so, to what extent? You may have noticed the ongoing controversies over Amtrak's services, library hours, parks, and city sports stadiums used by professional teams.

Quieter debates continue constantly about city services, public schools and universities, airports, golf courses, state liquor stores in 16 states, and all other public enterprises. In every case, the questions are: What is the valid social element? How much of it should the public pay for?

2. Subsidies and efficiency

The public pays by means of subsidies, which come from government tax revenues. The subsidy can be any amount, ranging from 100 percent to zero. Thus, the public schools are subsidized totally from taxes, while local water supply is paid for by the users. Most public universities are in between, supported partly by government subsidies and partly by students' tuition payments.

The subsidy ought to be fitted precisely to the social element of the public firm. A small social effect requires little or no subsidy, while a large social element might justify a total subsidy. Total subsidy means that the direct users pay nothing; the taxpayers pay for it all.

There are two dangers from subsidies to public firms.

Size.   One is that the subsidy will simply be too large, giving the users an undeserved free ride. Should library users, or local golfers on the public course, or bus riders, or students at public universities be subsidized heavily? Does the service meet a special social need? Are the users really needier than the cross-section of taxpayers?

Incentives.   The second risk from subsidies is that they will weaken the enterprise's incentives to cut costs. Whenever costs can be covered without effort, the firm may let them rise. The subsidy can become a self-creating device. Public firms as diverse as city transit, the Postal Service, and Medicare are regularly accused of such wasteful and demoralizing subsidies.

These dangers are real, and they have no universal solution. Society must struggle along with its public enterprises, trying to fit the subsidies to the true social element and trying to avoid wasteful incentives. If the political process works well, it may supervise the firms effectively and trim their subsidies to just the right patterns. Public enterprises can go beyond the narrow limits of profit to serve genuine public needs. But this capacity needs constant control to keep the firms from wasteful mistakes.

Public enterprises come under the same rules for efficient pricing that private firms do. Their prices should be aligned with their marginal costs (including social costs), just as for regulated utilities. Many public firms do, in fact, adopt efficient price structures, carefully measuring marginal costs and setting prices in line with them. The task is easier because the firms are not subject to the special biases—from monopoly power and cost-plus-profit regulation—that privately owned utilities have.

IV. THE PRIVATIZATION OF PUBLIC FIRMS[9]

The "publicness" of firms depends on their ownership, the degree of outside subsidy and control, and the kind of policies the firm takes (e.g., strict profit maximizing or pursuing some public purposes). During 1950–1980, the degree of public enterprise in the United States and Western Europe was roughly stable.

But the 1980s saw an ideologically inspired program in Britain to put public firms into private hands. The Thatcher government had made major changes by 1986, including privatizing the telephone system, gas supply, intercity buses, British Airways airline, the ports, the airports, and British Steel. As of 1989, there are plans to sell off even the electricity and water systems. This push to privatize was echoed in Japan and certain other countries. The United States made only modest changes, despite the ideological leanings of the Reagan Administration.

The experience suggests interesting lessons about the methods of privatizing public enterprises and the benefits realized from "getting the government out of the marketplace." The following summary only touches the main points of a large, growing literature.[10]

Privatizing can take either or both of two directions, in economic terms: (1) *ownership can be shifted to private hands* and/or (2) *entry by new private rivals can be permitted.* By itself, private ownership only shifts managements toward a tighter profit orientation. Unless competition is effective, the privatized firm's actions can be doubly harmful: there will be monopoly pricing and retarded innovation, *plus* a withdrawal of the public firm's allowances for social impacts. A pure sell-off is therefore only appropriate when competition will be effective and the social elements are negligible.

The alternative method of privatizing is simply to open up entry in a way that maximizes competitive pressure as new private firms come in. It will succeed only

---

[9] This section draws on William G. Shepherd, "Public Enterprise: Criteria and Cases," a chapter in Henry W. de Jong, ed., *The Structure of European Industry,* 2d ed. (Dordrecht, The Netherlands: Kluwer Academic Publishers, 1988).

[10] See H. Abromeit, *British Steel (New York: St. Martin's Press, 1986);* Y. Aharoni, *The Evolution and Management of State-Owned Enterprises* (Cambridge, Mass.: Ballinger, 1986); Beesley and Littlechild, "Privatisation: Principles, Problems and Priorities," pp. 1–20; S. Domberger, and J. Piggott, "Privatization Policies and Public Enterprise: A Survey," *Economic Record,* (June 1986), pp. 145–162; S. M. Jaffer, and D. J. Thompson, "Deregulating Express Coaches: A Reassessment," *Fiscal Studies,* 7 (November 1986), 45–68; J. A. Kay, and D. J. Thompson, "Privatisation: A Policy in Search of a Rationale," *The Economic Journal,* 96 (March 1986), 18–32; J. A. Kay, C. Mayer, and D. Thompson eds., *Privatization and Regulation: The UK Experience* (Oxford: The Clarendon Press, 1986); R. Molyneux and D. Thompson, "Nationalised Industry Performance: Still Third-Rate?," *Fiscal Studies,* 8 (February 1987), 48–82; D. Steel and D. Heald, eds., *Privatizing Public Enterprises: Options and Dilemmas* (London: Royal Institute of Public Administration, 1984); and J. Vickers, and G. Yarrow, *Privatization and the Natural Monopolies* (London: Public Policy Centre, 1985). See also the symposium on Privatization in the *Journal of Policy Analysis and Management,* 6 (Summer 1987).

if entry is really free and the new competitors are forceful. Paradoxically, that very situation makes a sell-off unnecessary: the existing tight competition will force an efficient and innovative result even if the firm's ownership remains public. Free entry is therefore both necessary and sufficient for successful privatization, while a sell-off is neither! The British literature has noted the need for competition, but the British government's policies have not succeeded in creating it.

British privatizing since 1979 has shrunk the set of failing firms that had been taken over in earlier rescues. That may provide public benefits, by reducing the costs of covering deficits incurred by poor private management. But the main change has been simply a selling off of ownership that is inspired chiefly by ideology and by pressures from investor groups seeking to make capital gains for themselves. Some privatized firms have indeed faced strong competition: British Rail Hotels and Jaguar (automobiles) are examples. The dominant firms have been much more numerous, however, and they have had it much easier. There are many optimistic predictions of powerful entry into their supposedly "contestable" markets, and the whole campaign is actually turning into a series of experiments in entry.

Still, in many of these cases actual entry has been slight and easily repelled. In both telephone service and equipment supply, for example, British Telecom has largely maintained its previous monopoly position. Its strategic pricing of service against new entry by the much smaller Mercury has successfully confined Mercury to a small, weak position. In equipment, British Telecom has reputational advantages that have also prevented any large rivals from emerging.

British Gas has had the same experience: competition against it is ineffective. In inner-city bus travel, the virtual monopoly of the incumbent National Express was not sold off, but new entry was opened in 1980. Though many small chartered bus firms existed as a source of new entry into regular lines, actual entry has been slight. National Express has controlled access to terminals and has applied strategic pricing effectively to minimize the inroads of new bus rivals.

The sell-off of British Airways has also failed to generate effective competition or new entry. The firm faces little competition on its domestic routes, and in 1987, it actually sought to buy out British Caledonian, its one rival. Its control of airport access in Britain as well as its use of strategic pricing has protected its virtual monopoly, with predictable results in keeping fares at high levels. British Airways has also continued the long-standing collusion with its rivals in international routes, so as to resist entry and maintain fare levels.

Taken together, the British experiments demonstrate that effective competition is unlikely to develop in monopolized markets, so the privatized incumbent is able to sustain monopoly behavior. The U.K. Monopolies and Mergers Commission has had little effect in overcoming these problems, while efforts to apply some form of regulation by government agencies have been largely empty. Therefore privatization has failed to deliver competitive results in markets with market power.

Moreover, the government has commonly underpriced the stocks issued to the private buyers, so that private investors have reaped windfall gains at the expense of the public treasury. The pressures to underprice the shares are strong, both from the prospective buyers and from the government's anxiety to ensure that all of the shares are sold.

On the whole, the privatizing programs have provided some improvements for firms operating in competitive markets that have small social elements. But these cases have been the relatively minor ones in Britain, and the selling off of firms with dominant positions (especially in utility markets) has not succeeded in establishing competitive conditions and benefits.

There is certainly a need for variety and experimentation in industrial markets, but the effort to convert utilities into unregulated competitive private firms is an exercise in illusion. It requires a very careful balancing of ownership, entry support and regulation, under favorable conditions.

V.   SUMMARY

Regulation is a unique U.S. policy. It attempts to limit private firms to zero excess profits and to efficient price structures. Although there are economic guidelines for these decisions, the regulatory commissions still have to make rough decisions and compromises much of the time.

Marginal cost pricing is usually the correct guide for efficient pricing, but it often conflicts with the utility's preferences. Peak-load pricing is being increasingly applied in electricity and telephones.

Regulation may induce various kinds of inefficiencies. It may also need to be removed as the sector evolves back toward natural competition. But that transition requires a delicate balance between competition and control.

Public enterprises commonly have a social element as well as commercial operations. Any public subsidy needs to be fitted to this social element. The danger is that the subsidy will diverge from that level and sap the firm's incentives for efficiency.

The actual performance of public enterprises ranges from excellent to poor. Good performance usually denotes careful supervision and clear economic guidance.

Privatizing is usually a complex task, not well achieved merely by selling assets or permitting new entry.

QUESTIONS FOR REVIEW

1. "Federal regulation uses reproduction cost in valuing the rate base because that method makes the best economic sense." True?
2. "Regulatory issues have grown more complex and intense since 1965." True?
3. "Regulation operates by an adversary process, with debate among the conflicting interests." True?
4. "In setting the floor under the permitted rate of return, the commission can consider risk-return conditions or other criteria." True?
5. "Utility firms are usually able to practice some discrimination in pricing." True?
6. "There are no simple criteria that clearly mark off the sectors that should be regulated." True?
7. "Marginal cost is usually the proper guideline for setting efficient price structures." True?

8. "Regulation can encourage X-inefficiency because it operates on a cost-plus basis." True?

9. "The rate-base effect is likely to reduce the amount of investment by regulated firms, but it has not as yet had a large impact." True?

10. "New entrants will naturally try to compete first in the 'creamy' markets." True?

11. "Utilities have no interest in discriminatory pricing because they have official monopoly franchises." True?

12. Does regulation operate by clear formulas about "fair" rates of return and "just and reasonable" price structures?

13. What types of industries should be regulated?

14. Why should prices for utility services usually be higher at peak than off-peak times?

15. Explain why regulation may induce waste of capital, as well as X-inefficiency.

16. The price of long-distance phone calls usually varies with the time of the call. Explain how this price variation could encourage an efficient allocation of resources.

17. Explain what "price caps" are and how they contrast with traditional "rate-base" regulation. Under what conditions will they work well (e.g., numbers and complexities of outputs, similarities of price trends in the economy, and knowledge about technological progress)? Or poorly?

18. For deregulation to be effective, what criteria must be met, especially about market shares? Do those standards square with the competitive conditions we have discussed throughout this book?

19. Explain how deregulation might eliminate service to small towns, such as for telephone, bus, electricity and airline service. Has this generally happened?

20. Discuss the two elements of successful "privatization:" private ownership *and* effective competition. Choose an actual public enterprise in the US. Do you think it could be effectively privatized? Should that be tried?

21 FURTHER STUDY

The field you have now surveyed is turbulent, important, and fascinating. Learning the current technical concepts and terms was just the first step. You also learned to see how they are evolving, and how they apply to changing industrial conditions. This book has, I hope, helped you to understand complex economic problems and feel the exhilaration of dealing with colossal corporations and immense interests as routine, everyday matters.

By completing this course, you have extended your knowledge on several planes. You have learned the greater part of a new language, with technical terms and standards. The main lines of a large body of literature are now familiar to you. You are beginning to know how to test concepts and where to go for data on the subject. And you have acquired a certain amount of factual knowledge about United States and foreign conditions.

This has helped you achieve a more professional level of understanding. You should now be able to make sense of many journal articles and monographs by specialists, except perhaps for the most advanced. Better, you can apply a critical sense to these writings, judging for yourself how valid they are. You should be able to design ways to test concepts and industrial conditions, fitting the methods to the kinds of evidence available. And, of course, you are now keenly aware of how ignorant the experts are on many issues.

It is your level of skill that matters, not the specific views you now hold about competition and its effects. One's ratings of the quantitative "answers" must always be provisional rather than final. The evidence is usually weak, requiring a careful weighing of probabilities. Also, as new data emerge, old opinions must often be revised, and sometimes discarded. One can only strive to use valid methods, on a professional level of quality. You are now able to do that. Some of your research papers (or "term papers") will be almost as good as some of those published in the journals.

Recognize this skill as a blessing, for it will enable you to handle the issues intelligently from now on. A few of you will go on to professional research careers in this field. Many of you will follow careers in law, business, accounting, or public agencies. They, too, will involve you deeply in the issues. The rest of you will face the problems described here month in and month out for at least forty years, as the issues develop and your own interests evolve. Understanding the nature of the "competitive system"—as it changes and you change—will be one of your continuing tasks. You can now approach it skillfully and skeptically.

APPENDIX 1

HISTORY OF THE FIELD

This appendix is only a bare summary of the fascinating, turbulent history of the economics of industrial organization. It tries to animate the details in the rest of the book and to give some perspective on where trends and events are heading.

1. Early Origins

We cannot go back to the true beginnings, because they are lost in antiquity. We must conjecture. Through many millennia the members of early tribes surely struggled over who should control their meager weapons, tools, and land. The growth of settled cultivation must have made it possible for some clever members to gain larger holdings. Trade in grains and implements would also have provided large gains, from price-fixing by concerted action or by outright monopoly.

As ancient towns and then cities grew in the Middle East and elsewhere, and as production diversified, the problem of monopoly undoubtedly became chronic. When the Code of Hammurabi, king of Babylon, included references to monopolistic practices in approximately 2100 B.C., these practices were already many centuries old.[1] The functioning of markets was also well advanced. The Egyptian kingdoms contained a variety of enterprises and conditions of market power, most of them under state and religious control. King Solomon's mines are just one example.

The preclassical Greek states—especially Corinth—began to develop true entrepreneurial ventures, and they also bristled with private and city-based efforts to seize control of markets. Military excursions became a form of enterprise, along with the more traditional trading. By 480–420 B.C., when Athens reached its zenith, operations of banking, industry, and public utilities were well advanced. There were also elaborate rules aimed at preventing monopoly exploitation, as frequent judicial hearings and penalties attest. The large-scale Athenian silver mines at Larium were under a measure of state control.

---

[1] Herodotus and Xenophon are among the few primary sources of information about early market conditions in the Greek city-states and elsewhere. Among good summaries, try Humphrey Mitchell, *The Economics of Ancient Greece* (New York: Macmillan, 1940); and George M. Calhoun, *The Business Life of Ancient Athens* (Chicago: University of Chicago Press, 1926).

The Romans greatly increased the range of "industrial" activities and the scale of production in the ancient world. And throughout early Rome, the Republic, and the Empire, problems of monopoly were routine and serious.[2] Much later, in A.D. 483, the edict of the Emperor Zeno prohibited all monopolies, combinations, and price agreements; the Code of Justinian in the year 533 attempted much the same, perhaps with no more success.

The Dark Ages were marked by a descent into localism, the eclipse of large-scale production and markets, a decline in entrepreneurship. Market controls were embedded throughout in feudal and religious systems of power. The early renaissance after 1000 had two main features: trading among areas, and merchant guilds and crafts. Though it was 1600 before coal and iron works in Britain brought early industrial growth, monopoly and collusion were chronic in the feudal setting and the Middle Ages. "Forestalling, engrossing and regrating" had long been held to be crimes under common law when a statute of Edward I in 1285 formally prohibited them.

The rising monarchies in Western Europe tended to replace the guilds by means of direct monopoly grants to nobles, corporations, and court favorites, as well as to inventors.[3] Queen Elizabeth did this frequently from 1560 to 1603. The tide did reverse enough so that in 1623 Parliament enacted a Statute of Monopolies forbidding most such grants. Still, the 1500–1770 period was "mercantilist," with a range of policies by which monarchs sought to control or alter markets. The restrictions were aimed at increasing the national treasure in gold, even at the expense of production and trade. Yet by 1700, the essential rudiments of modern markets were widespread in Western Europe and its colonies. Massachusetts, among others, in 1641 and 1779 formally opposed monopoly, and the common law firmly recognized the problem and prohibited it.

Events in the 1770s upset the mercantilist orthodoxy favoring restrictions. The British "Industrial Revolution" began, and Adam Smith's *Wealth of Nations* at one stroke established classical economics, with its stress on free trade.[4] Smith developed the *harmoniedoktrine* of the "invisible hand": If each individual sought personal gain, the economy would reach the best outcome for society as a whole. Yet this would work only if markets were competitive and free from political controls. Competition was therefore an essential part of classical economic thought.

America's breakaway from Britain also opened its markets to freer conditions of competition. By 1850, industrialization was stirring in the United States, France, and Germany. The railway booms of 1840–1890 bred heavy metalworking and engineering industries. They also widened local markets into national ones. Capital markets were rapidly developing. Though full of trickery and instability, especially in the United States, they were making the financing of large-scale industrial ventures possible. Certain "utilities" were already of long standing—town gas, water, highways, postal service, canals—but the modern electricity and telephone "utilities" burst on the scene in the 1870s.

[2] On Rome, one begins with Edward Gibbon's *Decline and Fall of the Roman Empire*. There are also several more recent surveys to choose from.
[3] See Charles W. Cole, *Colbert and a Century of French Mercantilism* (New York: Columbia University Press, 1939); and William H. Price, *The English Patents of Monopoly* (Boston: Houghton Mifflin, 1906).
[4] Adam Smith, *Wealth of Nations* (New York: Modern Library).

The widening of markets from 1865 to 1900 increased competition, often radically.[5] But western railroads themselves posed the classic monopoly problems, with extreme price discrimination, excess profits, and a degree of internal inefficiency that was often extraordinary. The main "evils of monopoly" were fully demonstrated and familiar to the public and to the handful of economists concerned with the problem.

By 1890, the western railroad monopolies had been joined by the Standard Oil Company and other new industrial monopolies. Indeed, railroad rebates had helped breed Standard Oil's monopoly. The struggle between Main Street and Wall Street—small business versus high finance and large industry—became intense. Each financial panic or genuine depression had a disastrous effect on small companies, as large firms used seemingly "unfair" tactics to increase their power. Tariffs and other public support seemed also to be directed mainly for the benefit of large firms.

In any event, by the 1880s, the preconditions of modern industrial society existed in the United States. Meanwhile, neoclassical economics had developed rapidly. *Marginal productivity* and *marginal utility* were the new language, and the competitive equilibrium conditions were worked out in great detail. This strengthened economists' belief that market processes would generate a social optimum. Monopoly was seen as an odd departure from what was essentially a competitive process. Wedded to social Darwinism, this belief led conservative economists to regard actual firms as fit and efficient, the products of an economic process of natural selection.

2.   To 1945

The next two decades (1890 to 1910) were crucial in three ways. (1) The emerging competitive conditions of industry shifted sharply toward monopoly, especially in the United States. (2) The study of industrial organization advanced quickly. (3) Public policies in the United States crystallized in antitrust and regulation, along lines sharply different from those in other countries.

From 1894 to 1901, an extraordinary series of mergers created near-monopolies in hundreds of industries, many of them small but some large.[6] Many of the mergers were arranged by large-scale financiers, such as J. P. Morgan and the Rockefeller brothers. A crisis in public concern and policy ensued. There were authoritative claims that "consolidation" was necessary to attain modern efficiency. But there was severe anxiety that the monopolists were simply setting out to exploit the populace (and, indeed, many of them were). Above the concerns about individual markets were deepening fears that a Morgan and Rockefeller "money trust" might come to control the whole economy. Actually, some of the new corporations formed by the mergers faded away rather quickly.

---

[5] For U.S. background, see Gilbert C. Fite and Jim E. Reese, *An Economic History of the United States,* 3rd ed. (Boston: Houghton Mifflin, 1973); Ralph Gray and John M. Peterson, *Economic Development of the United States,* rev. ed. (Homewood, Ill.: Irwin, 1974); and Hans Thorelli, *The Federal Antitrust Policy* (Stockholm: P. A. Norstedt and Sons, 1954).

[6] Some details of this first merger wave are given in Chapter 8. For background, see Frederick Lewis Allen, *The Great Pierpont Morgan* (New York: Harper & Row, 1949); William Z. Ripley, ed., *Trusts, Pools and Corporations* (Boston: Ginn, 1916); John Moody, *The Truth about the Trusts* (Chicago: Moody Publishing, 1904); and G. W. Stocking and M. W. Watkins, *Monopoly and Free Enterprise* (New York: Twentieth Century Fund, 1951).

The Sherman Act, passed in 1890, was applied in the 1890s to stop most collusive price-fixing, and in 1911 to take apart the very large Standard Oil and American Tobacco companies. Such "trust-busting" actions toward many other dominant firms also advanced between 1910 and 1917, but they were mostly ended by World War I and the 1920s shift back to "normalcy." From 1920 to 1937, antitrust activity virtually stopped.

State regulation of privately owned utilities had become the norm by 1920, often because the utility firms had lobbied for it. This policy prevented any major experiments with public ownership of electricity and telephones (though many city gas and light plants remained). The concept of "natural monopoly" in regulated utilities became firmly fixed.[7]

Meanwhile, the 1894–1901 trust wave stirred new thinking about the causes, forms, and effects of monopoly. At several universities such leading economists as J. B. Clark, Richard T. Ely, and William Z. Ripley began analyzing them in some depth.[8] The Bureau of Corporations made a series of thorough factual studies of the leading trusts—Standard Oil, American Tobacco, U.S. Steel, and others—as part of the antitrust effort. Yet many other economists regarded the monopoly problem as trivial. Their optimism reflected the attitudes of social Darwinism and the neoclassical marginal utility analysis.[9]

Most observers took it for granted that market share was the key element of monopoly. The concept of economies of scale was prominent, and many writers soon recognized the difference between technical and pecuniary economies. The role of the financial sector and of specific financiers in shaping market structure and behavior was given due weight. It was widely recognized that leading firms would often try to coordinate their prices and market shares, as they had in the steel, meatpacking, pipe, and many other industries. This predated the 1930s theories about oligopoly. The understanding of "utilities" was also quite sophisticated and realistic by 1915.

By 1921, there were two strands of thought and research. One was *neoclassical*. It stressed the efficiency of the competitive system. It also relied on highly abstract analysis.[10] The other approach was more *realistic*. It embraced the variety of conditions actually posed by monopoly and the mass of new information about its real-world roles. The neoclassical approach led to the complacent conviction that competition prevailed and that performance could not be improved.

The 1920s brought a second merger craze, fed by a stock market boom. Many industries were converted into tight oligopolies. There was also a bizarre, frantic

[7] See Martin Glaeser, *Public Utilities in American Capitalism* (New York: Macmillan, 1957); and Irston R. Barnes, *The Economics of Public Utility Regulation* (New York: Crofts, 1942). Chapter 20 of this textbook gives a concise review of regulatory policies.

[8] For a splendid summary, see Charles J. Bullock, "Trust Literature: A Survey and Criticism," *Quarterly Journal of Economics*, 15 (February 1901), 167–217, where many of the present-day concepts are lucidly covered. Other good studies of the time include William Z. Ripley, ed., *Trusts, Pools and Corporations*, rev. ed. (Boston: Ginn, 1916).

[9] The best known of these academic apologists for the trusts were William Graham Summer, Jeremiah Jenks, and John Bates Clark; see the excellent brief history of the field by Almarin Phillips and Rodney E. Stevenson, "The Historical Development of Industrial Organization," *History of Political Economy*, 6 (Fall 1974), 324–42.

[10] For a good survey, see George J. Stigler, "Perfect Competition, Historically Contemplated," *Journal of Political Economy*, 65 (February 1957), 1–17.

series of utility mergers and pyramiding. The stock market collapse in 1929 accentuated the descent into the Depression of the 1930s. This stirred an overreaction, in which oligopoly came to be emphasized as *the* problem.

The "realistic" approach now came to the fore, with new evidence and more detailed theories about the intermediate degrees of oligopoly. The importance of large corporations was explored by Adolf Berle and Gardiner Means. They argued that the largest firms were capturing an increasing share of the economy and that they were becoming units of unconstrained power. But technical analysis also began strongly. Edward Chamberlin and Joan Robinson staked out oligopoly and its price effects as the major new frontier for theory.[11] The Depression, the rise of the corporate state in Europe, and a seeming rise in American industrial monopoly lent the whole topic a stark urgency.

It is from this ferment of rethinking and rhetoric during the 1930s that the modern field of industrial organization emerged. Though the field has old roots, it took form only about six decades ago. It began to crystallize and grow in the 1930s as a major topic, with new theories, new measures of actual economic concentration, and a deep social concern about the nature of modern capitalism. In 1939, the first set of concentration ratios for industries (for the year 1935) were published. Data on prices, costs, output, and other industry features also began to be issued. All these fostered new statistical studies, with oligopoly concentration as the centerpiece.

Out of the 1930s, therefore, came a focus on industry conditions and on concentration. This differed from the earlier focus on individual firms and their market shares. In fact, the *industry* replaced the firm as the locus for thought and research. Meanwhile, Edward S. Mason was leading a group of young specialists at Harvard toward intensive case studies of specific industries, as a different mode of research.

Antitrust was revived after 1937, partly in the hope of turning back the seeming tide of monopoly and reducing the collusion that the new analysis of oligopoly had highlighted. The electricity and banking industries also underwent searching exposés from 1929 to 1935, and new laws had by 1940 largely frozen their structure and sealed them off from other sectors. World War II cooled the antitrust effort (just as World War I had cut off the earlier wave), and it fostered industrial controls, cooperation, and planning. In 1942, Joseph Schumpeter launched a powerful defense of monopoly: that it was a necessary part of the creative process of competition, not a mere distortion from efficient allocation.[12]

3. To the 1970s

The year 1945 marked a watershed, a change in context. The war's end started the long, unexpected postwar boom, which restored much of the shaken faith in the competitive private economy. The study of oligopoly spread, with the new theory of games as a focus.

---

[11] A. A. Berle and G. C. Means, *The Modern Corporation and Private Property* (New York: Macmillan, 1932; rev. ed., Harcourt, Brace & World, 1968); Edward H. Chamberlin, *The Theory of Monopolistic Competition* (Cambridge, Mass.: Harvard University Press, 1933; 8th ed., 1965); Joan Robinson, *The Economics of Imperfect Competition* (London: Macmillan, 1933); and Arthur R. Burns, *The Decline of Competition* (New York: McGraw-Hill, 1936).

[12] Joseph A. Schumpeter, *Capitalism, Socialism and Democracy* (New York: Harper, 1942).

The *Alcoa* decision in 1945 (convicting the Aluminum Company of America of monopoly) seemed to restore a strict antitrust policy against dominant firms. The *American Tobacco* decision of 1946 seemed to reach further, to prohibit even "tacit" or "implicit" oligopoly collusion. Here the Supreme Court moved to apply the "new" thinking about tight oligopoly, as a form of "shared monopoly." This was quick work. Usually, new research ideas take at least twenty years to be absorbed by the courts.

More major suits against dominant firms followed, involving IBM, AT&T, Du Pont, and others. Yet little was in fact accomplished and the whole effort petered out after 1952. Public confidence in the competitive economy was reviving, and George Stigler, Morris Adelman, Fred Weston, and Warren Nutter now sought to reverse the 1930s thinking by showing that the U.S. economy was still quite competitive. A study by Arnold Harberger suggested that the misallocation caused by monopoly cost the economy only 0.2 percent of national income—a trivial sum.[13] Such studies, and the temper of the times, bred faith in big business and confidence that economies of scale were actually large in many industries.

The two new beliefs—that there was low monopoly and that big business achieved high economies of scale—encouraged optimism, even complacency. These ideas became firmly fixed in the new Chicago-UCLA School, which has flourished ever since. Monopoly was said to be scarce, and to occur only where scale economies justified it. Furthermore, John Kenneth Galbraith's *American Capitalism* in 1952 extended Schumpeter's defense of monopoly into a version of praise for oligopoly. Tight oligopoly might be rigid, he noted, but it would be limited vertically by the countervailing power of powerful buyers. As a result, oligopoly prices could be forced down to competitive levels and oligopoly innovation would be rapid.

In a landmark book of 1956, Joe S. Bain developed certain parts of oligopoly theory and added the idea of barriers to entry by potential competitors.[14] The height of barriers would determine the scope for oligopolists to behave like shared monopolists. They could set prices to limit entry, but low barriers would keep such "limit prices" low. Gardiner Means and John Blair urged that large oligopolies did in fact behave like shared monopolies, setting "administered prices." In 1959, Carl Kaysen and Donald F. Turner's *Antitrust Policy* gave estimates that tight oligopoly was widespread and costly. They proposed major new laws and efforts to reduce it to loose oligopoly. Meanwhile, industrial growth faltered from 1957 to 1960, so doubts about the character of industry revived.

By 1960, the field was rich in concepts about the elements of structure—market shares, concentration, entry barriers, vertical power, and so forth. Opinions about

---

[13] These represent the best of the Chicago-UCLA School. The original Chicagoans—Henry C. Simons and Frank H. Knight—praised the competitive system, but by the 1930s, they had also come to see monopoly as a genuine threat. The new breed has a fuller faith: To them monopoly in real markets can only be a small, transient deviation unless "the state" reinforces it. See especially George J. Stigler, *The Organization of Industry* (Homewood, Ill.: Irwin, 1968); Morris Adelman, "The Measurement of Industrial Concentration," *Review of Economics and Statistics,* 33 (November 1951), 269–96; and Arnold Harberger, "Monopoly and Resource Allocation," *American Economic Review,* 44 (May 1954), 77–87.

[14] Joe S. Bain, *Barriers to New Competition* (Cambridge, Mass.: Harvard University Press, 1956); see also his *Industrial Organization,* rev. ed. (New York: Wiley, 1968). To place Bain's use of barriers in perspective, see W. G. Shepherd, "Bain's Influence on Research into Industrial Organization," in Robert T. Masson and P. David Qualls, eds., *Essays in Industrial Organization in Honor of Joe S. Bain* (Cambridge, Mass.: Ballinger, 1976).

the extent and burdens of monopoly were widely divergent. The 1960s brought a variety of large econometric studies, covering the hundreds of manufacturing industries defined by the U.S. Census Bureau. They relied heavily on census concentration ratios (the combined share of the top four firms in each industry). These ratios are defective, so a great deal of the research was shaky. Yet the studies did begin to build up strong hints that market power was extensive and its costs were large, after all.[15]

The research suggested that concentration does raise prices above costs. Also, it appeared, invention and innovation tended to lag in giant firms and tight oligopoly rather than to be unusually active. Harberger's estimate of the misallocation burden was revised up by others toward 2 percent of national income. The statistical causation of market power's negative effects was not tightly proved by studies in the 1960s, but the normative burden of proof had shifted—on topic after topic—against market power.

Oliver Williamson, Robin Marris, and others analyzed the organizational features of large corporations further, looking closest at managers' tendencies to seek extra growth and even extra expenditures instead of maximum profits. Harvey Leibenstein's concept of X-inefficiency in 1966 crystallized the growing awareness that market power bred internal slack.[16]

Meanwhile a merger boom and "go-go" activities on Wall Street from 1964 to 1969 brought conglomerate mergers to the fore as an issue. Were such mergers dangerous, reducing competition and increasing total concentration in the economy? Or were they flimsy and inconsequential? Or were they, perhaps, quite beneficial, applying takeovers to stir sluggish firms and to create "synergy" among their parts? The whole problem stimulated new theorizing to explain these mergers and to estimate their effects. Though the merger boom collapsed after 1969, an even bigger one in the 1980s revived the issues.

In short, the field advanced during the 1960s toward richer theories and fuller evidence. The normative case against economic concentration grew stronger, and indeed the 1952–1968 lull in antitrust action was followed by several new efforts. Major antitrust suits against IBM, cereals companies, Xerox, and AT&T were filed from 1969 to 1974. These and other attacks on corporate bigness were stirred by the turbulent Vietnam War atmosphere of protest, by sharp inflation and recession, and by new evidence of corporate corruption and political abuses.

All the while, econometric analysis was going quite far in some directions, such as correlations between concentration and profit margins. The newer effort sought to improve the data themselves and to select samples more carefully. The use of large-scale econometric studies may have peaked in the 1960s.

4. Recent Developments

The 1970s and 1980s were another watershed period, comparable to the 1890–1910 era. A parallel field of "IO Theory" developed, and Chicago-UCLA ideas gained popularity. The economy itself became much more competitive than before,

---

[15] See W. G. Shepherd, *Market Power and Economic Welfare* (New York: Random House, 1970), and sources noted there.

[16] See Harvey Leibenstein, "Allocative Efficiency vs. 'X-Efficiency,' " *American Economic Review,* 56 (June 1966), 392–415; Oliver E. Williamson, *The Economics of Discretionary Behavior* (Chicago: Markham, 1967); and his *Markets and Hierarchies* (New York: Free Press, 1975); and Robin Marris, *The Economic Theory of "Managerial" Capitalism* (New York: Free Press, 1964).

as Chapters 1 and 4 note, and that realization gave impetus to actions to deregulate many sectors, ranging from banking to railroads. Antitrust was cut back sharply by Reagan officials at the Antitrust Division and the Federal Trade Commission. Only the big AT&T case led to important changes.

The field of industrial economies itself became far more conservative and vulnerable to doctrinal attack. One group (see Chapter 11) even asserts that potential entry will usually dominate actual monopolies. Such extreme views add interest to the field, but their challenge to mainstream concepts needs to be examined carefully.

The flow of research continues to expand, including a wide range of theory, empirical studies, case-by-case industry studies, and other approaches. The conservative trends may continue or reverse, depending on economic and "IO theory" and political events. In any case, the rise of competition and the shifts of policy have created fascinating new conditions whose effects will become visible in the 1990s.

APPENDIX 2

THE SIC SYSTEM

This appendix treats the census "standard industrial classification" (SIC) system.

The census system evolved over many decades. Special efforts to fit "industries" to actual market conditions began with the 1935 set of ratios. The definitions are revised occasionally as industries themselves change. About half of the four-digit industries are likely to be redefined during any 15-year period. This makes it difficult to maintain continuity in analyzing industries and trends. Yet the degree of fineness of detail does stay about the same, and therefore broad comparisons over time of the average degree of concentration are reasonably safe.[1]

The SIC system and its relation to actual markets are suggested by Tables A2.1 and A2.2. Both industries in Table A2.2 (drugs and automobiles) include numerous real markets: for example, there are probably at least eight markets within the drug industry, and buses, trucks, and snow plows are distinct from ordinary cars. In both cases in Table A2.2, the four-digit industry concentration ratio would need adjusting. First, one reestimates the true product and geographic markets, making a reasonable estimate of the average concentration in local markets. Then one inserts imports, if any, in the denominator.

Using the census report on the full set of ratios, you can do sample studies of (1) levels of average concentration, (2) shifts of the ratios for individual industries, (3) changes in industry definitions, and (4) changes in average concentration.

---

[1] For current details, see Office of Management and Budget, *Standard Industrial Classification Manual* (Washington, D.C.: U.S. Government Printing Office, 1987).

TABLE A2.1   The Complete Set of SIC Two-Digit Classifications

A. Agriculture, forestry, and fishing
   01. Agricultural production—crops
   02. Agricultural production livestock and animal specialties
   07. Agricultural services
   08. Forestry
   09. Fishing, hunting, and trapping
B. Mining
   10. Metal mining
   12. Coal mining
   13. Oil and gas extraction
   14. Mining and quarrying of nonmetallic minerals, except fuels
C. Construction
   15. Building construction—general contractors and operative builders
   16. Heavy construction other than building construction—contractors
   17. Construction—special trade contractors
D. Manufacturing
   20. Food and kindred products
   21. Tobacco products
   22. Textile mill products
   23. Apparel and other finished products made from fabrics and similar materials
   24. Lumber and wood products, except furniture
   25. Furniture and fixtures
   26. Paper and allied products
   27. Printing, publishing, and allied industries
   28. Chemicals and allied products
   29. Petroleum refining and related industries
   30. Rubber and miscellaneous plastics products
   31. Leather and leather products
   32. Stone, clay, glass, and concrete products
   33. Primary metal industries
   34. Fabricated metal products, except machinery and transportation equipment
   35. Industrial and commercial machinery and computer equipment
   36. Electronic and other electrical equipment and components, except computer equipment
   37. Transportation equipment
   38. Measuring, analyzing, and controlling instrumentts; photographic, medical and optical goods; watches and clocks
   39. Miscellaneous manufacturing industries
E. Transportation, communications, electric, gas, and sanitary services
   40. Railroad transportation
   41. Local and suburban transit and interurban highway passenger transportation
   42. Motor freight transportation and warehousing
   43. United States Postal Service
   44. Water transportation
   45. Transportation by air
   46. Pipelines, except natural gas
   47. Transportation services
   48. Communications
   49. Electric, gas, and sanitary services
F. Wholesale trade
   50. Wholesale trade—durable goods
   51. Wholesale trade—nondurable goods
G. Retail trade
   52. Building materials, hardware, garden supply, and mobile home dealers
   53. General merchandise stores
   54. Food stores
   55. Automotive dealers and gasoline service stations
   56. Apparel and accessory stores
   57. Home furniture, furnishings, and equipment stores
   58. Eating and drinking places
   59. Miscellaneous retail
H. Finance, insurance, and real estate
   60. Depository institutions
   61. Nondepository credit institutions
   62. Security and commodity brokers, dealers, exchanges, and services
   63. Insurance carriers
   64. Insurance agents, brokers, and service
   65. Real estate
   67. Holding and other investment offices

TABLE A2.1 (*continued*)

I. Services
- 70. Hotels, rooming houses, camps, and other lodging places
- 72. Personal services
- 73. Business services
- 75. Automotive repair, services, and parking
- 76. Miscellaneous repair services
- 78. Motion pictures
- 79. Amusement and recreation services
- 80. Health services
- 81. Legal services
- 82. Educational services
- 83. Social services
- 84. Museums, art galleries, and botanical and zoological gardens
- 86. Membership organizations
- 87. Engineering, accounting, research, management, and related services
- 88. Private households
- 89. Miscellaneous services

TABLE A2.2 Selected Details of Two Sample SIC Classifications

2834 Pharmaceutical Preparations

Adrenal pharmaceutical preparations
Analgesics
Anesthetics, packaged
Antacids
Antibiotics, packaged
Antihistamine preparations
Antiseptics, medicinal
Astringents, medicinal
Barbituric acid pharmaceutical preparations
Botanical extracts: powdered, pilular, solid, and fluid
Cold remedies
Dextrose injection
Digitalis pharmaceutical preparations
Diuretics
Emulsions, pharmaceutical
Ether for anesthetic use
Fever remedies
Galenical preparations
Hormone preparations
Insulin preparations
Intravenous solutions
Laxatives
Lozenges, pharmaceutical
Medicines, capsuled or ampuled
Nitrous oxide for anesthetic use
Ointments
Parenteral solutions
Penicillin preparations
Pituitary gland pharmaceutical preparations
Poultry and animal remedies
Procaine pharmaceutical preparations
Proprietary drug products
Sirups, pharmaceutical
Sodium salicylate tablets
Spirits, pharmaceutical
Suppositories
Thyroid preparations
Tranquilizers and mental drug preparations
Veterinary pharmaceutical preparations
Vitamin preparations
Zinc ointment

3711 Motor Vehicles and Passenger Car Bodies

Ambulances (motor vehicles)
Assembling complete automobiles, trucks, commercial cars, and buses
Automobiles
Bodies, passenger automobile
Brooms, powered (motor vehicles)
Cars, armored
Fire department vehicles (motor vehicles)
Flushers, street (motor vehicles)
Hearses (motor vehicles)
Mobile lounges (motor vehicles)
Motor buses, except trackless trolley
Motor trucks, except off-highway
Patrol wagons (motor vehicles)
Reconnaissance cars
Scout cars (motor vehicles)
Snowplows (motor vehicles)
Station wagons (motor vehicles)
Street sprinklers and sweepers (motor vehicles)
Taxicabs
Tractors, truck: for highway use

FINANCE, ACCOUNTING, AND DISCOUNTING

This summary barely touches the main issues. The ambitious student should consult good finance and accounting textbooks.

The firm generates a tangible stream of profits, with the managers trying—at least approximately!—to maximize the value of the firm for its owners. Investors meanwhile appraise the company's prospects and buy and sell the company's stock in capital markets. The firm acquires new capital (1) by plowing back retained earnings, or (2) by borrowing directly from its bankers, or (3) by issuing new bonds or stocks on the market. Several technical points about this process need clarifying.

1. The Cost of Capital: Sources of Funds

Money is converted by the firm into real assets and other inputs, which then generate more money as profits. Money has its price, which is a cost to the firm.

What determines the cost of capital? Two basic factors: (1) money market rates generally (e.g., high interest rates when money is "tight," low interest rates when credit is "easy"), and (2) the specific prospects of the firm. A really secure, lucrative firm is a "better risk," and therefore can get capital cheaper, both from its bankers directly and from issues floated on the capital markets.

The several sources of funds—internal funds, borrowings, debt, and equity—may seem to have different prices. Yet their uses are mingled, so they are determined by the same basic conditions. The costs of these kinds of capital are not always precise.

1. *Internal funds* (or "cash flow") come from retained earnings and depreciation flows. They are not "free" to the firm, however, since they have opportunity costs. To use them in project X means to forgo using them in project Y, or investing them outside, or using them to pay off existing debt. Each of these alternatives would yield a return, and the return on the best alternative *not* taken is the opportunity cost.

2. *Borrowings* are at a set interest rate. But often the firm must keep "compensating balances" (some percentage of the bank loan) on deposit at the bank. This raises the real cost of the funds. Or the firm may get valuable extra services (advice, processing), which lower the real net costs of the funds. Firms can also get short-term borrowings from credit markets rather than just from banks.

3. *Long-term debt* promises fixed payments to the bondholder. Yet the rate of payment set when the bonds are issued may depend on how much the firm borrows. So even here the cost of capital may be imprecise!

4. *Equity* capital has an even more indefinite cost. It depends mainly on the earnings that investors will need to expect in order to get them to buy up a new stock issue. This often ranges between 8 and 16 percent. But usually it can only be guessed at, especially for the many firms that rarely issue new stock.

"The" cost of capital is not a constant. Rather it often varies with the amount of capital being taken. For any given level of funding, the cost of capital is some sort of weighted average among the several sources. Evidently, calculating the "embedded cost" of the firm's existing capital can be done, but with a margin of error. One sums up interest payments, assigns a cost to the equity capital, and then takes a weighted average of them both, divided by the book value of the debt and equity securities that are outstanding. That involves some guesswork. Calculating the *forward-looking* "cost of new capital" is much more speculative.

Yet managers must make choices that involve a known or estimated cost of capital. Rough estimates are often necessary and acceptable. After all, the cost of capital is rarely less than 8 percent or above 14 percent for any normal firm. This contrast between precise concepts and rough practical judgments is familiar. As before, you should learn the concepts precisely but be prepared for actual uses that are inexact but reasonably workable.

2. Capital Structure

Capital structure is the share of debt in the firm's entire capital.[1] This ratio—often called "leverage"—can vary from zero to over 90 percent. Debt is "cheaper," but it adds to the firm's degree of financial risk because the interest on it *must* be paid or the firm will be insolvent. Equity is the sum of (1) amounts gained by issuing stock in the past and (2) all retained earnings down the years.

What determines a firm's choice of capital structure? There are several factors, which vary from firm to firm. Innate technical conditions are often decisive. A *capital-intensive* firm will generally have higher leverage. A *risky* firm (say, one in an erratic market or facing other "real" hazards) will generally maintain lower leverage. This is to guard against fluctuations in earnings that would make it impossible occasionally to cover large interest payments. Yet managerial preferences can be decisive, and of course stockholder interests can play a strong role. Highly *risk-averse* managers will keep leverage low.

The "optimal capital structure" is a perennial topic in the literature, but no clear optimum may exist. As the ratio of debt rises, the cost of capital might seem to go down, because the interest costs on debt are usually thought to be lower than the costs of equity. If so, some minimum might be reached, beyond which increasing risk caused by the leverage itself would make the firm pay higher interest rates on additional bonds. This could raise the cost of capital. But instead, a rise in leverage may, throughout the range, raise the cost of equity capital at least enough to offset

[1] This is the most general measure. Other ways of defining *capital structure* have been tried, but they give results similar to the basic debt percentage ratio.

the seemingly lower cost of debt. A reasonably perfect capital market might cause the one effect to neatly offset the other. If so, the cost of capital would be roughly constant. The optimum structure would then not be definable.

For all these reasons, leverage varies greatly even among firms that otherwise seem identical. Preferences and differences in judgment are important, as well as some basic influences.

3. Depreciation

A physical asset is acquired at some cost (C), is used during its life (L), and then is either worthless or sold (V for final value). Its life is determined by (1) physical "wear and tear" and/or (2) obsolescence. The firm assigns expected lives to each physical asset, mainly on a physical basis. The firm then charges off the asset's value year by year on some specific basis. The resulting depreciation is a yearly cost item, which is part of the firm's cash flow (net income is the other part). The accrued depreciation is not a fund or a pool, but it does give an approximate basis for showing the net assets of the firm (gross assets minus depreciation).

The actual depreciation charges are set by the firm's choices of the asset life and the basis of depreciation. (These methods include "straight line, double declining, sum of the years' digits, service units," and various special "accelerations" of the write-offs. They are too complex to be presented here.) These charges may stray far from the true change in value of the asset (1) if obsolescence speeds up because of new innovations or (2) if special tax laws lead the firm to take rapid write-offs, and so on. Also, many machines stay in good working order even after their depreciable "lives" are over.

The standard rules give much room for variety. The firm can set its own reasonable basis for assigning asset lives and charging depreciation: all it must do is stick to it consistently. Figure A3.1 shows the differences that can occur for a given asset. Identical firms can show sharply differing net income and net assets by choosing different depreciation lives and rates. There are two blades to this scissors. Faster depreciation reduces the reported profits *now*, but it also reduces the nominal asset base for computing *future* profit rates. Accordingly, it may be difficult to measure the firm's "real" assets in a uniform way. Yet in the long run, such deviations will tend to even out.

Assets are listed at "book" values (gross and net). Their "true" economic value may differ from book values. One may measure what the assets could be sold for: their "market value." Or one could calculate what it would cost now to replace them: their "reproduction cost." Both concepts are plausible and have some uses, but they are irrelevant to the accounting for the firm as a "going concern." They are also virtually impossible to measure precisely. Any method involves some slippage between accounting and economic values. The standard methods are reasonably sound on economic grounds, and they give precise objective figures.

4. Inventories

Firms may choose any reasonable method for accounting the value of inventories, but they must adhere to it. If prices are changing, inventory values may change. Suppose 100 crates of X were produced for sale at $1,000 each and stored.

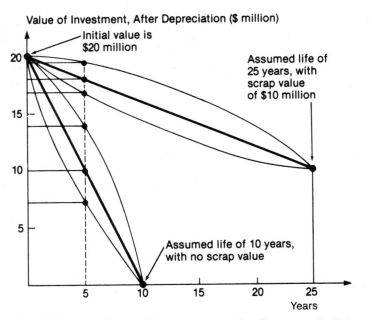

Value of Investment, After Depreciation ($ million)

Initial value is
$20 million

Assumed life of
25 years, with
scrap value
of $10 million

Assumed life of 10 years,
with no scrap value

Years

FIGURE A3.1.   Depreciation can vary; after five years, is the machine worth $19.5 million,
$7.2 million, or something in between?

Then costs rose to $2,000 each, and 100 more crates were stored. What are the first
100 crates "really worth" now: $100,000 or $200,000? If $200,000, the firm has a
paper gain of $100,000. Should that go directly into profits or should it be treated
as a special gain? After all, the firm's basic productivity is unchanged; only a windfall
profit occurred.

The standard methods for accounting inventory values are "first-in-first-out"
(FIFO) and "last-in-first-out" (LIFO). Their results can differ in times of inflation
or falling prices. They offer the firm some choice in taking such inventory gains or
losses now or later. Though inventories usually do not matter as much to overall
profits as depreciation does, they can be significant for businesses with very large
inventories and during inflationary periods.

5. Taxes and Special Items

Taxes are usually treated on par with other costs of doing business. Some (real
estate taxes, for example) are subtracted before figuring net income. Others (such
as profits taxes) depend on, and come out of, net income. Frequently Congress enacts
special tax write-offs to encourage more investment or to benefit certain kinds of
firms. (Examples: a shorter write-off period for assets; a doubling of the yearly
depreciation charge. This changes the accounting profits and—soon—the firm's
recorded assets, even though the firm's real conditions have not altered.) Such items
make profit comparisons among firms—or over time for the same firm—shaky.

Firms occasionally make special adjustments. (Example: a one-time write-off of a mistaken project or a failing division. That puts the year's profits out of line.) Such items can often be averaged. Averaging a big loss backward may fit the true trend toward losses that the firm was undergoing; but it changes history! Averaging it forward makes less economic sense. One remains alert for such special items and treats them carefully. Often a number of smaller special items are routinely included, so that the casual observer is not aware of the tricks they can play on profits.

6. Profitability

These and other special accounting choices leave much room for honest differences about the true levels of profits. Purposive choices can also be made in order to make profits look larger, smaller, or more steady than they "really" are. As one studies the methods, one develops a healthy skepticism about the actual accounts rendered by firms. In fact, U.S. firms keep two sets of accounts: one for public issuance and another one for tax purposes. The two often differ considerably. (Abroad, firms commonly keep three sets: one for the public, one for taxes, and a third private set of accounts so that the managers can keep track of what *really* happened!)

Still, these differences partly wash out over a period of years, so a six-, eight-, or ten-year average profit rate is often a fairly powerful statistic. It will mask differences among the firm's products: even a unified firm usually has several products or lines that yield differing returns. The wise observer remembers that firms wish to show the public that their profits are not excessive, while at the same time they wish to show their shareholders that the firm *is* profitable!

There remains the choice between returns on *assets* and returns on *equity*. Especially if leverage is high, the two can differ. The two methods are (net income is after tax):

$$\text{Returns on equity} = \frac{\text{Net income}}{\text{Equity}}$$

$$= \frac{\text{Net income}}{(\text{Value of shares when issued}) + (\text{Retained earnings})}$$

$$\text{Return on assets} = \frac{\text{Net income} + \text{Interest payments}}{\text{Equity} + \text{Debt}}$$

Since interest payments are usually only 10 to 12 percent of debt, the rate of return on assets is usually lower than that on equity. Both methods are plausible, and the careful observer uses them both. But equity has a broader validity. It represents the shareholders as the ultimate owners. And it is the rate most akin to what managers regard as their performance test: to maximize the shareholder's wealth.

As a final note, these issues are much the same for public firms as for private ones. Costs must be accounted, assets must be valued, and net revenue must be calculated for public enterprises. The methods are quite general, and one needs the same sense of reasonable skepticism.

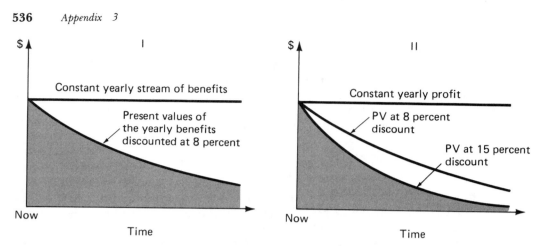

FIGURE A3.2.   Discounting future payments to present values.

In panel I, discounting for time reduces the present value of a future payment below its nominal value. The effect of discounting increases as the interval increases. The sum of the present values, shown by the shaded area, is the total present value of the entire stream. In panel II, a higher rate of discount reduces the present value even further, leaving a smaller shaded area representing present value.

7. Discounting

The firm has first to decide whether to invest at all. The cost is the outlay to acquire and install the capital. The benefits are the future stream of net returns (or profits) gained from selling the goods that are produced by using the capital. Future returns must be discounted for time, to reflect the fact that present dollars are more valuable now than future dollars. Panel I of Figure A3.2 illustrates the effect of discounting where the *constant money stream of benefits translates into a decreasing stream of present values of benefits.* The present values are obtained by the formula

$$\text{Present value} = \frac{\text{Future value}}{(1 + r)^T}$$

where r is the interest rate used to discount future values and T is the number of years into the future. The more distant benefits are discounted more heavily, because the yearly discounting process operates over more years. A $1 million profit expected next year has a present value of $925,900 when discounted at 8 percent; the $1 million expected in the tenth year has a present value of only $463,200; after fifteen years only $315,200, and so on.

These discounted present values (shown by the shaded area in panel I) are summed to obtain the total benefits (or profits) from this amount of investment. The total *PV* from period 1 forward is:

$$\text{Total present value} = \frac{\text{Profit}_1}{(1 + r)} + \frac{\text{Profit}_2}{(1 + r)^2} + \frac{\text{Profit}_3}{(1 + r)^3} + \cdots + \frac{\text{Profit}_n}{(1 + r)^n}$$

If the stream continues at a constant level for an indefinite number of periods, then the formula becomes much simpler:

$$\text{Total present value} = \frac{\text{Yearly profit}}{\text{Discount rate}} = \frac{\text{Yearly profit}}{r}$$

Thus a \$1 million yearly stream discounted at an 8 percent rate has a total present value of \$12.5 million. A higher discount rate gives a lower present value; for example, if r is 15 percent, then PV is \$6.7 million. In panel II of Figure A3.2, the higher discount rate leaves a smaller shaded area.

This calculation of total PV is called *capitalizing the value of future benefits*.

As for the firm's choice, the expected total PV must be at least as great as the cost of the investment, or else the investment will not be worth undertaking.

8. Rates of Return

Where investment returns are high enough to warrant some level of investment, the firm must decide *how much to invest*. The firm compares the cost and benefits of alternative amounts of investment. It arrays its investment projects from the most profitable to the least profitable. The task is to select the optimal level of investment, which is the level that will *maximize the firm's profits in the long run*.

The array is based on the *rates of return* expected from the investment levels. The rate of return for each project is the interest rate *that will just equate the capitalized value of an investment's future profits with the investment's initial cost*. It is called the *internal rate of return* of the investment project. For example, a \$10 million investment might generate \$3 million yearly in profits for an unlimited number of years. By the simple equation

$$\text{Investment cost} = \frac{\text{Yearly profit}}{\text{Rate of return } (r)}$$

we have

$$\text{Investment cost} = \$10 \text{ million} = \frac{\$3 \text{ million}}{r}$$

Transposing the \$10 million and r terms, we get:

$$r = \frac{\$3 \text{ million}}{\$10 \text{ million}} = 30 \text{ percent}$$

The project therefore has a rate of return of 30 percent. At an interest rate of 30 percent, it will just break even. For comparison, suppose that a \$13.8 million investment yields a yearly profit of \$3.73 million. Its internal rate of return is (\$3.73) ÷ (\$13.8 million) = 27 percent. If the profit stream is for a finite period, the calculation is only a bit more complicated.

INTERPRETING
STATISTICS

To be able to evaluate the "evidence" and methods of research in this field, one needs at least a course or two in econometrics. Yet a brief word here can help. There are two main tools: variance analysis and multiple regression. Beyond tools, one needs good sense in evaluating what the "results" really mean. One should ask: (1) Is the correct hypothesis or model being tested? (2) Do the data measure the right variables? (3) What is the quality of the data? (4) What true "significance" do the results have?

1. Trends

Often one must judge whether a trend is under way. (Examples: Is aggregate U.S. concentration rising? Is Xerox's market share declining?) The yearly data usually wiggle about, so one has to look for the underlying trend. Five-year moving averages are a standard way to show trends, but they still leave one wondering if the recent shifts are important and lasting or trivial and about to be reversed. Figure A4.1 shows the problem. Has the trend reversed, or not?

No easy solution exists. One must use judgment. The "experts" can be as wrong as anyone. You may believe that the process is *cyclical,* so that what goes up must come down, and vice versa. Or you may expect *steady* trends: new patterns will develop further. In fact, both kinds of trend occur, in various situations. The best approach is to look for the underlying *causes* of change. Are they about spent, or are they still strong? One might then try to fit basic shapes to the trend. These include straight-line projections, exponential curves, oscillating curves, and others. The more mature experts tend to be skeptical and to avoid rash predictions about trends.

2. Relationships

The more basic research questions usually involve two parts: Is X_1 related to X_2 and if so, what is the shape of the relationship? I will illustrate with a familiar hypothesis: that market power (X_1) yields excess profits (X_2). (This is evaluated in Chapters 4 and 5.)

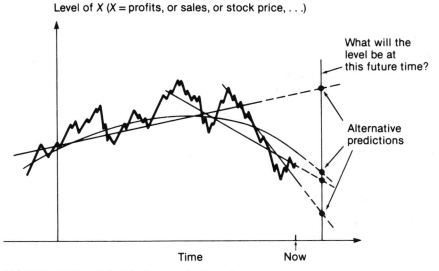

FIGURE A4.1.   What is the trend, if any?

Hypothesis

At its simplest, such a relationship would emerge in scatter diagrams, such as in Figure A4.2. Assume for the moment that accurate data can be used. They would simply be listed as in Table A4.1. Each "observation" is a firm, with a value both for X_1 and for X_2. The number of firms included is then the size of the "sample": this is labeled N.

These data can then be plotted in scatter diagrams, as in Figure A4.2. We believe that X_1 is the "independent" or "causative" variable, and so it goes on the horizontal axis. The "dependent" variable X_2 is on the vertical axis. If a relationship did exist and were "linear" (a straight-line form), panel I would result. If no relationship existed, the scatter diagram might look like panel II. The line in panel I is fitted in to summarize the pattern. The usual method for fitting it is "least-squares regression," but you can often fit the line on just about as well by hand. The equation for the fitted line is, in this illustration:

$$X_2 \text{ is a function of } X_1$$
$$= \quad a \ + \ bX_1 \qquad \text{(a linear form)}$$
$$X_2 = \ .05 \ + \ .08 \ X_1$$
$$\qquad (.02) \quad (0.2) \qquad (\leftarrow\text{standard errors})$$
$$\qquad [2.5] \quad [4.0] \qquad (\leftarrow t\text{-ratios})$$
$$N = 20 \quad r^2 = .55$$

This linear equation is a model; it has a definite form that may or may not

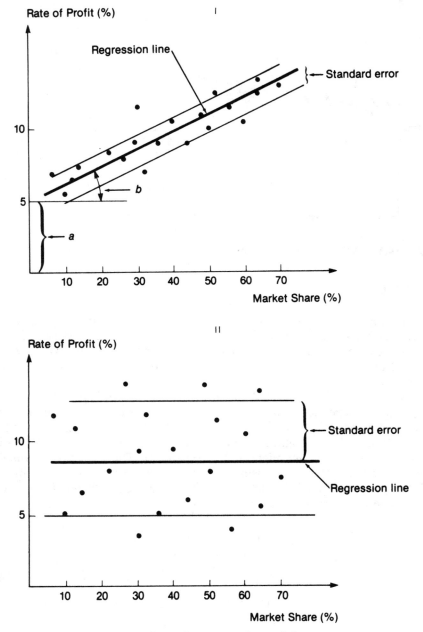

FIGURE A4.2. Illustrations of patterns of actual data.

TABLE A4.1 Illustrative Data Behind Figure A4.2

	PANEL I		PANEL II	
FIRM NUMBER	MARKET SHARE (%)	RATE OF PROFIT (%)	MARKET SHARE (%)	RATE OF PROFIT (%)
1	6%	7.0%	6%	12.0%
2	10	5.5	10	5.0
3	12	6.5	12	11.0
4	14	7.5	13	6.5
5	22	8.5	22	8.0
6	26	8.0	26	14.0
7	30	9.0	30	3.5
8	30	11.5	30	9.5
9	32	7.0	32	12.0
10	36	9.0	36	5.0
11	40	10.5	40	9.5
12	44	9.0	44	6.0
13	48	11.0	48	14.0
14	50	10.0	50	8.0
15	52	12.5	52	11.5
16	56	11.5	56	4.0
17	60	10.5	60	10.5
18	64	12.5	64	13.5
19	64	13.5	64	5.5
20	70	7.5	70	13.0

correctly fit the actual scatter of data. The term a is the "intercept" of the vertical axis, while b is the slope of the line, or "function." The dots seem to fit a linear function such as this. How closely they fit is shown by the r^2 term—the "correlation coefficient" r squared. It can range between 0 (no correlation at all) and 1.0 (a perfect correlation with all dots precisely on the line). The r_2 value (here .55) says that 55 percent of the variation in X_2 is statistically "explained" by X_1. The "standard errors" in the a and b coefficients are shown just below them in parentheses. The standard errors are defined to contain about 68 percent of the dots; they measure the dispersion. They are also drawn in panel I of Figure A4.2. So-called t-ratios are the coefficients divided by their standard errors, thus: (coefficient of a) ÷ (standard error of a), and so on. They are shown here in brackets.

Now, high r^2 and t-ratios indicate that there is a close statistical fit. This in turn suggests that X_1 and X_2 are genuinely related. One could see that clearly in this case, even without fitting the line and computing the ratios. But most cases are not so clear, so the r^2 and t-ratios provide objective, repeatable tests of statistical "significance." With small samples, only high r^2 and t-ratios can be accepted as being "significant." With larger samples (roughly speaking, over thirty observations is a large sample), r^2 of about .3 and t-ratios of about 2.5 pass the "significance" tests. In panel II of Figure A4.2, a fitted line is flat: X_2 does not vary with X_1. The t-ratio for a would be high, but r^2 and the t-ratio for b would approach zero. This would only confirm what is obvious to the eye. The two variables are unrelated.

Dependent Variable

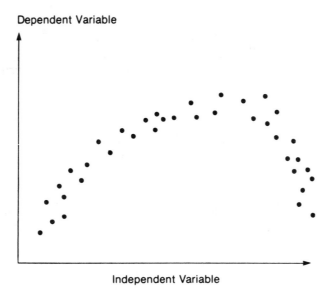

Independent Variable

FIGURE A4.3.   A nonlinear pattern.

3.   Two Cautions

First, suppose that the real pattern is not linear but, instead, curved as in Figure A4.3. Then we should fit a curve of some sort (using logarithms, a squared term, or some other form in the equation). The careful analyst plots out the data and inspects for this condition before trying to fit an equation or model to it.

Second, this "simple" regression, with two variables, may leave out the main factors at work. Does X_1 cause X_2? Not necessarily. Perhaps they are both influenced by some other factor, X_3. X_1 and X_2 are *correlated,* but we must look for other likely factors and include them if we can. That is, our model needs to be reasonably *complete.* We will think logically about the main likely variables, and we will then try to include perhaps the three or four most likely ones. In the present example, a likely third variable, labeled X_3, is economies of scale. An X_4 might be growth. An X_5 might be a "dummy" variable showing whether the firm makes producer or consumer goods. (Dummy variables have values of 1 or 0, rather than ranging along a scale. Producer-goods industries could be 0, and consumer-goods, 1.) We use our judgment—theory, plus a feel for relative importance—in deciding which factors to include. We would not, of course, try to include "everything" (say, twenty variables). Only the main variables are eligible.

The result might be an expanded equation, to be fitted by "multiple regression." In principle, the method isolates the relation between each independent variable and the dependent variable, *holding all the others constant.* The b, c, d, and e terms are called "partial correlation coefficients." As shown in Table A4.2, the X_3 and X_4 variables do "explain" some variation in X_2, while X_1 "explains" less. The total R^2 for the whole equation means the same as r^2 does for the small regression, and the

TABLE A4.2   Sample Multiple Correlations

$$X_2 = \underset{(.01)}{.05} + \underset{(.02)}{.07X_1} + \underset{(0.8)}{2.2X_3}$$
$$\quad\quad [5.0] \quad [3.5] \quad [2.8] \quad\quad \leftarrow\text{(standard errors)}$$
$$\quad\quad\quad\quad\quad\quad\quad\quad\quad\quad\quad\quad\quad \leftarrow\text{(}t\text{-ratios)}$$
$$N = 20 \quad\quad R^2 = .61$$

$$X_2 = \underset{(.01)}{.04} + \underset{(.02)}{.09X_1} + \underset{(0.7)}{2.3X_3} + \underset{(0.3)}{.9X_4} + \underset{(.01)}{.03X_5}$$
$$\quad\quad [4.0] \quad [4.5] \quad [3.3] \quad [3.0] \quad [3.0] \quad \leftarrow\text{(standard errors)}$$
$$\quad\quad\quad\quad\quad\quad\quad\quad\quad\quad\quad\quad\quad\quad\quad\quad\quad \leftarrow\text{(}t\text{-ratios)}$$
$$N = 20 \quad\quad R^2 = 66$$

where X_3 is economies of scale, X_4 is growth, and $X_5 = 1$ consumer goods firms and 0 for producer-goods firms.

t-ratios mean the same as before. Very roughly speaking, variables with higher t-ratios are likely to be more "important."

Multiple regression is more complete than simple regression, and therefore it helps avoid shallow and incomplete analysis. Yet it poses problems. Plotting out the data for inspection is not easy to do, so the researcher often tries to fit linear forms incorrectly to curved scatters. Also, a few freakish observations (often called "outliers") can shift all the coefficients strongly. These and other problems should make one skeptical of multiple regression results. Yet the basic concept is sound and the tool can be powerful.

4. Data and Variables

Some variables can be measured precisely (age, for example, or height), but most economic variables of real markets cannot. After framing the hypothesis correctly, one is usually forced to use data that are inaccurate and unreliable to some degree. In the illustration, one cannot measure market power directly—it is a complex phenomenon, and official figures are not kept on it. Market share may be the main element in it, but not the only one. Moreover, exact measures of market share are not readily available. So, instead, four-firm concentration in the industry is often used as an estimator of market power. But that is a rather different concept. The degree of profitability also poses tricky problems of measurement, as do economies of scale.

Lesson: One often—indeed, almost always—must use indirect, incomplete variables. Such tests are commonly better than nothing, but they are easy to misinterpret. Beware of approximations and "proxy" variables that differ in content from the true factors in the model.

5. Quality of the Data

Most data are shakier than they seem, and some are utterly worthless. Official data are often based on arbitrary definitions that miss the reality. (Example: The national four-firm concentration ratio for newspapers is 14 percent. In real [local] newspaper markets, the true average concentration is over 90 percent.) Data from private sources are often prepared with self-interest uppermost in mind. A general melancholy law holds: The most sensitive and important data are the most likely to be secreted and/or unreliable. Data prepared by objective academics are often faulty, too, because (1) academics are usually outsiders, unable to get direct information; and (2) they often have their own biases.

Data on industrial organization are especially prone to these defects. Often one needs to add a variable to make the analysis complete enough; and yet the data for that variable are so bad that they may increase the degree of error in the whole analysis. Many articles that include bad data do get published; a major task of "the experts" is to guard against wrong conclusions based on faulty data in one another's research!

6.   What Do the "Results" Mean?

Difficult as it is, processing data to test hypotheses is usually easier than interpreting what the "results" really mean. One must bear in mind the problems of incorrect models, indirect variables, and faulty data. Usually the statistical significance of the research findings (the r^2, R^2, t-ratios, and other results) is marginal. Suppose that X_1 is barely significant at the 1 percent level and "explains" only 7 percent of X_2 (leaving 93 percent of X_2's variation unexplained). Yet you know that the data contain much error, and you recall that theory strongly suggests that X_1 does influence X_2. The theory is not rejected, nor is it affirmed. Measurement error may be the culprit. The recurring question is: If you had perfect data, would the fit be closer? If bad data give at least some correlation, wouldn't good data give more?

Generally, errors in data do tend to make the observed patterns seem weaker than they really are. Research "findings" may therefore have a downward bias. The measured correlations are probably weaker and slope coefficients lower than the underlying processes themselves are. Does this bias make the scope and effects of market power seem weaker than they really are? Most say yes, but others claim no. Still, you must keep this possibility of downward bias constantly in mind.

There is usually room for divergent evaluations of any research "results." Even a very *tight* fit of observations to curves is grounds for doubt in this kind of cross-section analysis! An R^2 over 75 percent raises a little red flag: How can it be so *high* unless there is spurious correlation for some reason?

Research in this field is both a science and an art. There may be a pervasive downward bias in the measured results. Most issues are not tested and "settled." They are illumined in various degrees, often dimly. But further testing—with different models or new data—is always in order, and it can raise new doubts about even the most basic "settled" hypotheses.

Answers to Review Questions

(If a true-false statement contains any error, it is answered as "not true.")

CHAPTER 2

1. Not true   2. True   3. Not true   4. Not true   5. (3)

CHAPTER 3

1. Not true   2. Not true   3. Behavioralist   4. Not true   5. (a), (c), (e)   6. True

CHAPTER 4

1. Not true   2. True   3. True   4. Not true

CHAPTER 5

1. Not true   2. True   3. True   4. True   5. (a), (c), (d)

CHAPTER 6

1. True   2. True   3. Not true   4. True   5. True   6. Not true

CHAPTER 7

1. Not true   2. True   3. Not true   4. True

CHAPTER 8

1. True   2. Not true   3. True   4. True

CHAPTER 9

1. True   2. Not true   3. Not true   4. True   5. Not true   6. Not true   7. Not true   8. True   9. (1)   10. True

CHAPTER 10

1. Not true   2. True   3. Not true   4. True   5. Not true   6. True

CHAPTER 11

1. Shrink

CHAPTER 12

1. Not true   2. True   3. No   4. None are   5. True   6. Not true   7. Not true   8. Not true

CHAPTER 13

1. Not true   2. True   3. Not true   4. True   5. True   6. Not true   7. True   8. Not true   9. True   10. Not true

CHAPTER 14

1. Not true   2. Not true   3. Not true   4. Not true   5. Not true   6. Not true   7. Not true   8. Not true

CHAPTER 15

1. True   2. Not true   3. Not true   4. Not true   5. Not true   6. Not true   7. Not true   8. True   9. Not true   10. Not true   11. (1), (2), (4)   12. True   13. Not true   14. True   15. Not true   16. Not true   17. True   18. Not true   19. True

CHAPTER 16

1. (1), (2), (3)   2. Not true   3. Not true   4. True   5. Not true   6. True
7. True   8. Both   9. (1)

CHAPTERS 17, 18

(No true-false questions)

CHAPTER 19

1. Not true   2. True   3. True   4. True   5. True   6. Not true
7. True   8. Not true   9. Not true   10. True

CHAPTER 20

1. Not true   2. True   3. True   4. True   5. True   6. True   7. True
8. True   9. Not true   10. True   11. Not true

Index of Cases, Firms, and Industries

INDEX OF NAMES

INDEX OF SUBJECTS